ADVANCE PRAISE FOR *POLITICIZING ISLAM IN CENTRAL ASIA*

"Kathleen Collins achieves something extraordinary in this masterful and careful analysis of Islamism in Central Asia. Based on years of in-depth interviews, archival materials, and other sources, Collins traces the emergence of Islamist movements, from the moderate and democratic to the radical and militant in Kyrgyzstan, Tajikistan, and Uzbekistan. Along the way, she reveals the lived experiences of many Kyrgyz, Tajik, and Uzbek religious believers. Without demonizing Islam or sensationalizing Islamism, Collins enriches our understanding of both Soviet and post-Soviet religious repression and its unintended consequences: making Islam more resilient and fostering a religious basis for political opposition. Anyone endeavoring to understand the fabric of modern-day Central Asia should closely read Collins' scholarship."

—Steve Swerdlow, esq.,
Associate Professor of the Practice of Human Rights,
University of Southern California, and former
Senior Central Asia researcher at Human Rights Watch

Politicizing Islam in Central Asia

From the Russian Revolution to the Afghan and Syrian Jihads

KATHLEEN COLLINS

OXFORD
UNIVERSITY PRESS

Oxford University Press is a department of the University of Oxford. It furthers the University's objective of excellence in research, scholarship, and education by publishing worldwide. Oxford is a registered trade mark of Oxford University Press in the UK and certain other countries.

Published in the United States of America by Oxford University Press
198 Madison Avenue, New York, NY 10016, United States of America.

CIP data is on file at the Library of Congress
ISBN 978–0–19–768507–5 (pbk.)
ISBN 978–0–19–768506–8 (hbk.)

DOI: 10.1093/oso/9780197685068.001.0001

Paperback printed by Marquis Book Printing, Canada
Hardback printed by Bridgeport National Bindery, Inc., United States of America

For my children, Michael, Katie, and Elisa,
May you always be blessed with freedom, peace, and love

Contents

List of Figure

List of Images

List of Tables

List of Maps

Acknowledgments

One of the things I have often admired about Central Asians, from those living in remote villages to those in dense urban *mahallas* (neighborhoods), is their ability to persist despite adversity. Their faith and endurance motivated me to continue with this book, which has been a long time in the making. My Central Asian friends and I have often shared our hopes for a better future. I pray this book makes a small contribution to that future, both by remembering the past and by reminding readers of the basic human need for justice and religious freedom.

During the years that I have worked on this book, I have been able to observe Islamism in Central Asia as it has developed and changed. My project grew as Islamism of many forms evolved and spread across the region, from Tajikistan to Uzbekistan and Kyrgyzstan. I became all too aware of the complexity of the Islamist phenomenon. Some, like the Islamic Movement of Uzbekistan, shifted from an early focus on President Islom Karimov's regime to attacking U.S. forces in Afghanistan, and then waging jihad in Syria. Most Islamists in Tajikistan, by contrast, moderated and were willing to speak with me about their desire for democracy and religious freedom. My eyes were opened as they recounted how the "Red Terror" had triggered their demands for justice. Caught between the state's religious oppression and the violence perpetrated by some Islamists were ordinary Muslims, men and women seeking a better life for their children, as do people everywhere. As an Uzbek cab driver once told me, "You're Christian, I'm Muslim, but there's just one God."

Over the years, I have worked closely with wonderful colleagues and assistants throughout Central Asia; they have become dear friends. Together we have watched—and they have lived through—the turmoil of politics and everyday existence in the region. Throughout this time, I have relied on them and many other good people there for help. Given continued political oppression and uncertainty, I have chosen not to name most of them here. I hope that they know how grateful I am and how much I have learned from them. I truly appreciate the advice, knowledge, and friendship of Elvira Ilibezova and El-Pikr in Kyrgyzstan. I thank Saodat Olimova, Muzaffar Olimov, and Muhiddin Kabiri in Tajikistan. Ercan Murat, Emil Nasritdinov, Keneshbek, Esen, Hassan and his family, Hurmat, Dinara, Parviz, Murat, Dilbar, Tolekan, and many others shared their knowledge, helped arrange meetings, and got me safely from Bishkek to Kara-Suu, from Tashkent to Andijon, and from Khujand to Dushanbe, among many other places. Central Asian journalists and human rights activists who risk their lives every day offered me their assistance. Those who drove me around cities and villages, through the mountain passes, and across the steppe of Central Asia all deserve far more than my heartfelt thanks. Others poured me tea, brought me warm meals, kept me safe and healthy, and became my friends. Many took risks because they wanted me to tell their story.

The U.S. embassies, Organization for Security and Co-operation in Europe, and United Nations Development Programme in Tashkent, Bishkek, and Dushanbe provided support and insight, as did Robin Schulman, Greg Taubman, Kelly Kivler, Daniel Burghart, and David Abramson. Damon Mehl and Chris Borg offered a wealth of expertise on militants in Afghanistan. Ismail Yaylacı and Selçuk Köseoğlu assisted me in Turkey, and Valery Tishkov in Russia.

David Holloway nominated me for the Carnegie grant that funded the initial stages of this project. My mentor at Notre Dame, Jim McAdams, encouraged me never to forget the human side of my work. His wisdom and copious comments greatly improved this manuscript. Scott Mainwaring, Kathryn Sikkink, and Sid Tarrow were especially generous with their counsel. Bayram Balcı, Stéphane Dudoignon, Steve Fish, Fran Hagopian, Valerie Bunce, Laura Adams, Carrie Rosefsky, Kathryn Hendley, Amaney Jamal, Mark Tessler, Eric McGlinchey, John Heathershaw, Ted Gerber, and David Samuels, among others, offered advice. Adam Casey, Shoshanna Keller, Alisher Khamidov, Adeeb Khalid, and Jeff Sahadeo each thoughtfully read several chapters. My dear Uzbek friend and colleague provided feedback on the Uzbekistan chapters. I have learned so much from him over the years, and he has been a steady source of inspiration. Farhad greatly assisted me with Abu Saloh's videos. Esen translated Kyrgyz, Zamira and Marifat translated Tajik, and Mustafa Düzdağ translated Arabic sources. I am most grateful to the two anonymous reviewers for generously giving me their time and sage advice.

Lisa Hilbink, Teri Caraway, Nancy Luxon, Adrienne Edgar, and Bisi Agboola continually encouraged and reassured me. Bud Duvall, Joan Tronto, and Paul Goren always supported me. I have been blessed with many outstanding undergraduates and Ph.D. students. Niamh McIntosh-Yee, Margaux Granath, Alisher Kassym, Sasha Dunagan, Maya Mehra, Ethan Hoeschen, Natalie Melm, and especially Shawn Stefanik, Kamaan Richards, and Zamria Yusufjonova assisted at various stages. Ibrahim Öker, Selçuk Köseoğlu, and Luke Dykowski each generously read the entire manuscript and offered insight on every aspect of the book. Selçuk, more than once, painstakingly helped me proofread the text. Luke was a superb copyeditor. Their dedication has made this book far better.

The Carnegie Corporation of New York, the U.S. Institute of Peace, the National Council for East European and Eurasian Studies, the Kellogg Institute, the University of Notre Dame, the McKnight Land Grant, the Templeton Foundation, and the University of Minnesota each provided grants to finance my fieldwork and writing. I am indebted to David McBride and the production team at Oxford University Press for their superb advice, careful oversight, and cheer as they guided this project to completion.

I am especially beholden to my family—my parents, Megan, Ryan, and Tom—who have encouraged and supported my endeavors and lived through this project with me. Above all, I am infinitely grateful for my children's love, companionship, and inspiration. My eldest, Michael, was born not long after I began my research. Michael and his younger sisters, Katie and Elisa, have brought an abundance of joy into my life. They have often sat beside me in my office or at the kitchen table, writing their own books as I wrote mine. They went from knocking over my towering stacks of sources and colorfully scribbling on my books and notes, to solving my computer problems, helping me proofread chapters, and filing thousands of pages of interview transcripts. They endlessly encouraged me to press ahead. They cheered me on and told me they believed in me. They kept me grounded by reminding me to bake cookies and come play. I dedicate this book to them, with love.

Technical Note

Writing a book of this nature involves many complications. Uzbek, Tajik, and Kyrgyz have changed spellings and even alphabets multiple times over the past century. The names of cities, territories, countries, and institutions have changed as well. So too the geographical borders of the Central Asian states changed multiple times in the period discussed in this book.

Throughout I have sought to balance historical accuracy and cultural respect for local particularities with a reader-friendly manuscript. I have generally adopted the following guidelines for spelling and transliteration. I have retained the standard English spelling of names that are common (e.g., Ferghana, Kokand, Samarqand). For Uzbek words, I have followed the most recent Uzbek Latin script. For Turkish, I have used the Turkish Latin script. For languages written in Cyrillic (Russian, Tajik, Kyrgyz), I have transliterated titles of sources and other names and terms from the most recent spellings, using the Library of Congress system. Tajik and Kyrgyz transliterations follow the Library of Congress system for the modified Cyrillic alphabets. For example, as is common in transliteration for nonlinguists, I use gh for Ғ ғ, and j for Ҷ ҷ (e.g., Turajonzoda). I have used the most recent official spellings (e.g., Jalalabat, not Jalal-Abad). For Arabic terms or names, I have used those commonly recognized (al-Qaeda). I have dropped most diacritical marks to make the book more accessible to readers of English.

I have used the Oxford English Dictionary variant of Islamic terms that have become common in English (e.g., hijab, jihad, hajj without italics). For religious terms that differ across Tajik, Uzbek, and Kyrgyz, I have generally used the more well-known Arabic form (e.g., *hadith, kafir, zakat*). In deference to local culture, I have adopted the commonly used Central Asian variants of certain frequently used terms that are distinct from the Arabic (e.g., *shariat*, *da'watchi*, *namaz*).

There are some issues that simply have no easy answer. I resolved them by balancing the native language names and spellings, as much as possible, with the ease of the reader. Wherever possible, I replaced Russified names of people and places (even during the Soviet era) with the current Central Asian spelling. If a Central Asian author has published in English, I used the spelling of the given publication. Acronyms reflect the native language, unless there is a commonly used acronym in English-language sources.

I attempted to verify the transliteration of every Central Asian and Arabic word, phrase, name, and place in this book (and its variations in name over time), with multiple sources, including many native speakers.

Sometimes they themselves did not agree, so I defaulted to the principles above. My goal throughout the text has been to respect the Central Asian languages and cultures, maximize consistency, and ease the nonspecialist's burden. I hope the reader will forgive any errors and focus on the substance of the work.

List of Acronyms

AKP	Justice and Development Party, Turkey
ANF	Al-Nusra Front
AQI	Al-Qaeda in Iraq
ASSR	Autonomous Soviet Socialist Republic
AUIRP	All-Union Islamic Revival Party
BNSR	People's Soviet Republic of Bukhara
CA-ISIS	Central Asians in the Islamic State of Iraq and Syria
CPT	Communist Party of Tajikistan
CRA	Council on Religious Affairs
CTC	Combating Terrorism Center
DoD	Department of Defense
DPT	Democratic Party of Tajikistan
ETIM	East Turkestan Islamic Movement
FATA	Federally Administered Tribal Areas
FSB	Federal Security Service, Russia
GKNB	State Committee on National Security, Kyrgyzstan
GNR	Government of National Reconciliation, Tajikistan
Gulag	Main Directorate of Camps
GVU	Head Waqf Directorate
HTI	Hizb ut-Tahrir al-Islami (Islamic Liberation Party)
HTS	Hayat Tahrir al-Sham
ICCT	International Centre for Counter-Terrorism
ICSR	International Centre for the Study of Radicalisation and Political Violence
IED	improvised explosive devices
IJU	Islamic Jihad Union
IMU	Islamic Movement of Uzbekistan
IRPT	Islamic Revival Party of Tajikistan
IRPU	Islamic Revival Party of Uzbekistan
ISAF	International Security Assistance Force
ISIS	Islamic State of Iraq and Syria
ISIS-K	ISIS-Khorasan Province
JA	Jamoati Ansorulloh, Tajikistan
KA	Kokand Autonomy
KGB	Committee for State Security (USSR)
KIB	Katibat Imam al-Bukhari
KTJ	Katibat al-Tawhid wal Jihad
MIRT	Movement for the Islamic Revival of Tajikistan
MVD	Ministry of Internal Affairs (the police)

MXX	National Security Service, Uzbekistan (also known by the acronym SNB; since 2018, it is called the DXX, State Security Service)
NATO	North Atlantic Treaty Organization
NEP	New Economic Policy, USSR
NKVD	People's Commissariat for Internal Affairs, USSR
ODIHR	OSCE Office for Democratic Institutions and Human Rights
OGPU	Soviet secret police, predecessor to NKVD
OMI	Muslim Board of Uzbekistan
OMON	Interior Ministry's Special Purpose Police Unit (or the MVD's Special Forces), Tajikistan
OSCE	Organization for Security and Co-operation in Europe
RFE/RL	Radio Free Europe/Radio Liberty
SADUM	Spiritual Administration of the Muslims of Central Asia and Kazakhstan
SAMK	Spiritual Administration of the Muslims of Kyrgyzstan
SCO	Shanghai Cooperation Organization
SCRA	State Commission on Religious Affairs, Kyrgyzstan
SSR	Soviet Socialist Republic
SUJ	Seyfuddin Uzbek Jamaat
TTP	Tehrik-i-Taliban of Pakistan
USCIRF	U.S. Commission on International Religious Freedom
UTO	United Tajik Opposition
WMD	weapons of mass destruction

Map of Central Asia
Source: Wikimedia Commons

Map of Tajikistan
Source: United Nations Cartographic Section, Wikimedia Commons

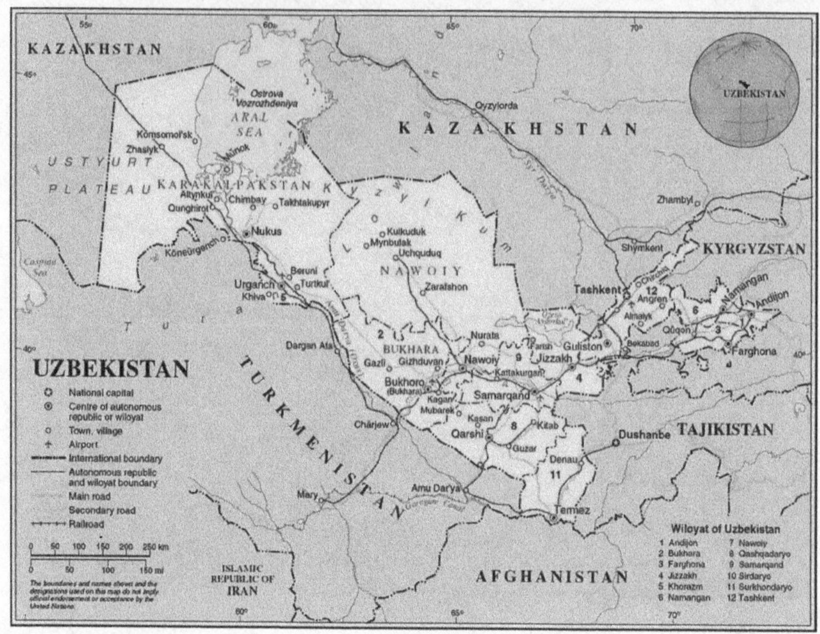

Map of Uzbekistan

Source: United Nations Cartographic Section, Wikimedia Commons

Map of Kyrgyzstan

Source: United Nations Cartographic Section, Wikimedia Commons

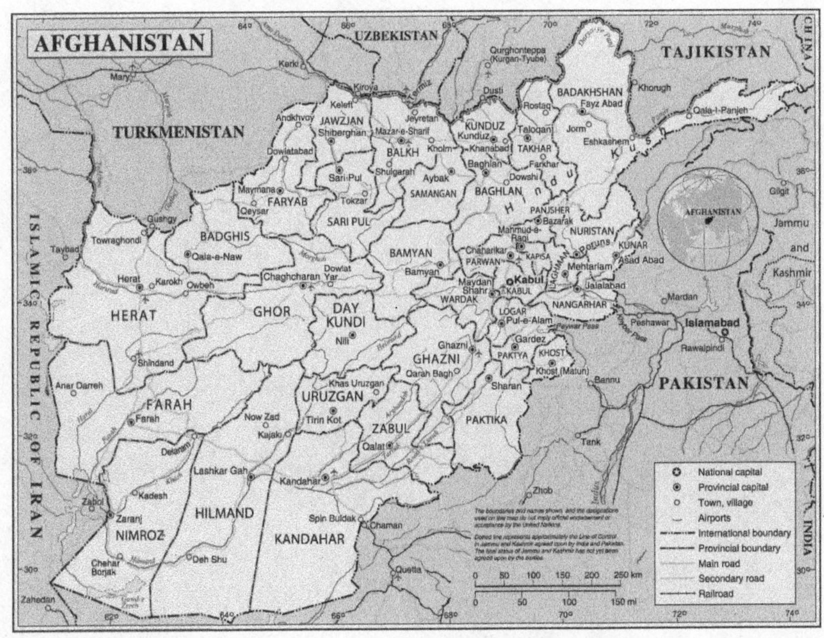

Map of Afghanistan
Source: United Nations Cartographic Section, Wikimedia Commons

PART I
UNDERSTANDING ISLAMISM

Introduction: An Overview of Islamism in Central Asia

Sitting in a cab from Tashkent to Bukhara, I chatted with my driver, Hurmat, for many hours as we crossed the dusty steppe. An Uzbek man in his twenties, Hurmat was dressed in jeans and a "New York" T-shirt. He sported short hair and a clean-shaven face. Although he had completed only a secondary education, he spoke intelligently about world affairs, from Russian-U.S. relations to the war in Afghanistan. He voiced strong opinions. He looked like someone who ought to have a bright future. Over the many hours of the trip, Hurmat expressed his overwhelming frustration with the conditions created by then-President Islom Karimov, whose degradation of ordinary Muslims was evident to him every day.

Hurmat had been born Muslim but had only recently pursued an Islamic education. Working in Russia, he had purchased many books about Islam and cassettes of imams' sermons. He played some of them while we drove. They were lectures on how to pray, how to fast, and how to be a good Muslim. Hurmat was not a member of the Islamic Movement of Uzbekistan (IMU) or a "Wahhabi" sect, the term the Uzbek government used to stigmatize and ban almost any independent form of Islamic practice, branding it as terrorism. However, much of the literature that Hurmat read originally came from Saudi Arabia, where Salafist sermons were published in Russian or Uzbek. He was not a member of any Islamist organization, but his religious and political views, which he conveyed passionately to me, were typical of those the Uzbek regime had branded "extremist." He was brashly disdainful of "government mullahs," who urged him "to be patient" with injustice. He explained, "Before 1999, women wore hijab and men had beards. People freely prayed. After 1999, everyone went to jail; women could not wear the hijab. They [the security services] closed all the small *mahalla* [neighborhood] mosques, only the big ones stayed open, fewer than ten. They [the government] prepare one lecture for all the imams. But the imam's sermon should be about religion, for example, about sins, not political propaganda." Hurmat's anger was palpable. After much thought and investigation of religion on his own, outside of "government mosques," he had concluded that Islam and law by *shariat*[1] would improve life in Uzbekistan: "For sins, you need *shariat* law,

[1] *Shariat* translates as "the path" of Islam or "Islamic law."

Politicizing Islam in Central Asia. Kathleen Collins, Oxford University Press. © Oxford University Press 2023.
DOI: 10.1093/oso/9780197685068.003.0001

cutting off hands for stealing and corruption. . . . Of course, it would be better with *shariat* law." *Shariat*, in Hurmat's view, was the clear solution. Influenced by his voracious consumption of Saudi publications, he was supportive of the *hudud* penalties,[2] which most Central Asians would decry as extreme and premodern. Repressive state policy had politicized Hurmat's Muslim identity.

Hurmat was far more explicit and puritanical than most Central Asians in endorsing *shariat* as state law. However, he was not alone in thinking that Islam was somehow the answer to decades of Soviet and post-Soviet state repression. A group of women from the Ferghana Valley recounted to me their fear and horror after the Andijon massacre of 2005, in which Uzbek government forces killed hundreds of ordinary Muslims protesting both shortages and the unjust imprisonment of their loved ones for "Islamic extremism."[3] Others gave examples of neighbors who had "disappeared" while going to mosque. These women, like Hurmat, sympathized with calls for a more just—and more Muslim—legal system. They did not support radical Islamist parties, and they expressed fear for youth in their neighborhoods, who were drawn to the ideas of Islamist opposition groups. Still, they too opposed Karimov's oppressive secular regime and believed Islamic law would bring justice.

The vast majority of Central Asians avoided politics, remaining silent out of fear. Some scholars expected that the Islamist phenomenon that has characterized politics in the Middle East and South Asia had bypassed Central Asia due to its unique Soviet historical legacy; decades of Soviet oppression of religion and destruction of religious knowledge, together with forced secular modernization, seemed to have a firm hold on societal views about religion and politics. For decades, Soviet "nationalities policy" had relegated Islamic practices to mere "culture" or ethnonational tradition.[4] Indeed, the Soviet regime eliminated Islam's role in law and political legitimacy. The growth of political Islam has thus been a strikingly unexpected phenomenon: since the Soviet collapse in 1991, Islamist movements have been a major form of political opposition in Central Asia. Many thousands of Tajiks, Uzbeks, and Kyrgyz have turned to Islamist ideologies and joined Islamist movements, and many others increasingly favor at least some Islamist ideas. In fact, for over forty years now, Central Asia has experienced several waves of Islamism. Islamism's first wave had roots in Tajikistan and Uzbekistan in the 1970s and 1980s. Over time, new

[2] *Hudud* refers to severe punishments specified in the Qur'an and sunna for certain offenses. The actual application of *hudud* penalties is rare and due to rigid standards for witnesses and evidence. See Wael Hallaq, *An Introduction to Islamic Law* (Cambridge: Cambridge University Press, 2009), 155–56.

[3] "'Bullets Were Falling Like Rain': The Andijon Massacre, May 13, 2005," *Human Rights Watch* 17, no. 5 (June 2005).

[4] Adeeb Khalid, *Islam after Communism: Religion and Politics in Central Asia* (Berkeley: University of California Press, 2007).

and highly varied Islamist organizations emerged. By 2013, the Islamic State of Iraq and Syria (also known as the Islamic State of Iraq and al-Sham, or ISIS) and al-Qaeda affiliates were recruiting young Central Asian men like Hurmat to fight for the caliphate in Syria.

Why and how did Islam become politicized in Central Asia? How did it become a source of political contention and subsequently an ideology at the core of various opposition movements challenging the secular authoritarian state? And why and how did Central Asians become mobilized to support Islamist movements? Understanding and explaining Islamism's root causes and varied paths in the post-Soviet space is the task of this book. Neither Hurmat nor those Tajiks, Uzbeks, and Kyrgyz who joined ISIS were born extremists. Muslims are not born extremists. Rather, political injustice—especially state repression of Islamic belief and practice together with forced secularization—breeds contention over the proper role of religion in the function of the state and society. In the context of such grievances, religious ideologues proffer Islamist ideas of justice as the solution. They promote a political interpretation of the religion. Ultimately, they drive Islamist opposition and mobilization, and sometimes foster violence.

The Longue Durée of Political Islam in Central Asia, 1917–2021

It was the Bolshevik Revolution and Soviet power that, ironically, both transformed Central Asia and politicized Islam, planting the roots of Islamism. From Vladimir Lenin and Josef Stalin to late communist and postcommunist dictators such as Islom Karimov, these leaders implemented the Communist Party's crushing antireligious policies—policies that were responsible for "making extremists," in the words of one of my Uzbek informants.

The Bolsheviks confronted a deeply Islamic society across Central Asia in 1917. Lying at the heart of the Silk Road with historical, theological, and cultural centers in Samarqand and Bukhara, this region was for many centuries a hub of the Muslim world. Islam shaped not only society but also the law, public life, and politics of the region.[5] Central town mosques and *madrasas* (Islamic religious institutes) defined the cultural landscape and education system. *Musulmonchilik* (Muslimness) characterized one's everyday existence and worldview. Shrines to Muslim saints dotted the landscape even where *madrasas* and mosques were fewer in number. Tombstones in clan cemeteries featured crescent moons. Throughout the region, *shariat* and *adat* (customary law) courts implemented the law. The political order of nineteenth-century Central Asia—which governed

[5] Ira Lapidus, *A History of Islamic Societies* (Cambridge: Cambridge University Press, 2014).

the region's settled people until the tsarist and then Bolshevik incorporation of the region eventually destroyed them—drew upon both Islam and lineage to construct their political legitimacy. Yet, the dominant Hanafi school of Islamic law was explicitly quietist following the advent of Russian colonial rule in the nineteenth century. Many Muslims made peace with secular rule so long as it did not repress Islam and force secularization on society.[6]

The Bolshevik Revolution destroyed the old political and religious order by the late 1920s. For decades, the Soviet party-state brutally attacked Islamic institutions and law, religious authorities, sacred literature, and even belief itself. It mandated Cyrillic script to eliminate access to Arabic, the language of the Qur'an. Soviet Muslims not only lost a great deal of religious knowledge and the possibility of fulfilling the core pillars of Islam; many even lost the fundamentals of Islamic doctrine and prayer, fearing the repercussions of passing faith and customary practice on to their children. Signs of children fasting at school could inadvertently expose the religiosity of their parents, who could lose their job or the privilege of Party membership and higher education. Thousands of *ulama* (Muslim religious scholars) were sent to the Gulag because they possessed a sacred authority that rivaled the Party's authority. Moreover, the Soviet party-state was intent upon—and almost totally succeeded in—severing Central Asian ties with the rest of the Muslim world for the seven decades of its existence. Consequently, until the USSR's demise, Soviet Muslims did not experience the trends pervading the rest of the Islamic world during much of the twentieth century.

Nonetheless, the past century has witnessed several periods of Muslim political mobilization in Central Asia, some of them violent and all of them in response to the state repression of Islam that began in 1917. Mass Muslim mobilization—albeit not shaped by Islamist ideology—took place during the Russian Revolution and early Bolshevik period (1917–1926) in opposition to communism and atheism. When decades of nearly total state control began to loosen, a new generation of Muslim underground opposition began networking; entrepreneurial religio-political activists gained access to and were profoundly shaped by the transnational diffusion of the ideology of political Islam. Their activism ushered in successive "waves" of Islamist mobilization.[7]

The first wave began in the 1970s, when Islamist ideology spread to the Tajik and Uzbek republics. Influenced by the Muslim Brotherhood, the Iranian Revolution, and the anti-Soviet jihad of the Afghan mujahidin, first-wave Islamists mobilized against communism during the Soviet collapse. When the

6 Khalid, *Islam after Communism*.

7 On mobilization waves, see Mark Beissinger, *Nationalist Mobilization and the Collapse of the Soviet State* (New York: Cambridge University Press, 2002).

communist regime responded with violence in Tajikistan, a bloody civil war erupted, killing up to 100,000 Tajiks. Both Tajik and Uzbek Islamists were driven into Afghanistan. The second wave of Islamist movements mobilized in the late 1990s and early 2000s in response to post-Soviet secular authoritarianism. Some worked within Tajikistan and Uzbekistan, while others remained based across the Afghan border. Some were nationally focused; others adopted a transnational ideology. A third Islamist wave, a wholly transnational foreign fighter movement, took off under escalating religious repression and in response to the call of al-Qaeda and ISIS from Syria. Central Asians followed extremist propaganda to pursue jihad and the promise of Islamic justice embodied in the new caliphate (see Table I.1). Central Asians, together with Muslims from Russia, comprised the most significant regional foreign fighter contingent in the Syrian jihad—also proving more durable than those coming from the Middle East or South Asia.

Across Central Asia, Islamism's precise content and political trajectory have varied over time and place. In late Soviet-era Tajikistan, Nahzat-i Islami (Islamic Revival), an Islamist youth organization, evolved into an anticommunist national Islamist party, the Islamic Revival Party of Tajikistan (IRPT). That party played a leading role in the anticommunist protests and then civil war of the 1990s. In a second wave of mobilization, the IRPT shifted to democratic, peaceful participation as a legal Islamist party. However, in a third wave, far more radical—violent and antisystemic—Islamists emerged, including those who joined ISIS.

In Uzbekistan, Islamism also varied. The Islamic Revival Party of Uzbekistan (IRPU), Adolat (Justice), and Islom Lashkarlari (Armies of Islam) were all rooted in 1970s underground study circles; they emerged openly around 1990, but the regime quickly eliminated some and drove others into exile. The second Islamist wave included Hizb ut-Tahrir al-Islami (HTI, Islamic Liberation Party), a nonviolent transnational party aiming to establish a caliphate; HTI spread for a decade but, like the first wave, was crushed by Karimov's nearly totalitarian control of Uzbekistan. Another second-wave movement emerged in the late 1990s, when Uzbek exiles formed the militant IMU in Kabul and expanded inside Afghanistan. By 2001, the IMU had become deeply intertwined with al-Qaeda and the Taliban, and for fifteen years it posed an ongoing threat to U.S. military efforts to stabilize Afghanistan. By 2014, in the third wave of Islamism, Uzbeks were also joining radical affiliates of al-Qaeda and ISIS in Syria and Iraq, and ISIS-Khorasan (ISIS-K) in Afghanistan.

Kyrgyzstan, by contrast, seemed immune to Islamism throughout the 1980s and 1990s. The Soviets had been less repressive of Islam there, if only because mosques and veiling were less common among the nomads. Moreover, 1991 had brought widespread religious freedoms and the development of civil Islam. But as President Kurmanbek Bakiyev began to repress certain purist imams and

Table I.1 Waves of Muslim and Islamist Mobilization, 1917–2022

Time Period	Type of Mobilization	Tajikistan	Uzbekistan	Kyrgyzstan
1917 to 1920s[a]	Muslim[b]	*Basmachi movement*	*Basmachi movement* *Kokand Autonomy*	*Basmachi movement*
1930 to mid-1970s	None	None	None	None
Wave 1: Late 1970s to mid-1990s	Islamist	*Nahzat/IRPT*	*IRPU* *Adolat* *Tavba* *IL*	None
Wave 2: Late 1990s to mid-2000s	Islamist	IRPT *HTI* *JA*	*IMU* *IJU* *HTI*	*HTI*
Wave 3: 2011 to 2022	Islamist	IRPT HTI JA *CA-ISIS/ISIS-K*	HTI *CA-ISIS/ISIS-K* IMU *KIB* IJU *KTJ*	HTI *CA-ISIS/ISIS-K* *KTJ*

Note: Groups in *italics* were newly formed in the given time period.

CA-ISIS: Central Asians in the Islamic State of Iraq and Syria

HTI: Hizb ut-Tahrir al-Islami

IJU: Islamic Jihad Union

IL: Islom Lashkarlari

IMU: Islamic Movement of Uzbekistan

IRPT: Islamic Revival Party of Tajikistan

IRPU: Islamic Revival Party of Uzbekistan

ISIS-K: Islamic State of Iraq and Syria-Khorasan Province

JA: Jamoati Ansorulloh

KIB: Katibat Imam al-Bukhari

KTJ: Katibat al-Tawhid wal Jihad

Nahzat: predecessor to the IRPT.

[a] The geographic boundaries were different at this point, before the Soviet national republic delimitation.

[b] The Basmachi movement and Kokand Autonomy are examples of high Muslim mobilization, not modern Islamism; some elements within these movements exhibited some characteristics and demands of later Islamists. The Basmachi were primarily based in the Ferghana Valley region of contemporary Tajikistan, Uzbekistan, and Kyrgyzstan and in eastern Bukhara (central and southern Tajikistan).

their communities, HTI took root there as well. By 2014, Kyrgyzstanis were also drawn into the third wave, becoming Syrian jihadis.

The vast majority of Central Asians have not become Islamist activists. Even fewer have engaged in violence. Nonetheless, most Central Asians seek greater freedom for Islamic practice, a moral state, and religiously oriented justice. Islamists promise those things.

Core Questions and Arguments

Two interrelated sets of questions orient the narrative of this book. First, I seek to understand Islamist emergence or nonemergence over time and space. Under what conditions does Islam become the language and the defining character of political opposition movements? Why has this Islamist mobilization taken place in Tajikistan and Uzbekistan, whereas in Kyrgyzstan civil Islam rather than Islamism has predominated? And why have three distinct waves of Islamist organizations and movements emerged and mobilized from the 1980s through the 2010s?

My second, closely related set of questions centers on whether and how Islamists attract popular support. Why do some Islamist organizations achieve relatively high mobilization, attracting a mass following, whereas many others remain fringe groups or disappear altogether? What strategies do Islamists employ to win a social base? Are ordinary people attracted to any of the multiple Islamist movements that have surfaced? Why are some Central Asians, like Hurmat, sympathetic to Islamist ideas? Islamists must recruit followers, much as any political party or social movement does. Yet in the former Soviet region, in contrast to the Middle East and South Asia, Islamist organizations generally enjoy little room to work in the social and civic spheres, much less to contest elections. They must mobilize followers in challenging and high-risk conditions.

Islam and Muslims are not inherently Islamist, much less militant or terrorist. I seek to explain Islamism in Central Asia, including its core religious motivations and goals, without demonizing either Islam or a political role for Islam. However, in addressing these two puzzles, I argue that the state can and often does politicize Islam. Based on an exploration of Soviet and post-Soviet Central Asia, I contend that the process of Islamist emergence begins when a secular authoritarian state oppresses Islam and imposes secularization. Such policies generate discontent and opposition and ultimately activism as religious entrepreneurs make Islam their ideology—a blueprint for melding Islam, state, and politics. With sufficient associational space, these entrepreneurs found organizations that seek to realize their Islamist ideology within the modern state apparatus. In Central Asia, Soviet repression of Islam and forced secularization, coupled with the diffusion of Islamist ideologies to Tajik and Uzbek entrepreneurs in the widening space of the post-Stalinist era, ultimately led to Islamist emergence and mobilization.

I further contend that popular support for Islamist movements cannot be assumed; it varies greatly. Islamists who employ certain strategies—adapting their ideas/ideology to the local context, building and exploiting sacred authority, and accessing not only local but also broad, transcommunal networks—are likely to generate greater social support and to sustain mass mobilization over time. Sacred authority endows Islamist leaders with status and legitimacy within the Muslim community, while also facilitating recruiting through religious ties, mosques, and *madrasas*. Networking beyond such local ties (for example, by developing ethnic, migrant, or transnational networks) enhances Islamists' potential for higher, nationwide, and even regional or transnational mobilization. Finally, Islamists—especially those who begin with transnational or foreign ideas—need to adapt to the local context in which they are recruiting. They need to integrate the political, economic, and religious grievances of their potential followers. In Central Asia, the IRPT mobilized greater support over time because it adapted its once purist Islamist message to a more Sufi-influenced society. It also incorporated multiple sources of sacred authority and broadened its networks beyond its regional base to include religious nationalists and Muslim democrats who were also aggrieved at the political conditions in Tajikistan. By contrast, ISIS had far less mass support in Central Asia, because it refused to adapt its violent and puritanical ideology, and it lacked indigenous sacred authority and networks for mobilization.

Core Concepts

Political Islam and Islamism

Political Islam and Islamism are concepts and phenomena that are poorly understood despite their growing salience in global politics for nearly a century.[8] I begin with a caveat: this book is not about Islam, one of the world's great religions and civilizations since the seventh century.[9] Rather, my focus is *political Islam*, a concept scholars use to refer to the political phenomenon of making

[8] Mohammed Ayoob, *The Many Faces of Political Islam: Religion and Politics in the Muslim World* (Ann Arbor: University of Michigan Press, 2008), 2; Shadi Hamid and William McCants, eds., *Rethinking Political Islam* (New York: Oxford University Press, 2017).

[9] On Islam as a religion and civilization, see, for example, Seyyid Hossein Nasr, *Islam: Religion, History, and Civilization* (New York: HarperCollins, 2003); Michael Cook, *Ancient Religions, Modern Politics: The Islamic Case in Comparative Perspective* (Princeton, NJ: Princeton University Press, 2014).

Islamic claims on the state in pursuit of religious political objectives.[10] The term broadly captures the variation and fluidity of Islamist actors and their goals, which often change or evolve over time.[11]

At the core of political Islam is the discourse of *Islamism,* a "modern ideology" and a "political program" that puts Islam at the center of its agenda for the state.[12] Islamists include an array of actors—mass organizations, political parties, popular movements, and also terrorist groups—that follow an ideology and pursue the goals of Islamism.[13]

Islamism is rooted in the late nineteenth-century ideas of Muslim critics of colonialism, who sought to re-create an idealized "golden age" of Islam. Historically, Islamism first emerged in 1928 in Egypt, with Hassan al-Banna and the founding of the Muslim Brotherhood. In the 1940s, Sayyid Abu al-Ala Mawdudi in South Asia articulated a similar political critique of secularism and colonialism. Their ideologies made Islam central to defining and controlling a modern state apparatus and its juridical system.[14] That system, they believed, should be based upon their specific political readings of Islamic doctrine. Islamist ideologies and organizations are characterized by the instrumentalization of Islam for political goals; for them, the state is not a domain independent of Islam.[15] Islamists generally seek a central or even a total political role for Islam in defining the constitution and the legal, judicial, economic, and executive apparatus of the state.[16] Islamists believe that the modern state's application and enforcement of *shariat*—God's revealed "divine law"—will bring justice. For Islamists, *shariat* is not only a guide for one's personal moral "path"[17] but also the basis of modern, codified law, which will rectify the injustices of secular authoritarianism. They thus explicitly reject Western-centric, "secular" understandings of modernity and the state.[18] Islamists' ultimate objectives vary, and most never explicitly define what their ideal "Islamic state," "caliphate," or political order would look like; they vary in

10 Hamid and McCants, *Rethinking Political Islam.*

11 Ayoob, *The Many Faces of Political Islam;* Gilles Kepel, *Jihad: The Trail of Political Islam* (Cambridge, MA: Belknap Press, 2002).

12 John Esposito, *The Islamic Threat: Myth or Reality?* (Oxford: Oxford University Press, 1999); Cook, *Ancient Religions, Modern Politics,* xviii.

13 Asef Bayat, "Islamism and Social Movement Theory," *Third World Quarterly* 26, no. 6 (2005): 891–908; Peter Mandaville, *Global Political Islam* (London: Routledge, 2007), 57–58.

14 Esposito, *The Islamic Threat*; Mandaville, *Global Political Islam.*

15 Ayoob, *Many Faces of Political Islam,* 2.

16 Maajid Nawaz and Sam Harris, *Islam and the Future of Tolerance: A Dialogue* (London: Harvard University Press, 2015); Ayoob, *Many Faces of Political Islam*; Shadi Hamid, *Islamic Exceptionalism: How the Struggle Over Islam Is Reshaping the World* (New York: St. Martin's Press, 2016).

17 Khaled Abou El Fadl, *The Great Theft: Wresting Islam from the Extremists* (New York: HarperOne, 2005), 150–52.

18 Talal Asad, *Formations of the Secular: Christianity, Islam, Modernity* (Stanford, CA: Stanford University Press, 2003).

their interpretation of *shariat* laws and penalties and are usually ambiguous in their governance programs.

Ironically, Islamists' state-centric vision departs from the more organic way in which Islam had historically affected public space, law, and political views.[19] As Abdullahi Ahmed An-Na`im argues, the Islamists' goal of re-creating the "Islamic state" is profoundly ahistorical; the "Islamic state" is actually a "post-colonial innovation based on a European model of the state," not an institution dating to the seventh century.[20]

Islamists are moving actors, and the phenomenon of Islamism has become highly variegated over the past century. Static terms to describe the broad range of Islamists are problematic, so we must use any designation with care. I employ the terms "radical/extreme" and "moderate/mainstream" analytically to capture the variation and describe the spectrum of Islamists. Using such terms does not endorse abuses in the name of counterextremism—all too common in Central Asia. Rather, as in a long-standing literature on communist movements and the growing literature on "right-wing radicalism" and "extremism" in the West, these terms describe a set of totalizing, exclusivist, and sometimes violent ideas and movements. Islamist movements or ideas that I describe as "radical" occupy one "extreme" end of the spectrum; they are not merely illiberal but are antisystemic and revolutionary in their endgame, the forced adoption of an exclusivist and often puritanical interpretation of *shariat* for the state. HTI, for example, has a radical vision of the caliphate, rejects all democratic law and elections, and holds extreme views about other religions, as is evident in its anti-Semitic propaganda.

Radical Islamist ideas have sometimes been influenced by Salafism or Deobandism, two Sunni "revivalist" movements that claim a monopoly on truth. They follow ultraconservative, puritanical practices, which they claim were practiced in seventh-century Arabia by the Salaf (the pious forebears, or companions and early followers of the Prophet).[21] Their ideas are typically intolerant of the rights, and even the lives, of minority religions (Christians, Jews, converts, and atheists), which they deem to be *kuffar* (infidels) or apostates. They reject any alternative interpretations or practices of Islam as *shirk* (polytheism). Radicals want to enforce women's purity and morality through strict forms of dress and limitations on their rights. Radicals often seek to enforce the *hudud* laws and penalties to use fear to maintain a pure society.[22]

[19] Asma Afsaruddin, "The Islamic State: Genealogy, Facts, Myth," *Journal of Church and State* 48, no. 1 (2006): 153–73; Noah Feldman, *The Rise and Fall of the Islamic State* (Princeton, NJ: Princeton University Press, 2008); Hallaq, *Introduction to Islamic Law*, 60–63.

[20] Abdullahi Ahmed An-Na`im, *Islam and the Secular State: Negotiating the Future of Shari'a* (Cambridge, MA: Harvard University Press, 2008).

[21] Abou El Fadl, *The Great Theft*, 45–94; Roel Meijer, ed., *Global Salafism: Islam's New Religious Movement* (London: Hurst, 2009).

[22] Abou El Fadl, *The Great Theft*, 194–95.

Only some radicals engage in violence. They reject mainstream Muslim understandings of jihad, an Islamic concept that means "striving in the path of God." Mainstream Muslims emphasize the "greater" (inner, spiritual struggle) over the "lesser" (militant) jihad, and justify the latter primarily in self-defense, according to centuries of Islamic doctrine. By contrast, some radical Islamists embrace and glorify an explicitly militant interpretation of jihad. They employ violence, terrorism, and even suicide bombing.[23] One of the most widely discussed forms of radical militant Islamism in the past fifty years has been Salafi jihadism, an ideology rooted in the extensive writings of Muslim Brother Sayyid Qutb. Qutb elaborated a theological justification of violence, claiming that jihad is a *fard al-Ayn*, an individual duty to wage militant jihad to defend the faith through armed struggle.[24] Qutb's ultimate goal was the abolition of *jahiliyya*, a term referring to the pre-Islamic age of ignorance, with which he equated modern society and the secular state. Through jihad, which he argued was a far broader duty than defensive war, Qutb envisioned the establishment of *hakimiyya*, true Islamic government or Allah's sovereignty on earth.[25] This idea evolved over time, carried on by extremely violent offshoots of the Muslim Brotherhood, even as their parent movement rejected the idea.[26] Salafi jihadism became a transnational ideology and movement in the 1980s during the Soviet-Afghan War. In calling all Muslims to fight in Afghanistan, the Palestinian Islamic scholar-activist Abdallah Azzam expanded on Qutb and "elaborated a modern Islamic legal argument for foreign fighting as an individual religious duty."[27] Transnational Salafi jihadism has characterized many groups—from al-Qaeda to ISIS—and has strongly influenced their followers.[28] In Central Asia, these include the IMU, the Islamic Jihad Union (IJU), Katibat al-Tawhid wal Jihad (KTJ), and ISIS-Khorasan Province, among others discussed in this book. Through revolutionary transnational jihad they have aimed to impose a radically puritanical understanding of *shariat* and a totalizing Islamic state or caliphate.

[23] Michael Bonner, *Jihad in Islamic History* (Princeton, NJ: Princeton University Press, 2008), 3–7; David Cook, *Understanding Jihad* (Berkeley: University of California Press, 2015).

[24] Sayyid Qutb, *Milestones* (New Delhi: Islamic Book Services, 2002), 53–76; Fawaz Gerges, *Making the Arab World: Nasser, Qutb, and the Clash That Shaped the Middle East* (Princeton, NJ: Princeton University Press, 2018), 250–51.

[25] Gerges, *Making the Arab World*, 245–48.

[26] Marc Lynch, "Islam Divided Between Salafi-jihad and the Ikhwan," *Studies in Conflict & Terrorism*, 33, no. 6 (2010): 467–87.

[27] Thomas Hegghammer, *The Caravan: Abdallah Azzam and the Rise of Global Jihad* (Cambridge: Cambridge University Press, 2020), 499.

[28] Shiraz Maher, *Salafi-Jihadism: The History of an Idea* (Oxford: Oxford University Press, 2016); Hegghammer, *The Caravan*, 474–78; Assaf Moghadam, "Motives for Martyrdom: Al-Qaida, Salafi Jihad, and the Spread of Suicide Attacks," *International Security* 33, no. 3 (2008): 46–78; Assaf Moghadam, *The Globalization of Martyrdom: Al Qaeda, Salafi Jihad, and the Diffusion of Suicide Attacks* (Baltimore, MD: Johns Hopkins University Press, 2008).

The majority of Islamists are often referred to as "moderate," in contrast to the extremists, but they might better be considered "mainstream."[29] Mainstream Islamists are a broad and heterogeneous group, but in recent decades they have typically proven willing to work within the existing national political system. They accept some democratic rules of the game and do not demand a total Islamic state, but they still oppose secularism and a secular political order. Some of them formerly envisioned more extreme ideological ends, and have moderated on certain issues over time. Whether they genuinely envision or just pragmatically accept the partial implementation of *shariat* varies across groups, and often remains unknown.[30] Mainstream Islamists do typically hold certain illiberal ideas about marriage, women, religious minorities, sexual behavior, and blasphemy, but mainstream Islamists strictly condition the application of the harsh *hudud* punishments or argue that they were not meant to be applied because evidentiary standards are impossible to meet.[31]

In contrast to radicals, mainstream Islamists endorse gradual, peaceful methods of Islamizing society and law. They work through proselytization, education, elections, and parliament. They eschew violence as necessary except in self-defense, and reject the idea of an individual duty to wage militant jihad at home or abroad. They generally condemn terrorism and suicide terrorism.[32]

Finally, Islamists' ideologies and strategies often vary over time, making it necessary to recognize that these labels are at best conceptual tools. For example, both the IRPT and Tunisia's Ennahda Party now identify as Muslim democratic parties that fully accept a secular democratic state, whereas most mainstream Islamists reject secular democracy.

Muslim Politics and Civil Islam

Distinct from political Islam or Islamism are two other concepts that I use to discuss alternatives to Islamism: *Muslim politics* and *civil Islam*. I use the former concept broadly to characterize the use of Muslim symbols and rhetoric in politics and also to define some Muslim organizations or movements that play an activist and political role; however, Muslim politics as such, following Dale

[29] Hamid and McCants, *Rethinking Political Islam*, 2–3.

[30] Moderation theory mistakenly assumes a unidirectional process of "moderation" along multiple dimensions of the ideology and strategy. See Carrie Rosefsky Wickham, *The Muslim Brotherhood: Evolution of an Islamist Movement* (Princeton, NJ: Princeton University Press, 2013); Jilian Schwedler, *Faith in Moderation: Islamist Parties in Jordan and Yemen* (Cambridge: Cambridge University Press, 2006).

[31] Abou El Fadl, *The Great Theft*, 194–95; Shadi Hamid, *Temptations of Power: Islamists and Illiberal Democracy in a New Middle East* (Oxford: Oxford University Press, 2014).

[32] Lynch, "Islam Divided Between Salafi-jihad and the Ikhwan."

Eickelman and James Piscatori, excludes Islamist movements that seek state control.[33] In Muslim politics—much as in the United States, where Christianity is not strictly separated from the public or political sphere—individuals and social or political actors bring Muslim beliefs, values, and identity into the public discourse and political realm.[34] Islam at least in part shapes political preferences and goals. These actors and this discourse may be illiberal, but they do not necessarily constitute Islamism.

I demonstrate the growth of Muslim politics of multiple forms during and for several years after the Russian Revolution. We again see varieties of Muslim politics emerge in Kyrgyzstan in relatively liberal periods since 1991, as an array of Muslim actors, from the *mufti* (chief Muslim legal expert) to Muslim aid organizations, debated political issues or sought to influence the public sphere. By contrast, in Uzbekistan and Tajikistan for most of the Soviet and post-Soviet periods, such discourse has been banned.

Relatedly, this work explores the growth of *civil Islam,* a concept that captures a phenomenon that sharply contrasts with Islamism. Building upon Robert Hefner's foundational work, I define civil Islam as an array of Muslim social organizations, associations, formal and informal networks, and behavior that occupies the communal space outside the state and does not seek to control but rather to influence the state through employing a discourse of Muslim politics.[35] Civil Islam is neither theocratic nor necessarily liberal. As Hefner writes, civil Islam seeks "to imbricate Islamic values and practices with those of a democratic and religiously undifferentiated citizenship. Muslim actors aspire to do so in an effort to ensure that democratic institutions are accorded religious legitimacy and are vernacularized and strengthened through their enculturation with Islamic religiosity. In attempting this synthesis, the proponents of civil Islam promote the co-construction of Islamic and democratic values."[36]

Such civil Muslim organizations have thrived in Kyrgyzstan since independence, and they are beginning to emerge in Uzbekistan. They often provide benefits for society, such as education or the defense of Muslim rights. They sometimes engage in the discourse of Muslim politics rather than overt political contestation for power. Like Islamism, civil Islam is also varied. As we shall see, these actors and discourses may be tolerant, pluralist, and democratic in some respects; however, Muslim civil organizations and associational life may also be

[33] Dale Eickelman and James Piscatori, *Muslim Politics* (Princeton, NJ: Princeton University Press, 2004).

[34] Geoffrey Layman, *The Great Divide: Religious and Cultural Conflict in American Party Politics* (New York: Columbia University Press, 2001).

[35] Robert Hefner, *Civil Islam: Muslims and Democratization in Indonesia* (Princeton, NJ: Princeton University Press, 2000).

[36] Robert Hefner, "Whatever Happened to Civil Islam? Islam and Democratization in Indonesia 20 Years On," *Asian Studies Review* 43, no. 3 (2019): 380.

deeply illiberal, conservative, and even seek to limit individual rights within a democracy as they promote a religious form of democracy.[37] Civil Islam, an alternative to Islamism, is likely to emerge when Islam is relatively free from repression; in such conditions, Islamists fail to gain ground.

Why Central Asia?

Studies of Islamism have largely ignored Soviet and post-Soviet Central Asia for three reasons: because scholars of Islam and politics long saw the USSR as peripheral to the Muslim world, because extremely oppressive security services have made this region tremendously challenging to study, and because of a general perception that the USSR had successfully secularized the population. As bastions of secular authoritarianism almost wholly cut off from the rest of the Muslim world for seven decades, the former Soviet republics seemed the least likely cases in which to find the emergence and mobilization of an Islamist opposition. Explaining why and how such mobilization has nonetheless taken place is consequently of theoretical and historical importance because it demonstrates the resilience and potential trajectory of religion politicized through repression.

This book is a comparative case study that explores Tajikistan, Uzbekistan, and Kyrgyzstan over the longue durée, from the Russian Revolution and founding of the Soviet Union through the post-Soviet present day. I examine high Muslim mobilization from the revolutionary years and the early Bolshevik government (1917–1926), then total demobilization under high Stalinism. In the post-Stalinist era, I trace the germination and emergence of Islamist movements across the Soviet republics, as well as the rise of new post-Soviet movements. Table I.1 displays the country cases and the emergence or nonemergence of Islamism, details all major Islamist organizations, movements, and parties, and notes each period of Islamist emergence and mobilization.

A comparative study of these cases controls for many potential causal factors, such as similar Soviet and post-Soviet economic and social conditions and the absence of Western colonialism, cultural Westernization, and economic liberalism—factors often seen as generating Islamism in the Middle East. These cases share a relatively similar cultural context, characterized by the integration of Hanafi Islam with strong Sufi traditions, upon which was imposed seven decades of Soviet atheist modernization. However, these cases exhibit distinct trajectories. Islamist movements emerged earliest and strongest in Tajikistan

[37] Jocelyne Cesari, *The Awakening of Muslim Democracy: Religion, Modernity and the State* (Cambridge: Cambridge University Press, 2014); Jeremy Menchik, *Islam and Democracy in Indonesia: Tolerance without Liberalism* (Cambridge: Cambridge University Press, 2016).

and continued through three successive waves; in Kyrgyzstan, weaker Islamist movements emerged only in the 2000s; in Uzbekistan, early emergence was crushed, but Islamism reemerged in stronger second and third waves. Within each country, I find that a particular subnational region or regions became the heart of Islamist movements. Thus, at both the national and subnational level, I trace the conditions and process leading to Islamist emergence and I highlight variation across and within the country case studies and over time. This variation is associated with three critical factors: differing implementation of Soviet antireligious policy and distinctly different post-Soviet religious repression, varying levels of associational space, and varying exposure to Islamist ideas.

In addition to national and subnational comparisons that isolate the causes of Islamist emergence and mobilization, I compare the relative success of the multiple Islamist movements that emerged. Table I.2 organizes basic information describing each specific Islamist group (location and origins, national or transnational agenda, and ethnic basis) that emerged and mobilized in the first, second, and third waves. The table also includes the Islamist groups' relative levels of mobilization—the second outcome this book seeks to explain. Excepting the IRPT, most groups have never achieved high mobilization, despite having a sizable impact on politics in some of these countries.

Bringing in Society: Field Methods and Data

In my narrative, I draw on multiple types of sources, including extensive primary sources from published archives and original data from years of fieldwork. Thousands of pages of Soviet Communist Party and secret police archival materials document repression and resistance. I used oral histories to reveal the persistence of religious belief, practice, and networks, and the emergence of Islamist ideas from the Brezhnev to the Gorbachev years. The research for this book took me on many extended trips to Tajikistan, Uzbekistan, and Kyrgyzstan, as well as to Russia, Azerbaijan, and Turkey, between 2004 and 2019. My fieldwork encompassed both participant observation and 378 open-ended interviews to understand the process and mechanisms by which Islamist organizations emerge and mobilize. My interviews with religious and political actors—including Islamist leaders and activists, Islamic NGOs, state and nonstate imams and religious teachers, government officials, and secular party leaders—aimed to explore the ideas and motivations of the Islamist opposition and the state. These methods help to uncover the identity and meaning of Islamists' ideas and agendas. Additionally, I studied Islamist websites, their print and digital literature, books sold at mainstream and opposition mosques, and more than 150 propaganda videos by their leaders and figures of sacred authority. Online

Table I.2 Islamist Organizations, their Characteristics, and Relative Level of Mass Mobilization, 1990–2022

Islamist Organizations	Location (Origins, If Different)	National or Transnational	Ethnic Basis[a]	Relative Level of Mass Mobilization (Noting Change over Time)[b]
IRPT	Tajikistan	National	Tajik	High (1990–1997); low (1997 to early 2000s); moderate (mid-2000s to 2015)[c]
IRPU Adolat, Tavba, IL[d]	Uzbekistan	National	Uzbek	Moderate (1990 to mid-1992)
IMU	Afghanistan, Pakistan (Uzbekistan)	National, then transnational	Uzbek + Tajik	Moderate (1998–2015); low (2016–2022)[c]
IJU	Afghanistan (Uzbekistan)	Transnational	Uzbek + Chechen, German, Turkish	Low (2004–)[c]
HTI	Kyrgyzstan, Uzbekistan, Tajikistan (Palestine)	Transnational	Kyrgyz, Uzbek, Tajik	Moderate then low in Uzbekistan/Tajikistan (late 1990s–2000s); low then moderate in Kyrgyzstan (2000s–2022)[c]
JA	Afghanistan (Tajikistan)	National, then transnational	Tajik	Low (mid 2000s–2022)[c]
KIB	Syria (mostly Uzbekistan, Afghanistan)	Transnational	Uzbek + Kyrgyz, Uyghur	Low to moderate (2013–2022)[c]
KTJ	Syria (mostly Kyrgyzstan and Uzbekistan)	Transnational	Uzbek + Kyrgyz, Uyghur	Low to moderate (2013–2022)[c]
CA—ISIS; ISIS-K	Syria (originating mostly in Tajikistan, Uzbekistan, Kyrgyzstan); Afghanistan	Transnational	Tajik, Uzbek, Kyrgyz + Kazakh, Turkmen	Low to moderate (2013–2022)[c]

[a] Ethnic basis denotes the main ethnic composition of the group plus ethnic minority members.

[b] Relative level of mobilization is a qualitative assessment that takes into account membership, activism, and durability. Mobilization level varies over time. Years in parentheses denote periods corresponding to high, moderate, and low mobilization. Membership numbers are debated and are discussed in the case chapters.

[c] End dates are uncertain. The IRPT was presumed to be largely defunct as of late 2015, although its top leader was active abroad and members may simply be underground or may have joined other organizations. The IMU, IJU, JA, KIB, KTJ, ISIS, and ISIS-K had declined but were still operating in early 2022.

[d] These groups were loosely related in one movement in Uzbekistan in 1990–1992.

activism has spread Islamist ideas around the globe and has contributed to the proliferation of Islamist foreign fighters in Syria and Iraq.

Most studies of Islamist movements pay minimal attention to ordinary Muslims. Because I sought to capture a societal perspective on Islamic belief and practice, sacred authority, and the ideas and messages of various Islamist groups, my local research teams and I carried out seventy-nine focus groups with ordinary Uzbek, Kyrgyz, and Tajik citizens throughout each country. We also conducted 154 semi-structured interviews with religious leaders (imams, mullahs, and *otinchas*—female religious teachers), village or neighborhood leaders and elders (*oqsoqols*, *aksakals*), prominent local businessmen and notables, party members, regional government bureaucrats, and regionally based journalists. I designed, and my research team conducted, two original national surveys in Kyrgyzstan in 2006 and 2010; these data supplement and reinforce my qualitative findings. Finally, I incorporated the knowledge of local experts in each country.

My fieldwork offers insight and nuance to the sharply polarized debate between perspectives that see violent Islamism as inevitable and theories that dismiss Islam's role and meaning in politics. Islamist movements are not inevitable, but due to Soviet and post-Soviet policies and the power of Islamist ideas, such movements have emerged to challenge unjust governments and must be taken seriously.

Overview of the Book

The book proceeds in several parts. Part I develops my arguments and analytical framework, laying out more explicitly the elements of an ideational approach to religion and politics, and then the process through which Islamist groups emerge, mobilize, and draw a following.

Part II examines Soviet Central Asia, the critical historical and institutional context of this book. During the twentieth century, the Communist Party of the Soviet Union laid the foundations of Islamist opposition through its antireligious policies. Chapter 2 shows that from 1917 to 1926 the onset of atheism and religious repression, together with competing Muslim ideas about Islam's proper role, triggered the emergence of multiple forms of Muslim mobilization. Chapter 3 examines the impact of Soviet persecution of Islam from 1927 through 1943; the *hujum* (assault) decimated Islam, yet beginning in the 1940s incremental increases in associational space allowed Islam to persist. Islamic teachers released from the Gulag formed underground study circles to pass on belief and knowledge. These religious activists would ultimately give rise to Islamist entrepreneurs, discussed in later chapters. Chapter 4 examines

Central Asian society during the later Soviet era. My oral histories and focus groups reveal that ordinary people engaged in "everyday" religious resistance.[38] An unintended consequence of the Soviet Union's antireligious policy was the politicization of Islam, particularly for those deemed more religious because of their attempt to preserve religious study. Part II thus describes the conditions—state repression and politicization of Islamic identity, alongside growing associational space to disseminate Islamist ideas—that fostered the emergence of Islamist entrepreneurs.

Parts III through V develop three case studies of Soviet republics/post-Soviet states: Tajikistan, Uzbekistan, and Kyrgyzstan. In each case study, I investigate several waves of Islamism. Part III develops the case of highest Islamist mobilization—Tajikistan—over nearly fifty years. Chapter 5 traces the emergence of a first wave of Islamism, with the Nahzat-i Islami in the Tajik republic during the 1970s. I explain its transformation into the IRPT during *perestroika*, and then its mobilization against the communist regime and its role in the five-year civil war that killed 50,000 to 100,000 people. In Chapter 6, I explain the second wave of Islamism in Tajikistan. This wave entailed the rebirth of the postwar IRPT, which became a legal party until President Imomali Rahmon's regime banned it in 2015. Chapter 6 also explains the emergence of more radical and violent Tajik Islamists in the postwar era. Chapter 7 uses my focus groups and interviews with communal leaders to make the case that most Tajiks were overwhelmingly religious but not radical. Many supported the IRPT in the 2000s because of its call for Muslim religious freedom, justice, and national Islamic revival through nonviolent means.

Part IV turns to the Uzbek case, one of less widespread but long-lasting Islamist mobilization. Chapter 8 explains why and how an Islamist movement emerged; Islamists formed in opposition to communism and atheist repression, inspired by Salafist imams, radical ideas of an Islamic state, and the Afghan jihad. Chapter 9 explains how Karimov's brutal repression of independent Islam in the 1990s led to a second Islamist wave, including the IMU and IJU. These groups, formed by Uzbek exiles in Afghanistan, were influenced by the Salafi jihadist ideology of al-Qaeda and the militant Deobandi ideology of the Taliban. After 9/11, these Islamists became a threat to both U.S. interests and the Afghan government. In Chapter 10, I again turn to society, drawing on dozens of focus groups and interviews with communal leaders in Uzbekistan. Radical Islamist ideas have not

[38] James C. Scott, *Weapons of the Weak: Everyday Forms of Peasant Resistance* (New Haven, CT: Yale University Press, 1985).

resonated, but grievances about religious repression, injustice, and corruption remain powerful.

Part V explores the case of Kyrgyzstan, where Islamism was slow to emerge. Chapter 11 demonstrates that religious liberalization precluded the birth of an Islamist movement in the 1990s; instead, ordinary Muslim politics and civil Islam developed. Chapter 12 explores the shift in Kyrgyzstan from 2005 to 2020, as the country's political and religious environment gradually became more repressive and Islamist ideas were disseminated throughout the Ferghana Valley, particularly through HTI. In Chapter 13, focus groups and interviews show that the majority of Kyrgyzstanis opposed radical Islamism, but where religious repression and exclusion increased by the mid-2000s some respondents were open to Islamist ideas.

In Part VI, Chapter 14 examines the surprising rise of the foreign fighter movement, the exodus of Central Asians to Syria and Iraq. This movement's root causes are similar to those of earlier waves of Islamism: secular states' unjust repression of Muslims and the diffusion of Salafi jihadist ideology by radical entrepreneurs, this time through online associational space. The ideas of ISIS and al-Qaeda–linked foreign fighter groups in Syria did not resonate with most Central Asians. Nonetheless, these groups strategically used social media to amplify anger about injustice, enhance their sacred authority, and develop networks that enabled them to mobilize thousands of fighters. Chapter 15 considers cases beyond Central Asia and trends in the wake of the Taliban's victory in Afghanistan.

Islamism is varied and complex, and the process of Islamist mobilization in Central Asia, as elsewhere, is embedded in the region's historical and political context. Studying these successive waves of Islamism—from their roots in the USSR to contemporary Tajikistan, Uzbekistan, and Kyrgyzstan—reveals that religious repression and the idea that Islam will bring political justice continually interact to generate Islamist movements. Most Central Asians merely seek the right to believe and practice their faith under a just state—not militant jihad or a caliphate. Yet decades of state repression, injustice, and the shuttering of Islam from the political sphere have bred and continue to breed radicalization. Radicalization in turn has triggered a cycle of contention and violence that not only risks political destabilization but continues to have tragic consequences for ordinary Muslims merely professing their faith.

Studying Central Asia provides novel insights into why Islamists sometimes emerge and mobilize and why the majority of Muslims reject radical and violent forms of Islamism. A better understanding of Islamism's root causes and dynamics over time is crucial for the policy community, scholars, and the general public, all of whom still struggle to address the instability and conflict associated with some variants of Islamism in Central Asia, Afghanistan, Syria, and, increasingly, the West. Finally, a more realistic understanding of Islamism's forms and trajectories and of many Muslims' desires to integrate Islam and democracy is essential to improving the lives of Central Asians themselves.

1
Secular Authoritarianism, Ideology, and Islamist Mobilization

I wasn't a radical, but now, sure, I'll take up a Kalashnikov.
—Abdulaziz, Uzbekistan, 2003

A number of years ago, an Uzbek friend recounted an incident that was unfortunately too commonplace in President Islom Karimov's Uzbekistan. The police stopped an acquaintance from his neighborhood, a young man in his twenties—I will call him Abdulaziz. They questioned him because he had been attending religious lessons in someone's home. Private study of the Qur'an had been banned. The police warned him that such "meetings" were illegal. So too was his religious clothing, which they mocked. They approached him again a few days later. This time, they threatened to arrest him and rape his wife for the crime of wearing an "extremist hijab" if he did not pay them $5,000. He knew the money would go "v karman" (into their pocket), and he had no such money. In desperation, he borrowed from relatives and friends to pay them off. The police left him alone after collecting the bribe, but Abdulaziz was enraged. He declared, "I wasn't a radical, but now, sure, I'll take up a Kalashnikov."[1] Those may have just been hotheaded words, but his experience motivated him to sympathize with, if not join, Islamist groups claiming to rectify such religious repression and injustice.

As I would learn, Abdulaziz's experience was not isolated. An Uzbek journalist accompanied me through the forlorn streets of several Ferghana Valley towns, which were among the hardest hit by both Soviet and post-Soviet government assaults on Islam. She explained, "These men are very angry, and they are not afraid. Even their children want violence."[2] An Uzbek friend explained the situation this way: "You are not free to be Muslim in Uzbekistan. There is no freedom. Uzbekistan is a prison for thirty million people."[3]

This chapter explains the causes of Islamist emergence and mobilization in Central Asia, and it explains the role of religion in that process. Taking the

[1] Personal communication with Uzbek informant, August 2014.
[2] Interview with journalist, Ferghana Valley, Uzbekistan, n.d.
[3] Personal communication, Tashkent, Uzbekistan, n.d.

Politicizing Islam in Central Asia. Kathleen Collins, Oxford University Press. © Oxford University Press 2023.
DOI: 10.1093/oso/9780197685068.003.0002

potential political role of Islam seriously is not to assume that being Muslim or pious determines support for Islamism. For many, Islam is only about piety, practices, and traditions, but for a growing number, Islam has had political implications. Across the Muslim world, from Egypt to the Caucasus, Pakistan, Afghanistan, and Central Asia, Islamist mobilization became a prominent form of opposition politics during the twentieth century. The entrepreneurs and ideology of Islamism gave birth to Islamist groups, movements, and parties that sought to fuse Islam and the modern state in various ways. The result has been the emergence of multiple forms of political Islam in Central Asia, from the illiberal but democratic IRPT (in the 2000s) and the nonviolent but antisystemic party HTI to the militant jihadists of the IMU, KTJ, and ISIS. How and why did Muslim belief and identity become politicized in Central Asia, and under what conditions have Islamist oppositions emerged and mobilized a following? Of the many Islamist groups that formed, why are some more successful than others at gaining support and sustaining themselves over time?

In this chapter, I first develop the book's argument about the causes of Islamist emergence and mobilization in Central Asia. Fundamental to that process is the repression of Islam that Abdulaziz experienced, particularly when mixed with the diffusion of religio-political ideologies—whether of the Muslim Brotherhood, the Jamaat i-Islami, the Taliban, al-Qaeda, or ISIS. I further contend that several strategic factors affect the relative level of mass social support for Islamist movements—building sacred authority, constructing networks of mobilization, and adapting ideologies to local grievances.

However, I begin by addressing the limitation of existing theories about Islamism, and I explain why and how we need to bring religion, carefully, into the study of Islamism.

Alternative Approaches to Studying Islamist Movements

For decades, numerous theories have purported to explain Islamist mobilization. The Orientalist worldview, once prevalent in scholarship, still holds sway in the media and policy circles. Orientalism presumed the theocratic nature of Islam and argued that Islam was uniform, unchanging, inherently political, and both antimodern and antidemocratic.[4] It portrayed Islamic societies and states as invariably caliphate-centered and driven to violent promulgation of the faith.[5] Orientalist scholarship on Central Asia anticipated, incorrectly, that

[4] Ernest Gellner, *Muslim Society* (Cambridge: Cambridge University Press, 1983); Elie Kedourie, *Democracy and Arab Political Culture* (London: Frank Cass, 1984).

[5] Bernard Lewis, *The Crisis of Islam: Holy War and Unholy Terror* (New York: Random House, 2004), 21–22.

"fundamentalist" Islam would bring down Soviet power.[6] In the post-Soviet era, many scholars and journalists advocated similarly deterministic arguments about Islam's inherently radical and anti-Western nature.[7] Samuel Huntington boldly asserted that Islam is a "civilization" inevitably in a "clash" with Western values and democracy.[8] Huntington's theory resonated widely, from Washington to Uzbekistan and Russia. The rise of al-Qaeda and the attacks on 9/11 solidified the West's narrow focus on militant jihadist Islamism.[9] The subsequent failure of the Arab Spring to bring democracy and the stunning emergence and extreme brutality of ISIS revived public and policymaker convictions about a transnational, violent Muslim agenda to reestablish a premodern caliphate.

Among scholars, Edward Said's trenchant critique of Orientalism led to a radical rethinking of the nature of Islam and its relation to politics.[10] Orientalism, in both its earlier and its more recent forms, ignores the underlying causes of Islamism and the significant variation in when and where it emerges, as well as variation in the extent to which Islamists attract a following. Islam does not inevitably breed Islamism, much less violent Islamism, as subsequent chapters will demonstrate.

Other explanations of Islamism, by contrast, attribute little if any role to Islam. From Enlightenment thought to Marxism and Leninist ideology and contemporary Western social science, most scholars have treated religion as something irrational, a relic of the past, eventually to be overcome by development. Modernization theory, for example, long expected religiosity and belief to decline and lose any political relevance in economically advancing societies, explaining religious durability as a response to socioeconomic insecurity.[11] Olivier Roy and Gilles Kepel, among others, prominently situated Islamism as the consequence of socioeconomic grievances of a young, urban, educated, but economically frustrated underclass, a "lumpen proletariat."[12] Cihan Tuğal has emphasized the effects of neoliberal economic policies.[13] Kristen Ghodsee has argued that

[6] Alexandre Bennigsen and Marie Broxup, *The Islamic Threat to the Soviet State* (New York: Routledge, 1983).

[7] Aleksei Malashenko, *Islamskoe vozrozhdenie v sovremennoi Rossii* (Moscow: Moscow Carnegie Center, 1998), 200; Boris Rumer, *Central Asia: A Gathering Storm* (London: Routledge, 2002); Aleksander Ignatenko, "Epistemologiia islamskogo radikalizma," in *Religiia i globalizatsiia na prostorakh Evrazii*, ed. A. Malashenko and S. Filatov (Moscow: Moscow Center Carnegie, 2009), 176–221; A. Malashenko and L. Polonskaia, *Islam in Central Asia* (Reading, UK: Ithaca Press, 1994).

[8] Samuel Huntington, *The Clash of Civilizations and the Remaking of World Order* (New York: Simon & Schuster, 1996), 121.

[9] Ahmed Rashid, *Jihad: The Rise of Militant Islam in Central Asia* (New Haven, CT: Yale University Press, 2002).

[10] Edward Said, *Orientalism* (New York: Vintage Books, 1979).

[11] Ronald Inglehart and Pippa Norris, *Sacred and Secular: Religion and Politics Worldwide* (New York: Cambridge University Press, 2004).

[12] Olivier Roy, *The Failure of Political Islam* (Cambridge, MA: Harvard University Press, 1994); Kepel, *Jihad*.

[13] Cihan Tuğal, *Passive Revolution: Absorbing the Islamic Challenge to Capitalism* (Palo Alto, CA: Stanford University Press, 2009).

acceptance of the new "Arab" Islam is a postsocialist response to "capitalism, consumerism, and exploitative relations of production."[14]

Historians and Middle Easternists have emphasized the complex historical and social context of Islamism, but they too have downplayed the role of religion. Some have explained Islamism as a response to Western colonialism; others emphasize U.S. support of Israel and the U.S. invasions of Iraq and Afghanistan.[15] While these factors are central to Islamism in the Middle East, they are peripheral to Islamism's birth in Soviet Central Asia.

Rational choice theorists have generally argued that economic conditions, self-interest, and resources—not religion, religious identity, or religious ideas—drive political behavior, whether voting for Islamist parties, joining Islamist movements, or engaging in suicide terrorism.[16] To the extent that religion matters, this approach argues that it does so because religious institutions pursue social or political power and their own self-interested survival.[17] Such works commendably treat Muslim voters as rational. They recognize that the Muslim Brotherhood, Ayatollah Khomeini, and Osama Bin Laden are not irrational fanatics. They recognize the role of agency and possibilities for change in the Muslim world. Yet, the prevailing rational choice theories in political science fail to explain why people engage in high-risk activism, which may be detrimental to their own economic, or even physical, security. However, recent work by Timur Kuran has challenged scholars to integrate Islamic culture and institutions into our explanations by demonstrating how Islam has shaped economic development throughout Middle Eastern history.[18]

Nonetheless, existing scholarship does not explain why some political oppositions have adopted specifically *Islamist* ideas instead of nationalist, fascist, or liberal democratic ideas. Why have the strongest opposition groups

[14] Kristen Ghodsee, *Muslim Lives in Eastern Europe: Gender, Ethnicity, and the Transformation of Islam in Postsocialist Bulgaria* (Princeton, NJ: Princeton University Press), 33.

[15] Juan Cole, *Engaging the Muslim World* (New York: St. Martin's Press, 2009), 50; Said, *Orientalism*; Esposito, *The Islamic Threat*; Nikki Keddie, *Modern Iran: Roots and Results of Revolution* (New Haven, CT: Yale University Press, 2006).

[16] Robert Pape, *Dying to Win: The Strategic Logic of Suicide Terrorism* (New York: Random House, 2005); Lisa Blaydes and Drew Linzer, "The Political Economy of Women's Support for Fundamentalist Islam," *World Politics* 60, no. 4 (July 2008): 576–609; Eli Berman and David D. Laitin, "Religion, Terrorism and Public Goods: Testing the Club Model," *Journal of Public Economics* 92, nos. 10–11 (October 2008): 1942–67; Thomas B. Pepinsky, R. William Liddle, and Saiful Mujani, *Piety and Public Opinion: Understanding Indonesian Islam* (Oxford: Oxford University Press, 2018); Aisha Ahmad, *Jihad & Co.: Black Markets and Islamist Power* (Oxford: Oxford University Press, 2017); Mark Tessler, *The Origins of Popular Support for Islamist Movements: A Political Economy Analysis*, Issue 93, Part 4 of Occasional Papers (Milwaukee, WI: Center for International Studies, University of Wisconsin–Milwaukee and Marquette University, 1993); Tarek E. Masoud, *Counting Islam: Religion, Class, and Elections in Egypt* (Cambridge: Cambridge University Press, 2014).

[17] Anthony Gill, *Rendering unto Caesar: The Catholic Church and the State in Latin America* (Chicago, IL: University of Chicago Press, 1998).

[18] Timur Kuran, "Islam and Economic Performance: Historical and Contemporary Links," *Journal of Economic Literature* 56, no. 4 (2018): 1292–359.

in Tajikistan and Uzbekistan, as in Egypt and Afghanistan, distributed religiously grounded texts rather than Václav Havel's *Power of the Powerless,* which influenced the democratic opposition in Eastern Europe in the 1980s? Why do these groups use Islamic ideas, literature, symbols, historical precedents, and rhetoric to legitimize and sanctify the types of political institutions or laws that they seek to establish? Why do Islamists assert religious claims and justifications, usually with a commitment to a long-term time horizon? Political science struggles to answer these questions.

Historians and anthropologists of Central Asia offer a deeper examination of Islam and Islamism in Central Asia, but their arguments suggest contrasting hypotheses about the legacy of the Soviet effect and the role of Islamic identity in Central Asia today. Several studies have revealed the brutality of the USSR's campaigns against Islam. Shoshana Keller's work on the Leninist and Stalinist eras has demonstrated that the eradication of religion was central to Soviet ideology and policy.[19] Gregory Massell and Douglas Northrop have revealed the devastating effects of Soviet social engineering in Central Asia, while Marianne Kamp has countered that many Uzbek women joined the Party's revolutionary effort.[20] Adeeb Khalid's groundbreaking study of Uzbekistan's formation has uncovered the complexity of Central Asian responses to Soviet rule and the power of Jadidist ideas in shaping modern Uzbekistan.[21] Scholars of the later Soviet era debate how successful the USSR was in eliminating Islam.[22] Eren Tasar suggests that after World War II, being both "Soviet and Muslim" was not nearly as problematic as scholarship on the Stalinist era suggests.[23] Yet anthropologists have shown us that a significant revival has been underway since about 1990.[24] This

[19] Shoshana Keller, *To Moscow, Not Mecca: The Soviet Campaign against Islam in Central Asia, 1917–1941* (Westport, CT: Praeger, 2001).

[20] Douglas Northrop, *Veiled Empire: Gender and Power in Stalinist Central Asia* (Ithaca, NY: Cornell University Press, 2004); Gregory Massell, *Surrogate Proletariat: Muslim Women and Revolutionary Strategies in Soviet Central Asia, 1919–29* (Princeton, NJ: Princeton University Press, 1974); Marianne Kamp, *The New Woman in Uzbekistan: Islam, Modernity, and Unveiling under Communism* (Seattle: University of Washington Press, 2006).

[21] Adeeb Khalid, *Making Uzbekistan: Nation, Empire, and Revolution in the Early USSR* (Ithaca, NY: Cornell University Press, 2015).

[22] Yaacov Ro'i, *Islam in the Soviet Union: From World War II to Perestroika* (New York: Columbia University Press, 2001).

[23] Eren Murat Tasar, *Soviet and Muslim: The Institutionalization of Islam in Central Asia, 1943–91* (Ithaca, NY: Cornell University Press, 2017).

[24] Mathias Pelkmans and Chris Hann, "Realigning Religion and Power in Central Asia: Islam, Nation-State and (Post)Socialism," *Europe-Asia Studies* 61, no. 9 (October 2009): 1517–41; Johan Rasanayagam, *Islam in Post-Soviet Uzbekistan: The Morality of Experience* (Cambridge: Cambridge University Press, 2010); Maria Louw, *Everyday Islam in Post-Soviet Central Asia* (London: Routledge, 2007); Morgan Y. Liu, *Under Solomon's Throne: Uzbek Visions of Renewal in Osh* (Pittsburgh, PA: University of Pittsburgh Press, 2012); Julie McBrien, *From Belonging to Belief: Modern Secularism and the Construction of Religion in Kyrgyzstan* (Pittsburgh, PA: University of Pittsburgh Press, 2017); Emil Nasritdinov, Zarina Urmanbetova, Kanatbek Murzakhalilov, and Mametbek Myrzabaev, "Vulnerability and Resilience of Young People in Kyrgyzstan to Radicalization, Violence and

study builds on and contributes to these debates, all of which highlight contestation over the role of Islam in Central Asian and Soviet politics.

Khalid's work provides a critical starting point for my claims. Khalid convincingly argues that we must understand Islam and Islamism in a particular historical context. The Soviet period profoundly shaped Central Asia. Soviet Muslims were cut off from the rest of the Muslim world and Soviet policies decimated Islamic learning and institutions. Consequently, "the meaning of being Muslim changed quite radically. . . . Being Muslim came to mean adherence to certain local, cultural norms and traditions rather than adherence to strictures that were directly validated by the learned tradition."[25] Although Khalid is primarily interested in explaining the post-Soviet " 'return' to Islam . . . [as] a way of reclaiming the national cultural patrimony and decolonizing,"[26] and is less concerned with explaining the emergence and trajectories of political Islam, he makes two critical observations. First, Central Asian Islamism is not merely an offshoot of a global Islamist phenomenon. Second, Central Asian Islamist opposition is tied to hatred of the regimes whose largely antireligious views are rooted in the Soviet legacy.[27] Recognizing the importance of regional history compels caution against global explanations of Islamism. Khalid's work also raises a critical question: If Islam became relegated to tradition, then why and how did Islamism become a significant form of political opposition in some republics by 1990, and throughout the post-Soviet era? Moreover, why has the vibrant religious revival underway since the 1990s been so politically contentious?

Bringing Religion into the Study of Islamism

The USSR devoted decades to razing mosques, silencing Islamic leaders, and forcing secularization on the population, but it could not fully transform Central Asia's identity, which was deeply intertwined with Islam. As Aziz, an Uzbek businessman I interviewed, reminded me, "[Uzbeks] were Soviet for seventy years but Muslim for over twelve hundred." Central Asian societies have historically been characterized by the centrality of Islam, which arrived with Arab conquests in the ninth century.[28] Islam spread over the next few centuries through the growth and networking of several Sufi brotherhoods. A rich and dynamic syncretism

Extremism: Analysis across Five Domains," Central Asia Program, Working Paper No. 213, Research Institute for Islamic Studies, Bishkek, Kyrgyzstan, January 2019.

[25] Khalid, *Islam after Communism*, 83.

[26] Khalid, *Islam after Communism*, 158.

[27] Khalid, *Islam after Communism*, 144.

[28] Lapidus, *History of Islamic Societies*; John Voll, *Islam: Continuity and Change in the Modern World* (Syracuse, NY: Syracuse University Press, 1994).

of Hanafi Islam with Sufism also integrated pre-Islamic traditions and customs with regional and local characteristics, from the mountain valleys to the densely populated agricultural center in the Ferghana Valley and the nomadic steppe. Instead of eradicating Islam, the Russian Revolution and the subsequent century of religious oppression across much of Central Asia forced the political role of Islam to change.

Religious Identity and Ideas

In contrast to a substantial body of existing scholarship, this book brings Islam into an explanation of Islamism by drawing on insights from religious studies and a "constructivist" theoretical approach; both emphasize the role of culture, identity, ideas, ideology, and informal institutions in politics. Constructivists have shown that all identities are socially and institutionally constituted by narratives, beliefs, values, and community.[29] So too Islamic identity is neither homogeneous nor unchanging. Although usually assumed at birth and rooted in specific, monotheistic beliefs, Muslim identity is also deeply embedded in intentional practice, which forms one's "habitus" and moral character.[30] Islamic identity is also carried through centuries of traditions and customs, whether among Persians, Uzbeks, or Kazakhs. As Talal Asad has argued, we must understand Islam not as a fixed theology but as a set of evolving "discourses," constituted and reconstituted, and embodied in narratives and lived practices that define a moral system and community.[31] Devin DeWeese has similarly argued that we need to recognize "the richness and complexity of religious life" and practice, "which traditionally trumps 'orthodoxy'" of doctrine.[32] For most, Islam is a "mode of collective belonging" as well as believing.[33]

Across Central Asia, as elsewhere in the Muslim world, Islam comprises identity, practice, and belief, even though it is manifested differently in different regions. For settled Tajiks and Uzbeks, historically, Islam was textually and canonically centered, resulting in more strictly observant practice, whereas for nomadic peoples of the Central Asian steppe, narratives of lineage were central to

[29] Benedict Anderson, *Imagined Communities: Reflections on the Origin and Spread of Nationalism* (London: Verso, 1991); Rogers Brubaker and Frederick Cooper, "Beyond Identity," *Theory and Society* 29, no. 1 (February 2000): 1–47.

[30] Saba Mahmood, *The Politics of Piety: The Islamic Revival and the Feminist Subject* (Berkeley: University of California Press, 2005), 136.

[31] Talal Asad, "An Anthropology of Islam," *Qui Parle* 17, no. 2 (Spring/Summer 2009): 17–20; Talal Asad, *Genealogies of Religion: Discipline and Reasons of Power in Christianity and Islam* (Baltimore, MD: Johns Hopkins University Press, 1993).

[32] Devin DeWeese, "Islam and the Legacy of Sovietology: A Review Essay on Yaacov Ro'i's *Islam in the Soviet Union*," *Journal of Islamic Studies* 13 (2002): 305.

[33] McBrien, *From Belonging to Belief*.

the communal understanding of Islam and identity.[34] For twentieth- and twenty-first-century revivalists, whether urban, rural, or steppe, pious Islamic practices have aimed at creating the ideal "ethical self" by adhering to and demanding others adhere to what they view as orthodoxy and orthopraxy.[35] Challenging other interpretations of Islam and contestation for "authority" in interpreting and enforcing the "correct" Islam has continued.[36]

While piety may be personal in some contexts—that is, without an explicit political agenda—religious belief and piety often have a political effect. Islamic praxis occurs in a particular political context and has particular political implications.[37] Merely attending mosque or wearing the hijab may trigger the state to brand individuals as "bad Muslims" in a secular authoritarian context.[38] Saba Mahmood has argued that under such circumstances, piety *is* political; it has political implications within states that seek to impose secularism, a modern, Western worldview at odds with believers' goals of observance and self-purification.[39] The secular narrative and framework imposed by modern states force the faithful, directly or indirectly, into contention of a regime's political order.

Other strands of religious studies and constructivist theory point to the central role of ideas and ideology in driving politics, asserting that ideas—whether communism, nationalism, liberalism, or Islamism—have political consequences.[40] Religion, as Charles Taylor writes, shapes the values, beliefs, and ideas of the "social imaginary."[41] Many religions designate certain places as sacred and define when violence is legitimate.[42] Religious ideas embody conceptions not only of God and morality but also of society and "justice."[43] As Alfred Stepan has argued,

[34] Devin DeWeese, *Islamization and Native Religion in the Golden Horde: Baba Tükles and Conversion to Islam in Historical and Epic Tradition* (University Park, PA: Pennsylvania State University Press, 1994); Bruce Privratsky, *Muslim Turkistan: Kazak Religion and Collective Memory* (London: Routledge, 2001).

[35] Mahmood, *Politics of Piety*, 25–35; Pierre Bourdieu, *The Logic of Practice* (Palo Alto, CA: Stanford University Press, 1990), 55.

[36] Pierre Bourdieu, "Social Space and Symbolic Power," *Sociological Theory* 7, no. 1 (Spring 1989): 14–25.

[37] Mahmood, *Politics of Piety*.

[38] Rasanayagam, *Islam in Post-Soviet Uzbekistan*; Mahmood Mamdani, *Good Muslim, Bad Muslim* (New York: Pantheon, 2004).

[39] Mahmood, *Politics of Piety*.

[40] James C. Scott, *Seeing Like a State* (New Haven, CT: Yale University Press, 1998); Sheri Berman, *The Primacy of Politics: Social Democracy and the Making of Europe's Twentieth Century* (Cambridge: Cambridge University Press, 2006); Stephen Hanson, *Post-Imperial Democracies* (Cambridge: Cambridge University Press, 2010); A. James McAdams, *Vanguard of the Revolution* (Princeton, NJ: Princeton University Press, 2017).

[41] Charles Taylor, *Modern Social Imaginaries* (Durham, NC: Duke University Press, 2003), 194.

[42] Bruce Lincoln, *Holy Terrors: Thinking about Religion after September 11* (Chicago: University of Chicago Press, 2006); John Kelsay, *Arguing the Just War in Islam* (Cambridge, MA: Harvard University Press, 2007); Ron E. Hassner, *War on Sacred Grounds* (Ithaca, NY: Cornell University Press, 2009).

[43] Abou El Fadl, *The Great Theft*.

however, religious traditions—and therefore, such social imaginaries—are not uniform nor inherently democratic or autocratic; they are "multi-vocal."[44] Religious leaders and activists may articulate different "political theologies" to justify political agendas in religious terms.[45] Like Islamic identity, Islamic ideas about politics, justice, and the modern state are not one static "tradition" of the past but are debated, vary widely, and change over time.[46] The *ulama* (Islamic scholars), the state, and Islamist leaders, both local and foreign, often compete for authority and offer differing visions of "true Islam" and of what Islam means for law, government, and society.

Religious Resources for Mobilization: Sacred Authority and Networks

Insights from social movement theory further help us to understand how religion becomes politically mobilized. In this theory, Islamism is one type of social movement, a phenomenon that involves a "collective challenge, based on common purposes and social solidarities, in sustained interaction with elites, opponents, and authorities."[47] Islamist social movements typically engage in a range of contention: everyday praxis, network formation and dissemination of religio-political ideas and underground religious education, party formation, and, sometimes, violent confrontation with the state. While most scholarship has assumed such religious resources are only material or financial, associated with formal organizations,[48] social movement theory has emphasized not only material but nonmaterial resources as necessary to mobilization.[49]

In secular authoritarian contexts, in particular, religious resources can have a powerful effect in contending political order. Religions are endowed

[44] Alfred Stepan, "Religion, Democracy, and the 'Twin Tolerations,'" *Journal of Democracy* 11, no. 4 (October 2000): 37–57.

[45] Daniel Philpott, "Explaining the Political Ambivalence of Religion," *American Political Science Review* 101, no. 3 (August 2007): 505–25.

[46] Muhammad Qasim Zaman, *The Ulama in Contemporary Islam: Custodians of Change* (Princeton, NJ: Princeton University Press, 2007).

[47] Sidney Tarrow, *Power in Movement: Social Movements and Contentious Politics* (Cambridge: Cambridge University Press, 1998), 4–5; Quintan Wiktorowicz, *Islamic Activism: A Social Movement Theory Approach* (Bloomington, IN: Indiana University Press, 2004).

[48] Gill, *Rendering unto Caesar*.

[49] Charles Tilly and Sidney Tarrow, *Contentious Politics* (London: Paradigm, 2006); Carrie Rosefsky Wickham, *Mobilizing Islam: Religion, Activism, and Political Change in Egypt* (New York: Columbia University Press, 2002), 5; Doug McAdam, Sidney Tarrow, and Charles Tilly, *Dynamics of Contention* (Cambridge: Cambridge University Press, 2001); James M. Jasper, "Emotions and Social Movements: Twenty Years of Theory and Research," *Annual Review of Sociology* 37 (August 2011): 285–303.

with unique, nonmaterial resources that influence society and can affect politics. Anthropologists and scholars of religious studies have highlighted the role of "sacred authority"—religious leaders' distinctive social standing and influence rooted in sacral knowledge and lineages, personal piety, and charisma.[50] Sacred authority provides an important alternative to secular legitimacy and leadership for local, national, and transnational communities.[51] Those with sacred authority offer religiously oriented meaning, moral guidance, and order for a community. Sacred authority is often sought by groups or states vying for influence with a pious public. Those holding sacred authority are likely to enjoy high social trust; as Pierre Bourdieu has argued, religious knowledge and authority are the principal elements of "cultural capital" or "symbolic capital."[52] Religious entrepreneurs can potentially draw on sacred authority as tools of mass mobilization when challenging a secular regime.

Those holding sacred authority often have other resources—namely, formal or informal relationships with networks of followers. Indeed, leaders with sacred authority are embedded in "social networks and the norms of reciprocity and trustworthiness that arise from them," which scholars have argued are the foundation of civic and political life.[53]

Religions are often endowed with both formal institutions (e.g., the Spiritual Administration of Muslims of Central Asia and Kazakhstan) which control financial and organizational resources, as well as informal institutional resources. Many Muslim networks involve informal connections made through mosques, *mahalla*s (neighborhoods), *hujra*s (religious study circles), Sufi master-disciple relationships, or extended kinship ties.[54] Religion thus has potential for far-reaching grassroots mobilization.[55] Indeed, formal and informal social networks may broaden the authority and trust in Islamists and thereby facilitate grassroots mobilization.

[50] Eickelman and Piscatori, *Muslim Politics*, 57–58; Hassner, *War on Sacred Grounds*, 88, 106–7.

[51] Ronald Aminzade and Elizabeth Perry, "The Sacred, Religious, and Secular in Contentious Politics," in *Silence and Voice in the Study of Contentious Politics*, ed. Ronald Aminzade, Jack A. Goldstone, Doug McAdam, Elizabeth J. Perry, William H. Sewell, Sidney Tarrow, and Charles Tilley (Cambridge: Cambridge University Press, 2001), 162.

[52] Bourdieu, "Social Space and Symbolic Power."

[53] Robert Putnam, *Bowling Alone: The Collapse and Revival of American Community* (New York: Simon & Schuster, 2020), 19.

[54] Eickelman and Piscatori, *Muslim Politics*.

[55] Scott Mainwaring, *The Catholic Church and Politics in Brazil, 1916–85* (Palo Alto, CA: Stanford University Press, 1986), 14–16.

Islamist Movements and the Contentious Politics of Secularism

The work of both Asad and Mahmood has reminded us that Islam today exists within a modern world in which "secularism" has become a hegemonic[56] condition of "modernity," which seeks to limit "religion" to the private sphere and personal life.[57] Religion and secularism are therefore inevitably in conflict within various secular authoritarian regimes—the USSR; Turkey; Communist China; postcolonial Egypt, Iraq, and Syria; and post-Soviet Central Asia—that use the state forcibly to impose secularism, whether only in the state and law or in the totality of the public sphere. Communist states sought to impose secularism in private life as well. Islamism challenges the legitimacy and power of secular authoritarianism.[58]

Islamist activists in such regimes risk threats, financial penalties, arrest and prolonged detention without rights, and even their lives. As journalists and human rights activists have repeatedly documented, scores of Islamists in Tajikistan and Uzbekistan were "disappeared" or brutally tortured to death in prison camps dubbed "the place of no return."[59] Islamists engage in "high-risk activism" with little chance of reward. By linking social movement theory with religious studies and constructivism's understanding of the power of ideas and identity, we can better explain high-risk activism. Religious ideas unite movement members and serve as the basis of ideological outreach.[60] Islamists construct religious "meaning" as a motivation for mobilization and use sacred authority and religious networks to mobilize.[61] Building on such work, I now turn to my core arguments.

[56] Talal Asad, "Religion, Nation-State, Secularism," in *Nation and Religion: Perspectives on Europe and Asia*, ed. P. van der Veer and H. Lehmann (Princeton, NJ: Princeton University Press, 1999).

[57] Asad, *Formations of the Secular*, 14–15; Saba Mahmood, *Religious Difference in a Secular Age: A Minority Report* (Princeton, NJ: Princeton University Press, 2016).

[58] Modern Christian political movements also challenge secular hegemony, albeit typically in the West. On types of secularism, see José Casanova, *Public Religions in the Modern World* (Chicago: University of Chicago Press, 1994).

[59] "Disappeared" refers to the secret arrest and imprisonment or execution of someone targeted by the state security services. Bagila Bukharbayeva, *The Vanishing Generation: Faith and Uprising in Modern Uzbekistan* (Bloomington, IN: Indiana University Press, 2019).

[60] Kathleen Collins, "Ideas, Networks, and Islamist Movements: Evidence from Central Asia and the Caucasus," *World Politics* 60, no. 1 (October 2007): 64–96.

[61] Rosefsky Wickham, *Mobilizing Islam*, 13–20, 119–20; Nathan Brown, *When Victory Is Not an Option: Islamist Movements in Arab Politics* (Ithaca, NY: Cornell University Press, 2012); Michael Kenney, *The Islamic State in Britain: Radicalization and Resilience in an Activist Network* (Cambridge: Cambridge University Press, 2018).

Explaining Islamism: From Emergence to Mobilization

Islam can be politically salient but is not always politicized, much less mobilized. What drives the politicization of Islam? How do we explain the phenomenon and process of Islamist emergence and mobilization?

The Process of Islamist Emergence and Mobilization

Islamist emergence entails the birth or formation of an organization of religious entrepreneurs who pursue a religio-political agenda and ideology to define the state. They work toward reversing the secularization of the state, its legal system, and the public sphere. They seek to bring Islam into both the political sphere and public life in some manner. Under a secular authoritarian state, Islamist emergence usually takes place underground and is but the first step of a long process of mobilization. *Islamist mobilization* refers to the generation and activation of widespread societal support for the movement. Mobilization may involve open political contention, either in fits and starts over a long period of time or at a steady pace. Demobilization occurs when Islamist entrepreneurs are arrested, killed, or dispersed, giving up their demands.

Four key factors explain Islamist emergence and Islamist movements' mobilization over time. *Religious repression*, *religious ideology* and *religious entrepreneurs*, and *associational space* interact over time in a dynamic process, which I illustrate in a general form in Figure 1.1. In the first phase of this process (T1), state repression of Islam triggers contention, political exclusion, and latent politicization of Muslim identity under conditions of virtually no associational space. In the next phase (T2), with low but increasing associational space, Islamist ideas spread, inspiring religious entrepreneurs to emerge and organize an underground opposition. In this process, the perception of increasing associational space and political opportunity is likely to trigger open mass mobilization in the third phase (T3). Either a massive closure of associational space or, alternatively, sufficient inclusion may in turn lead to demobilization.

Two background conditions bound my argument. First, the presence of a shared Muslim identity among a significant segment of the population is critical for mobilization. Islamist entrepreneurs cannot simply create a Muslim identity to serve their political purposes. Islamists like Egypt's Muslim Brotherhood and Tunisia's Ennahda first pursued a longer-term strategy of reviving Muslim

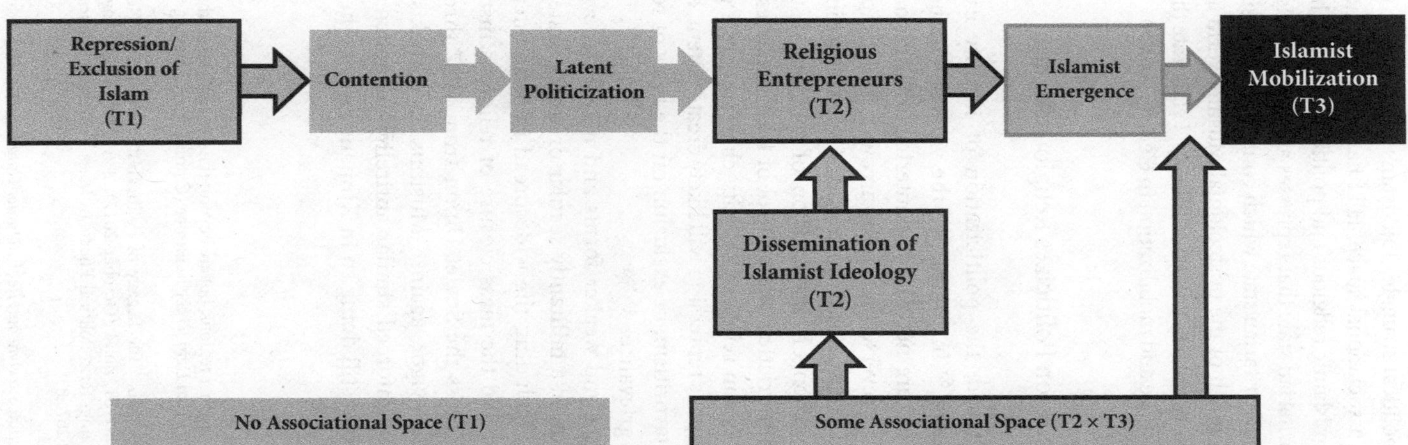

Figure 1.1 The process of Islamist emergence and mobilization

Background conditions: Muslim society and a secular authoritarian state.

Key:

- Arrows indicate temporal and substantive links in the causal chain.
- T1, T2, T3: timing/phases of the process.

identity before turning to political struggle. Tajikistan's IRPT sought to do the same, albeit with even less associational space. HTI has likewise concentrated on forming or awakening an Islamic religious and political identity. The second condition is a secular authoritarian state that represses and threatens Islam. The all-encompassing modern authoritarian state which conjoins secularism and repression is characteristic of much of the postcolonial Muslim world and is the root cause of Islamism in the modern era. In what follows, I elaborate the logic of the process of Islamist emergence and mobilization in Central Asia.[62]

Religious Repression Politicizes Religious Identity

As Stathis Kalyvas has argued, the politicization of identity cannot be assumed; it must be explained.[63] In contrast to the view that authoritarian repression and secularization are necessary counterterrorist responses to a preexisting Islamist threat, I reverse the causal arrow. Islamist movements are a response to state secularization and repression of religion, which entails the state's threats to, oppression of, or exclusion of religious institutions, leaders, and followers, and restriction and control of their practices and belief. In conditions where Muslim religious identity characterizes a group or society as a whole, state religious repression will likely create potent, enduring grievances.[64] Corruption, favoritism, or exclusion on the basis of religiosity further magnifies religious grievance.

Repression takes stronger and weaker forms and may be uneven in its targets and implementation. In a militantly secular or atheist state, repression is particularly harsh, including the widespread imprisonment of religious leaders or activists and the mass closure of religious institutions. "Militant atheism" raged across the Soviet Union from 1917 through the mid-1940s, with particular vigor against Muslims in Uzbekistan and Tajikistan.[65] China brutally enforced similar antireligious policies during its Cultural Revolution and is still doing so in Xinjiang against the Uyghur Muslim population.[66]

62 Other paths to Islamism exist in other regions, but are beyond the scope of this study.

63 Stathis Kalyvas, *The Rise of Christian Democracy in Europe* (Cambridge: Cambridge University Press, 1996).

64 Noam Lupu and Leonid Peisakhin, "The Legacy of Political Violence across Generations," *American Journal of Political Science* 61, no. 4 (October 2017): 836–51; Yuri Zhukov and Roya Talibova, "Stalin's Terror and the Long-Term Political Effects of Mass Repression," *Journal of Peace Research* 55, no. 2 (February 2018): 267–83.

65 Keller, *To Moscow, Not Mecca.*

66 Fenggang Yang, *Religion in China: Survival and Revival under Communist Rule* (Oxford: Oxford University Press, 2012).

Religious repression might also take the form of the exclusion—formal or informal—of religious adherents from political or economic power. Certain communities, regions of the country, or sects may be marginalized because the state perceives them to be orthodox, which it equates with extremism. Secularizing and modernizing states often force religion out of the public sphere and secularize education.[67] For example, in Turkey (from the 1920s to the 1950s) and in Iran (from the 1920s to the 1970s), modernizing authoritarian leaders—albeit not atheist ones—imposed secularizing reforms, marginalized the *ulama*, and oppressed Islam, although to a lesser extent than the Bolsheviks did.[68] Where the previous regime had defended or integrated Islamic elites and law, as had the Ottoman Empire and the Bukharan and Kokand khanates of Central Asia, the *ulama* had once held great influence; state legitimacy largely depended on upholding Islam. Forced secularization threatened Islam's political and economic primacy.

Where repression of religion was brutal, resistance was high in Central Asia. Sustained societal contention, including militant resistance in the 1920s to 1930s, led to longer-term tension with the state. As Soviet state officials used policies of exclusion, discrimination, and forced modernization against some Muslims, social elites and ordinary believers preserved their religious identity by passing on narratives of repression to keep salient the experiences of their loss. "Everyday resistance"—routine activity that quietly defies and subverts state policy, rather than protest or violence—became common.[69] Many ordinary Muslims, although "powerless" in most respects, engaged in what James Scott has called "hidden transcripts": they criticized and disobeyed the state in private, even while in public they mouthed the official discourse.[70] Simply maintaining an Islamic identity became a political act. Islamist emergence eventually followed this initial politicization.

In such areas of high contention, resistance could range from these hidden transcripts to outright militancy. Such responses, however, were not the only paths for a religious group facing repression. In some areas, resistance was weak or less militant because of limited leadership and resources or because state repression was more limited. Lower contention tended to depoliticize religious identity, making the task of a religious entrepreneur much more challenging. Islamist emergence was consequently less likely. These paths represent two ends of a spectrum; other cases may fall in between them. The key point is that the

[67] Ahmet Kuru, "Passive and Assertive Secularism: Historical Conditions, Ideological Struggles, and State Policies toward Religion," *World Politics* 59, no. 4 (July 2007): 568–94.

[68] M. Şükrü Hanioğlu, *The Young Turks in Opposition* (Oxford: Oxford University Press, 1995).

[69] Scott, *Weapons of the Weak*.

[70] James C. Scott, *Domination and the Arts of Resistance* (New Haven, CT: Yale University Press, 1990), 15–16.

initial state-society interaction—be it one of high or low contention—set in motion a path-dependent process, illustrated in Figure 1.1. In Soviet and post-Soviet Eurasia, severe repression of Islam and high contention characterized certain regions (e.g., the Ferghana Valley of Uzbekistan and Kyrgyzstan, Tajikistan, Dagestan, and Chechnya), leading to greater politicization of Muslim identity. By contrast, in other areas (i.e., other parts of Uzbekistan, Kyrgyzstan, Kazakhstan, and Azerbaijan), the implementation of antireligious measures was less brutal, mainly because the Bolsheviks perceived those populations to be superficially Muslim. Muslim identity there was consequently less politicized.

Religious Entrepreneurs and Religious Ideology

Religious repression alone does not create Islamism; whether in its stronger or weaker forms, repression is a necessary but not sufficient condition to produce political Islam. Salient ideas and agency are critical. Religio-political entrepreneurs (for simplicity, religious entrepreneurs) are those who turn such repression into activism and seek to rectify repression by articulating an ideology of a political order defined by religious justice: Islamism. Particular individuals and their ideologies and actions are critical to Islamist mobilization.

Islamist entrepreneurs may include prominent *ulama*, as in Iran in 1979 or in Pakistan in recent decades. As Muhammad Qasim Zaman has argued, far from being antiquated keepers of Islamic tradition, many *ulama* have increasingly turned to religio-political activism, and even Islamism.[71] Religious entrepreneurs also include underground religious teachers, such as Sayid Abdullohi Nuri in Tajikistan. They include, most prominently, Abdallah Azzam, the Palestinian preacher turned transnational jihadist in 1980s Afghanistan, who became "one of the most influential jihadist ideologues of all time," as Thomas Hegghammer has shown.[72] Islamist entrepreneurs also include figures acting in the name of Islam but possessing limited religious training, such as the IMU's leaders or HTI's activists. Albeit often lacking in depth and sophistication in their religious interpretations, these entrepreneurs generally share a belief that state action has harmed their religion and values and that Islam can resolve social and political issues. They therefore turn to underground networking, organizational formation, and ultimately mobilization with the aim of fulfilling their agenda in either the near or long term. Islamism becomes the dominant "frame"[73] that

[71] Zaman, *Ulama in Contemporary Islam*.

[72] Hegghammer, *The Caravan*, 3.

[73] Doug McAdam, John McCarthy, and Mayer Zald, *Comparative Perspectives on Social Movements: Political Opportunities, Mobilizing Structures, and Cultural Framings* (Cambridge: Cambridge University Press, 1996), 261; Emmanuel Karagiannis, *Political Islam in Central Asia: The Challenge of Hizb ut-Tahrir* (London: Routledge, 2010).

entrepreneurs use to found religio-political movements challenging the secular authoritarian regime. Because Islamic symbols and ideas resonate with people's identity and values, Islamism can become a compelling, motivating discourse that captures the imagination of Muslim followers. The persistence of Islamist activism under secular authoritarian regimes—where there is little reasonable chance of political success or financial reward, but where the risks are exceedingly high—strongly suggests that a religious ideology, rather than economic or other rationalist considerations, is central to their motivation and to that of their followers.[74] Indeed, the groundbreaking work of Carrie Rosefsky Wickham on the Muslim Brotherhood, Thomas Hegghammer on the Saudi jihadist movement, and Michael Kenney on British recruits to ISIS suggests that Islamists' ideological outreach and networking facilitated high-risk activism and social mobilization in these cases.[75] Recent scholarship on the Taliban, al-Qaeda, ISIS, and foreign fighters has similarly highlighted both leadership and religious ideology to explain these movements' origins and support.[76]

Islamism, as noted in the introduction, was rooted initially in the idea of a modern Islamic state, espoused by religious entrepreneurs of the twentieth century. Beginning with Hassan al-Banna's founding of the Muslim Brotherhood in Egypt and continuing with Sayyid Abu al-Ala Mawdudi's establishment of the Jamaat-i Islami on the Indian subcontinent, early Islamists advocated a gradualist path, using education and religious revival to achieve a vaguely defined Islamic state.[77] By the 1960s, however, the Muslim Brotherhood ideologue Sayyid Qutb was explicitly urging the violent overthrow of apostate regimes and the creation of an Islamic state to eradicate ignorance and establish divine law. Qutb's highly influential tract, *Milestones*, was the ideological spark of the militant Salafi jihadist turn in Islamism.[78] Azzam's ideas, activism, and writings were the driving force of the transnational Salafi jihadist movement; Azzam further radicalized Islamism, making its means a transnational militant jihad.[79] For nearly a century, successive Islamist entrepreneurs have adapted and reconceived and often

[74] Brown, *When Victory Is Not an Option*, 52–53.

[75] Rosefsky Wickham, *Mobilizing Islam*, 19–20; Thomas Hegghammer, *Jihad in Saudi Arabia: Violence and Pan-Islamism since 1979* (Cambridge: Cambridge University Press, 2010); Kenney, *The Islamic State in Britain*.

[76] Fawaz Gerges, *The Far Enemy: Why Jihad Went Global* (Cambridge: Cambridge University Press, 2005); Thomas Hegghammer, "The Rise of Muslim Foreign Fighters, Islam and the Globalization of Jihad," *International Security* 35, no. 2 (Winter 2010–11): 53–94; Charles Lister, *The Syrian Jihad: Al-Qaeda, the Islamic State and the Evolution of an Insurgency* (Oxford: Oxford University Press, 2015).

[77] Charles J. Adams, "Mawdūdī and the Islamic State," in *Voices of Resurgent Islam*, ed. John L. Esposito (Oxford: Oxford University Press, 1983), 99–133; Irfan Ahmad, "The Genealogy of the Islamic State: Reflections on Maududi's Political Thought and Islamism," *Journal of the Royal Anthropological Institute* 15, no. 1 (2009): 145–62.

[78] Sayyid Qutb, *Milestones* (New Delhi: Islamic Book Services, 2002).

[79] Hegghammer, *The Caravan*.

radicalized Islamist ideology to suit their particular political circumstances and ends.

A critical caveat is that Islamist entrepreneurs across space and time reflect the "multi-vocality" and diversity of Islamist ideas and ideologies, from nonviolent to violent, from national revolutionary to "pan-Islamist" and transnational jihadist.[80] The Turkish Justice and Development Party's cautious and self-limited entrepreneurs, intending to avoid a backlash from the secular military, long advocated gradualism in increasing Islam's public and state role and anchors one end of the spectrum of Islamism. Global Salafi jihadism, represented by al-Qaeda's transnational network aimed at destroying the West, marks the other.

Islamist entrepreneurs make choices and can change the direction of movements. Over time some have disavowed an Islamic state entirely to seek justice through democracy and human rights. During Tunisia's Arab Spring, Ennahda transformed itself into what some consider to be a "post-Islamist" party; now only "guided by" Islam, Ennahda espoused democracy and a "civil," secular state.[81] Within Central Asia, we shall see that varied Islamist identities, ideas, and ideologies were central to opposition movements from the 1980s to the present. IRPT leaders Mullah Nuri and Muhiddin Kabiri became more committed to peace and a Muslim version of democracy even in the face of an oppressive regime. By contrast, Tohir Yo'ldosh was uncompromising when he led Adolat, and he chose to become steadily more radical in ideology and violent in strategy as he led the IMU down the path of al-Qaeda.

Although driven by a religious ideology, Islamists are not irrational fanatics; as we shall see, the IRPT, IMU, HTI, and others rationally respond to institutional constraints and opportunities as they strategize. Yet, they also risk persecution and death, knowing that their goals may not be achieved in their lifetime.

Associational Space

Any opposition also needs some associational space, the realm of private and civic space in which individuals and groups can operate, de facto or de jure, free of persistent state control or monitoring. Islamist ideational diffusion and religious entrepreneurship depend on a minimum level of associational space for the networking needed to build an opposition organization—even an underground one.[82] Under a secular totalitarian state that engages in massive religious

[80] Hegghammer, *Jihad in Saudi Arabia*, 6.

[81] Asef Bayat, *Post-Islamism: The Changing Faces of Political Islam* (Oxford: Oxford University Press, 2013).

[82] Deborah J. Yashar, *Contesting Citizenship in Latin America: The Rise of Indigenous Movements and the Postliberal Challenge* (New York: Cambridge University Press, 2005), 76. Yashar specifies

repression, Islamist organizing is virtually impossible. However, under a softer authoritarian state that implements more sporadic, limited tactics in repressing religion, the state no longer totally controls nonstate activity in the civic and private realms. The introduction of minimal associational space triggers the dissemination of alternative ideas, including the political theologies that motivate religious entrepreneurs. Greater shifts in associational space, sometimes triggered by a shock to the political system, explain the move from underground activism to open contentious politics and mass mobilization, including party formation and competition, peaceful protest, and violent conflict.[83]

Associational space varies significantly across nondemocratic regimes. The totalitarian era under Stalin (especially 1927–38) was vicious in targeting Islam and eliminated all associational space. Yet by the Brezhnev era, increased private space meant that underground Islamist networking was possible. Repression continued but was more sporadic, with variations from republic to republic. In Tajikistan, for example, Communist Party bosses in some rural areas even protected Islamist teachers and activists.[84] Gorbachev's reforms in the late 1980s created the expectation among religious and political entrepreneurs that open activism was becoming possible. The seismic institutional change from 1990 to 1992 did loosen control and increase space as the USSR collapsed, an event which triggered a shift to open mass mobilization by Islamists in Tajikistan and Uzbekistan.

The state's attempt to crush Islamism through a return to religious and political repression does not always succeed; it can motivate even more intense Islamist-state contention, and even a turn to violence, as in Afghanistan, Algeria, Tajikistan, Chechnya, Dagestan, and most recently Syria.[85] Nonetheless, the sharp and total closure of associational space and the use of mass repression often results in demobilization. Stalin demobilized a Muslim opposition movement in Central Asia in the 1920s to 1930s. Karimov demobilized Islamists in Uzbekistan in the 1990s, killing many and driving most others into exile, as did Rahmon of Tajikistan after 2015.

"*political* associational space." I argue any associational space allows networking and dissemination of ideas.

[83] Tarrow, *Power in Movement*; McAdam, Tarrow, and Tilly, *Dynamics of Contention*.

[84] Stéphane A. Dudoignon and Sayyid Ahmad Qalandari, "'They Were All from the Country': The Revival and Politicisation of Islam in the Lower Wakhsh River Valley of the Tajik SSR (1947–97)," in Stéphane A. Dudoignon and Christian Noack, *Allah's Kolkhozes: Migration, De-Stalinisation, Privatisation and the New Muslim Congregations in the Soviet Realm (1950s–2000s)* (Berlin: Klaus Schwarz Verlag, 2014), 47–122.

[85] Fawaz Gerges, *ISIS: A History* (Princeton, NJ: Princeton University Press, 2016).

Explaining Nonemergence

I have argued that three conditions interacted to foster Islamist emergence in Central Asia. Absent one of those conditions, Islamism did not emerge. Subsequent chapters illustrate this argument by comparing the cases with each other, and also over time. For example, religious repression motivated opposition, and sufficient associational space existed for opposition from 1917 to 1926, yet Islamist ideology was missing. Chapter 2 will show that the consequence was a proliferation of Muslim politics and even high Muslim opposition mobilization, but without Islamism. Chapter 3 will demonstrate that religious oppression and secularization were brutal, but the Party's near total control of associational space for over four decades meant that religious entrepreneurs and ideas could not begin to take root until the late 1970s.

Notably, the path to Islamism is not fixed once a state initiates religious repression and secularization. There are always points when a state may reverse its policies. Substantial liberalization of religion and concessions to Islam's public role will likely decrease the chance of Islamist mobilization; it undercuts Islamists' core grievances. There are continual opportunities for religio-political entrepreneurs to adapt, soften, or even abandon Islamist ideologies. In Kyrgyzstan, broad religious freedom in the 1990s defused religious grievances and mollified potential Islamist entrepreneurs—despite a history of religious repression and secularization and despite ample associational space for mobilization.

Explaining Relative Levels of Islamist Mobilization

Islamist groups vary widely in their success at mass mobilization, even when external conditions are similar. If all Islamist movements lay claim to religious ideas, why do they vary in their relative levels of mobilization? Islamist mobilization may be high, even if the movement does not achieve its ultimate political ends. Or Islamists may remain marginal, largely shunned by society. High Islamist mobilization involves organizational activity, sustained over time with widespread public participation. Such activity could include protesting, lobbying, disseminating the movement's message and literature to the masses, or campaigning in elections. Low Islamist mobilization entails sporadic activism or mere episodes of contention, involving relatively few adherents and diminishing over time.

To explain relative levels of mobilization in high-risk environments—in terms of both mass support and its endurance over time, even as associational space closes—we must look to religious entrepreneurs and their mobilization strategies. Three strategies—*ideological adaptation* emphasizing congruence with a local religious and historical context, *building sacred authority*, and *developing both local and transcommunal networks*—are critical to broader mass mobilization in an authoritarian context.

Adapting Ideologies to Local Contexts

More successful religious entrepreneurs develop, propagate, and adapt their ideology to their target base, which is generally more moderate than radical. Society does not simply accept any Islamist ideas about politics; ideational "congruence"[86] and "localization"[87] within a particular context are critical. Islamist activists must adapt their ideas to induce local elites and society to accept and support them. Islamist movements that are more successful in recruiting and in sustaining themselves over the long term under repressive conditions are those that develop powerful ideas which resonate in the particular cultural and historical context they face. They draw on indigenous Islamic norms, practices, and beliefs rather than impose a foreign cultural interpretation of Islam. Adaptation to local customs and concerns allows Islamists to appeal to the broader religious base of society, which in Central Asia is a centuries-old syncretism of Sufism, Hanafi Islam, and local identities rather than a purist, *madrasa*-centered, scripturalist Islam.

Adapting to the target population usually means giving precedence to national identities and concerns over transnational ones. Successful Islamist groups offer a religious interpretation of and solution for local political conflicts, corruption, or economic inequality, as did the Muslim Brotherhood in Egypt. By contrast, al-Qaeda had difficulty convincing "national" jihadists in Sudan or Afghanistan to adopt "global" jihadism.[88] Inside Central Asia, only the IRPT's platform was nationally focused and broadly consistent with local interpretations of Islam; as such, it resonated with many in Tajik society. The IMU, HTI, KTJ, and ISIS, among other groups, adapted in part, but ultimately their core ideology was too radical; they alienated the majority of Central Asians.

86 Richard Price, "Reversing the Gun Sights: Transnational Civil Society Targets Land Mines," *International Organization* 52, no. 3 (Summer 1998): 613–44; Collins, "Ideas, Networks, and Islamist Movements."

87 Amitav Acharya, *Whose Ideas Matter?* (Ithaca, NY: Cornell University Press, 2009).

88 Gerges, *The Far Enemy*, 29.

Building Sacred Authority

In addition to a compelling message, Islamists need sacred authority. A resource unique to religious groups, sacred authority is rooted in communally recognized religious knowledge and deeds, and often martyrdom. Sacred authority endows Islamist entrepreneurs with greater legitimacy,[89] enabling them to articulate their message from a position of significant social standing that commands trust and respect from Muslims. Sacred authority is accompanied by other resources, such as organizational ties associated with mosques, *madrasas*, Sufi networks, and Islamic charities. Such ties enable entrepreneurs to network and disseminate information, much as religiously rooted "social capital" fosters mobilization in the West.[90]

Islamist entrepreneurs vary substantially in their possession of religious resources. Some entrepreneurs are deeply embedded in social and religious organizations imbued with significant societal legitimacy, sometimes by virtue of birth into an esteemed religious family and sometimes by their education, teaching, or suffering under state repression. Transnational religious entrepreneurs, as outsiders to the community, often lack societal roots. The absence of such social ties limits their authority and their ability to attract adherents and effectively mobilize.

In short, high sacred authority facilitates higher Islamist mobilization, so many Islamist entrepreneurs invest in cultivating this resource. In Tajikistan, for example, the Islamist opposition drew on both Sufi lineages associated with Haji Akbar Turajonzoda, as well as on Mullah Nuri's authority as an underground Islamic teacher. The IMU drew on the sacred authority of the martyred Shaykh Abduvali Qori. By contrast, HTI lacked any such figurehead and authority in Central Asia.

Developing Networks: Local and Transcommunal

Social networks are essential to sustaining Islamist movements and are a chief mechanism by which more successful mobilization takes place.[91] As sets of interconnected nodes, networks operate informally, outside the easy purview of the state, and consequently can evade authoritarian control more easily than formal

[89] Alexandre Papas, *Soufisme et politique entre Chine, Tibet et Turkestan* (Paris: Librarie d'Amérique et d'Orient, Jean Maisonneuve successeur, 2005); Eickelman and Piscatori, *Muslim Politics*.

[90] Robert Putnam, *Making Democracy Work: Civic Traditions in Modern Italy* (Princeton, NJ: Princeton University Press, 1993).

[91] Rosefsky Wickham, *Mobilizing Islam*, 19–20.

organizations such as opposition parties.[92] Personal ties and small numbers make cohesion within the core network of activists easier.[93] Networks are more likely to be influential if they are rooted in trusted and dense local ties. In Central Asia, as in many Muslim societies, kinship, clan, village, *mahalla*, mosque, and collective farms all provide such ties. Religious organizations, student groups, and professional associations also constitute networks.[94] Carriers effectively transmit ideas through face-to-face contact that further builds ties, educates, and recruits.[95] Transnational networks, by contrast, lack such embeddedness and trust. Nonetheless, entrepreneurs need to disseminate their ideas across a national political space; they need to transcend exclusivist local networks to gain access to wider, "inclusive,"[96] and "transcommunal" networks[97] and broader ties which enable widespread mass mobilization. Forming coalitions with other Islamic groups or with a democratic opposition is one way to widen networks.

In Central Asia, the indigenous ties of particularistic networks are dense and strong but often narrow.[98] Transcommunal ties are difficult to build, especially in the Soviet and post-Soviet cases, where the state was historically effective in preventing the formation of broader movements. The long-term presence of Islamic religious networks, albeit not politically active ones, in some Soviet republics since the 1950s endowed them with greater social capital than the hastily developed and narrowly based democratic or nationalist networks that emerged as opposition movements in the late 1980s and early 1990s. Where Islamists could also draw on transcommunal networks, as did the IRPT when it partnered with both democrats and state Islam, they were better poised to mobilize nationally.

. . .

The following chapters will reveal that Islam is not inevitably political but can become politicized. Islamist entrepreneurs can use Islamic identity and Islamic

[92] Miles Kahler, *Networked Politics: Agency, Structure, Governance* (Ithaca, NY: Cornell University Press, 2009), 3–7; Collins, "Ideas, Networks, and Islamist Movements."

[93] James Gibson, "Social Networks, Civil Society, and the Prospects for Consolidating Russia's Democratic Transition," *American Journal of Political Science* 45, no. 1 (January 2001): 53; Mark Granovetter, "The Strength of Weak Ties," *American Journal of Sociology* 78, no. 6 (May 1973): 1361.

[94] Quintan Wiktorowicz, *The Management of Islamic Activism: Salafis, the Muslim Brotherhood and State Power in Jordan* (New York: SUNY Press, 2000); Diane Singerman, *Avenues of Participation: Family, Politics, and Networks in Urban Quarters of Cairo* (Princeton, NJ: Princeton University Press, 2004), 149.

[95] Kathleen Collins, "The Political Role of Clans in Central Asia," *Comparative Politics* 35, no. 2 (January 2003): 171–90.

[96] Collins, "Ideas, Networks, and Islamist Movements."

[97] Margaret Keck and Kathryn Sikkink, *Activists beyond Borders* (Ithaca, NY: Cornell University Press, 1998).

[98] Kathleen Collins, "The Logic of Clan Politics: Evidence from the Central Asian Trajectories," *World Politics* 56, no. 2 (January 2004): 224–61.

ideas about justice to mobilize a base and advance their goals. We shall see that, from the Bolshevik Revolution through the Syrian Civil War, the process of Islamist mobilization is rooted in religious repression; such conditions of religious injustice provided a powerful motive for organizing Islamist opposition against the USSR, and then against the post-Soviet Tajik and Uzbek regimes. In each case, religious entrepreneurs used gradual openings in associational space to spread Islamist ideologies and recruit supporters in their pursuit of a religious political order. Moreover, the Islamist order sought by the IMU or KTJ, whose ideologies were influenced by Salafi jihadism, proved to be distinct from the Islamic order sought by the IRPT in either its early or later programs.

Accordingly, we shall also see that not all Islamists gained a mass following. Under the high-risk political conditions of Karimov's Uzbekistan or Rahmon's Tajikistan, or even the soft secular authoritarianism of Kyrgyzstan in the 2000s, recruiting and mobilization were dangerous and religious actors were severely restricted. We shall see that the mainstream views of Central Asian society—normative opposition to antisystemic, revolutionary Islamist goals and to the use of violence—limit Islamism's growth. Only those Islamist organizations that flexibly adapted their ideas to the local context and concerns, that constructed sacred authority, and that developed both local and transcommunal networks were successful in mobilizing and sustaining followers.

PART II
THE USSR POLITICIZES ISLAM

2
The Russian Revolution and Muslim Mobilization

> Religion is the sigh of the oppressed creature, the heart of a heartless world, just as it is the spirit of a spiritless situation. It is the opium of the people.
>
> —Karl Marx, "Contribution to the Critique of Hegel's Philosophy of Right"

> "Religion is the Opium of the People" was written on a banner that greeted us at the school entrance every day.
>
> —Oqsoqol, Tashkent, Uzbekistan, 2017

To understand the origins of Islamism in Soviet Central Asia in the 1970s and 1980s, we need to understand the social order that existed before 1917 and how the Russian Revolution of 1917 attempted to destroy that order.[1] Determined to create an atheist, communist society and state, the Bolsheviks unleashed radical political, economic, and social change, central to which was a policy of religious oppression. Bolshevik policy, although implemented only with difficulty for the first decade, aimed to use massive force to destroy religion, despite Lenin's avowed desire to "liberate" Central Asians from Russian imperialism. Repression by the state made practicing Islam an act of political opposition. That politicization of Islam, beginning in 1917, sowed the seeds of the later emergence of Islamist opposition movements.

In the first part of this chapter, I present the pre-Bolshevik context: Islam's role in Central Asian society and politics prior to 1917. Second, I sketch the political dynamics of the Russian Revolution and the establishment of Soviet rule in the region. Third, I discuss emergent Muslim activism in the revolutionary period and demonstrate that religious repression and associational space triggered widespread mobilization in some regions. However, I show that in the 1920s,

[1] Keller, *To Moscow, Not Mecca*; Northrop, *Veiled Empire*; Jeff Sahadeo, *Russian Colonial Society in Tashkent, 1865–1923* (Bloomington, IN: Indiana University Press, 2007); Khalid, *Making Uzbekistan*; Paul Bergne, *The Birth of Tajikistan: National Identity and the Origins of the Republic* (London: Tauris, 2016); Boatkaz Kassymbekova, *Despite Cultures: Early Soviet Rule in Tajikistan* (Pittsburgh, PA: University of Pittsburgh Press, 2016).

Politicizing Islam in Central Asia. Kathleen Collins, Oxford University Press. © Oxford University Press 2023.
DOI: 10.1093/oso/9780197685068.003.0003

Islamist ideology was absent; the mobilization that unfolded preceded the birth of modern Islamism, which would occur in Egypt in 1928. With no expressly Islamist ideational influence, Central Asian Muslim activists did not pursue a modern Islamic state. Instead, they engaged in multiple forms of Muslim politics—activism and debates concerning the role of Islam and the *ulama* (religious scholars and the moral elite of society) in the new political order and the use of Islamic symbols and rhetoric to justify alternative political agendas. The goals of these movements were varied, including demands for a return to the pre-1917 Islamic order, Muslim nationalism, autonomy within Russia, and even parliamentary governance that incorporated *shariat.* An investigation of this era underscores an overarching theme of this book: Islamism is not inevitable. Even when religion is oppressed, Islamist mobilization requires a particular set of ideas and entrepreneurs which do not exist under all conditions. Historical contingencies, such as timing and exposure to specific political ideas, have significant effects on the type of mobilization that takes place.

In the final section, I trace the varied paths by which the Bolsheviks incorporated different regions of Central Asia into the USSR. I argue that Soviet antireligious policies were more brutal and generated more resistance and conflict in areas where the *ulama* had greater influence (i.e., certain regions of contemporary Tajikistan and Uzbekistan, especially Tashkent, the former Bukharan Emirate, and the Ferghana Valley).[2] The dynamics of this period set the stage for either a cycle of repression and contention over Islam well into the 1930s or, conversely, for greater inclusion within the USSR, with less politicization of Islam.

The Context: Pre-Soviet Muslim Central Asia

A brief overview of the historical context of Islam in Central Asia reveals why the Bolshevik Revolution of 1917 began a century of Islam's repression and consequent politicization. From its very early history, Islam was intricately associated with the identity of Central Asian polities and peoples. Through changes of name, shifting boundaries, and the rise and fall of various dynasties, Central Asia's population became Muslim from the seventh century onward. Islam initially spread to Central Asia when Arab armies captured Bukhara in 709 and Samarqand shortly thereafter, bringing Transoxiana into the Umayyad caliphate (661–750) less than a century after the time of the Prophet Muhammad (622–632). Later conquests of these territories were part of the rise and consolidation

[2] The Ferghana Valley includes the densely populated southeastern portion of contemporary Uzbekistan, northern Tajikistan, and southern Kyrgyzstan. Much of the Ferghana Valley population is ethnic Uzbek.

of the Abbasid dynasty and caliphate (750–1258). The period ushered in a flowering of Islamic civilization that included the development of Islamic law and a Perso-Islamic culture and *ulama*, together with extensive urban growth and trade.[3] The region was home to great centers of Islamic philosophy, law, theology, and science in the cities of Bukhara and Samarqand. The renowned Abu Ismoil al-Buxoriy (810–870) lived and worked in Bukhara while he compiled his influential *hadith*.

In Central Asia's steppe, Islamization proceeded more slowly, through different mechanisms, as an array of Turkic tribes converted.[4] The nomadic tribes inhabiting contemporary Kyrgyzstan accepted Islam over time, from the eighth through the twelfth centuries. Islamization of the nomads of the Kazakh steppe began in the tenth century and continued into the nineteenth.[5] Islam there created a sense of belonging to a broader Muslim *umma* (the global community of Muslims) but also anchored one to the local community. Islam was not an esoteric theology and doctrine, but rather, as Devin DeWeese has argued, the lived morals, practices, rituals, discourse, way of life, and shared communal traditions of Central Asians.[6]

Islamic ideas and institutions—predominantly Sunni Islam and the Hanafi school of jurisprudence—pervaded the region.[7] The major cities of Transoxiana—Bukhara, Samarqand, Kokand, and Khiva—boasted a dense array of institutionalized Islam, in mosques and *madrasas* (Islamic schools). As in the Middle East, the *ulama* of Central Asia were the religious and learned elite of society and wielded enormous influence. They were schooled primarily in the Islamic classical tradition, including Arabic, Persian, *fiqh* (Islamic jurisprudence), and Islamic history.[8] The court system operated on a very local, communal, and informal basis, with *qazis* (judges trained in Islamic law) making decisions on the basis of both *shariat* and *adat* (customary law).[9]

Islam was also a resource; sacred authority was held in great esteem. Religious leaders not only led prayers and issued *fatwas* (nonbinding legal opinions issued by a *mufti*) but were also negotiators in familial, communal, and even tribal and political conflicts. Religious leadership included the *ulama* and Sufi leaders; sacred authority was manifest in various forms: the learned *muftis* (legal scholars

[3] James Pickett, *Polymaths of Islam: Power and Networks of Knowledge in Central Asia* (Ithaca, NY: Cornell University Press, 2020).

[4] Khalid, *Islam after Communism*.

[5] Privratsky, *Muslim Turkistan*.

[6] DeWeese, "Islam and the Legacy of Sovietology."

[7] Lapidus, *History of Islamic Societies*, 414; Ashirbek Muminov, "Traditional and Modern Religious Theological Schools in Central Asia," in *Political Islam and Conflicts in Russia and Central Asia*, ed. Lena Jonson and Murad Esenov (Stockholm: Utrikespolitiska Institutet, 1999), 101–11.

[8] Adeeb Khalid, *The Politics of Muslim Cultural Reform: Jadidism in Central Asia* (Berkeley, CA: University of California Press, 1998); Pickett, *Polymaths of Islam*.

[9] Wael Hallaq, *An Introduction to Islamic Law* (New York: Cambridge University Press, 2009).

of Islamic law), mullahs (religious leaders), imams (mosque prayer leaders), *qazis*, *domlas* (respected teachers), *eshons* (Sufi masters), *pirs* (Sufi patrons), and *otinchas* (female religious teachers for women). The honorifics shaykh (leader or master) and *ustod* (learned master) were often given to such individuals. Comprising a substantial portion of the 2 to 3 percent who were educated prior to the twentieth century, the *ulama* were enormously influential; they held significant spiritual, social, and legal authority in the interpretation and implementation of *shariat*. Mullahs and *muftis* preached in the thousands of Friday mosques that were the center of urban life; smaller daily prayer mosques were also located in every *mahalla* (neighborhood) and in every *aiyl* or *qishloq* (village). They also ran *maktabs* (Qur'anic primary schools) and *madrasas*, which were the only form of education prior to Russian colonialism. Social categories and hierarchy were not defined by wealth, ethnicity, nation, or even birth, but by mastery of sacred knowledge.[10]

Besides the traditional Hanafi *ulama*, the region became home to several important Sufi orders, whose spiritual masters also possessed sacred authority. In fact, the *ulama* and Sufi *eshons* were intersecting and overlapping categories rather than rivals.[11] Both were keepers of many forms of knowledge, from medicine and healing to the study of Arabic texts and Persian poetry and literature—all of which was deemed Islamic.[12] Sufism took many forms in Central Asia, as elsewhere, including mystical rituals, such as the *zikr* (a repetitive devotional recitation), shrine visitation, and a political role. In some regions, Sufi orders legitimized and guided the sovereign.[13] The Naqshbandi *tariqat* (order) exerted influence over political life and society into the 1900s, particularly in Bukhara and among the khans of Kokand in the Ferghana Valley.[14] The Qadiri *tariqat* became prominent throughout much of eastern Bukhara (contemporary Tajikistan).

Among the Kazakh, Kyrgyz, and Turkmen nomads, Sufi shaykhs were particularly instrumental in spreading Islam, as was the Yassaviy *tariqat*, founded by the Sufi shaykh Ahmad Yassaviy.[15] Sufism among the nomads was centered on narratives of lineage and demonstration of a genealogical connection to saints or the Prophet Muhammad.[16] *Khojas* claimed descent from the Prophet himself.

[10] Pickett, *Polymaths of Islam*, 197.
[11] Pickett, *Polymaths of Islam*, 130–45.
[12] Pickett, *Polymaths of Islam*, 16–17.
[13] Alexander Knysh, *Sufism* (Princeton, NJ: Princeton University Press, 2017).
[14] Thierry Zarcone, "Naqshbandi-Khalidi Influence in Twentieth Century Central Asia, Including Afghanistan and Xinjiang," *Journal of the History of Sufism* 5 (2007): 216.
[15] Anvarbek Mokeev, "Rol' Sufiiskikh sheikhov v rasprostranenii Islamskoi religii v Kyrgyzstane," *Journal of Turkic Civilization Studies* 2: 125–36.
[16] DeWeese, *Islamization and Native Religion*, 216; Allen Frank, *Gulag Miracles: Sufis and Stalinist Repression in Kazakhstan* (Vienna: Austrian Academy of Sciences Press, 2019), 33.

Other Sufi lineages maintained *mazars* (shrines), many of which were burial places for holy persons and saints and connected communities with their ancestors.[17] Across the region, such sacred places were intertwined with sacred lineage and authority. As Robert McChesney writes, "Shrines, the imputed final resting places of saintly figures or relics, play[ed] a major role in imagining the landscape."[18] For example, the shrine of Naqshbandi (1318–1389), the fourteenth-century Sufi shaykh and mystic for whom the Naqshbandi *tariqat* was founded, was a place of veneration and pilgrimage. Closely connected to shrines was the *waqf* system of religious endowments (public or private), the major source of funding for mosques, *madrasas*, and public buildings, as well as for communal feasts, the indigent, and travelers. *Waqf* administrators were typically shaykhs of the shrine's lineage.[19]

Cultural interpretation and practice of Islam varied greatly within Central Asia, as across the Islamic world, reflecting urban, rural, or nomadic economies. In Transoxiana, Islam was highly institutionalized. Islamic education was largely conducted at the mosque or in a *madrasa*; lessons were textually and canonically oriented. Emphasis was given to studying commentaries of renowned Islamic scholars rather than the Qur'an itself. Compared to nomadic areas, society observed a strict, scripturalist interpretation of Islam. Women were usually secluded in urban areas, and the *paranji* (the body-length robe to cover women) and *chachvon* (face veil) characterized their dress when they ventured into public.[20] Among the nomadic Muslims of the steppe and mountains, by contrast, mosques and *madrasas* were few. Although a tradition of textual learning was uncommon among the nomadic peoples, they nonetheless considered themselves Muslim.[21] Learning took place with itinerant Sufi preachers, and shrine visitation was more central to Muslimness than strict adherence to *shariat*. Women were neither secluded nor veiled, and they were integrated into the economy.[22] Both the Russian colonizers and the Bolsheviks considered the long-settled populations of Central Asia (Tajiks and Uzbeks) to be more deeply Islamic than nomads or recent nomads (northern Kyrgyz, Kazakhs, Turkmen), whom they considered superficially Muslim.[23] Everyday discourse in post-Soviet Central Asia still reflects this stereotype, albeit less so than in the 1990s.

[17] Privratsky, *Muslim Turkistan*.

[18] Robert McChesney, *Central Asia: Foundations of Change* (Princeton, NJ: Darwin Press, 1997), 15.

[19] Robert McChesney, *Waqf in Central Asia: Four Hundred Years in the History of a Muslim Shrine, 1480–1889* (Princeton, NJ: Princeton Press, 1991), 319.

[20] Northrop, *Veiled Empire*.

[21] DeWeese, "Islam and the Legacy of Sovietology"; Privratsky, *Muslim Turkistan*.

[22] Adrienne Edgar, "Bolshevism, Patriarchy, and the Nation: The Soviet 'Emancipation' of Muslim Women in Pan-Islamic Perspective," *Slavic Review* 65, no. 2 (Summer 2006): 252–72.

[23] Jeff Sahadeo, *Russian Colonial Society in Tashkent, 1865–1923* (Bloomington: Indiana University Press, 2007); David Tyson, "Shrine Pilgrimage in Turkmenistan as a Means to Understand Islam

Throughout nineteenth-century Central Asia, political order and law in both the nomadic tribal regions and the urban city-states of Transoxiana still centered around Islam. The Bukharan Emirate and the khanates of Kokand and Khiva were by no means "Islamic states" in the modern, twentieth-century understanding of the term, but the sovereign upheld Islamic law, which was enforced by *shariat* courts, and depended upon the *ulama* for legitimacy.[24] Islamic charitable and educational systems thrived. Rulers maintained societal legitimacy by manipulating Islam, attempting to demonstrate their sacred lineage while also forming alliances with influential Sufi brotherhoods, such as the Naqshbandiya-Mujaddidiya *tariqat*, a Sufi reformist movement associated with the South Asian Islamic scholar and *mujaddid* (renewer) Shaykh Ahmad Sirhindi (1564–1624).[25] The movement introduced Central Asia to puritanical ideas about cleansing un-Islamic innovations, ideas later spread by the Deobandis in reaction to British colonialism.[26]

Weakened by elite infighting, civil and ethnic conflicts, and economic volatility, Central Asia became incorporated into the advancing tsarist empire beginning in the 1850s, leading to the conquest of Tashkent in 1865 and Samarqand in 1868. The Russian colonial period in Central Asia altered the Muslim political order most significantly in the region that became Russian Turkestan—which expanded over time to include the sedentary *oblasts* (administrative regions) of Samarqand and Syr Darya. After defeating the Kokand Khanate in 1876, Russia subsumed Ferghana as well. The empire further included the mostly nomadic steppe of Semireche and Transcaspia.[27] The Bukharan Emirate and Khivan Khanate became Russian protectorates but retained internal legal and political autonomy. The Bukharan emir continued to rely on the *ulama* for legitimacy through the Russian Revolution. The Kokand Khanate preserved Islamic norms throughout society.[28] While Russian domination brought notable changes, it did not uproot the *ulama* or secularize society, public space, or the existing political order. The *madrasa* and court system remained. The *ulama* even "acquired a

among the Turkmen," *Central Asia Monitor* 1 (1997); McBrien, *Belonging to Belief*; Sebastien Peyrouse, *Turkmenistan: Strategies of Power, Dilemmas of Development* (New York: M. E. Sharpe, 2012).

[24] Pickett, *Polymaths of Islam*; Scott Levi, *The Rise and Fall of Khoqand* (Pittsburgh, PA: University of Pittsburgh Press, 2017).

[25] Baxtiyor Babadzhanov, "On the History of the *Naqshbandiya mujaddidiya* in Central Mawaraannahr in the Late 18th and Early 19th Centuries," in *Muslim Culture in Russia and Central Asia from the 18th to the Early 20th Centuries*, ed. Michael Kemper, Anke von Kügelgen, and Dmitry Yermakov (Berlin: Klaus Schwarz Verlag, 1996), 412–13; Aziz Ahmad, *Studies in Islamic Culture in the Indian Environment* (Oxford: Oxford University Press, 1999).

[26] Barbara Metcalf, *Islamic Revival in British India: Deoband, 1860–1900* (Princeton, NJ: Princeton University Press, 2014).

[27] A. Morrison, *Russian Rule in Samarkand, 1868–1910* (Oxford: Oxford University Press, 2008), 281–82, 286–87.

[28] Levi, *Rise and Fall of Khoqand.*

position of social preeminence unprecedented in earlier Central Asian history," as Russian colonial rule had eliminated tribal and military elites but generally exercised a policy of "noninterference" in religion and culture.[29]

Continuity with its pre-Russian Islamic history continued until the cataclysmic events of 1917. Far from being confined to the mosques and *madrasas*, Islam pervaded everyday life and society throughout the colonial era. *Musulmonchilik* (Muslimness) defined individual and societal identity. By contrast, modern identities—ethnicity or nation (i.e., Tajik, Uzbek, Kyrgyz) and citizenship—were at most nascent in the early twentieth century, before the Soviet creation of national republics across the region. For most, kinship, clan and tribe, localism, and being Muslim were salient and closely interwoven identities. No theocracy nor any ideology of political Islam had existed in Central Asian history, but Islamic leaders still shaped much of the legal system and influenced political order in the sedentary regions on the eve of the Russian Revolution. More broadly, Islam was part of a rich social fabric of everyday grassroots civic activity, including Sufi networks, business associations, and mosque communities. Islamic social organization took diverse forms and was organic, diffuse, informal, and not tied to movements, parties, or political ideologies. Yet, Islamic identity, sacred authority, religious institutions, and networks all provided potential resources for political mobilization.

The Russian Revolution and the Creation of Soviet Central Asia

One of the first acts of the new Bolshevik regime was the Declaration of the Rights of Nations and Russia in November 1917, which was followed in December by a special appeal to "all working Muslims of Russia and the East."[30] Lenin urged the "awakening" and "emancipation" of the "Peoples of the East," calling on them to join the international proletariat.[31] Yet Soviet consolidation of power in Central Asia proved extremely difficult. Communists were virtually nonexistent in Central Asia. As elsewhere in non-Russian lands, indigenous resistance was high. For many, the Russian Empire's collapse was an opportunity for autonomy.

[29] Adeeb Khalid, "Tashkent 1917: Muslim Politics in Revolutionary Turkestan," *Slavic Review* 2 (1996): 273; Khalid, *Making Uzbekistan*, 30.

[30] L. C. Gatagova, L. P. Kosheleva, and L. A. Rogovaia, "Vvedenie," in *TsK RKP(b)-VKP(b) i Natsional'nyi Vopros, Kniga 1, 1918–33gg.*, ed. L. C. Gatagova, L. P. Kosheleva, and L. A. Rogovaia (Moscow: ROSSPYEN, 2005), 6.

[31] V. I. Lenin, "Address to the Second All-Russia Congress of Communist Organizations of the Peoples of the East" (November 22, 1919), *Bulletin of the CC.R.C.P.(B.),* no. 9 (December 20, 1919), https://www.marxists.org/archive/lenin/works/1919/nov/22.htm, from Lenin's Collected Works, 4th English Edition, Vol. 30 (Moscow: Progress Publishers, 1965), 151–62.

Across the empire, 1917 did not herald unity with the establishment of the first communist state. Rather, the revolution was just the start of several years of civil wars, many of which involved non-Russian insurgencies opposing forced incorporation into the Russian-dominated USSR.[32] Central Asians did not unanimously welcome the Bolsheviks as liberators. The Red Army had to crush Kokand into submission in 1918, and it took Bukhara only by force in 1920.

"War Communism"—a term coined by Lenin to describe Bolshevik policy during the civil war, from 1918 to 1921—involved the rapid, uncompromising implementation of Bolshevik policies of land and property expropriation, grain requisitioning, and cessation of the free market so as to achieve a communist economy more quickly. In Central Asia, War Communism not only triggered widespread violence but also caused mass starvation in the Ferghana Valley and prompted the flight of thousands of Muslims to Afghanistan, Turkey, and China.[33] In fact, in 1914–22 the Ferghana Valley suffered more than any other area of Central Asia, with the population dropping by about 550,000 people; an estimated 20 to 33 percent of the population perished.[34]

War Communism's failure was followed by a strategic retreat; the New Economic Policy (NEP) introduced in 1921 was an "interlude" in the Bolshevik onslaught that reintroduced the free market in an effort to alleviate the economic disaster gripping the country.[35] The NEP's calculated retrenchment of Soviet power consequently opened up economic, social, and, to some extent, contested political space. Even as it adjusted its economic plan, however, the Party resumed its efforts to transform Central Asia by establishing new governance structures. This process was often chaotic and multifaceted, as political divisions had emerged among the European population, as well as among the Muslim population, along altogether different axes.[36] Although Soviet rule had been imposed by late 1917, as resistance grew, the Party sought local counterparts and supporters—including among Central Asian Muslims.

The most significant example of Muslim integration into the new political order was the rise to prominence by the early 1920s of Muslim modernist ideas, disseminated by a new group of activists who came to be known as the Jadids.[37] Jadidism had begun as a modernist intellectual movement for cultural

[32] Jonathan Smele, *The "Russian" Civil Wars, 1916–1926: Ten Years That Shook the World* (New York: Oxford University Press, 2017).

[33] Ashirbek Muminov, Uygun Gafurov, and Rinat Shigabdinov, "Islamic Education in Soviet and Post-Soviet Uzbekistan," in *Central Asian Studies: Islamic Education in the Soviet Union and Its Successor States*, ed. Michael Kemper, Raoul Motika, and Stefan Reichmuth (Florence: Routledge, 2009), 232.

[34] Sergey Abashin with Kamoludin Abdullaev, Ravshan Abdullaev, and Arslan Koichiev, "Soviet Rule and the Delineation of Borders in the Ferghana Valley, 1917–1930," in *Ferghana Valley: The Heart of Central Asia*, ed. S. Frederick Starr (London: M. E. Sharpe, 2011), 102.

[35] Sheila Fitzpatrick, *The Russian Revolution* (Oxford: Oxford University Press, 2017).

[36] Khalid, "Tashkent 1917," 270.

[37] Khalid, *Making Uzbekistan*, 32–38.

reform. Originating in Crimea in the 1890s with the reformist writer Ismail Bey Gasprinskiy (1851–1914),[38] it had spread to Turkestan, where it sought to remake Central Asian culture through educational reform. Its program advanced "new method" schools to replace the static, *ulama*-dominated system. Abdurauf Fitrat (1896–1938), one of the most influential Jadids, copiously wrote and disseminated Jadidst ideas, which provided a counterpoint to *ulama*'s traditionalism; Fitrat advocated modernism, ethnic belonging, the unity of the Turkic peoples and languages, Muslim nationalism (specifically for the sedentary "Muslims of Turkestan"), and ultimately an "Uzbek nation."[39] The Jadids, comprised of some wealthy merchants, a small, educated Muslim elite in urban centers such as Tashkent, and a handful of *ulama* reformers, pursued an agenda of progress, modernity, and enlightenment for Muslims.[40]

After 1917, the Jadids came to occupy positions of cultural and even political influence.[41] While not communist, as modernists and advocates of the nation, the Jadids shared many Bolshevik ideas and therefore became extremely influential in the People's Soviet Republic of Bukhara (BNSR), the temporary republic created in 1920 after the Bukharan Emirate was forced into the Bolshevik state. Yet, in his groundbreaking study of the Jadids' influence in the revolutionary period, Adeeb Khalid has argued that, "[The BNSR] was rooted in discourses of Muslim modernism much more than those of Marxism or Leninism; it was a Muslim republic."[42] However, the BNSR did not last, for the Bolsheviks did not truly support autonomy. In 1924 the Party imposed new "national" (i.e., ethnically defined) administrative borders on Soviet Central Asia, and the BNSR was forced into the new Uzbek republic. Indeed, the National Territorial Delimitation, when finally completed in 1936, had carved out five Central Asian republics within the USSR: the Uzbek, Tajik, Turkmen, Kazakh, and Kyrgyz Soviet Socialist Republics (SSRs). The formation of new "nations" and "national cadres" aimed, at least rhetorically, to be internationalist and inclusive and to mobilize indigenous support for the Party.[43] The Party sought to stem nationalism and secession and retain the economic assets of the tsarist empire; they therefore created an "empire of nations" rather than allow self-determination.[44] Despite the blow to their goals in Bukhara, the Jadids cooperated with the Party and proved to have great effect in influencing the establishment of the new Uzbek

[38] Khalid, *The Politics of Muslim Cultural Reform*, 35.

[39] Khalid, *Making Uzbekistan*, 42, 54.

[40] Khalid, *Making Uzbekistan*, 38, 54.

[41] Khalid, "Tashkent 1917," 275.

[42] Khalid, *Making Uzbekistan*, 118.

[43] Ronald G. Suny, *Revenge of the Past: Nationalism, Revolution, and the Collapse of the Soviet Union* (Stanford, CA: Stanford University Press, 1993).

[44] Francine Hirsch, *Empire of Nations* (Ithaca, NY: Cornell University Press, 2005); Terry Martin, *The Affirmative Action Empire* (Ithaca, NY: Cornell University Press, 2001).

republic. The new borders, modernizing cultural and educational reforms, the secularization of the public sphere, the diminishing of the *ulama*, and the creation of the Uzbek nation all reflected Jadidist goals.[45]

By contrast, the Tajiks and others deemed fanatically Muslim or mere tribesmen were largely excluded from the process, were subsumed within the Uzbek SSR until 1929, and continued to be marginalized in the governance of their new national republics for some time.[46] In fact, the new borders and institutions had, in part, established modern national identities to replace and disempower religious and other indigenous elites the Soviets deemed premodern and opposed to their rule.[47]

This brief sketch of the pre-1917 sociopolitical order, Bolshevik political goals for Central Asia, and the Russian Revolution's unfolding allows us to comprehend why 1917 represented a fundamental break with the past for Central Asia. Despite some limited support from the modernist Jadids, the revolution triggered significant opposition from the religious elite and pious, ordinary Muslims whose political order and social norms were throttled by Bolshevik atheism.

Conditions Fostering Muslim Mobilization in Opposition to the Revolution, 1917–26

Growing Associational Space: Pre-1917 and Post-1917

By the early twentieth century, crucial changes were already underway that would shape the nature of Muslim mobilization that emerged in 1917. Tsarist power had been declining since at least 1905, and there had been a notable opening in civic space in some urban centers (far more so in Turkestan than in the *ulama*-dominated Bukhara) for discussing ideas, local and transnational. The growth of education and an active Turkic-language press in the early twentieth century led to the spread of new concepts about society, education, identity, and ultimately politics in Central Asia.

The February 1917 Russian Revolution brought the end of the tsarist regime and introduced a relatively liberal period under the provisional government, which triggered a sudden expansion of associational space in Central Asia. The indigenous Muslim population seized the moment to articulate its interests. In addition to the pro-revolutionary Jadids, other forms of Muslim politics emerged, facilitated by an active Muslim press. Muslim congresses began to

45 Khalid, *Making Uzbekistan*.

46 Martin, *Affirmative Action Empire*, 181.

47 Bergne, *Birth of Tajikistan*, 62; Beatrice Penati, "The Reconquest of East Bukhara," *Central Asian Survey* 26, no. 4 (2007): 52.

assemble across the former Russian Empire, and Muslim organizations of many stripes appeared in Tashkent.[48] Such space declined once the Bolsheviks seized power in Petrograd on October 25, 1917—the October Revolution. Six days later in Tashkent, the Bolsheviks announced they held power in Turkestan through the Tashkent *soviet*. Yet, political uncertainty, lack of centralized state control, and ongoing upheaval continued to make associational activism possible; protest movements and insurgencies grew. Throughout the ensuing decade, the lack of strong Party control over much of Central Asia was reflected in ongoing resistance; such turbulent conditions increased the associational space that had developed in the previous two decades as tsarist control had weakened. Into this space, as we shall see, multiple types of activism emerged, some modernist, some nationalist, and some reactionary. Counterintuitively, even as state control over associational space loosened across Central Asia, space for religious activity was immediately under threat.

Religious Repression: The Bolshevik Assault on Muslim Social Order

Bolshevik rule initiated a dramatic transformation of Central Asia. It ushered in religious oppression, a key factor in Islamist emergence. The Bolshevik Party's ideology was rooted in the *Communist Manifesto* of Karl Marx and Friedrich Engels, adapted and implemented by Vladimir I. Lenin, the Bolshevik leader of the Russian Revolution and head of the Soviet government (1922–24). Religiosity and belief in the divine were, according to Marx, the "opium of the people." The Communist Party[49] proposed a radical alternative: an atheist society, party, and government that would break the people free of religious chains and reorder society according to the modernist, materialist principles of communism. This goal was directly threatening to Muslim elites and society.

While repression initially targeted the Russian Orthodox Church, the Bolsheviks soon turned to Islam. Lenin's ideas regarding "the East" reflected a contradictory plan to integrate and liberate the "oppressed" indigenous population of Central Asia from Russian imperialism, while also eradicating Islam. Ironically, the Bolsheviks' understanding of Islam in many ways mirrored the "Orientalism" of the Russian colonialists whom they had overthrown.[50] Ignorant

[48] Khalid, "Tashkent 1917," 276–83.

[49] VKP(b) is the acronym used at the time for the Party; the name for the Communist Party shifted frequently in the 1920s. Throughout discussion of the 1920s, I use "Bolshevik" and "communist" interchangeably.

[50] Vladimir Bobrovnikov, "The Contribution of Oriental Scholarship to the Soviet Anti-Islamic Discourse: From the Militant Godless to the Knowledge Society," in *The Heritage of Soviet Oriental Studies*, ed. Michael Kemper and Stephan Conermann (London: Routledge, 2011), 73–78.

and afraid of Islam, the Bolsheviks suspected "cults" and "religious fanaticism" among observant Muslims, who allegedly forced women to wear the *paranji*, sold girls into arranged marriages, and deprived them of education.[51] They viewed Muslim clerics as obscurantists, impeding the road to modernity. They saw their mission among Muslims of the East as both liberalizing and civilizing, "conquering" the Central Asians, who in their view were the "embodiment of backwardness."[52] Soviet Orientalist discourse about Islam justified and required a violent cultural revolution, which meant crushing religion, its institutions, personnel, values, and practices.[53]

The Bolshevik seizure of power entailed decrees that abolished private property, including that of religious organizations and leaders. Local Party organs rapidly seized centuries-old *waqf* property which sustained the *ulama* and its Islamic schools. The July 1918 Soviet Constitution denied clergy the right to vote. It later revoked the right to freedom of conscience and to disseminate religious "propaganda." Early decrees also dissolved religious marriages, put Islamic family law under civil court jurisdiction, and banned Islamic marriage rituals. In 1919, another decree abolished legal pluralism and *shariat* courts, replacing them with Soviet versions, which were initially military tribunals. Bolshevism thus attempted to quickly overthrow the central role of Muslim civil and societal organizations, especially the *ulama*. Granting women suffrage further upended the existing social hierarchy.

Shoshana Keller has argued that this policy on Islam amounted to brutal social engineering, but antireligious measures were not fully implemented until 1927.[54] Shifting policy on Islam reflected the broader context of the NEP's strategic retreat after the failure of War Communism. Between 1921 and 1923, the Bolsheviks made tactical concessions to Muslims, issuing decrees that reestablished the *shariat* courts; however, further decrees limited their authority and the number of such courts significantly decreased within a few years.[55] The government returned the *waqfs* but established the GVU, the Head Waqf Directorate, to put *waqf* lands and properties under the Ispolkom (Executive Committee). Cooperative clergy were brought into the institution to administer the property, while a new spiritual administration co-opted and strengthened the "progressive *ulama*" and advanced school reform.[56] However, in addition to traditional *ulama* resistance, the state simply lacked the capacity, funds, and

51 Bobrovnikov, "Contribution of Oriental Scholarship," 76.

52 Khalid, *Making Uzbekistan*, 213; Adeeb Khalid, "Russian History and the Debate over Orientalism," *Kritika*, n.s. 1 (2000): 697.

53 Michael Kemper, "The Soviet Discourse on the Origin and Class Character of Islam, 1923–1933," *Die Welt des Islams*, n.s., 49, no. 1 (2009).

54 Keller, *To Moscow, Not Mecca*.

55 Khalid, *Making Uzbekistan*, 232–33, 237.

56 Keller, *To Moscow Not Mecca*, 36.

personnel to force the new secular system on the population. The ban on Islamic schools was temporarily abolished, as Party leaders urged caution in more conservative areas.[57] Nonetheless, the forced shift to Soviet schools escalated after 1923. Whereas before 1917 there were 10,072 traditional, *ulama*-run schools, by 1927 only 1,305 remained; resistance to the shift was highest in the Ferghana Valley.[58]

Because the Red Army conquered the Bukharan Emirate only in 1920, oppressive measures began later there. The Bolsheviks created the BNSR under the newly established Bukharan Communist Party and unleashed a sweeping assault on the long-standing social and legal order. French and Turkish anticlerical ideas heavily influenced the state takeover of schools and *waqfs*. The Bukharan press printed extensive propaganda against religion. Theater presented Muslim clerics as immoral, corrupt, backward, and puppets of capitalist foreign powers. *Shariat* courts were put under the Ministry of Justice. Islamic education came under the oversight of the secular and modernist Ministry of Education. The Party even destroyed shrines and banned the practice of holding elaborate life-cycle celebrations, such as Muslim funerals—rituals core to Muslim identity.[59]

In short, across the region, but especially among the Muslims of the Ferghana Valley and the former Bukharan Emirate, whose lives were strictly oriented around the mosque and institutions of Islamic learning, the Bolshevik agenda was destructive and rapidly triggered fear and anger as the *ulama* and Muslim elites saw their way of life come under frontal attack.

Ideas and Entrepreneurs

In just a few months, a flurry of modernist, nationalist, and even democratic ideas about political order, along with traditionalist ideas, surfaced across the region, propagated by indigenous elites, activists, and political entrepreneurs. Notably, neither communist nor Islamist ideologies were among those ideas.

While Jadidist ideas in many ways aligned with the Bolshevik Revolution, other ideas motivated significant Muslim political activism in opposition to Bolshevism. One set of ideas could be described as proto-democratic: the notion that parliamentary governance might be combined with Muslim norms was circulating throughout parts of the Middle East and Eurasia in the early 1900s,

[57] No. 82, "Tsirkularnoe pis'mo OGPU polnomochnym predstaviteliam OGPU i oblastnym otdelam OGPU vostochnykh okrain o prepodavanii islama v shkolakh" (before May 12, 1924), in *TsK RKP(b)-VKP(b) i Natsional'nyi Vopros, Kniga 1, 1918–33gg.*, 202–3; Muminov, Gafurov, and Shigabdinov, "Islamic Education," 230.

[58] Muminov, Gafurov, and Shigabdinov, "Islamic Education," 244.

[59] Khalid, *Making Uzbekistan*, 137–38.

from Iran to Azerbaijan and the territory of the new Uzbek SSR. Jadidist ideas of educational reform and modernism were also blended with the idea of territorial autonomy. The entrepreneurs who advocated such ideas would mobilize to establish the Kokand Autonomy.

Yet, the idea of governance most widely supported might be called traditionalist—a desire to return to the old order, to the political and social system that had existed in Bukhara until 1920 or in Kokand prior to Russian colonialism. This was not an Islamist idea of establishing a caliphate or a modern Islamic state, and not centrally about theological debate, but instead concerned restoring the long-standing prominence of the *ulama* and *shariat* in law and society. Traditionalists sought to reestablish the authority and property of societal elites, especially of clerics but also of the tribal *bai* (feudal lords), communal elders, and urban notables. Throughout the region, various entrepreneurs would mobilize followers behind movements that attempted to restore versions of this sociopolitical order—some through the Tashkent *duma* (legislature) and others by joining the Basmachi insurgency.

The growing threat of religious oppression, but with adequate associational space to organize, engendered religio-political entrepreneurs who articulated multiple and competing ideas about Muslim autonomy and *shariat*. They would contribute to widespread anti-Soviet mobilization in the decade following the 1917 Revolution.

Cases of Opposition Mobilization, 1917–26: Muslim but Not Islamist

Although Central Asia officially became part of the new Bolshevik state between 1917 and 1920, it did so only through violence and civil war, which continued in some areas for up to six years.[60] In this context, multiple forms of Central Asian mobilization emerged. I do not offer an exhaustive overview of all activism during this period; rather, I sketch several cases of Muslim opposition mobilization. In doing so, I emphasize two points. First, in line with my core argument, absent an Islamist ideology to influence activists' views, no expressly Islamist movement emerged in 1917; however, "Muslim politics"—debate and contestation over Islam's role in the new order—was prominent. Second, evidence of the varied Muslim activism that did emerge sustains another core argument of this book: that Muslims do not inevitably or homogeneously support an Islamic state.

[60] Smele, *"Russian" Civil Wars*, 36–37.

The Turkestan Ulama

Throughout Turkestan, the *ulama* and other Muslim elites generally opposed the October Revolution; Bolshevism posed a threat to their religion, social order, and hierarchies of power. Opposition took various forms, including the formation of new Muslim congresses, whose debates revealed the growing importance of Muslim politics.

In early 1917, Muslim activism escalated in Turkestan, particularly in elections to the Tashkent city *duma*, where many used that forum to disseminate ideas about Muslim autonomy. Members of the Turkestani *ulama* formed the Ulamo Jamiyati (Society of Ulama), a modern organization that functioned as a party and represented the interests of traditional elites. With over forty thousand votes, the Society successfully won the largest *duma* bloc in August 1917.[61] While progressive in its electoral participation, the Turkestani *ulama* generally viewed *shariat* as inseparable from law and governance. They wanted to revive their traditional social role, political influence, and hierarchy of power, justified by *shariat*, and sought to restore the *shariat* courts. They opposed Bolshevik ideas about cultural change and women's suffrage.[62] To counter more liberal factions within the *duma*, the ulama convened a congress, declaring that "the affairs of religion and of this world should not be separated, that is, everything from schools to questions of land and justice should be solved according to the *shariat*"; moreover, "women should not have rights equal to those of men, but everyone should have rights according to one's station as adjudged by the *shariat*."[63]

Nonetheless, the Ulamo Jamiyati advocated Muslim autonomy *within* the new Russian-dominated federation but called, unsuccessfully, for the Tashkent *soviet* to include Muslims. Tashkent, where Russians and Europeans were most numerous, had become the seat of Bolshevik power in Central Asia, and by November 1917 the Bolsheviks ruled the region through the city's *soviet*. Highly distrustful of Muslim activism, the Bolsheviks of Turkestan excluded Muslims from Party meetings and governance,[64] arguing that they were neither "workers" nor culturally prepared to be in the new administration.[65] The Third Regional Congress of Soviets on November 15, 1917, declared, "Muslim participation in the highest revolutionary bodies is for now unacceptable. . . . [There is] no proletarian class organization of the kind that the Bolsheviks would be prepared to

[61] Khalid, "Tashkent 1917," 287.

[62] Marianne Kamp, "Debating Sharia: The 1917 Muslim Women's Congress in Russia," *Journal of Women's History* 27, no. 4 (Winter 2015): 29.

[63] Khalid, "Tashkent 1917," 289.

[64] Khalid, *Making Uzbekistan*.

[65] Interview with Davlat Usmon, Dushanbe, Tajikistan, 2010; Sahadeo, *Russian Colonial Society*, 218.

welcome into the highest regional authority."[66] Ultimately, the Tashkent *soviet* dissolved the existing city *duma* in which the Society of Ulama had been dominant.[67] Despite Lenin's exhortations to increase native participation,[68] as the Bolsheviks consolidated control in Turkestan they excluded those insufficiently supportive of their antireligious and modernizing agenda. Moreover, Bolshevik policies also differentially targeted Muslims; frequent Red Guard requisitions left the Muslim population near starvation,[69] triggering protests in which large numbers of Muslims were arrested.

The Kokand Autonomy

The Ferghana Valley soon became the center of anti-Bolshevik Muslim activism as the Bolsheviks tightened their control over Tashkent.[70] Motivated by Russian exclusion, some Jadids and *ulama* left Tashkent for Kokand. In the heart of the Ferghana region, Kokand became a center of counterrevolution as Muslim regional congresses challenged the Tashkent *soviet*, advancing a mix of Muslim nationalist, democratic, and traditionalist ideas about governance.

On November 26, 1917, the Fourth Extraordinary Regional Congress of Muslims convened in Kokand. The Ferghana Valley's population had been brutally repressed during the 1876 Russian colonial takeover,[71] and again following a bloody but failed 1898 Andijon uprising against Russian imperial soldiers. The uprising, led by a Sufi shaykh known as Dukchi Ishan, a follower of a puritanical and anticolonial Sufi order, has been interpreted by some historians as a jihad.[72] Proponents of the pre-Russian sociopolitical order hoped 1917 would finally return their autonomy; however, disillusioned with the exclusionary policies of the Tashkent *soviet*, the Fourth Congress instead elected the Provisional Government of Autonomous Turkestan and the Provisional People's Council, which they entrusted with planning an elected parliamentary council. The new "self-proclaimed Muslim government," a "symbol of anti-Bolshevik opposition," became known as the Kokand Autonomy (KA).[73] The KA enjoyed significant

66 Abashin et al., "Soviet Rule and the Delineation," 95.
67 Sahadeo, *Russian Colonial Society*, 211–12.
68 Gatagova, Kosheleva, and Rogovaia, "Vvedenie," 8.
69 Sahadeo, *Russian Colonial Society*, 218.
70 Paul Bergne, "The Kokand Autonomy, 1917–18," in *Central Asia: Aspects of Transition*, ed. Tom Everett-Heath (London: RoutledgeCurzon, 2003), 30; Abashin et al., "Soviet Rule and the Delineation," 96.
71 Victor Dubovitskii and Khaydarbek Bababekov, "The Rise and Fall of the Kokand Khanate," in Starr, *Ferghana Valley*, 49–50.
72 Hisao Komatsu, "The Andijon Uprising Reconsidered," in *Muslim Societies: Historical and Comparative Aspects*, ed. S. Tsugitaka (London: RoutledgeCurzon, 2004), 29–61.
73 Abashin et al., "Soviet Rule and the Delineation," 97.

popular backing, although its leadership was divided among those Jadids who had rejected Bolshevism, nationalist reformers, moderate socialists, and a small *ulama* representation. Seeking the European population's support, the council demanded equality for Muslims and non-Muslims; influenced by Jadidist ideas, it advocated cultural and educational reform, and proclaimed national territorial autonomy for Turkestan, a move that caused division within the *ulama*. Still, the KA did not claim full sovereignty and most delegates remained open to the possibility of a union with a democratic Russian federation; it hoped for the fulfillment of the liberal promises of the February Revolution.[74] At the same time, other KA delegates sought freedom from the control of Bolshevik unbelievers and supported the preservation of Islam's traditionally wide sociopolitical role in Kokand. KA leader Mustafa Chokaev pronounced an agenda strongly influenced by at least some conservative Muslim ideas: "[We want] *shariat* courts, our system of land tenure . . . women to remain veiled and subordinate," unlike "Europeans."[75]

Backed by Kokand's strictly observant Muslim bourgeoisie, the magnates of financial power in Central Asia,[76] the KA organized demonstrations throughout Turkestan, unnerving the Bolsheviks. In a protest in Tashkent in December 1917, on the Prophet's birthday, tens of thousands of KA supporters carried green Islamic flags as they marched toward the Russian quarters of Tashkent.[77] Bolshevik troops opened fire and the event ended in bloodshed. By early 1918, the Bolsheviks were determined to crush the KA. The Red Army slaughtered an estimated ten thousand to fourteen thousand people in Kokand, including many civilians, and ransacked and then leveled the city.[78] The KA was short-lived but would generate long-lasting mistrust and contention with Bolshevik power, especially in the Ferghana Valley.

The Basmachi Insurgency

The consequence of Bolshevik repression—from the destruction of Kokand in 1918 to the overthrow of the Bukharan Emirate in 1920—was the birth of another form of Muslim activism, a militant movement motivated to restore a traditionalist political order that would uphold Islam and defend Muslims. Branded the "Basmachi" (bandits) by the Bolsheviks, these insurgents continued to mobilize

74 Khalid, *Making Uzbekistan*, 73–74.
75 Khasanov, cited in Bergne, "Kokand Autonomy," 38.
76 Bergne, "Kokand Autonomy," 31–37.
77 Stephen Kotkin, *Stalin: Paradoxes of Power, 1878–1928* (New York: Penguin, 2014), 254.
78 Abashin et al., "Soviet Rule and the Delineation," 97–98; Bergne, "Kokand Autonomy," 31; Kotkin, *Stalin*, 255.

into the early 1930s, primarily in the Ferghana Valley and eastern Bukhara (regions that became incorporated into the Uzbek and Tajik SSRs in the 1920s).[79] Jonathan Smele has argued that the Basmachi movement was an insurgency so significant that it amounted to "an armed civil war against Soviet supremacy."[80]

The Basmachi movement was in fact a loose collection of multiple armed factions with no central organization; it included elements of resistance from the Ferghana Valley, Bukhara, eastern Bukhara, and even the former Khivan Khanate. The Basmachi, known locally as the *qo'rboshi* (commanders of local militias) aimed to defend the population from Bolshevism.[81] Its membership included village mullahs, the Bukharan *ulama*, the emir's forces (estimated at some thirty thousand to forty thousand) calling for "holy war,"[82] former activists of the Kokand Autonomy, landowners, Turkmen tribal and religious leaders, prominent Sufi shaykhs, and even some Jadids angered by Bolshevik betrayal.[83] Various religious, clan, and tribal leaders used their networks and sacred authority to mobilize the insurgency.[84] Peasants supported the opposition, both in defense of their religion, customs, and land and also to resist food confiscation. Mercenaries and adventurists also joined.[85]

Contrary to the claims of contemporary Islamists, the Basmachi were not a pan-Islamic and pro-caliphate movement. They had no Islamist ideology. Yet they did include a strong religious element; their leaders were often *ulama*, aggrieved by the overthrow of the old order in which Islam played a central role. They sought to defend societal religious practices and traditional forms of power. Basmachi appeals to the population for support in resisting the Bolsheviks were made at least in part on religious grounds and grievances, which increased with the intensified Soviet attack on Islam. According to OGPU (Soviet secret police) reports, the *bai* claimed that Russians sought "to destroy their Islamic religion" and that "without the Basmachi, the Russians would establish their own religion."[86] The Basmachi drew upon Islamic symbols and the sacred authority of religious leaders—including *qazis*, mullahs, *eshons*, and *khojas*—to enhance the movement's support. One legendary Basmachi leader, known as Ibrohim

[79] No. 41, "Zakrytoe pis'mo sekretaria TsK KP(b) Turkestana M. S. Epshteina v TsK RKP(b) po itogam poezdki v Ferganu" (March 17, 1923), in *TsK RKP(b)-VKP(b) i Natsional'nyi Vopros, Kniga 1, 1918–33gg.*, 102; Alfred Rieber, *Stalin and the Struggle for Supremacy in Eurasia* (Cambridge: Cambridge University Press, 2015), 75.

[80] Smele, *"Russian" Civil Wars*, 234.

[81] Memoir, shared by the author's brother, Tashkent, Uzbekistan, 2014, 5; Petr Kokaisl and Emirbek Usmanov, *Istoriia Kyrgyzstana glazami ochevidtsev: Nachalo XX veka* (Prague: Institut etnologii, 2012), 55–56.

[82] Teresa Rakowska-Harmstone, *Russia and Nationalism in Central Asia: The Case of Tadzhikistan* (Baltimore, MD: Johns Hopkins University Press, 1970), 23; Smele, *"Russian" Civil Wars*, 234.

[83] Khalid, *Making Uzbekistan*, 230; Peyrouse, *Turkmenistan*, 32.

[84] Kassymbekova, *Despite Cultures*, 26–31, points out that some switched sides.

[85] Smele, *"Russian" Civil Wars*, 235.

[86] *Sovershenno Sekretno* 5 (1927): 531.

bek, articulated religious grievances against the "Satanic Government" of the Bolsheviks, decrying its destruction of mosques, houses of prayer, and religious books, its laws forbidding religious burial and wedding ceremonies, the rise of prostitution, disregard for the *shariat*, the corruption of the younger generation, and the destruction "of all those who dare even to speak the name of God."[87] He claimed to be fighting to defend Islam and the homeland against invaders. However, religion was not the only motivating force. Confiscated land, the use of tractors, and heavy taxes were also included prominently in Ibrohim *bek*'s proclamation against the Bolsheviks.[88]

The Ferghana Valley initially became the center of Basmachi operations. By the summer of 1919, the region was "virtually cut off from Soviet control." Some eight thousand to fifteen thousand Basmachi remained in the Ferghana Valley region,[89] even after the Red Army forced them to flee into eastern Bukhara. In February 1922, the Basmachi successfully seized Dushanbe, but several months later they waged a failed assault on Bukhara. In April 1922, Fayzulla Xo'jayev, a Jadid who had become head of the BNSR in 1920, estimated the armed Basmachi forces to be up to four thousand in eastern Bukhara, with another twelve thousand supporters in different places, following various shaykhs. He added, "Ibrohim *bek*, the former aide of the emir, has 4000 persons, as do others."[90] They were, he asserted, receiving arms from Afghanistan.[91] By 1923–24, Bolshevik concessions and military successes had weakened popular support for the Basmachi resistance, driving them from the Ferghana region. Yet, particularly strong Basmachi bases remained in Matjo, Darvoz, Gharm, the Qarotegin Valley, Qurghonteppa, and Kulob.[92] Fazel Maqsum, a famed Basmachi leader in Gharm, is known to have led the last major Basmachi battle against the Red Army in 1929.[93] The Bukharan emir himself fled to Afghanistan with his fighters and waged attacks from across the Amu Darya border until 1931. Ibrohim *bek* continued small-scale but frequent attacks on the Bolsheviks from mountainous areas of the Tajik republic until his arrest and execution in 1932.

87 "Proclamation of Ibrohim bek, 1931," text printed in Rakowska-Harmstone, *Russia and Nationalism*, 297–98.

88 "Proclamation of Ibrohim bek," 297–98.

89 Sahadeo, *Russian Colonial Society*, 212.

90 No. 155, "Telegramma I. V. Stalina–G. K. Ordzhonikidze" (May 14, 1922), in *Bol'shevistskoe Rukovodstvo: Perepiska: 1912–1927* (Moscow: ROSSPYEN, 1996), 252–53. The document includes a letter from Xo'jayev to Karakhan.

91 No. 155, "Telegramma I. V. Stalina–G. K. Ordzhonikidze," 253.

92 Rakowska-Harmstone, *Russia and Nationalism*, 26; Stéphane Dudoignon and Sayyid Ahmad Qalandar, "They Were All from the Country," in Stéphane Dudoignon and Christian Noack, *Allah's Kolkhozes: Migration, De-Stalinisation, Privatisation and the New Muslim Congregations in the Soviet Realm (1950s–2000s)* (Berlin: Klaus Schwarz Verlag, 2014), 65–66.

93 Monica Whitlock, *Land beyond the River* (New York: Thomas Dunne Books, 2003), 55.

Like the KA, the Basmachi movement illustrates that religious repression, in the context of sufficient associational space, generated high Muslim mobilization. However, absent an ideology, the Basmachi did not advance a modern Islamist agenda; they merely sought a return to what they viewed as the traditional Islamic order.

Differing Paths of Incorporation into the USSR and Consequences for Islam

As we have seen, individuals, groups, or regions the Bolsheviks deemed more amenable to their modernizing and transformative aims, such as the Jadids, were expediently brought into Soviet governance—at least for a time. By contrast, those areas where opposition, especially of an Islamic nature, was particularly strong—the south-central Tajik republic and the Ferghana Valley of the Uzbek republic (e.g., Kokand)—were violently repressed and excluded from Soviet governance.

High Contention and Exclusion Further Politicizes Islam (the Tajik Republic; the Ferghana Valley of the Uzbek Republic)

The Basmachi movement was the source of the most violent contention between the Muslim population and the Soviet state. That contention reinforced Soviet Orientalist views, which justified the exclusion of certain Muslim groups and thus continued to politicize Muslim identity over the longer term. Stalin personally expressed such views in a March 1919 *Pravda* article: "Our tasks in the East . . . present . . . culturally backward peoples, either stuck in the middle ages or only recently entered into the realm of capitalist development."[94] Likewise, a Soviet report by a local commissariat of justice referred to the "2½ million-strong dark and fanatical Muslim population."[95] Consequently, by 1923, Stalin had begun reducing the power of national-minority party cadres and using the OGPU Eastern Department for the close surveillance of Soviet Muslim communists.[96]

The Basmachi and the resistant *ulama* thwarted Soviet goals so forcefully in the Ferghana Valley that for some time the Soviets retracted their agenda and did not even attempt to implement their decrees on *waqf*s and courts in those regions.[97]

[94] Kotkin, *Stalin*, 369.
[95] Khalid, *Making Uzbekistan*, 233.
[96] Kotkin, *Stalin*, 502.
[97] Paolo Sartori, "What Went Wrong: The Failure of Soviet Policy in Shari'a Courts in Turkestan, 1917–1923," *Die Welt des Islams* 50 (2010): 397–434.

A communication from A. A. Ioffe, the chairman of the Turkestan Bureau of the Central Committee of the Russian Communist Party (known as the Turkbiuro), to Vyacheslav Molotov, secretary of the Party's Central Committee, discussed Basmachi activism as driving the "complete collapse" of Party governance there; Ioffe observed that "there have been instances of [those who] leave Party organizations to join the Basmachi."[98] BNSR leader Xo'jayev was so concerned that he recommended "convoking an emergency congress of all the ringleaders of the tribes and authoritative persons and spiritual leadership with a friendly attitude to Soviet power," which "will be the base of our revolutionary actions against the Basmachi."[99]

In April 1922, Stalin sent the Cheka (secret police) to Tashkent to "liquidate the Basmachi movement in the districts of Ferghana and Bukhara . . . [and] ascertain . . . the condition and number of the Basmachi fighters and information about the progress of the political struggle against the Basmachi movement by the local powers and Party organizations."[100] A leading Party member close to Stalin, G. K. Ordzhonikidze, reported several weeks later that "the situation in Bukhara can be characterized as a general uprising," especially in eastern Bukhara,[101] which was almost in a state of "civil war" due to the Basmachi insurgency.[102] Ordzhonikidze further emphasized that "the Basmachi are undoubtedly connected with dissatisfied urban groups. . . . The Basmachi make up songs about defense of religion, Muslimhood, against the Russians. . . . [T]here's been a rising up of feudal lords [*bai*] and khans, who have their military people wage strikes [against us]." He recommended using the Cheka "to dilute them."[103] Consequently, on May 14, 1922, Stalin declared that war in Bukhara was "unavoidable" and that "the occupation is inevitable, the sooner the better."[104]

Realizing that Muslim backlash was exacting a heavy toll on Soviet forces and resources, later in 1924 the Party became more careful in "reactionary" areas and made temporary concessions in the implementation of secular schools for Tajik and Uzbek Muslims of Turkestan and former eastern Bukhara (and likewise for Chechens and Dagestanis in the Caucasus). By contrast, it quickly eliminated religious schools in the regions which had offered little resistance.[105]

[98] No. 152, "Shifrotelegramma predsedatelia Turkbiuro TsK RKP(b) A. A. Ioffe sekretariu TsK RKP(b) V. M. Molotovu o polozhenii v Ferganskoi oblasti" (November 30, 1921), in *Rossiia i Tsentral'naia Aziia 1905–1925 gg.: Sbornik dokumentov*, ed. D. A. Amandolova (Karagandi: KarGU Press, 2005), 335.

[99] No. 155, "Telegramma I. V. Stalina–G. K. Ordzhonikidze," 253.

[100] No. 152, "Telegramma I. V. Stalina–G. K. Ordzhonikidze" (April 21, 1922), in *Bol'shevistskoe Rukovodstvo*, 247.

[101] No. 154, "Telegramma G. K. Ordzhonikidze–I. V. Stalinu" (May 12, 1922), in *Bol'shevistskoe Rukovodstvo*, 250.

[102] Khalid, *Making Uzbekistan*, 139–40.

[103] No. 156, "G. K. Ordzhonikidze–I. V. Stalinu" (May 18, 1922), in *Bol'shevistskoe rukovodstvo*, 255.

[104] No. 155, "Telegramma I. V. Stalina–G. K. Ordzhonikidze," 251.

[105] No. 82, "Tsirkularnoe pis'mo OGPU," 202–3.

In 1925, the Politburo was still discussing the Basmachi in connection with defending its Afghan border. It commissioned the Central Asian Bureau (which had replaced the TurkBiuro in 1922) of the Party's Central Committee to put "energetic military pressure on the Basmachi," to improve economic conditions, and to use "the most decisive measures—repression" against the "Basmachi shaykhs who ha[d] not given up their weapons."[106] The decision gave a "special department of the [secret police] the right . . . to use the highest measures of punishment toward the Basmachi who have been captured with weapons in their hands; to establish on the whole territory of eastern Bukhara emergency sessions of military tribunals with the right of carrying out final sentences about the highest measures of punishment within twenty-four hours."[107] The OGPU was further charged with "expelling [Basmachi] from the bounds of Turkestan" and was entrusted in the Uzbek SSR and Tajik Autonomous SSR with "carrying out the cleansing of the Soviet apparat of the Emirate's bureaucrats."[108]

The lack of political and military control of the Ferghana and eastern Bukhara region resulted in reports of "banditry," allegedly perpetrated by Islamic leaders; such reports persisted into the 1930s. Party officials also reported widespread survival of Islamic institutions (especially *madrasas*, *hujras*, mosques, and courts). They insisted that reactionary elements of the Uzbek and Tajik republics—including Basmachi, *bai*, village leaders, Muslim bankers and traders, and religious leaders whom they called "enemy-*kulak* mullahs"[109]—were resisting the Revolution.[110] Prayer, reopening of mosques, closing of women's clubs and Jewish centers, and veiling continued in mountainous regions and on the *kolkhozes* (collective farms) of the Ferghana Valley—with Namangan mentioned as particularly problematic—into the late 1930s.[111] The Party therefore unambiguously perceived the regions that would become the Tajik republic and the Uzbek Ferghana Valley as fanatically Islamic and incompatible with the Party's ideals. Consequently, indigenous Party membership was negligible in the

[106] No. 184, "Postanovlenie Politbiuro TsK RKP (b) po voprosam Sredne-Aziatskogo Biuro TsK RKP(b)," including "Protokol zasedaniia komissii Politbiuro TsK po voprosu ob okhrane granits s Afganistanom, Persiei, Zapadnym Kitaem i o basmachestve s Vostochnoi Bukhare" (January 19, 1925), in *Rossiia i Tsentral'naia Aziia 1905–1925 gg.*, 411–12.

[107] No. 184, "Postanovlenie Politbiuro," 412.

[108] No. 184, "Postanovlenie Politbiuro," 413.

[109] These terms are used in multiple OGPU documents: *Tsk RKP(b)-VKP(b) i Natsional'nyi Vopros, Kniga 1, 1918–33gg.*.

[110] No. 41, "Zakrytoe pis'mo sekretaria TsK KP(b) Turkestana M. S. Epshteina v TsK RKP(b) po itogam poezdki v Ferganu," 101–3.

[111] No. 199, "Iz spravki sektora informatsii organizatsionno-instruktorskogo otdela TsK VKP(b) sekretariu TsK VKP(b) G. M. Malenkovu o diskriminatsii zhenshchin v Namanganskom, Andizhanskom, Izbaskentskom raionakh Ferganskoi oblasti Uzbekskoi SSR" (dated after December 19, 1939), in *Tsk VKP(b) i Natsional'nyi Vopros, Kniga 2, 1933–45*, ed. L. C. Gatagova, L. P. Kosheleva, L. A. Rogovaia, and Dj. Kadio (Moscow: ROSSPYEN, 2009), 512–13.

1920s and remained low for decades.[112] In the Tajik republic, most Party leaders were nonindigenous until 1946.[113]

Indeed, through World War II the Party still considered the Tajik republic to be a problem for Soviet rule. The NKVD (the People's Commissariat for Internal Affairs, successor to the OGPU) believed Germans and Turks had funded nationalist and Islamist opposition movements, including the KA and the Basmachi exiles in Afghanistan. In 1941, Soviet intelligence was still claiming a threat from "the activation of the Basmachi movement" in Afghanistan.[114] One Party official, A. V. Stanishev, recommended that the NKVD be directed to focus on "breaking down the Basmachi shaykhs from within," drawing on the Cheka's experience in the 1920s, and "strengthening the Chekists' work . . . by creating farmers' self-defense groups in the border regions" of Central Asia.[115] Such rhetoric was part of Stalin's overall "war scare" tactics, which he used to justify purges, deportations, and forced migrations in the 1930s to 1940s and to spur ambivalent Central Asians into fighting against fascism.[116]

The USSR People's Commissar for Internal Affairs Lavrenti Beria portrayed the situation in the Tajik republic as dire; he claimed that in the first four months of 1943, the NKVD arrested 4,177 deserters in just one border detachment and another 1,704 deserters in the mountains, especially in the Gharm and Kulob *oblasts*. Beria recommended significantly increasing border guards in the southern Tajik republic to stem emigration to Afghanistan.[117] A memo sent to Georgy M. Malenkov, who at the time was close to Stalin and served as a secretary of the Central Committee, reported that in Gorno-Badakhshan, especially on the Afghan border, part of the population was engaged in "counterrevolutionary" activity under the guise of custom; an espionage organization reportedly existed in a *qishloq* (village) in the Pamirs, "masking its work under religious customs."[118] In a related memo, another Party member acknowledged that in the highland border regions "before 1940, there was no collectivization" and "no liquidation of the *kulaks* [*bai*]. . . . In the internal life on their *kolkhoz*,

[112] Bergne, *Birth of Tajikistan*, 62–63.

[113] Khalid, *Making Uzbekistan*, 277; Kathleen Collins, *Clan Politics and Regime Transition in Central Asia* (New York: Cambridge University Press, 2006), 110.

[114] No. 268, "Pis'mo A. V. Stanishevskogo sekretariu TsK VKP(b) G. M. Malenkovu o polozhenii v Srednei Azii v sviazi s usileniem raboti nemetskoi razvedki na Vostoke i merakh po okazaniiu protivodeistviia organami NKVD SSSR" (dated not later than July 13, 1941), in *TsK VKP(b) i Natsional'nyi Vopros. Kniga 2, 1933–45*, 646–47.

[115] No. 268, "Pis'mo A. V. Stanishevskogo," 649.

[116] I thank Shoshana Keller for this point.

[117] No. 314, "Zapiska narodnogo komissara vnutrennikh del SSSR L. P. Beriia sekretariu TsK VKP(b) A. A. Andreevu ob uklonenii ot prizyva v Krasnuiu armiiu v Tadzhikskoi SSR" (June 5, 1943), in *TsK RKP(b) i Natsional'nyi Vopros, Kniga 2, 1933–45*, 753–54.

[118] No. 330, "Iz informatsionnoi spravki sektora informatsii organizatsionno-instruktorskogo otdela TsK VKP(b) sekretariu TsK G. M. Malenkovu, o faktakh vrazhdebnoi deiatel'nosti ismailitov na Pamire" (February 1, 1944), in *TsK RKP(b) i Natsional'nyi Vopros, Kniga 2, 1933–45*, 799–800.

clan relations have strong influence. . . . Party-political work among the population . . . is found in a frightening state" due to the "disarray of the Party."[119]

As we have seen, high contention and difficulty in establishing control shaped the USSR's incorporation of most of the Tajik republic, as well as the Uzbek republic's Ferghana Valley. It was in areas of high but incomplete repression, contention, and violence that the Soviets distrusted and excluded more rigidly observant Muslims decades into the twentieth century. Islam, as an institution and identity, became most deeply politicized there.

Lower Contention, Easier Incorporation, Inclusion: Parts of Turkestan and the Steppe

By contrast, the Bolshevik co-optation strategy fostered the far less contentious incorporation of Turkestan and the steppe into the USSR. The Bolsheviks deemed the "progressive *ulama*" and the Jadids, who were influential in Turkestan, as well as the nomads, less "fanatical" than the Tajik and Ferghana Valley *ulama*. By splitting the clergy and co-opting those progressives, the Bolsheviks expected to more easily eliminate all the *ulama*.

The Kazakh and Kyrgyz regions, Tatarstan, Bashkiriya, Crimea, the Urals, Siberia, and Astrakhan were all specified as places where, by 1926, "the struggle between the conservative or reactionary part of the clergy and the progressive part was complete, and the progressive wing was victorious."[120] This perceived success was compounded by the Party's belief that the inhabitants of these regions identified less strongly with Islam than did those of the Tajik republic or the Ferghana Valley. Among the Kyrgyz, Kazakh, Turkmen, and Karakalpaks it was uncommon to find a powerful *ulama*, mosques, *madrasa*s, and sedentary Islamic practices, such as veiling.[121] Although historians and anthropologists have convincingly demonstrated otherwise, in Bolshevik eyes these nomadic Muslims were therefore only *superficially* Islamic.[122] They could thus, in theory, be more easily modernized, transformed, and integrated into the Soviet system.[123] Consequently, the antireligious assault in 1927 would not target these

[119] No. 337, "Iz informatsionnoi spravki zamestitelia zaveduiushchego sektorom informatsii organizatsionno instruktorskogo otdela TsK VKP(b) L. A. Slepova sekretariu TsK G. M. Malenkovu o polozhenii v pogrannichnykh Murgabskom i Alichurskom rayonakh Tadzhikskoi SSR" (March 11, 1944), in *Tsk VK(b) i Natsional'nyi Vopros, Kniga 2, 1933–45*, 809–10.

[120] No. 8, *Islam i Musul'mane po materialam vostochnogo otdela OGPU. 1926 godu* (Nizhnii Novgorod: "Medina," 2007), 80. "Reactionary" clergy refers to the *qadimchilar* or conservative clergy.

[121] Adrienne Edgar, *Tribal Nation: The Making of Soviet Turkmenistan* (Princeton, NJ: Princeton University Press, 2004); Ali Igmen, *Speaking Soviet with an Accent: Culture and Power in Kyrgyzstan* (Pittsburgh, PA: University of Pittsburgh Press, 2012), 123–25.

[122] DeWeese, "Islam and the Legacy of Sovietology."

[123] Abashin et al., "Soviet Rule and the Delineation," 106–8; Devin DeWeese, "Ahmad Yasavi and the Divan-I Hikmat in Soviet Scholarship," in *Heritage of Soviet Oriental Studies*, 281–82.

regions as viciously as it did the Tajik republic and the Uzbek Ferghana Valley. Even the widely popular Sufi shrine of Khoja Ahmad Yassaviy in the southern Kazakh republic was neither destroyed nor closed like so many shrines in the Uzbek, southern Kyrgyz, and Tajik republics.[124] Less repression meant less contention and politicization of Islam.

In the nomadic steppe, the attack on Islam was more commonly understood, by both the Party and the nomads, as an attempt to change patriarchal norms and foster women's emancipation, a broader Soviet policy exercised across the USSR. Moreover, enforcement of women's liberation among the nomads was not one of the Party's primary goals. According to Adrienne Edgar, in Turkmenistan "[l]ocal officials . . . quickly learned that Moscow's priorities were elsewhere," such as meeting "the regime's quotas on collectivization or rooting out *kulaks*."[125] So long as local officials recognized these economic priorities, the Party was content to simply escalate modernizing propaganda rather than brand these republics as religiously reactionary.

So too in the Kazakh and Turkmen steppe, of far greater concern to the Party than their saintly lineages, shrine visitation, or faith healing was premodern nomadism. The Bolshevik sedentarization campaign, which began in 1928, unleashed a different form of destruction in the Kazakh SSR from 1930 to 1933: a devastating famine triggered by government confiscation of livestock. The death toll has been estimated at 1.5 million.[126] Tribe, clan, and land relations became highly politicized as Soviet authorities targeted the wealthy tribal or clan elders for deportation and execution; they were seen as agents preserving feudal and personalistic relations antithetical to communism.[127] While even nomadic religious leaders were sent to the Gulag in the 1930s, overall, other political cleavages proved more salient than Islam.[128]

Within the new Uzbek republic, the situation was mixed; some progressive and pro-Bolshevik Muslim leaders did exist. In Tashkent, Samarqand, and Bukhara (after the emir fled), the Bolsheviks had temporarily used the Jadids to win Muslim support in state-building. Tashkent became "the economic, cultural, and political center of all Central Asia,"[129] home to the Tashkent *soviet*

[124] Tasar, *Soviet and Muslim*, 9.

[125] Edgar, "Bolshevism, Patriarchy, and the Nation," 269.

[126] Sarah Cameron, *The Hungry Steppe: Famine, Violence, and the Making of Soviet Kazakhstan* (Ithaca, NY: Cornell University Press, 2018), 2.

[127] Edgar, *Tribal Nation*; Collins, *Clan Politics*; Edward Schatz, *Modern Clan Politics: The Power of "Blood" in Kazakhstan and Beyond* (Seattle, WA: University of Washington Press, 2004).

[128] Communication with grandson of arrested Sufi leader, Kazakhstan, June 2021; Frank, *Gulag Miracles*.

[129] No. 86, "Zapiska zamestitelia narkoma po delam natsional'nostei G. I. Broido v TsK RKP(b) po voprosu o natsional'no-territorial'nom razmezhevanii Srednei Azii" (June 4, 1924), in *TsK RKP(b)-VKP(b) i Natsional'nyi Vopros, Kniga 1, 1918–33gg.*, ed. L. C. Gatagova, L. P. Kosheleva, and L. A. Rogovaia (Moscow: ROSSPYEN, 2005), 219.

and the locus of the OGPU's and NKVD's operations against the Basmachi. The Communist Party grew in the Uzbek republic with an indigenous cadre of new Muslim recruits; however, indigenous participation included only those without clerical ties and assiduously excluded those from more strictly observant Muslim regions such as Kokand, Andijon, and Namangan in the Ferghana Valley. Ultimately, even the Jadids and other pro-Bolshevik Muslims would be purged and replaced by a new postrevolutionary cadre who had neither Islamic ties nor a national project in potential conflict with Soviet goals.[130] Nonetheless, Soviet co-opting of those Muslims who supported—or at least did not oppose—the Bolsheviks, as well as a less aggressive antireligious policy in more nomadic regions, helped prevent violent resistance and facilitated Turkestan's smoother incorporation into the Soviet system.

Overall, as Khalid writes, "over the next decade, party authorities routinely conceptualized Uzbekistan as comprised of advanced and backwards regions, and calibrated the implementation of its policies accordingly."[131] Bolshevik assessments of "Muslimness" dictated the severity of their revolutionary programs, which resulted in varying degrees of contention over Islam. Here, perceived "Muslimness" and contention were both relatively low.

The origins of Islamism within the Soviet sphere lie in the very foundation of the USSR. The Bolshevik Revolution's religious repression was an assault on the deeply Islamic society, culture, and legal order that characterized most of Central Asia. The atheist Marxist-Leninist regime sought to radically transform a millennium of Muslim social relations and eliminate the *ulama*'s influence on personal and civic life, law, and state. From 1917 onward, Islam was oppressed as an obstacle to Party policy. To be openly observant of Islam—to have a religious marriage, attend Islamic schools, or even visit shrines and perform other Muslim customs—was seen as reactionary and even fanatical; the Bolsheviks targeted and excluded such behavior. A consequence of Bolshevik religious repression was high Muslim mobilization, at least until 1926, when the new regime would consolidate power and shutter associational space. Most anti-Soviet Muslim activists, such as the Ulamo Jamiyati, the KA, and the Basmachi, advocated a prominent role for Islam in politics and society. Nonetheless, studying the early Soviet period demonstrates that Muslim politics and activism in Eurasia was *not Islamist*—much less radically and militantly jihadist. As argued in Chapter 1, religious repression does not invariably generate Islamist mobilization. Absent an ideology, Islamist movements did not emerge in the early Soviet period.

[130] Khalid, *Making Uzbekistan*, 387–88.
[131] Khalid, *Making Uzbekistan*, 277.

We have also seen that the first decade of Soviet rule in Central Asia established different paths of Muslim-state relations in different republics and regions. Greater resistance by Central Asians led to a more contentious path of incorporation into the Soviet state. Such high contention would foster the underground survival of religious activists and the simmering politicization of religious identity over time. This was particularly true in the Tajik republic and the Uzbek Ferghana Valley. I now turn to the escalated assault on Islam under Stalinism and the Cultural Revolution, as the state again targeted areas deemed "fanatical" and ruthlessly eliminated the forms of Islamic activism that had survived the first decade of Bolshevik rule.

3

The Atheist State

Repressing and Politicizing Islam

Lenin was God.

—Uzbek respondent, Tashkent, 2017

It was the time of the Red Terror.

—Tajik respondent, Dushanbe, 2013

Repression of Islam dramatically escalated in 1927, as Josef Stalin consolidated power and resolved that God would no longer be a rival for legitimacy nor a barrier to Soviet modernization policies. Frustrated at the slow pace of change in the USSR's Muslim territories, from 1927 to 1942 the Communist Party waged an unprecedented assault on Islam, seeking both to eliminate all religious institutions and to create a nation of atheists whose loyalty would be to the Party. Recognizing only Marxist-Leninist ideology as legitimate, the Party treated religion as a political enemy. All aspects of religious life were politicized; simply being a believer, much less practicing Islam, meant defying the Party.

Total state repression of religion and the closure of all associational space under high Stalinism led to the demobilization of early Muslim activism, discussed in the previous chapter. Militant atheism, as it was known, also resulted in the destruction of Islamic institutions and the elimination of public expression of Islamic belief and identity, but also generated significant and ongoing contention and resistance, still primarily in the Uzbek Ferghana Valley and Tajik republic.

Soviet policy also, paradoxically, created the possibility for Islam to revive. Despite its brutality, militant atheism wavered over time, and by the 1940s allowed for minimal associational space. During World War II, Stalin decided to accommodate a state-controlled version of Islam in Central Asia, which opened channels for the spread of Islamic literature from the Middle East. Nikita Khrushchev again renewed religious persecution, even while his Thaw eroded total state control of ideas. Under Brezhnev, Party leaders declared victory over God while silently recognizing de facto defeat in eradicating Islam and other religions. Incomplete repression together with marginal increases in space allowed the reemergence of religious actors. They became agents of Islamic

Politicizing Islam in Central Asia. Kathleen Collins, Oxford University Press. © Oxford University Press 2023.
DOI: 10.1093/oso/9780197685068.003.0004

revival, often credited with "saving Islam." While these religious actors stayed out of politics, by the 1980s their students would challenge the Soviet state, initially only in discourse but eventually through opposition mobilization.

High Stalinism: Religious Persecution and the Closure of Associational Space

Stalin's rise to power in the late 1920s and 1930s brought unmitigated state violence against the entire Soviet population.[1] His forced collectivization of land and sedentarization of nomads would restructure, modernize, and control the economy at the cost of staggering famine and death. However, Stalin first launched the Cultural Revolution in 1927 that began in Central Asia with the *hujum* (assault) on religion. The *hujum*'s effort to remake society as *Homo Sovieticus* (Soviet man) continued through the Great Terror of 1937–38, with its purges, show trials, and killing or expulsion to the Gulag of millions, and even into the early 1940s. From 1927 to 1941, Stalin's dictatorship left virtually no space for Islam to exist, legally or illegally. Muslims, especially in post-Soviet Tajikistan, often refer to this period as the "Red Terror."[2] Stalin's policy demobilized the vigorous Muslim activism of the previous decade and nearly destroyed all visible and institutionalized elements of Islam.

The Shift to Militant Atheism: Increasing Repression and Closing of Associational Space

In 1926, a lengthy OGPU (secret police) report assessed the religious situation as a grave threat to Soviet plans. The Muslim Congress of 1926 had demonstrated that the Muslim leaders of each region were active, continually pressing the Bolsheviks and local government representatives to make various concessions and to keep some space open for religious activity. Moreover, the OGPU accused the clergy of trying to mobilize peasants and even Muslim women against the Bolsheviks[3] through religious education. The OGPU characterized the situation in the Tajik and Uzbek republics as "a struggle between numerous conservative clergy in alliance with the *bai* [wealthy communal leaders] on one side, and on the other side, a small number of progressive clergy." It carped, "Conservative

[1] Stephen Kotkin, *Stalin: Paradoxes of Power: 1878–1928* (New York: Penguin Press, 2014).

[2] Interview with Haji Akbar Turajonzoda, former deputy leader of the Movement of Islamic Revival of Tajikistan and former *qozikalon* of Tajikistan, Dushanbe, Tajikistan, December 2011.

[3] No. 8, "Nastuplenie Musdukhovenstva i mery borby s nimi," in *Islam i musul'mane po materialam Vostochnogo otdela OGPU, 1926 godu*, ed. D. Iu. Arapov and G. G. Kosach (Nizhnyi Novgorod: "Medina," 2007), 82–83.

clergy [are] struggling against Soviet power, agricultural reforms, and the reorganization of religious schools. . . . [They are] especially strong in the *qishloqs*, where the *bai* actively speak out in alliance with the clergy."[4] There were "attempts by the clergy to strengthen their influence through offering economic services for the masses" and thereby "to return authority over property to the mosque."[5] The report also noted the struggle against "Eshonism," the sacred authority of Sufi masters among their *murids* (disciples) and society more broadly. The report contrasted the Tajik, Uzbek, Chechen, and Dagestani republics with the more favorable situation among the still-nomadic Kazakhs and Kyrgyz. Even among the latter, however, Party officials warned that a new class, a "national bourgeoisie" ("NEP men" in cities and *kulaks* in rural areas) was financing a religious movement.[6] The OGPU claimed that even the "progressive clergy" were demanding more rights and the reopening of religious schools, religious book publication, and religious curricula.[7] Although cooperating with the government, the progressives' religious practices and beliefs still remained antithetical to the Soviet system.

The OGPU faulted the "low-level Soviet apparat in our districts; insufficient attention by the Party to religious questions . . . the quantitative and qualitative weakness of the Soviet schools, the weakness of cultural enlightenment work in general and especially in the countryside."[8] It continued, "All local organs of Soviet power have insufficiently regulated, and sometimes even did not regulate" the theology and activity of the clergy.[9] The 1926 OGPU report laid the groundwork for a major policy change, including "strengthening attention to Soviet schools," working "against religion and religious schools," "raising the cultural level . . . of the peasants," increasing the role of "cultural and political enlightenment organizations, especially in the cities," and "strengthening anti-religious work." This last objective entailed "supplying the countryside with anti-religious and scientific publications in the local language," "enforcing the law against teaching theology," and "relentless repressive measures against the conservatives."[10] The OGPU recommended: "(a) complete repression of religious schools for educating adults; (b) limited opening of [youth] religious schools; (c) repression of mullahs . . . who violate the laws about separation of church and state; (d) merciless repression of mullahs . . . (e) deprivation of electoral

[4] No. 8, "Nastuplenie Musdukhovenstva i mery borby s nimi," 89–90.

[5] No. 8, "Nastuplenie Musdukhovenstva i mery borby s nimi," 83.

[6] No. 165, "Postanovlenie biuro Tatarskogo obkoma o musul'manskom religioznom dvizhenii" (August 10, 1926), in *TsK RKP(b)-VKP(b) i Natsional'nyi Vopros, Kniga 1, 1918–33gg.*, ed., L. C. Gatagova, L. P. Kosheleva, and L. A. Rogovaia (Moscow: ROSSPYEN, 2005), 417–21.

[7] No. 8, "Nastuplenie Musdukhovenstva i mery borby s nimi," 82–83.

[8] No. 8, "Nastuplenie Musdukhovenstva i mery borby s nimi," 82–83.

[9] No. 8, "Nastuplenie Musdukhovenstva i mery borby s nimi," 82–83.

[10] No. 8, "Nastuplenie Musdukhovenstva i mery borby s nimi," 87–89.

rights for the *muezzins* and *azanchy* . . . and . . . decomposition of the clergy by [O]GPU methods."[11] The head of the Anti-Religious Commission of the Central Committee of the All-Union Communist Party E. M. Yaroslavsky assessed that Soviet schools must be strengthened to increase "the struggle against the Muslim religious movement."[12] In a secret memo, the Central Committee directed "the OGPU and NKVD to coordinate repression" especially against "the most evil persons," as they referred to mullahs and imams.[13] Clearly, the suffocation of religious leaders and institutions was paramount and the secret police's brutal methods were sanctioned.

Between 1926 and the 1930s, Party policy went "from control and regulation" to "five-year atheist plans [using] direct repression,"[14] much like Stalin's devastating five-year plans for the economy. By 1927, Stalin had concluded that a full-scale attack on Islam was now possible and necessary for the Cultural Revolution. Tremendous use of force replaced earlier half-measures;[15] associational space and "pseudo-liberalism" had disappeared.[16] Stalin demanded the cessation of Muslim congresses, liquidation of mosques and Islamic courts and schools, and thereby the end of the clergy's influence, the modernization of Muslim women, and an end to Islamic and tribal customs.[17]

"Militant atheism" was launched in Central Asia in 1927. As in Russia, it was far-ranging, violent, and extremely destructive.[18] Concessions to reformist clergy ended, and many were arrested and imprisoned in the Gulag. The Jadids were purged and replaced by those believed to be true communists. In areas previously considered too strongly Muslim to change, transformation by force was deemed necessary. The Uzbek republic (which in 1927 still included Tajikistan as the Tajik ASSR) became the "epicenter" of the *hujum*, the anti-Islamic onslaught.[19]

Unveiling women was key to the campaign. The Bolsheviks pursued a "civilizing mission," and the Party decided that the veil represented fanatical religiosity.[20] In the Uzbek and Tajik republics in particular, where women veiled

[11] No. 8, "Nastuplenie Musdukhovenstva i mery borby s nimi," 88. *Muezzins/azanchy* are those who call Muslims to prayer from the minaret of a mosque.

[12] No. 197, "Proekt postanovleniia Orgbiuro TsK VKP(b) 'O merakh borby s musul'manskom religioznym dvizheniem'" (August 8, 1927), in *TsK RKP(b)-VKP(b) i Natsional'nyi Vopros, Kniga 1*, 500–501.

[13] No. 197, "Proekt postanovleniia Orgbiuro," 502.

[14] A. Khabutdinov and D. Mukhetdinov, "Vvedenie," in *Islam i musul'mane*, 11.

[15] Gatagova, Kosheleva, and Rogova, "Vvedenie," 10–11.

[16] Gatagova, Kosheleva, and Rogova, "Vvedenie," 12.

[17] No. 197, "Proekt postanovleniia Orgbiuro," 501–3.

[18] Keller, *To Moscow, Not Mecca*; Alexander Yakovlev, *A Century of Violence in Soviet Russia* (New Haven, CT: Yale University Press, 2002).

[19] Khalid, *Islam after Communism*, 71. The Tajik ASSR was an Autonomous Soviet Socialist Republic until 1929.

[20] Christian Teichmann, "Cultivating the Periphery: Bolshevik Civilising Missions and 'Colonialism' in Soviet Central Asia," in *Ordering the Colonial World around the 20th Century. Global*

completely, unveiling women would advance modernization and secularization and liberate women from Islamic patriarchy and *shariat*, which the Bolsheviks blamed for inequality. Soviet propaganda argued that Muslim men—the *bai*, khans, and religious leaders—were oppressive, backward, and capitalist. OGPU reports proclaimed progress in unveiling, especially in urban, Russified centers such as Samarqand and Tashkent. For example, in Samarqand *okrug* (district), the head of a *sel'sovet* (rural council) directed all members of the *sel'sovet* to bring their unveiled wives to the plenum. He decreed, "All women in the course of ten days must remove the *paranji*; for non-fulfillment of this [order] they will be arrested."[21] Overzealous European and indigenous Party officials implemented the *hujum* through forced public unveilings, and were sometimes even reprimanded by Moscow officials for using too much violence.[22]

Beyond the veil, militant atheism attempted to eliminate the institutional basis of Islam and its associational spaces for men to gather and potentially speak against the state. There was a sweeping attack on mosques, *madrasas*, *maktabs* (Muslim primary schools), *mazars* (shrines), and a broad array of Muslim spiritual authorities. Closing sacred spaces denied the *ulama* their major venue of influence. Few records were kept, as Party officials destroyed mosques at a furious pace, so data are incomplete. Keller's study estimates that in the Uzbek republic, of 10,489 known mosques before 1917, 6,544 (about 40 percent) were closed by 1936. Of the 60 percent remaining open, however, only 686 (17 percent) were legally registered; the other 3,259 (83 percent) existed illegally.[23] Thus, 93.5 percent of the pre-1917 total were either closed or functioning illegally. Many mosques were desecrated, boarded up, dismantled, or, at best, turned into libraries or museums.[24] The highest numbers of mosque closures took place in the Ferghana Valley and Bukhara *oblast*; they were primarily ethnic Uzbek and Tajik and more conservatively observant and canonically educated than elsewhere.[25] The cities of Kokand and Marg'ilon, both in the Ferghana Valley, experienced the highest number of mosque closures recorded. The assault on Islam

and Comparative Perspectives, ed. Hrsg. von Sebastian Conrad, Nadin Heé, and Ulrike Schaper (Leipzig: Leipziger Univ.-Verl., 2009), 34–52.

[21] "No. 7, Obzor, politicheskogo sostoianiia SSSR za iiul' 1927 g. (po dannym Ob'edinennogo gosudarstvennogo politicheskogo upravleniia), Prilozhenie No. 3, Vostochnye natsional'nye respubliki i avtonomnye oblasti, Uzbekistan," in *Sovershenno Sekretno: Lubianka—Stalinu o Polozhenii v Strane (1922–1934gg.)*, ed. V. S. Khristoforov, A. N. Sakharov, et al. (Moscow: Institute of Russian History of the Russian Academy of Sciences and the Central Archive of the Federal Security Service of Russia, 2003), 5 (1927): 530.

[22] Northrop, *Veiled Empire*; Khalid, *Making Uzbekistan*.

[23] Keller, *To Moscow, Not Mecca*, 220–22.

[24] Keller, *To Moscow, Not Mecca*, 223–24.

[25] The data actually include "houses of worship" for all major faiths, but in the rural *oblasts* places of worship were almost 100 percent Muslim; data from the cities are harder to disaggregate and are not included in these figures.

also meant completing the closure of *shariat* courts. The Ferghana region, for example, had 122 *shariat* courts in 1922; by 1927, just two remained.[26]

Together with the decimation of Islamic institutions, militant atheism aimed to destroy religious leadership. While they had been legal during the previous decade, in 1927 imams and mullahs were stripped by the OGPU of their previous "authority" in family law and communal disputes. They had no educational and a limited spiritual role.[27] Soon, the *ulama*—*mufti*s, mullahs, Sufi shaykhs, and itinerant *eshon*s who taught in the old schools, gave sermons in mosques or ran *hujra*s (study circles) or *khanqah*s (Sufi retreats)—were overwhelmingly killed, imprisoned, or forced into hiding or exile.[28] Partial data indicate a 72.8 percent decline in Islamic leaders in Ferghana *oblast* and a 79 percent decline in Andijon. Such figures very likely underreport the death toll. Some survived by hiding in rural areas, working on collective farms to mask their identity.[29] The Party sent thousands to the Gulag in Siberia or Kazakhstan after brief trials, usually a *troika* of three Bolshevik judges.[30] Many others were executed without trial.[31] The overall toll was devastating; about fourteen thousand were killed or disappeared between 1927 and 1939, almost three-fourths of the *ulama*.[32] By 1936, only 108 imams and fourteen mullahs were registered in all of Central Asia. Unregistered imams reportedly numbered merely 1,151.[33]

As Keller demonstrates, militant atheism also involved "smashing the pillars of Islam."[34] The *hajj* (pilgrimage to Mecca) became illegal. Fasting during Ramadan was outlawed. Party officials forced children to eat during the day in school and observed workers to ensure that they consumed lunch. *Zakat* (compulsory charitable giving of a portion of one's salary) was also banned to undermine private charity, an important source of religious leaders' livelihoods and funds to maintain shrines. *Namaz* (prayer) became nearly impossible. The campaign against circumcision and repression of *janaza* (funeral rites), like unveiling, struck at the core of Muslim identity and traditional practice.

The Party also established a monopoly over the public discourse about Islam. It attacked the Muslim clergy and culture in newspapers, periodicals, and satirical publications. The Union of Militant Godless, established in 1925, organized atheist education[35] under slogans such as "The struggle against religion is the

26 Keller, *To Moscow, Not Mecca*, 148.
27 No. 197, "Proekt postanovleniia Orgbiuro," 502–3.
28 Muminov, Gafurov, and Shigabidinov, "Islamic Education," 245–47.
29 Interviews with multiple imams in Tajikistan and Uzbekistan, 2005–6.
30 Interview with Turajonzoda.
31 Muminov, Gafurov, and Shigabdinov, "Islamic Education," 247.
32 Keller, *To Moscow, Not Mecca*, 241.
33 Keller, *To Moscow, Not Mecca*, 227–30.
34 Keller, *To Moscow, Not Mecca*, 147.
35 Daniel Peris, *Storming the Heavens: The Soviet League of the Militant Godless* (Ithaca, NY: Cornell University Press 1998).

Image 3.1 Atheist propaganda against mosques
Source: Calvert Journal, https://www.calvertjournal.com/features/show/11386/godless-utopia-how-the-soviet-union-launched-its-war-against-religion.

struggle for socialism."[36] In 1927, the Central Committee directed "local Party and Komsomol organizations to develop educational work among the remaining Party members and candidates, directed at the final elimination of a religious disposition."[37] A typical cover of the journal *Bezbozhnik* (Atheist) shows anti-Islamic propaganda interwoven with Bolshevik slogans such as "Who [will conquer] whom?" (Image 3.1).

Destruction of Islamic knowledge also meant that the Party banned the creation of new religious schools while concocting multiple pretexts, such as substandard sanitation, to close existing schools. A secret Central Committee memo of August 8, 1927, placed multiple restrictions on religious teaching outside of already beleaguered schools. Theology could be studied for two years only, after age fourteen, with a controlled curriculum in vernacular languages. The Party explicitly undermined Islamic knowledge by limiting Arabic study.[38] According

[36] Arif Yunusov, *Islam in Azerbaijan* (Baku: Zaman, 2004), 139.
[37] No. 197, "Proekt postanovleniia Orgbiuro," 502.
[38] No. 197, "Proekt postanovleniia Orgbiuro," 501.

to some data, before 1917 there were over 10,000 religious schools in the Uzbek SSR; in 1927, there were only 1,305.[39] By the late 1920s, all *maktabs* and *madrasas* were closed, at least officially. Lessons in mullahs' homes were also banned, and personal libraries of Islamic literature were confiscated. The Muslim Spiritual Directorates and local boards of "progressive *ulama*" were also closed. "Scientific atheism" pervaded the new educational system. Religion was taught only as a premodern "cult," and Soviet values replaced religious values.

A core goal of educational reform was to create a new, more loyal, and genuinely revolutionary Soviet youth from which to draw a national cadre for the Muslim republics.[40] In the 1920s, a Latinization campaign replaced the Arabic and Persian scripts to separate Muslims from their religious literature and history.[41] By 1940, the Politburo had ordered the Latin script replaced with "Russian script" (Cyrillic), a further barrier to attaining Islamic knowledge.[42]

Varying Forms of Repression and Resistance to the *Hujum*

Throughout the 1920s, secret police and Party reports continued to discuss the Tajik regions and the Ferghana Valley (as well as Dagestan, Chechnya, and Ukraine) as the most resistant to the Cultural Revolution. Hence, Soviet policymakers determined that they should begin the *hujum* in areas believed to be less "backward," such as Tashkent and Samarqand.[43] According to Douglas Northrop, "central authorities knew virtually nothing about the most basic conditions on the ground in Tajikistan," so they postponed the *hujum* there for several years.[44]

Although targeted later, the Tajik SSR and the Uzbek Ferghana Valley continued to be the most difficult places to implement antireligious measures. The very threat of further Party incursions increased Basmachi resistance during the unveiling campaign.[45] In 1927, multiple OGPU reports claimed anti-*hujum* activity involving both Basmachi commanders and *qazis* (Islamic judges) in

[39] Muminov, Gafurov, and Shigabdinov, "Islamic Education," 244.

[40] Peris, *Storming the Heavens*.

[41] Kemper, Rotika, and Reichmuth, *Islamic Education*; Martin, *Affirmative Action Empire*, 188.

[42] No. 227, "Postanovlenie Politbiuro TsK VKP(b) 'O perevode kirgizskoi pis'mennosti s latinizirovannogo na russkii alfabit" (July 6, 1940), in *TsK VKP(b) i Natsional'nyi Vopros, Kniga 2*, 559; No. 232, "Dokladnaia zapiska zaveduiushchego otdelom shkol TsK VKP(b) A. B. Bushueva sekretariu TsK VKP(b) A. A. Andreevu 'O khode perevoda pis'mennostei soiuznykh respublik s latinizirovannogo alfabita na russkii'" (September 26, 1940), in *TsK VKP(b) i Natsional'nyi Vopros, Kniga 2*, 563–64.

[43] Northrop, *Veiled Empire*.

[44] No. 261, "Postanovlenie Politbiuro TsK VKP(b) 'O predsedatele TsIKa SSSR i TsIKa Tadzhikskoi SSR N. Maksume i predsedatele SNK Tadzhikskoi SSR A. Khodzhibaeve'" (December 1, 1933), in *TsK RKP(b)-VKP(b) i Natsional'nyi Vopros, Kniga* 1, 723.

[45] Northrop, *Veiled Empire*, 15.

the Tajik ASSR,[46] along the Afghanistan border, and in the Uzbek and Kyrgyz Ferghana Valley regions, such as Osh, Jalalabat, and Kara-Suu.[47]

Because the Uzbek- and Tajik-populated regions of Central Asia were home to learned Islam, and because they had proved most contentious and resistant to the Bolshevik Revolution, they became the central target of severe repression during militant atheism.[48] Unveiling, mosque, *madrasa*, and *maktab* closures, and the attack on the *ulama* were to be far more devastating there than in the nomadic and recently nomadic areas that had few such institutions. Yet despite the all-encompassing assault on religion and the total closure of associational space, OGPU records from the 1920s to the 1940s reveal significant "everyday resistance" among Central Asians.[49] Islamic spiritual leaders and their families frequently moved and hid to avoid arrest.[50] They fled to remote villages in the Ferghana Valley and to southern and central Tajik regions.[51] This led to a concentration of the more conservative population, religious leaders, and those most resistant to Bolshevism inside the Tajik republic, where they remained out of reach for some time.[52] Throughout the revolutionary years and again during World War II, many Tajiks migrated to Afghanistan. Party officials worried about the potential for mobilization of the roughly two million Tajiks in Central Asia, many of them on the Afghan-Tajik border or inside northern Afghanistan; the Party saw the Afghan-Tajik nexus as a threat and a potential source of aggression against the USSR.[53]

While some Muslim women welcomed unveiling and joined the Party, as Marianne Kamp and Zamira Yusufjonova have each argued,[54] resistance to unveiling was generally high. Available OGPU reports document multiple forms of anti-*hujum* resistance and consequent contention with the state through the early 1940s, especially in the Ferghana Valley and Tajik ASSR. There were

[46] Bergne, *Birth of Tajikistan*.

[47] "No. 5, Obzor, politicheskogo sostoianiia SSSR za Mai 1927 (po dannym Ob'edinennogo gosudarstvennogo politicheskogo upravleniia), vostochnye natsional'nye respubliki i avtonomnye oblasti," 5: 373–74. As discussed in Chapters 13 and 14, Kara-Suu was a center of puritanical Islamic practice.

[48] Khalid, *Islam after Communism*, 71–73.

[49] The term comes from Sheila Fitzpatrick, *Stalin's Peasants: Resistance and Survival in the Russian Village After Collectivization* (Oxford: Oxford University Press, 1996).

[50] Northrop, *Veiled Empire*.

[51] Muzaffar Olimov, "Islam in Contemporary Tajikistan: Role of Muslim Leaders," in *Religion and Security in South and Central Asia*, ed. K. Warikoo (New York: Routledge, 2011), 150–63.

[52] Qazi Akbar Turajonzoda, "Religion: The Pillar of Society," in *Central Asia: Conflict, Resolution and Change*, ed. Roald Sagdeev and Susan Eisenhower (Chevy Chase, MD: Center for Post-Soviet Studies, 1995), 265–74.

[53] No. 86, "Zapiska zamestitelia narkoma po delam natsional'nostei G. I. Broido v TsK RKP(b) po voprosu o natsional'no-territorial'nom razmezhevanii Srednei Azii" (earlier than June 4, 1924), in *TsK RKP(b)-VKP(b) i Natsional'nyi Vopros, Kniga 1*, 218.

[54] Kamp, *The New Woman in Uzbekistan*; Zamira Yusufjonova, "Coerced Liberation: Muslim Women in Soviet Tajikistan," unpublished manuscript, 2019.

frequent reports of local officials working against state policy. In some villages, there were also reports of *sel'sovet* members reveiling their wives.[55] In Kokand, three Party members reportedly attended a meeting with their wives unveiled, then left for home, where the women reveiled.[56] One report claimed that women removed their *paranji* but substituted the *chador*.[57] According to another report, when a "people's judge" came to a village to begin an election campaign, the *bai* urged "the population [to] meet him with hostility and shouted that it would not allow the election of women," which they deemed unacceptable for Muslims.[58] In Andijon region, a *bai* also urged mosque attendees "not to forget God and their customs and not to believe the atheists."[59] In Qashqadaryo, an imam reportedly made a speech to a mosque gathering in which he argued that "open [uncovered] women" and "the policy of Soviet power contradict the psychology of the population"; he added that "he can't wait for the English to declare war and destroy the USSR," because the Soviets were "against the laws of *shariat*."[60] In Andijon, there were reports of similar statements from a Muslim religious leader.[61] Muslim men interrupted women's meetings and forced unveilings. Local Party organizations in turn disrupted mosques to "agitate for unveiling," in some cases arresting those resisting the campaign.[62]

Inhabitants of the Tajik Panjakent district held a vote about the unveiling policy, the majority voting against it; even a local Communist Party member opposed it.[63] Imams in the region refused Party demands that they promote unveiling because it contradicted *shariat*. The chairman of Shulaginskii *sel'sovet* threatened to jail local farmers for three years if they did not bring their wives to

[55] "No. 7, Obzor, politicheskogo sostoianiia SSSR za iiul' 1927 g. (po dannym Ob'edinennogo gosudarstvennogo politicheskogo upravleniia), Prilozhenie No. 3, Vostochnye natsional'nye respubliki i avtonomnye oblasti, Uzbekistan," 5 (1927): 530.

[56] "No. 4 Obzor, politicheskogo sostoianiia SSSR za aprel' 1927 g. (po dannym Ob'edinennogo gosudarstvennogo politicheskogo upravleniia), Prilozhenie No. 3, Sredniaia Aziia," 5 (1927): 344.

[57] "No. 7, Obzor, politicheskogo sostoianiia SSSR za iiul' 1927 g. (po dannym Ob'edinennogo gosudarstvennogo politicheskogo upravleniia), Prilozhenie No. 3, Vostochnye natsional'nye respubliki i avtonomnye oblasti, Uzbekistan," 5 (1927): 531.

[58] "No. 7, Obzor, politicheskogo sostoianiia SSSR za iiul' 1927 g. (po dannym Ob'edinennogo gosudarstvennogo politicheskogo upravleniia), Prilozhenie No. 3, Vostochnye natsional'nye respubliki i avtonomnye oblasti, Uzbekistan," 5 (1927): 531.

[59] "No. 7, Obzor, politicheskogo sostoianiia SSSR za iiul' 1927 g. (po dannym Ob'edinennogo gosudarstvennogo politicheskogo upravleniia), Prilozhenie No. 3, Vostochnye natsional'nye respubliki i avtonomnye oblasti, Uzbekistan," 5 (1927): 530.

[60] "No. 4 Obzor, politicheskogo sostoianiia SSSR za aprel' 1927 g. (po dannym Ob'edinennogo gosudarstvennogo politicheskogo upravleniia), Prilozhenie No. 3 Sredniaia Aziia," 5 (1927): 344.

[61] "No. 7, Obzor, politicheskogo sostoianiia SSSR za iiul' 1927 g. (po dannym Ob'edinennogo gosudarstvennogo politicheskogo upravleniia), Prilozhenie No. 3, Vostochnye natsional'nye respubliki i avtonomnye oblasti, Uzbekistan," 5 (1927): 529.

[62] "No. 4 Obzor, politicheskogo sostoianiia SSSR za aprel' 1927 g. (po dannym Ob'edinennogo gosudarstvennogo politicheskogo upravleniia), Vostochnye natsional'nye respubliki i avtonomnye oblasti, Sredniaia Aziia," 5 (1927): 325.

[63] "No. 4 Obzor, politicheskogo sostoianiia SSSR za aprel' 1927 (po dannym Ob'edinennogo gosudarstvennogo politicheskogo upravleniia), Prilozhenie No. 3 Sredniaia Aziia," 5 (1927): 344.

the meeting. Around two hundred women showed up wearing *paranjis*; none unveiled. Even in Khujand—the Tajik region where Party control was strongest—the *bai* and religious leaders reportedly held a secret meeting and discussed means of opposing the *hujum*.[64] In Khujand city, a thousand women had reportedly unveiled, but about five hundred reveiled once surveillance declined.[65]

Reports claim that opposition to the unveiling campaign in the Uzbek and Tajik regions came from Muslim leaders in the spiritual directorate, the *bai*, and "anti-Soviet elements in the villages, [who were] inflaming religious fanaticism."[66] Such activity was particularly noted in the Ferghana Valley. Women were regularly prevented from attending women's Party meetings, and *bai* murdered a woman activist, triggering further "repression."[67] Thousands of ordinary women who unveiled were violently attacked, even murdered, by their own communities.[68] Religious leaders and *bai* reportedly "terrorized" even the "more dedicated campaign activists."[69] The Party accused Basmachi of killing Urkuya Saliyeva (1910–1934), an advocate for social change in the Kyrgyz republic's Ferghana Valley, where Islam was more strictly practiced than in the north. In 1927, reports continued of Basmachi resistance in the Ferghana Valley of both the Kyrgyz and Uzbek republics.[70]

Small-scale acts of resistance also indicated the ongoing struggle of Islamic spiritual leaders, ordinary Muslims, and even Muslim Party members to preserve their identity, beliefs, and customs. One Party report about the work among women in the Ferghana Valley of the Uzbek republic stated that conditions of "feudal enslavement" continued; "some communists and Komsomol members keep their wives under the *paranji*." Some were even returning to veiling, including the "second secretary of the Komsomol committee Ro'zixon Rahmonova, [who] threw away her school texts, married, and covered herself in a *paranji*."[71]

[64] "No. 5 Obzor, politicheskogo sostoianiia SSSR za mai 1927 g. (po dannym Ob'edinennogo gosudarstvennogo politicheskogo upravleniia), Prilozhenie No. 5, Vostochnye natsional'nye respubliki i avtonomnye oblasti, Sredniaia Aziia," 5 (1927): 399.

[65] "No. 7, Obzor, politicheskogo sostoianiia SSSR za iiul' 1927 g. (po dannym Ob'edinennogo gosudarstvennogo politicheskogo upravleniia), Prilozhenie No. 3, Vostochnye natsional'nye respubliki i avtonomnye oblasti, Uzbekistan," 5 (1927): 531.

[66] "No. 4 Obzor, politicheskogo sostoianiia SSSR za aprel' 1927 g. (po dannym Ob'edinennogo gosudarstvennogo politicheskogo upravleniia), Vostochnye natsional'nye respubliki i avtonomnye oblasti, Sredniaia Aziia," 5 (1927): 325.

[67] "No. 4 Obzor, politicheskogo sostoianiia SSSR za aprel' 1927 (po dannym Ob'edinennogo gosudarstvennogo politicheskogo upravleniia), Vostochnye national'nye respubliki I avtonomnye oblasti, Sredniaia Aziia," 5 (1927): 325–26.

[68] Northrop, *Veiled Empire*, 96.

[69] "No. 4 Obzor, politicheskogo sostoianiia SSSR za aprel' 1927 (po dannym Ob'edinennogo gosudarstvennogo politicheskogo upravleniia), Vostochnye natsional'nye respubliki i avtonomnye oblasti, Sredniaia Aziia," 5 (1927): 325.

[70] "No. 4 Obzor, politicheskogo sostoianiia SSSR za aprel' 1927 (po dannym Ob'edinennogo gosudarstvennogo politicheskogo upravleniia), Vostochnye natsional'nye respubliki i avtonomnye oblasti, Sredniaia Aziia," 5 (1927): 326.

[71] No. 199, "Iz spravki sektora informatsii organizatsionno-instruktorskogo otdela TsK VKP(b) sekretariu TsK VKP(b) G. M. Malenkovu o diskriminatsii zhenshchin v Namanganskom,

As late as December 1939, reports were sent to the Central Committee about weak antireligious propaganda in Namangan, Andijon, and rural districts of Ferghana *oblast*, the widespread continuation of fasting in rural areas, and the need for antireligious work among women.[72] Another Party document on women stated that in the Uzbek and Tajik republics during World War II, "the number of women veiling increased . . . even the wives of communists and Soviet workers. In the Urateppe district of Leninabad *oblast* of the Tajik SSR, they work under the *paranji*: the wife of the newspaper editor, the second secretary of the district Ispolkom, the deputy chief. The same facts are also verified in Ganja district of this *oblast*."[73]

Reports also deplored the continuing frequency of polygyny. The All-Union Leninist Young Communist League "observed great abnormalities in the situation of women in Central Asia. Here, especially in rural areas, polygyny still has a place."[74] Their investigation found that "[d]irectors of *kolkhoz*es have two to three wives, force the cohabitation of girls, and for not submitting, they threaten neighboring *kolkhoznik*s. . . . The district Party and the Soviet organizations only fight very weakly against these occurrences. Komsomol workers from all the Central Asian republics report these facts, in one voice."[75] The report further condemned the continuation of early marriages and other pre-Soviet practices. It recommended "mass political work among women" and more "cultural-enlightenment institutions."[76]

Even in the late 1930s and 1940s, everyday resistance to secularization continued. Local leaders' nonimplementation of Party regulations against Islam still constituted an important form of everyday resistance in the Ferghana Valley. Namangan and Marg'ilon officials were extremely frustrated with failed antireligious measures and reported cases of Party members allowing their wives to veil.[77] Namangan, Andijon, and Izbaskent districts were accused of "weakly carry[ing] out anti-religious propaganda. The spiritual leadership, using this situation, [had] activated its enemy activity," including "recently repair[ing] thirteen mosques used for *namaz*, and at the same time closing clubs for women and

Andizhanskom, Izbaskentskom raionakh Ferghanskoi oblasti, Uzbekskoi SSR" (after December 19, 1939), in *TsK VKP(b) i Natsional'nyi Vopros, Kniga 2*, 512.

[72] No. 199, "Iz spravki sektora informatsii organizatsionno-instruktorskogo otdela," 512–13.

[73] No. 396, "Dokladnaia zapiska sekretaria TsK VLKSM O. P. Mishakovoi sekretariu TsK VKP(b) G. M. Malenkovu o polozhenii zhenshchin v Srednei Azii" (September 18, 1945), in *TsK VKP(b) i Natsional'nyi Vopros, Kniga 2*, 987–88.

[74] No. 396, "Dokladnaia zapiska sekretaria TsK VLKSM O. P. Mishakovoi sekretariu TsK VKP(b) G. M. Malenkovu," 987.

[75] No. 396, "Dokladnaia zapiska sekretaria TsK VLKSM O. P. Mishakovoi sekretariu TsK VKP(b) G. M. Malenkovu," 987.

[76] No. 396, "Dokladnaia zapiska sekretaria TsK VLKSM O. P. Mishakovoi sekretariu TsK VKP(b) G. M. Malenkovu," 988.

[77] Keller, *To Moscow, Not Mecca*, 174.

Jews. The majority of the *kolkhozniks* follow the fast. In the Yusupova *kolkhoz* in Namangan district, about 300 gathered in a field and participated in prayer. On Voroshilov *kolkhoz*, Party candidate members Kenjayev and Ishinatov fasted and attended mosque."[78] Party officials particularly noted this problem in the Tajik republic, where loyal Party cadre were considered few in number. In Kyrgyzstan, the Party reported that officials in the Ferghana Valley's Osh *oblast* had "low knowledge of Marxist-Leninist theory" and "huge inadequacies in agit-prop work," especially "in anti-religious propaganda."[79]

There were fewer OGPU reports of resistance to unveiling among the northern Kyrgyz, Kazakhs, and Turkmen. Most nomadic women had never veiled or been secluded. There were far fewer mosques and *madrasas* there to close. Even in the 1930s, atheist brochures to create a "new man" consumed much of the Party's focus.[80] Consequently, opposition to the *hujum* was undeniably less frequent. The target of the women's campaign became "crimes of custom," such as early marriage, bride price, and polygyny, practices associated more with patriarchal, tribal, and nomadic societies than with Islam.[81] Yet even in these republics, liberating women aroused opposition from both clan and religious leaders into the 1940s.[82]

Shifting Policy: Religious Repression with Limited Associational Space, 1943–85

Multiple factors—local resistance, lack of Russian-language skills in the Central Asian republics, and a shortage of skilled cadre—impeded the success of the Cultural Revolution. The most critical factor in ending militant atheism, however, was World War II, which triggered a tactical shift. Hitler was decimating the Red Army, and Stalin desperately needed all citizens behind the war effort.[83] Soviet intelligence believed that Hitler was making deals with Muslim leaders, in Afghanistan and elsewhere, to turn the USSR's Muslim population against

[78] No. 199, "Iz spravki sektora informatsii organizatsionno-instruktorskogo otdela," 512.

[79] No. 359, "Iz dokladnoi zapiski komissii TsK VKP(b) sekretariu TsK VKT(b) G. M. Malenkovu o nedostatkakh ideologicheskoi i agitatsionno-propagandistskoi raboty TsK KP(b) Kirgizii" (no later than September 18, 1944), in *TsK VKP(b) i Natsional'nyi Vopros, Kniga 2*, 860.

[80] Nazira Kurbanova, *Islam v obshchestvenno-politicheskoi zhizni Kyrgyzstana* (Bishkek: Institut istorii i sotsial'no-pravogo obrazovaniia, 2009), 19–20.

[81] Edgar, "Bolshevism, Patriarchy," 269.

[82] No. 219, "Pis'mo sekretaria TsK KP(b) Turkmenii M.M. Fonina sekretariu TsK VKP(b) A. A. Andreevu ob izmenenii v Turkmenskoi SSR zakona o brachnom vozraste dlia zhenshchin" (April 30, 1940), in *TsK VKP(b) i Natsional'nyi Vopros, Kniga 2*, 549.

[83] Jeff Eden, "A Soviet Jihad against Hitler: Ishan Babakhan Calls Central Asian Muslims to War," *Journal of the Economic and Social History of the Orient* 59, nos. 1–2 (2016): 237–64.

communism.[84] NKVD reports claimed that Tajiks, especially from the Pamirs and along the Tajik-Afghan border, were deserting or emigrating to Afghanistan to avoid fighting for the USSR; they were accused of being in close correspondence with Afghanistan's intelligence agency and participating in "counterrevolutionary organizations" and subversive activity along the border.[85] The NKVD also reported that Crimean Tatars, Chechens, and Tajiks were being courted by both Hitler and Afghanistan's intelligence agency, which promised a caliphate. Yet while Stalin punished some suspect groups with forced deportations, he also sought to motivate Muslim support by demonstrating, domestically and abroad, that Islam not only legally existed in the USSR but was a recipient of state sponsorship.

Late Stalinism: Creating State Islam

Stalin began easing restrictions on religion in 1943. Repression continued, albeit in differing and usually less violent forms, together with a gradual, although very small increase in associational space.

On June 10, 1943, a Politburo decision signed by Stalin directed the NKVD to allow the organization of the Spiritual Directorate of Muslims of Central Asia and Kazakhstan (SADUM). This effectively sanctioned Islam within a narrow, state-controlled framework, giving the regime the ability to co-opt Muslims, monitor and shape state-approved Islam, and, they hoped, prevent the growth of independent Islam. In some aspects, Stalin's scheme worked: the first *mufti*, Eshon Boboxon ibn Abdulmajidxon (1943–57), used Qur'anic references and appeals to jihad to rally Muslims to fight for the USSR against "the fascists."[86] Central Asian mullahs reportedly turned over their children to serve in the Red Army and gave money to aid families of those fighting; however, the Party still questioned Tajiks' loyalty to the USSR.[87] SADUM's purpose was not limited to wartime mobilization, and consequently opened up some associational space for the diffusion of religious ideas. The Party used SADUM to justify other Soviet

[84] Roger Reese, *Why Stalin's Soldiers Fought: The Red Army's Military Effectiveness in World War II* (Lawrence: University Press of Kansas, 2011), 142.

[85] No. 330, "Iz informatsionnoi spravki sektora informatsii organizionno-instruktorskogo TsK VKP (b) sekretariu TsK G. M. Malenkovu o faktakh vrazhdebnoi deiatel'nosti ismailitov na Pamire" (February 1, 1944), in *TsK VKP(b) i Natsional'nyi Vopros, Kniga 2,* 799–800; No. 340, "Dokladnaia zapiska zamestitelia zaveduiushchego organizatsionno-instruktorskim otdelom TsK VKP(b) L. A. Slepova sekretariu TsK VKP(b) G. M. Malenkovu o vystuplenii sekretaria TsK KP(b) Tadzhikistana o patrioticheskoi roli musul'manskogo dukhovenstva v gody voiny" (April 10, 1944), in *TsK VKP(b) i Natsional'nyi Vopros, Kniga 2,* 815.

[86] Eden, "A Soviet Jihad," 254–57.

[87] No. 340, "Dokladnaia zapiska zamestitelia zaveduiushchego organizatsionno-instruktorskim," 814–15.

policies to Muslims as well. Stalin further expected SADUM to present the USSR to the rest of the Muslim world as a place where Muslims thrived.[88] SADUM officials traveled to various Muslim-majority countries, establishing contacts and good relations, presenting a positive image of Soviet Islam in "the East."[89]

After a period in which religious education was virtually impossible, SADUM opened several narrow opportunities. Several dozen students per year were allowed to study at the only two legal Islamic institutions of the USSR: the Mir-i Arab *madrasa* in Bukhara and the Islamic Institute of Imam al-Bukhari in Tashkent. In the 1950s, there was a cohort of just eighty students at the *madrasa*, and their education was tightly controlled. One graduate explained, "I studied there for nine years, secular and religious subjects. It was all under state control. The same propaganda and strict surveillance were everywhere, but the local cadre was strong."[90] An imam recalled that in the 1970s, when he studied at the Islamic Institute, there were only forty students from the entire USSR. Meanwhile, both religious education in the home and mosque attendance were illegal for anyone under the age of eighteen, despite religious obligations. "It was a very difficult, impoverished time for our religion. The Soviet Union was completely against religion. It [Islam] got weaker, but they [communists] did not destroy it."[91] Yet compared to the pre-1927 period, only a tiny number of mosques were registered and openly functioning, at least until the 1980s.

The establishment of SADUM opened restrictive but important avenues for the flow of new ideas and the maintenance of Islamic knowledge. A handful of students would have the opportunity to study in Libya, Syria, Jordan, and Egypt. They included the head *mufti* of Central Asia, Muhammad Sodiq Muhammad Yusuf (appointed 1989–93), and the Tajik republic's *perestroika*-era *qozikalon* (supreme Islamic judge), Akbar Turajonzoda (1989–92). Both became open critics of the communist regime in the late 1980s. As its capacity grew over time, SADUM established contacts, developed student exchanges, and even brought back literature from the Arab world.[92] Some of these materials were puritanical, originating from the Hanbali school in Saudi Arabia. Other literature—possibly unbeknownst to those tasked with its monitoring—was explicitly political, including the writings of the Muslim Brotherhood and Mawdudi, which were rapidly spreading in the Middle East at the time.

[88] Abdujabar Abduvakhitov, "Islamic Revivalism in Uzbekistan," in *Russia's Muslim Frontiers: New Directions in Cross-Cultural Analysis*, ed. Dale Eickelman (Indianapolis, IN: Indiana University Press, 1993), 80.

[89] Interview with a former *mufti* of Central Asia, Muhammad Sodiq Muhammad Yusuf, Tashkent, Uzbekistan, January 2003; interview with Turajonzoda.

[90] UZ-oral history #18, imam, Marg'ilon, Uzbekistan, 2004.

[91] UZ-oral history #17, imam, Marg'ilon, Uzbekistan, 2004.

[92] Interview with Muhammad Sodiq Muhammad Yusuf.

Unregistered *hujras*, Sufi *khanqahs*, and unofficial mosques were the only remaining opportunities for education outside of SADUM. All increased in number after 1943, though such teachers remained illegal and at perpetual risk of secret police raids and imprisonment. Life-cycle practices such as *janaza* were forbidden but sometimes tolerated during the last decade of Stalinism. Stalin renewed repression of religion a few years before his death in 1953, but the era of mass killing or incarceration of religious leaders had passed.

Khrushchev's Renewed Religious Repression and the "Thaw"

The decade after Stalin's death was a period of "post-totalitarianism," to borrow Havel's term for the late socialist era, but it paradoxically liberalized associational space and speech while renewing the campaign against religion. The amnesty of March 27, 1953, shortly after Stalin's death, pardoned many thousands of prisoners in the Gulag, including thousands of former religious leaders, teachers, and others imprisoned for their religious beliefs.[93] Released prisoners from Central Asia were allowed to return to their homeland, yet they were not legally certified by SADUM as religious teachers. Instead, most were sent to work on collective farms or became forced labor migrants. Nonetheless, many became unregistered Islamic teachers, operating in the informal Islamic sphere. At first, some started literary circles that passed on Persian Islamic culture rather than directly engaging in religious instruction.[94] Some later returned to teaching Islam at home to their children and neighbors. "Some Sufi masters or representatives of sacred lineages even again gathered and taught numerous *murids* around the republic."[95]

Khrushchev, who succeeded Stalin as the Communist Party's general secretary (1953–64), exposed many of his predecessor's crimes and excesses in his famed "Secret Speech" of 1956. He initiated a "Thaw"—as Ilya Ehrenburg's novel dubbed this era—policies that increased associational space in several ways, including greater cultural freedom, reduced surveillance and dramatically fewer arrests, and limited possibility for travel and student exchange. Ideas and information (from Eastern Europe as well as Iran) became accessible with the introduction of short-wave radios. Although not democratic political liberalization, the post-Stalinist period was a significant shift away from Stalin's attempt at total control. De-Stalinization inadvertently encouraged a dissident movement in

[93] Stéphane Dudoignon, "From Revival to Mutation: The Religious Personnel of Islam in the Tajik SSR, from De-Stalinisation to Independence (1955–1991)," *Central Asia Survey* 50, no. 1 (2011): 58.

[94] Dudoignon, "From Revival to Mutation," 58.

[95] Interview with Davlat Usmon, Dushanbe, Tajikistan, November 2010. *Murids* are followers or disciples of a Sufi master.

Eastern Europe and more limited "sedition" in the USSR—various forms of private discussion and public complaints from ordinary people dissatisfied with the Soviet system.[96] In effect, this meant that Central Asians began to voice, at least within their kinship circles, discontent about religious repression and desire for Islamic education.

Despite the easing of political persecution, the Tajik religious leader Haji Turajonzoda recalled that "until 1963, even after Stalin had died and even after many of those arrested had returned from prison, fear remained. We still hardly performed *namaz*. Only a few were brave enough to pray as a community together and at home, with children. There wasn't any [prayer] in the mosques."[97] Turajonzoda has contested that "official Islam . . . operated under the omnipresent supervision of the KGB," while "the universality of Islamic teachings was completely ignored. [Yet] these teachings in their entirety were taught and studied in underground *madrasa*s and groups."[98] Activists and ordinary mullahs complained that only ten to fifteen Muslims per year could make the *hajj* from Central Asia; it was still effectively banned. No ordinary Muslim could hope to fulfill this Islamic obligation. All *haji*s were under close supervision of the KGB. Other pillars and practices remained either forbidden or severely restricted.[99]

Khrushchev also renewed repression of religion in a campaign launched in 1958. Eren Tasar has detailed the viciousness of Khrushchev's campaign, the extreme measures it involved, and the "volatile and unsystematic execution" of those measures.[100] Sufism, still pervasive in the Tajik republic, became the prime target of Khrushchev's campaign against "survivals," as the Party dubbed religious forms and rituals that persisted despite four decades of oppression; the regime sought to eliminate Sufi *eshon*s, shaykhs, faith healers, and rural mullahs leading practices of circumcision, funeral rites, and shrine visitation, among others. In 1958, the Central Committee issued decrees both intensifying antireligious propaganda and directing attacks on shrine pilgrimage.[101] SADUM also strongly opposed Sufis, who rivaled its sacred authority. The *mufti*'s *fatwa*s attacked Sufi shrines and undercut the financial basis of Sufi activity in the Uzbek republic, SADUM's stronghold. Major Sufi shrines in Bukhara and Samarqand were destroyed. Others became mere tourist attractions. Knowledge of Sufism and Sufi leaders dramatically weakened, even though some still made pilgrimages to shrines.[102] In the Tajik SSR, the traditional hierarchical order of

[96] Vladimir Kozlov, Sheila Fitzpatrick, and Sergei Mironenko, *Sedition: Everyday Resistance in the Soviet Union under Khrushchev and Brezhnev* (New Haven, CT: Yale University Press, 2011).

[97] Interview with Turajonzoda.

[98] Turajonzoda, "Religion."

[99] Interview with Mullah Zubaydullo Roziq, Dushanbe, Tajikistan, June 2011; interview with Sayidibrohim Gadoev, Dushanbe, Tajikistan, March 2011.

[100] Tasar, *Soviet and Muslim*, 304.

[101] Tasar, *Soviet and Muslim*, 304.

[102] Personal communication with religious expert, Tashkent, Uzbekistan, November 2004.

murids around a Naqshbandi shaykh, the *khanqahs* and their property holdings, and the practice of performing *zikr* (devotional recitations) dramatically declined.[103] Sufi teachers were still influential underground, but engaged in strict self-censorship.[104]

The attempt to reduce official Islam's growth again involved mosque closures. According to some reports, thousands of mosques which had functioned unofficially since 1943 were shuttered; 3,567 mosques (mostly unregistered) were again closed in the Uzbek republic alone between 1961 and 1963. Only 312 registered mosques remained there in 1964.[105] Krushchev's campaign also targeted *hujras*, clandestine study circles, typically for small groups of young men in late-night sessions.[106] The confiscation of religious materials continued. Surveillance and intimidation of those attending prayer escalated. In contrast to the *hujum*, however, arrests were not widespread; they took place almost exclusively in the Tajik and Chechen republics.[107]

Khrushchev further renewed attacks on patriarchy, which he associated with Islam and blamed for undermining the modernization of women. Practices of veiling, bride payment, polygyny, and early marriage were associated with both patriarchal and Islamic customs. These practices still existed widely in rural areas, where fewer women had adopted Soviet norms than in the urban, Russian- or European-populated areas of Central Asia (e.g., Tashkent, Samarqand, or Bishkek).

From the 1950s onward the state's antireligious policy was primarily manifest through propaganda, atheist education, a godless workplace, and Soviet "houses of scientific atheism."[108] The Party used the Academy of Sciences to publish "scientific atheist" propaganda.[109] Atheism pervaded plays, concerts, films, museums, and clubs.[110] In formerly nomadic areas, where Islam had always been less textually and canonically centered, Soviet propaganda was particularly powerful. In the Kyrgyz republic, there was a substantial and effective Party

[103] Muriel Atkin, *The Subtlest Battle: Islam in Soviet Tajikistan* (Philadelphia, PA: Foreign Policy Research Institute, 1989), 23; Razia Sultanova, *From Shamanism to Sufism: Women, Islam and Culture in Central Asia* (London: I. B. Tauris, 2011).

[104] Kirill Nourzhanov and Christian Bleuer, *Tajikistan: A Political and Social History* (Canberra: ANU E Press, 2013), 104; Martha Brill Olcott, *Whirlwind of Jihad* (Washington, D.C.: Carnegie Endowment for International Peace, 2012), 98–99; Baxtiyor Bobojonov quoted in S. M. Prozorov, ed. *Islam na territorii byvshei Rossiskoi imperii* (Moscow: RAN, 1998).

[105] John Anderson, *Religion, State, and Politics in the Soviet Union and the Successor States*, (Cambridge: Cambridge University Press, 1994), 58.

[106] Prozorov, *Islam na territorii byvshei Rossiskoi imperii*, 428–29.

[107] V. Alekseev, *Shturm nebes' otmeniaetsia* (Moscow: Rossiia molodaia, 1992), 235, cited in Anderson, *Religion, State and Politics*, 58.

[108] UZ-oral history #14, imam, Tashkent, Uzbekistan, 2017.

[109] Personal communications with academicians in Tashkent, Uzbekistan, 2005, and Osh, Kyrgyzstan, 2013, 2019.

[110] Tasar, *Soviet and Muslim*; Igmen, *Speaking Soviet*.

investment in atheist propaganda and the atheist educational system, especially in the 1960s to 1980s.[111] As Ali Igmen has shown, many Kyrgyz actively took part in the new Soviet culture.[112] Women in particular relished educational and workplace advances due to the Soviet system.[113] Yet, elsewhere Party propaganda was weak. The campaign's foot soldiers were half-hearted; they exaggerated their success, even while religious leaders rejected their ideas.[114]

The Khrushchev era also notably renewed the forced migrations of Tajiks and, to a lesser extent, Uzbeks, which had begun during the *hujum*. While these population transfers had economic aspects—from the 1920s to the 1940s earlier forced migrants had been sent to work on the cotton collective farms—Stéphane Dudoignon has compellingly argued that the policy also had religio-political motivations and consequences. While not as devastating in lives lost as the Chechen and Crimean Tatar deportations during World War II, the Tajik forced migrations numbered over 100,000 households by the 1950s, with more relocated in the 1960s.[115] As with the Chechens, the migrations reflected both Party punishment of the perceived opposition and antimodernism of the targeted groups, which was tied directly to religious observance and the continued authority of religious elites. The migrations served to uproot these peoples, severing ties with their ancestral homelands, which were often home to sacred shrines.[116] Those transferred were mostly "mountain Tajiks," removed from the highland villages of Matja, Gharm, Qarotegin, Urateppa, Dang'ara, Fayzobod, and Tavildara, and sent to work the lowlands of the Vakhsh River Valley (in Qurghonteppa).[117] The deportations took place as a post-Stalinist generation became aware of growing space for sedition.[118] Resettling entire kinship groups reinforced their networks and identity[119] and created especially strong narratives of oppression among those who would come of age during the Brezhnev era and *perestroika*.

Mahmadali Hayit, like others who would eventually found the Tajik Islamic Revival Party, was a child of the 1950s migrations, which he described as a form of religious "purge": "In those years, the 1950s, some people were thrown out or exiled from [their homes] in Rasht, Vakhsh, and other places, and were

111 Kurbanova, *Islam v obshchestvenno-politicheskoi zhizni Kyrgyzstana*, 20–21.

112 Igmen, *Speaking Soviet*.

113 Personal communications with Kyrgyz women, former Party members, Bishkek and Osh, Kyrgyzstan, June 2019.

114 Personal communication with Uzbekistani scholar/son of an atheist propagandist, Tashkent, Uzbekistan, August 2017; Peris, *Storming the Heavens*.

115 Valentin I. Bushkov, "Population Migration in Tajikistan: Past and Present," in *Migration in Central Asia*, ed. Hisao Komatsu, Chika Obiya, and John Schoeberlein (Osaka: JCAS, 2000), 149–50.

116 Dudoignon, "From Revival to Mutation."

117 Sh. Kurbanova, *Pereselenie: Kak eto bylo* (Dushanbe: Irfon, 1993), 58; O. Ferrando, "Soviet Population Transfers and Interethnic Relations in Tajikistan: Assessing the Concept of Ethnicity," *Central Asian Survey* 30, no. 1 (2011): 41–42.

118 Kurbanova, *Pereselenie*, 71–73, 80–81.

119 Olivier Roy, *The New Central Asia: Creation of Nations* (New York: I. B. Tauris, 2000), 85–87.

relocated to other places. They were Muslims. A great part of the mullahs and *eshons*. . . . They were [sent] too . . . to 'red districts' [those under strict party control]." According to Hayit, the goal was to eliminate the religious leadership: "Let's take the Qarotegin Valley and Gharm—except for Domullo Hikmatullo [who would also become an Islamist activist], no other well-known mullahs remained. . . . The situation was the same in other districts nearby. . . . [N]ew mullahs—Eshon Numonkhon, and several other *eshons*—came only in 1985. This period had a huge influence on the thinking of the Tajik people."[120] Davlat Usmon, another leading Tajik Islamist, held a similar view: "[The forced migrations] became one factor of the civil war."[121] According to Islamist Party leader Muhiddin Kabiri, "the tragedy of the migration resulted in the migrants rallying around several hundred spiritual leaders, including Mullah Nuri's father."[122] The dislocations strengthened "solidarity dynamics" as Sufi *eshons* developed strong followings in both their new locale as well as their home region.[123] Dudoignon and Qalandar argue that the migrations had an enormous impact on the transmission of Sufi networks across the Tajik republic, as well as on attachment to what Tajiks understood as their "sacred territory."[124] For example, some Tajik respondents recalled how those Gharmi migrants forced to Qurghonteppa returned in 1989 to build a mosque, still without legal permission, to solidify their religious and local ties.[125]

The tumultuous Khrushchev era blended growing space for criticism with reinvigorated repression of Islam, particularly in the form of attacks on Sufi shrines, mosque closures, and forced migrations that continued to disproportionately affect more strictly observant Tajiks and Uzbeks. One consequence of these conditions was an aggrieved younger generation that would ultimately be more willing to oppose the state.

Brezhnev's Relaxed Repression

With Khrushchev's ouster, Leonid Brezhnev assumed Party leadership, reversed the "Thaw," and presided over nearly two decades of relatively stable and consistent authoritarian rule (1964–82). Brezhnev was less driven by antireligious

[120] Interview with Mahmadali Hayit, Dushanbe, Tajikistan, November 2013.
[121] Davlat Usmon, "*Tadzhikskii konflikt i mery doveriia*," *Postroenie Doveriia Mezhdu Islamistami i Sekuliaristami-Tadzhikskii Eksperiment*, ed. Jan-Nikolai Bitter and Vol'fgang Tsel'ner (Dushanbe: Devashtich, 2004), 244.
[122] Interview with Muhiddin Kabiri, November 2012.
[123] Ferrando, "Soviet Population Transfers," 49.
[124] Dudoignon and Qalandar, "They Were All from the Country"; Zevaco, "From Old to New Macha," in Dudoignon and Noack, *Allah's Kolkhozes*, 167–70.
[125] Interview with Kurbon, imam, Gharm, Tajikistan, July 2006.

fervor than his predecessor, but he institutionalized many of Khrushchev's policies. As Tasar observes, the state was "virtually omnipresent" in monitoring religious activity, while "less severe" in punishment.[126] Yet Brezhnev ran the USSR—and especially Central Asia—through patronage, cadre stability, and indirect rule; the indigenous communist cadre in Central Asia had great control so long as it turned over raw materials, kept order, and did not challenge the regime. These practices left room for local officials to decide how strictly to implement antireligious policies. Some officials ignored Islamic practice. In remote regions where the state apparatus was minimal, religious practice often went unnoticed;[127] elsewhere, powerful individuals in the state and private sector even contributed money and protection for Islamic revival.[128] Brezhnev's long-serving first secretary of the Uzbek Communist Party, Sharof Rashidov, allowed more registered religious communities, largely to buy local support.[129]

Throughout the 1970s, repression could be harsh, but implementation oscillated. The surveillance of mosque attendees and sermons and punishment for fasting continued. Mosque communities were harassed or badgered for paperwork to prevent legal registration. Fear that attending mosque would pose risks for education and employment remained widespread. Far fewer arrests occurred; many received fines or were subjected to taxation rather than prison sentences.[130] As under Khrushchev, the Party renewed efforts to spread "scientific atheism" through education, modernization, and antireligious propaganda rather than violence.[131] As Vladimir Bobrovnikov has convincingly argued, the "scientific atheism" of the 1950s to 1970s, while not militant, was decidedly oppressive.[132] It involved many of the same goals, slogans, and ideological tropes of the 1920s to 1940s, violated religious identity and national custom, instilled fear, undermined belief, and bred resentment among some.

From Andropov to Gorbachev: Religious Policy in Turmoil

Little improved after Brezhnev's death under the ossified Party leadership of the early to mid-1980s. John Anderson argues that the Council on Religious Affairs (CRA) chairman expressed the need for vigilance due to the Iranian Revolution

[126] Tasar, *Soviet and Muslim*, 241.

[127] Ro'i, *Islam in the Soviet Union*; personal communications with a former Party official from Gharm, Tajikistan, August 2007; academician, Tashkent, Uzbekistan, November 2004; historian from Osh, Kyrgyzstan, August 2014.

[128] Dudoignon and Noack, *Allah's Kolkhozes*.

[129] Anderson, *Religion, State and Politics*, 216.

[130] Tasar, *Soviet and Muslim*, 106–7.

[131] Atkin, *The Subtlest Battle*, 1989.

[132] Bobrovnikov, "The Contribution of Oriental Scholarship," 77.

and the Soviet war in Afghanistan; the CRA's "perception" of an Islamic threat was notable, if unsubstantiated.[133] As early as 1983, Soviet leaders in both Moscow and Tashkent were concerned with the effect of the Soviet-Afghan war on the Soviet public, which was writing letters of protest.[134] Artemy Kalinovsky, however, argues that actual resistance to the war among Muslims was minimal, and antireligious policy changed little.[135] Under the Party's general secretary Yuri Andropov (1982–84), who had long served as chief of the KGB, state monitoring and the periodic arrest of religious activists continued. Andropov attempted to reinvigorate control over Islam at the regional and local level, but his death in 1984 cut short such efforts.

As the Soviet system stagnated, illegal religious belief and activity increased as associational space, de facto if not de jure, marginally expanded, primarily in connection with the policies of the USSR's last general secretary, Mikhail Gorbachev (1985–91), and the unravelling and collapse of the USSR during 1991. Gorbachev's *glasnost'* (openness) and *perestroika* (reform, restructuring) programs significantly increased associational space—for the media, civil society, and even protest. Gorbachev also liberalized Russian Orthodoxy and celebrated its thousand-year anniversary in 1988. By contrast, little changed with regard to Central Asia, especially Islam. The dynamics of the Gorbachev era will be discussed in detail in each case study in the following chapters. Here I note that in the mid- to late 1980s, limits on mosque registration, a key indicator of continued oppression of Islam, remained a significant grievance.

As evident in Table 3.1, very few Juma (Friday) mosques had been legally registered in Central Asia by 1987. When comparing the number of registered mosques across the region, we see that the disparities in treatment of Islam by republic had a cumulative effect over time. Mosques were less restricted in the Kyrgyz SSR, which had thirty-four mosques for its population of about 4.4 million, of whom about 71 percent were Muslim. By contrast, state suspicion and control of Uzbek and Tajik Islam continued to create obstacles to mosque registration. The Uzbek republic had the largest Muslim population, but the number of legal mosques there had declined from ninety to sixty-seven under Khrushchev.[136] That number increased by only twenty, at least legally, under *perestroika*. Namangan city still had only four registered mosques (one mosque for roughly every seventy-one thousand Muslims), despite the puritanical observance of Islam there.[137] There had been thousands of mosques before 1917—360

[133] Anderson, *Religion, State and Politics*, 96.

[134] Anatoly Chernyaev, "The Diary of Anatoly Chernayev, 1985," National Security Archive 2006, https://nsarchive2.gwu.edu/NSAEBB/NSAEBB192/, 38–39.

[135] Artemy Kalinovsky, *A Long Goodbye: The Soviet Withdrawal from Afghanistan* (Cambridge, MA: Harvard University Press, 2011), 47–51.

[136] John Anderson, "Islam in the Soviet Archives," *Central Asian Survey* 13, no. 3 (1994): 384.

[137] UZ-oral history #19, imam, Namangan, Uzbekistan, 2004.

Table 3.1 Registered Friday Mosques in Several Muslim-Majority Republics

Republic	Total Population (millions), 1989	Muslim Population (est. millions), 1989	Number of Legal Friday Mosques, Jan. 1958	Number of Legal Friday Mosques, Jan. 1964	Number of Legal Friday Mosques, Jan. 1987	Mosques per 1 million Muslims, 1987
Kazakh	16.5	7.4	26	25	25	3.4
Kyrgyz	4.4	3.1	34	33	34	7.7
Tajik	5.3	4.5	34	18	17	3.8
Turkmen	3.7	3.1	4	4	4	1.2
Uzbek	20.5	18.45	90	67	87	4.7

Sources: Columns 2–3: Demoscope, http://www.demoscope.ru/weekly/2022/0965/index.php; CIA worldfactbook, https://www.cia.gov/the-world-factbook/; Columns 4–6: Dmitry Trofimov, database on mosques, "Friday Mosques and Their Imams in the Former Soviet Union," *Religion, State, and Society*, 24, no. 2–3 (1996): 217.

mosques in Marg'ilon alone, for a population of forty thousand. During *perestroika*, only two mosques remained in Marg'ilon, and only four in the entire densely populated Ferghana province.[138] The Tajik SSR had even fewer legal mosques—only seventeen for over five million Muslims, the majority of whom were observant. Haji Turajonzoda complained that "the religious administration [SADUM] . . . allowed only three or four mosques in Dushanbe city" for a population of several hundred thousand, even while churches were being built.[139]

Despite high birth rates among Muslims of Central Asia, especially in the Ferghana Valley and the Tajik republic, the number of legal Friday mosques actually declined from 1958 to 1987, even as Gorbachev was allowing church registration. Gorbachev's contradictory policies would trigger renewed contention over mosques in this region. As under Khrushchev, growing expectations of greater religious liberalization, due to more open associational space elsewhere, were met by a recalcitrant, anti–Islamic Party leadership both in Moscow and locally. Like Moscow leaders, the republic-level Party first secretaries under Khrushchev and Brezhnev, and also those newly appointed by Gorbachev (especially Islam Karimov in the Uzbek SSR and Saparmurat Niyazov in the Turkmen SSR) in the 1980s viewed Islamic authorities and mosques as potential rivals to their own power.

[138] UZ-oral history #17, imam, Marg'ilon, Uzbekistan, 2017.
[139] Interview with Turajonzoda.

The Agents of Islamic Revival and Ideational Diffusion

On the one hand, the repressive and exclusionary policies of the Soviet state obstructed most forms of Muslim practice, precluded any form of Muslim politics, and demobilized Muslim opposition activism for decades. On the other hand, the de facto and de jure growth of associational space, in fits and starts, from World War II onward created enough space for limited Islamic revival. Within this space, both registered and unregistered Islamic actors—*ulama*, *hujra* teachers, and Sufi masters—were vital to Islam's endurance and revival. While some unregistered religious leaders were critical of those who collaborated with the regime, contrary to common perceptions the registered and unregistered often collaborated and protected each other in the common interest of preserving Islam.[140] In oral histories and interviews, both religious entrepreneurs and ordinary Muslims recalled those religious activists who had kept Islam alive from the 1950s to the 1980s.

After the opening of the Gulag, there were thousands of mullahs but only a handful of registered mosques, so many began teaching illegally in private *hujras*.[141] *Hujra* networks were most extensive in the towns of the Uzbek Ferghana Valley, especially in Andijon, Namangan, Marg'ilon, and Kokand, and of the central and southern Tajik republic—areas, as noted already, characterized by high contention over Islam from the 1920s to 1930s. Many *ulama* moved to smaller towns in the Ferghana Valley (of the Uzbek SSR), and in Dushanbe, Kulob, and Gharm (in the Tajik SSR), areas more distant from Soviet control. Here, *hujra*s sought to study and practice with less fear of rearrest.[142] Multiple elderly male respondents revealed that they met in *choyxona*s (teahouses) and in rooms on the *kolkhoz*es that were often unmonitored.[143] Sometimes each brigade had its own prayer room.[144] In some cases, these *hujra*s took place with the tacit compliance of the *kolkhoz* and local officials.[145] Such study circles attracted students and created networks of followers who studied Islamic texts and debated interpretations of Islam's role in society and state.[146] Rajab Mirzo,

[140] Parviz Mullojonov, "The Islamic Clergy in Tajikistan since the End of the Soviet Period," in *Islam in Politics in Russia and Central Asia*, ed. S. Dudoignon and H. Komatsu (London: Kegan Paul, 2001), 221–50.

[141] Interview with Turajonzoda; Bakhtiyar Babadjanov and Muzaffar Kamilov, "Muhammadjân Hindûstânî (1892–1989) and the Beginning of the Great Schism among the Muslims of Uzbekistan," in Dudoignon and Komatsu, *Islam in Politics in Russia and Central Asia*, 195–219; Dudoignon and Qalandar, "They Were all from the Country."

[142] Dudoignon and Qalandar, "They Were all from the Country"; interview with Turajonzoda.

[143] TAJ-FG#10, Qurghonteppa, 2009.

[144] Interview with pensioner, former collective farm brigadier, Andijon, August 2004.

[145] Dudoignon and Qalandar, "They Were all from the Country"; Ro'i, *Islam in the Soviet Union*, 355–57.

[146] Bobojonov and Kamilov, "Muhammadjân Hindûstânî," 117–18.

a Tajik journalist and democratic activist who grew up in the 1970s, recalled the role of *hujras*: "One *eshon* lived in our village. He taught unofficially, and people brought their children to him. . . . About eighty to ninety percent of acting mullahs studied in unofficial groups, *hujra* lessons. Mullahs receiving an official education in Bukhara and Tashkent were very few. . . . Each mullah had five to six students in a group. With each group, at one time in one place, and another time in another place, the mullah conducted lessons for two hours . . . which they carried out at night."[147] *Hujras* met a growing demand for religious education that the state refused to accommodate. Haji Akbar Turajonzoda credited these scholars and *hujras* with "carrying on Islamic belief" through the "dark Soviet era. . . . Despite their old age and the terrible conditions of Stalin's labor camps, they preserved an unbending Islamic spirit, which helped them to pass on their encyclopedic knowledge of Islam."[148] SADUM's Mufti Muhammad Sodiq Muhammad Yusuf, appointed during *perestroika*, resolutely agreed.[149]

Domla Muhammadjon Hindustoniy was the most renowned Soviet-era Islamic scholar and *hujra* activist in Central Asia. He reportedly studied in the renowned Deobandi Islamic center in India, as well as in Bukhara's famed *madrasa*, before 1917. He returned to the USSR in the 1920s and attempted to teach. Hindustoniy opposed political activism, but the authorities nonetheless viewed his religious teaching as political and anti-Soviet. He was thrice imprisoned, but after his release from the Gulag, SADUM appointed Hindustoniy imam of a mosque in Dushanbe. Although later removed, probably due to his widespread sacred authority, he was not rearrested, and he maintained contact with both SADUM and unregistered Islamic teachers. His underground *hujra* passed on a deep, classical Hanafi study of Islamic knowledge which was not legally obtainable in the USSR.[150] He taught the history of Islam, Arabic Islamic literature, Persian poetry, and other subjects excluded from SADUM's curriculum.[151] Over the course of five to six decades he mentored generations of students; most came from the Tajik SSR and the Ferghana Valley, and some would later become Islamist entrepreneurs. One IRPT activist recalled that in the 1950s and 1960s, Hindustoniy and other Islamic scholars reopened possibilities for studying Islam; most considered him "an exceptional and unparalleled Hanafi scholar of the Qur'an, *shariat*, and Islamic history."[152] Another activist said, "Domla Hindustoniy was a good teacher, person, and scholar for Islam in Tajikistan. He played an enormous role. . . . Hindustoniy himself was an intellectual and a

[147] Interview with Rajab Mirzo, activist and journalist, Dushanbe, Tajikistan.
[148] Turajonzoda, "Religion," 268.
[149] Interview with Muhammad Sodiq Muhammad Yusuf, Tashkent, January 2003.
[150] Interview with Turajonzoda; Bobojonov and Kamilov, "Muhammadjân Hindûstânî"; Olimov, "Islam in Contemporary Tajikistan."
[151] Interview with Gadoev.
[152] Interview with Roziq.

visible light." Haji Turajonzoda recalled Hindustoniy's lessons: "I went to such lessons several times, and my brother Eshon Nuriddin studied with Haji Domla Hindustoniy sixteen [to] seventeen years. . . . Their night lesson was . . . not far from the flour factory. . . . The lesson began at two in the morning and continued [for] two to three hours. They gathered and performed the morning *namaz* together. Whoever studied at that time received the very best education. . . . Hindustoniy explained everything very well. . . . He taught four subjects . . . *tafsir, hadith, usul*, and [Persianate] literature. . . . He commented beautifully on [the poetry of] Hafiz."[153] Students took notes or tape-recorded the lectures to pass them on.

Hindustoniy was not alone in his teaching. Domla Abdurashid, another scholar originally from Kokand with an esteemed pre-Soviet Islamic education, had a similar following. Mufti Muhammad Sodiq Muhammad Yusuf's own father, son of a renowned shaykh, also taught Islam illegally.[154] Yet another esteemed teacher, Domla Hikmatullo, formed a *hujra* in the Tajik center of Gharm and Qarotegin Valley. One mullah recalled, "We all brought every question to Domla Hikmatullo. [He was] a great religious authority."[155] An Uzbek imam reported, "During the Soviet era there were many who helped save [Islam]. I personally know that here in the entrance to this mosque, there were secret *hujras* and in these places they [*ulama*] taught people. There was a small courtyard in the basement where people gathered and secretly performed *namaz*. There was a time when twenty young guys were arrested and put in prison for this, around 1980. Such *hujras* were in the Ferghana Valley and far-off villages. Teachers told children in the *hujras* not to tell anyone about it, even their parents. . . . Everything was secret."[156] Also associated with the *hujras* was the illegal sale of the Qur'an, which, according to one Uzbek imam, "cost at that time [about 1980] from one thousand to ten thousand rubles. . . . My father bought one for one thousand rubles. At that time, you could buy a car for some two thousand rubles. There was a deficit of Qur'ans, and also of cars. . . . One had to hide such books when outside. So, you see what difficulties we had in the Ferghana Valley, in Andijon, Kokand, and Marg'ilon."[157]

Sufi *eshons* and shaykhs were also central religious actors in the post-Stalinist Islamic revival. Sufism persisted around individual spiritual leaders and families, who were often the guardians of shrines,[158] especially in remote, less tightly controlled areas. Sufi teachers and their *murids* (followers) had also

[153] Interview with Turajonzoda.
[154] Interview with Muhammad Sodiq Muhammad Yusuf.
[155] Interview with Kurbon, imam, Gharm, Tajikistan, July 2006.
[156] UZ-oral history #16, imam, Marg'ilon, Uzbekistan, 2017.
[157] UZ-oral history #16.
[158] Sergei Abashin, "The Logic of Islamic Practice: A Religious Conflict in Central Asia," *Central Asian Survey* 25, no. 3 (2006): 267–86; Kemper, Motika, and Reichmuth, *Islamic Education*.

fled to villages and settled on collective farms during the turmoil of the 1920s and 1930s.[159] Like more mainstream Hanafi clerics, they too subsequently reestablished religious networks there.[160] Sufism's dispersed Islamic authority and informally rooted Islamic learning, practices, and networks were harder to control than the mosque-centered Hanafi *ulama*. Sufi shaykhs—including Abdurahim Eloqi, Abdukarim Romiti, and Eshoni Turajon—devoted themselves to Islam's survival through unofficial education.[161]

Sayidibrohim Gadoev, an IRPT activist, recalled that in the Tajik republic Sufis were instrumental in teaching "pure prayer and a pure heart. . . . They were strong advocates of the force of Islam."[162] He claimed that they consciously avoided the political realm, shunning newspapers and television, so that they would be immune to Soviet propaganda. Gadoev himself had initially studied with a Sufi *eshon*: "He gave me a religious education that I couldn't find with anyone else. It's the power of Allah. As a believer I know that it's all from the wisdom and power of Allah. . . . Sufis served Islam and I respect that."[163] Sufi hostels and networks reemerged, but without organized brotherhoods.[164] Individual Sufi shaykhs still had significant sacred authority through *murid*s and their reputation, though their influence was weaker than in the past. As victims of recent religious repression and perpetually excluded from SADUM, many such religious adherents were discontented. Their students—the children of the 1950s and 1960s, who had less fear of the Party and greater access to Islamist ideologies—would ultimately mobilize, infusing the enduring faith of their teachers with political ambitions.

As we have seen, Soviet policy after 1917–27 continued to create both the motivation and, if unintentionally, the means for Islamism to emerge. First, the Soviets' brutal repression of religion politicized Islam; it made the practice of Islam an act of resistance to the Communist Party's policies of atheism and social engineering. Beginning in 1927, Stalin's regime devoted massive force to eliminating virtually all public traces of religion and to creating atheist citizens loyal to the Party. It was immensely destructive, but, in the face of high resistance, it did not wholly succeed.[165] State policy shifted multiple times, from intense religious repression throughout most of Stalin's rule and under Khrushchev to softer forms under Brezhnev and Gorbachev. Yet, from executions and imprisonments of

159 Zevaco, "From Old to New Macha."
160 Vladimir Bobrovnikov, Amir Navruzov, and Shamil Shikhaliev, "Islamic Education in Soviet and Post-Soviet Dagestan," in Kemper, Motika, and Reichmuth, *Islamic Education*.
161 Turajonzoda, "Religion: The Pillar of Society," 268.
162 Interview with Gadoev.
163 Interview with Gadoev.
164 Interview with Turajonzoda; Bobrovnikov et al., "Islamic Education."
165 Keller, *To Moscow Not Mecca*, 247.

religious leaders to mosque raids and closures, bureaucratic strangulation, exclusion, and forced migrations, oppression of Islam continued to politicize religious identity.

Second, assessing the Soviet period over time reveals the importance of shifts in associational space due to inconsistent implementation of these policies. In the first decade of Soviet power, emergent threats to religion in the context of relatively high associational space had led to multiple forms of Muslim mobilization which were not Islamist. Then, from 1927 to 1943, Stalin's complete closure of associational space demobilized Muslim activists across Eurasia. Marginal openings fostered by Khrushchev's "Thaw" and Brezhnev's patronage system inadvertently allowed a gradual reemergence of Islamic activism. Emboldened and enabled by gaps in state repression, unregistered *ulama* and Sufi leaders who had survived the *hujum* defied state policy to preserve and pass on Islamic knowledge and faith at considerable risk to themselves and their families.

Thus, motivated by religious repression, which was both ongoing and remembered through narratives of the 1920s to the 1940s, and then enabled by the limited associational space of the post-Stalinist period, religious actors and activism revived. Concentrated in the Tajik and Uzbek Ferghana Valley regions, where contention over Islam had long been high, unregistered *ulama* and Sufi teachers played a key role in Islam's endurance through decades of Soviet oppression. Tajik Islamist Hikmatullo Sayfullozoda's words exemplify this phenomenon. Excoriating Soviet attempts to create "a new man, free from religion," he declared, "Even the Soviets could not find the means to forbid the transmission of Islamic values from generation to generation. Islam, with the help of underground *hujra* study, was able to pass on its values to the next generation."[166] Many like him would form a new generation of religio-political entrepreneurs who emerged from the *hujra*s armed with some religious knowledge and new opportunities to express their ideas and share experiences of repression. The next chapter will explore this survival and politicization of Muslim identity and practices through the personal narratives and memories of ordinary people who lived through the 1960s–to the 1980s.

[166] Interview with Sayfullozoda, IRPT activist, Dushanbe, Tajikistan, 2010.

4

Muslim Belief and Everyday Resistance

> If we fasted, they came to us and said, "Religion is the opium of the people. Why do you fast?" They put bread in your mouth and forced you to eat.
>
> —Mullah, Jalalabat, Kyrgyzstan, 2005

> Elders taught the youth. . . . But the children said it's forbidden. They'll kick us out of the Komsomol. . . . But what did old people have to be afraid of? What should they do? So, they did not hide their faith. Those who were not communists performed *namaz*.
>
> —Oqsoqol, Marg'ilon, Uzbekistan, 2005

> There was no religious freedom, no cultural freedom . . . but many people performed *namaz* anyway, during the time of Brezhnev and Gorbachev.
>
> —Otincha, Namangan, Uzbekistan, 2004

The mullah, *oqsoqol* (respected elder), and *otincha* (female religious teacher) quoted above, like many other Central Asians, described themselves as "believers" despite the decades of Soviet propaganda, atheist education, and assaults on religious institutions and practices discussed in previous chapters. My interviews throughout Central Asia revealed the widespread endurance of Muslim identity, practice, and belief. As historians and anthropologists have increasingly recognized, decades of state religious repression failed to eradicate either faith or *Musulmonchilik* (being Muslim).[1] Repression instead politicized religion by making most Islamic practice illegal and by forcing secularization on an unwilling population. By the late Soviet era, many Muslims resisted the state by practicing Islam behind the walls of their courtyard or apartment in "hidden transcripts," exercising "everyday resistance."[2] They did so even though

[1] Khalid, *Islam after Communism*; Judith Beyer, *The Force of Custom* (Pittsburgh, PA: University of Pittsburgh Press, 2016); Marlene Laurelle, ed., *Being Muslim in Central Asia: Practices, Politics, and Identities* (London: Brill, 2018); David Montgomery, *Practicing Islam: Knowledge, Experience and Social Navigation in Kyrgyzstan* (Pittsburgh, PA: University of Pittsburgh Press, 2016).

[2] Scott, *Domination*; Fitzpatrick, *Everyday Stalinism*; Kozlov, Fitzpatrick, and Mironenko, *Sedition*.

Politicizing Islam in Central Asia. Kathleen Collins, Oxford University Press. © Oxford University Press 2023.
DOI: 10.1093/oso/9780197685068.003.0005

they accepted the Soviet system as inevitable, and even approved of it in other respects. This situation reflects in some ways the paradox with which anthropologist Alexei Yurchak characterized "the last Soviet generation": *Everything was forever until it was no more.*[3] As Yurchak implies, few Soviet citizens—Muslim or otherwise—expected the USSR's collapse. They repeated Soviet hegemonic discourse and performed Communist Party rituals for decades, assuming the system was forever. Yet, as pockets of associational space slowly appeared, ordinary people found opportunities to be Muslim as best they could. They engaged in small-scale, hidden resistance to Soviet antireligious policy by performing Muslim funeral rites or sending their sons to *hujras*. Yet, they did not do so to challenge state power. They accepted the "normality" of Soviet circumstances and envisioned nothing better. But when the Soviet state suddenly collapsed, they openly reflected on the Soviet era as a time of severe repression of their religious identity, whether or not they had lived through the Red Terror of the 1920s and 1930s.

Yurchak has astutely observed that former Soviets often displayed a remarkable ability to rapidly adapt to post-Soviet life, even after seventy years of state socialism. They could do so, despite the cataclysmic shock of the USSR's collapse, because of the skills they had acquired underground or informally during the late socialist era. In the post-Soviet era, as we shall see in subsequent chapters, Central Asians who for decades had been denied opportunities to practice their religion suddenly became openly and actively Muslim. This rapid transition was possible because, as Scott has argued elsewhere, a long-term engagement in "hidden transcripts" enables a rapid resurgence and mobilization. Performing hidden transcripts had preserved fundamental Islamic belief, identity, and networks, if not deep scriptural knowledge.

In this chapter, I first establish that shared Muslim belief and identity, which I have argued is a precondition for Islamist emergence, endured into the late Soviet era. Central Asians did not simply claim to be believers. Ordinary people living through the final three decades of the USSR regularly engaged in both public Soviet and hidden Islamic practices. They proclaimed atheism in school or at work but continued to perform at least some Muslim rituals in private.

Second, although ordinary Muslims, like Soviet citizens more generally, were not espousing political change throughout most of the Soviet era, engaging in hidden transcripts implied opposition. Hidden transcripts constituted "everyday forms of resistance," the "prosaic" but constant struggle of the weak to defend their interests.[4] Such quotidian acts of seemingly powerless citizens defied the all-powerful state and its hegemonic discourse. Central Asians' own

[3] Alexei Yurchak, *Everything Was Forever Until It Was No More: The Last Soviet Generation* (Princeton, NJ: Princeton University Press, 2006), 16–28.

[4] Scott, *Domination*, 4, 15–16; Scott, *Weapons of the Weak*, 29.

narratives reveal that religious repression and exclusion from the Party continued into the 1980s; Soviet religious policy remained a significant grievance against the state.

Third, this chapter addresses ongoing debates about the extent to which Islam survived under communism. Adeeb Khalid has argued that the Soviet destruction of learned Islam, together with Soviet "nationalities policy," resulted in Islam becoming little more than ethnic custom, an aspect of Uzbek or Tajik "national" tradition.[5] Eren Tasar has posited that the Soviet creation of SADUM (see Chapter 3) enabled Central Asians to become both "Soviet and Muslim"; using archival sources on SADUM's activities, he concludes that after Khrushchev, repression had largely ended.[6] The interview-based evidence I present reinforces Khalid's claim that Soviet "nationality" categories and Islamic custom became deeply intertwined, but also reveals that nationality and Islam were mutually reinforcing. Islamic identity never withered away and was not rendered apolitical, for it was still oppressed.

The few scholars who have examined late Soviet-era Islamic practice have relied primarily on limited state archives, Soviet-era surveys conducted under authoritarian conditions, and state newspapers. These sources provide one perspective but have serious omissions, reflect Party propaganda, and give limited insight into individual opinions and experiences. Devin DeWeese has advocated going beyond archival sources to understand the ways in which Soviet antireligious policies profoundly and negatively affected individual lives. We need to recognize the effect of atheist propaganda and the pervasive indoctrination of antireligious ideology that citizens experienced "in virtually all cultural, educational, and political venues"; we need to grasp the pervasive fear and "the atmosphere of harassment and intimidation that could envelop anyone engaged in religious practice."[7]

In this chapter, I rely instead on various types of interviews conducted during fieldwork, including oral histories with elders (both former Party members and nonmembers) who lived through much of the 1950s to the 1980s, interviews with societal elites (including religious leaders, *mahalla* leaders, former Communist Party bureaucrats, and businessmen who sponsored mosques), and twenty-four focus group interviews with ordinary citizens who grew up and were educated under Soviet rule. These conversations are a rich source of material on an era with limited archival access. Moreover, interviews provide perspectives that are unlikely to ever be documented in archives. Rather than simply a record of a

[5] Khalid, *Islam after Communism*.
[6] Tasar, *Soviet and Muslim*.
[7] DeWeese, "Islam and the Legacy of Sovietology," 308.

mullah's arrest or mosque closure, interviews provide the context and insight into the emotional effects of such events on those involved. While requiring careful interpretation, interviews are a crucial means of documenting the past before the last Soviet generations pass away.[8]

The use of interviews is not unproblematic, of course. Memory and perceptions of the past may be faulty or biased or shaped by later experiences. Many Central Asians, however, could speak about religion during the bygone Soviet era with relative freedom, especially in contrast to speaking about the present, which was more likely to induce fear and self-censorship. Given the general nostalgia for the Soviet past, amplified by post-1991 political turmoil and economic hardship, it is notable that many respondents favorably recalled certain qualities of Soviet life and yet overwhelmingly resented the treatment of religion. (See the appendix for a full discussion of interview methodology.)

Overall, my interviews reflected Yurchak's view of the late Soviet generation. Individuals rarely exhibited binary opinions about the Soviet system; most were neither dissidents nor communists.[9] Instead, they accepted and even approved of many aspects of Soviet socialism—its patriotism, equality, education, and respect for elders, values they saw as compatible with Islam. One Kyrgyz imam contrasted Soviet times with the present this way: "We lived very well. Everyone was employed. There were no rich and poor, and it was very good. And now everyone has their own property, but youth are unemployed. There are rich and poor. . . . I think that's the bad side [of the USSR's collapse]."[10] An Uzbek imam from Jalalabat said, "In those times, everything was in abundance—patience, goodwill, attentiveness to the needs of others. Now, even relatives don't help each other."[11] Similar views were shared by many other respondents. Yet, even while they had enjoyed some aspects of Soviet life, most had remained Muslim, fearful of practice and discontented with Soviet antireligious policy. Interviews also revealed that contention and politicization of Islam was typically higher in the Tajik republic and the Uzbek Ferghana Valley. As we shall see in Chapter 5 and later, the ideas and actions of late Soviet Islamist entrepreneurs in those specific areas would appeal to deep religious grievances, rooted in targeted state repression.

[8] Adrienne Edgar, *Intermarriage and the Friendship of Peoples: Ethnic Mixing in Soviet Central Asia* (Ithaca, NY: Cornell University Press, 2022), 7.

[9] Yurchak, *Everything Was Forever.*

[10] Interview with ethnic Kyrgyz imam, Batken, Kyrgyzstan, June 2005.

[11] Interview with ethnic Uzbek imam, Jalalabat, Kyrgyzstan, June 2005.

Muslim Belief, Identity, and Practice in the Later Soviet Years

Muslim Believers

A precondition for Islamist emergence is a society, or at least a substantial segment of a society, that identifies as Muslim in a meaningful way. Previous chapters have demonstrated, through archival documentation, the strength of Islamic identity throughout the early Soviet era, as well as the widespread resistance to militant atheism into the 1940s. Here, interviews offer a different—but complementary—perspective on the endurance of Muslimness under later Soviet rule.

Most people did not readily admit to belief in Allah publicly during Soviet times, and they were cautious about doing so in post-Soviet Uzbekistan and Tajikistan.[12] In fact, one *mahalla* leader whom I interviewed insisted at first that he was an atheist. After several hours of conversation over green tea, he admitted that he was and had always been "a believer."[13] As they recalled the Soviet era, most of my hundreds of respondents claimed to always have been believers. For some, there was likely an element of memory falsification or reconceptualization of history as they spoke of the past. Nonetheless, respondents almost universally considered themselves Muslim believers. Many saw little distinction between supposed nonbelief before 1991 and the revival of belief after 1991.[14] When I asked about Islamic "revival" in the 1990s, for example, Mukarram, a Tashkent resident, stated, "In principle, God was always in my life. . . . When did I begin to breathe?" She was clearly puzzled by the suggestion that she had somehow become Muslim only after the USSR's collapse, merely because she had previously been unable to participate in many Islamic rituals.[15] Subxinisso, a Tajik businesswoman in Dushanbe likewise said, "We Tajiks have faith and it will remain within our bones even if they [the political powers] exterminate it."[16] An Uzbekistani respondent explained, "We did not [need to] 'come back' to religion [after independence because] faith was always there." The vast majority of Tajik and Uzbek respondents felt the same.

For most Central Asians, Islam was not about scriptural studies but, as Talal Asad has argued, customary practices and identity; Islam was a lived tradition. DeWeese similarly has shown that among formerly nomadic Muslims, Muslimness centers on lineage, shrines, and life-cycle rituals, not theological precepts.[17] In addition to SADUM, the unregistered *ulama*, and the Sufi

12 Personal communication with academic, Tashkent, Uzbekistan, July 2015.
13 Interview with *mahalla* leader, Ferghana, Uzbekistan, June 2004.
14 Louw, *Everyday Islam*.
15 UZ-oral history #3, 2017.
16 TAJ-FG#18, Khujand, 2013.
17 DeWeese, "Islam and the Legacy of Sovietology," 305.

masters who passed on Islamic knowledge, many ordinary people were also responsible for saving Islam amid Soviet conditions. In over 90 percent of focus groups (including participants raised before 1991), respondents claimed to have learned about Islam "from childhood" and from grandparents.[18] In only four groups did respondents admit being raised as Party members—"as atheists."[19] Overwhelmingly, it was parents or "grandparents and great-grandparents" who passed on belief and the basics of "hidden prayer." One Uzbek *oqsoqol* recalled that his grandfather, who had joined the Party in the 1920s (before the mass repression of Islam began), still "performed *namaz* [prayer] five times a day . . . learned prayers like verses of poetry, fulfilled all rituals, and had a beard. No one bothered him."[20]

Religious teaching at home usually took place without a Qur'an or religious texts. Belief was taught through oral tradition and participation in community religious rituals. As Sobira, a university-educated woman from Dushanbe, observed, "All parents want to acquaint their children more closely with national and religious values. . . . When I was seven years old, my grandfather and grandmother taught me *sura* [chapters of the Qur'an]."[21] Her grandparents were born in the early 1940s but still learned and passed on the faith. Another Uzbek *oqsoqol*, Erkin, born during World War II, said, "*Oqsoqol*s taught faith in our family, in the evening, after dinner. They sat nearby and said, 'You must know this, otherwise you will be a *kafir* [nonbeliever].' They told us about the *duo* [prayer] that you must say when you have a bad dream, to prevent the devil, and so forth."[22] For most, exposure to Islamic teaching took place in these limited, familial ways. In private, elders often adhered to religious obligations with little or no explanation to youth. Ulfat's father-in-law went to perform *namaz* in the mosque two times every day in the 1970s, and at night he read the Qur'an to the family in Arabic; they understood little, and he did not teach them more "because," he said, "for right now, our life conditions are not conducive to it."[23] He feared for their persecution.

Some respondents in Tajikistan, Uzbekistan, and southern Kyrgyzstan had also clandestinely studied with a mullah or *otincha* in the Brezhnev years. Those with connections to learned *ulama* had access to Arabic-language books, carefully hidden from Soviet authorities. For others, access to Islam was at best through their poorly educated local mullahs, who passed on Islamic knowledge, primarily during *janaza* (the Muslim burial rite) gatherings. Bahodir emphasized

[18] TAJ-FG#14, Kulob, 2009.
[19] KY-FG#11, Issyk-Kul, 2005.
[20] UZ-oral history #7, 2017.
[21] TAJ-FG#15, Dushanbe, 2013.
[22] UZ-oral history #7, 2017.
[23] UZ-oral history #4, 2017.

that "the elders, *oqsoqols*, people who knew the Qur'an well, talked about faith at events and community gatherings. Yes, it's in our blood to be Muslim."[24]

Many others studied again, more rigorously, after the Soviet collapse, through exposure to religious literature, new mosques, and new teachers. Only then was the possibility of deeper Islamic instruction more widespread. Nonetheless, despite these limitations, one respondent expressed the view of many: "In substance, nothing has changed. Those same traditions and customs were not as strong then, but we saved them."[25] Being Muslim, a religious identity and belief, was still widespread by the 1980s. The drive to create *Homo Sovieticus* had failed. Oral histories thus reveal the decisive impact of the everyday efforts of ordinary religious persons to preserve Islam, not only as national custom but also as belief and identity. As a Tajik woman from the Ferghana Valley asserted, "In Soviet times, atheism did not spread. The religious leaders and mosques were banned, but in the villages, people saved Islam's foundations. Mullahs secretly performed rituals and taught spiritual values."[26] Another Tajik, Mahinakhon, agreed: "Local mullahs played a big role in out-of-the-way villages where the government power and security organs could not always pay attention."[27]

Respondents' religious knowledge, particularly theological instruction, was typically low under socialism. Yet, their accounts of covertly performing religious customs, rituals, and traditions before 1991 reveal that religious identity had endured across generations, despite Soviet atheist policy.

Hidden Transcripts: How Ordinary Muslims Defied Atheism

Many people participated in Islamic practices during later Soviet decades. These actions took the form of "hidden transcripts," the repertoires and discourse by which ordinary people engaged in the deception of the regime.[28] Without wholly rejecting the state, and even without pushing political change, both religious leaders and ordinary people would perform religious rituals in private. To borrow Lisa Wedeen's term for Syrians living under Hafez al-Assad's dictatorship, Central Asians acted "as if"[29] they believed the all-pervasive state propaganda, but their acts of everyday resistance pushed back against the regime's encroachment on their identity, faith, and sacred space.

[24] UZ-oral history #5, 2017.
[25] UZ-FG#6, Ferghana, 2005.
[26] TAJ-FG#18, Khujand, 2013.
[27] TAJ-FG#18, Khujand, 2013.
[28] Scott, *Domination*, 18–19.
[29] Lisa Wedeen, *Ambiguities of Domination: Politics, rhetoric, and symbols in contemporary Syria* (Chicago, IL: University of Chicago Press, 2015), 67.

Doing so contrasted sharply with their own public discourse before the Komsomol or Party, or at work, where most put on the appearance of supporting atheism. The widespread phenomenon of hidden transcripts strongly suggests that Soviet policies were largely unsuccessful in instilling atheism or transforming religiosity, at least among the majority rural population or in small towns in the Ferghana Valley. Professing one's faith, performing circumcision feasts, burial rites, marriage rites, and ritual prayer, and fasting demonstrated Soviet Central Asians' Muslimness.[30] One elder said that people "consciously deceived" the state: "It was the politics of the time."[31]

Life-Cycle Rituals

In the Tajik and Uzbek republics, life-cycle rituals such as the circumcision ceremony for young boys (Tajik/Uzbek: *sunnat to'yi*; Kyrgyz: *sunnöt toi*) were considered so central to the Muslim way of life that they continued, often unpunished by local officials. Ulfat recalled that even in the early 1960s when Khrushchev was cracking down on surviving Muslim customs, her family held the ritual circumcision and prayer for her young son. Defying the Party, they performed this ritual, which they agreed "was absolutely necessary." Such ceremonies were imbued with religious meaning and teaching. According to Alisher, a manual laborer who was a child in Dushanbe in the 1970s and early 1980s, "When a person comes of age, he recognizes God, and can understand heaven and hell. Mullahs told us about this at circumcision ceremonies."[32]

Janaza continued almost universally across the region. They were sometimes even public, given the difficulty in hiding the communal ritual. "At *janaza*, elders and mullahs said prayers. Everyone knew that it was a sin to not bury a person without reading *janaza*. . . . The soul of the person will not rest in peace."[33] When Ulfat's family held *janaza*, verses of the Qur'an were recited, *palov* prepared, men gathered, an *otincha* came, and "women loudly wailed."[34] Some officials tolerated *janaza* so as not to alienate the population.

With the dawn of the Soviet era, weddings were supposed to be modern, secular, and Soviet, performed and certified by the state civil registry office, known as ZAGS (*otdel' zapisi aktov grazhdanskogo sostoianiia*); in 1917, the Party had banned religious marriages. Nonetheless, some respondents claimed that they

30 Atkin, *The Subtlest Battle*; Ro'i, *Islam in the Soviet Union*. Many scholars, however, viewed such rites as merely communal customs. See: T. S. Saidbaev, *Islam i obshchestvo: opyt istoriko-sotsiologicheskogo issledovania* (Moscow: Nauka, 1984).

31 UZ-oral history #4, 2017.

32 TAJ-FG#16, Dushanbe, 2013.

33 UZ-oral history #5, 2017.

34 UZ-oral history #4, 2017.

also arranged religious marriages, secretly. Sanobar, an *otincha* from Ferghana, insisted that Islamic marriage rites (Tajik/Uzbek: *nikoh*; Kyrgyz: *nike*) were an essential part of both *O'zbekchilik* (being Uzbek, Uzbekness) and *Musulmonchilik* (Muslimness). "The Qur'an demanded *nikoh*," she said.[35] Even outside the Ferghana Valley, many Uzbeks followed the religious norm. One woman, married around 1960, said her father had died in World War II and her mother had very little money, so "a Soviet wedding" was "more practical." The factory director also encouraged "a Komsomol wedding" for career advancement. Nonetheless she exclaimed, "Of course, we also had *nikoh*! Our wedding was legal—we went to ZAGS. Then at home we said *nikoh*. . . . My mother would not have allowed it! . . . Without *nikoh*, marriage is *haram* [forbidden]!"[36] Likewise, Erkin described his "Soviet red wedding," which included alcohol and music. Yet they also "called the mullah to the house to say *nikoh*." In rural areas, such as the predominantly Tajik and Uzbek Qashqadaryo region, *nikoh* was not a secret, said one respondent: "It was our tradition. All Muslims did this. Otherwise [marriage] would have been a sin."[37] *Nikoh*, like *sunnat-to'yi* and *janaza*, was more than ethnic custom; it was a religious practice. Those ceremonies were a rare venue for passing on religious truths, values, and identity.

Performing *Namaz*

Performing *namaz*, the Islamic pillar of ritual prayer five times a day, was a particularly risky and uncommon practice. Leaving work or school to perform *namaz* was forbidden, said the men in one focus group. "People rarely performed *namaz*," reported a former Party member. Another disagreed: "People performed it secretly."[38] A third said it was harder to perform *namaz* in Namangan, because "Namangan was generally repressed."[39] An Uzbek businessman from Namangan emphasized that "Friday *namaz* was only for men in their fifties [i.e., pensioners]. For youth it was forbidden."[40] According to one *otincha*, also from Namangan, "There was no religious freedom, no cultural freedom, [but] many performed *namaz* anyway, in the time of Brezhnev and Gorbachev."[41]

In some regions, families prayed secretly at home, when possible, concentrating on early morning and evening prayer. Abduholiq, growing up in Dushanbe, learned *namaz* in the 1980s despite restrictions: "Performing *namaz*

35 Interview with unregistered mullah, Ferghana, Uzbekistan, 2005.
36 UZ-oral history #4, 2017.
37 UZ-oral History #7, 2017.
38 UZ-FG#3, Marg'ilon, 2005.
39 UZ-FG#3, Marg'ilon, 2005.
40 Interview with businessman, Namangan, Uzbekistan, 2005.
41 Interview with *otincha*, Namangan, Uzbekistan, 2005.

begins in the family, then in the mosque. For example, when I was eleven, youth from our *mahalla* went to the mosque and learned with the mullah. I wanted to go too."[42] Most began *namaz* only as pensioners, when they no longer feared reprisals at work. In Kulob, Tajikistan, a respondent said, "We even had to pray in secret so that the KGB wouldn't arrest us. They prosecuted all the mullahs."[43] In Andijon, a former collective farm brigadier told me that men used to perform *namaz* in the field or in farm buildings.[44]

The proliferation of unsanctioned mosques after World War II became a new way of defying the regime's ban on unregistered prayer.[45] Tajik respondents in some regions described "*choyxona* [teahouse] mosques built by *hashar* [the tradition of mutual communal assistance]" during the USSR. They could gather there to talk and pray under the guise of drinking tea.[46] Haji Mansur, an unregistered mullah who taught and led *namaz* during the Soviet era, said, "We always had a mosque, secretly. We only began building this big official one [in use at the time of the interview] during Gorbachev's *perestroika* and only finished after the tragic events [the Tajik Civil War]. Our mosque was built on the donations of the population and businessmen who financed it."[47] Officially, *zakat* (compulsory religious donation) was banned, but informally people "gave *sadaqa* anyway," helping family and neighbors as required by Islam.[48]

Shrine Visitation and Other Sufi Practices

Elements of Central Asian Sufism both survived and served to preserve an Islamic communal identity. The vast majority of respondents did not use or even know the term "Sufi" or "Sufism." Few respondents mentioned knowledge of or participation in Sufi practices such as *zikr* (performing mystical devotions). Although many had personally encountered an *eshon* (Sufi master) as a village spiritual elder, especially in Tajikistan, organized Sufi brotherhoods were rare. Nonetheless, Sufi engagement with sacred space was essential to broader Muslim tradition and belief.[49] Visiting the *mazars* (shrines) of saints or holy persons was a common form of practicing Islam in Muslim Eurasia before, during, and after

[42] TAJ-FG#16, Dushanbe, 2013.
[43] TAJ-FG#14, Kulob, 2009.
[44] Personal communication, Andijon, Uzbekistan, July 2004.
[45] Ro'i, *The New Central Asia*.
[46] Interview with Tajik former Communist Party official in Gharm, Dushanbe, Tajikistan, August 2005.
[47] Interview with unregistered mullah, Dushanbe, Tajikistan, 2006.
[48] UZ-oral history #8, 2017.
[49] Louw, *Everyday Islam*.

the Soviet era.[50] According to Paolo Sartori, shrines "acquired meaning through an interpretive framework provided by Sufi narratives about saints and their miracles. Therefore, shrines represented for Central Asia a collective memory space. . . . [T]he past was preserved for mobilization in the present through narrative."[51] Pilgrimages to holy places or shrines still existed in the 1980s[52] and rapidly revived in the 1990s. In a focus group with well-educated women raised in the Soviet era, Sanoat explained, "Visiting shrines is considered a very important spiritual value." Subxinisso agreed: "To visit the burial stone of the dead is an extremely vital and essential Muslim tradition."[53]

Knowledge and practice of Sufi rituals were also passed on by elders. As Otamurod said, "Some say that it's forbidden to worship the dead, but it's not worship. It's remembering, respect for their memory. The goal is to remember our ancestors."[54] One man who grew up on a *kolkhoz* near Tashkent recounted that his father had told him about the renowned Shakyh Ahmad Yassaviy; they often went to Turkestan to visit Yassaviy's mausoleum, a Sufi shrine. "Holy places were banned," he recalled, "but people came anyway, because he was from the Prophet's clan. . . . Some shrines were destroyed during Soviet times, but they [the authorities] were afraid to touch others."[55] Many such shrines, dating back centuries, had survived destruction by Stalin and Khrushchev. Others were long closed and only later rehabilitated by Brezhnev or Gorbachev.

Among the Kyrgyz, teaching by Sufi *eshons* was less common. An elderly imam, Tochubai, recalled that in the 1970s there were "Sufi *jamaats* [congregations]" in the south, "but only secretly. They passed on special Islamic education. They taught Muslimhood and *shariat*."[56] Yet the Sufi practice of shrine visitation was still common. Moreover, for the Kyrgyz, *mazars* were not only mausoleums but also rock formations, creeks, trees, and nomads' cemeteries—any place associated with saints, holy relics, and the ancestors. In the Kyrgyz republic, especially in the mountains, people visited tombstones of Sufi saints and honored their forefathers at Shamanist holy sites. Even Kyrgyz living in the north, who did not typically attend mosque or perform *namaz*, much less study in *hujras* or *madrasas*, passed on knowledge of these sites and rituals to their children. They were a habitual part of *Musulmonchilik*.

[50] Bruce Grant, "Shrines and Sovereigns: Life, Death, and Religion in Rural Azerbaijan," *Comparative Studies in Society and History* 53, no. 3 (July 2011): 654–81; Montgomery, *Practicing Islam*.

[51] Paolo Sartori, "Of Saints, Shrines, and Tractors: Untangling the Meaning of Islam in Soviet Central Asia," *Journal of Islamic Studies* 30, no. 3 (2019): 367.

[52] Atkin, *The Subtlest Battle*, 25.

[53] TAJ-FG#18, Khujand, 2013.

[54] UZ-FG#31, Termiz, 2013.

[55] UZ-oral history #2, 2017.

[56] Interview with Imam Tochubai, Jalalabat, Kyrgyzstan, 2016.

Narratives of Religious Repression and Exclusion

There was a large gap between the public "authoritative discourse" about Lenin and atheism and the hidden transcripts that occurred behind the doors of Soviet-era apartments or the courtyard walls in the old city *mahallas* and villages.[57] Personal accounts—narratives of respondents' own experiences or those of their parents and grandparents—reveal painful memories of Soviet-era repression of Islam and of exclusion from the Party as a consequence of one's faith.

Non-Party Muslims' Narratives of Repression

At a minimum, most Soviet-generation oral history respondents were critical of Soviet religious repression, even if they remembered other aspects of the USSR positively. Likewise, in every Soviet-generation focus group in Tajikistan, in most Soviet-era groups in Uzbekistan, and in about half such groups in Kyrgyzstan,[58] participants complained that "religion was not free during Soviet times." One Tajik *mahalla* leader summed up the Soviet government this way: "It was bad. The Soviet system was totalitarian. The individual person was prohibited from having a point of view or thoughts or faith. . . . It was a regime with certain benefits and order, but it was a mistake."[59] Many others also remembered the Red Terror with anger; they said that Islamic knowledge, family, and acquaintances disappeared. Sadriddin, a Tajik from Gharm, described the period as "witnessing the danger of liquidating religion, from the 1930s to the 1990s. . . . Many books were burned . . . books on morals, poetry, on philosophy and religion. . . . [T]hey [communists] were illiterate and just burned them."[60] Mukarram, an educated, urban, and pious woman, recalled hearing about the Stalinist years from her grandmother. Born in 1956, her grandparents studied Islam before the Revolution; her grandmother's parents had been religious teachers. They were rounded up in Tatarstan in the 1920s and sent to the camps because they possessed Islamic texts. Her grandmother fled with other family to the Uzbek SSR, where she married an Uzbek. Her own parents grew up religious, performing *namaz* at home, but did not encourage their children to do so before adulthood since they feared being revealed and that their children would suffer consequences.[61] Bahodir, an Uzbek factory worker born in 1946, recalled

57. Yurchak, *Everything Was Forever*, 15.

58. All Soviet-generation ethnic Uzbek groups in Kyrgyzstan reported religious repression under the USSR, whereas many ethnic Kyrgyz groups did not.

59. Interview with Abdulfatoh, unregistered imam, Gharm, Tajikistan, 2006.

60. TAJ-FG#11, Gharm, 2009.

61. UZ-oral history #3, 2017.

learning that before the 1920s and 1930s, "everyone was raised in religion's soul. When the Soviets came to power, they began to cleanse religion. They repressed a lot. Many imams and believers were sent to the Gulag. You know of course what took place in this time of repression! My grandfather and others hid their faith. But my father's family observed all the *farz* [pillars] of Islam, secretly."[62] Alisher, a businessman from Marg'ilon, Uzbekistan, bitterly recalled, "My grandfather, a mullah, was sent to the Gulag and died there—for stealing bread during the famine."[63] In one of my focus groups, the women complained, "The Soviet Union stopped the state from being Muslim."[64]

Assadullah was born in 1949. He was Uzbek and the son of Abu Bakr, who came from a religious family in Marg'ilon. They taught Assadullah his faith and rituals at home. He had only a high school education. Most of his life he had lived and worked on a *kolkhoz* in the south of the Kyrgyz republic. After independence he became imam of a mosque in Osh region. Assadullah recalled that "in those times [the 1930s to the 1960s] prayers were repressed. Reading the Qur'an was also forbidden. If they caught you praying anywhere the atheists came and said, 'Will you have eternal rest or not?' They very seriously reprimanded us and forced us to take an oath to not say prayers again." He continued:

> I need to tell the history so that you understand. My grandfather was a religious person, and in 1931 they sent him to prison because he was accused of carrying religious propaganda. . . . He was shot and we don't even know where his grave is. Grandmother and his sister remained in the house. . . . Then in the spring Abdulla [our uncle] came one day and said "If you don't leave tonight, then tomorrow they will come for you and send you to Ukraine."[65] And we all had to leave our home. We went and hid in a field of wheat during the day and then at night we walked. We did that for three or four days. We came to the *kolkhoz* Frunze [near Osh] and stayed. We still live there. . . . Ever since 1970, we had wanted to return to our homeland, our house, to remember our parents and have a memorial. But when we finally arrived there, an invalid, a miner, lived in our house. Stalin had transferred our home to him. So, we said prayers and just gave him our home. We figured we were already foreigners there, so we never returned. Look, understand that in one hand I have a fire, and in the other a Qur'an. Look how we saved and carried our Qur'an. Yes, we were very strong and carried our faith with us. And since 1992 [in Kyrgyzstan] we have been able to read our Qur'an openly.[66]

[62] UZ-oral history #5, 2017.
[63] UZ-FG#3, Margi'lon, 2005.
[64] UZ-FG#3, Margi'lon, 2005.
[65] Ukraine was then stricken by collectivization-induced famine, causing four to seven million deaths.
[66] Interview with Assadullah, imam, Osh region, Kyrgyzstan, 2016.

Erkin, from a Qashqadaryo village on the Uzbek-Tajik border, remembered that "in those times, many people had a Qur'an, but some of them were so afraid of Soviet power . . . that after the searches began, many burned the Qur'an and other religious books. They arrested people if they found their Qur'an. I remember that in 1947 or 1950. I was young. I remember Stalin. That's how it was in those times."[67] By the late 1940s, few still possessed a Qur'an, and even if they did, it was in Arabic, so fewer still could read it. An elderly Uzbek mullah, originally from Marg'ilon in the Ferghana Valley, recalled, "They arrested all who were rich or religious, killed them, and took their houses. In 1932 they sent our family to Ukraine for resettlement, and only after the war . . . we returned, got permits and were assigned to work on the collective farm, in [the neighboring Kyrgyz town] Kara-suu. I have about ten books left from that time."[68]

The destruction of religious knowledge and mosques did not end with the Stalin years, or even after Khrushchev's anti-survivals campaign. Repression went far beyond mosques, forcing family and private Islamic education deep underground. Given that so few possessed substantive religious knowledge after the *hujum* (assault), parents who sought an Islamic education for their children sent them to unofficial mullahs or *otins* (female religious teachers for women and girls) after school or in the evening, to the extent it was possible without attracting government surveillance. One elder from a village outside Tashkent recalled that he would have had to travel through several villages to find a *hujra* teacher. He consequently had little religious instruction until after communism's collapse.[69] Although by the 1970s *hujra* education had become more widespread than in earlier decades, police harassment of unregistered mullahs and the closing of *hujras* continued, especially in the Tajik and Uzbek republics.

Some Stalinist-era tactics also continued into late socialism, especially the confiscation of religious books. Aziza, for example, recounted the treatment of her father, who came from a religious family in Andijon. Born in 1949, he had memorized thirty *sura* of the Qur'an. "He always raised us this way: 'Be good. Do only good for people, nothing bad. . . . Study always.'" However, she had to work so much, even as a child, that she had little time to study in school and none to learn about religion. She recalled, "Father had a lot of religious books." Around 1960–61, she said, "members of the internal police found out and took them. They knew he was a religious man and had books. They took very valuable books, the works of Ibn Sino. . . . Father healed people with these books. They took away all of them except one Qur'an. They slandered my father and defamed him."[70] Another Uzbek, a registered mullah in Namangan, born in 1936, was

[67] UZ-oral history #7, 2017.
[68] Interview with Uzbek mullah, Osh *oblast*, June 2005.
[69] UZ-oral history #2, 2017.
[70] UZ-oral history #8, 2017.

permitted to study abroad in Syria in the Brezhnev era. Having obtained religious texts there, he was later detained by Soviet police for making and selling copies of those works.[71] One Uzbek man from the Ferghana Valley of Kyrgyzstan recalled a guest who "came and gave [my] neighbor religious books, which he then hid away. That guest had previously been in prison many years, and then in a Siberian labor camp. Probably it's the strength of his faith that helped him survive. When people don't have such faith, I don't know how they could be happy. My grandfather was Tatar, which in Central Asia meant he was educated following an Islamic curriculum. He knew Arabic. Hundreds of thousands of people suffered violence only because they were educated or had their own opinion. They [the secret police] shot a large number of people who were not guilty of anything."[72]

Soviet constraint of Islam went well beyond these obvious forms. Most respondents who lived through the late socialist period recounted repression in the form of pervasive atheist indoctrination and obstacles to performing *namaz*, fasting, and observing *janaza*—in schools, universities, the army, and at work. While relatively few attended mosques or *hujra*s, many respondents or their family members personally experienced these broader constraints, even into the 1980s. Atheist indoctrination was a subtle but transformative form of oppression of the whole society. One man summarized the experiences of his cohort at school and work, growing up in the 1970s and 1980s in Tashkent: "It was difficult with religion. If you even uttered 'There is no God but God,' you would become an enemy of the people, because of atheism. If you said there is a God then they said 'No, there's not; there's communism, and Lenin.'"[73]

Indeed, the Party viewed schools as a crucial means of forming atheist citizens. Teachers prevented the ritual daily prayer and the fast, both obligatory in Islam. One former administrator recalled rounding up the students during Ramadan with bread in his hand. If he learned that a teacher or student was fasting, he forced the individual to take a bite of bread and to drink water.[74] Schools also indoctrinated the younger generation. Maryam said, "In school there were posters everywhere [instilling] atheism. Everywhere were posters against religion."[75] Mukarram recalled that in the 1960s and 1970s, atheist instruction directly contradicted how they were raised at home and necessitated their adopting a different discourse in public: "In school they told us there is no God. Nature created everything. We asked Grandma and Father and they said, 'Say yes to them in school, but when you come home, God exists, so you will

[71] Interview with imam, Namangan, Uzbekistan, 2005.
[72] KY-oral history #4, 2016.
[73] UZ-oral history #10, 2017.
[74] UZ-oral history #1, 2017.
[75] UZ-FG#3, Marg'ilon, 2005.

perform *namaz*.' . . . Some said we must adjust to the circumstances in which we live, but father did not want to accommodate himself to it."[76] Prayer at home had to be hidden from friends and teachers at school.

Some laughed and others expressed disgust as they recalled the omnipresent Marxist slogan "Religion is the opiate of the people." One Uzbek elder said, "To believe in God was forbidden. Religion [was] deceit, opium. They raised us in this atmosphere."[77] Bahodir, like most others, was disturbed by the transformative effect of Soviet teaching: "Atheism had a strong effect on Soviet citizens. All the children joined the Pioneers and then the Komsomol. For us, Lenin was God! Many children believed there was no God, that communism brings everyone to a heavenly life. . . . A communist activist, a Komsomol member in each class, reported on us for going to *namaz*, and Father was summoned to school. Because of that the Komsomol would not admit me."[78] For a time, he was prevented from going to the institute. When finally admitted in 1967, he admitted, "I threw away performing *namaz* for a time . . . but I returned to performing *namaz* after getting married." He and his wife worked in factories in Tashkent; both hid the fact that they performed *namaz*.

Indoctrination also took the form of denigrating religious authority and custom. One respondent reflected on how she was brought into Soviet culture: "I studied in school, in the Russian language. They told us a lot about the Pioneers, the Komsomol, those who fought to establish Soviet power in the USSR and Central Asia. So we tried to resemble them. They talked about our national traditions and customs. They said that some remained and that it was necessary to be ashamed of them, and that the mullahs and *bai* exploited simple people and repressed them." She continued, critically, "The younger generation, especially the Russian-speaking Uzbeks and Kyrgyz, tried to take on Soviet appearances and rejected the advice of their parents."[79]

Resentment of scientific atheism was also high. According to one man, a highly educated ethnic Uzbek born in Osh in the early 1960s, "Atheism negatively affected family relations. According to *shariat* and *adat* [customary law], relatives must help each other, respect each other. But many have forgotten these principles. Soviet atheism destroyed the national culture and religion and changed the mentality of the people," primarily the urban, Russian-speaking Muslims he engaged with, many of whom became Party members.[80] Although he noted that "in the *qishloq*s [villages] three traditions were generally practiced

76 UZ-oral history #3, 2017.
77 UZ-oral history #2, 2017.
78 UZ-oral history #5, 2017.
79 KY-oral history #4, 2016.
80 KY-oral history #4, 2016.

among Muslims: *sunnat to'yi*, *nikoh*, and *janaza*," he maintained that "atheism caused the collapse of the Soviet state."[81]

Conflicts between generations took place as children were caught between the school's teaching and their religious upbringing at home. One Tashkent *oqsoqol* recalled:

> Elders taught the youth, their children, and grandchildren. But the children said "It's forbidden. They'll kick us out of the Komsomol. They'll kick us out of school." Children were told . . . to read books about Lenin at home and school. But what did old people have to be afraid of? . . . So, they did not hide their faith. Those who were not communists performed *namaz*. . . . But children sang about Grandpa Lenin and Stalin. Communists not only did not perform *namaz*; they did not believe in God! . . . Everyone lived in sin. They rejected God.[82]

Enforcement of atheist doctrine was particularly strict in the institutes of higher education. Belief could affect one's entry to the institute and later career path. The Komsomol monitored institute students for religious violations and expelled believers. A respondent from mountainous Naryn, Kyrgyzstan, recalled:

> In first grade, I joined the Octobrists and later became a Pioneer. . . . In school they taught us both Soviet and national values. At that time the Octobrists, Pioneers and Komsomol learned the moral code of building communism, which was far removed from religion. . . . After school, I entered the Polytechnical Institute, and after first year, I served in the Soviet Army. In the second year, I became the representative of the ProfSoiuz [union] Committee. They taught us "Atheism" in the institute. . . . People rarely talked about religion. Islamic knowledge was low. The spirit of socialism and communism was everywhere. Atheism had a directly negative effect on our national culture and religion.[83]

For men, the military was also a place for further indoctrination of atheist ideology and Soviet values, and fasting or prayer were next to impossible. Some men recalled having no choice but to eat pork, and of course, there was no place to pray.

Work was also a place of surveillance by both bosses and peers. Religious violations could prevent advancement and lead to reduced financial compensation. Neighbors or schoolmates sometimes knew of a family's private religious practices, and some even tried to expose them at work. For example, Matluba

[81] KY-oral history #4, 2016.
[82] UZ-oral history #7, 2017.
[83] KY-oral history #1, 2016.

recalled, "One of my aunts taught geography. Students sometimes approached her and asked, 'Zilola, is there a God or not?' She looked the student straight in the eye and said, 'There is no God.' And then she came home, prayed for forgiveness, and fasted."[84] In southern Kyrgyzstan as well, an Uzbek *oqsoqol* and *mahalla* leader "feared going to the mosque under Brezhnev. If work found out, they could seriously punish us or even fire us," he complained.[85]

Recalling her father's experience, Matluba recounted how his decision to be a committed Muslim cost him dearly, even though in the post-Stalinist period he did not face serious risk of arrest or deportation to the camps because he was an engineer. His supervisors pressured him to join the Party. He refused because of his religious convictions, and he paid a heavy price.[86] His daughter recalled,

> "The ideology [of communism] hindered one's faith. . . . It destroyed people. Those who believed, for them the ideology was like hell. I know from my father, when they told him not to perform *namaz*—saying that 'It makes no difference. . . . God will give you nothing anyway'—it was very difficult for Father to hear. In those conditions, it was very difficult to believe. Now I understand him. It was so difficult when from all sides they were telling him 'There is no God.' For Father it was like this: 'If I join the Party it means I am renouncing God.'"[87]

Because he refused to join, which would have entailed directly denying his belief in God, her father was denied promotions and opportunities for advancement at work. For years, the large family lived on a small salary in poor conditions, while his peers received much higher wages and benefits. They also used their positions to line their pockets. According to his daughter, "Of course, he wanted to rise in his career, but he wanted to do so together with his faith. And they [the Party] said 'No.'"[88] Often there was not enough to eat. Conditions were sometimes so difficult that his wife accused him of hurting the family because of his principles. There were constant arguments among adults in the extended family about how to remain believers and whether to go along with the Party, at least in public, or whether directly to refuse cooperation.

While not physical persecution, these cases reveal that such believers did experience repression of other, agonizing forms—fear, psychological pressure, deprivation, exclusion, and discrimination—in addition to the continuing legal restrictions on religious practice. This may have been a reprieve after the brutality of the 1930s, but it unquestionably still constituted religious repression.

84 UZ-oral history #3, 2017.
85 Interview with ethnic Uzbek *mahalla* leader, Jalalabat, Kyrgyzstan, June 2005.
86 UZ-oral history #3, 2017.
87 UZ-oral history #3, 2017.
88 UZ-oral history #3, 2017.

One *oqsoqol* said of the 1960s and 1970s, "In those times, exclusion from the Komsomol and Party—it was horrible, worse than death! They gave you no job. You had to be a farm worker or a simple bazaar trader."[89] In short, all economic and educational opportunities, much less political ones, could be ended for those known as Muslim believers.

It is often assumed that religious repression decreased markedly under Gorbachev, but in the Tajik and Uzbek republics many endured escalating restrictions on Islamic practice during the 1980s. Former Party member Aziza reported that whereas previously her friends, family, and neighbors had been able to secretly participate in funeral rites, from the late Brezhnev years onward everyone feared repercussions: "They went to *janaza*, but with trepidation. I saw it with my own eyes. Because Moscow forbade *janaza* and *nikoh*, not just the Uzbek [Party] leaders. There was a decree from Moscow which everyone had to fulfill, and in Uzbekistan it was fulfilled in all the regions according to the Party line."[90] In 1983, she said, "they again increased repression of religion, using more force. They banned *janaza* and *sunnat to'yi*" and even forbade the custom of "baking on *Eid-al-Fitr*," the Muslim feast at the end of Ramadan.[91] "We were Party members, we had to enforce [the rules]."[92] In Ferghana, focus group participants told of continued oppression after Brezhnev: "In the USSR you were forbidden to go to a funeral. I remember that in Tashkent a professor could not even go to his mother's funeral."[93] They emphasized that, nonetheless, *O'zbekchilik* continued; everyone helped during funerals—except for those in government "who thought about jobs and power."[94] In enforcing a ban on funeral rites, the Party struck at the core of Muslim identity, said one elder.[95]

Others noted that mosque and *hujra* closures also continued through the 1980s.[96] Inhabitants of the Ferghana Valley resorted to secret "cemetery mosques," where people feigned visiting gravestones in order to perform *namaz*.[97] Aziza recalled the excessive repression under Andropov and Gorbachev throughout the Andijon region, where her father's family originated. Her disillusionment with the Party—it was then the late 1980s—was followed by her decision to take up *namaz* and follow her father's example. She began to read his Qur'an, a priceless edition from 1289, saved and kept hidden by the family.[98] In Tajikistan as

89 UZ-oral history #5, 2017.
90 UZ-oral history #8, 2017.
91 UZ-oral history #8, 2017.
92 UZ-oral history #8, 2017.
93 UZ-FG#6, Ferghana, 2005.
94 UZ-FG#6, Ferghana, 2005.
95 UZ-oral history #2, 2017.
96 UZ-oral history #1, 2017.
97 UZ-oral history #2, 2017; interview with unregistered mullah, ethnic Uzbek, Jalalabat, Kyrgyzstan, June 2005.
98 UZ-oral history #8, 2017.

well, the Gorbachev years were not liberating for Islam. One Tajik businessman recalled, "Even though there was no more terror against believers, nonetheless there was still fear among most people."[99] One unregistered mullah remembered that in the late 1980s, "believers still did not have the possibility to openly carry out their religious ceremonies, and the KGB often summoned us."[100] A group of Tajik women discussed how they learned to perform *namaz* in the early 1980s, as young adults, but Mastona reminded them that "freedom"—specifically "to go to mosque without fear"—came only after independence, after 1991.[101]

Kyrgyzstani respondents' views about the late Soviet era were more positive, however, especially in the 1980s. One imam of a mosque in Jalalabat, born in 1943, learned Islam from his parents, when "everyone was forbidden to study the Qur'an." He was educated as a zoo technician but later studied to become a mullah. He recalled that in Soviet times, the 1960s to the 1980s, "there was agitation and propaganda—the Party, newspapers, and radio. Atheism of course was against religion. But we observed *namaz*. And in 1989 there was a *jamaat* [community] created in the mosque and they began to get interested in religion and to teach religion. I myself was interested in history and books. There were several cases of people being sent to court, but everything turned out well. Religion teaches justice.... After independence those who had practiced religion came out into the open."[102]

Another recalled, "In 1985–89, religious literature began to circulate. Mosques were opening. I began to get interested in religion, to learn prayers, to read Qur'an. In my family it was praised of course."[103] An Uzbek from Osh, Kyrgyzstan, recounted how his father had worked for a communist boss for many years but nonetheless sent his children to *hujras* to get the Islamic education that they could not receive in school. When they were young adults during *perestroika*, they began attending unregistered mosques.[104]

Recalling the late 1980s, an imam explained, "In Kyrgyzstan we have division into clans, and there were conflicts because of those. But no one was arrested and sentenced to prison because of religion."[105] Another Kyrgyz imam, also from southern Kyrgyzstan and born in 1948, recounted repression of *namaz*, the Qur'an, and mosques in the 1920s and some restrictions on visiting shrines in the 1970s. Still, he professed that in his lifetime "no one was arrested." He said that by 1990, "[President Askar Akayev] supported religious freedom. They established freedom and all possibilities [for religion] existed."[106] Religious

99 Interview with businessman/mosque donor, Dushanbe, Tajikistan, 2006.
100 Interview with unregistered mullah, Dushanbe, Tajikistan, 2006.
101 TAJ-FG#18, Khujand, 2013.
102 Interview with Imam Tochubai.
103 KY-oral history #4, 2016.
104 KY-oral history #6, 2016.
105 Interview with Imam Tochubai.
106 Interview with Imam Torokul, Kara-suu, June 2016.

freedom, even according to ethnic Uzbek citizens of Kyrgyzstan, began "with *perestroika*. . . . From the mid-1980s, one could pray openly, go to mosque, without any problem."[107]

Narratives of the Communist Party's Exclusion of Practicing Muslims

Respondents also revealed a large gulf between ordinary people and Party and Komsomol members. Non-Party members often engaged in hidden transcripts with few repercussions. However, Party members faced a constant struggle; local Muslim norms required attendance and participation in hidden transcripts, but Party regulations strictly prohibited members from participating in Islamic rituals. Some defied the Party and did so anyway, for community and identity, if not for faith alone. Others feared losing their Party membership card and stayed away, risking social opprobrium. Where the presence of the Party was greater, there was correspondingly less religious activity, open or private. According to Aziza, who worked in the Komsomol, the Party, and later as director of a school, "The Party was first. . . . When we finished the university [in the early 1970s] and were getting jobs, the Party organization had us fill out a form where there were questions such as: 'Do you believe in God? Is there a God?' I heard that if a person became religious or conversed with religious people, they would be excluded from work in the Party and Komsomol organizations."[108] At work and in the institutes, coworkers, supervisors, and other Komsomol members monitored and observed those not eating during Ramadan and sneaking out for prayer, as "communists were forbidden to perform *namaz*."[109] Those caught might face harsh repercussions, even beyond being expelled from the Party. In one case, some student Komsomol members were arrested for reading religious books and then accused of stealing so as to mask the fact that piety continued.[110] Aziza recalled that in the Uzbek republic, even though some communists attended *janaza* rituals for a member of their community, they did so "with fear in their eyes."[111] Some even reported that Party members were afraid to circumcise their children, although many in the Tajik and Uzbek republics did so anyway.

There are also many who once had bought into the Soviet system but later returned to Islam. A group of Uzbek women who had belonged to the intelligentsia and were former Party members recalled, "A lot was forbidden under

107 KY-oral history #4, 2016.
108 UZ-oral history #7, 2017.
109 UZ-oral history #4, 2017.
110 UZ-oral history #8, 2017.
111 UZ-oral history #8, 2017.

communist governance. . . . If you were a member of the CPSU, then each step was monitored. You were followed. Wherever you went, whatever you did, they knew about everything. They would kick you out of the Party. You were forbidden to pray."[112] According to one respondent, "When I was young [in the 1950s and 1960s], none of the older women performed *namaz*. They did not even fast. In those days the teachers and professors were communist. Everyone wanted to keep their positions, to become bosses, and no one was interested in religion. . . . In Soviet times there was no teacher, mullah, or *otincha* to show [us] how to perform *namaz* or how to fast." She continued, "People forgot about God. The [political] power was so strong that everywhere, on TV, they said that faith was an old-fashioned mentality. They always talked about Lenin and Stalin. When we were Pioneers in ties, we believed that Grandpa Lenin created a happy life for us. We believed what the government, the bosses, said. Our state was Soviet. We had to believe in Lenin and communism. No one anywhere talked about God, about religion."[113]

Fasting was nearly impossible for the intelligentsia. Respondents from such families in Termiz recalled that they did not fast, but villagers did; as student Komsomol members in Tashkent in the 1970s, they "were forbidden to fast. They were forced [to drink] water—it was forced into their mouths" if they were caught.[114] Another respondent revealed that a "communist boss" was "expelled from work because he observed the fast during Ramadan. He hid it from everyone, but someone reported it to the *raikom* [district committee], and they fired him. So, he lived very poorly, working as a trainee in a factory."[115] Mirfayoz claimed that communists in the *raikom* were "sneaky." They tried to trick those suspected of fasting by inviting them for a meeting and serving them tea and bread to see what they would do. His family discussed whether it was permissible to break the fast in order to hide one's faith. In one such situation, his friend had taken a piece of bread: "He coughed it out, but [his family] said, 'He broke the fast.'" However, he passed the *raikom*'s test. "The young were more afraid for their future. But the middle-aged and old people never feared."[116]

Although no longer faced with the Gulag, religious violations could lead to expulsion from the Komsomol or Party, as well as job loss, salary cuts, and public denigration. Respondents stressed the repercussions for Party members if they went to *janaza* or were found at prayer or fasting, much less attending mosque. Well after the 1930s there were still serious repercussions for communists who partook in religious rituals. One mullah in Osh said, "Now [since the 1990s]

112 UZ-FG#5, Marg'ilon, 2005.
113 UZ-oral history #4, 2017.
114 UZ-FG#31, Termiz, 2013.
115 UZ-oral history #4, 2017.
116 UZ-oral history #6, 2017.

religion is not repressed. A lot of new mosques have been built recently. But then religious people might be excluded from the Party, or might lose their job. Thanks to Allah, that has passed into history."[117] Respondents from Uzbekistan told of people losing their jobs and careers although Party officials sometimes pretended that religion was not the cause of the punishment. An Uzbek, Mirfayoz, recalled that when a neighborhood elder died, "the family held *janaza* and for three days his neighbor's son stood by the door of the house and fulfilled all the rules of Islam [for the funeral]. He was a Party member. After that they kicked him out of his job. They didn't say it was because of his religiosity. They found an excuse."[118] In the Kyrgyz republic as well, an informant revealed that the repercussions of holding *janaza* for the Party member in her family were harsh. When her husband's grandfather died, the sons organized *janaza*: "As a result of this, my husband's uncle was punished for it. They removed him from his job, kicked him out of the Party, demoted him at work, and assigned him to . . . a less prestigious position. There was a big negative article about our family in the paper and about our prayer, *janaza*."[119] This was in the 1980s. Religious freedom, she said, "only began with *perestroika*."[120]

In some rural areas of Tajikistan, it was somewhat easier for a communist to partake in Muslim rituals. My interviews revealed examples of Party members sympathizing with—or at least not cracking down on—neighbors or coworkers who were found to be observing religious rituals. Occasionally, Party elites even performed such rituals openly. Bahodir recounted how the director of his *kolkhoz* performed *namaz*: "He was a Party member. Yo'ldosh Oxunboboyev [an early communist activist and head of the Uzbek SSR's government] personally gave him [the *kolkhoz* director] a medal for building the *kolkhoz* after the war [World War II]. He'd been wounded. He didn't hide his religion. He performed *namaz* five times a day and fasted. . . . You'd go to his house and his son would say, 'He's busy performing *namaz*.'" Bahodir continued, "I don't know why he wasn't afraid. Probably because he had great authority among the population. He died in the 1980s. No one punished him."[121] But such cases were not the norm.

For most in Tajikistan and Uzbekistan, even if inconsistently enforced, Soviet oppression of Islam was tangible, threatening, and remained a potent source of grievance against the state, well into the Gorbachev era.

117 Interview with unregistered mullah, ethnic Uzbek, Osh, Kyrgyzstan, June 2005.
118 UZ-oral history #6, 2017.
119 KY-oral history #2, 2016.
120 KY-oral history #2, 2016.
121 UZ-oral history #5, 2017.

Becoming "National" and Muslim

These narratives add nuance to the prevailing scholarship on Central Asia, which has argued that Soviet repression of Islam was overwhelmingly successful in eliminating religious knowledge and in transforming Islamic belief and practice into mere "national" or ethnic custom. Soviet "nationalities policy" had created the officially recognized ethnonational categories of Tajik, Uzbek, and Kyrgyz, among others. As mentioned in Chapter 2, by creating these "nations" the Bolsheviks meant to modernize and replace Islam, tribe, and clan, which they viewed as premodern identities.

Over time, Central Asian Muslims did come to view themselves as Tajik, Uzbek, or Kyrgyz. Yet, Soviet nationality categories did not replace Muslim identity; they proved to be compatible with Muslimness. Religious practices became even more deeply intertwined with custom, and extensive theological knowledge became rare, but individual accounts reveal that an understanding of the importance of being Muslim survived. Religious and Soviet-defined "national" traditions were interwoven with Islam. Birth, circumcision, marriage, and funeral rites were commonly perceived as having *both* Islamic and national content. Sufi traditions continued to be integral to being Muslim. In fact, for most Uzbeks and Tajiks, religion and nationality—*Musulmonchilik* and *O'zbekchilik* or *Tojikchilik* (and to a lesser extent *Kyrgyzchilik*)—were intimately intertwined; they saw little distinction. For example, respondents emphasized that funerals were not just a national custom but included a mullah's religious instruction and prayers.[122] One Uzbek pensioner said, "At work we observed the rules of the state and at home we observed our national traditions";[123] like many, he gave a national label to the hidden transcripts of covert Islamic observance. In Namangan, respondents were emphatic that despite Soviet policy, nothing had changed: "All Uzbeks are Muslims."[124]

Likewise in Tajikistan, respondents overwhelmingly discussed religion and nationality as closely enmeshed. One respondent declared, "Islam flows in our blood." Another claimed, "Tajiks are more religious than all others when it comes to bowing to God."[125] One said, "We must preserve both *urf-adat* [national and tribal custom] and religious rituals. You should not separate circumcision, *nikoh*, *Eid-al-Adha,* Ramadan, and *Navruz.*"[126] A Tajik businesswoman, Mutriba, remembered, "They [grandparents] saved *urf-adat* of our people even in the hardest times. Before the Revolution we celebrated national holidays like

122 UZ-FG#20, Andijon, 2005; UZ-FG#11, Namangan, 2005.
123 UZ-oral history #4, 2017.
124 UZ-FG#11, Namangan, 2005.
125 TAJ-FG#14, Kulob, 2009.
126 TAJ-FG#18, Khujand, 2013.

Navruz and *Eid-al-Fitr* everywhere, and we observed *Eid-al-Adha*."[127] For nearly all, learning Islam was "essential to being Tajik."[128] Another said proudly, "We preserved Islam in Soviet times despite the ideology."[129]

In Soviet-generation Kyrgyzstani focus groups, ethnic Kyrgyz respondents also overwhelmingly described *Kyrgyzchilik* as being about *urf-adat*, "hospitality," "respect for elders," and "traditions,"[130] but fewer ethnic Kyrgyz considered fasting and performing *namaz* to be part of *national* identity; for many, such Islamic practices were relatively new. By contrast, in focus groups with ethnic Uzbeks of Kyrgyzstan, participants universally emphasized *namaz*, fasting, *shariat*, and belief as central to *O'zbekchilik*, which was both national and Islamic.

Saba Mahmood has argued that when respondents claim that their religious practices are about piety and belief—not just nationalism or anticolonialism—we should take them seriously.[131] The performance of such customs should be understood both as a manifestation of ethnonational tradition and as part of religious belief and identity. Given that most Soviet Muslims were forced to maintain belief and perform religious rituals in secret or the close privacy of family and friends, many who dared to do so were dissatisfied with Party restrictions on their identity and traditions—even if the era of mass arrests and killing was over. Even many of those who were less devout participated in life-cycle celebrations in defiance of Soviet policy. These religious customs survived to a far greater extent than theological knowledge. Thus, the narratives here demonstrate that Soviet national identities did not replace Muslim identity. Rather, "Islamic" practices came to be central to the content of each national category, especially Tajik and Uzbek. Islam and nation reinforced each other.

Becoming Soviet and Muslim

The evidence further suggests caution in accepting an alternative argument often made, that Central Asians were comfortably "Soviet and Muslim."[132] Certainly, not all Soviet values were antithetical to Islam. Many respondents were nostalgic for some aspects of the USSR. Since World War II, many had reconciled being Muslim with being Soviet; during the war, the whole country had mobilized against fascism. Mavjuda, an educated Tajik woman, said, "Everyone knew how

127 TAJ-FG#18, Khujand, 2013.
128 TAJ-FG#12, Qarotegin, 2009.
129 TAJ-FG#13, Kulob, 2009.
130 KY-FG#11, Issyk-Kul, 2005; KY-FG#14, Bishkek, 2005.
131 Mahmood, *Politics of Piety*.
132 Tasar, *Soviet and Muslim*.

to defend the homeland, the fatherland. One was proud to serve in the army." But she continued, "My parents are Muslim and I'm Muslim. . . . I should never do anything against religion to shame them."[133] Women, former Party members, from Marg'ilon, the heart of the Uzbek Ferghana Valley, agreed with Nodira, who said, "There was a lot of focus on education then. . . . Communism was good. We went everywhere, studied, and our children studied. We saw the world. Then we built communism."[134] Respondents praised the Soviet emphasis on learning, paralleled in Islam. As Umid put it, "The USSR's values, education, and [scientific] knowledge" were all positive qualities of the Soviet system.[135] The Soviet emphasis on "respect for elders" and "helping the poor" also reflected Muslim values. A Tajik respondent from Isfara observed, "In the USSR there was justice; rich and poor were equal. There was no difference."[136] A small business owner, Imomiddin, concurred: "In the USSR everything was good except we couldn't fulfill our religious traditions."[137]

A Tajik former Party member described the Soviet period this way: "There were good values, like humanism, respect for elders, and love of the homeland, monuments to the past, but it was bad that they did not permit us to carry out our religious rituals and events."[138] Likewise, Bahodir, who came from a family of former *bai* and lived in a village outside Tashkent, remarked:

> One can't say that the idea of communism was itself bad. Children were brought up well, and studied. . . . But it was terrible that they repressed faith and declared that there is no Allah. Indeed, that was the position of the USSR not only on Islam but on all religions. . . . Russians directed the Party organs, in all institutions. At one event a student was exposed performing *namaz* and he was expelled from the institute. I could not fast. On vacations, I performed *namaz* at home. In the city [living in the dormitory], I lived by city [Party] rules. . . . In Tashkent, even the elders were afraid to go to show their faith. And youth—they completely repressed youth faith everywhere.[139]

Non-Party members also embodied such contradictions. An Uzbek mullah living in the Ferghana Valley of Kyrgyzstan fondly remembered the "Soviet value" of "respect for mothers," which, he explained, "was also an Islamic value. . . . I consider that [Soviet] generation of people honorable and I respect them." Yet,

133 TAJ-FG#4, Dushanbe, 2009.
134 UZ-FG#3, Marg'ilon, 2005.
135 TAJ-FG#12, Qarotegin, 2009.
136 TAJ-FG#5, Isfara, 2009.
137 TAJ-FG#5, Isfara, 2009.
138 Interview with National Democratic Party of Tajikistan activist, Qurghonteppe, Tajikistan, May 2006.
139 UZ-oral history #5, 2017.

he continued, it "was bad that there were atheists among them. They set Islam on fire."[140] Multiple respondents also complained about the rise in prostitution and stressed that in Soviet times women were pure—despite the ban on the hijab. Many bemoaned the decline of education; in Soviet times, they explained, the quality of education was high, even if the study of Islam was banned. One businessman who supported the Islamist opposition in Tajikistan reflected, "We lived in a socialist construction. The most important values then were friendship and brotherhood between peoples and social justice. There were no problems with Soviet values—except for the destruction of religion and the religious leadership."[141] These remarks reflect complicated assessments of the Soviet era, and the absence of polarized support for or opposition to state socialism in the later decades, as Yurchak has argued.[142] Despite partial approval of Soviet values and satisfaction with Soviet life by the 1970s, for many, religion remained an area of intractable disagreement with the USSR.

Variations in Islamic Practice within Soviet Central Asia

As anticipated in previous chapters that sketched different paths of incorporation into the USSR, respondents' discourse also revealed regional variation, both in Islamic practice and in experiences or narratives of repression. Respondents themselves regularly contrasted northern Kyrgyzstan or northwestern Uzbekistan with the predominantly Uzbek Ferghana Valley and Tajikistan, commonly portraying the latter two regions as "more Islamic," at least until Muslim proselytization spread into northern Kyrgyzstan in the 2000s. One imam explained that, in the Soviet era, "religion was strongest in Marg'ilon and the Ferghana Valley, because the *ulama* and intellectuals were there. They were not afraid. Even before *perestroika*, on *Eid-al-Fitr* the square was full of people for prayer."[143] Osh city at the time, said one former resident, was "about sixty percent Uzbek." Islam, he recalled, revived quickly among the Uzbeks even though many had lost interest in religion in the 1960s to the 1980s due to Soviet policy and desire to join the Party.[144] Few reported *hujra*s existing in the Kyrgyz republic, although some did say that by the time of independence, ethnic Uzbeks living in southern Kyrgyzstan went to Andijon [in the Uzbek republic] to hear the sermons of new, independent Uzbek preachers.[145] Like many, an Uzbek

140 Interview with ethnic Uzbek imam, Osh, Kyrgyzstan, June 2005.
141 Interview with businessman/mosque donor, Dushanbe, Tajikistan, May 2006.
142 Yurchak, *Everything Was Forever*.
143 Interview with imam #2, Marg'ilon, Uzbekistan, May 2004.
144 KY-oral history #5, 2016.
145 Interview with ethnic Uzbek imam, Jalalabat, Kyrgyzstan, June 2005; KY-oral history #6, 2016.

mullah from Kyrgyzstan, educated in Andijon and Namangan in the 1980s, criticized Kyrgyz as less devout.[146] Another Uzbek imam said, "We [Uzbeks] are close to Allah. . . . [O]ur ancestors, thanks to Allah, performed *namaz*. They were Allah's people. . . . Kyrgyz slaughter a sheep for a funeral, and even take a loan to do it. . . . This is against Allah. It's a sin."[147] The ethnic Uzbek minority within Kyrgyzstan prioritized Islam and religiosity as part of their identity, as one ethnic Uzbek businessman from Jalalabat described: "Our religious values are Muslim traditions, fasting, going to mosque, prayer five times a day, taking spiritual and theological lessons, and going to graves of dead ancestors."[148]

Kyrgyz respondents often characterized the south (Osh, Batken, and Jalalabat provinces), heavily populated by ethnic Uzbeks, as "more religious" during the Soviet era.[149] Kyrgyz religiosity took less purist, as well as less scripturalist, forms; mosques and *madrasas* were few among the nomads even in the pre-Soviet era.[150] Many Kyrgyz regularly repeated the Russian and Soviet Orientalist discourse that stereotyped them as only nominally Muslim because of their recently nomadic past.[151] Even in the south, many Kyrgyz described their values in this way: "Kyrgyz have good traditions, generosity, hospitality, humanity, justice. Unfortunately, in our lifetime, by comparison with other peoples, we have less belief in religion, in Islam."[152] In northern Kyrgyzstan, according to an elderly resident of Naryn, "*namaz* was seldom performed." She added, "My grandmother told me about God. . . . I accepted God despite the propaganda of atheism." Yet she admitted, "I know very little about Islam." She knew no mullahs and had no exposure to religious education in Soviet times: "I'm a simple woman who believes in God."[153]

Kyrgyz respondents emphasized values "coming from our ancestors" and rarely mentioned *hujras* or mosques. Religious workers among Kyrgyz were often those who "performed miracles" or cured illnesses rather than those who taught or recited the Qur'an.[154] Kyrgyz emphasized lineage and tradition rather than Islamic knowledge. "We follow our ancestors," said one Kyrgyz mullah.[155] Yulduz, for example, a typical northern Kyrgyz woman, had only "heard of the five pillars of Islam"; she had never learned anything about them. She sometimes tried to fast and said that Kyrgyz "should be ashamed of not following Islamic laws," but she emphasized "tolerance" of other religions, especially "shamanism."[156]

146 Interview with ethnic Uzbek imam, Jalalabat, Kyrgyzstan, June 2005.
147 Interview with ethnic Uzbek imam, Osh, Kyrgyzstan, June 2005.
148 Interview with ethnic Uzbek businessman/mosque donor, Jalalabat, Kyrgyzstan, June 2005.
149 This view was expressed in most oral histories in Kyrgyzstan.
150 Montgomery, *Practicing Islam*, 87–89.
151 Igmen, *Speaking Soviet*; Liu, *Under Solomon's Throne*, 66.
152 Interview with ethnic Kyrgyz businessman/mosque donor, Jalalabat, Kyrgyzstan, June 2005.
153 KY-oral history #3, 2016.
154 Interview with unregistered mullah, ethnic Kyrgyz, Osh, Kyrgyzstan, June 2005.
155 Interview with unregistered mullah, ethnic Kyrgyz, Osh, Kyrgyzstan, June 2005.
156 Interview with ethnic Kyrgyz businesswoman, Issyk-Kul, Kyrgyzstan, May 2005.

A Kyrgyz imam, influenced by the new purism being proselytized, criticized lack of Islamic knowledge among the Kyrgyz: "It's wrong that our Kyrgyz only follow the real rules of Islam a little. . . . During funerals, they follow *Kyrgyzchilik* and slaughter a fat cattle, sheep, or goat. In Islam, for three days you must not entertain guests."[157]

These stereotypes reflect an orthopraxy-centered idea of being Muslim that does not admit the variety of forms of religiosity and the many ways that Muslims practice or understand their faith.[158] Yet, this discourse also facilitated a generally less contentious relationship between northern Kyrgyz Muslims and the state during the Soviet period. Interviews, oral histories, and focus groups in much of Kyrgyzstan further revealed less sense of exclusion from the Party as a result of one's Muslimness. By contrast, ethnic Uzbeks from southern Kyrgyzstan remembered parents' and grandparents' stories of the deportation of Islamic teachers to the Gulag, the destructiveness of atheism, and secret gatherings with unofficial mullahs.[159]

Ultimately, despite being one of the strongest and most repressive states in modern history, and despite its ideological vision of liberating workers from religion, the Soviet Union failed to turn most Muslims into atheists. By exploring Muslim narratives about practicing Islam under communism, I have shown the complexity of Muslim life in the USSR. The widespread preservation of *Musulmonchilik* in some regions and the ongoing importance of Islam in the private sphere were surprising given Soviet policies. Prayer and ritual continued, albeit in a less learned, scripturalist, or purist form than it had in the settled regions during the pre-Soviet period. Few engaged in political resistance, given the lack of opportunity, yet many were dissatisfied with the regime's ongoing repression and exclusion of practicing Muslims—even if Soviet policy in the 1950s through the 1980s was less destructive of Islam than previously. Hence, many ordinary Muslims engaged in everyday resistance. They mouthed Marxist-Leninist atheist rhetoric, looking and acting like secular Soviet citizens in public, even as they rejected Party truths by praying, fasting, or celebrating Muslim rituals in private. People defied Communist Party ideology and regulations and risked consequences for their well-being, education, or career.

James Scott has argued that "hidden transcripts" foster rapid transformation when political conditions change and allow those once-veiled scripts to become public demonstrations that challenge the state. In the late 1980s and early 1990s,

[157] Interview with ethnic Kyrgyz imam, Karakol, Kyrgyzstan, May 2005.
[158] Montgomery, *Practicing Islam*.
[159] KY-oral history #5, 2016; KY-oral history #6, 2016.

as associational space increased and fear of the state dissipated, a rapid shift to open Islamic practice began. In the Tajik and Uzbek republics especially, a strong sense of Islamic identity, religious repression, and exclusion made some Muslims more prone to support a religiously framed opposition during *perestroika*. Subsequent chapters will show that religious entrepreneurs in both those republics were motivated by and appealed to widespread grievances about the USSR's atheist ideology and policy.

PART III

TAJIKISTAN

From Moderate Islamists to Muslim Democrats

5
The Islamic Revival Party Challenges Communism

> Believers tried to fulfill all religious rituals secretly.... It was during those years that ideas began to grow, ideas about creating a religious-political group for defending the interests of Muslims.
>
> —Nahzat member, 2011

> [During the war], those who supported the "Red" [communist] government [fought] under red signs or red headscarves, and Russian machinery.... If they found in some house or apartment anything that was in Arabic or Persian, they destroyed it. I'll never forget [it].
>
> —Mahmadali Hayit, deputy chairman, Islamic Revival Party of Tajikistan, 2011

Tajikistan witnessed the earliest and ultimately the most successful Islamist movement to emerge in the former Soviet territories.[1] During *perestroika*, the Hizbi Nahzati Islomii Tojikiston (the Islamic Revival Party of Tajikistan, IRPT) formed underground and illegally convened its founding congress just outside the republic's capital of Dushanbe. In 1991, the IRPT joined forces with democrats, nationalists, the *qozikalon* (head Islamic official), and Sufi networks to become the core of the political opposition to communism during and after the Soviet Union's collapse. This period constituted what I have called the first wave of Islamism in Tajikistan, the wave that set into motion forty years of Islamist contention in Central Asia.

In this chapter, I investigate the actors, goals, and dynamics of this movement. I first review the longer-term factors that led to Islamist emergence: religious repression and exclusion that began with the Bolshevik seizure of power, escalated under Stalinism, and extended through the late 1980s. Repression of Islam, paradoxically, paralleled a second factor: marginally growing associational space

[1] The Tajik SSR (discussed in Chapters 2–4) became the independent state of Tajikistan in August 1991. This chapter spans the late Soviet and post-Soviet periods; for simplicity, throughout this chapter and going forward, I refer to Tajikistan.

Politicizing Islam in Central Asia. Kathleen Collins, Oxford University Press. © Oxford University Press 2023.
DOI: 10.1093/oso/9780197685068.003.0006

from the 1950s onward, which proved critical for the development of Islamist ideas and entrepreneurship. Next, I delve into the ideological influences and personal narratives of these entrepreneurs during the 1970s and 1980s. I then analyze the rise and mobilization of the Tajik Islamist movement from 1989 through 1997. Finally, I consider the instrumentalization of Islam during the Tajik Civil War, which ranged from 1991 to 1997.

Conditions Breeding Islamist Emergence and Mobilization

Ongoing Religious Repression

The Tajik Islamist movement was the result of decades of religious repression: the initial Soviet assault and contention over Islam in the 1920s, militant atheism in the 1930s and 1940s, Khrushchev's crackdown on Sufism, and Brezhnev- and Gorbachev-era closures of *hujras*. Repression was also manifested as exclusion. Those areas of Tajikistan deemed more religious and fanatical, a consequence both of more conservative dress and strict adherence to Islamic norms and of the long Basmachi resistance, were excluded from political and economic power for decades. They were further targeted during waves of forced migrations which continued into the 1960s. I have already sketched the broad contours of state policy in Chapters 2 and 3, as well as many ordinary Tajik Muslims' experiences and perceptions of exclusion in Chapter 4. Here, I turn to the narrative of oppression as seen in the eyes of Tajik religious activists and entrepreneurs of the 1970s and 1980s.

Haji Akbar Turajonzoda, the chief Islamic leader of Tajikistan just before the civil war, for decades articulated the religious opposition's narrative of Soviet persecution. In his chilling words: "The anti-Islamic Terror in Tajikistan began after 1929. The *ulama* were sent, as they said in those times, 'in a *troika*' to Siberia. Along with the rich, thousands were sent, craftsmen, scholars, mullahs, and social leaders—to Siberia and the steppes of Kazakhstan, including my grandfather. . . . [A] great loss fell upon us, a great devastation for our Islamic culture, [and] Islamic education. We prayed secretly because they destroyed all the mosques." Describing the desecration of holy places and books, he explained, "They [the Bolsheviks] even turned the mosques into palaces for cattle and sheep. . . . On the *kolkhozes* they used them for storing produce. In the countryside, the most uneducated, ignorant people were entrusted [by the Soviets] with the fate of the people and the nation. Naturally, it was a big blow to us. . . . Many, many books were lost."[2] The *qozikalon*'s condemnation of the Bolsheviks was unflinching: "The cruelty of tsarist colonialism fades to insignificance in view of

[2] Interview with Haji Akbar Turajonzoda, former deputy leader of the Movement of Islamic Revival of Tajikistan and former *qozikalon* of Tajikistan, Dushanbe, Tajikistan, December 2011.

the horrors the Bolsheviks brought with them. . . . [T]he Bolsheviks . . . began to methodically destroy everything. They admitted application of *shariat* for some time, only to replace it with their revolutionary laws, i.e. lawlessness. . . . [T]hey began to implant idolatry by covering the country with monuments, busts, and portraits of the leaders of the revolution. . . . All the nations of the Soviet Union were trapped in a common Gulag."[3] Turajonzoda was not alone. Those who became activists were mostly of his generation, born in the late 1940s through the 1960s. Unlike Domulla Hindustoniy's generation, they had not personally been imprisoned in the Gulag, though they were aware of fathers, grandfathers, kin, or village leaders who had been so sentenced or executed.

The politicization of Muslim identity was evident in the narratives of repression recounted by other activists as well. In my interviews, they spoke of how the mass arrests in earlier Soviet decades, forced migrations, and ongoing systematic restrictions on Islam motivated their generation of revivalists. Although decades had passed, like Turajonzoda, they still reflected upon the "Red Terror" of the 1920s and 1930s. Mahmadali Hayit, who joined the IRPT around 1990 and would himself later be imprisoned, recalled, "Here [in Tajikistan], we experienced the 'Red Terror.' . . . We remember that when Russian power structures, especially the new Soviet power structures conquered Bukhara, then Samarqand, and other places, and then Dushanbe and Gissar, they destroyed a great part of our history, all that was connected with Islam. . . . Most of the spiritual leadership was destroyed or sent to Siberia or Stavropol in exile." Hayit admired "the Basmachi [as] a movement standing up against the *kuffar* [unbelievers], that is, the Russians—against those who wanted to seize this region and subordinate us to them."[4] Davlat Usmon, another *hujra* student and IRPT activist, also viewed the Basmachi as representing "the population which saw Soviet power as a threat to their faith and religious values." He explained that there was "an ideological war against spirituality and religious people . . . to liquidate the very roots of spirituality. . . . If it weren't for the Second World War, who knows what would have happened to Islam and the mullahs! But the 'Powers' [Stalin and Party leaders] knew that without the help of the people it would not be possible to defeat Fascism . . . so in 1943, they created the *muftiyat* [SADUM]. . . . The [Communists] didn't end the war against religion and Islam then, but it became less aggressive."[5]

Nonetheless, the 1940s were remembered as difficult years. Islamist Sayidibrohim Gadoev recalled there was almost no possibility for religious study. Soviet concessions to Islam did not appease many *hujra* members.[6] They

[3] Turajonzoda, "Religion: The Pillar of Society," 267.

[4] Interview with Mahmadali Hayit, deputy chairman, IRPT, Dushanbe, Tajikistan, December 2011.

[5] Interview with Davlat Usmon, former IRPT activist and deputy prime minister, Dushanbe, Tajikistan, November 2010. See also Usmon, "Tadzhikskii konflikt i mery doveriia," 241–44.

[6] Interview with Sayidibrohim Gadoev, IRPT activist, Dushanbe, Tajikistan, March 2011.

emphasized that despite the state's legalization of the Tajik Qoziyot (the Tajik SSR's branch of SADUM), by the 1970s there were still only seventeen mosques legally functioning in the entire Tajik republic and no *madrasas*.[7] According to Usmon, the government-run Islamic Institute allowed "only twenty-six persons from the whole USSR to study there. . . . [W]ith such a small number of students it could not satisfy the demand of the whole country for religious education. So spiritual persons taught their students secretly."[8] Moreover, many disparaged "official" Islam. Another former *hujra* student turned Islamist, Hikmatullo Sayfullozoda, stated that "the graduates of the [state-controlled] *madrasa* in Bukhara and higher institute in Tashkent were KGB students."[9] Hayit agreed: "Except for Haji Turajonzoda, the majority of imams and mullahs were under the KGB's direction, and cooperated with them. Most imams, mullahs, and *eshons* were agents of the state security apparatus and special organs. . . . [E]veryone responsible for Friday mosques, the central mosques of each *raion* (district), was appointed by KGB approval."[10] Usmon claimed that because of this, from the 1950s onward, "secret religious schools began to open in Tajikistan."

Even Turajonzoda, who studied in SADUM's Islamic Institute, realized that no genuine liberalization of Islam had taken place after World War II. In his view, SADUM was essentially "a KGB-controlled religious institution."[11] Moreover, SADUM and the Tajik Qoziyot were dominated by ethnic Uzbeks; ethnic Tajiks were excluded from its patronage.[12] SADUM had also pushed a purist Islam which the Party considered more "modern," thereby marginalizing the culturally rich "Persian traditions" typical of Tajiks, as well as the Sufi practices and heritage of many other Central Asians.[13]

Khrushchev's campaign against religion targeted Tajikistan more harshly than other republics. It entailed the imprisonment of unregistered religious leaders and teachers, especially Sufis, and the raids and closures of both registered and unregistered mosques. For Tajiks, Khrushchev's "Thaw" meant a ban on visiting shrines, a particularly harsh blow, both financially and spiritually, to Sufi shaykhs prevalent in Tajikistan.[14] Throughout this time, Turajonzoda said, "there were great *domullo*s [such as Hindustoniy] living under harsh surveillance"[15] but who

[7] Interviews with imam, Haji Yakub Mosque, Dushanbe, Tajikistan, July 2005.

[8] Interview with Usmon.

[9] Interview with Mullah Hikmatullo Sayfullozoda, editor in chief, IRPT journal *Najot*, Dushanbe, Tajikistan, December 2011.

[10] Interview with Hayit.

[11] Turajonzoda, "Religion," 267.

[12] Stéphane Dudoignon, "Local Lore, the Transmission of Learning, and Communal Identity in Late-20th-Century Tajikistan," in *Devout Societies vs. Impious States*, ed. Dudoignon (Berlin: KS Verlag, 2004), 213–41.

[13] Interview with Turajonzoda.

[14] Dudoignon and Qalandar, "They Were All from the Country."

[15] Interview with Turajonzoda.

nonetheless remained "committed" to reviving Islamic belief and the "moral" and "just society" that the communists, in their view, had destroyed. Under Brezhnev, they witnessed a renewed crackdown on political dissidence and occasional targeting of their own *hujras*.

Fear had kept public opposition to religious repression muted through the late 1980s. Nonetheless, especially under Brezhnev, everyday resistance and hidden transcripts became widespread. For many, as we saw in Chapter 4, religious oppression constituted a deep grievance against the regime. For a few, this oppression would become the chief motivation for opposition and a means of mobilizing support. Harsh but incomplete religious repression had fostered the likelihood that religious entrepreneurs would emerge in Tajikistan, especially among regionally targeted groups in Gharm and Qurghonteppa.

Minimal Associational Space

It was a gradual shift in associational space, more de facto than de jure, that made religious activism, and later the spread of Islamist ideas and religious entrepreneurship, possible in Tajikistan.

Several factors opened space for networking and sharing Islamist ideas. Khrushchev's opening of the Gulag had allowed many religious teachers to return to Tajikistan. Under Brezhnev, the Party exerted less control over local cadres. There was less monitoring of remote villages, and *hujra*s began to form and thrive in Gharm, Qurghonteppe, and regions bordering Afghanistan. Even in Dushanbe, this marginal relaxation of control meant that Hindustoniy and other Islamic teachers could reach a growing number of students. Both local government and Qoziyot officials sometimes sympathized with unregistered Islamic teachers and the community's participation in religious rituals. Meanwhile, official Islam had opened up limited travel to and exchanges with the Middle East. Underground black markets emerged and new networks allowed access to books and literature that was banned.

As we will see more clearly in the IRPT's evolution, the policies of Gorbachev created a significant increase in associational space Union-wide after 1986, even though Tajikistan's Party leaders were both slow to liberalize religion and wavering in political reform.[16] Highly dependent upon Moscow to maintain control and their privileged position, many of the Tajik Party elite aligned with hardliners to prevent change. After the USSR's collapse in August 1991, associational space widened and became highly contested as Tajik Party leaders struggled to respond to mass demonstrations. The newly independent republic's

[16] Collins, *Clan Politics*.

acting president allowed protests and new party registration during August and September 1991, while a coup brought the former communist boss back to power and again closed space. Yet contestation over the first presidential election in post-Soviet Tajikistan brought more uncertainty through the spring of 1992, as the government struggled in vain to reassert control.

As argued in Chapter 1, religious repression and associational space are necessary—but not sufficient—conditions for Islamist mobilization. Islamist ideas and entrepreneurs are critical to Islamist emergence and mobilization. In the 1920s, such ideas did not exist; by the 1960s, however, Islamist ideology was influential among underground networks of *hujra* students, inspiring them to become religious entrepreneurs and to advance an Islamic political order.

Religious Entrepreneurs and Ideologies: The Young Mullahs Form Nahzat

Most religious entrepreneurs began as *hujra* students and underground religious scholars, merely seeking an Islamic education under Soviet conditions. They often came from devout families, sacred lineages, and villages oppressed for their beliefs. Some were well-educated theologically, while others were not. Some had an extensive secular Soviet education, while others had little. They were students or worked as engineers, mechanics, collective farm laborers, or journalists by day, and attended *hujras* at night. Most were part of the unregistered Islamic sector, although Turajonzoda worked within SADUM.

They shared a common desire for freedom for Islam. They had observed and interacted with the older generations of unregistered mullahs, who maintained a political quietism but whose religious teaching constituted acts of everyday resistance to the regime. Dubbed "the young mullahs," they broke away from the apolitical Hanafi or Sufi *hujras* of the older religious scholars and teachers, whom we met in Chapter 3.[17] One of these "reformers" recalled disapprovingly, "Domla Hindustoniy always urged his followers not to contradict the Soviet system . . . only to study Islam, avoiding politics."[18] In contrast to this quietism, the young mullahs formed their own *hujras* to disseminate not only Islamic teaching, but also *political* theology.[19]

In April 1973, the young mullah Sayid Abdullohi Nuri (1947–2006), according to his own account, created the Harakat (movement), otherwise known as Nahzat-i Javonon (Islamic Youth), together with four other young mullahs. It

[17] Dudoignon, "From Revival to Mutation."
[18] Interview with Sayfullozoda.
[19] Interview with Turajonzoda.

was hardly a movement at the time, but by 1978 they had drawn in others and renamed themselves the Nahzat-i Islami (Islamic Revival) to emphasize their core mission: the cultural, educational, and political revival of Islam.[20]

Nuri had been born in 1947 in the village of Oshtiyon, near Tavildara in the central Tajik highlands. As a youth, he knew that his grandfather had been deported to the Gulag during the Red Terror because of his religious commitment and refusal to abide by atheist policies.[21] Like many from the highlands, Nuri and his family had been relocated to the Vakhsh district of Qurghonteppa to work on the Turkmenistan *sovkhoz* (state farm) in 1953. They were among the region's forced migrants whom the regime attempted to dislocate from their sacred space, and use as labor on new state farms. Yet they maintained strong kinship and regional ties to Gharm, a region known for being rigidly Islamic and culturally conservative decades into the Soviet era, and for being excluded from Soviet political and economic power. Nuri trained to be an engineer, but also studied theology at home with his grandfather and father. His father, emblematic of the paradoxes and complexities of the time, was a Communist Party member, a *sovkhoz* (state farm) director, and an Islamic teacher;[22] however, like many Tajiks who used the Party for their own ends, he engaged in everyday resistance. His official position allowed him to protect unofficial Islam.[23] The young Nuri continued his religious studies in the most renowned *hujras*, including those of the Domla Hindustoniy and Mullah Siyomiddin Najmiddinov. He became expert in a vast range of Islamic sciences largely inaccessible through Soviet Islamic institutions, including: Logic, the History of Islam, *Fiqh* (Islamic law and jurisprudence), *Usul al-Fiqh* (the science of the sources of Islamic law and its relation to legal rulings), *Hadith*, and *Tasfir Qur'an* (the science of explanation of and commentary on the Qur'an).[24] By the early 1970s, then in his twenties, Nuri was given the titles of *ustoz* (master) and *ustod* (mentor, respected teacher) by his followers and students, for he had developed a reputation for Islamic learning. He had also become a leader among the young mullahs in the Vakhsh region. Nuri's cofounders (Qori Muhammadjon, Nematullah Eshonzoda, Holidi Abdusalom, and Qalandar Sadriddinov), as well as many of their followers, came from Gharm, Vakhsh, and Qurghonteppa—forced migrant communities.[25] They shared both many experiences and motivations.

[20] Interview with Sayid Abdullohi Nuri, Dushanbe, Tajikistan, August 2002. Some contend the group was not really an organization until about 1978.

[21] Sayid Abdullohi Nuri, "Diruz, imruz va fardoi HNIT," in *HNIT–Zodai ormoni mardum (ba iftihori 30-solagii ta'sisi Hizbi nahzati Islomii Tojikiston* (Dushanbe: ShKOS, 2003), 4–44.

[22] Dudoignon and Qalandar, "They Were All from the Country."

[23] Thanks to Stéphane Dudoignon for sharing this with me.

[24] Interview with Nuri; Nuri, "Diruz, imruz va fardoi HNIT," 6.

[25] Nuri's biography is based on my interviews with IRPT members, 2005 through 2022.

A figurehead in the movement was Muhammadsharif Himmatzoda, whose *hujra* joined Nuri's in 1978, and brought the Nahzat key religious and political activists. Himmatzoda hailed from Tavildara in the Rasht Valley, not far from Gharm. According to early Nahzat members, he was trained as a mechanic and worked as a guard for the local MVD (Ministry of Internal Affairs), but he wrote religious commentaries and taught Islam by night. He too was a Hindustoniy student, as well as the disciple of a Naqshbandi Sufi shaykh, and thus deeply learned in Islamic studies. Himmatzoda went on to study law in Peshawar University in Pakistan in the 1970s, a highly unusual opportunity.[26] There he was likely exposed to both Mawdudi's ideas and Pakistani state-led Islamization; *shariat* was gaining salience in Pakistan's legal system. Himmatzoda taught in his own *hujra* and influenced dozens of students, including Sayidumar Husayni; both men would vastly extend their underground *madrasa* network in the 1980s.[27] Himmatzoda was known as a prolific theologian, and like Nuri he was given the title *ustod* by those within the movement. IRPT activists also note that Himmatzoda was more interested in theorizing religion's role in politics than in strictly theological matters.[28] Himmatzoda and Husayni were early leaders during the movement's shift to party formation. Himmatzoda would become the first chairman of the IRPT, and both men ultimately became the IRPT's deputies in the country's legislature. Another of Himmatzoda's students, Mullah Zubaydullohi Roziq, also came from central Tajikistan, near Gharm, and was instrumental in the late 1970s in connecting the Gharm-Qurghonteppa networks to expand their reach.[29] Three decades later, he was still one of the leading ideologues of the IRPT.

Sayidibrohim Gadoev, like Nuri, came from a collective farm. Gadoev's father had dreamed of becoming an Islamic scholar, so he studied the Qur'an in *hujras*. Over the course of more than four decades he secretly gathered religious scholars and mullahs to discuss Islam. He sent his son, Sayidibrohim, to a *hujra* in Kulob, where he learned Farsi and Arabic, the Qur'an, and the *Chahar kitob*, a classic text merging theology and the Sufi Persian poetry of Mirza Abdul-Qader Bedil (1644–1721). From his early years as a Soviet factory worker, Sayidibrohim went on to become a leading party activist.[30]

[26] Majlisi olii jumkhurii Tojikiston, Biography of Deputy Himmatzoda for the Parliament of Tajikistan, accessed December 30, 2008, www.majlisi-oli.by.ru/index.shtml?/doc/en/dip/himmatzoda_m.

[27] See the biography of Husayni and discussion of Himmatzoda on the IRPT's website: HNIT, "A Lion Captured by Jackals," n.d., https://en.nahzat.org/a-lion-captured-by-jackals/.

[28] Interview with Muhiddin Kabiri, Chairman, IRPT, Exeter, UK, November 2012.

[29] Interview with Mullah Zubaydullohi Roziq, IRPT activist, Dushanbe, Tajikistan, 2011; Zubaydullohi Roziq, *HNIT dar masiri ta'rikh* (Dushanbe: Muattar, 2013), 53.

[30] Interview with Gadoev.

Davlat Usmon, who would eventually become the Islamic Party's key political representative and a deputy prime minister in the temporary 1992 coalition government, also grew up on a farm of forced migrants. Like Nuri, he too had studied with Hindustoniy. While a university student he founded a *hujra* in Dushanbe. He joined the Nahzat around 1977–78 and connected the *hujra* of Dushanbe with those from Qurghonteppa, helping further expand their network. Usmon, like Himmatzoda, was keenly interested in the political implications of the ideas Nahzat members were debating.[31]

With shared Muslim identity, a deep anger at repression and exclusion by the Communist Party, and desire to learn Islam more deeply, these individuals began to network in pursuit of their goals. As Gadoev explained, "together" these underground "religious leaders and students played a large role in the development of the Nahzat, and later the IRPT."[32]

From Sirhindi to Qutb and Mawdudi: Ideas of Islamic Revival and an Islamic State

The core leaders of the Nahzat claimed above all to have been inspired by Islam; theirs was a religious grievance and a religious agenda. In the 1970s, the organization's main focus was developing their religious knowledge in small Islamic study circles, where they critiqued the religious interpretations of the Hanafi *ulama* (registered and unregistered).[33] Roziq recalled, "In the beginning, it was a cultural, religious, educational, and scholarly movement, not a political [one]." Their "education sector" provided books, organized lessons, and gave exams to the group's members. They spread the *da'wat*, the call to Islam; they aimed to bring Soviet Muslims back to the true *shariat*. They collected membership dues to cover the costs of acquiring Islamic literature and travel.[34]

In his memoir of the IRPT, Nuri wrote, "The idea of founding the Islamic movement began in our youth. . . . The main factor . . . was Islamic teaching itself. When we understood the Qur'an, when we became aware of the orders of the Prophet of Islam (peace be upon him), as well as having learned the Islamic books, then we compared it to society around us and we saw the lack of conformity with Islamic teachings. Therefore, we came up with the idea that we should create an organization, and through it spread Islam's teachings in society."[35] Aware of the tension between religious and political goals, he wrote, "Of

[31] Interview with Usmon.
[32] Interview with Gadoev.
[33] Interview with Nuri; Tim Epkenhans, *The Origins of the Civil War in Tajikistan: Nationalism, Islamism, and Violent Conflict in Post-Soviet Space* (Lanham, MD: Lexington Books, 2006), 188–90.
[34] Interview with Roziq.
[35] Nuri, "Diruz, imruz va fardoi," 7.

course, founding an organization had a political meaning," even though "religious teaching did not have much political meaning."[36] Nuri fully realized that the USSR had politicized any independent religious organization; state atheism inevitably made religion political.

According to a journalist familiar with Nahzat's origins, Nuri wanted to "educate youth according to religious law, to agitate, and spread religious propaganda and ideas."[37] He acted in a context in which "communist ideology . . . was fighting a war against religion" and the state constantly watched and pressured unregistered Islamic teachers.[38] Usmon claimed that Nahzat's aims were the "regeneration of the faith after seventy years of anti-religious attacks."[39] He said they "hoped that Islam could address the spiritual upbringing of youth, and serious problems of immorality in the country."[40]

Nahzat's religious program was originally modeled on that of their teachers, a blend of traditional Hanafi scholarship, Sufi and Persian Islamic literature, Arabic study, and the Qur'an. Yet over time, the young mullahs challenged their elder teachers. They advocated a far stricter interpretation of Islam and a cleansing of *bid'ah* (un-Islamic accretions or heresies) and *shirk* (polytheism). Nahzat members were initially influenced by a small—but long-present—reformist and modernist strand in Central Asian Islam.[41] These purists had drawn inspiration from the Naqshbandi Shaykh Ahmad Sirhindi (1564–1624), who was active in South Asia in the seventeenth century. A contradictory figure, Sirhindi was a Sufi who advocated revivalism of purist Sunni belief and the cleansing of false rituals. He was posthumously given the highly esteemed title, Mujaddid-i Alf-i Thānī (Renewer of the Second Millennium of Islam). So too, the Nahzat called themselves Mujaddidi to indicate their commitment to puritanical renewal of Sunni Islam under Soviet oppression.[42] Further influenced by the Deobandi school which Sirhindi had inspired, the young mullahs initially rejected both national and traditional Sufi practices as *bid'ah* and *shirk*. They wanted to renew the *shariat* and *sunna* in pure form.

Sirhindi's criticism of Muslim political systems led the Nahzat from religious purism to activism. They believed that Soviet conditions had encouraged

[36] Nuri, "Diruz, imruz va fardoi," 7.

[37] Interview with Rajab Mirzo, Tajikistani journalist and activist, Bishkek, Kyrgyzstan, May 2013.

[38] Sulton Hamadov, "Mezhdunarodnyi Kontekst—Afganskii Faktor," in *Religioznyi ekstremizm v Tsentral'noi Azii* (Dushanbe: OSCE, 2002), 137.

[39] *Komsomolets Tadzhikistana*, November 21, 1990, cited in Anderson, *Religion*, 201–2.

[40] Interview with Usmon.

[41] Bakhtiyar Babajanov, Ashirbek Muminov, and Anke von Kügelgen, *Disputy musul'manskikh religioznykh avtoritetov v Tsentral'noĭ Azii v XX veke (Kazakhstanskie vostokovednye issledovaniia)* (Almaty: Daĭk-Press, 2007).

[42] On the ideas of Sirhindi and the Mujaddidiya, see Yohanan Friedmann, *Sheikh Ahmad Sirhindi: An Outline of His Thought and a Study of His Image in the Eyes of Posterity* (Montreal: McGill, 1971).

widespread idolatry. Hayit described their focus on purification this way: "Look at Arab countries, Iran, and Afghanistan. There were no such customs there. They only say prayers, read the Qur'an. . . . [F]anatical elements are Soviet-era traditions."[43] Roziq recalled, "We talked a lot about *shirk*, honoring *mazars*, and places of burial . . . [so] the KGB called us 'Wahhabi.'"[44] Another member explained, "The Nahzat existed in the 1970 to 1980s. It conducted its activity underground. . . . [I]t had an 'enlightenment' character, first and foremost directed towards revival of Islam. [Members] opposed giving out money, [Tajik] funeral traditions—seven- and forty-day remembrances—and sought to regulate all this," in conformity with pure Islam.[45]

Nuri further emphasized that the political oppression of Islam motivated them: "[T]he absence of free thinking, of the expression of free thought, and the pressure . . . on Muslims developed their [Nahzat's] ideas about founding an Islamic reform movement. This was the main factor . . . the idea of freedom and the creation of a political and social organization. We were always under the KGB's watchful eye, pursuit, and pressure. . . . That [pressure] created the idea of awakening and of freedom."[46] Nuri personally recounted how his father had studied in *hujras* and was widely respected for his religious knowledge and freethinking. Despite being a Party member, his father had listened to news about the Iranian Revolution on Radio Farda on his short-wave radio—news that was banned in the USSR, but accessible given the spread of technology, coupled with the fact that Tajik and Farsi were mutually intelligible. He was deeply interested in the possibility of such a revolution for Islam.

Defending Islam and freedom for Muslims motivated the young mullahs. As Sulton Hamadov, editor of the IRPT's newspaper, explained, "During those years . . . believers were trying to fulfill all religious rituals secretly . . . and ideas arose about creating a religious-political group to defend the interests of Muslims. . . . The right to study and freedom of religious belief and practices was then trampled on by the 'Powers' [the Party and security apparatus], officially, in the constitution. The [state] viewed the formation of an Islamic religious-political group . . . as the spread of extremism and radicalism. It was a criminal action that had to be punished."[47] Nonetheless, "the absence of freedom of conscience, religious belief, and practice, pushed the young Muslim spiritual leaders to break the law and fight for their rights and freedoms."[48]

[43] Interview with Hayit.
[44] Interview with Roziq.
[45] Interview with Hayit.
[46] Nuri, "Diruz, imruz va fardoi," 8–9.
[47] Sultan Hamadov, "O faktorakh perestaniia umerennogo Islama v radikal'nyi," in *Postroenie Doveriia Mezhdu Islamistami i Sekuliaristami-Tadzhikskii Eksperiment*, ed. Jan-Nikola Bitter and Vol'fgang Tsel'ner (Dushanbe: "Devashtich," 2004), 322–35.
[48] Hamadov, "O faktorakh perestaniia."

The Nahzat realized that freedom for Islam would come only through opposition to the atheist Soviet regime. Their internal debates led them to condemn both collaboration with the communist regime and political quietism as anti-Islamic. According to Hayit, "Except Akbar Turajonzoda, the majority of imams and mullahs were under the direction of the KGB and cooperated with them. . . . [E]veryone responsible for Friday mosques was appointed only with the 'approval' of the KGB's committee." Hayit pointed to the fate of "Muhammadjon Hindustoniy Qori [who] was never against [state] power and never uttered anything that was forbidden. Yet, he was put into prison only because he was Muslim and studied Islam a great deal."[49]

Islamist ideas shaped their political thinking.[50] Although Nuri repeatedly denied foreign influences, he and Nahzat members acknowledged they had access to books obtained from abroad. These included the writings and lectures of major twentieth-century Islamists: Hassan al-Banna, Sayyid Qutb, and Muhammad Qutb, the major ideologues of the Egyptian Muslim Brotherhood. They read not only Sirhindi but also Mawdudi, the influential South Asian revivalist and Islamist activist who founded the Jamaat-i Islami.[51] As Davlat Usmon recalled:

> At the time, they became acquainted with books, those which were spreading different religious political movements, the books of Sayyid Qutb, Muhammad Qutb, Muhammad Abdu. Then little by little they brought these books to Tajikistan. . . . In 1973, I myself was a witness to it . . . the first little book of Sayyid Qutb . . . which Iranians had translated into Persian. This book discusses the political essence of Islam, the role of Islam in politics and in the economy. . . . Also [we read] the political views of Sayed Jamaluddin Afghani. Because of this, our youth group formed and organized with political and religious views, and a political and religious movement emerged here at the end of the 1970s.[52]

Afghani (1838–1897) was a Persian scholar, a critic of imperialism, and an early pan-Islamic political activist. He and other authors of interest to Nahzat advocated Islamic revival and strict adherence to Islamic principles and law, as well as modernization. Some advocated pan-Islamism as well as nationalism and anticolonialism.

[49] Interview with Hayit.
[50] Dudoignon and Qalandar, "They Were All from the Country," 58; they also identify Abdurahmon Hitobov's writings (1958–1992) as a source of inspiration. I have been unable to obtain a copy of his work, *The Cadet*.
[51] Interview with Roziq; interview with Usmon.
[52] Interview with Usmon.

Thus, despite their public denials, Nahzat's members became increasingly affected by Islamist literature, which shaped their worldview.[53] Muhiddin Kabiri, Nuri's successor as of fall 2006, explained to me that "Ustod Nuri was strongly influenced by the ideas of [Sayyid] Qutb and Mawdudi."[54] Hayit also acknowledged the significance of this factor: "No one spoke openly about it; however, the sources of our political thinking brought us closer to the Muslim Brotherhood [than to Hindustoniy]."[55] Sayfullozoda also admitted this influence: "We were very swayed by the new methods and ideas of the Ikhwan [the Muslim Brotherhood]. We studied their works in the early 1980s."[56] While they did not adopt wholesale the Brotherhood's methods, especially Sayyid Qutb's call for militant jihad, access to such ideas, among other Islamist and modernist thinkers, was a decisive factor in shaping the Tajik entrepreneurs' ideology and agenda.[57] Nuri himself even claimed that it was from books he had obtained and studied in the 1970s that he learned how to form a political organization.[58]

The books came from multiple sources, their path revealing that foreign ideas were penetrating the Iron Curtain and reaching even into the depths of Soviet Central Asia. Some books, *tamizdat* (banned publications published abroad), came from connections with Arabs in Moscow; Syria, Yemen, Iraq, and Egypt all sent students there.[59] Mullah Roziq described how photocopies of books were then circulated through *samizdat* (underground publishing), much as copies of the Qur'an and books on religious knowledge and practice were disseminated.[60] Such books were also sold on the black market.[61] Kabiri, who in his youth was an entrepreneurial black market bookseller, explained that banned literature of all kinds was smuggled into Tajikistan: "Everything from Bulgakov to Solzhenitsyn, to the Qur'an and Qutb was sold in the underground."[62] According to Kabiri, "[Central Asia] could not long hold off in isolation from everything going on in the Islamic world. In the beginning of the 1970s some radical Islamist ideas filtered in together with literature." The Soviet context was critical, noted Kabiri: "The limitations on religious rights and freedoms of Muslims, together

[53] Interview with Turajonzoda; Epkenhans, *The Origins of the Civil War in Tajikistan*, 202; Dudoignon and Qalandar, "They Were All from the Country."

[54] Interview with Kabiri, 2012.

[55] Interview with Hayit.

[56] Interview with Sayfullozoda.

[57] Hamadov, "Mezhdunarodnyi Kontekst," 136–37; Epkenhans, *The Origins of the Civil War in Tajikistan*, 201–3.

[58] Interview with Nuri.

[59] Epkenhans, *The Origins of the Civil War in Tajikistan*, 192.

[60] Interview with Roziq.

[61] Epkenhans, *The Origins of the Civil War in Tajikistan*, 201–3.

[62] Interview with Kabiri, 2012.

with the events in Iran and Afghanistan, created favorable conditions for the growth of religious radicalism" in the USSR.[63]

Somewhat paradoxically, ideas of Tajik national identity and sovereignty were also influential with the young mullahs and became central to the movement's ideology.[64] Despite its purism, Nahzat sought to resurrect Tajik national Islam from Soviet oppression, not eliminate the Tajik culture or nation-state. Nuri believed that "Islam is the spine of the Tajiks' culture, and no nation can live without a culture."[65] Ironically, he pointed to the influence of *The Tajiks,* a landmark of Soviet scholarship written by the communist academic Bobojon Ghafurov (from 1946 to 1956 the first secretary of the Central Committee of the Communist Party of the Tajik SSR). Ghafurov's narrative constructed and glorified the history of the Tajik nation; although written in conformity with Soviet nationalities policy, the work perhaps unwittingly laid the foundations for conceiving of an independent Tajik nation. Nuri was inspired by and drew on Ghafurov's national conception: "Until 1972, we had read in school books that the Tajik people had nothing, [that] they were illiterate, and without civilization, and that thanks to the October Revolution and to the Russian people, advancements came [here]. When *The Tajiks* was first published in Moscow and became available for the first time, I read it attentively several times . . . about the ancient past, culture, and civilization of our great nation. I discovered important points for myself in the history of our nation, including national struggle and freedom, national religious movements. . . . That helped a great deal in developing my thoughts about freedom."[66] Mahmadali Hayit, who would eventually become the IRPT's deputy chairman, eloquently observed that they firmly believed Islam could not be divorced from the Tajik nation and culture: "Islam is not only a prayer, but also a way of behavior, traditions and custom. The foundation of Tajik culture is Islam. . . . [N]ational responsibility can only be carried out with the help of the Islamic religion. . . . Islam flows in my blood from the time of my birth."[67] Nahzat's leadership thus increasingly believed that the Tajik people could unite as a political entity only through Islam. Unsurprisingly then, Muhammad Iqbal (1877–1938), the renowned poet, philosopher, and political leader whose nationalist ideas inspired the Muslim movement seeking national independence from British colonial India, also influenced the Nahzat's Islamic nationalism. Both the Tajik nationalist and Islamist movements embraced Iqbal's writings, especially his poem "Awake from the Deep Sleep."[68] Iqbal's verses

[63] Muhiddin Kabiri, "Islamskii radikalizm: Faktori voznikoveniia," in *Religioznyi ekstremizm v Tsentral'noi Azii* (OSCE: Dushanbe 2002), 125.
[64] Roziq, *HNIT dar masiri ta'rikh.*
[65] Nuri, "Diruz, imruz va fardoi."
[66] Nuri, "Diruz, imruz va fardoi," 9.
[67] Interview with Hayit.
[68] Epkenhans, *The Origins of the Civil War in Tajikistan*, 147–48.

appear prominently in the first pages of the IRPT's autobiographical history.[69] Such ideas would, importantly, push Nuri to build bridges with the secular national-democratic movement and support an independent Islamic nation-state, while rejecting the ideas of transnational Islamists.

The Qozikalon's Shift to Religious Activism

Before we turn to Nahzat's formation of the IRPT, it is necessary to dwell on the most influential Islamic activists during this era and through the 2000s: Akbar Turajonzoda. Appointed *qozikalon* (chief Muslim official of the Tajik republic) in 1989, Turajonzoda would play an important role in the Islamist opposition movement, albeit not as early as the Nahzat entrepreneurs and not within the Islamic Revival Party. Turajonzoda was not the driving force behind Islamism's emergence in Tajikistan, but his role was crucial in its development from 1990 onward—in broadening the movement, legitimizing it, and fostering its mobilizational success.

Cold War–era scholarship long assumed Islam was either registered (legal and pro-state) or underground (illegal and anti-state); however, this binary ignores important complexity in the Islamic sphere. Many unregistered mullahs accepted the Soviet state or simply remained quietist, while some registered *ulama* were discontented and entered the political arena.[70] In Tajikistan, one such cleric was Akbar Turajonzoda, who was raised in a devout family with a prominent Sufi lineage. His grandfather, an esteemed Sufi shaykh of the Qadiriyya order, had been persecuted in the 1930s. The family elders—his father and two brothers, all Sufi masters—were excluded from official Soviet Islam. Akbar at first studied informally with them and other renowned Sufi masters but later decided to continue his education inside the official Soviet Islamic institutions of the 1970s and early 1980s. Yet, he found that education limited, and SADUM to both be Uzbek-dominated and anti-Sufi.

SADUM did, however, open a critical opportunity to him. In the late 1970s, the young Akbar was appointed as a local guide for a Jordanian imam who had been invited to visit Central Asia; the visit was part of the Soviet state's campaign to demonstrate to the Muslim world the socioeconomic prosperity enjoyed by "Muslims of the Soviet East." One evening over a private dinner that included Turajonzoda's father, the Jordanian imam spoke frankly to his hosts about the appalling condition of Soviet Islam. This conversation opened Turajonzoda's

[69] *HNIT–Zodai ormoni mardum (ba iftihori 30-solagii ta'sisi Hizbi nahzati Islomii Tojikiston* (Dushanbe: ShKOS, 2003).
[70] Dudoignon and Qalandar, "They Were All from the Country," 314.

eyes to Soviet oppression. He recalled, "After that conversation with [the imam], we realized that our information, our religious education in Bukhara was of the Middle Ages; we were not allowed to read the commentaries [on the Qur'an].... There were a lot of limitations and restrictions. Sixty percent of the subjects at our Islamic Institute were not even religious subjects. We studied philosophy, Russian, English. I suddenly understood what I was lacking. I needed a real religious education."[71] The imam invited Akbar to study in Jordan, and he was finally granted state permission to travel to Amman. Turajonzoda recalled that while there, between 1982 and 1987, he had finally "plumbed the depths of true Islamic learning." While in Jordan, Turajonzoda also "read everything"—including writings of Russian democrats, liberal newspapers such as *Ogonyok, and* the works of the Muslim Brotherhood. He explained:

> I admit I read a lot of political literature, almost all those [works] of the Muslim Brotherhood, not only Sayyid Qutb ... [the Brotherhood's] path, methods: *not* to use force, *not* to hurry, the lesson of an Islamic state, not to establish an Islamic regime, but the lesson of creating an Islamic society so people would become Muslim, so they would want to demand Islam themselves. The people, through elections, slowly, step by step. This teaching is close to my soul. When I was in Jordan, I began to understand the absurdity of the USSR's ideology. During *perestroika*, many people were publishing anticommunist articles.... As an Islamic, religious-thinking person, I began to understand that ... we needed a religious consciousness, a national consciousness.[72]

The exposure to new ideas led him to reevaluate his decision to work quietly within a system that he knew had caused so much destruction of Islam.

Not long after returning from Jordan, Turajonzoda drew closer to Nuri. Like the IRPT, he recognized the "very low authority of the official mullahs, [while] the unofficial mullahs' authority began to rise everywhere." He even aided Nuri after the latter's release from the Gulag in 1988 and invited him to work under the Qoziyot.

In 1989, Turajonzoda was, surprisingly, appointed *qozikalon*—a decision that reflects the curious role of contingency in the political process of Islamist mobilization. Gorbachev's reforms, together with protest against the long-standing corrupt Uzbek *mufti* of SADUM, had triggered the appointment of a new *mufti*. The latter then appointed Turajonzoda, possibly because they shared similar views about increasing Islam's public role and influence on the state. As an "official" religious leader willing to challenge the Communist Party, Turajonzoda

[71] Interview with Turajonzoda.
[72] Interview with Turajonzoda, my italics.

subsequently became a key activist for Islamic revival, one of the most vocal critics of Soviet religious repression, and an advocate for both a public and a political role for Islam.[73] His ideas about Islam, politics, and law increasingly intersected with Nuri's as the Islamist movement evolved in the growing associational space of *perestroika*.

The Outcome: First-Wave Tajik Islamist Mobilization

From Religious Revival to Politics

Coming mostly from the politically and religiously marginalized regions, these Nahzat members, as Usmon explained, "became, during the following years, the living, breathing activists of political Islam in Tajikistan."[74] Ongoing repression coincided with new pockets of space for religious entrepreneurs to meet, debate, and discuss their political direction. Over a decade or more, this led to Nahzat's shift from teaching Islamic revival to advocating and mobilizing to form an Islamic sociopolitical order.[75]

As they prepared to enter politics, Nahzat members needed to keep vigilant. The KGB had learned of the organization's existence from informants. They searched Nuri's home and confiscated religious books. Nahzat developed "security protocols" to ensure that the leadership was safe and that no members betrayed the organization to the police.[76] There was at least one attempt to "disappear" or possibly kill Nuri in the early 1980s.[77] He was abducted by the KGB but ultimately released after a large number of his followers protested at the district Party headquarters—a rare open display of opposition. Such threats increasingly politicized them.

The Effect of Iran's Islamic Revolution and Afghanistan's Jihad

Growing awareness of Islamist models from abroad—the practical implementation of the Islamist ideologies that they had been reading—shaped the Nahzat's thinking. Nahzat studied the examples of Islamism in action in Iran and Afghanistan with great interest. In 1979, two major regional events—the Islamic revolution in Iran and the Soviet invasion of Afghanistan—prompted

73 Turajonzoda, "Religion: The Pillar of Society."
74 Interview with Usmon.
75 Interview with Mirzo; interview with Gadoev.
76 Interview with Roziq.
77 Interviews with Roziq, Gadoev, and Mirzo.

discussions about political theology, the role of Islam in politics, and concrete political action. Although there appears to have been no direct contact with Iranian or Afghan Islamists before 1991, their actions and ideas inspired Nahzat to form a more direct political agenda to establish an Islamic order.

While Nuri and other leaders insisted that the Tajik Islamic Party was entirely "self-grown,"[78] key Nahzat activists cited the Iranian Revolution's success as inspirational. As Hayit explained, "All revolutions have an effect on the thinking and ideas of people. What happened there [in Iran] revived our memories of the [forced] migrants."[79] Sayfullozoda similarly noted, "All revolutions are influenced by others. The revolution in Iran had an influence . . . even on thinking in Islamic societies with a secular worldview."[80] According to Tajik journalist and democratic activist Rajab Mirzo, Tajiks wondered why a neighboring country with a similar language, culture, and shared history "had such possibilities and we do not. . . . [In Tajikistan] everything was controlled."[81] They began to envision a Tajikistan that followed the path of Iran, or at least, what they knew of that path.

The Soviet invasion of Afghanistan had a stronger and more direct effect on the ideas of the Tajik Islamist movement. The Afghan mujahidin's example hit closer to home for many Tajiks.[82] According to Sayfullozoda, "At the end of the 1980s, jihadist thinking there influenced Muslims of Tajikistan. When our Tajik military servicemen returned home [from fighting in the Soviet-Afghan War] they spoke about the bravery of the mujahidin against the Russians."[83] While too little is known about the Soviet-Afghan War's effect on Soviet Muslims, the statements of Nahzat members reveal that at least among those already disaffected with the Soviet regime and its religious policy, the war intensified their anger at the Party.[84] Hayit, for example, had deployed to Afghanistan as a senior lieutenant in the Soviet Army at the height of the war. While there he realized "that the Soviets were trying to do there [in Afghanistan] what they had already done in the Tajik republic." He declared, "It was a war with Islam. Their plan was to create a division internally in Islam, between Muslims."[85]

Nahzat members spoke of shared "Muslimness" with Afghans, especially the northern ethnically Tajik Afghans led by the mujahidin Burhanuddin Rabbani and Ahmed Shah Massoud. They constructed a narrative of an "imagined community" based on ethnic, kinship, and religious ties.[86] Gadoev claimed that

78 Interview with Nuri.
79 Interview with Hayit.
80 Interview with Sayfullozoda; Roziq, *HNIT dar masiri ta'rikh.*
81 Interview with Rajab Mirzo.
82 Interview with Usmon; interview with Roziq.
83 Interview with Sayfullozoda.
84 Hamadov, *Mezhdunarodnyi Kontekst*, 137.
85 Interview with Mahmadali Hayit, Dushanbe, Tajikistan, May 2007.
86 Anderson, *Imagined Communities.*

Massoud's kin had been among the first Tajiks to flee to Afghanistan to escape Bolshevik repression after 1917. Thus, the Nahzat had a shared identity with Massoud and interest in his success. While serving in Afghanistan in 1984, Hayit had been the Soviet Army's point of contact with Massoud during a ceasefire negotiation with the mujahidin. Some eight years later, the Tajik Islamists would be seeking Massoud's aid and shelter in Afghanistan, in their own fight against communism.

Moreover, Soviet attempts to hide the nature of the Afghan war were only partially successful. The Afghan war "revealed" what Gadoev called "the truth, the true face of the USSR."[87] Like the Iranian Revolution, the Soviet-Afghan War intensified their belief in the necessity and possibility of political Islam:

> Iran and Afghanistan did not help us [with Nahzat's formation], but when the war in Afghanistan and the revolution in Iran began, we knew about it; it was impossible to not know. A person could not close his ears and block out the information about these events. They were positive moments. . . . I personally didn't know who Khomeini was before 1979–1980. We didn't know who Rabbani and Ahmed Shah Massoud were. But of course, the revolution in Iran influenced our thoughts and ideas. . . . The Soviet war in Afghanistan influenced Mullah Sayid Nuri's thoughts and ideas, and those of other leaders and members of the IRPT. [But] . . . these events were not the foundational source of Mullah Nuri's ideas. Ustod Nuri was an idealist.[88]

Usmon said, "The success of the mujahidin against the Soviet occupation and the communist regime of Najibullah in Afghanistan had a great psychological effect on the actions and convictions of the opposition in Tajikistan."[89] The Afghans' resistance and success in 1989 inspired the Islamist opposition in Tajikistan.[90]

Indeed, Afghanistan became the subject of heated debate in *hujras* in Tajikistan and Uzbekistan. Before his death in 1989, Hindustoniy distributed a letter in which he stridently denounced those mullahs advocating "jihad" and calling themselves "*mujahids*" while criticizing his own nonmilitant resistance to the USSR. Videotapes of Hindustoniy debating the issue of the Soviet invasion of Afghanistan were disseminated throughout Tajik and Uzbek *hujras*. One video included critical commentary from a leading Naqshbandi shaykh in Tajikistan, Domla Sharif Hisari (1893–1990).[91] Afghanistan had pushed many

87 Interview with Gadoev.
88 Interview with Gadoev.
89 Usmon, "Tadzhikskii konflikt i mery doveriia," 250.
90 Roziq, *HNIT dar masiri ta'rikh*.
91 Hisori was a shaykh in the Hisor area of Tajikistan; he played a role in the transmission of Persian and Islamic learning and disseminated tapes in the Tajik and Uzbek republics. See Dudoignon and Qalandar, "They Were All from the Country," 68.

Tajiks to believe that "it was necessary to put forth more radical ideas."[92] Some, however, insist that even after Afghanistan the Nahzat never envisioned anything but peaceful change and gradual Islamization, never violence or an Islamic state.[93] Nonetheless, the movement was edging closer to a political challenge to the Soviet regime.

Religious Repression into the Gorbachev Era

Repression of Islam had continued into the mid- and late 1980s, with intense propaganda and targeted arrests.[94] Religio-political discussions were particularly perilous. During the 1980s, and well into the first few years of Gorbachev's tenure, there was a new anti-Wahhabi campaign (1982–86), which was reminiscent of 1920s Soviet policy.[95] According to one Nahzat member, "[I]n 1986 . . . the leadership of the central apparat of the USSR KGB carried out 'special operations' for curtailing the actions of the 'reactionary part of the Muslim spiritual leadership' . . . [These policies were] responsible for serious violations of [our] rights. . . . [They] even brought criminal charges against us for [allegedly] possessing narcotics. . . . Such actions by the law enforcement agencies incited more extreme indignation . . . even among our neighbors. That influenced the development of extremism. . . . Radical tendencies increased among most of those who had been imprisoned."[96] Mirzo explained, "[The Nahzat] worked under harsh repression. . . . They used remarkable underground methods."[97] Fear was still pervasive. Nahzat members were at times threatened, and in the 1980s arrests increased. Dozens of trials of unofficial mullahs took place in 1986 and 1987. The KGB head himself reported that such trials inadvertently "stimulated religion" and "an anti-Soviet jihad."[98] KGB claims about the threat from these mullahs were likely exaggerated. Still, the arrests reveal that the religious repression of Muslims, at least those believed to be independent and political, continued through the mid- to late 1980s, supporting IRPT claims of an anti-Wahhabi campaign against them. Nahzat leaders complained that Gorbachev was even more anti-Islamic than Brezhnev. The gap between expectations and reality further politicized them, as Sayfullozoda explained: "Under Gorbachev's *perestroika*, we witnessed the first signs of Islamic freedom, but [the Tajik Communist Party leaders] Nabiev and especially Mahkamov opposed religious freedom. . . . To the

92 Hamadov, "O faktorakh perestaniia," 325.
93 Interview with Hayit.
94 Atkin, *The Subtlest Battle*.
95 Dudoignon and Qalandar, "They Were All from the Country," 100.
96 Hamadov, "O faktorakh perestaniia," 324–25.
97 Interview with Mirzo.
98 *Daily Report, Soviet Union*, FBIS-SOV-88, January 11, 1988, cited in Atkin, *Subtlest Battle*, 62.

contrary, these atheists stirred up hatred against the Islamic movement. Under the pretext of 'forbidding Islamization' these two atheists caused the civil war's eruption."[99] According to one of the IRPT's spiritual leaders, Zubaydullohi Roziq, it was during *perestroika* that "Ustod Sayid Abdullohi Nuri and Ustod Himmatzoda were speaking out against the Communist Party. We understood then that communist power and atheists were outcasts and damned."[100]

Nuri's public speaking, which took place mainly in wedding ceremonies where the community gathered to learn about Islam, led to his arrest in February 1987. He was charged with "spreading false news" that "stigmatized socialist government" and was sentenced to eighteen months in Siberia and the Soviet Far East.[101] About forty other members of the Nahzat were also arrested, and some were given prison terms. According to an IRPT activist enraged by the incident, "They imprisoned Ustod Nuri, claiming he was an American spy. But we value one gram of our soil more than a million American dollars."[102]

Nuri's imprisonment delayed, but also contributed to, the Nahzat's political mobilization. According to his closest Nahzat followers, Nuri was moved from place to place in prison so as to sever his network and undermine his proselytization efforts among inmates; Nahzat members reported that he continually prayed and gained widespread respect even when he could not directly teach. In March 1988, Gadoev and his brother traveled the long distance to Amursk in Khabarovsk *krai* (in the Far East of Siberia) to visit Nuri. Gadoev recounted how the prison guard, upon learning whom they were seeking, released Nuri for a week, because even the guards "held our *ustod* in high respect."[103] By Gadoev's account, Nuri had many followers in prison among forced migrants and deportees. Another IRPT activist explained that, "To imprison Nuri was an invitation to create an Islamic movement. . . . Little by little, in whichever prison he was transferred to, Nuri created followers and became accepted as the spiritual leader. Even some Russians became Muslim under his influence."[104] Whether or not this narrative is wholly accurate, Nuri's incarceration triggered further resistance. Shortly after his release, Nuri and other Nahzat members returned to activism.

February 1990 saw the first wide-scale protests against the regime, which appear to have been instigated by Rastokhez, a nationalist movement. Students were angry over food and housing shortages, plus the rising cost of bread. Even though the Nahzat was not the orchestrator, it joined the demonstrations, which

99 Interview with Sayfullozoda.
100 Interview with Roziq.
101 Interview with Nuri.
102 Interview with Roziq.
103 Interview with Gadoev.
104 Interview with IRPT activist.

spread to their stronghold in Qurghonteppa. Party First Secretary Qahhor Mahkamov used the incidents to blame "extremists," among them the Islamists, for the deadly unrest. He cracked down on all meetings and political activity, even while Gorbachev's *demokratizatsiia* (democratization program, 1988–91) was escalating elsewhere in the USSR.

Meanwhile, Qozikalon Turajonzoda intervened to quell the violence, and his negotiating role enhanced his societal authority. Turajonzoda, who had also become an elected deputy to the Tajik Supreme Soviet (a consequence of Gorbachev's electoral reforms), subsequently made several demands of the republic's parliament: that Muslim holidays and Fridays be declared national nonwork days to allow for prayer, that livestock be slaughtered in accord with Muslim law, and that mosques and other religious structures be exempt from land tax. Turajonzoda was also furious that Christian churches had greater freedom than mosques. He suggested that if the Party conceded to his demands, he would not join the political opposition challenging the communist regime. But several months later, legislators agreed only to accept national Islamic holidays. Contention ensued as Turajonzoda responded by refusing to bury Communist Party members according to Muslim ritual. Ironically, this infuriated the Party. The *Qozikalon* and his imams stood their ground in an escalating confrontation with the Party-state.[105] Turajonzoda drew increasingly closer to the IRPT as he realized that entering politics might be the only way to diminish the Party's power.

Nahzat's Move to Party Formation

As Nahzat members became increasingly politicized, they shifted from discourse to action. About eighteen years after its birth, the religious organization transitioned into a religious party. Its aim was to change the communist ideology it deemed responsible for the suppression of Muslims' religious freedom. According to Sayidibrohim Muhammadnazar, an early Nahzat member, the Tajik Islamists were not extremists, as they have often been labeled; rather, they were challenging the "extremist regime of communism and the so-called 'secular' regime."[106]

[105] "Ban on Tajik Islamic Party Counterproductive," *Komsomolskaya Pravda*, March 23, 1991, 2, *Daily Report, Soviet Union*, FBIS-SOV-91-2, April 1, 1991.

[106] Sayidibrohim Muhammadnazar, "Rol' i mesto religioznykh organizatsii v natsional'nom gosudarstve," in *Postroenie Doveriia Mezhdu Islamistami i Sekuliaristami–Tadzhikskii Eksperiment*, ed. Jan-Nikolai Bitter and Vol'fgang Tsel'ner (Dushanbe: "Devashtich," 2004), 186; interview with Sayidibrohim Muhammadnazar, cultural department chief, IRPT, Dushanbe, August 2004.

From the late 1980s through 1990, Nahzat's entrepreneurs had connected with Islamist activists throughout the USSR. Gadoev traveled to meet and recruit members and spent two years living in Moscow for that purpose. They connected with Islamists from across the Union, especially from Tatarstan, Dagestan, Chechnya, Ingushetia, and Uzbekistan. In June 1990, Gadoev and Usmon met activists from these other republics—about two hundred strong—in Astrakhan. There they formed an All-Union Islamic Revival Party (AUIRP).[107] The party activists established a council of *ulama* to advise them and they elected Akhmedkadi Akhtaev, an ethnic Avar physician, as president. Harassed by the police and refused registration in the predominantly Muslim Soviet republics, the AUIRP registered as a political organization in Moscow. Gadoev, who was elected first deputy of the AUIRP at its founding, recalled that Tajiks were the most numerous and active of the AUIRP's members because of Himmatzoda's and Nuri's long-established organization. For two years, the Nahzat attempted to spread the AUIRP's influence in the Tajik and Uzbek republics. Though they were blocked at the Tashkent airport from entering Uzbekistan, they had some success at home, albeit illegally, inside Tajikistan.[108]

The AUIRP's program, like that of many nascent political organizations at the time, and like many Islamic parties in the Middle East, was vague. However, its leaders showed a close identification with the Nahzat's concerns in Tajikistan. They demanded religious freedom for all, political reform of the USSR by peaceful means, and a restructuring of the economy. The official platform stated that the AUIRP "is a religious and political organization which unites Muslims who are actively disseminating Islam, who fulfill the prescriptions of Islam, and who participate in religious, cultural, social, political and economic life on the basis of Islam's principles."[109] The program referred to their plan to "regulate the excessive accumulation of wealth . . . on the basis of the *shariat*."[110] Party ideologist Valiakhmed Sadur told the *glasnost*-era Soviet media that the AUIRP supported peaceful, constitutional reform and Islamic revival for Soviet Muslims, *not* independence.[111] However, other party members were growing discontented. One activist advocated the creation of Islamic republics in Central Asia and the Caucasus.[112] The AUIRP lacked a clear position on Gorbachev's democratization. One salient article in the party's newspaper, *Al' Vakhdat*, argued that "democracy [is] for democrats and Islam for Muslims."[113]

[107] Interview with Gadoev.

[108] Interview with Gadoev.

[109] Alexei Malashenko, "Islam versus Communism," in *Russia's Muslim Frontiers: New Directions in Cross-Cultural Analysis*, ed. Dale Eickelman (Bloomington, IN: Indiana University Press, 1993), 73.

[110] Cited in Malashenko, "Islam versus Communism," 73.

[111] *Izvestiya*, January 8, 1991, cited in Anderson, *Religion*, 202.

[112] Anderson, *Religion*, 202.

[113] *Al' Vakhdat* paper of IRP, cited in Malashenko, "Islam versus Communism," 74.

Meanwhile, Tajik AUIRP members were working actively to establish their own republic-level branch of the party. When they sought government permission to meet, the Tajik Supreme Soviet summoned and interrogated both Usmon and Gadoev, accusing them of wanting to establish an Islamic state. Despite their denial of such a goal, in November 1990, the Central Committee of the Communist Party of the Tajik SSR banned the Tajik branch of the AUIRP. In an attempt to divide the Islamic opposition, the December 8, 1990, Law of the Tajik SSR on Freedom of Conscience and Religious Organizations allowed the right to freedom of conscience, the existence of religious organizations, and even the independence of religious authority, but still barred all religious political activity and any parties based on religion (Article 7).[114] Finally, on December 14, 1990, the Tajik Supreme Soviet adopted a resolution ordering the Prosecutor's Office, the KGB, and the MVD to take immediate steps against the Islamic Party. It was banned in March 1991 by the still overwhelmingly communist Tajik legislature. Nonetheless, that spring, the AUIRP claimed thirty thousand members across the USSR, including thousands of Tajiks, despite the ban.[115] As the USSR disintegrated over the summer of 1991, however, so too did the AUIRP. The Tajik branch, thenceforth known as the Islamic Revival Party of Tajikistan (IRPT), carried on and joined in mass anticommunist protests.[116]

Ultimately, nearly seven hundred members and three hundred guests—a large cadre recruited by Nahzat's religious entrepreneurs—would attend the IRPT's founding congress on October 26, 1991, after Tajikistan had declared independence. Longtime religious entrepreneur Himmatzoda was elected the party's first chairman.

The IRPT's Shifting Ideology: Adapting to Its Context

The Nahzat's political theology, developed over a decade or more, shaped the IRPT's program. The party was a distinctly Islamist opposition with religious grievances, appealing to those who identified as Muslim and felt oppressed or excluded by Soviet atheism. Yet, like the Muslim Brotherhood, its vision of what role Islam would play in the state remained unclear. The IRPT was rapidly adapting its ideas to the Tajik national context.

[114] V. I. Bushkov and D. V. Mikul'skiy, *Tadzhikskaia revoliutsiia i grazhdanskaia voina (1989–1994 gg.)* (Moscow: Institut etnologii i antropologii, 1995), 131–32; "Zakon Tadzhikskoi SSR 'O svobode sovesti v religioznykh organizatsiiakh,'" December 8, 1990, in *Vedomosti Verkhovnogo Soveta Tadzhikskoi SSR, 1990g.*, no. 24, 418.

[115] Malashenko, "Islam versus Communism."

[116] Interview with Gadoev.

First, anticommunism was central to the IRPT's agenda. A quarter of the IRPT platform, adopted by its First Party Congress on October 26, 1991, was devoted to discussing the crimes of the communist period and Soviet system: "For over seventy years, the Muslim peoples have been unable to satisfy their political, economic, and social, moral, and cultural needs. . . . The pernicious policy of the communist leaders destroyed society—almost to its very foundations. . . . As a result of atheist propaganda, the moral foundation of all classes of society and all peoples was undermined. . . . The Muslim peoples of Central Asia were cut off from other Muslim peoples around the world; they were not represented in a single Muslim international organization. The IRPT sees the communist system's unnatural theories, inhuman foundations, and anti-ethnic structure as the cause of its downfall."[117] The program condemned the communist regime's lies, false use of Islamic slogans, and false promises of freedom of worship: "For seventy years our Muslims did not have these rights"—to worship; build mosques, Sufi convents, and *madrasas*; to perform *namaz* and the fast; and to discuss religious problems.[118] To rectify this situation, the party program turned to Islam: "To us, the followers of Islam, it is well known that the Prophet Muhammad, may the prayers and blessings of Allah be with him, was an outstanding political figure. He built a just society, which rested on the laws of truth. He brought people piety and the purification of the spirit."[119] An Islamist political order was their solution to impiety and injustice.

Second, the IRPT elaborated its core mission as creating a party "on the basis of pure Islam. . . . For the party, Islam is the law and the guide in all political matters. The aim of the IRPT is to enlighten the people with regard to the principles of the Muslim religion."[120] Yet, instead of emphasizing the language of puritanical renewal, the program directly connected this goal to the need for freedom, to "build a society founded on the basis of faith, a just, free, independent society in which, while preserving its national and religious character, will enable each member, regardless of nationality or religious affiliation, to live or work freely."[121] This proclamation notably did not preclude democracy. The program specifically called for a "multi-party system and free competition of parties," claiming that it maintained ties with all democratic forces in the republic.[122]

Third, the IRPT party platform condemned communist destruction of private property with the false promise of "creating a communist paradise on earth."[123]

[117] IRPT programme, translated in Vladimir Babak, Demian Vaisman, and Aryeh Wasserman, eds., *Political Organization in Central Asia and Azerbaijan: Sources and Documents* (London: Frank Cass, 2004), 299.
[118] IRPT programme, 300.
[119] IRPT programme, 300.
[120] IRPT programme, 300.
[121] IRPT programme, 301.
[122] IRPT programme, 301.
[123] IRPT programme, 300.

They painted communist policies as those of a "colonial" state expropriating the property and wealth of Muslims and turning it over to non-Tajiks[124] and wanted to rectify Soviet seizure of *waqfs*.[125] They called for an Islamic economy, banking, working week and holidays, and taxes as a just alternative to the state's regulations.[126] They declared, "[T]he IRPT opposes monopolies, speculation, and usury."[127]

Fourth, reflecting the original ideas of the Nahzat, the IRPT demanded the legal recognition and respect of Islamic culture and the ability to create an Islamic society through the educational system, both of which were still completely under communist atheist control. The IRPT demanded "restructuring the system of education" to include Islam and national values. While the party program specifically recognized the importance of "technical education" and "non-Muslim literature," it also called for elevating national and Islamic values, including "teaching the native Tajik language," instituting "the teaching of religion, intensifying the study of national-Islamic culture . . . in keeping with Islam."[128] As Sayfullozoda emphasized, many of the IRPT's demands were about "sovereignty and recognition of [Tajik] national mentality." The party also promised prosperity, equality, guaranteed work, housing, free elections, eliminating corruption, preserving the family and spiritual health, and using Islam to solve environmental problems.[129]

Finally, the program included a section on "ideology," devoted to core Islamist issues that revealed a renewed focus on a return to pure Islam. Its ideology came from "belief in the Creator and in the Prophet Muhammad's mission . . . [and that] our national traditions do not differ at all from Islam or contradict it in any way." They set forth their core principles:

- No one should be worshipped but Allah;
- Aside from Allah no one, neither an absolutist monarchy nor an elected government, can determine the law;
- Every Muslim is obligated to do his utmost so that the axis and aim of his entire life is finding grace in the eyes of Allah;
- The IRPT in a variety of ways, both in the sphere of religion itself, and in the spheres of culture, civilization, everyday life and politics, and also in all

124 IRPT programme, 301.

125 Interview with Dr. Abdullo Hakim Rahnamo, aide to Haji Akbar Turajonzoda, Dushanbe, Tajikistan, August 2005.

126 Henry Dunant Center, "Humanitarian Engagement with Armed Groups: The Central Asian Islamic Opposition Movements," February 2003, https://www.hdcentre.org/wp-content/uploads/2016/07/Humanitarian-engagement-with-armed-groups-The-Central-Asian-Islamic-opposition-movements-February-2003.pdf, 12.

127 IRPT programme, 302.

128 IRPT programme, 303.

129 IRPT programme, 304–5.

matters of vital importance, proceeds from divine inspiration and does not acknowledge any law which contradicts the *shariat*.[130]

Much like the Muslim Brotherhood, this program mixed the goals of a religious movement urging spiritual purity with those of a political party demanding social and economic reform. While it did not clearly endorse the adoption of *shariat* as law, Allah, not the people, was the ultimate legal authority. The party never clarified how these principles would be adjudicated in a parliamentary system. The program explicitly endorsed *both* free elections and adopting law in accordance with *shariat*.

The IRPT's position on an "Islamic state" has been a source of much debate. The Communist Party's goal was to tarnish the IRPT as an extremist organization whose endgame was an Iranian-style revolution and state; hence, state-run media claims that Mullah Nuri was preaching an Islamic state are questionable. However, lack of consensus within the party, the need to balance strategy and ideology, and simply an inability to speak openly fomented confusion about its actual goals. The IRPT program reflected themes central to the Muslim Brotherhood and Jamaat-i Islami: anticolonialism, Islamic revival, Allah's sovereignty, and the primacy of *shariat*. But it did not specifically call for an "Islamic state." Nonetheless, Gadoev admitted that their "early leaders" spoke "too openly" during *perestroika*, igniting fear among the population and a backlash from the government. Russian journalist Igor Rotar published an interview with Himmatzoda in 1991, in which the party leader said, "[W]e hope—it is the dream of every Muslim—that Islam will be recognized as the state religion and that we shall live in accordance with the laws of Islam. But we are going to have to prepare the people for this, and the Islamic state must come about through peaceful means."[131] Tajik scholar Saodat Olimova claims that the IRPT leader Himmatzoda publicly stated both before and after the war that the party's "goal is to create an Islamic state," and "in this Islamic state only male Muslims could be representatives in elected bodies."[132] Other scholars also emphasize their commitment to an Islamic state. Nourzhanov and Bleuer argue that, "as late as 1991–92, the IRP[T]'s goal was the creation—but not immediately—of an Islamic state. This would be achieved, according to the IRP[T], through an election victory and then a referendum."[133]

[130] IRPT programme, 303.

[131] Rotar's interview was published in *Nezavisimaya gazeta* on September 18, 1991, and then reprinted in the official Tajik newspaper, *Narodnaya gazeta*. See Igor Rotar, "Under the Green Banner," *Religion, State, and Society* 30, no. 2 (2002): 124.

[132] Saodat Olimova, "Political Islam and Conflict in Tajikistan," *Central Asia and the Caucasus*, CA&C Press, Sweden, 5 (1999).

[133] Nourzhanov and Bleuer, *Tajikistan*, 265.

Others disagree. Mirzo became familiar with the IRPT, both as a journalist and in his democratic activism. He believed that "Nuri's views were close to those of Domla Hindustoniy. They were not supporters of an Islamic state, but worked for an Islamic society where people would be knowledgeable about their religion . . . not more."[134] In speaking with me, Mullah Nuri denied ever advocating an Islamic state himself, but he also spoke favorably of the Muslim Brotherhood's idea and of its moderate and gradual path to an Islamic state; he contrasted that idea and method with "extremists like the Taliban"; both Nuri and Himmatzoda clearly wanted to dissociate the IRPT from the Taliban's radical and violent version of an Islamic state.[135] From 1990 on, the core IRPT leaders advocated a parliamentary electoral system within a vaguely defined Islamic moral framework.[136] Gadoev insisted, "When we registered the party officially, our goal became making a contribution to the political life of society, [but] there was no mission to create an Islamic state in the program of the party."[137] Usmon, the IRPT's deputy chairman in its early years, challenged the government's "propaganda":

> In one session of parliament [the Supreme Soviet of the Tajik SSR], they discussed the problem of permitting the party to participate in elections. I spoke out to defend the position of the party. The deputy head of the Supreme Soviet asked me, "Will you create an Islamic state?" I answered, "No," but in the end I said that every party has a goal. If we say that we are not gathering to create an Islamic state, it will be a lie. But to create an Islamic state—it's a difficult business; we cannot tomorrow, or the day after tomorrow, create an Islamic state; it's not possible. Like the Communist Party also, we will participate in a political struggle. If we are victorious in elections, then we will not force the people to accept an Islamic state. If the people freely want to accept an Islamic regime, then please go ahead. But if they do not want this [an Islamic regime], then no. We do not want armed methods or the path of revolution to fight or seize power. From our viewpoint, creating an Islamic state is not possible for the next fifty years.[138]

Himmatzoda speculated that the regime painted the IRPT as proponents of an Islamic state to tarnish them as fundamentalists before the West. Given that the

134 Interview with Mirzo.

135 Interview with Nuri; Muhammadsharif Himmatzoda, "Faktory provedeniia religioznogo ekstremizma i mery po ego predotvrashcheniiu: iavliaetsia li islam ekstremistskoi religiei?" in *Postroenie Doveriia Mezhdu Islamistami i Sekuliaristami–Tadzhikskii Eksperiment*, ed. Jan-Nikolai Bitter and Vol'fgang Tsel'ner (Dushanbe: "Devashtich," 2004), 306.

136 Epkenhans, *The Origins of the Civil War in Tajikistan*, 363.

137 Interview with Gadoev.

138 Interview with Usmon.

IRPT never gained control of the state, it is difficult to assess the true meaning of these statements, if indeed a clear understanding of the party's vision and agenda to achieve it did exist. However, even when Usmon served as vice premier in the brief power-sharing coalition of May–June 1992, the IRPT did not propose any *shariat* laws, much less push forward the creation of an Islamic state of any form. The party only sought to reverse Soviet-era restrictions on Islam.

Nonetheless, uncertainty remained. Gadoev acknowledged in my interview that some IRPT members had made "careless statements," sparking fear of their motives. He added, also with some ambiguity: "We did not want to take power or seek the creation of a Muslim state. We set our goal as the defense of Muslims and the building of a national state. *At that time*, we didn't want to create a movement for an Islamic state, as it was not fruitful. The communists would not have allowed it. And we knew this: that our nation was not ready for this."[139]

In the early to mid-1990s, various IRPT statements took pains to emphasize that the party did not seek an Islamic state in the near term. As vice premier in June 1992, Usmon publicly stated, "The republic is not yet ready to become an Islamic state." Yet even these leaders—arguably the most moderate in the Islamist coalition—continued to imply that creating an Islamic state, by the will of the people, was a long-term ideal, if not goal. They specified that after fifty or sixty years of Islamizing society, Tajik voters themselves might demand an Islamic state.[140]

Qozikalon Turajonzoda, who would join forces with the IRPT in a broader Islamic movement in 1992, was initially concerned that the IRPT was moving too quickly into politics, but he too has insisted that neither the IRPT nor the Qoziyot "had plans to impose a theocratic state on our people and send the country down the drain of obscurantism."[141] He too left open the possibility of eventually creating an Islamic state.[142] Turajonzoda declared that "decades of communist rule have killed the trust of many people in Allah, and they'd take more than a year to accept the idea of an Islamic republic on their own."[143] He emphasized that "the Sacred Qur'an proclaims that there is no compulsion in religion," but that "preaching Islam does not exclude the domains of politics, economy and legislation. These were and will remain spheres of our activities."[144]

The Islamist movement thus remained sharply at odds with the Tajik regime's "secularism."[145] Despite the collapse of the USSR and the demise of the

[139] Interview with Gadoev. Those are my italics. Some IRPT members left their future agenda vague.

[140] Henry Dunant Center, "Humanitarian Engagement with Armed Groups," 9.

[141] Turajonzoda, "Religion," 271.

[142] Interview with Turajonzoda.

[143] "Tajikistan Not Yet Ready to Become Islamic Republic," *Interfax, BBC*, June 6, 1992.

[144] Turajonzoda, "Religion: The Pillar of Society," 271.

[145] People's Party of Tajikistan, "Path for Resolving Economic Crisis," *Vecherniy Dushanbe*, December 20, 1993, FBIS. *Report, Central Eurasia*, February 2, 1994.

Communist Party in mid- to late 1991, the atheist ideology of the ruling elite and its fear of independent religion had not changed.

Open, Mass Islamist Mobilization

Demokratizatsiia and the Turn to Mass Protests

I argued in Chapter 1 that an Islamist organization often shifts to open, mass mobilization with the onset of growing associational space. In the Tajik case, the process of the Soviet Union's unraveling created greater—albeit still limited—opportunity for both Islam and independent parties.

The institutional context of the mid- to late 1980s was confused and contradictory. Under *glasnost* (openness), associational space had begun to grow, but Gorbachev's reforms did not immediately radiate to the regions.[146] While political Islam was still repressed, some restrictions on Islamic belief and practice had eased, according to Hayit: "In comparison with previous years, an atmosphere was created for practicing faith. The number of mosques and those performing *namaz* increased. . . . Beginning in 1985, mosques began to work. Islam little by little began to revive. In Soviet times, mosques had been turned into places for cows, others into red tea houses or public tea houses. The IRPT played a large role in the resurrection of Islam in Tajikistan. . . . Gorbachev's *perestroika* was a breath of fresh air for the spiritual being of Muslims."[147] Gorbachev's democratization further opened space. The religious revival already underway in the private sphere took off publicly as well. Qozikalon Turajonzoda used his position, with some success, to appeal to Gorbachev to grant religious freedom for Muslims as well as Orthodox Christians. With Turajonzoda's sponsorship, the number of registered mosques increased from just seventeen in 1987 to about two thousand to three thousand by 1992.[148] Still other mosques existed unofficially as well. With too few officially trained imams to serve in them, unofficial religious leaders expanded in numbers. The *qozikalon* also established relations with Middle Eastern states, including Saudi Arabia, which donated fifty thousand copies of the Qur'an in March 1990. Central Asian émigrés living in Saudi Arabia since the 1920s were allowed to visit. Many brought donations for mosque construction. Growing space also motivated the IRPT to take advantage of these conditions. Nahzat's proselytization and recruitment expanded. Its

[146] Interviews with IRPT members, Dushanbe, Tajikistan, August 2004; interview with Mirzo.
[147] Interview with Hayit.
[148] Interview with Turajonzoda; V. I. Bushkov and D. V. Mikul'skiy, *Anatomiia grazhdanskoi voyni v Tadzhikistane (ethnosotsial'nie protsessi i politicheskaia bor'ba 1992–1995)* (Moscow: Institut etnologii i antropologii RAN, 1992), 28.

Islamic publications, *Hidoyat* (Guidance) and *Haqiqati Islom* (Truth of Islam), advanced its ideas of reform and societal Islamization.[149]

The failure of the August 19, 1991, coup to restore the Union triggered mass pro-democracy movements in Russia, a wave of independence declarations by the republics, and soon the USSR's complete collapse. The Tajik republic's communist leadership, however, initially clung to the Party and declared independence only after it was inevitable. In this fluid context, the IRPT and other opposition groups turned to ongoing, open mass demonstrations. The IRPT and four other opposition movements—the Democratic Party of Tajikistan (DPT); Rastokhez, the nationalist movement; and Lal'i Badakhshon, an ethnic Pamiri autonomous movement—all of which had recently formed during *perestroika*, combined forces. They pressured Tajik First Secretary Mahkamov to agree to their common demands, including a ban on the Communist Party of Tajikistan (CPT), direct presidential elections, and legalization of other opposition parties. They were joined by Qozikalon Turajonzoda, who announced that six of the most authoritative religious figures in the republic would launch a hunger strike on Dushanbe's Shahidon Square, named by the opposition for the twenty-one individuals who had perished as *shahid*s (martyrs) in the 1990 student protests. The hunger-strikers included Turajonzoda's father and other renowned Sufi *eshons*.[150] One party member said, "I remember it well, the hunger strike on the Square. Sufi shaykhs gathered and joined."[151] By some estimates, these shaykhs had 100,000 followers each throughout Tajikistan.[152] Even if that number is exaggerated, their very presence brought large crowds and lent sacred authority to the protests. Some two hundred others joined the hunger strike.[153] In a symbolic challenge to communism, the Islamists, nationalists, and democrats together removed Lenin's statue.[154]

Succumbing to the unprecedented protest, First Secretary Mahkamov resigned. Power passed to an interim president, Kadriddin Aslonov, who allowed other parties to register. The IRPT held its first legal party congress, discussed earlier in this chapter.[155] The legislature lifted the ban on religious parties, paving the way for the IRPT's legalization. Yet, a hardline coup orchestrated by former Communist Party First Secretary Rahmon Nabiev, interrupted the reforms. On

[149] Epkenhans, *The Origins of the Civil War in Tajikistan*, 193.

[150] "Emergency Session over Dushanbe," Dushanbe Radio Dushanbe Network, September 30, 1991, FBIS-SOV-91-189; "Civil Disobedience Continues," Dushanbe Radio Dushanbe Network, September 26, 1991, FBIS-SOV-91-189.

[151] Interview with Hayit.

[152] "Emergency Session over Dushanbe."

[153] "Presidential Election Postponement Likely," *Izvestiya*, October 7, 1991, 2, FBIS-SOV-91-195.

[154] "Emergency Session Over Dushanbe."

[155] Interview with Himmatzoda, 1998, International Foundation for Electoral Systems, IFES.org (link now defunct).

September 23, 1991, Nabiev declared himself "acting president" and reversed the ban on the CPT.

Over ten thousand protestors massed in Dushanbe day after day. Ultimately, Nabiev agreed to schedule Tajikistan's first popular presidential elections for November 24, 1991. He ran as a hardliner from the old-guard Communist Party. The IRPT and other opposition groups united in a "democratic-nationalist-Islamist" coalition that supported a pro-democracy candidate, Davlat Khudonazar. Although Khudonazar had little in common with the IRPT platform, the Islamist leadership publicly declared that they could achieve their Islamic goals through a parliamentary democracy. Qozikalon Turajonzoda, whose authority had been rising amid the turmoil, briefly considered running for the presidency, but in the end he too supported the opposition coalition's choice against Nabiev.[156]

In what many considered a fraudulent election, Nabiev declared himself victor with about 57 percent of the vote, versus Khudonazar's 30 percent. Unsurprisingly, the ex-communist leader rapidly cracked down on political competition and associational space, putting parliament and the former KGB under his cronies and arresting opposition activists.[157] By spring 1992, Nabiev was again excluding Gharmis, Badakhshanis, and other groups from power. These moves sparked a rapid return to mass mobilization.

Again, in March 1992, the opposition coalition organized rallies. Lal'i Badakhshon bused in Pamiri supporters from distant Gorno-Badakhshan to stage demonstrations on Shahidon Square. Reports describe the growing participation of the IRPT as it drew supporters from Gharm and other rural regions. One woman, a student in Dushanbe during the 1992 protests, recalled that the Islamists' message and presence were compelling: "Every person and family began discussing their ideas."[158] In March and April 1992, protests of several hundred to several thousand per day gathered on the Square or in front of government buildings and the president's residence.

Each opposition organization had a distinct agenda and base. The DPT and Rastokhez were urban intellectual movements that emphasized democracy and Tajik nationalism.[159] Yet, during months of cooperation, both organizations notably adopted more Islamic rhetoric, while the IRPT amplified its nationalist focus and accepted some democratic ideas. Some activists, such as Hayit, began as Rastokhez members, but also joined the IRPT. An influential Gharmi leader and longtime follower of the IRPT described the opposition's shared goals and their

[156] FBIS, "Emergence Session Over Dushanbe."
[157] Collins, *Clan Politics*.
[158] Personal communication, 2012.
[159] "Democratic Party of Tajikistan Registered," *Izvestiya*, July 11, 1991, *Daily Report, Soviet Union*, FBIS-SOV-91, July 16, 1991.

strategic collaboration: "In the beginning of the 1990s, the intelligentsia rose up with the goal of independence and self-realization of the nation. At the same moment, the representatives of religion and their party [the IRPT] . . . also took the path of national revival. . . . And some [national intelligentsia] with a secular view realized that if they also were based on religion, they would have even greater strength, that 90 percent of the population is Muslim."[160] The protests themselves had a distinctly Islamic flavor. According to Muhiddin Kabiri, who would later lead the party, in the early 1990s most of the slogans used by the IRPT members and supporters were about Islam.[161] Islam became a rallying cry as IRPT leaders used the discourse of Islam to mobilize activists and supporters from rural regions where the population had long resisted Soviet antireligious policies. The protesters began the day with communal ritual prayer on the square at about 5:00 a.m. According to one journalist who witnessed the events, the "Islamic opposition leaders publicly demanded *shariat*."[162] Many men, young and old, wore beards in a sign of stricter Islamic practice. Few women were present.

The culturally Islamic aspect of the protest was welcomed by many. The opposition provided tea and water and kept order, whereas pro-government protesters threatened women passersby. One Tajik observer, a woman who identified herself as Muslim and pro-democratic, recalled:

> I used to defend the Shahidon side [the Islamic Party and democrats][163] because the crowd was very well organized, well-mannered without any profanity. They treated those passing by with respect. The prayer would start at the Square and I would just sit and wait on one corner until it finished because there was absolutely no space to walk. . . . I was never bothered for not wearing a [head] scarf and walking around alone, and never harassed by men on this side. My clothes were long and modest. Right before the war, they started to examine bags, but they would ask permission before searching. It was done with so much courtesy and care. Even when they spit, they had to cover it with dirt. The Ozodi [Square] protest, on the other hand, was totally opposite of what I have just described, very hostile, disorganized, and very bad mannered, profanity all the way, and spit everywhere. I couldn't recognize Lenin's statue because trash was all over the place. . . . It was dangerous! The guys would harass ladies. Most of them were drunk. When they checked bags, they would say something to make you uncomfortable or embarrassed.[164]

[160] Interview with *mahalla* leader, Gharm, July 2009. See also Usmon, "Tadzhikskii konflikt i mery doveriia," 244.

[161] Interview with Kabiri, November 2012.

[162] Interview with Firuz Iskander, BBC, Dushanbe, Tajikistan, October 2004.

[163] The opposition was in Shahidon Square. Nabiev's supporters were in Ozodi Square.

[164] Personal communication with former Tajik government employee, Dushanbe, Tajikistan, June 2016.

According to many informants, the moral conduct and civic and religious ideas articulated by the Islamist and national-democratic opposition induced many to join the protest.

In the context of *Eid-al-Fitr* that April, Nuri played a growing role; as Tim Epkenhans observes, Nuri "skillfully blended religious and nationalist sentiment" to "generate unity" among the diverse protesters.[165] On April 11, at the IRPT's urging, Turajonzoda agreed to join the opposition protest and brought in a much broader Islamic network of support. Again, Turajonzoda used his sacred authority and resources as *qozikalon* and his ties to eminent Sufis to support the demonstrations. He openly condemned the atheist regime and blamed it for past oppression of Islam.

By contrast, Nabiev's support came originally from communist hardliners and his clan and patronage network. Yet he increasingly drew support from convicts he released from prison or hired to form militias to serve him. All of these had a direct interest in maintaining Nabiev's political hegemony. Moreover, they used fearmongering to portray Turajonzoda and the IRPT and their supporters as extremists. Hayit recalled the pro-government protesters of spring 1992 in this way: "I'll never forget that time. I found myself in Dushanbe. On Ozodi Square, when Sangak [Safarov] and Rustam Abdurahim came there before the Supreme Soviet they waved banners: on the left side [on the banner was written] 'Down with Islam'; on the right side 'Down with Turajonzoda!' Many Muslims, mullahs, and *eshons* died under these slogans."[166]

By late April and early May, the number of demonstrators was estimated to be 50,000 to 100,000.[167] Although most opposition activists peacefully demanded inclusion in the government and new elections, some in the Islamist camp were becoming radicalized and, according to Bleuer and Nourzhanov, made "demands that were not supported by IRP[T] leader Himmatzoda. On May 7, Mullah Qiyomiddin, going by the title 'General Sayid Qiyomuddin Ghozi,' led 10,000 protesters in a chant, 'What do you want?' 'Islam, Islam, Islam!' 'Do you want an Islamic state?' 'Yes, Yes, Yes!' "[168] When the regime distributed weapons to pro-Nabiev protesters and a Kulobi militia led by Safarov, violence ensued.[169] Fearing he would be overthrown, Nabiev agreed to form a coalition Government of National Reconciliation (GNR) in May 1992. He retained the presidency and

[165] Epkenhans, *The Origins of the Civil War in Tajikistan*, 229.

[166] Interview with Hayit.

[167] "Decisions Will Mean Nothing," *Moscow Interfax*, April 30, 1992, FBIS-SOV-92, May 1, 1992.

[168] Bleuer and Nourzhanov, *Tajikistan*, 310. Even some IRPT members admit that radicalization took place. See Hamadov Hamadov, "O faktorakh perestaniia," 326–27.

[169] Iskandar Asadullaev, "The Tajikistan Government," in *The Politics of Compromise: The Tajikistan Peace Process, Accord*, ed. Kamoludin Abdullaev and Catherine Barnes (London: Conciliation Resources, 2001), 10, 24; interview with former U.S. ambassador to Tajikistan, Stanley Escudero, Baku, Azerbaijan, 1999.

ceded the post of prime minister and several others to the opposition. IRPT leader Usmon became deputy premier.

Despite their prominent presence in the ill-fated GNR, Islamists did not attempt to adopt Islamic laws, much less an Islamic state. They set aside most of the core elements of their platform to sustain the compromise. They were opposed to keeping the term "secular" in the Constitution and sought to give Islam a role in state education, but they achieved neither. They sided with the democrats in promoting free elections. However, neither the IRPT nor the democrats had experience with national governance, and Nabiev had little will to cooperate.

Demonstrations resumed when it became clear that the GNR was no more than a stall tactic for Nabiev. The opposition again demanded nullification of the election, a new constitution, and the resignation of both President Nabiev and Safarali Kenjaev, chief of the Committee of National Security. It also insisted upon the release from prison of pro-opposition government ministers. The IRPT and the *qozikalon* again mobilized supporters from their provincial and religious networks.[170] Order rapidly deteriorated as various groups in the country—government and opposition forces—began to arm themselves.

Violent Mobilization: The Islamists' Role in the Civil War, 1992–97

In June 1992, bloodshed erupted in Dushanbe, and from there radiated to central and southern Tajikistan. The fragile coalition government collapsed and violence spiraled. It is beyond the scope of this book to detail Tajikistan's five-year civil war. Most scholars have focused on economic grievances, clan and regional power struggles, local warlord dynamics, or criminality[171] in explaining the war's causes and dynamics. While neither Islam nor the IRPT caused the conflict, understanding the Islamists' role and how religion was used during the war is critical. Here, I build on more recent studies of the war that emphasize the Islamic nature of the main opposition faction.[172] Freedom for Islam and a political role for Islam were core to the IRPT's demands and a central feature of the war; however, militant jihad was not part of the IRPT's ideology, nor its preferred strategy of contesting power. Yet, the regime had responded violently to opposition mobilization challenging its monopoly on power. The result was the opposition's

170 Interview with Escudero.

171 Olivier Roy, "The Civil War in Tajikistan: Causes and Implications," USIP Report, Washington, D.C., December 1993; Collins, *Clan Politics*; Olimova, "Political Islam and Conflict in Tajikistan"; Lawrence Markowitz, *State Erosion: Unlootable Resources and Unruly Elites in Central Asia* (Ithaca, NY: Cornell University Press, 2013); Jesse Driscoll, *Warlords and Coalition Politics in Post-Soviet States* (Cambridge: Cambridge University Press, 2015).

172 Epkenhans, *The Origins of the Civil War in Tajikistan*, 360; Nourzhanov and Bleuer, *Tajikistan*.

militarization. Islam did not cause the violence, but during the ensuing conflict, it continued to be a tool of mobilization. As Abdullo Hakim Rahnamo, an aide to Turajonzoda, explained, "Religion was involved in the civil war from the very beginning. The religious feelings of the population were used."[173]

Government forces used criminal bosses and their militias to raze villages in IRPT strongholds. Militias targeted and "cleansed" the opposition; antigovernment leanings were assumed by location, dialect, and visible religious practice or dress. One man from Dushanbe said, "I remember that if they found a Qur'an in your house, they would kill you."[174] Violent purges led to the death, flight, and expulsion of tens of thousands.[175] Fear and desire for retribution escalated the spiral of violence and atrocities.[176]

At the end of 1992, in the face of unchecked brutality and with insufficient arms, the IRPT led a mass migration of its followers and anyone fleeing the government militias across the border to northeastern Afghanistan. They numbered over 200,000 (by some accounts, 600,000) civilians and militants together.[177] It would become a five-year exile. Various strands of the Islamist opposition joined the IRPT, including Turajonzoda and multiple Sufi *eshons*. Most came from the opposition's base (Gharm, Qarotegin Valley, Qurghonteppa, and Dushanbe), but others came from Kulob and Mastchoh, formerly a source of forced labor migrants. Islamists fleeing Uzbekistan, where President Karimov was then jailing supporters of the Islamist movement, joined the exodus to Afghanistan.

The Islamist opposition continued its campaign from across the Amu Darya River, based in camps in the Takhar and Badakhshan regions of Afghanistan. They reorganized into a broader movement, the Movement for the Islamic Revival of Tajikistan (MIRT). Led by Nuri, with Turajonzoda as his deputy, the MIRT provided a government-in-exile for the Islamists' followers and refugees. The MIRT also became the leader of an even broader opposition coalition, the United Tajik Opposition (UTO). The latter included some elements of the Democratic Party, nationalists, a range of Islamists, and various militia leaders. Yet the mostly urban democrats and nationalists had largely fragmented; many fled during the early stages of the war.[178] By contrast, the Islamists remained

[173] Interview with Rahnamo; "Islam in Tajikistan—Interview with Abdullo Hakim Rahnamo," *Religioscope*, April 25, 2004, https://english.religion.info/2004/04/25/islam-in-tajikistan-interview-with-abdullo-hakim-rahnamo/.

[174] TAJ-FG#3, Dushanbe, Tajikistan.

[175] Human Rights Watch, *Return to Tajikistan: Continued Regional and Ethnic Tensions*, May 1, 1995, https://www.refworld.org/docid/3ae6a7d30.html.

[176] Markowitz, *State Erosion*; Driscoll, *Warlords and Coalition Politics*; Epkenhans, *The Origins of the Civil War in Tajikistan*, 258–68.

[177] Abdullaev and Barnes, *The Politics of Compromise*, 8–14. Tajik journalist Bakhtiyor Sobiri uses the upper figure.

[178] Abdunabi Sattorzoda, "The Democratic Party," in Abdullaev and Barnes, *The Politics of Compromise*, 28–30.

organized and continued to wage military strikes on government forces.[179] Religious leaders played a major role in militia leadership; an emir (a commander) and a *mufti* led each armed group.[180] Militants in the MIRT numbered over fifteen thousand, of whom Nuri's IRPT alone were over eight thousand; the rest fought under allied Islamist commanders.[181]

Many mullahs played a significant role in the opposition, not only lending sacred authority but also sometimes engaging in brutality. In one case, Mullah Ajik Aliev, the IRPT chairman in the Xatlon district, together with the Islamist field commander Rizvon Sodirov, reportedly declared an Islamic republic in Gharm in 1992;[182] it lasted until they were driven out by the government in February 1993. Sodirov and his brother engaged in atrocities throughout the war, including taking UN workers hostage and killing a French aid worker. According to both the IRPT and local journalists, Sodirov frequently did so in opposition to the wishes of Nuri and the MIRT. By 1996, he abandoned his Islamist veneer, becoming a tool of the government and Russia in striking the IRPT; money was clearly also a factor in the war.[183]

Undoubtedly, IRPT members and their affiliates were not always unified in what an Islamic state entailed and to what extent they supported establishing one. Even Kabiri has emphasized that they had no clear vision of the state in the 1980s or during the war in the 1990s.[184] Nonetheless, the government painted the opposition as "Wahhabi" (*Vovchik*)—belonging to a puritanical Islamist sect seeking a Saudi Arabian–style theocracy; the designation was ill-fitting given that the MIRT was Hanafi and Sufi, as well as Tajik nationalist.[185] Calling someone "*Vovchik*" was equivalent to branding him a Muslim extremist and terrorist. The opposition, in turn, called government supporters "*Yurchiki*," a derogatory term that implied they were KGB communists (so named after former KGB head Yuri Andropov) and allied with Russia.[186]

An important element of the Islamist role in the war was the IRPT's understanding of jihad. Despite the influence of the Muslim Brotherhood, the decision to pick up arms was not part of a planned militant jihad to establish an Islamic state. Both before and after the war's end, Nuri avoided using the term "jihad." He justified the IRPT's turn to war in 1992 as necessary "defense."[187] It was a reaction

179 Interview with Mirzo; interview with Nuri.

180 Muzaffar Olimov, "Islam in Contemporary Tajikistan: Role of Muslim Leaders," in *Religion and Security in South and Central Asia* (London: Routledge, 2010), 161–62.

181 Interview with Hayit; Abdullaev and Barnes, *The Politics of Compromise*, 91.

182 U.S. State Department, Country Report on Human Rights Practices for 1994: Tajikistan.

183 Rotar, "Under the Green Banner," 125; interview with IRPT activist, Dushanbe, Tajikistan, August 2002; interview with representative, UNTOP, Dushanbe, Tajikistan, August 2002; Nancy DeWolf Smith, "Caught in a Tajik Web of Lies," *Wall Street Journal*, February 18, 1997.

184 Interview with Kabiri, November 2012.

185 Interview with Rahnamo.

186 Rotar, "Under the Green Banner," 95.

187 Interview with Nuri.

to the conditions imposed on the party—the government's turn to violence instead of debate. Rahnamo explained that they responded to the government's escalation of violence in 1993–94, "years of blind murder."[188] According to one Tajik journalist, writing under a pseudonym, "The number of abuses was so extreme. . . . One example was the massacre at the village of Sumbulak in Fayzabad region on December 26, 1993, where pro-government fighters murdered seventy-one civilians, including children."[189]

However, during the conflict, the IRPT and MIRT did refer to the war as a jihad and they selectively used jihadist rhetoric and the Islamic jurisprudence of jihad to garner legitimacy.[190] Mirzo recalled that at least some IRPT activists "called a jihad at that time [in the early 1990s]. . . . For example, Mullah Abdurahim said that 'we are fighting jihad against atheists.' "[191] Gadoev said, "Ustod Nuri always tried to avoid war. . . . Our leaders said they'd meet the government with a bouquet of flowers, if they want to sit at a negotiating table. . . . But they evicted the people from our homeland. So, it was necessary to organize a jihad for our defense, and it was correct."[192] Hayit said the war did not fit a "classical" definition of "another country invading a Muslim country"; however, he emphasized that in the 1920s, the USSR "sought the destruction of Tajik Muslims . . . so jihad was permitted." He continued, "In the 1990s, before the negotiations, I consider this a jihad—if you had a beard, or were from such a region that is a more spiritual region, or [were] a mullah from Qarotegin or Vakhsh, or because your home had religious books, the government [militias] killed you."[193]

IRPT leaders have further emphasized that Nuri turned to war and used the language of jihad only as a last resort, and that he always sought to deescalate: "Before 1997, Afghans came to us in groups asking that we permit them to cross the border and wage jihad. However, Ustod [Nuri] did not sanction either Afghans or Arabs or any others to enter into Tajikistan" to radicalize the conflict.[194] Similarly, Sayfullozoda claimed, "Our understanding of jihad emerged only after they forced us out of the country. We used this understanding to draw attention to ourselves in the international arena."[195] Very conscious of public perception, they emphasized that "the leaders of the IRPT never wanted violence and civil war in Tajik society."[196] It is probable that most IRPT leadership viewed the war as a defensive jihad, much like the Afghan mujahidin's war against the

[188] Interview with Rahnamo.
[189] Bakhtiyor Sobiri, "The Long Echo of Tajikistan's Civil War," *openDemocracy*, June 23, 2017.
[190] Abdullaev and Barnes, *The Politics of Compromise*, 91.
[191] Interview with Mirzo.
[192] Interview with Gadoev.
[193] Interview with Hayit.
[194] Interview with Hayit.
[195] Interview with Sayfullozoda.
[196] Interview with Sayfullozoda.

USSR. They saw their militant response to the government as religiously justified, and used that justification to bolster morale and gain external political and material support. While the IRPT later had an interest in minimizing its violent turn in 1992, jihad was neither their preferred strategy nor their ideology.

Nonetheless, the IRPT honored those fighters who died in the war as *shahids*, saying, "Martyrs are the Beloved of Allah."[197] They published their obituaries, which totaled 1,223. Over a decade later, anthropologist Sophie Roche found that youth in Gharm, like Afghan jihadis who fought against the Soviets, proudly called themselves "mujahidin" (those fighting militant jihad for Allah).[198]

While the core IRPT leadership held themselves to a classical jurisprudential interpretation of jihad—understanding it as legitimate defense of Islam, with violence limited to combatants—some opposition Islamists and their field commanders adopted more extreme means of fighting. The broader UTO umbrella included radical Islamists, especially an Uzbekistani faction that later joined forces with the Taliban, as well as warlords such as the Sodirovs, who used the cloak of Islamic legitimacy to justify their actions. These included assassinations of unarmed aid workers and hostage-taking. They attacked peacekeeping units operating in Tajikistan as well—for example, killing seventeen Kazakh troops in one battle near the Afghanistan border. They launched a campaign of terrorism, shooting noncombatants at bazaars or blowing up vehicles in towns and cities, including Dushanbe.[199]

Islamic Identity and External Support

The MIRT's Islamic identity, goals, and networks would aid in mobilizing external support throughout the conflict as well. Inside northern Afghanistan, the MIRT developed close ties with the ethnic Tajik mujahidin, particularly the Jamiat-i Islami, which was led by Rabbani and his military commander, Massoud. They were "moderate Islamists" within the spectrum of Islamist factions inside Afghanistan, and had recently won their war against the Soviet Union and defeated the communist government of Afghanistan. They too sought a state ordered around *shariat* but rejected the extreme puritanism of many Saudi- and

[197] Suchandana Chatterjee, *Politics and Society in Tajikistan in the Aftermath of the Civil War* (Kolkata, India: Hope India Publications, 2002), 102; D. V. Mikul'skiy, "*Opyt Analiza Nekrologov Chlenov Islamskoi Partii Vozrozhdeniia Tajikistana: Traditsionnoe i Sovermennoe*," *Vostok*, no. 1 (1996): 56–58; Igor Rotar, "V Kraiu Modzhakhedov: Reportazh korrespondenta 'NG' iz gornogo Tadzhikistana," *Nezavisimaia Gazeta*, November 16, 2000.

[198] Sophie Roche, *Faceless Terrorist: A Study of Critical Events in Tajikistan* (Heidelberg: Springer 2019).

[199] Bruce Pannier, "Tajikistan's Civil War: A Nightmare the Government Won't Let Its People Forget," *Radio Free Europe Radio Liberty*, June 23, 2017, https://www.rferl.org/a/qishloq-ovozi-tajikistan-civil-war/28575338.html.

Pakistani-backed factions in the country, which were expanding their influence inside Afghanistan in the 1980s and 1990s. Dubbed the "Lion of Panjshir," Massoud was legendary among Tajik Islamists for his role in the Soviet-Afghan War. Massoud and Rabbani, who became Afghanistan's transitional president in a 1992 peace agreement, provided the MIRT both weapons and training. MIRT continued its affiliation with the Jamiat-i Islami even as Afghanistan quickly descended into an internecine civil war.

So too the "Afghan Arabs"—Arab citizens who had migrated to Afghanistan to participate in the anti-Soviet jihad and then remained after 1989—provided support to the Tajik Islamists. The nascent al-Qaeda organization ran "the Tajikistan Project," which supplied the Tajik opposition with leftover arms from the Soviet-Afghan War, as well as trainers.[200] Claiming success against the USSR, they sought to spread jihad to Central Asia. According to Michael Scheuer, U.S. intelligence reports suggested that al-Qaeda viewed former Soviet Central Asia as fertile ground.[201] One al-Qaeda missive declared, "Allah facilitated our delivering weapons and ammunition to [the Tajiks]. . . . We need to cooperate together to continue this matter, especially in jihad's continuation . . . [which] will keep the enemies busy and divert them away from the Afghan issue."[202] Al-Qaeda viewed post-Soviet Central Asia, starting with Tajikistan, as important both for acquiring weapons of mass destruction and for narcotics-trafficking to fund their more ambitious, anti-Western jihad.

Precise numbers are unknown, but some report that in the early 1990s, 120 Afghan Arab fighters and perhaps several thousand Afghans made the trek across the Amu Darya to Tajikistan to aid the IRPT in fighting the ex-communist regime.[203] An increasingly influential Saudi jihadist who had fought with Osama Bin Laden in the battle of Jaji,[204] known by his nom de guerre Khattab, began training Tajiks, Uzbeks, and Chechens in al-Qaeda camps in Afghanistan. Khattab reportedly coordinated attacks with the IRPT[205] but eventually became disillusioned by the difficulty of the terrain and the lack of broad support for his Islamist goals, which were more radical than the Tajiks'; he moved on

[200] Anne Stenersen, *Al-Qaida in Afghanistan* (Cambridge, UK: Cambridge University Press, 2017), 40–43.

[201] Michael Scheuer, "Central Asia in Al-Qaeda's Vision of the Anti-American Jihad, 1979–2006," *China and Eurasia Forum Quarterly* 4, no. 2 (2006): 7.

[202] Document AFGP-2002-600321, letter from Osama Bin Laden to Mullah Mohammed 'Umar discussing the situation in Afghanistan, continuation of Jihad in the Islamic Republics, and the situation in the Arabian Peninsula, Combating Terrorism Center at West Point, Harmony Database, June 5, 2002, Letter to Mullah Muhammed `Umar from Bin Laden – Combating Terrorism Center at West Point.

[203] Bushkov and Mikul'skiy, *Anatomiia grazhdanskoi voini*. They report that several thousand Afghans were fighting in Tajikistan.

[204] Daniel Byman, *Road Warriors: Foreign Fighters in the Armies of Jihad* (New York: Oxford University Press, 2019), 81.

[205] Byman, *Road Warriors*, 82.

to Chechnya, where his extreme methods and goals met greater success.[206] Al-Qaeda's training camps meanwhile continued to welcome those fighting the post-Soviet regimes for over twenty years. Cooperation between al-Qaeda and Nuri ended when the IRPT entered peace negotiations in mid-1994, but only after an estimated ten tons of weaponry were delivered.[207] Nonetheless, in his 1996 "Fatwa against America," Bin Laden still cited Tajikistan as one front of al-Qaeda's attack against nonbelievers.[208]

In addition to their military operations, the Tajik Islamist opposition opened a diplomatic front to garner international support and funding. Turajonzoda and Nuri traveled to Iran, Pakistan, and other parts of the Middle East. Tehran provided shelter for a time. Outside support also provided crucial military and political assistance for the MIRT once the war had started. Their fighters were well-funded and -supplied with weapons and tanks, lacking only air power.[209]

Although they took aid from Iran, Massoud, Afghan Arabs, and even al-Qaeda during the war, the MIRT appears to have rejected connections with the Taliban, which launched its violent jihad to take control of Afghanistan in 1994 and was pushing steadily into northern Afghanistan's Tajik areas by 1996. Nuri adamantly declared, "We rejected the Taliban [even though] they sought an alliance with us [MIRT] in the mid-1990s. . . . The Tajiks were taking refuge in Afghanistan, but we refused to cooperate with the Taliban, even after they forced down [my] plane."[210] Nuri recounted how the Taliban had done so to compel him to meet with them; they attempted to co-opt him. But the Tajik leader, despite once being influenced by Deobandi thought, opposed the Taliban's radically puritanical and militant interpretation of the Deobandi school of Islam. The Taliban were also Pashtun-dominated and the MIRT chose to continue its alliance with the Afghan Tajiks, Rabbani and Massoud. The Taliban's rise was one factor that motivated the MIRT to make peace so that they could return to Tajikistan.

The war continued into 1997, leading to horrendous atrocities and costing tens of thousands of lives. Reasonable estimates of deaths range from 40,000 to 100,000; most sources agree that at least 50,000 perished.[211] The war was

206 Byman, *Road Warriors*, 80–82; Charlie Winter and Abdullah K. Al-Saud, "The Obscure Theologian Who Shaped ISIS," *The Atlantic*, December 4, 2016.

207 Stenersen, *Al Qaida in Afghanistan*, 44–45; Scheuer, "Central Asia in Al-Qaeda's Vision," 7–8.

208 The full text of the 1996 *fatwa* is found at "Bin Laden's Fatwa," *PBS Newshour*, August 23, 1996, https://web.archive.org/web/20140419014901/http://www.pbs.org/newshour/updates/military-july-dec96-fatwa_1996/#.

209 Interview with Hayit.

210 Interview with Nuri; Whitlock, *Land beyond the River*.

211 *Radio Free Europe/Radio Liberty* has estimated the death toll on the higher end: "Tajikistan: Senior Member of Islamic Party Dies in Jail," *Radio Free Europe/Radio Liberty*, January 30, 2008, Tajikistan: Senior Member Of Islamic Party Dies In Jail (rferl.org); Human Rights Watch, "Tajikistan," Helsinki (hrw.org), Human Rights Watch puts the toll on the low side, between 20,000 and 50,000. Shirin Akiner and Catherine Barnes, "The Tajik Civil War," in *The Politics of Compromise: The Tajikistan Peace Process, Accord*, ed. Kamoludin Abdullaev and Catherine Barnes (London: Conciliation Resources, 2001), 16–23, suggest 20,000 to 60,000. Epkenhans, *The Origins*

the second bloodiest conflict in the former Soviet Union. Only the fifteen-year Russian-Chechen War (1994–2009) was more deadly.[212] In the escalating cycle of violence, all sides targeted noncombatants. More than forty journalists were assassinated or killed covering the war.[213] The conflict internally displaced up to one million Tajiks. It devastated the economy and infrastructure before a peace agreement was signed.[214] Ultimately, Nuri claims, a desire to save Tajik lives led him to peace talks; Russian and Iranian government pressure, driven by fear of regional instability, was also crucial to the peace process.[215]

In this chapter I have explained the first wave of Tajik Islamism from the 1970s through the early 1990s. It emerged from the USSR's religious repression, which had created deep grievances and politicized Muslim identity going back to the Red Terror. That repression of Islam continued into the 1980s, as Nuri was "disappeared" and sent to the Gulag, while the USSR invaded Afghanistan. In that context, the diffusion of various Islamist ideas—from Iran, Afghanistan, Egypt, and South Asia—played a crucial role in forming Islamist entrepreneurs. The young mullahs thus shifted over time, from seeking Islamization of society to making Islamist demands of the state through protest and party formation. Even so, the Islamists were open to coalition-building with the democratic-nationalist front. While they went to war and used jihad to mobilize, they did not choose violence as a strategy; they turned to war because the communist regime sought to eliminate their communities.

Chapter 6 turns to the peace negotiations in 1997, which were followed first by Islamist demobilization, but then by a second wave of mobilization. In this wave, a legalized IRPT would position itself as a moderate, Islamic-democratic party that wholly rejected violence.

of the Civil War in Tajikistan, 347 suggests 40,000 to 100,000; Bushkov and Mikul'skiy, *Anatomiia grazhdanskoi voini*; Nourzhanov and Bleuer, *Tajikistan*.

[212] The death toll in the interstate war between Ukraine and Russia is still unknown.

[213] Pannier, "Tajikistan's Civil War."

[214] Relief Web, "Emergency International Assistance for Peace, Normalcy, and Rehabilitation in Tajikistan," UN General Assembly, August 31, 2000, https://reliefweb.int/report/tajikistan/emergency-international-assistance-peace-normalcy-and-rehabilitation-tajikistan, 6.

[215] Interview with Nuri; Kathleen Collins, "Tajikistan: Bad Peace Agreements and Prolonged Civil Wars," in *The Prevention of Violent Conflict*, ed. Chandra Sriram (Boulder, CO: Lynne Reinner, 2003), 267–306.

6
A Democratic Islamic Party Confronts an Extremist Secular State

> The republic is 99 percent Muslim, so we need a party [like the Islamic Revival Party]. One should exist in any democratic state.
>
> —University student, Khujand, Tajikistan, 2009

> We cannot be an Islamic state. We have had seventy years of socialism. But the Islamic movement is our history. We cannot deny that. We want freedom to practice Islam. Democracy is the best protection for religious freedom. . . . But some do not want to cooperate peacefully. They are losing patience, and some join radical groups.
>
> —Muhiddin Kabiri, 2012

After five years of civil war, Tajikistan lay in ruins politically, economically, and socially.[1] On June 27, 1997, several years of peace talks culminated when IRPT leader Sayid Abdullohi Nuri led the opposition in signing the General Peace Accord with Tajikistan's President Imomali Rahmon. Rahmon had come to power in a rigged election in November 1994, during the war. The Islamist opposition fragmented, with some former members joining the new coalition government and others further radicalizing and remaining in Afghanistan. War weariness initially led many Islamist supporters to demobilize. However, within a few years after the war political conditions fostered the resurgence of a second wave of Islamism that took multiple forms.

This chapter demonstrates that conditions similar to those generating the first wave of Islamism led to a second wave during the 2000s. Multiple Islamist groups—differing in their goals for the political system and law, in their societal goals, and in their views about jihad—offered distinct and competing visions for Tajikistan. Most prominent among Islamist actors during this wave was the IRPT, which itself would enter a wholly new wave of activism in 1999, after finally being legally registered. For the next sixteen years it struggled to compete

[1] Interview with UN official, Dushanbe, Tajikistan, August 2005; Open Society Institute, "Tajikistan: Refugee Reintegration and Conflict Prevention," Forced Migration Project, September 30, 1998, https://reliefweb.int/report/tajikistan/tajikistan-refugee-reintegration-and-conflict-prevention.

Politicizing Islam in Central Asia. Kathleen Collins, Oxford University Press. © Oxford University Press 2023.
DOI: 10.1093/oso/9780197685068.003.0007

as a democratic party. Like several Islamist parties in the Middle East,[2] it publicly rejected its one-time goal of an Islamic republic and *shariat* law and vocally supported democracy.[3] After being severely weakened by the war, the IRPT would rebuild itself with a modified Islamist agenda; it would become the leading challenge to Rahmon's authoritarian regime and a force for democracy in the 2000s.

Meanwhile, other second-wave Islamists also emerged in response to religious repression and new ideologies advocating Islamic justice. Hizb ut-Tahrir al-Islami (HTI), Jamoati Ansorulloh (JA, or the Society of Allah's Soldiers), and the Islamic Movement of Uzbekistan (IMU) appeared, often as radical splinters that left the IRPT because they were critical of its co-optation to a democratic and nonviolent path. They instead proffered radical—antisystemic, antidemocratic, and sometimes violent—ideologies. JA and the IMU espoused militant jihadism as an ideology and strategy. HTI, a transnational Islamist party, was nonviolent but extremist and antidemocratic.

This chapter also sustains the second core argument of this book: the IRPT was relatively successful in mobilizing large numbers and remaining durable for about twenty-five years, between 1990 and 2015, because it held high sacred authority, accessed both local and transcommunal Tajik networks, and adapted its originally purist Islamist ideas to appeal to Tajikistan's particular religious and political context, which generally practiced Sufi-Hanafi syncretism over puritanism and prioritized freedom for Islam and just government over antisystemic goals such as an Islamic state. By contrast, radical Islamist movements lacked sacred authority, networks, and ideational congruence; consequently, they could not mobilize public support and remained marginal to politics.

Ending the War: The 1997 Peace Accord

The first wave of Islamist mobilization ended with the internationally brokered peace deal signed in 1997 in Moscow under the auspices of the UN, between Rahmon's government and the UTO. The latter was primarily represented by the Islamist leaders Sayid Abdullohi Nuri of the IRPT and the former *qozikalon*

[2] Jillian Schwedler, "Democratization, Inclusion and the Moderation of Islamist Parties," *Development* 50, no. 1 (2007): 56–61; Carrie Rosefsky Wickham, "The Path to Moderation: Strategy and Learning in the Formation of Egypt's Wasat Party," *Comparative Politics* 36, no. 2 (2004): 205–28.

[3] Interview with Muhiddin Kabiri, Dushanbe, Tajikistan, July 2005. Arguably, the 2010 program painted an IRPT that was shifting toward what Asef Bayat has called "post-Islamism," the rejection of the core political goal of Islamists, the Islamic state, in favor of democracy. However, this term is difficult to assess in practice. Asef Bayat, *Post-Islamism: The Changing Faces of Political Islam* (Oxford: Oxford University Press, 2013).

Akbar Turajonzoda, who stated that he no longer believed continuing war served the interests of Islam and Muslims.[4] Not all factions of the UTO agreed to the government's terms, but Nuri and Turajonzoda sought to end the violence and return home.[5] The war in Afghanistan had a major impact on their decision. According to Nuri, the Taliban "wanted us to join them, but their ideas about Islam were not correct. I refused. I was responsible for so many people. I saw the destruction of the war still ongoing in Afghanistan. I realized that we must make peace."[6] He claimed that the Qur'an taught him the need for peace. Sayidibrohim Gadoev explained, "While continuing the war was clearly in our favor, the country and the nation could have been destroyed. We saw this in practice in the example of Afghanistan. Ustod Nuri said, 'I have a command from the Qur'an for peace and reconciliation, as is written there.' Our *ustod* gave up the majority of our successes in order to allow reconciliation."[7] Whether or not their narrative is wholly accurate, they were war-weary, their ability to maintain the resources to continue fighting was questionable, and the Taliban's steady push toward their haven in northern Afghanistan was perilous to the 200,000 Tajik refugees under their governance and protection.

Rahmon's government, on the other hand, was still weak and lacked full control of much of its territory, including the Afghan border. It was highly dependent upon Russia, which pushed the now former communist leadership to compromise. Both Russia and Iran, which had backed the MIRT, was concerned about the expansion of the Taliban and expected that peace in Tajikistan would foster regional stability.

The peace agreement ended most of the violence and allowed the opposition to return. It led to a revised constitution in 1999 that guaranteed the legality of all UTO parties, including the IRPT as the first and only legal Islamic party in Central Asia. The accord initiated a democratic transition; that process, if it had been implemented as the UN had intended, and as understood by the opposition, would have led to the first free, competitive elections in 1999–2000, democratization of all areas of the political system, and power-sharing.[8] The UTO was slated to get 30 percent of key government executive posts.

[4] Hikmatullo Sayfullozoda, "Ozhidaniia otnositel'no novoi kontseptsii, osnovannoi na sovremennoi natsional'nom ponimanii otnoshenii svetskogo gosudarstva i religii (Islama)," in *Postroenie Doveriia Mezhdu Islamistami i Sekuliaristami–Tadzhikskii Eksperiment*," ed. Jan-Nikolai Bitter and Vol'fgang Tsel'ner (Dushanbe: "Devashtich," 2004), 205–6.

[5] The UTO umbrella initially included the MIRT (including the IRPT), the Democratic Party of Tajikistan, and several other militias. The MIRT was the UTO's leading faction.

[6] Interview with Mullah Sayid Abdullohi Nuri, Dushanbe, Tajikistan, August 2002.

[7] Interview with Sayidibrohim Gadoev, IRPT activist, Dushanbe, Tajikistan, March 2011.

[8] Interviews with representatives of UN Development Programme, Organization for Security and Co-operation in Europe, and Democratic Party of Tajikistan, Dushanbe, Tajikistan, 2003–7.

Image 6.1 IRPT leader Mullah Sayid Abdullohi Nuri (center) at peace talks
Source: rferl.org, https://www.rferl.org/a/1077337.html.

Conditions Breeding Second-Wave Islamism

Despite initial improvements, the postwar period reproduced many of the same conditions that had led to first-wave Islamism during the late Soviet era. In a second Islamist wave, the IRPT revived itself as a party and competed in ever more challenging conditions, while other Islamist groups emerged to challenge its legitimacy.

Associational Space, from Liberalization to Steady Decline

Between 1997 and 2003, elements of political liberalization progressed, including minor improvements in the electoral process, civil society, media freedom, and governance. Rahmon invited some UTO members into the power structure, although never the number promised, and most were subsequently removed. The government, teetering from the war and subsequent economic collapse, exercised little control at the local level throughout much of the country. Consequently, religious organizations—mosques, *madrasas*, and charities—became widespread.

Yet political liberalization was limited and short-lived. Independent media emerged but faced problems when critical of the government. During the presidential election in 1999, IRPT candidate Davlat Usmon withdrew when it was clear that the vote would be fraudulent. The 2000 parliamentary election was only a marginal improvement.[9] The Organization for Security and Co-operation in Europe (OSCE) criticized the 2005 electoral conditions, and all subsequent votes—parliamentary and presidential—as having serious violations.[10] The next decade witnessed a steady decline in freedoms and retrenchment in commitment to democratization. The National Security Committee regularly harassed not only the opposition but also voters supporting opposition candidates.[11] Although it continued to compete in parliamentary elections, despite extensive electoral violations, the IRPT still declined to contest the presidency. Leaders said the country was "not ready" for an Islamic party winning the presidency.[12] According to party activist, Mahmudjon Faizrahmonov, "We wanted to send a message to society that the party is not in favor of monopolizing power. . . . By not monopolizing the power, we were sending a message to all strata of society and the world community that we were not seeking to Islamize the government and power should remain in the hands of secular people. . . .And even in the 2013 elections, we did not participate with our own candidate from within the party, but we still proposed a female candidate who is purely secular, Oynihol Bobonazarova, as our presidential candidate to the post."[13] More pragmatically, like some Islamist parties in the Middle East, they presciently feared retribution should they win.[14]

Religious Repression Recedes, Then Resurges

Despite quickly shrinking associational space, for the next five to ten years religion and religious activity enjoyed more opportunities than during the Soviet era and early 1990s. Both domestic control and international borders were now porous. This had significant unintended consequences in the religious sphere, opening up channels for the diffusion of new political theologies from the Middle East, South Asia, and neighboring Central Asian republics. Independent religious leaders, such as Turajonzoda, established ties throughout the Muslim world. The Iranian government, Arabs, and Turks also entered the scene, offering programs that sponsored Tajiks to study abroad. Many accepted, given that families could not afford the growing costs of a collapsing state school system in which bribery was the norm. At least several thousand young men studied Islam

[9] OSCE/ODIHR, Parliamentary Elections, Report, February 27, 2000.

[10] OSCE/ODIHR, Parliamentary Elections, Report, February 27 and March 13, 2005.

[11] Mas'uli Somona, "V Kuliabe dvoe zhenshin vyzvany v Komitet bezopasnosti," October 23, 2013, posted on Nahzat's Facebook page (link now defunct).

[12] Interview with Kabiri, November 2012.

[13] Interview with Mahmudjon Faizrahmonov, IRPT Secretariat, Director, Foreign Affairs Department, virtual, December 2022.

[14] Brown, *When Victory Is Not an Option.*

in this way, unregulated by Rahmon's government.[15] Many Tajiks, mostly from opposition regions, had already studied in Pakistan or Iran during the war because it was their only option while living as refugees in Afghanistan.[16]

For a while, the government allowed greater space for mosques to operate than during most of the Soviet era; some independent Islamic education and publications were allowed, and there was a drastic decline in monitoring those who attended mosque and religious rituals. By mid-2011, the State Committee on Religious Affairs had registered 39 central mosques, 338 Friday prayer mosques, and 3,352 mosques for daily prayers.[17] Many more mosques functioned without registration.

Yet the Tajik government also indirectly controlled Islam by endorsing official Hanafi Islam in an attempt to legitimize itself. It sought to co-opt the opposition's Islamic base. It brought Turajonzoda into the government as a deputy prime minister, a move the former *qozikalon* saw as an important concession to Islam. By contrast, the IRPT viewed Turajonzoda's conciliatory measures as abandonment of their cause. Rahmon also sponsored education about Islam in schools.[18] The government welcomed Saudi and Qatari financing of mosques. Qatar spent about $100 million in constructing the grandiose mosque of Dushanbe, meant to house 115,000 worshipers. President Rahmon himself launched construction in 2011. The parliament passed a 2014 law on Islamic banking.[19]

Yet, institutions such as the new Council of Ulama and Council on Religious Affairs also served to control religious activity.[20] Government suspicion of religion remained strong.[21] The state increasingly restricted all Muslim belief and activity that fell outside its narrowly defined limits. It returned to the prosecution of independent Islam (as well as of other unregistered faiths) as criminal and extremist. As Edward Lemon and Hélène Thibault have argued, the state regularly used rhetoric about "counter-extremism" as a form of "disciplinary power."[22] Following Russian president Vladimir Putin's success in Chechnya,

[15] David Abramson, "Foreign Religious Education and the Central Asian Islamic Revival: Impact and Prospects for Stability," Report, Central Asia-Caucasus Institute & Silk Road Studies Program, Johns Hopkins University-SAIS, March 2010, 38–40.

[16] Interview with Kabiri, 2012.

[17] Mavjouda Hasanova, "11 New Central Mosques Registered in Tajikistan," *Asia-Plus*, July 12, 2011, http://news.tj/en/news/11-new-central-mosques-registered-tajikistan.

[18] Hakim Zainiddinov, "The Changing Relationship of the Secularized State to Religion in Tajikistan," *Journal of Church and State* 55, no. 3 (2013): 456–77.

[19] "Law on Islamic Banking in Tajikistan Comes into Force," *Asia-Plus*, August 7, 2014, https://asiaplustj.info/en/news/tajikistan/economic/20140807/law-islamic-banking-tajikistan-comes-force.

[20] Interview with Council for Religious Affairs and Council of Ulama staff, Dushanbe, Tajikistan, August 2005. Members of those organizations clearly feared speaking independently in interviews, and most even refused to meet with me.

[21] Hélène Thibault, *Transforming Tajikistan: State-Building and Islam in Post-Soviet Central Asia* (London: Tauris, 2018).

[22] Edward Lemon and Helene Thibault, "Counter-extremism, Power, and Authoritarian Governance in Tajikistan," *Central Asian Survey* 37, no. 1 (2018): 137.

Rahmon adopted Russian-inspired discourse about terrorism to instill fear of independent Islam.

Government attacks on the IRPT went well beyond electoral violations. The government barred Nuri from being both a spiritual leader and head of the party, and subsequently barred the IRPT from having a mosque on its party property. The state practiced both de jure and de facto discrimination against women wearing the hijab, which it associated with the IRPT or other forms of "political" or "foreign" Islam. Schoolgirls were frequently denied diplomas because they wore the hijab,[23] and by 2007 the Ministry of Education was expelling students for wearing the hijab. Some young women challenged the ban in court, but all lost.[24] Police rounded up men and forcibly shaved their beards.[25] New mosques in villages or towns required 3,500 membership signatures for approval, a number that often exceeded the population of a village.[26] Large Friday mosques had to demonstrate they had fifteen thousand members.[27] Mosques were banned in mountainous regions that the state perceived as "Wahhabist." Hence, access to *juma namaz* became far more difficult. In 2005, the state barred women from attending mosque, a move that undercut much of the audience for widely popular Islamic scholars such as Turajonzoda and his brother. In 2007, security services began raiding and closing mosques and religious centers. The adoption of a new law on religion, passed in January 2009, was the most significant step in the Rahmon government's general repression of religious freedom. The law revived Brezhnev-era policies of religious control, intimidation, and oppression. Only state-registered Hanafi Islam remained legal. Salafism, a puritanical religious trend growing since the 1990s due to the influence of Arab-educated Tajiks, fell prey to a government ban. Tablighi Jamaat, a South Asian–based revival movement, was also banned, even though it too had stayed out of politics. Independent imams and religious teachers, and literature not produced under state control, were considered "unregistered" and "illegal." The state shuttered many more unauthorized *madrasa*s, used new exams to dismiss "undesirable" Islamic teachers,[28] and banned minors from any religious education or mosque attendance. The state assumed control over the content of all official Islam; preaching from the Qur'an was lawful only in large central, urban mosques. State imams and religious literature promoted Rahmon and pro-regime propaganda about the virtues of a secular state, especially during elections. Such propaganda

23 Igor Rotar, "New Moves against Muslims in the North," *Forum 18 News*, March 7, 2006.

24 "Tajikistan: Muslims and Protestants are the Latest Targets," *Forum 18 News*, June 12, 2009.

25 Mushfiq Bayram, "Tajikistan: My Police Shave Me," *Forum 18 News*, May 6, 2015.

26 Interview with Rajab Mirzo, journalist and activist, Dushanbe, Tajikistan, October 2004.

27 Interview with Dr. Saodat Olimova, Sharq Center, Dushanbe, Tajikistan, October 2004.

28 Mavzouna Abdulloyeva, "10% of Vetted Teachers at the Tajik Islamic University Dismissed," *Asia-Plus*, July, 1, 2015, https://www.asiaplustj.info/en/news/tajikistan/society/20150701/10-percent-vetted-teachers-tajik-islamic-university-dismissed.

also attacked the IRPT. Anything but state-run Hanafi Islam became criminal. The regime's strategy was eerily reminiscent of the USSR's policy of legalizing and co-opting "good" Islam while controlling and oppressing alternative practices and any semblance of independent worship. The "War on Terror" became the regime's trope for cracking down on religious activity.[29] Further, the government once again restricted the hajj to prevent citizens from making contacts in the Muslim holy land.

By 2012, the U.S. Commission on International Religious Freedom (USCIRF) had listed Tajikistan as a "country of particular concern" due to the escalating violations of religious freedom.[30] IRPT Deputy Chairman Mahmadali Hayit compared the repression of Islam under the Rahmon regime to early Soviet-era repression: "Under Soviet power, the Red Terror continued for a very long time, and today it's here again, for [the past] twenty years."[31]

Such religious oppression returned in the context of widespread Islamic revival among a younger, post-Soviet generation who did not share Soviet norms of separating religion and state, keeping religion in the private sphere, and accepting political quietism. The sizable post-Soviet generation—50 percent of the population was under twenty-five in 2020—was less influenced by Soviet norms and had little memory of the war. Some did not share the IRPT leadership's caution in resorting to violence. High youth unemployment and dependency on migrant labor (estimated at 1 million to 1.5 million annually in the 2000s) had created a demographic group that both attended mosque outside Tajikistan and got online, where a plethora of Islamist messages was spreading.

Old and New Islamist Ideologies and Entrepreneurs

As in the 1980s, Islamist religious entrepreneurs seeking justice were instrumental in mobilizing in the postwar period. This time, in large part due to a weaker state and borders, associational space still existed and multiple types of religious entrepreneurs entered the political scene.

Most notably, the IRPT leadership, especially a younger cohort among them, reemerged after a period of decline at the end of the war and gradually redefined itself as advocates of Muslim rights and democracy. Their agenda was moderate in comparison to new entrepreneurs who emerged. The latter included both

29 Tim Epkenhans, "Regulating Religion in Post-Soviet Central Asia: Some Remarks on Religious Association Law and 'Official' Islamic Institutions in Tajikistan," *Security and Human Rights* no. 1 (2009): 94–99.

30 U.S. Commission on International Religious Freedom, Tajikistan chapter, 2012, https://www.uscirf.gov/annual-reports.

31 Interview with Mahmadali Hayit, deputy chairman, IRPT, Dushanbe, Tajikistan, November 2013.

those who had broken away from the IRPT and MIRT when they accepted the 1997 accord and also foreign activists. One such group, which would achieve more success in Uzbekistan and Kyrgyzstan, was Hizb ut-Tahrir al-Islami. HTI activists were sponsored from abroad—the Arab world and HTI's transnational organization in Europe. They promoted a radical antisystemic idea—establishing a caliphate—by using revolutionary but nonviolent methods. HTI's ideas were mostly derived from its regional bases in Uzbekistan and its Palestinian founders. The IMU and JA, by contrast, were armed radicals. They sought an Islamic state through militant jihad. Their ideas and methods were influenced during the 2000s by the Taliban and al-Qaeda in Afghanistan.

Turajonzoda, no longer *qozikalon*, split with the IRPT after the opposition returned to Tajikistan, as did other Sufi leaders; consequently, the MIRT dissolved. Turajonzoda advocated a public role for Islam but generally cautioned against a direct role in parties and political competition. While they would remain outside Islamist movements in this period, their ideas, sacred authority, and networks significantly influenced the dynamics of this period.

The Outcome: Second-Wave Islamism

The IRPT's Second-Wave Mobilization

The most notable second-wave Islamist actor was again the IRPT, which declined, then steadily revived, until it was ultimately banned.

Postwar Decline and Peaceful Mobilization under Authoritarianism

Despite finally becoming legal, the IRPT went into a period of postwar decline after returning to Tajikistan. The government media monopoly relentlessly blamed the Islamists for the war.[32] Many became suspicious of religion's role in politics. Young women in one focus group said, "During the war, the Islamic party used religion for their own interests."[33] In another focus group, young men commented, "Different powers used religion for fulfilling their own goals. They discredited religion."[34] Zukhra, a student from an IRPT stronghold, confessed, "I am afraid that they will again bring calamity."[35] Such concerns were not isolated.

Other problems, however, resulted from internal divisions within the overarching Islamist movement. First, some more radically inclined Islamists had refused the peace terms and remained in Afghanistan. Some transformed

32 Interview with informal mullah, Kulob, Tajikistan, August 2006.
33 TAJ-FG#9, Qurghonteppa, 2009. See the Appendix for details.
34 TAJ-FG#7, Khujand, 2009.
35 TAJ-FG#9, Qurghonteppa, 2009.

themselves into, or later joined, the IMU, and others would form JA. Some retained their militias and attempted to live in the Tavildara region and Qarotegin Valley outside of government control. More IRPT defectors would join HTI.[36] Turajonzoda, as noted, briefly served as deputy premier, during which time he split with the Islamic party. Turajonzoda later withdrew from any overt political role to focus on Islamizing society. The core IRPT leadership, however, remained intact, but conflicts and debates about the party's direction nevertheless emerged. In August 2006, Mullah Nuri, their spiritual leader, passed away from cancer. Muhammadsharif Himmatzoda, another leading political and religious figure, died a few years later. Muhiddin Kabiri, the new party chairman, had joined the movement only during the peace negotiations. He was an Orientalist by training, not a religious scholar. Likewise, his deputy chairman, Hayit, was not a religious scholar but a journalist and nationalist before joining the IRPT in 1989. They sought to transform the IRPT organization from an underground movement to a competitive, democratic political party.[37] At first, it was not clear whether they had the unqualified support of many old-guard Islamists.

Government oppression would help reinvigorate the party and shape its new agenda and strategy. In violation of the peace accord, elections never proved to be fair. Rahmon's electoral manipulation, using media control and intimidation and vilification of IRPT candidates, all but guaranteed electoral losses; the IRPT won only two seats in each of the parliamentary elections held in 2000, 2005, and 2010. Like Islamist parties in the Middle East, the IRPT seemed to accept that it would not win.[38]

With its electoral agenda stalled, the party focused on social change and longer-term goals. It engaged in ideational outreach and adaptation of its message to varied social bases. As in the past, the party redoubled its message of religious repression to its traditional rural base in the central and southern regions, with moderate success.[39] The party also extended its base by establishing an organizational presence through fifty-eight regional offices by 2006, although local governments made it difficult to campaign through formal channels.[40] Further, it used students, mosques, and *mahallas* to network. The party emphasized organization, training, the publication of newspapers and journals, and the creation and regular updating of its social media to reach youth. It recruited a new base among educated women by emphasizing, as one publication stated, "equality of rights and freedoms for all women," especially through education

36 Interviews with Muhiddin Kabiri, chairman of the IRPT (since 2006), Dushanbe, Tajikistan, March 2002 and July 2005.

37 Interview with Kabiri, July 2005; Kabiri, "Uchastie Partii Islamskogo," 53–54.

38 Brown, *Winning Is Not an Option*.

39 Interview with Kabiri, 2012.

40 Interview with Kabiri, 2012; interview with NGO representatives, Dushanbe, Tajikistan, July 2006.

and job opportunities that, as Kabiri emphasized to me, extended "beyond the cotton fields, cleaning, and being waitresses" (common Soviet-era employment for women).[41] But as in the 1980s, the IRPT was cautious about pushing too far; it avoided using protest, and concentrated efforts on spreading the *da'wat*, the missionary work of calling society to Islam, together with their political message about corruption and unjust government.

The party did not call for Islamic law but still emphasized societal, not state, Islamization—calling society to Islam—as a long-term strategy for building its base and more moral and just government. Although little was possible through parliament, the IRPT's core activities in the 2000s involved legal defense of Muslim rights.[42] Himmatzoda resigned from parliament to protest the 2009 law on religion, which reinstated harsh, Soviet-era restrictions.[43] The party defended the right to wear the hijab in all places and men's right to a beard in observance of *shariat*. It condemned the eviction of youth from schools and universities for Islamic dress.[44] Party activists became vocal critics of government restrictions on religious education as well. Kabiri argued, "[T]he teaching of Islamic knowledge is a necessity, because the majority among us are Muslims and every self-aware Muslim has to know the principal foundations of his religion."[45] The party emphasized rights and choice in Islamic norms, including the hijab and Islamic study, not mandatory *shariat*.

Kabiri lambasted other government interference in religion as well, such as the regulation banning the call to prayer, mosque closures, and the ban on women attending mosque. He vocally opposed the government's return to Brezhnev-era state control over the appointment of imams and the Council of Ulama.[46]

Yet, party leaders accepted that achieving justice through elections and laws was a long-term process and so focused on re-Islamization of society first. Its social media propaganda—through Facebook postings and Twitter messages—emphasized Tajikistan's connection with the Islamic world. Party events, for example, included a Forum for the Defense of Muhammad (Peace Be Upon Him). Revealing the party's purist Islamic values, IRPT leaders removed their own newspaper editor for printing photographs of women without headscarves. But in contrast to its 1970s Islamist emphasis on cleansing idolatry, the IRPT now

41 "The Program of the IRPT, 2010," obtained from journalist, Dushanbe, Tajikistan, August 2014.

42 Interview with Mahmadali Hayit, IRPT activist, deputy head, Dushanbe, Tajikistan, August 2006.

43 U.S. Commission on International Religious Freedom, Tajikistan chapter, 2012.

44 Interview with Hikmatullo Sayfullozoda, Dushanbe, Tajikistan, August 2004.

45 Cited in Tim Epkenhans, "The Islamic Revival Party of Tajikistan: Episodes of Islamic Activism, Postconflict Accommodation, and Political Marginalization," *Central Asian Affairs*, no. 2 (2015): 344.

46 Muhiddin Kabiri, "Vozmozhnosti i predely integratsii islamskikh organizatsii v ebroaziatskoe prostranstve," in *O sovmestimosti politicheskogo Islama i bezopasnosti v prostranstve OBSE*, ed. Zaifert and Kraikemaier (Dushanbe: "Sharki Ozod," 2003), 271–72; Kabiri, "Islamskii radikalizm: faktory vozniknoveniia," 122–29.

exhibited theological flexibility, continuing to adapt to the local Muslim context, which overwhelmingly rejected purism and radicalism.

The party positioned itself as defender of traditional Tajik Islam. Kabiri directly attacked the government's growing co-optation of Islam under the guise of promoting state Hanafism. He firmly rooted the party in the Islamic social and political ideas of Abu Hanifa, the founder of the Hanafi school of Islamic law. Challenging Rahmon, he asked, "Why are we afraid to say that the majority of us are Sunni Muslims of the Hanafi school of law and that everyone who respects the Hanafi school . . . should struggle to comply in his behavior, speech, and religious thought with the Hanafi school of law to the extent possible?"[47] Kabiri also condemned "foreign" Islamic movements.[48] Turajonzoda and Kabiri informally supported each other's actions and statements against HTI. The IRPT organized seminars against extremism, while the former *qozikalon* used mosques, Sufi networks, and online methods to do so.

The IRPT's Evolving Ideology

Despite Rahmon's steady return to authoritarianism throughout the postwar period, the IRPT committed itself to parliamentary democracy and nonviolence. In choosing this path, IRPT leaders turned away from Iran's model of a republic, and observed the models of Islamist parties in Turkey, Egypt, and Tunisia. Initially, Turkey's Justice and Development Party (AKP) was attractive to IRPT leaders. Having departed from the overt Islamist ideology of its predecessors, the AKP had won power through democratic elections and gradually advanced Islamic rights in the name of "conservative democracy,"[49] at least before President Recep Tayyip Erdoğan's authoritarian turn after 2009. Kabiri consequently came to oppose the AKP's model. IRPT leaders also closely observed the Muslim Brotherhood's Freedom and Justice Party (FJP) as it came to power during the 2011 Arab Spring but was subsequently crushed in a military coup.[50] The FJP's fate indicated to many Tajiks that they should not push an Islamist agenda too far, and that a secular democratic state would best defend their religious and other freedoms.[51] The Tunisian model was also of interest. Rachid Ghannouchi, leader of Tunisia's Ennahda, had rejected that party's early goal of establishing an Islamic state. In 2011, Ennahda espoused the compatibility of Islam and democracy. Once Tunisia's authoritarian regime fell, Ennahda competed electorally, won a plurality, cooperated with secular parties to govern, and supported

47 Quoted in Epkenhans, "The Islamic Revival Party of Tajikistan," 343.

48 Interview with Nuri; interviews with Kabiri, January 2003, July 2005, and November 2012.

49 Tuğal, *Passive Revolution*; Vali Nasr, "The Rise of 'Muslim Democracy,'" *Journal of Democracy* 16, no. 2 (2005): 13–27.

50 Interviews with group of IRPT leaders, Dushanbe, Tajikistan, August 2005.

51 Interviews with Kabiri, November 2012 and December 2022.

the adoption of a "civil"—secular—democratic constitution.[52] Kabiri also cited Indonesia and Malaysia as positive examples of protecting the religious freedom of Muslims and religious minorities.[53]

Both the IRPT's discourse and its behavior similarly reflected a commitment to democratic participation and rejection of an Islamic state. In 2005, Kabiri stated:

> We know that it is impossible to set up an Islamic state or republic in Tajikistan in the foreseeable future. Tajikistan is a member of the OSCE. We also have a seventy-year history of . . . existence within the USSR. At the same time our pre–Bolshevik Revolution past shows that Tajikistan has its own traditions and a specific form of governing. . . . Our ultimate goal is to create a free, democratic, and secular state. I personally came to the conclusion that religious values can only be practiced in a democratic society and can only be observed in a society where the supremacy of law is in place.[54]

While he was not unopposed within either the party or society, Kabiri was proposing a "new model" for the Muslim world: "Tajikistan's own model" for Islam "within the democratic, secular state."[55] The IRPT's 2003 and 2010 party programs, in contrast to its prewar program, defined Islam as a quintessential part of Tajik national identity rather than as the basis of law or the political system.[56] Postwar IRPT leaders continued to promote local Islamic interpretations and "national Islam." Party ideologist Hikmatullo Sayfullozoda argued, "Much of what is national is Islamic. . . . [C]arrying out our national traditions without carrying out Islamic ones is not possible."[57] The 2003 charter still expressed a clear commitment to "Islamic values" and "the resurrection of the culture and spirituality of the citizens of Tajikistan based on the supreme Islamic and national values."[58] By contrast, the 2010 program barely mentioned

[52] Kasper Netterstrom, "The Islamists' Compromise in Tunisia," *Journal of Democracy* 26, no. 4 (2015): 13. Ennahda's democratic participation in parliamentary governance continued for a decade, until the July 25, 2021, military-backed coup.

[53] Interview with Muhiddin Kabiri, IRPT Chairman, virtual, December 2022.

[54] "Party Leader Denies Aim to Create Islamic State in Tajikistan," *Tojikiston*, Dushanbe, June 30, 2005, text in *BBC Monitoring*, August 8, 2005.

[55] Interview with Kabiri, 2022.

[56] Tim Epkenhans, "Muslims Without Learning, Clergy Without Faith: Institutions of Islamic Learning in the Republic of Tajikistan," in *Islamic Education in the Soviet Union and Its Successor States*, ed. Michael Kemper, Raoul Motika, and Stefan Reichmuth (London: Routledge, 2009), 337.

[57] Hikmatullo Sayfullozoda, "A Modern, National Understanding of Relations between the Secular State and Islam," in *From Confidence-Building towards Co-operative Co-existence: The Tajik Experiment of Islamic-Secular Dialogue*, ed. Jean-Nicholas Bitter, Frédérique Guérin, Delia Rahmonova-Schwarz, and Arne C. Seifert (Baden-Baden: Nomos Verlagsgesellschaft 2005), 159–77, 219.

[58] Quoted in Epkenhans, "The Islamic Revival Party of Tajikistan," 342.

Islam. It only emphasized, symbolically, that Tajiks have an "Islamic school of culture and civilization."[59] Both revised programs were a far cry from before the war; they removed the party's original statements about *shariat* and "Allah's sovereignty." The only exception was support for Islamic banking in place of both failed socialism and "immoral capitalism."[60]

Furthermore, instead of *shariat*, justice became the party's central theme. The 2010 IRPT program began, "The Tajik nation has always been in search of a *just* political and people's system. . . . [I]t is the constant struggle to achieve this justice that has always put our nation to the test."[61] Deputy Chairman Hayit emphasized that "Muslimness is the foundation of the *justice* of the Tajik nation. . . . The Tajik nation is well-known for its national and religious values, customs and traditions."[62] The program stressed "national unity" rather than Islam, and also emphasized opposition to "clannism," corruption, and abuse of power;[63] these were critical issues given that one family controlled most of the state and its wealth.

Human rights and democracy took center stage. Kabiri wrote that "radical slogans" were associated with the civil war, but because "the IRPT failed to fulfill the idea of a sacred society to its hundreds of thousands of refugees and fighters waiting for their fate to change . . . slogans concerning the establishment of an Islamic republic . . . were excluded from the lexicon of leaders and officials of the IRPT after the peace process and the beginning of its official activities. . . . The IRPT, which [formerly] had favored the establishment of a theocratic state in Tajikistan, has set in its program the goal of forming 'a humane, democratic and legal society.' "[64] He admitted, however, that "[i]t is true that the leadership of the IRPT has not yet declared that its members do not intend to create an Islamic state"[65] because to do so would be internally controversial. Despite intra-party debate, in its 2010 program the party's commitment to democracy as "the rule of law," "balance of power between the branches of government," and "transparency and free elections" was unambiguous.[66]

Democracy, however, remained a controversial issue within the party and among its supporters. The 2010 program also enshrined the more conservative IRPT view that "if democracy is understood in the sense of allowing immoral

59 IRPT Program 2010.
60 IRPT Program 2010.
61 IRPT Program 2010, my italics.
62 Interview with Hayit, 2006, my italics.
63 IRPT Program, 2010.
64 Muhiddin Kabiri, "Tadjikistan: Analyse comparative du Parti de la renaissance islamique et du Hizb al-Tahrir al-islami," *Cahiers d'Asie centrale*, no. 15 (2007): 27. See also Muhiddin Kabiri, "The Hermeneutics of the Dialogue to Achieve a Secular-Islamic Compromise in Tajikistan," in *From Confidence-Building towards Co-operative Co-existence*, ed. Bitter et al., 199–213.
65 Kabiri, "Tadjikistan," 27.
66 IRPT Program 2010.

and inhuman phenomena in society, and cultural instability, we declare our opposition to such a misconception. We claim that has nothing to do with democracy and human rights."[67] Many party leaders viewed true democracy as Muslim or Islamic democracy. Yet, Kabiri simultaneously emphasized the need for a *Muslim democratic* party—a party based on values, along the lines of Christian democratic parties of Europe. According to Kabiri, the IRPT retained an "Islamic ideology."[68] The IRPT pointedly opposed "Western democracy," what they described as the full separation of church and state and secularization of the public square. Islam, argued Kabiri, should play a wide role in society, politics, and the state, so long as the party rejected an Islamic state or caliphate.[69]

Despite accepting the secular constitution during the 1997 peace accord, the IRPT consistently opposed the very principle of a secular state, enshrined in Articles 1 and 100. Kabiri argued that "secularism" had become equivalent to "anti-religious"; the "secular state . . . reflected the legacy of Soviet thinking and atheism, merely substituting secular for atheist."[70] While the IRPT accepted the secular state initially as a step away from the "anti-religious slogans and understandings in society," Kabiri argued, "[t]he majority of the Tajik population are believers, so religion must play a role in addressing contemporary problems with government and society."[71] Himmatzoda even more directly rejected Western secularism: "The sources of Islamic thought bear witness to the fact that 'religion and politics are mutually connected, fulfill each other, and it's not possible to divide them.' Religion is important to an equal degree, for the purification of the soul, spirituality, and the fulfillment of individual piety, and for peace in society. The stronger the authority of religion and its influence on the people's convictions, the cleaner, more honest, more noble and correct, will be politicians and society in general."[72] He emphasized the interconnectedness of Islam and politics throughout history and opposed "secular democracy" being imposed on Muslim countries.[73] The party linked its discourse about the state's "human rights violations"[74] and the ills of secularism to its support of certain

67 IRPT Program 2010.

68 Interview with Kabiri, 2012.

69 Interview with Kabiri, 2003; interview with Kabiri, 2012.

70 Muhiddin Kabiri, "HT and the Islamic Revival Party of Tajikistan," in *The Challenge of Hizb ut-Tahrir: Deciphering and Combating Radical Islamist Ideology*, ed. Zeyno Baran (Washington, D.C.: Nixon Center, 2004), 75–81.

71 Kabiri, "Vozmozhnosti i predely integratsii islamskikh organizatsii v evroaziatskoe prostranstve," 278.

72 Muhammadsharif Himmatzoda, "Faktory provedeniia religioznogo ekstremizma i mery po ego predotvrashcheniiu: iavliaetsia li islam ekstremistskoi religiei?" in *Postroenie Doveriia Mezhdu Islamistami i Sekuliaristami–Tadzhikskii Eksperiment*," ed. Jan-Nikolai Bitter and Vol'fgang Tsel'ner (Dushanbe: "Devashtich," 2004), 301–2.

73 Muhammadsharif Himmatzoda, "Vopros o svetskoi sushchnosti gosudarstva," in *O sovmestimosti politicheskogo Islama i bezopasnosti v prostranstve OBSE*, ed. A. K. Zaifert (Dushanbe: "Sharki Ozod," 2003), 89–99.

74 Interview with Hayit, 2013.

shariat-based laws, such as legalizing polygyny. Hayit argued that polygyny was legal throughout the Muslim world.[75] Others claimed polygyny would solve socioeconomic problems for unmarried women.[76] Indeed, polygyny was becoming widespread and socially accepted.[77] Party conservatives used these issues to push Islamization of society.

Despite its shift away from some Islamist goals of the past, the IRPT's religious identity still clearly distinguished it from secular democratic parties. Its Islamic core was evident in its congresses, its leaders' interviews and speeches, and its publications, which promoted Islamic values. Its journal *Najot* remained devoted to religious, cultural, and political issues. As noted, the IRPT's actions at all levels were overwhelmingly focused on defending religious rights and religion's role in the public sphere and state. The party's Twitter account, aimed at young supporters, promoted religious issues—Islamic values, obedience to the Islamic "canon," reading the Qur'an, opposition to the hijab ban, and freedom of religion—together with secular concerns such as a free media, pluralism, the rights of migrants, and democracy.[78] Although accepting democracy, the IRPT rejected secularism.

The IRPT's Revival in the Run-up to 2015

Despite the uneven playing field, the IRPT's membership grew during the 2000s. In 1999, following the war, it claimed about 20,000, and that number remained steady through 2005.[79] In 2009, the IRPT reported 32,200 registered members.[80] By late 2014, various sources estimated membership to be about 40,000 to 50,000.[81] Party sympathizers were more numerous; mullahs in many regions continued to lend sacred authority to the IRPT.[82] Although small, it boasted about ten to twenty times greater support than any other democratic party in Tajikistan. One study found that from 2013 to 2015, the IRPT's Facebook page received more than double the "likes" of President Rahmon's party, and far more

[75] Interview with Hayit, 2006.

[76] Interview with Sayfullozoda.

[77] Michele Commercio, "A Woman without a Man Is a Kazan without a Lid," in *Tajikistan on the Move: Statebuilding and Societal Transformations*, ed. Marlene Laurelle (Lanham, MD: Rowman & Littlefield Publishing Group, 2018), 171–94.

[78] Nahzat.tj, http://twitter.com/nahzat_tj (now defunct). From April 2012 through September 2014, the IRPT posted 1,561 tweets.

[79] Bruce Pannier, "Tajikistan: Lone Islamic Party Pursues Dual Path to Challenge Incumbent," *Radio Free Europe/Radio Liberty*, May 19, 2006, http://www.rferl.org/articleprintview/1068519.html.

[80] Kabiri interview with *Radio Free Europe/Radio Liberty*, September 15, 2009.

[81] www.Nahzat.org; *Asia Plus*, April 3, 2015 (link now defunct); Oleg Salimov, "Tajikistan's Islamic Revival Party Struggles to Survive," June 24, 2015, http://www.cacianalyst.org/publications/field-reports/item/13241-tajikistans-islamic-resistance-party-struggles-to-survive.html; Abdulfattoh Shafiev, "A New Move in Digital Wars in Central Asia: The Tajik Islamic Party under 'Digital Porn' Attack," CERIA Brief No. 4, Central Asia Program, November 2014.

[82] Interview with OSCE expert on parties, Dushanbe, Tajikistan, June 2007.

than any other opposition party.[83] Thousands viewed YouTube videos posted by the IRPT, which portrayed the party responding to national problems, such as flooding, and as the founder of peace, supporter of national unity, and ally of the Democratic Party's 2013 presidential candidate, Oynihol Bobonazarova. Another video showed the ruins of an IRPT office, attacked in the 2015 campaign. The number of online followers was low; video hits ranged from a few dozen to about twenty thousand. The government monitored or blocked opposition sites. Assessing precise support is difficult. Nonetheless, the party was both the most popular and the most active political opposition in Tajikistan for nearly twenty-five years, so much so that in 2015 the regime decided to eliminate it.

The 2015 Election: A Death Knell for the IRPT and Moderate Political Islam?

By 2014, the regime was eliminating associational space and consolidating authoritarianism under the Rahmon family and the security forces. The IRPT's campaign for the March 1, 2015, parliamentary election centered on its demand for democratic reforms. Its slogan was a slap at the corrupt presidential cabal: "Tajikistan belongs to all, not one family."[84]

Party activists had for at least five years, since the IRPT's strong showing in 2010, been facing sustained pressure, intimidation, office raids, arrests, and beatings.[85] In 2010, security services had closed the party's central mosque. Party leader Shamsuddin Shamsuddinov had been arrested on charges of organizing a criminal group and practicing polygyny. In the run-up to the 2015 election, a government propaganda and smear campaign used the dirtiest tactics yet, including posting multiple internet videos and news broadcasts that claimed IRPT members and independent mullahs were either licentious or pedophiles. More activists were physically beaten or had mysterious "accidents." Several regional party offices were boarded up and members were intimidated into resigning. Some candidates were deregistered or denied registration.

The IRPT turned to social media—Facebook, Twitter, Odnoklassniki, Telegram, Instagram, and YouTube—and its website pages to reach the populace. But most Tajiks had limited internet access, blockages were frequent, and surveillance of those visiting its sites increased. The 2015 election commission results declared that the IRPT had won only 1.6 percent of the vote—not a single seat in parliament. Yet independent exit polls suggested anywhere from 28 to

[83] Abdulfattoh Shafiev, "The 2015 Tajik Elections Online," CERIA Brief No. 25, Central Asia Program, May 2015.
[84] Shafiev, "The 2015 Tajik Elections."
[85] Interview with Faizrahmonov.

57 percent of respondents had voted for the IRPT, despite the uneven playing field.[86]

By June, the party's situation was dire. Kabiri went into self-imposed exile due to rumors of pending charges. The party's regional offices were shuttered in June, and members were forced to make online announcements expressing support for President Rahmon.[87] In July, the Ministry of Justice dissolved the party, alleging that forty-five party members had committed crimes, ranging from illegally storing firearms, extremism, and inciting inter-religious hatred, to corruption and lethal assault. Prosecutions began.

That summer, the Interior Ministry launched a crackdown on all alleged "extremists"—the IRPT, ISIS, the Egyptian Muslim Brotherhood, HTI, the Caucasus Emirate, and the Salafi movement.[88] The Ministry's arrests escalated into outright persecution. After pinning a coup attempt on the IRPT with no evidence, the state incarcerated or detained hundreds to thousands more.[89] Party leaders sent an urgent appeal to the UN. They accused Tajik authorities of violating the Constitution and peace accord and threatening Tajikistan's security.[90]

In late 2015, the Supreme Court branded the IRPT an "extremist" and "terrorist organization" and outlawed it. Husayni, shortly before his arrest, told IRPT members, "This is the determination of Allah, that one group of people should be imprisoned in order for the truth to triumph and for the people to attain freedom."[91] From 2017 to 2019, the courts handed down *in absentia* sentences on multiple party leaders, including Kabiri, who was charged with terrorism. Husayni and Hayit, Kabiri's two deputies, both received life sentences. Hayit was tortured and denied critical medical care. Dozens of other party members received lengthy sentences of up to twenty-five years. For the crime of teaching Islam to other prison inmates, the IRPT's eighty-year-old Mullah Roziq was locked in the prison's notorious isolation wing, where torture is reportedly more common.[92] Five other IRPT prisoners are known to have died.[93] Some detainees

86 "Election Exit Polls," *Asia-Plus*, http://news.tj/ru/node/204041/resultsTojnew (link now defunct); Shofiev, "The 2015 Elections." The independent Tajik Asia-Plus news agency, once a source of reliable news, came under attack from the Tajik government in 2018, and has been blocked since November of that year.

87 "IRP's Office in Sarband Handed Over to Local State-Run Weekly," *Asia-Plus*, June 30, 2015, http://dev.news.tj/en/news/irp-s-office-sarband-handed-over-local-state-run-weekly (link now defunct).

88 "Tajikistan Blacklists Dozens of Islamist Websites, One Opposition Website," *Interfax-Religion*, July 6, 2015, http://www.interfax-religion.com/?act=news&div=12163.

89 Communication with human rights NGO and U.S. government official, Washington, D.C., October 2019.

90 "IRP Launches Appeal to Guarantors of the Inter-Tajik Peace Agreement," *Asia-Plus*, July 2, 2015, https://asiaplustj.info/en/news/tajikistan/politics/20150702/irp-launches-appeal-guarantors-inter-tajik-peace-agreement.

91 HNIT, "A Lion Captured by Jackals," n.d., https://en.nahzat.org/a-lion-captured-by-jackals/.

92 Interview with Faizrahmonov.

93 Interview with Kabiri, 2022.

were released, but only after paying bribes, making confessions, or renouncing the IRPT on video. Other IRPT prisoners were subjected to electrical shocks, having their nails ripped off or clothes removed, regular beatings, and threats to rape their wives. One party activist explained, "The torture . . . cannot be imagined by a human being."[94] Relatives of party members were threatened; sons and fathers were arrested. Some activists disappeared. Arrests have continued, information on those sentenced has not been released by the regime, and many of the arrested were still waiting in pre-trial detention years later. According to Kabiri, a precise count of their members has been impossible to ascertain.[95]

Many were charged merely with affiliation with the party or, alternatively, with the banned Salafi movement. Mere sympathizers were detained and charged as well. One man received nine and a half years for simply "liking" and sharing IRPT social media. One man was reportedly tortured for complaining about President Rahmon's picture hanging in a mosque. According to the IRPT, in one case prisoners begged, "Have mercy in the name of Allah," but a police officer working for the prosecutor general responded, "I [curse word] your Allah. Where is your Allah? You destroyed the world by saying Allah."[96] Even IRPT defense lawyers received lengthy prison sentences; lawyer Buzurgmehr Yorov was sentenced to twenty-three years in solitary confinement—horrifying psychological torture.[97] Soviet-era tactics characterized the regime's trumped-up charges, show trials, draconian sentences, and flagrant use of torture.[98]

The prosecution of the Islamic party had most likely been planned for several years.[99] It enabled Rahmon to consolidate his power, unopposed, in a constitutional referendum on May 22, 2016, which effectively compelled Tajik citizens to make him president for life. He claimed a landslide victory of 94.5 percent. Yet his unchecked power engendered no mercy. In 2022, over two hundred IRPT activists remained imprisoned, many with sentences of over twenty years. Over three thousand party members had gone into exile in Europe.[100] Thousands

[94] Interview with Faizrahmonov, 2022; Farangis Najibullah, "Tajikistan's Banned Islamic Party Claims Former Members Hit by Wave of Arrests," *Radio Free Europe/Radio Liberty*, June 18, 2018, https://www.rferl.org/a/tajikistan-s-banned-islamic-irpt-party--members-hit-by-wave-arrests/29283941.html.

[95] Interview with Kabiri, 2022; Payom.net (IRPT news site), "There Was No Bread," 2020 (no date), https://payom.net/en/there-was-no-bread-ex-prisoner-who-was-poisoned-with-bread-exposed-the-truth-video/.

[96] Payom.net, "There Was No Bread."

[97] Payom.net, "New pressure on Buzurgmehr Yorov: It is forbidden to talk to him," 2020 (no date), https://payom.net/en/new-pressure-on-buzurgmehr-yorov-it-is-forbidden-to-talk-to-him/.

[98] Human Rights Watch, "Tajikistan: Verdicts of Opposition Activists a Travesty of Justice," June 7, 2016, https://www.hrw.org/news/2016/06/07/tajikistan-verdicts-opposition-activists-travesty-justice.

[99] "Answer of the Prosecutor's Office to the IRPT: 'Protocol 32-20 has no Grounds,'" April 13, 2012, *Radio Ozodi*, https://rus.ozodi.org/a/24547674.html.

[100] Muhiddin Kabiri, presentation to Central Asia Program, George Washington University, virtual, September 16, 2020.

more had fled to Russia, but hundreds of them were later extradited to Tajikistan. Party Chairman Kabiri continued to resist the regime from abroad, through social media, international contacts, and the creation of the National Alliance of Tajikistan, a new coalition of all Tajikistan's democratic opposition groups, secular and religious. However, seven years after full-scale crackdown began, the regime showed no prospect of liberalizing. Despite the IRPT's commitment to peaceful change, Rahmon's unmitigated repression had spurred some Tajik youth to wonder whether violent resistance might be their only option.[101]

Radical Second-Wave Mobilization

The Islamist field grew beyond the IRPT in this period. Even as the IRPT became mainstream or even "post-Islamist" in some ways,[102] several radical Islamist movements emerged—the result of religious repression coupled with new political theologies and entrepreneurs who entered through more porous borders. They often attracted those angry at or fleeing Rahmon and disillusioned with the IRPT. All were opposed to democracy, whether the virtual democracy offered by Rahmon or substantive democracy, as it functioned in the West. All were antisystemic; they pursued a pure Islamic state or caliphate. HTI professed nonviolence, but the others were militant.

Hizb ut-Tahrir al-Islami

HTI was a transnational Islamist movement that first spread to Central Asia in the mid-1990s. The Palestinian judge and activist Shaykh Taqiuddin an-Nabhani had founded HTI in 1952–53 as a response to the repression of Muslims in the Middle East. He had experienced the collapse of the Ottoman caliphate and he lived in Palestine during the creation of Israel in 1948. The Palestinians' plight shaped his worldview.[103] Religious repression and exclusion, centered on the "sacred space" of Palestine, politicized him.[104] At the time, al-Ikhwan al-Muslimin (the Muslim Brotherhood) was propagating a new political theology and ideology in Egypt: the idea of an Islamic order in which religion and state are intertwined and "Islam is the solution."[105] The Muslim Brotherhood's ideology profoundly influenced an-Nabhani's thinking.

The quintessential religious entrepreneur, Shaykh an-Nabhani established HTI, which defined itself as "a political party whose ideology is Islam. . . . [HTI]

[101] Interview with Kabiri, 2022.
[102] Bayat, *Post-Islamism.*
[103] Mohamed Nawab Bin Mohamed Osman, "Hizb ut-Tahrir," in *Routledge Handbook of Political Islam*, ed. Shahram Akbarzaheh (New York: Routledge, 2011), 89–104.
[104] Hassner, *War on Sacred Grounds.*
[105] Richard Mitchell, *Society of the Muslim Brothers* (Oxford: Oxford University Press, 1993); Rosefsky Wickham, *The Muslim Brotherhood*, 23–24.

calls all people to Islam." Its program declared that Islam is political, *shariat* must be law, and the caliphate must be restored. The shaykh created HTI with the goal of liberating Muslims worldwide through the establishment of the caliphate and the reestablishment of Islamic law.[106] Restoring the caliphate would bring back God's divine order and "resume the Islamic way of life by establishing an Islamic State that executes the systems of Islam and carries its call to the world."[107] Core to its platform was its nonviolent strategy.

HTI came to Tajikistan from Uzbekistan's Ferghana Valley in the late 1990s and early 2000s. Given its primarily ethnic Uzbek activists, HTI recruited largely among the ethnic Uzbek minority of northern Tajikistan. It faced difficulty spreading to heavily ethnic Tajik regions, where the IRPT already had a strong base. Yet, disaffection with IRPT led some to shift to HTI, which was uncorrupted by the war. HTI focused on underground networking and disseminating its propaganda. In Tajikistan, as elsewhere, HTI preached the necessity of reestablishing the caliphate through cadre formation, Islamization, and the peaceful takeover of the state.

On the one hand, HTI faced the wrath of the state that it threatened. On the other hand, HTI triggered the enmity of traditional Tajik Islamic leaders like Turajonzoda, and entrenched Tajik Islamists such as Nuri and Kabiri. Moreover, its ideas were too radical for the Tajik mainstream Muslim populations. Its numbers topped at about five thousand adherents, many of whom were jailed. The organization did not last inside Tajikistan.

The UTO, IMU, and JA

From 2009 onward, a more pernicious form of Islamism emerged, one that is not only radical in its goals but also militant and jihadist. A series of attacks and clashes between the government and militants, including at least one suicide bombing, took place inside Tajikistan. The perpetrators included ex-UTO Islamists, the Islamic Movement of Uzbekistan (a radical jihadist group originating in Uzbekistan and fighting with the UTO in the Tajik Civil War), and JA, a newer jihadist network linked to the IMU.

As in the first wave, religious oppression and the influence of new ideas of Islamist justice meant that these groups, like the IRPT, drew on Islam to articulate

[106] See: Hizb ut-Tahrir, "Definition," posted at: http://www.hizb-ut-tahrir.org/index.php/EN/def. All by T. an-Nabhani: *Thinking* (London: Khilafah Publishers, 1973); *Economic System of Islam* (London: Khalifah Publications, 1997); *The Islamic State* (London: Khilafah Publications, 1998); *The Structuring of a Party* (London: Khilafah Publications, 2001); *The Concepts of Hizb ut-Tahrir* (London: Khilafah Publications, 2002). All are available on HTI's website: http://www.hizb-ut-tahrir.org/. Hizb ut-Tahrir, *Dangerous Concepts to Attack Islam and Consolidate Western Culture* (London: Khilafah Publications, 1997).

[107] Material posted on one of HTI's internet sites, http://www.hizb-ut-tahrir.org/index.php/EN/def, last accessed August 20, 2018.

their grievances and shape their vision of politics. Furthermore, weak government control over opposition territory and the relatively porous border with Afghanistan allowed ex-UTO militants, and sometimes their Uzbek or Afghan counterparts, to enter Tajikistan. The internet provided associational space for diffusing jihadist propaganda and the political theology of transnational Salafi jihadism, which had been escalating since 9/11 both in adjacent Afghanistan and globally.

Ex-UTO militant Mullah Abdullo, born Abdullo Rahimov, was the leader of one such group of second-wave Islamist militants. Abdullo had led Islamist fighters during the Tajik Civil War, in alliance with the IRPT, but considered the peace accord a betrayal of Islamist goals. He subsequently became affiliated with the emergent IMU, a group of Uzbek nationals who had fought with the UTO during the war. They too had rejected the peace agreement. Abdullo reportedly returned to Tajikistan with the IMU in 1999 but refused to submit to government control. The IMU and its UTO allies remained in hiding in Rasht, the MIRT/UTO base in the 1990s, and the same region where Basmachi opposition to Soviet power had continued into the 1930s.

The IRPT claims that Nuri urged the militants to leave Tajikistan. Some reports suggest that Abdullo was acting for al-Qaeda in Afghanistan and Pakistan and that his followers, estimated at about a hundred, were sheltered by the Taliban in the early to mid-2000s.[108] By 2009, the Afghan National Army and the International Security Assistance Force were taking more territory in Afghanistan, and the Pakistani government was driving Taliban and foreign fighters from its tribal areas. Abdullo reportedly again returned to Tajikistan in spring of 2009 with a larger force, about three hundred militants, probably recruited from others fleeing Rahmon's regime. In July, the Islamist militants clashed with Tajik government forces in Tavildara and the Rasht Valley, still strongholds of the Islamist opposition.[109]

The following August, in 2010, Abdullo's militants supported a jailbreak of several dozen men convicted on terrorism charges. Some detainees were IMU members; the leader of the jailbreak reportedly had been extradited to Tajikistan from Guantanamo Bay, Cuba, where he had been incarcerated following his capture with IMU fighters attacking U.S. forces in Afghanistan.[110] Ultimately, government soldiers entered the Rasht Valley to track down the escapees and clean

[108] International Crisis Group, "Tajikistan: The Changing Insurgent Threats," *Europe & Central Asia Report*, no. 205, May 24, 2011, https://www.crisisgroup.org/europe-central-asia/central-asia/tajikistan/tajikistan-changing-insurgent-threats.

[109] "Large Armed Group Attacks Tajik Police Post," *Radio Free Europe/Radio Liberty*, July 9, 2009, http://www.rferl.org/content/Gunmen_Attack_Police_Post_In_Tajikistan/1772955.html.

[110] Michael Schwirtz, "Tajikistan Says Militants Were Behind Attack on Troops," *New York Times*, September 20, 2010.

up the militants, but on September 25, 2010, Abdullo's fighters ambushed the convoy, killing at least twenty-five.[111]

The IMU claimed responsibility for the attack in a video restating its religious motivation: "The attack was in retaliation for Tajik government policies, such as closing mosques, jailing Muslims, and banning Islamic forms of dress."[112] The events revealed the interconnectedness of militant Tajik Islamists and the IMU. According to Kabiri, "It's no secret that . . . IMU fighters fought on the side of the UTO in the war against the governing powers" and that they split with the IRPT over whether to continue fighting in 1997.[113] Kabiri, explaining the split, emphasized that the IRPT had a "national goal," whereas the IMU had a transnational one. We shall see in Chapter 9 that over time, the IMU's endgame of achieving an Islamic state would shift from its once Central Asian, national focus to a transnational focus. Although limited in its strikes, it threatened Tajikistan's precarious stability. Tajik security forces finally killed Abdullo with many of his fighters in April 2011.[114] The government has since claimed to have tried fifty-three alleged IMU members inside Tajikistan.

A more mysterious organization calling itself Jamoati Ansorulloh in Tajikistan appeared openly with the nation's first recorded suicide bombing, which took place in Khujand on September 3, 2010. The car bombing killed three police officers of the organized crime squad and injured twenty-eight; JA claimed responsibility on the jihadist site, Kavkazcenter.com.[115] JA had its roots in factions that had left the UTO when Nuri signed the peace accord. Amriddin Tabarov, a former commander in the Islamist opposition during the 1990s and known as Mullah Amriddin, had joined the IMU after the peace accord that he, like IMU leaders, rejected. Amriddin later split to found JA, an ethnic-Tajik jihadist movement. Its numbers were initially estimated to be no more than a few hundred,[116] of whom several dozen were captured and tried for JA membership in 2015.[117] Mullah Amriddin himself was killed in Afghanistan in July 2015. Absent its

[111] Lola Olimova, "Killing of Veteran Militant Seen as al-Qaeda Emissary Has Eased But Not Removed Security Threat in Central Asian State, Analysts Say," *Institute for War & Peace Reporting*, May 5, 2011, https://iwpr.net/global-voices/few-tears-shed-tajik-bin-laden.

[112] Bill Roggio, "25 Tajik Soldiers Killed in Islamist Ambush," *FDD's Long War Journal*, September 19, 2010, https://www.longwarjournal.org/archives/2010/09/40_tajik_soldiers_ki.php; Lola Olimova and Nargis Hamrabaeva, "Tajik Authorities Struggle to Quell Militants," *Institute for War & Peace Reporting*, October 4, 2010, https://iwpr.net/global-voices/tajik-authorities-struggle-quell-militants.

[113] Kabiri, "Islamskii radikalizm," 127.

[114] International Crisis Group, "Tajikistan," 13.

[115] Tilav Rasulzoda and Parvina Khamidova, "New Militant Force in Tajikistan," *Institute for War & Peace Reporting*, October 21, 2010.

[116] Interview with expert, U.S. State Department, Washington, D.C., August 2018.

[117] Mavlouda Rafiyeva, "Tajikistan Tries 23 Alleged Members of Jamoati Ansorulloh," *Asia-Plus*, May 6, 2015, http://news.tj/en/news/tajikistan-tries-23-alleged-members-jamaat-ansarullah (link now defunct).

charismatic leader, JA faced schisms; some members left to join ISIS and others went to fight with al-Qaeda in Syria. Dozens more were jailed over the next few years. Amriddin's two sons were captured and sentenced in 2019 to sixteen and twenty-three years in Tajik prisons.[118]

Nonetheless, JA established itself as the primary militant Islamist movement operating inside Tajikistan and on its Afghan border since the end of the war. Following the 2010 attack on Khujand, JA was involved in some joint attacks with the IMU in Afghanistan and on Tajik border posts. It reportedly possessed arms supplied by the Taliban. Its websites, Irshod.com and Irshod.net, and its Telegram channel suggested an active virtual life as well. The sites featured romantic images and video clips of militants marching through the Pamir Mountains of Tajikistan or Afghanistan. Several videos called for jihad against "infidels,"[119] and one reportedly declared their intention to "use arms to make the norms of the Qur'an in Tajikistan higher than democratic and international regulations."[120] In sharp contrast to the IRPT, JA posted jihadist tracts and jihadi poetry. Many postings were in both Russian and Tajik; some even discussed Russian governmental abuses or jihad in the Middle East. However, the websites were not regularly accessible, and by 2015 were defunct.

Islamist Demobilization

Over nearly two decades, using threats of prosecution, imprisonment, the closure of mosques, rigged elections, and media control, the government had eliminated every possibility for open Islamist organization, much less mobilization. The IRPT, some Salafis, Tablighi Jamaat, and many ordinary Muslims, as well as any democratic opposition, had been marginalized, destroyed, imprisoned, or forced into exile. Under such conditions, it was hardly surprising that little potential for Islamism, especially of a nonviolent and mainstream form, existed inside Tajikistan. Instead, as we shall see in Chapter 14, some Tajiks would gravitate to ISIS and other transnational groups offering "justice" and a "dream of life in a 'real Islamic state.' "[121]

[118] "Two Sons of Banned Islamic Group's Late Founder Jailed in Tajikistan," *Radio Free Europe/Radio Liberty*, October 23, 2019, https://www.rferl.org/a/two-sons-of-banned-islamic-group-s-late-founder-jailed-in-tajikistan/30232121.html.

[119] "IS Militants Asked Baghdadi for Permission to Fight Infidels in Tajikistan," *Radio Free Europe/Radio Liberty*, January 5, 2015, https://www.rferl.org/a/isis-tajikistan-syria-jihad-fighters-repatriated/26777220.html.

[120] "Jamoati Ansorulloh Declared 'Outside Law' in Tajikistan," *Avesta.tj* (link now defunct), May 3, 2012.

[121] Anna Dyner, Arkadiusz Legiec, and Kacper Rekawek, "Ready to Go: ISIS and Its Presumed Expansion into Central Asia," Policy Paper, *The Polish Institute of International Affairs* 19, no. 121 (June 2015): 2–16.

Explaining Relative Levels of Mass Mobilization

In this final section, I turn to the theoretical question of relative Islamist success. Despite the repression it faced, before 2015 the IRPT was not only the most successful Islamist organization in Central Asia, but also the most successful opposition party in Tajikistan, as measured by its durability and membership.

High Mobilization: The IRPT/MIRT

Membership estimates of Islamist organizations are imprecise, particularly given the authoritarian conditions in which they operate and the need for secrecy. Yet the IRPT notably grew from a handful of young, underground mullahs in the 1970s to a peak of about fifty thousand registered members by 2015.[122] While other parties dissipated during the war, the IRPT was able to form its own militia of up to fifteen thousand, adding more forces from the MIRT. A comparison with other militant Islamist groups offers some perspective on their strength. In the Algerian Civil War, which began in late December 1991, the Islamist force was about thirty thousand fighters, only two times larger than the IRPT's, though its population was almost six times larger than Tajikistan's. Chechen Islamist militants in the Russian-Chechen wars (1994–2009) comparably numbered 1,600 to 1,800, with a population of 1.2 million.[123] Despite small numbers of Islamist fighters in each case, the violence and death toll in each conflict was high; estimates are contested but hover around 100,000 for Tajikistan, Algeria, and Chechnya (in the 1990s war).

The IRPT, unlike purely militant groups, had a broad public following. In 1991–93, in the protests before the Tajik Civil War broke out, the IRPT and its allies drew tens of thousands onto the Square to protest. The IRPT/MIRT led about 200,000 followers (not registered party members) during their exile from 1993 to 1997. After a postwar slide, the IRPT rebounded. While it never won more than two seats in manipulated parliamentary elections, journalists and local experts believe the party actually polled at least 10 to 15 percent of the vote in 2000 and 2005. The IRPT and some analysts believe that it won about 40 percent in 2010.[124] Independent exit polls in 2015, as well as local observers, suggest that if results had been fairly reported, the party would have won close to

[122] Henry Dunant Centre for Humanitarian Dialogue, "Humanitarian Engagement with Armed Groups," 2003, https://www.hdcentre.org/wp-content/uploads/2016/07/Humanitarian-engagement-with-armed-groups-The-Central-Asian-Islamic-opposition-movements-February-2003.pdf.

[123] Joss Meakins, "The Other Side of the COIN: The Russians in Chechnya," *Small Wars Journal*, January 13, 2017.

[124] Interview with Faizrahmonov; Ilya Lozovsky, "The Death of Tajikistan's Islamic Renaissance," OCCRP, June 5, 2018, https://www.occrp.org/en/moneybymarriage/the-death-of-tajikistans-islamic-renaissance.

30 percent of the vote.[125] By comparison, secular-democratic opposition parties throughout this time ranged from three thousand to ten thousand members. While some Islamist parties in the Middle East polled higher than the IRPT, in Tunisia's Arab Spring in 2011, Ennahda won 41 percent, and in 2019 took 24 percent. But those elections were free and competitive. Under conditions closer to the IRPT's in Tajikistan, the Egyptian Muslim Brotherhood–affiliated candidates won 20 percent in the regime-dominated 2005 parliamentary election in Egypt.

Here, I examine two factors that help explain the IRPT's relatively high mobilization and durability despite ongoing state oppression, intimidation, and media control, and the absence of any genuine electoral opportunity: sacred authority and transcommunal networks. The next chapter will address the third factor, ideational adaptation.

Sacred Authority

Sacred authority was crucial to the IRPT/MIRT's mobilizational success. Despite the damage to Sufi brotherhoods and Islamic learning, the sacred authority of both the *ulama* and Sufi lineages had remained central to Tajik society, identity, and social networks.[126] Much of Tajikistan could be "divided into spheres of influence of various Sufi families."[127] Sufi leaders were guardians of sacred places. Sufi master-student networks were important for the transmission of religious knowledge. As Tajik historian Muzaffar Olimov has written, "Islamic intellectuals, hereditary *eshons*, *xo'jas*, or *pirs* . . . are the bearers, keepers and communicators of traditions, spiritual values, ordinance, rites and knowledge. . . . [They] exercise their influence through organization and participation in rites which represent the main organizing force in personal, public, and to a great extent, political life of Muslim society."[128] Many Sufi *hujras* traced their heritage to pre-Soviet communities of the Bukharan Emirate. Masters had fled from Bukhara to Dushanbe, Rasht, or Kulob in the 1920s.[129] Many Tajiks revered Sufi shaykhs for preserving Islamic traditions during Soviet repression.[130] In both the

[125] "Агар якшанбеи наздик интихобот баргузор шавад, ба кадом ҳизб райъ медиҳед?," *Tojnews*, January 30, 2015, http://tojnews.org/tj/node/2470/results (link now defunct).

[126] Interview with Dr. Abullo Hakim Rahnamo, aide to Haji Akbar Turajonzoda, Dushanbe, Tajikistan, August 2005; Ismail Abdulvahhobzoda Kahhori, "Qadiriya v Tadzhikistane i ee vklad v sozdanie doveriia naroda," in *Postroenie Doveriia Mezhdu Islamistami i Sekuliaristami–Tadzhikskii Eksperiment*, ed. Jan-Nikolai Bitter and Vol'fgang Tsel'ner (Dushanbe: "Devashtich," 2004), 286; Turajonzoda, "Religion: The Pillar of Society"; interview with Turajonzoda; Dudoignon, "From Revival to Mutation," 62–64; Tim Epkenhans, "Defining Normative Islam: Some Remarks on Contemporary Islamic Thought in Tajikistan—Haji Akbar Turajonzoda's Sharia and Society," *Central Asian Survey* 30 (2011): 81–96.

[127] Rahnamo, "Islam in Tajikistan," 14.

[128] Olimov, "Islam in Contemporary Tajikistan," 162.

[129] Bushkov and Mikul'skiy, *Anatomiia grazhdanskoi voini*, 98–99.

[130] Interview with Rahnamo.

late Soviet era and after 1991, Tajik parents commonly sent a son to study with a Sufi teacher.[131] Sufi masters typically taught a hundred students or more.

Participants in multiple focus groups mentioned having great respect for *eshons* and rural mullahs, who were not state appointees. They professed admiration for Haji Turajonzoda, Eshon Nuriddinjon, Ustoz Sayid Nuri, and Domla Hindustoniy—referring to each by their honorific title. One young man, a teacher from a village outside Dushanbe, said, "The mullah is the most respected person in our *qishloq*."[132]

The IRPT's sacred authority was mainly associated with the personae of its key leaders, Ustoz Nuri and Mullah Himmatzoda. Both were spiritual leaders, scholars of many years of religious study; in fact, they arguably had far better religious training in underground *hujras* than was possible in SADUM's two institutions. Hayit described Nuri this way: "Ustoz Sayid Abdullohi Nuri was a unique person. [He was] a cultured and religious person. He achieved great things."[133] They called him *ustoz* because of his revered teaching. Although born into a very religious family, Nuri did not come from a sacred lineage. Nonetheless, his followers gave him the honorific title *sayid* (a descendant of the Prophet Muhammad). Anthropologist Sophie Roche has found that Nuri's followers and former combatants treated his life story as a "master narrative" of "Muslim suffering under the Soviet era."[134] A former high-ranking Communist Party official of the Gharm region recalled meeting Nuri "many times" while working there. Although not a supporter, he said, "I have a lot of respect for him. He was strong, quiet, soft-spoken. He never engaged in swearing and name-calling. He held the IRPT together."[135] Nuri's charisma clearly even impressed his opponents. If Nuri was the spiritual figurehead, Himmatzoda was arguably even more well-known for his Islamic scholarship and political ideals, recalled Kabiri.[136] The spiritual charisma of both men enhanced the IRPT's sacred authority.

Qozikalon Akbar Turajonzoda provided the second base of sacred authority for the Islamist movement. His family lineage went back generations in the Qadiriyya line, one of the two most widespread orders in pre-Soviet Tajikistan. His father was a renowned shaykh.[137] Akbar and his brother Eshon Nuriddinjon were among the most respected spiritual authorities in Tajikistan.[138] Multiple

[131] Epkenhans, *Origins of the Civil War in Tajikistan*, 184.

[132] TAJ-FG#19, Dushanbe, 2013. See the Appendix for detailed information on the focus groups.

[133] Interview with Hayit, 2013.

[134] Sophie Roche, *Domesticating Youth: Youth Bulges and Their Socio-political Implications in Tajikistan* (New York: Berghahn, 2014), 101, 89.

[135] Interview with Tajik former Communist Party official in Gharm, Dushanbe, Tajikistan, August 2005.

[136] Interview with Kabiri, 2012.

[137] Rahnamo, "Islam in Tajikistan," 14.

[138] TAJ-FG#15, Dushanbe, 2013; TAJ-FG#16, Dushanbe, 2013; TAJ-FG#3, Dushanbe, 2009; TAJ-FG#19, Dushanbe, 2013.

Image 6.2 Haji Akbar Turajonzoda, deputy head of the MIRT
Source: rferl.org, https://www.rferl.org/a/tajikistan-slander-clerics-trial/24932321.html.

Sufi *eshons* were active in leading the antiregime hunger strike and protests in 1991–92. They too lent sacred authority to the Islamist opposition movement.

Turajonzoda had commanded further authority and resources due to his state appointment in 1989 as the *qozikalon* of Tajikistan and official leader of mainstream Hanafi Tajiks. He was the first ethnic Tajik to achieve a high rank in the Uzbek-dominated Soviet religious hierarchy. Turajonzoda had achieved national prominence as a spiritual leader during the February 1990 protests, when he served as a mediator between protesters and the regime.[139] The IRPT credited him with preventing greater bloodshed.[140] In contrast to other state imams, Turajonzoda had fostered the building and legalization of some two thousand to three thousand *mahalla*s and village mosques between 1989 and 1992, and 130 large, central Friday mosques.[141] He had pressed the Tajik Supreme Soviet for greater freedoms for Muslims. He had arranged gifts of the Qur'an from Saudi Arabia, the opening of Iranian and Saudi bookstores, and even a $500,000 grant from the Islamic Bank for an Islamic institute in Dushanbe.[142]

When Turajonzoda united with Nuri against the regime in 1992, their religious networks enhanced their ability to mobilize a broader Islamist movement. When Turajonzoda and his family joined the IRPT in exile in Afghanistan, many of their followers went as well. When they returned to Tajikistan, they

139 Nourzhanov and Bleuer, *Tajikistan*, 186.
140 Interview with Hayit, 2013.
141 Interview with Rahnamo; Bushkov and Mikul'skii, *Anatomiia grazhdanskoi voini*, 97.
142 Interview with Haji Akbar Turajonzoda.

were also met with great fanfare.[143] The family proceeded to build large mosque communities, where over ten thousand attended Friday prayers. During the 2000s, Akbar's brother, Eshon Nuriddinjon, became one of the most respected figures in Tajikistan; his mosque overflowed with thousands of men and women who came from throughout the country to hear his sermons.[144] The Turajon brothers developed a major online presence as well. Eshon Nuriddinjon's YouTube postings drew 70,000 to 175,000 viewers, and Haji Akbar's postings some 15,000 to 36,000 viewers within a few years.[145] When asked which spiritual leaders they most respected, focus groups immediately identified Turajonzoda. Muzaffar, a university student, observed, "In the end of the 1980s, despite the atheist ideology, Haji Akbar Turajonzoda took on the leadership of the republic Qoziyot and with his authority united Muslims. He was an active player in the world's attempt to stop the conflict in Tajikistan."[146]

As noted earlier, Haji Turajonzoda's postwar estrangement from party leaders in the 2000s depleted the IRPT's base. The deaths of Nuri a few years later, in 2006, and then of Himmatzoda in 2010, were powerful blows to the IRPT organization, which depended heavily on sacred authority. Videos posted on YouTube showed many thousands attending traditional *janaza* in mourning. Tens of thousands more viewed the events online,[147] where other videos glorified their lives of spiritual and political leadership.[148]

When Kabiri assumed the IRPT chairmanship in 2006, he had initially struggled to maintain authority.[149] More conservative party members had hoped the mantle would pass to Nuri's son, to carry on the lineage and spiritual legacy of his father. Moreover, Kabiri's training and experience could not have been more distinct from their own. Yet, Nuri himself had chosen Kabiri.[150]

[143] "Hayoti Eshoni Turajon 4," July 10, 1998, www.isloh.page.tl, accessed September 2010 (link now defunct).

[144] Roche, *Domesticating Youth*, 2014.

[145] For example, see Haji Akbar Turajonzoda's presentation to the presidential journal *Elite*, February 25, 2010, 35,935 views; "Eshoni Nuriddinjon, Hukmi Benamoz," 93,644 views; "Eshoni Nuriddin 2014 New!!!," 142,540 views; "Eshoni Nuriiynon 2012 Posuhi Pursishxo 001," 175,799 views.

[146] Muzaffar, participant, TAJ-FG#19, Dushanbe, 2013.

[147] "Ustod Said Abdullohi Nuri," part 2, YouTube, May 1, 2008, https://www.youtube.com/watch?v=1uUgg_DSoJU.

[148] "Ustod janozai Nuri02," YouTube, September 27, 2009, https://www.youtube.com/watch?v=yOBfRCml6Nc; "Ruhat shod bod, ustod Himmatzoda," YouTube, March 20, 2010, https://www.youtube.com/watch?v=5CZRZk4SZRQ (24,652 viewers); "Ustod Nuri onoza3," YouTube, September 28, 2009, https://www.youtube.com/watch?v=bgMTuwIOAMk (129,755 viewers by July 2015).

[149] It is notable that Eshon Turajonzoda's many YouTube videos often have thirty thousand to sixty thousand viewers. His online presence gives the appearance that he maintains widespread spiritual leadership in Tajikistan, as do reports that over ten thousand attend his mosque and that of his brother, Eshon Nuriddin. Multiple YouTube videos of Eshon Nuriddin registered even more viewers, from 60,000 to 176,000 (last accessed July 4, 2015).

[150] Interview with Mirzo, 2013.

Image 6.3 Funeral ceremony for Muhammadsharif Himmatzoda, the IRPT's first political leader

Source: rferl.org, https://www.rferl.org/a/Spiritual_Leader_Of_Tajikistans_Islamic_Party_Dies/1986626.html.

Image 6.4 Leaders of the IRPT (Kabiri is second from the left.)

Source: Facebook screenshot

Kabiri came from the Fayzobod district, also in the Rasht Valley, the heart of much of the Islamic opposition; his family was devout and he had studied Islam with Himmatzoda during the late Soviet years. However, he presented a very different face for the party. He was younger (born in 1965), clean-shaven, and appeared Western in dress and comportment. Well-educated in the secular Soviet system in the 1980s, he had completed a university education in the Faculty of Oriental Studies, rather than extensive Islamic learning in the *hujra*s of Tajikistan. He was not among the Nahzat's members or the IRPT's founders in the 1980s. Kabiri left

Image 6.5 Muhiddin Kabiri's Outreach on Twitter (Kabiri is in the center.)
Source: Twitter screenshot

for Yemen to study at Sana'a University in 1992, as the war began, an indication of his growing interest in Islamic issues. He then pursued a graduate degree at the Diplomatic Academy in Moscow, from 1993 through 1996. Yet, Kabiri shared the IRPT's view of Soviet and post-Soviet repression, and he became involved in the Tajik peace process in 1997. He gained prominence and Nuri's favor by serving on the National Reconciliation Commission from 1997 through 2000. While becoming active in the postwar party, Kabiri continued his graduate education in Russia, receiving his doctorate in Political Studies at the Diplomatic Academy, in 2005. Fluent in his native Tajik, as well as Russian, Persian, and Arabic, Kabiri also learned English; he thereby developed a good relationship with the West, in addition to fostering the party's longer-standing ties with Iran.[151]

To build Kabiri's sacred authority, party postings and videos skillfully linked him to their revered Ustod Nuri and Ustod Himmatzoda. Multiple images showed them seated together in discussion and prayer. Meanwhile, the IRPT posted extensive information for the younger generation on Facebook, Twitter, Najot.tj, and Nahzat.org to reinforce Kabiri's image as a modern Islamic world leader, so as to target a new urban and educated base.

Focus groups in the 2010s revealed that Kabiri had made progress in rebuilding the IRPT's spiritual authority in the years after Nuri's death. For example, numerous younger respondents agreed with the statement, "The IRPT, in the face of its leader M. Kabiri, reflects its great authority not only in the republic and region, but in the Islamic world."[152] Kabiri raised the national and international standing of the IRPT. For many, the IRPT had a national presence, was the strongest and most widely recognized opposition party, was still known for its spiritual leadership, and had the sympathy or support of many,

[151] Interviews with Kabiri; interview with Mirzo, 2013; interview with Hayit, 2013; interview with Faizrahmonov, 2022.

[152] TAJ-FG#19, Dushanbe, 2013.

including the younger generation and the educated. When asked about religious authority within Tajikistan, multiple participants in each of five groups, including women, identified Kabiri as one of the most respected religious and political authorities in the country. For example, one graduate student, Behru, praised him this way: "Kabiri speaks beautifully and talks about religion, and its essence. . . . He has a good command of religious and secular knowledge."[153] Even beyond the IRPT's original base and strongholds, some participants listed IRPT leaders Kabiri, Nuri, and Himmatzoda as respected spiritual authorities for Tajiks. Komronjon, a university student in Khujand, observed, "The IRPT under Muhiddin Kabiri's leadership has great authority not only in the republic but in the Islamic world. Such parties are necessary." He emphatically added, "It [the IRPT] follows the laws."[154] Some respondents mentioned Kabiri alongside the Ayatollah Khomeini as the religious authorities whom they respected most.[155] In the 2000s, such individuals turned to Kabiri and the IRPT as a trusted opposition, much as the earlier generation had trusted in Nuri and Turajonzoda.

Networks

The IRPT had emerged from underground *hujra* networks, which enabled it to draw in activists across several regions. *Hujra* students in the Tajik republic also communicated with those in the Uzbek republic, as well as in Tatarstan and the North Caucasus. They exchanged ideas, information, and strategies for mobilization.[156]

Mobilization went beyond the *hujras*; it drew on family, kinship, and localism, all trusted personalistic networks built over decades.[157] In Tajikistan, sacred authority was inextricably connected to personal, educational, and kinship networks between teachers, students, Sufi leaders, and family lineages.

Networks of forced migrants were particularly important to IRPT mobilization. Identities and informal ties had been reinforced by the trauma of migrations in the 1930s to the 1950s and had created the potential for a potent mix of regional, religious, and economic resentment against the Soviet state.[158] Nuri, as the son of forced migrants, drew support from the migrant communities in Qurghonteppa as well as from his homeland in Gharm and Qarategin. These

[153] TAJ-FG#15, Dushanbe, 2013.

[154] TAJ-FG#17, Khujand, 2013.

[155] TAJ-FGs#15–19, Dushanbe and Khujand, 2013.

[156] Interview with Gadoev.

[157] Interview with Usmon; interview with Gadoev; Roy, *The New Central Asia*; Kathleen Collins, "Tajikistan: Bad Peace Agreements and Prolonged Civil Wars," in *The Prevention of Violent Conflict*, ed. Chandra Sriram (Boulder, CO: Lynne Reinner, 2003), 267–306; Collins, *Clan Politics*; Bleuer and Nourzhanov, *Tajikistan*; Saodat Olimova and M. Olimov, "Public Opinion, Democracy, and Authoritarianism in Central Asia," *Central Asia & the Caucasus* 15, no. 2 (2014): 142–60.

[158] Kurbanova, *Perseselenie*; Dudoignon and Qalandar, "They Were All from the Country," 63, 70–78.

connections helped to bus in thousands of demonstrators during the 1991–92 protest cycles.[159]

However, these local and regional identities and networks also played a role in limiting the IRPT's mobilizational power. In Tajikistan's clan-oriented and regionally divided society, the IRPT quickly became associated with "Gharmis," which, like most narrow identity networks, lacked national legitimacy.[160]

Consequently, the IRPT's alliance with Turajonzoda—and access to his Sufi lineage and the Qoziyot—provided critical transcommunal networks for mobilization. As *qozikalon*, Turajonzoda had influence over thousands of new mosques, their mullahs, and their congregations. Focus group participants in Qurghonteppa recalled that the IRPT disseminated religious literature and ideas through such mosques between 1990 and 1992.[161] Born into a prominent Sufi lineage, Turajonzoda had extensive informal networks as well. When he and half a dozen prominent Sufi leaders joined the antiregime demonstrations, support for hunger strikers and protesters increased—symbolically and numerically; the numbers of opposition protesters increased from some 35,000 to 50,000 to 100,000.[162] By contrast, pro-government rallies were estimated to be 10,000 strong.[163]

After the war, Turajonzoda's split with the IRPT was a blow to its ability to mobilize. As we have seen, networks from Gharm and Qurghonteppa remained the core of the party, but they had been disrupted by both the war and the outflow of hundreds of thousands of migrant workers in the 2000s. Kabiri therefore engaged in new transcommunal network building. Kabiri's emphasis on a more modern party structure began to transform the once personalist and religious base of the party, thereby including broader constituencies. By the mid-2000s, the party had an organizational presence in almost every region and subregion, although local governments made it difficult to spread the party's message.[164] Nonetheless, it pursued grassroots organization, training, the publication of newspapers and journals, developing ties with mosques, and the active use of internet and social media. The IRPT formed youth groups to attract the younger generation, including women, in universities and rural areas.[165] It even built networks among Tajik migrant laborers in Russia and Turkey. The result of skillful construction

[159] Interview with Sayfullozoda; interview with Stanley Escudero, former U.S. ambassador to Tajikistan, 2004.

[160] Interview with Rajab Mirzo, Dushanbe, Tajikistan, 2002.

[161] TAJ-FG#10, Qurghonteppe, 2009.

[162] "Further on Continuing Rallies in Dushanbe," *Moscow POSTFACTUM*, April 20, 1992, and "Roundup of 29 April Events," *Moscow POSTFACTUM*, April 30, 1992, *Daily Report. Central Eurasia*, FBIS-SOV-92-085, May 1, 1992.

[163] "Roundup of 29 April Events," *Moscow POSTFACTUM*, April 30, 1992, *Daily Report. Central Eurasia*, FBIS-SOV-92-085, May 1, 1992.

[164] Interview with Kabiri, 2012; interview with Rajab Mirzo, Dushanbe, Tajikistan, July 2005; interview with NGO representatives, Dushanbe, Tajikistan, October 2004.

[165] Interviews with Kabiri, 2005, 2012.

of sacred authority and building transcommunal networks was slow but steady growth until 2015, when the party was banned, if not annihilated.

Low Mobilization: The JA, the IMU, and HTI

The media has made much of the bouts of violence in Tajikistan between 2009 and 2015, but an empirical perspective suggests that support for jihadist violence, in any of these groups, is relatively minimal. Indeed, they are competing among each other for supporters. JA had a few hundred followers at its height. The IMU was mainly an Uzbek force in Afghanistan with a few dozen Tajik followers, although it did coordinate with Mullah Abdullo and JA. HTI very likely had a few thousand adherents reading its leaflets in the north in the early 2000s, but they never mobilized.[166]

Why was the threat of transnational militant jihadism, more specifically Salafi jihadism—as propagated by the IMU and JA—from about 2000 to 2015 so limited? We have seen that opposition movements that can draw on widespread religious authority have an advantage in mobilizing and sustaining a following. Democratic parties, by contrast, had no such authority. Nor did foreign Islamists, such as HTI. Discussed in more depth in Chapter 12, HTI had difficulty making headway in Tajikistan. While HTI did use aggrieved ethnic Uzbek networks in northern Tajikistan to expand, it lacked sacred authority. It claimed to be a religious party but had no religious leader. HTI even faced religious denunciations from Nuri, Kabiri, and Turajonzoda.

Notably, Mullah Abdullo had both narrow regional networks and spiritual credibility in Rasht, where he had been an opposition mullah in the early 1990s. For years, he had also led his militant following in both Tajikistan and Afghanistan. Kavkazcenter.com, a mouthpiece for the Chechen jihad, posted a tribute to the militant leader shortly after his death. The message reportedly came from the "mujahidin of Tajikistan." They mourned Abdullo as a *shahid*:

> We the mujahidin of Tajikistan, seek to speak to the Muslims of Tajikistan about *shahid* (*Insha'allah*) Mullah Abdullo, first of all, we want to call on you so that you our brothers and sisters do not mourn. Our brother, Emir Mullah Abdullo waged Jihad against the enemies of Allah for nineteen years, without stopping. And now Allah has taken him to Himself. We ask Allah to accept him as a *shahid* and to carry him to the Garden of Paradise. So, we want to say to the *kafir* and *munafiq* that they should not rejoice. . . . In our ranks there are still many brothers ready to sacrifice themselves on the Path of Allah, *Insha'allah*.[167]

[166] Discussion of HTI's transnational party and mobilization is found in Chapter 13.

[167] "ТАДЖИКИСТАН: Моджахеды Таджикистана выступили с обращением в связи с Шахадой амира Мулло Абдулло," Kavkaz Center, April 21, 2011, http://www.kavkazcenter.com/russ/content/2011/04/21/80912.shtml.

They sought to motivate jihad by emphasizing state injustice and also the glory and honor of becoming a *shahid* for Allah. The message also revealed that the transnational networks from Chechnya to Afghanistan had likely sustained Abdullo and his associates in the IMU.

By contrast, JA leader Amriddin Tabarov was not a recognized spiritual authority. JA sought sacred legitimacy by posting Salafi jihadist literature and jihad poetry on its websites, which had a very limited following in Tajikistan. Linked to their low sacred authority was their lack of transcommunal networks in the country: JA's followers appeared to be drawn from Rasht. Tabarov had a network in the Nurobod district, through support from a prominent mullah.[168] Yet broader UTO networks were frayed after years of being in Afghanistan. JA had no national appeal. Unlike the IRPT or HTI, JA and the IMU offered a militant jihadist political theology with the aim of establishing a radical Islamic state. They disseminated that theology via the internet—translating propaganda from Arabic sources into Tajik, Russian, and Uzbek—but did not engage in *da'wat* and did not adapt to local Islamic norms. JA disseminated its message almost exclusively via the websites Irshod.com and Irshod.net.

. . . .

We have seen that the conditions leading to the emergence of a second Islamist wave in Tajikistan in many ways paralleled conditions breeding the first wave. The regime was now postcommunist and had a façade of reverence for Hanafi Islam, yet its legislation and practices, especially by 2009, had revived Soviet-era antireligious institutions. The Tajik state responded to its population's growing religiosity with renewed repression of religion. Any associational space that had opened in the postwar era steadily closed. Only de facto space—porous borders, limited state capacity to monitor, and some internet access—allowed a range of religious and political theological ideas, brought by diverse religious entrepreneurs to penetrate its territory and sow the seeds of new Islamist political movements. Foreign and local Islamist ideas promised justice and spurred networking among both new Islamist entrepreneurs and long-present activists. These conditions again sparked Islamist opposition from the IRPT's robust revival to low-level mobilization by HTI, JA, and the IMU.

Over time, the IRPT's platform, rhetoric, and policy proposals became increasingly "Muslim democratic," shifting away from its earlier Islamist goals. Instead of an Islamic political order, they sought justice, religious freedom, an end to corruption, and democratic participation and competition.[169] The IRPT

[168] International Crisis Group, "Tajikistan," 8.

[169] Asef Bayat refers to such a shift in the Middle East as "post-Islamism." Bayat, *Post-Islamism*.

still advocated a society guided by Islamic morals and values, but emphasized that societal Islamization should take place within a democratic context. Not all members agreed with this shift, and even those who did so were not necessarily liberal in their understanding of democracy. Yet, the IRPT repeatedly committed itself to nonviolent means of democratic competition for power, despite Rahmon's reneging on the peace accord, and even after the IRPT was unconstitutionally shuttered by the government in 2015. It was no doubt for this reason—the IRPT's potential for success—that Rahmon finally crushed the party.

The case of the IRPT also underscores the central role of sacred authority and transcommunal networks in mobilization. The IRPT's ideas, adapted over time to focus on Islamic rights and justice, resonated with the majority of the population. The next chapter will use focus groups and interviews with ordinary Tajiks to investigate in more depth how society viewed these and other Islamist ideas.

7
Society and Islamist Ideas in Tajikistan

> No one should interfere with the religion of the people, not even the state.
>
> —Dilbar, university student, Dushanbe, 2009

> Suicide-bombers are terrorists.
>
> —Muhiddin, *mahalla* leader, Fayzobod, 2009

> Religion must be separate from politics. But politics must take into account the *shariat*, as it pertains to the law.
>
> —Parviz, accountant, Khujand, 2009

> Islamic democracy exists in Iran, for example. It's different from other democracies. If people fully understand the meaning of the word [democracy], then they'll see Islamic democracy is better.
>
> —Mirali, labor migrant, Qurghonteppa, 2009

These brief excerpts from lengthy conversations with ordinary Tajiks reveal a plethora of reasons for sympathy with the IRPT's ideas. Dilbar's remark reflects a widely held view, more than a decade after the Tajik Civil War had ended: Tajiks opposed the state's interference, control, and repression of Islam. Muhiddin, a *mahalla* community leader from the Qarotegin Valley, long the heart of the Islamic opposition, favored the strict adoption of *shariat* law but also staunchly opposed suicide bombing and killing innocents through terrorism. From rural Gharm to Dushanbe, most respondents expressed views that opposed Islamist radicalism but simultaneously rejected secular, liberal-democratic governance. Most wanted a more Muslim government, not one built on a Western model, which they characterized as secular. Understanding what type of government Tajiks want demands that we listen to ordinary people.

A core argument of this book is that not all Islamist organizations gain a mass following, much less exhibit durability over time. In Chapter 6, we saw that the IRPT, in contrast to other Tajik Islamist groups, achieved relatively successful mobilization as the result of two strategies: establishing sacred authority and developing local and transcommunal networks, both before and after the war.

Politicizing Islam in Central Asia. Kathleen Collins, Oxford University Press. © Oxford University Press 2023.
DOI: 10.1093/oso/9780197685068.003.0008

This chapter turns to the third strategy that was critical to the IRPT's high mobilization: adapting its ideas so as to resonate with Tajik society, its target base. I demonstrate that the IRPT's mainstream Islamist message, particularly as localized and adapted to Tajik society in the 1990s and 2000s, resonated widely with a populace that favored mainstream interpretations of Islam and its role in politics. Most Tajiks favored defending Islamic rights in private and public spaces, as well as a nationally grounded synthesis of Islam with law and democratic politics.

In this chapter, I briefly recap the core ideas of the range of Islamists in Tajikistan (discussed in Chapter 14). Then I present the words and views about Islam and politics generally held by ordinary Tajiks (focus group participants) and by Tajik communal elites (interviews with those holding influence in Tajik society). I examine their discourse about ideas and issues that the IRPT and other Islamists propagated, from their opinions about national versus puritanical Islamic revival to Islamic education, Islamic dress, an Islamic state or caliphate, and democracy.

Core Ideas Propagated by Islamists in Tajikistan

In the two previous chapters, I examined the ideas and strategies of Islamists in Tajikistan over nearly fifty years. The only movement advocating moderate Islamist ideas in this era was the IRPT, a mainstream Islamist organization in its ideology, goals, and strategies.[1] Despite its puritanical origins in the 1970s among Deobandi and Salafi revivalist thinkers, by the early 1990s the IRPT had adapted to Tajik society's fusion of Hanafi and Sufi practices, in part due to its alliance with Turajonzoda's network. The IRPT had also long embraced Tajik nationalism as deeply intertwined with Islam. By the 1990s, the IRPT was focusing its ideology against communism. The IRPT defended the right to wear the hijab by choice; it did not seek to enforce puritanical dress. Some party leaders still spoke of establishing an Islamic state—albeit only by parliamentary vote and only, *possibly, if the people want it*, after many decades. Kabiri later very explicitly rejected that idea altogether. After the end of the war, the IRPT had categorically rejected violence, and after 9/11 it took a strong stance against terrorism and suicide bombing. Leaders embraced democracy and human rights, but also advocated a Muslim form of democracy that might include some laws by *shariat* (such as marriage law). The party proposed a synthesis of Islam and politics that rejected secularism. It sought state-funded religious education and demanded religious freedom, just government, and an end to authoritarianism.

Far more "radical" Islamist ideas were propagated by other Islamists. Militants (the IMU, JA, and ISIS) propagated ideas justifying violent jihad and martyrdom,

[1] See the introduction for a discussion.

including suicide bombing, and making law according to a rigid interpretation of *shariat* (including the *hudud* penalties, such as amputation for theft and stoning for adultery—penalties which were never part of the traditional Sufi and Hanafi understanding of *shariat*) that had prevailed in Tajikistan. The revolutionary Islamic state or caliphate they envisioned would violently overthrow the existing order. It would expunge practices deemed impure (*shirk* and *bid'ah*), such as *urf-adat* and Soviet influences, and would denounce Jews and Christians as *kuffar* and restrict their rights. HTI's ideas were similarly radical in their goals; also antisystemic, HTI sought to overthrow the existing nation-state and create a total Islamic political order, a caliphate, based on *shariat*. However, HTI rejected radical means or revolutionary violence to achieve those goals.

Profiles of Focus Groups in Tajikistan

Too little research has examined societal reaction to Islamists' ideas and messages, or more generally, what Muslims think about the relationship between Islam and the state, about secularism, democracy, justice, corruption, women's rights, religious freedom, and other salient religious and political issues. Focus groups help us better understand which, if any, Islamist ideas resonated with society. In this section, I draw on findings from nineteen focus groups across five regions; my Tajik research team conducted the groups in two waves, before the IRPT was banned. Groups were divided by gender and representative of different ages and classes (university students, white-collar or blue-collar workers, migrant laborers, and small business owners/traders). Additionally, I draw on insights from fifty interviews with societal elites (mullahs, imams, *mahalla* leaders, and wealthy local businessmen, party activists, journalists, and local government officials well informed on the local religious and political dynamics), also in five regions (see the appendix for full details). The discussion in this chapter presents general trends that emerged in conversations with hundreds of Tajiks. Only pseudonyms were used, as discussed in the Appendix.

Individuals are complex, and their views are sometimes wavering, contradictory, or unclear; unlike surveys, focus groups capture some of this fluidity and nuance. Focus groups do not necessarily produce a single viewpoint, but they do reveal how people think about and debate the ideas and issues posed. Here, I present specific groups representing the range of responses about Islam and its relationship to politics: mainstream/moderate ideas, mixed (mainstream/radical-leaning) ideas, and secular ideas. Profiling these groups as a whole gives a sense of how identity and norms, issues, views, and ideas are often mutually constitutive. No groups expressed primarily radical views, and only a few expressed secular views about governance. Those who were pious and complained of religious repression and injustice typically sought some Islamic influence in the public sphere, parties, and law—issues and ideas central to the IRPT. The discussions revealed no clear correlation between piety and radicalism; even those most strictly observant did not necessarily advocate creating a caliphate, aggressive jihad, or suicide bombing.

Groups Exhibiting Mainstream Views about Islam and Politics

Most respondents, across groups, saw Islam as a core part of their identity. Islam and Tajik nationality were also deeply interconnected, and Tajik national practices and customs, many Sufi in origin, were considered central to being Muslim. They rejected purism. Most also saw a synthesis of Islam and politics as normal and necessary. Governance should integrate and uphold Islam, protect morality, and defend Muslim rights to prayer, dress, education, and practice.

Men, Small Business Owners, Thirty-five to Fifty Years Old, Kulob, 2009

A group of middle-aged men, small tradesmen and entrepreneurs from Kulob,[2] held many views in line with the IRPT's ideas. Islam was also central to their identity, and some of them still remembered Soviet repression and restrictions on the fast and *namaz*. Majid recalled, "In the times of Soviet power we even prayed silently. We prayed so that the KGB did not arrest us. They accused all the mullahs [of being anti-Soviet]." They were angered by President Rahmon's oppression of Islam as well. Pulod demanded Islamic freedom: "Believers must be allowed to believe, to be free." Ergash said, "The government should not restrict Islam, only propagandists." He considered HTI to be mere propagandists, not devout Muslims.

The men all fasted and prayed and urged others to perform *namaz* and give *sadaqa* (alms). They themselves had become more religious since 1991, and hoped others would as well. Alihon said, "People are 100 percent more religious. My neighbors even built two mosques by *hashar* [voluntary, communal labor] in our *qishloq*." They noted that the mosques and mullahs offered assistance to people in the community. They sent their children to study with mullahs and wanted religious education to be offered in state schools. They all planned to make the hajj. Like many pious Muslims, they were not radical, and in fact they were tolerant of non-Muslims, saying only "It's their choice" or "Let Allah judge them." Their views on women were mixed. Respondents were angry about harassment of women who wore the hijab, but most claimed they did not believe the hijab should be mandatory; like the IRPT, they insisted it should be

2 TAJ-FG#14.

"a woman's choice." They simultaneously approved of legalizing polygyny for religious and economic reasons, but also advocated for women's right to attain higher education and to work in any profession.[3]

On the one hand, most of them blamed Islamists—specifically "Wahhabis" and "extremists"—for the Tajik Civil War, but politically most were sympathetic to the IRPT. Sayfiddin said, "Intelligent youth are members of the Islamic Revival Party of Tajikistan. Maybe not today, but in the future, everyone will rise up and become members of this party." However, Alihon added, "Our fathers and grandfathers were Muslim and didn't need a document to show it. It was in their heart. The party is for the younger generation." Pulod insisted, "All the youth of our Muslim people became members of this party out of their heart and soul. They just don't have a paper showing their membership registration" due to fear of repercussions from the government.

However, one of them, a former IRPT supporter, criticized Nuri's betrayal of Islam in order to sign the peace deal: "[Nuri] agreed to only thirty percent of the government. If he were a real defender of Islam, he would not have sold out our faith and for nothing." He also said, more ambiguously, "It's not possible to implement their [the IRPT's] intentions without force." His words suggested that he had supported continuing the war to achieve the IRPT's initial goals.

The participants' specific views on governance were difficult to elucidate, and they seemed to fear responding. They generally expressed some support for mainstream ideas of political Islam but were mostly concerned with establishing justice, in contrast to Rahmon's regime. As one respondent, Gairat, said, "We need justice in society." Sayhomid clarified that "religion leads to justice." The men approved of a secular court system but were also dismayed at its corruption. Even so, Hayrullo said, "Religious leaders should not get involved in politics. They should only spread moral propaganda about purification." Nonetheless, the men leaned toward a Muslim style of democracy that would respect *shariat* in all things. "Islamic democracy," said Sayhomid, "is better [than Western democracy] because Islam is the essence of democracy." All agreed that the current political system was rife with corruption.

Their views on jihad were mainstream; that is, they rejected radical Islamists' justification of violence to achieve an Islamic state, but they did not consider jihad to be restricted to inner purification. They described jihad as something that was allowed only "when there is a war on your wife and children, as in Iraq, to save them." They adamantly agreed that "setting off a bomb among civilians is a crime." This was the view espoused by the IRPT and widely shared by Central Asian Muslims.

[3] For similar findings on polygyny, see Commercio, "A Woman without a Man."

Alihon summed up their views: "We want peace, justice, and respect for our children, and money in our pocket." Their views were pious and skeptical of liberal democracy, but not radical.

Women, White-Collar, Twenty-five to Thirty-five Years Old, Dushanbe, 2009

A group of university-educated women holding white-collar jobs[4] openly shared their views. Despite their atheist education and secular upbringing in the late Soviet era, these women were also outwardly pious. They wanted their children to study Islam regularly, after school, and independently of government control. Mavdjuda declared, "I think that I should never do anything against religion so as not to shame my parents." The women stridently opposed the influx of Western influence in Tajikistan—which they equated with "drugs" and "discos"—as opposed to more respectable Soviet-era morals and forms of sociability which some of them remembered with a certain nostalgia. Their views on both converts and other religions, particularly Christians and Jews, were remarkably liberal for Tajikistan. "Everyone is free to choose religion," they unanimously agreed. Nigina said, "They are people of the Book." A third agreed: "I respect them because they also accept the prophets."

The women were politically motivated by state religious oppression, such as the state ban on women performing *namaz* in mosques. They claimed that religiosity had grown in the 1990s, but they said that at the time of our conversation (in 2009), few Tajiks were openly practicing due to fear of being persecuted. They sought Islamic education virtually instead, but Mavdjuda claimed that the Tajik government allowed religious television programs to air only during *Eid-al-Adha* (the festival of the sacrifice), whereas in Iran, according to their information, Islam was freely promoted. In Iran, life was better. One young woman declared that "people living in Iran say that there, they don't have to scold their children, [because] religion is stronger." Turkey, she said, was also better: "Religion has its own defined place there, even though Turkey is a secular state." Another participant, Nizoramoh, added, "When the government messes in religious affairs, it's not good, because there is no religious freedom."

These respondents did not respect most of their local mullahs because "ninety-nine percent teach Islam for personal profit," said Huma, whereas "In Iran, they actually teach us Islam . . . not fanatic[ism], but pure Islam. People there teach it from the heart. People there sincerely believe and do not pretend. We have leaders at the top who all perform *namaz* but then they carry on with their bad actions and words. In Iran there is no evil, only kindness to each other." It was not

[4] TAJ-FG#4.

clear if all or some of them had direct experience with Iran, but they idealized it as truly Islamic and good.

The women's religious identity and frustration with religious restrictions influenced their political choices. They did not recognize a division between a private religious sphere and a public secular one. Instead, all agreed that religion and religious leaders should "without a doubt" play a role "in all spheres," from education to law and politics. Mehrangez said, "Our government isn't Muslim because in real Islamic states, like Saudi Arabia and Iran, all the laws are [made] on the basis of the Qur'an." Olufta criticized the Tajik court's sentencing of Wahhabis who, she said, sympathetically, just "clearly live by Muslim laws." Their views were shaped by the corruption of the Tajik government, which they viewed as secular, like the Soviet system. All agreed that a Muslim court system would be better for them, because the Tajik courts were corrupt. They consistently idealized Iran's Islamic republic. Mavdjuda said, "Islamic democracy is better for us because there is less corruption and crime. In Western countries, there is more crime." Everyone agreed that the "Iranian model is better for us. We have the same language and culture." But Elena moaned, "We are a poor copy of Iran!"

While they preferred a more Islamic government, when asked about specific Islamist parties, the women claimed that "only fanatics joined the IRPT" and that HTI followers "only joined for money." Mavdjuda proclaimed, "Both parties proved to be no help to the people. Corruption has developed inside both parties!" They declared that they had no knowledge of secular democratic parties. Iran, to them, embodied the merger of Islam and democracy to which Tajikistan should aspire. How such a system would work was unclear; it would entail laws based on the Qur'an and also tolerance and equal rights for minorities. Overall they seemed to endorse an Islamic party in principle, or better, an Iranian Islamic republic, but they were disillusioned with the IRPT and dismissive of HTI.

Their views on jihad were similarly nuanced. Most understood jihad as militant self-defense: they were supportive of the Afghan and Iraqi "jihads," which they considered justified, because they viewed those wars as self-defense against U.S. invasion. Yet they also decried suicide bombers as deranged, "persons under hypnosis."

Men, Small Business Owners, Twenty-five to Thirty-five Years Old, Qarotegin/Gharm, 2009

A group of young traders and entrepreneurs from Qarotegin[5] articulated extremely negative views about their current government. They viewed the Rahmon regime as failing to uphold morals, control alcohol and prostitution, reduce corruption, and provide work. One young man angrily declared,

[5] TAJ-FG#12.

"Corruption lives in the highest echelons of power and has only strengthened [under President Rahmon]." Another added, "The government can only prevent conflict if it will be honest and just." Others contended that it was "not religion," as the government falsely charged, but rather "corruption" and "unjust elections that cause conflict." No one believed that Rahmon would address these problems.

The men agreed, as Shohmurod said, that Muslims must follow "Muslim ways, praying five times a day, giving *sadaqa*, saying *shahada*, fasting, and making the hajj if possible." Sherali insisted, "All people who recognize Islam follow these rules." Another added, "Islam is necessary in all spheres of life, that is, in the political sphere, just as in the social sphere. It must also play a role in education and in marriage because marriage cannot take place without *nikoh*. That is against *shariat*." According to Vahid, "Without the influence of religion, marriage isn't possible, and in the courts if there are no Islamic rules and principles, if people don't fear and obey Allah everywhere, there will be no justice."

The men carefully considered their own government and, hypothetically, a better government for Tajikistan. Their discourse went as follows:

NEGMATULLO: Although we all criticize Soviet power, there was less corruption under the USSR than now.

FIRUZ: Our state is democratic, secular, and legal. I think, it's not necessary to have an Islamic state.

SHOMUROD: Our state is not Islamic by name, but in reality, it should be Islamic. Nothing should be irreligious in our state. Since we are Muslim, it would be better to be a Muslim state.

ILHOM: In Western democracy there is corruption. In an Islamic democracy, bad things like corruption, bribery, and violence . . . would be punished. Our democracy should not depart from our Eastern core. First of all, it's respect to our elders, and parents.

SHERALI: We need the sort of democracy that they have in Iran.

FIRUZ: Again, I say that the Turkish variant is good, because they both develop the state and also adhere to religion.

SHERALI: The Iranian model is better for all Muslims, because they wear proper clothes for an Islamic state.

ILHOM: The Turkish and Arab models are also good for Muslims.

SAFARALI: [We need] Islamic *shariat*.

UMED: Islamic *shariat* is necessary for all Muslims.

The respondents, who had been teenagers during the protests in 1990–92, remembered the communist regime and the war and openly supported the IRPT. Shohmurod stated, "Those youth who join or follow the Islamic party are those who want to carry out correct, just actions and their good deeds through the party." By contrast, they unequivocally denounced HTI, which they saw as merely using Islam for their own ends. In Kudrat's words: "[HTI] is not connected . . . with any religion!" Ilhom likewise condemned the "Wahhabis" (he used the government's negative term), who in his view had appeared because of the civil war and repression in Tajikistan, as in Chechnya and Uzbekistan. He said, "I oppose them [Wahhabis] because in the end, it's only the innocent peaceful population who die." His characterization assumed Wahhabis were those employing violence, which he opposed. In fact, all the participants agreed that jihad was really "a call to people for kind actions," to "be on the right path with your family and neighbors," and that "in Islam suicide is forbidden and will be judged [as such by Allah]." In sum, their views were generally consistent with mainstream Islamist ideas. But a few of the men were open to the possibility of an Islamic state, following either Iran or Saudi Arabia, at least on the basis of their limited knowledge and experience of such models.

Women, University Students, Twenty to Twenty-four Years Old, Dushanbe, 2013

One group of women university students[6] held views consistent with many of the IRPT's Islamist ideas. They detested atheism, recalling that their parents and grandparents had preserved *Eid-al-Fitr* and *Eid-al-Adha* and other religious values "despite the Soviet atheist state." Sobira's grandmother had taught her the Qur'an when she was seven years old. Tahmina read Islamic books, like those of Husain Voizi Koshifi, about a proper Muslim woman's role. Behru also emphasized reading the Qur'an, and Robiya said it must "begin in the family, with grandparents, and then [continue] in kindergarten."

Marhabo said they had learned from their parents that "some Soviet values were good." Both Islam and the USSR valued "education" and "respect for elders," which had rapidly declined after the Soviet collapse. "But," she said, "we were not free." Tahmina emphasized, "It's not possible to destroy the faith. . . . [T]he older [Soviet] generation still prayed." Things improved after communism ended, but one woman claimed that, "from 2005 onwards, those not following Islam increased from fifty percent to eighty-five percent." They opposed renewed restrictions on religiosity and clearly disagreed with government policies.

Umeda said, "It's good that we have a party like the IRPT, because our society is democratic [even though the state is not]." However, their idea of a democratic society and party was neither liberal nor secular. The women agreed that a religious party was needed to raise the quality of life, education, rule of law, and justice. Tahmina added, "Since we generally have a religious worldview, politicians should use examples from the Qur'an," and laws "should not

[6] TAJ-FG#15.

contradict the Qur'an." Marhabo complained bluntly, "The Constitution of Tajikistan contradicts Islam." However, they opposed religious intolerance, another hallmark of the radicals.

More concretely, all but one woman in the group advocated for *shariat* courts. As Behru said, "I agree one hundred percent that *shariat* courts work. We are all Muslim. Most of our population acts on the basis of *shariat* law. If there were such a possibility, to have *shariat* courts, then many family conflicts and divorces could be decided." Several women suggested having both *shariat* and secular courts. What specific *shariat* laws they sought was less clear; about half thought polygyny should be legal, and all wanted the state to provide religious education. The young women concurred with one student who lamented, "Muslim democracy doesn't exist in our society. . . . Today, as a small example, I tell you, youth are not permitted to go to mosque. Where is democracy, or human rights?" Most of them expressed support for the idea of "Muslim democracy."

Their views on jihad were mixed. Some opposed all militancy, while others were sympathetic and viewed Palestine and the wars in Afghanistan and Iraq as Christian-versus-Muslim conflicts. Marhabo unequivocally declared, "Christians are at fault. . . . [T]hey wish us evil." Umeda replied, "They know that Islam is a great religion and they want to destroy it." Robia added, "They specially prepare such operations against Islam." But a fourth woman interjected that in Islam "jihad is for defense. Today jihad is incorrectly used, and it's to the detriment of Muslims."

Some women were sympathetic to those who committed suicide-terrorism, but not one of them endorsed the method. Marhabo, for example, sympathized with the mental trauma of such women: "Suicide bombers sprang up only recently, maybe because their husbands were killed before their eyes." Behru articulated well the mainstream Muslim view: "Those people today who call jihad and kill themselves as martyrs are not *shahids*. In Islam it's written that you must defend yourself. . . . Today they use jihad the wrong way, for harm to Muslims and other states." Muhayo even more explicitly rejected violence, saying, "Jihad, as I understand it, means that when someone criticizes Islam, I should explain to him how he is mistaken. We shouldn't repeat jihad as it was in the seventh century." Tahmina added, "That just allows other countries to see Islam's weak side, and to criticize it for supporting bloodshed." Marhabo contended that "suicide bombers are fairly new. . . . [M]aybe suicide-bombing has no relation to Islam at all. Maybe it's prepared by the secret police of other countries, not Islamic countries." In short, the women generally held views congruent with the IRPT's ideas. Like the postwar IRPT, the women sought a tolerant and inclusive marriage of Islam and democracy, and they were critical of the militancy of contemporary jihadists. That young educated women held such views was testimony to the IRPT's inroads with urban youth and educated women.

Mixed Views about Islam and Politics

In other groups, participants held some of the mainstream Islamist ideas discussed above. Yet, on certain issues, the same individuals also held exclusivist ideas, similar to the messages propagated by more extreme Islamists. For example, they might oppose puritanical laws, but also condemn Jews or advocate an Islamic state without any democratic rights. A range of participants, men and women across age groups and regions, albeit more typically in the Islamist opposition's strongholds, held these mixed views.

Women, University Students, Twenty-one to Twenty-four Years Old, Qurghonteppa, 2009

A group of devout young women from Qurghonteppa gathered in one focus group.[7] Like the mainstream groups discussed already, these female students praised the building of new mosques and religious revival. One student's uncle had given $500 to erect a mosque, a sum far higher than the average monthly wage in Tajikistan. Others professed that their village had gathered money to finance new mosques. They believed in pursuing Islamic and national revival through education. Many felt that "in school, religion should be treated equally with other subjects." They were skeptical of the education and teaching of some Tajik mullahs, whom they viewed as ignorant or government-trained, and they professed greater faith in those imams who had studied in Pakistan or Saudi Arabia.

The students held mixed and sometimes contradictory political views, heavily shaped by their anger at corruption and nepotism under the Rahmon regime. Participants agreed with Salomat, who said, "The government only works for its own ends." Bibijon lamented, "We need to eliminate clannism. It's the tragedy of our nation." They widely endorsed the idea of bringing Islamic values and morality into politics and society to counter corruption.

Respondents were angry at injustice. Some believed following *shariat* in one's personal life was sufficient to improve society, but others claimed that greater justice existed in places with strong Islamic laws. The group favored having Islamic courts impose the *hudud* penalties of the *shariat* as a solution. Bunafsha said, "When you cut off a hand or leg, then this affects the upbringing of everyone in society." Salomat and others agreed that Muslim courts "create fear," which was good for decreasing crime. They were also intolerant of Christian missionaries and converts, for as Salomat argued, "Tajikistan should be a Muslim state, because most [citizens] are Muslims." She and others emphasized that

[7] TAJ-FG#9.

Tajikistan should be a "Muslim state," because such a state should "respect all their [Muslim] traditions and customs."

Yet, in other areas, their ideas about law and the state were liberal. They agreed, in a view somewhat at odds with their support for adopting *shariat* courts, that "religious freedom should exist for all. We need to respect the freedom of other religions." Most of them opposed legalizing polygyny. All emphasized the importance of education for women. Bibijon thought Tajiks "themselves, [not the current regime] should decide [on the state], but without violence."

The women all supported the IRPT, which they said was very popular with youth, mainly because they "call people to prayer, to be Islamic, Muslim." Bibijon added that the "people turned to the IRPT for leadership during our civil war." Salomat, an Islamic party member, criticized other democratic parties for doing nothing. The women were skeptical of democracy. As Bibijon said, "They [the government] say we are a democracy but it's in name only. So, I don't know." Sadbarg added, "I haven't seen what Western democracy is, but I think it's better. In Western democracy there's a little justice." Olufta and several others responded that they "really liked Iranian democracy, despite its problems." Overall, they were less willing than IRPT leader Kabiri to settle for a secular democracy.

They were even more negative about HTI, which several panned as a party of "uneducated people" seeking a caliphate; achieving such a state, they agreed, would entail bloodshed. They opposed jihad as "bloodletting." Salomat agreed: "It's a division between religions and nations." Typical of the majority in Tajikistan, they all denounced suicide bombers, whether Chechen, Palestinian, or al-Qaeda and Bin Laden, as "terrorists." Apart from Salomat, they repeatedly emphasized that they were "afraid" that Islamists would bring the country back to war.

Men, White-Collar, Thirty-five to Fifty Years Old, Qarotegin/Gharm, 2009

A group of well-educated Gharmi men, white-collar professionals,[8] held similarly mixed views—moderate on some issues and leaning radical on others. A decade older than the female students, they had come of age in the late Soviet era in Gharm, the IRPT's base, and lived through the Tajik Civil War. They denounced Soviet religious repression. Sadriddin recalled that "throughout the twentieth century, Islam was in danger of liquidation . . . from the 1930s to the 1990s. Many books were burned. . . . They were books for teaching morals and [Sufi] books of poetry, philosophy, and religion. . . . No one learned their contents, so we became almost illiterate. They burned everything." Kamol added, "In the socialist period, there were many specific limits on religious issues. However, the people who believed used every possibility to say prayers, read

[8] TAJ-FG#11.

religious books, and teach their children. There were few mosques. There were times when they forbade us to observe the fast, *Eid-al-Fitr*. They monitored religious leaders. Still, to this day our elders preserved our religion." The men were equally angry at Rahmon's repression of religion. They had participated in a vigorous religious revival, which the IRPT had supported, in spite of government policy. They had built a mosque by *hashar* in 1990, with help from their network of fellow Gharmis in Qurghonteppa. "Now there are ten to fifteen mullahs per village in Gharm region," said one respondent proudly.

The men complained bitterly about their current government—about bribery for everything, nepotism, and economic difficulties. Salim said that, to ensure stability, the government must "first stop corruption and the practice of regional patronage," which excluded them. Shuhrat said, "There is no justice in whatever does not belong to *Musulmonchilik*." "Nowadays you can't solve any problems without bribes," said Kamol. Concerned about violence, Sadriddin said, "If there won't be an end to bribery and corruption in our republic, that path will lead to colossal casualties for the republic's leaders."

As they considered what sort of Muslim rules or qualities they would like to adopt to rectify injustice, the men were divided. Most participants wanted Tajikistan to become "a Muslim state," which, they explained without detail, would be "based on the Qur'an and *shariat*." Others only sought to incorporate some elements of *shariat* into a democracy. Kamol believed that "in an Islamic democracy there wouldn't be any corruption, killing, stealing, and deceit even if there is a place for those harsh punishments [*hudud* penalties]."

Some leaned toward more radical Islamist ideas—an Islamic state with strictly interpreted *shariat*, including the *hudud* penalties—agreeing with Alisher: "Maybe several practical measures of an Islamic state are necessary for us, for example, cutting off the hand of a thief." He emphasized an "Islamic state," not an "Islamic democracy": "In the Qur'an everything is there. Democracy—it's power of the people; however, in an Islamic state the people don't have the right to govern [Allah does]. . . . [S]o from what I know, democracy can't be Islamic." Ali declared, to affirmative nods from all, "The democratic parties in our region do nothing." Their illiberalism went further. High intolerance of Jews and converts in the group also indicated radical tendencies. The men again agreed with Alisher, who accused converts of selling themselves and their religion for money.

The men did not support a caliphate. Yet when asked whether they preferred an Islamic or a secular court system, all the participants preferred Islamic courts. Alisher responded, "In 1993, in the center of Gharm, I remember how they [religious leaders] made a decision to cut off a thief's hand. This example remained in people's memory for a long time. But today a thief is arrested and tomorrow he is free. So, I think a Muslim court is better, because it acts on *shariat* principles." Furthermore, the men agreed that religious leaders should have more influence, not only "in [leading] rituals and traditions" but also "in schools. Texts on religious study would have a positive effect on the relations between religion and state." The men believed that religious leaders should take part in "elections. . . . [They] would maintain peace. They'd have a positive influence." Some suggested Iran as a model for Tajikistan, because they had "learned about Iran from those [Tajiks] who had studied in Pakistan, Iran, and Turkey." However, some also cautioned that "they [themselves] had not been there" and they were not ready to adopt an Islamic state. Such a state was still very abstract to them.

Several men decried recent arrests of Salafis and alleged "Wahhabis." Sadriddin said, favorably, "Salafis are purer [than others]. . . . [P]eople will accept those [groups] that are pure." They disagreed with Tajik court rulings banning Salafis and Wahhabis. Sadriddin continued, "Judging their belief . . . it's not right." Their views toward religious freedom and minorities leaned radical as well. They not only perceived a "threat" from Christian missionaries but also stridently opposed the legal right to convert. One man declared, "No one here would ever sell out their religion."

The men revealed further conflicting views as they reflected on the Gharmis' goal of an Islamic state in the 1990s, as well as on more recent radicalism. As he talked about the Tajik Civil War, Sadriddin pointed out, "Each revolution has its slogans . . . like the October Revolution. . . . There are those who say that Tajikistan is ready to have an Islamic state . . . but it can't change in the course of two months. . . . Tajikistan is not ready to become an Islamic state. It takes decades of work. The initiators of our [Tajik] revolution adopted the Iranian Revolution's example. However . . . the Iranians were preparing for much longer. . . . After seizing power, they had the means to govern. We were not ready for this." He continued, "I recall reading Haji Turajonzoda's article before 1992. He said: 'To grab power is easy, but to govern the state is difficult.' " Kamol added, "An Islamic state is not necessary. . . . The people will come to Islam on their own. But it's necessary that they completely follow Islam." Skeptical of the IRPT's turn under Kabiri, they were unanimous in opposition to democracy of any form because "it is Western." Indeed, most considered *shariat* and an Islamic state to be better, even though—with the hindsight of the war—they were cautious about adopting an Islamic state too quickly.

They did view jihad as sometimes necessary. "It's a demand in the *hadith*," Kamol said. He explained, "In the 1990s this idea of jihad came to us from the Arabs, and it took root in the ideas of people. It meant war with the *kuffar*. . . . Jihad is a struggle against one's inadequacies, and also a struggle against injustice." Although admitting that such views had been salient in Gharm in the past, they now shunned the militant road to an Islamic state and supported Haji

Turajonzoda's path, patience and nonviolence: "It will take a hundred years. You can't succeed by war." They professed to follow the *fatwa*s of Domla Hikmatullo Tojikobod, a traditional Islamic leader educated by Hindustoniy and close to the IRPT. As Abubakr said, he was "the mullah closest to them. No one else could issue better *fatwas*." Thus, despite their support for some radical Islamist ideas, the men preferred traditional sacred authority and moderation over radicalism.

Men, Migrant Workers, Twenty-five to Thirty-five Years Old, Kulob, 2009

A group of Kulobi migrant workers[9] likewise exhibited mixed views about both Islam and governance. Respondents told of brutal Soviet repression of Islam, a policy that continued after 1991. Sayid remarked, "Religion is necessary, [but] in Soviet times, the [communist] ideology limited the rights of the religious person. [But] Tajiks still saved their religion. We can say with certainty that our nation cannot be divided from religion." Aziz recalled, "My father worked in the [USSR's] government. For him there should [have been] no Islam. But in the evening after work and dinner, he performed *namaz*, prayed, and taught us what he knew about Islam. All this he did secretly. Thankfully, because of him, today I am acquainted with the rules of *Musulmonchilik*." The men spoke proudly of "preserving the faith in Soviet times, despite the ideology." Tohir bitterly summed up Soviet policy: "For seventy years, there was nothing but blows against Islam." Ahmad decried Tajikistan's ongoing religious repression: "If there is [constitutional] separation of religion and state, why then does the state interfere with religion? Where is our democracy?" Darvon replied, "Islam is democracy."

The men firmly believed that Islam and Tajik nationhood were intertwined. One participant, Muhammadsharif, said, "Religion preserves the nation." Another said, "Islam flows in our blood." Tajik migrant laborers often turned to piety and ethnic solidarity "in the face of discrimination and violence against them as they worked degrading jobs in Russia. When killed there, imams and Tajiks at home considered them '*shahids*.'"[10] In such difficult conditions, some were drawn to the Islamist opposition; Muhammadsharif was expressly sympathetic to the IRPT, and most of them named the IRPT as the party they trusted: "Its goal is the moral improvement of Tajikistan." However, they agreed that religious leaders had pushed for "too much in 1992." They believed, mistakenly, that the Islamist movement had "wanted immediately to take power. . . . They realized their mistakes." They favored gradualism.

Yet, their ideas about law and the state were more radically Islamist than the IRPT's postwar goals. Tohir said, "Let our country be Islamic and act according to Islamic laws. Iran is an Islamic state and is one of the most developed

9 TJ-FG#13.

10 Sophie Roche, "Illegal Migrants and Pious Muslims," in Laurelle, *Tajikistan on the Move*, 259.

countries of the world." All agreed, expressing approval of the Iranian model, except Sayid, who preferred a "Tajik Sunni model of a state," as opposed to a Shia one. It was not entirely clear what this state entailed. They went on to explain that "Islam is equality," in contrast to the current corruption and inequality. However, Abdulmumin said passionately, "I want Tajikistan to become a Muslim country and for all its citizens to be Muslim." Presumably, that meant evicting or converting religious minorities, or denying them equal rights. Indeed, the group voiced extremely illiberal ideas about minorities and women; they denounced Jews as "the first enemy," rejected the right of conversion, and agreed that "a woman is second after her husband."

The men blamed corruption for the absence of justice and proposed that Islamic courts would improve the legal system. They were almost unanimous in calling for all law by *shariat*, including legalizing polygyny and the *hudud* penalties. Ahmad said, "If a thief steals the meal of a child, why not cut off his hand? It's the best upbringing. If you take off the hand of one thief, you stop a thousand from this path." Only Bahrom disagreed, saying, "It's not correct; it's extreme." Sayid disagreed: "It's not extreme. It's the most just punishment. It's Islamic democracy. And why not throw stones? Excuse me, if it happens with your wife or child, how would you react? Who wouldn't want to throw stones?" They all favored giving religious leaders greater influence in the government. They were sympathetic to HTI; one declared, "[HTI] isn't terrorist." Another affirmed, "HTI would not be radical if it were not underground." Another added, "Islam and its parties are completely distinct from terrorist parties. The IRPT isn't terrorist. Only Jews and Christians and those in power say this."

Their views on jihad were more militant than most of the other focus groups, and aligned with some elements of Salafi jihadist ideology. Most of the men agreed that jihad was "war against *kuffar* [unbelievers]" and consistently supported what they considered to be jihads against the infidels from Afghanistan and Iraq, Chechnya, and Palestine. "Jihad [there] is just," said Ahmad. Others voiced agreement. U.S., Israeli, and Russian violence against Muslims made militancy justifiable in their view. One migrant worker said, "The U.S. adopts policies that are against Muslims. This is wrong! . . . They always want to destroy Muslims." Sayid explained their support for anti-U.S. jihads in Afghanistan and Iraq: "The United States' foreign policy is all war. . . . U.S. policy is against Muslims. America is governed by Jews. They are constantly threatening and violating Muslims." Ahmad and Bahrom agreed: "Everyone knows that Israel wants to wage a third world war." All of the men even characterized Chechens fighting Russia as "heroic."

A few group members favored using suicide bombing in just wars, but only so long as innocents were not hurt. Darvon explained, "If they [Chechens] blow themselves up among innocent people, it's not right. If they blow themselves up by the court or prosecutor's office, then it's okay. It's a just struggle." Others agreed with Farhod, who justified Palestinian suicide bombers, because "the Jews have been waging war against Islam for years already. . . . [The Palestinians] fight for the love of their homeland. The Jews don't have the right to live on the territory of Arabs." Sayid insisted that Osama Bin Laden was "America's agent," just an excuse for the United States to take Afghanistan.

Some further sympathized with those fighting their own unjust government. For example, Ismoil believed that the Tajik state had wrongly punished those it branded "Salafis" and "Wahhabis." He meaningfully queried, "Maybe these people aren't even Wahhabis or Salafis? These people are fighting against injustice in society. They are patriots of their country. Western Europe and the rulers of Uzbekistan call them Wahhabis, Salafis, and extremists out of fear. . . . If I were judging them [in court] I would support them completely." He continued, "Jihad is the best means of defending Islam." Also sympathetic to HTI, he said, "Those who have endured a lot of brutal events in their lives join HTI." However; he was skeptical of HTI's commitment to nonviolence: "Without violence it's not possible to take power."

Men, Blue-Collar, Thirty-five to Forty-five Years Old, Dushanbe, 2013

Echoing others who had emphasized the role of *Musulmonchilik* in Tajik identity, a group of blue-collar workers[11] in Dushanbe considered Islamic and national values to be interwoven, passed on "from century to century." They had learned from grandparents, teachers, and books in the 1970s and 1980s. Farhod, a Tajik manual laborer, stated, "All [Tajik] parents are required to circumcise a boy, to marry a son and daughter according to Islam. Each man must perform *juma namaz* (Friday prayer). We must fulfill that which came before us." Most of the men decried "foreign emissaries" imposing an "Arab style" of Islam. As Jamshed said, "We only need religion." As Tajiks had been for centuries, they were tolerant of legal rights for non-Muslims, although they too strongly opposed Christian missionaries and converts.

All were angry at state repression of their Islamic identity and practices. Shohrukh recalled, "Under Soviet power, they taught that national and religious values were not necessary . . . but now we study everything." They said, even "during the Soviet era we studied with a *domla*" privately and "learned about *sadaqa* and Ramadan and *namaz*" because "religion is necessary for everyone." In the last days of the USSR, they recalled, religion became freer. But now, said Saidabror, "they want to forbid *juma-namaz* again. I think they want to prevent Muslims from uniting." Abduholik agreed: "The people who are preventing it [*namaz*] are the same who oppose Muslim unity." The numbers of those publicly

[11] TAJ-FG#16.

practicing Islam had grown in the early 2000s, they explained. However, ten years later, they complained, "in Rasht [Valley], restrictions began again." Their mosques were increasingly under state control. Atam said, "Until 2008, [mosque numbers] were increasing, but they have closed them again. The mosque is critically important. . . . It brings people to purity and oneness." They complained of police harassing women in hijab. Muzaffar insisted, "There's nothing bad in [the hijab]. Let them wear it."

The men expressed their respect for certain mainstream spiritual leaders, such as Haji Turajonzoda. "All believers know and respect him," said Muzaffar. They believed that IRPT leader "Sayid Abdullohi Nuri and his successor [Kabiri] were great scholars." They also expressed admiration for Ayatollah Khomeini, a radical, but seen by many Tajiks as the great founder of a Persian Islamic republic.

The group was united in supporting the IRPT and legalizing Islamic parties. Other parties, they said disparagingly, only "wanted a chair [profitable position in government]" and did nothing for the people. While the IRPT's moderate ideas about Islam's role generally resonated with them, the men were divided about the right state for Tajikistan. Saidabror, who came from Gharm, argued, "*Shariat* must be in all spheres an indicator of morality. If people would work according to *shariat*, then many problems in our country would be resolved—including corruption." Others complained of "corruption" and the lack of "justice," and proposed that Islamic courts and parties would decrease abuses in the legal system. Some articulated much more radical ideas than the IRPT, agreeing that "religion and state should be totally united," since politicians "must believe in Allah." Suhrod declared that "democracy is dangerous for religion," and Jamshed said, "*Shariat* is the law of the Almighty." Atam complained that "the laws of *shariat* are required [by Allah] of each Muslim and currently we can't fulfill them." Many were impressed by Iran's example. Muzaffar explained that Iran was better than Tajikistan because "in Iran the courts are Islamic." Several added that "in Iran there is no prostitution" or bribery, while "in Tajikistan corruption is widespread" and is "only fined twenty-five *somoni*" (about $2). Corrupt officials went unpunished and sexual immorality was rising.

The men interpreted democracy in Islamic terms. Alisher said, "Islamic democracy is freedom, [being] free to carry out all the demands of *shariat*, and the state can't interfere in the religious affairs of Muslims." Indeed, like other groups, the migrants were skeptical of democracy—especially of a Western, secular form, which they viewed as immoral and threatening. "Western democracy brings atheism. It's a danger for our religion," said Holik. But "Muslim democracy," said Saidabror, "is freedom of faith and religion. No one can interfere with or forbid the religiosity of people. Even the state's power organs can't do that." Parviz added, "Western democracy is dangerous . . . for our religion and . . . our culture." Muzaffar summed up the consensus: "The state must adopt laws that defend faith and religion." Drugs and other crimes, they complained, are "too weakly punished" in Tajikistan "under our [secular] democratic state."

Atam declared, "Religious freedom and religious laws must be active in society." He meant Islamic religious laws, such as legalizing polygyny. Some respondents supported more extreme interpretations of *shariat*, such as using *hudud* penalties to punish homosexuality, fornication, adultery, prostitution, and drug use—punishments which are not widely applied in the Muslim world, much less in Central Asia. Their statements reflected a positive view of Iranian application of Islamic law. Still, participants remained divided on the necessity of implementing the *hudud* penalties like amputation and stoning. Some wanted only a more limited *shariat* influence on state law and sought their "own Tajik model," as opposed to copying Iran.

Despite their sometimes extreme interpretations of Islamic law, the respondents' views on jihad were not revolutionary but in accord with classical, mainstream Islamic teaching. Muzaffar and others thought that jihad was necessary in some circumstances, for "defense of the homeland." Sunob agreed: "Jihad is [fighting] for freedom, like the Chechens." Saidabror added approvingly, "The Palestinian jihad and the Uyghurs' struggle—that's [correct] jihad." Farhod explained, "You can't just wage jihad anywhere and everywhere. A fatwa is necessary, a decision of the *mufti*. . . . All the requisite conditions are in the Qur'an." Although they confused the theological difference between the "greater" and "lesser" jihad, they specified that only the proper authority, in proper conditions, could call for jihad. They therefore agreed that "Bin Laden's [war] is not a jihad." Jamshed declared, "They [al-Qaeda] are terrorists." Alisher explained their opposition to the concept of suicide bombing: "It is forbidden to perform *janaza namaz* for those who commit suicide." Such violence, they believed, was fundamentally against Islam.

Some of their views reflected the IRPT's postwar ideas. Yet, the men arguably still sought an Islamic government and a puritanical version of *shariat* that the party's leadership had rejected by the late 1990s.

Secular Political Views

Finally, a small minority of focus group participants—only one group unanimously, and a handful of respondents in five other groups—wanted secular governance and were often democratically oriented. Such views were more common among the Soviet-born intelligentsia, such as the highly educated in urban Khujand.

Women, White-Collar, Thirty-five to Fifty Years Old, Khujand, 2013

A group of Khujandi women, born in the 1960s,[12] advocated secular political views, although they were personally pious. They had learned Islamic rituals since childhood, together with *urf-adat* (customs) They did not recall facing religious oppression. They opposed "Western values," which destroyed "respect for elders." Favorable to the USSR's influence, they believed, as Sanoat put it, that "for working women and women studying in universities, wearing the hijab is not appropriate." They believed in a "strong educational system, with secular subjects, because youth need scientific knowledge." They wanted morality, but not religion, to be taught in school, as in Soviet times. Suspicious of foreign Islam, they followed some local Islamic leaders, such as Haji Kalonzoda, known to be traditional and quietist.

They viewed Islam "as important for morality, personal matters, and children's upbringing," but most opposed any role for Islam in law and politics. Only Mahinahon was sympathetic to religion having a role in law because "the rural population, seventy percent [of Tajiks], is very religious." Mutriba countered, "But a Muslim country must be different from an Islamic republic as, for example, exists in Afghanistan. Our country is secular and democratic, and according to the constitution every person can choose his religion." The women opposed *shariat* courts too. According to Hafiza, "Nothing from the *shariat* should be in the law. We have a secular state, and in the constitution our rights are there."

Subhinisso agreed, emphasizing women's rights and expressing fear of what Islamic law might bring: "According to *shariat*, a man is higher than a woman and he uses that right to take all the property. The fate of a woman and children depends on the father and husband. . . . [I]n divorce too. . . . A woman is not defended under *shariat*." Hafiza added, "There are laws in *shariat* that say a woman can't work in business. Market competition doesn't work under *shariat* rules." She added sarcastically, "The just laws of *shariat* will drive a business into bankruptcy." Moreover, the women recognized that corruption was a problem everywhere, but believed that Islamic laws would not solve it. Strongly opposed to religious parties, one said, "You receive your religious values from books, in the mosque, in social, communal places, and in the family. Religious parties act only for politicians, not the people."

Their views included tolerance of other religions, which they believed should have broad and equal rights. They leaned toward democracy, which they defined as "freedom of speech" and "freedom of the individual." Mahinahon expressly argued for a secular democracy because "women must have equal rights to vote. These rights are in our constitution." However, others were skeptical of

[12] TJ-FG#18.

democracy because in neighboring Kyrgyzstan, they believed, democracy had descended into "chaos." Muhabbat declared, "Kyrgyz democracy is not for us" because of its political instability. Without expressly endorsing secular authoritarianism, either Soviet- or Russian-style, most agreed that "elections are unnecessary," that "a strong leader is critical, but not a parliament."

Unsurprisingly, this group of women viewed jihad as primarily internal: "Many people incorrectly interpret jihad," which they agreed is necessary only "if something threatens Islam." They viewed wars in Afghanistan, Palestine, and elsewhere as being about territory, not defending the faith. They blamed "other countries" for creating a division between Muslims and Russians in Chechnya. They opposed U.S. and NATO bombings, but also criticized Saddam Hussein and Osama Bin Laden "because people suffered and died as a consequence" of their actions. They were sympathetic to the people of Palestine and Afghanistan, but generally thought of jihad as something from ancient Islamic history. They expressed empathy for "the ordinary people caught in their bombs and terrorist acts, as in Afghanistan," and they opposed all violence.

Their views on wholly separating Islamic teaching and religious leaders from politics were arguably typical of the very small, urban Tajik elite, who were Muslim believers but strongly influenced by Soviet education, which had benefited them.

Societal Leaders: Not Secular, Not Radical

Social leaders, especially religious and communal elders, played a key role in shaping the views of their community during the Soviet era and the civil war. They still do today. Interviews revealed a range of opinions: puritanical, traditionally conservative, occasionally liberal. Most favored the integration of Islam into public life, politics, and law. One imam from Qurghonteppa explained, "In my view, democracy is freedom, but better to have an Islamic [democracy], since in an Islamic one there's no bribery or alcoholism. For us there should be an Islamic democracy, because in Islamic countries it's necessary to follow the *shariat*."[13] His view was not uncommon. Most societal elites, especially religious and *mahalla* leaders, were wary of democracy. Yet, they did not seek an Islamic state in the near term, much less a renewal of jihad inside Tajikistan. A few examples of those who identified as Islamists or IRPT supporters are worth considering, because they suggest the limits of Islamism in Tajikistan.

The views of a *mahalla* leader from Gharm, who was about thirty-five when the USSR dissolved, were typical of societal elites in that region. He recalled the

13 Interview with religious leader, Qurghonteppa, Tajikistan, 2006.

USSR as "the system of totalitarianism.... [It] restricted one's thoughts and one's faith."[14] Despite Soviet repression, he had learned Islam with his father, who had attended a *hujra*. He said, "Nowadays [the 2000s], people again fear the legal system and power organs [the president and secret police].... But they should respect the law, not fear it." He criticized Islam as practiced by Tajiks for allowing Soviet and Sufi or national influences. Devout and purist, he preferred those Tajik imams who had studied Islam abroad, "in Arabia." He did not advocate an "Islamic state," primarily because "the Tajik people are not ready." But he still wanted *shariat* to be law. He strongly advocated legalizing polygyny, but he was vague about how Islamic law would govern. He insisted the origin of democracy was in Islam, not the West, so some sort of Islamic democracy was appropriate.

Another communal elder, also a Gharmi, who considered himself more committed than the IRPT to Islamist ideas, viewed jihad as a "duty . . . to defend Islam against foreign religions."[15] He also expressed sympathy for the Chechens, Palestinians, and Afghans, each of whom he described as waging jihad for Islam and freedom. He approved of militant jihad in defense only. However, reflecting HTI's preoccupation with the Palestinian issue, he said, "They called [chairman of the Palestine Liberation Organization Yasser] Arafat a terrorist, but he won the Nobel Peace Prize. The Palestinians want freedom and independence. The Jews, with U.S. help, kill innocent people. Palestinians want peace and Israel wants violence." More radical than most, he not only sympathized with but also glorified suicide bombing: "They [bombers] have lost relatives. They have become *shahids*. It's bravery." This sympathy for extremist ideas and methods was tied to his anger at corruption, an immoral government, and the courts' sentencing of "good Muslims" as "Wahhabis." He was angry at those he deemed "internal enemies": the government itself. Yet, when he considered militants' (IMU's and JA's) calls for jihad in Tajikistan in 2009, he recalled living through the Tajik Civil War. He cautioned against using violence: "Society has been burned up and no one should use force any more, it won't accomplish anything.... [Since the war] fear has remained in our blood."

Also of note was the occasional liberal voice among religious leaders. Ahmadjon, an unregistered mullah of the Soviet era,[16] was open and tolerant. He did not view Jews, Christians, or converts as a threat to Islam. Instead, he said, "Everyone has a right to choose this or that religion. I don't view them negatively. Maybe no one had the chance to explain in depth the essence of the Islamic religion to them." Ahmadjon argued that "religious leaders should never have influence [on the government].... Religion is the faith, the dream of the people....

[14] Interview with *mahalla* leader #1, Gharm, Tajikistan, 2009.
[15] Interview with *mahalla* leader #2, Gharm, 2009.
[16] Interview with Ahmadjon, unregistered mullah, Qurghonteppa, Tajikistan, 2008.

The state and system of government can change. . . . So religion must not be integrated into the state." His opinions on law and social issues were also liberal: men and women were equal, and polygyny "was a violation of women's rights." *Shariat* applied to personal life, not law, he said; he strongly opposed the puritanical influence of foreign-educated imams in Tajikistan. Rejecting all political Islam, he claimed that "religious leaders, because of their [political] positions," had been the cause of the civil war. He concluded that secular democracy was best for Tajikistan.

Support for the IRPT

Respondents, as we have seen, voiced both open approval of the IRPT and also agreement with its message and goals, if not direct support of the party. In many interviews, and in fourteen of the nineteen focus groups—cutting across regional, gender, occupational, and educational differences—multiple participants expressed a favorable view of the IRPT or reported positive views from their community about the IRPT, either from its inception during *perestroika* or in its reincarnation under Kabiri.

Besides its high sacred authority and extensive networks, discussed in Chapter 6, the IRPT had adapted its ideas and platform to the mainstream Muslim norms and values of Tajik society, which did not support an Islamist version of the state, including purist forms of dress or imposition of the *hudud* penalties, much less puritanical bans on Sufi practices and national customs. Focus group participants often openly expressed their approval of the party, especially its defense of nationalism, its focus on state-funded religious education, defending Islamic rights, and eradicating corruption. Many believed that some implementation of that *shariat* in the law and courts would eradicate corruption and solve multiple social problems; this was especially true in opposition regions (e.g., Gharm and Qurghonteppa), but was true even in Dushanbe and Khujand a decade after the civil war had ended.

Likewise, the IRPT's approach to synthesizing Islam and democracy resonated with some, especially the urban and educated among the younger generation. For them, an Islamic party need not be Islamist, much less radically Islamist; it did need, however, to counter secularism. The IRPT stood for a different form of democracy than did the West or Tajikistan's secular-democratic parties, a more moral and national form: Muslim democracy. Zamira, when asked about whether a religious party was a good idea for Tajikistan, responded, "Our society is democratic, so it's good that we have such a party as the IRPT working [here]."[17]

[17] TAJ-FG#15.

As a mullah from Gharm explained, the IRPT and Islamic parties generally "could improve life," "decrease corruption," and "teach love of Islam."[18] Reflecting general opposition to secular politics, one young man from Khujand declared, as had many others, "Such parties are necessary." Others simply stated, "The republic is ninety-nine percent Muslim, so we need such a[n Islamic] party. It should exist in any democratic state."[19]

Tajik sociologist Saodat Olimova's 2008 survey (conducted when such work was still possible without fear overwhelmingly biasing responses) supports my qualitative findings. Olimova found that about 65 percent of Tajik respondents claimed they would support a party of moderate Islamic ideas.[20] That number was more than double the response in 2005, when 25 to 35 percent (varying by age groups in 2005) supported a moderate Islamist party.[21] Olimova also reported that nearly half, 44 percent, supported (and 52 percent rejected) a party that could "unite all the Muslim clergy."[22]

Through an examination of Tajik respondents' discussions in focus groups and interviews, this chapter has documented societal attitudes about the particular issues and messages central to Islamist movements. I found support for mainstream Islamist ideas among a portion of the Tajik population, such as those propagated by the postwar IRPT. Many Tajiks wanted to blur the boundaries between religion and public life, law, and even the state, albeit to varying degrees. They wanted a party and state that would support a national Islamic revival, state-funded Islamic education, opening mosques, wearing the hijab, and some laws in accordance with *shariat*. They wanted an end to repression of Islam and secularism. For many, Islamist calls for justice and an end to government corruption were also critically important.

Surprisingly, at least to many Western observers who assume that the desire for liberal conceptions of freedom is universal, most Tajiks shared the IRPT's critique of democracy.[23] They too perceived existing forms of democracy as too Western, immoral, permissive of apostasy, and chaotic. Despite the Soviet influence, the vast majority of Tajiks rejected secularism both in personal matters and

[18] Interview with unregistered mullah, Buston, Tajikistan, 2009.

[19] TAJ-FG#17.

[20] Saodat Olimova and Farkhod Tolipov, "Islamic Revival in Central Asia: The Cases of Uzbekistan and Tajikistan," documentos CIDOB, Asia 26 (Barcelona: Barcelona Centre for International Affairs, March 2011), 7, https://www.cidob.org/en/publications/past_series/documents/asia/islamic_revival_in_central_asia_the_cases_of_uzbekistan_and_tajikistan; Olimova and Olimov, "Public Opinion," 158–78.

[21] Saodat Olimova, "Youth of Tajikistan Facing Islam and Islamism," *Cahiers d'Asie Centrale*, nos. 15–16 (2007): 196–222.

[22] Olimova and Tolipov, "Islamic Revival"; Olimova and Olimov, "Public Opinion."

[23] Mahmood, *Politics of Piety*.

in governance; to the extent that they wanted to live in a democracy, they preferred a strong Islamic influence on democracy.[24]

Respondents' discourse further demonstrates that the IRPT's ideational adaptation—moderation over time on the issue of an Islamic state and national, syncretic Islam, as well as its defense of local concerns, as opposed to focusing on its earlier goal of an Islamic state that enshrined "Allah's sovereignty"—enabled it to broaden its social base significantly in the decade leading up to the 2015 election. The idea of a more Islamic society and government—one that could uphold religious values, end religious repression, and rectify injustice—resonated. The affinity of a significant portion of Tajik society for the IRPT's ideas was a key factor in the party's growth and durability despite oppression. By contrast, extremely few endorsed the ideas of more radical Islamists. Almost no one expressed the desire to establish a caliphate. Only a handful clearly favored an Islamic state, typically of a form exemplified by Iran. Support for militant jihad was highly qualified; most viewed jihad as legitimate only in self-defense. Nearly all opposed suicide bombing in all circumstances.

Even so, we have seen that politically extreme ideas were not anathema to all. As previous chapters have suggested, given ongoing state repression, Islamist radicalism was limited but not disappearing. In fact, as Mr. Kabiri had warned, radical ideas were gaining influence among those who demanded justice and were frustrated with the IRPT's inability to counter Rahmon peacefully, through democratic means. Chapter 14 will show that the diffusion of ISIS's ideology in such conditions and its active recruiting inflamed anger and incited thousands to join its violent movement.

[24] Kathleen Collins and Erica Owen, "Islamic Religiosity and Regime Preferences: Explaining Support for Democracy and Political Islam in Central Asia and the Caucasus," *Political Research Quarterly* 65, no. 3 (September 2012): 499–515.

PART IV

UZBEKISTAN

From Salafists to Salafi Jihadists

8
Seeking Justice and Purity
Islamists against Communism and Karimov

> I was born on the Kolkhoz Ordzhonikidze in 1954. My father said *namaz.* So did my mother. But our ideology was atheism, and young people were all afraid to talk about religion. . . . In school, they forced me to eat during the fast. . . . I had a wake-up call in the 1970s, a man from Namangan came. . . . He had suras from the Qur'an. . . . It was forbidden, from above. . . . After independence the state started opening mosques, and celebrating Islamic holidays. . . . But I told you, we were raised in communist air, and in communist air we will die.
>
> —*Oqsoqol* and unregistered mullah, Tashkent, 2004

While Tajikistan has been widely known since 1991 for its instability and conflict over the role of Islam in politics, Uzbekistan has typically been seen as a country where heavy-handed communist rule kept stability and maintained secularism.

A large and diverse country of almost thirty-five million, Uzbekistan is a land of many paradoxes. In the 1990s and 2000s, Uzbek men donned dark tracksuits and leather jackets, many striking a mafioso air. Russian vodka was widely sold. Young women strolled downtown in miniskirts and stilettos. Central Tashkent became crowded with shiny new high-rises, fast-food restaurants, opulent cars, and lavishly refurbished apartments. To the casual visitor, Uzbekistan seemed strikingly secular, at least through the end of the nearly twenty-eight-year dictatorship of Islom Karimov (1989–2016). In the old city of Tashkent or in the Ferghana Valley, by contrast, behind the closed gates that wall in the houses along narrow streets, life was very different. People sat at a *dasturxon* (traditional woven tablecloth), eating hot *tandir non* (bread from a tandir), and drinking *choy* (tea). Even in the Soviet-style buildings, however, and among those many Uzbeks wearing Soviet garb, many rose to eat before sunrise during the *ro'za* (fast) of the holy month of Ramadan or to perform morning *namaz* at sunrise, as my landlady did every day, despite being highly educated and living in the center of Tashkent. She brought me breakfast, usually a hearty stew, shortly after

Politicizing Islam in Central Asia. Kathleen Collins, Oxford University Press. © Oxford University Press 2023.
DOI: 10.1093/oso/9780197685068.003.0009

prayers. Throughout the Karimov era, most men feared to grow a beard, a sign of Islamic piety, much less wear Islamic dress. Yet, some clean-shaven men would nonetheless interrupt their work to pray if they could find a safe mosque and their employer did not report them to the security services.

For most, practicing Islam had never been a political statement, but a belief, identity, and way of life. Islamic revival reflected conservative, traditional norms in society, but not intolerance or violence. But some Uzbekistanis felt enormous anger at the Karimov regime. The president's response to the Islamic revival of the late 1980s and early 1990s was successive waves of religious and political oppression. My acquaintance Hurmat, a young driver from Tashkent, who had turned to foreign Islamic literature for religious and political solutions, explained, "I'm tired of the government imams saying 'Be patient and wait for the day of judgment, when you will have all you wish.' "[1] From the Islamic lectures he listened to in his car throughout the day he had learned that "revolution is the law of Allah."[2]

Since the early 1990s, Islam has been at the heart of political contention in Uzbekistan, guiding the demands of the most durable political opposition movements to challenge Karimov's post-Soviet regime. Three waves of Islamism have emerged in Uzbekistan, the later waves increasingly more radical—both antisystemic and violent. The first wave, centered around the Islamic movement Adolat (Justice) and the Islamic Revival Party of Uzbekistan (IRPU), developed before Uzbekistan's independence from the USSR on August 31, 1991. A second wave of Islamism emerged in the mid- to late 1990s; it began with the appearance of Hizb ut-Tahrir al-Islami (HTI), a clandestine, transnational party that first took root in the Uzbek Ferghana Valley, and then spread.[3] A few years later, the Islamic Movement of Uzbekistan (IMU), an outgrowth of Adolat, appeared as a militant and revolutionary movement that sought to overthrow the Karimov regime (Chapter 9). A third wave involved a transnational movement of foreign fighters in Syria, Iraq, and Afghanistan that began in 2011 and had not fully ended in 2022 (Chapter 14).

Previous chapters have discussed how Soviet-era religious repression politicized Islamic identity and how a marginal opening of associational space allowed political theologies and Islamist ideologies from the Middle East and South Asia to spread to the USSR—both unintended consequences of Soviet policy. This chapter turns to the conditions—religious entrepreneurs inspired by activist political theology, within growing associational space—that ultimately led to the first and second waves of Uzbekistani Islamist mobilization in the early

[1] Communication with Hurmat, Tashkent, Uzbekistan. See the introduction for my previous discussion of Hurmat's views.

[2] Interview with Hassan, Andijon, Uzbekistan, May 2003.

[3] HTI subsequently emerged in Tajikistan (see Chapter 6) and in Kyrgyzstan (see Chapter 12 for more detail).

1990s. I explore the content and limited success of Adolat and the IRPU, the key actors of the first wave. I then turn to the mobilization and demobilization of HTI, a more radical party at the beginning of the second wave. I demonstrate that Karimov's oppression of all Islamist opposition and of independent Islam laid the groundwork for more violent second- and third-wave Islamists.

Conditions Breeding the First Wave of Uzbek Islamism, 1980s–1992

Associational Space: *Perestroika* Leads to the Spread of Islamist Ideas

For decades, there had been no possibility for public Muslim activism. Soviet control was even tighter in Uzbekistan than in Tajikistan. Yet, the level of associational space finally grew during the late *perestroika* years. Although later than elsewhere, limited religious liberalization led to mosque openings, both registered and unregistered. By late 1991, the eighty-seven legal Friday mosques had multiplied to about four thousand (registered as well as unregistered but functioning).[4] A new *mufti*, Muhammad Sodiq Muhammad Yusuf, initially appointed some independent-thinking imams to lead major mosques. The *muftiyat* distributed tens of thousands of Qur'ans, gifted by Saudi Arabia.[5] Unofficial mullahs taught and led prayers, and Muslim missionaries could operate, circumventing official permission. In some towns of the Ferghana Valley, local Islamic elites even gained enough influence to prevent alcohol sales.[6]

Together with the proliferation of mosques came a growing market in Islamic and nationalist *samizdat* (clandestine publications, produced within the country), much of which was readily available for sale outside mosques during the *perestroika* period and early 1990s. A voluminous quantity of sermons and pamphlets about Islam was distributed and sold, in print and on audiocassette. Although not legally produced and sold, the materials were not well-known or understood by the government for several years and thus evaded the censorship of the press.[7] Men frequently gathered at such sellers, in private homes,

[4] Human Rights Watch, "Creating Enemies of the State: Religious Persecution in Uzbekistan" (New York: Human Rights Watch, 2004), 20, https://www.hrw.org/reports/2004/uzbekistan0304/uzbekistan0304.pdf.

[5] Communications with residents, Andijon, May 2004.

[6] Communication with resident, Kokand, Uzbekistan, June 2002.

[7] David Tyson, "The Role of Unofficial Audio Media in Contemporary Uzbekistan," *Central Asian Survey* 13, no. 2 (1994): 283–93.

or at safe teahouses during *gap* sessions (meetings of a group of male friends).[8] Some materials were focused on Uzbek national identity, which usually included an Islamic emphasis as well. The widely popular Ferghana Valley *hofiz* (master singer of traditional songs) Dadaxon Hasan used music to convey social and political messages. Each song had a didactic aspect, informing listeners about the meaning of being Uzbek, the connection between Islam and nation, and the negative qualities of their Soviet rulers.[9] Hasan openly lambasted the colonial Russians who enslaved Uzbeks, but also took on Soviet rule. As David Tyson writes of Hasan's songs, "If the enemies of the recent past were the Russians, the individuals representing oppression and evil today are often members of the present 'system.' [Hasan] cites concrete examples of injustice and repression and offers accounts of recent events which portray the present leadership (or at least elements thereof) as villains."[10] Hasan regularly intertwined his themes of awakening national pride, a return to Islamic morality, and a calling for Islamic and political unity.[11] Given his national standing, Hasan's call to be more Muslim was influential across society.

A related genre of pamphlets recounted the lives of Ferghana Valley Basmachi, treating them as national and religious heroes who fought Soviet power, and reviving the idea of seeking Muslim self-rule. Many other materials were meant to encourage Islamic revival. Titles such as *What Is Islam?* offered answers to basic questions from a population eager to explore its Islamic identity. Often print publications and cassettes, and the imams who produced them, adopted a political tone as well, linking the return to pure Islam with rejection of communist rule.[12]

Religious Entrepreneurs and Ideologies

In the context of *glasnost* of the late Soviet era, various "modernist" and "reformist" ideas of Islam—dubbed either Wahhabist or Salafist by those who opposed them[13]—were becoming politically influential in Uzbekistan.[14] In fact, they had taken root decades earlier. The journal *Shura,* disseminated by Tatar intellectuals in the 1800s, had first introduced Turkestan to the puritanical thought of the

[8] Interview with David Tyson, former instructor of Central Eurasian Studies, Indiana University, Washington, D.C., July 2022. Tyson was doing doctoral research in the Namangan region of Uzbekistan at the time.

[9] Tyson, "The Role of Unofficial Audio Aedia," 287.

[10] Tyson, "The Role of Unofficial Audio Aedia," 287.

[11] Tyson, "The Role of Unofficial Audio Aedia," 287–88.

[12] Interview with Tyson.

[13] On similarities between these movements, see Abou El Fadl, *The Great Theft*, 75–79.

[14] Vitaly Naumkin, *Radical Islam in Central Asia: Between Pen and Rifle* (Oxford: Rowman & Littlefield, 2005).

thirteenth-century Syrian thinker Taqi al-Din Ahmad Ibn Taymiyyah (d. 1328).[15] Ibn Taymiyyah was known for rejecting all idolatrous innovations and Sufism and calling for militant jihad. He was an influential figure in the writings of Sayyid Qutb and political Islam in the Middle East. In the 1920s, the Arab missionary Shami Damulla (1867–1932) disseminated puritanical ideas more widely. Considered the "founding father" of Salafism in modern Uzbekistan—a purist interpretation of Islam subsequently branded "Wahhabism" by both the KGB and Hanafi traditionalists—Shami Damulla taught unofficially in Tashkent and elsewhere, until being arrested and exiled in 1932.[16] His ideas were carried on by followers in clandestine religious communities, including the Ahli Hadith, and later the Ahli Qur'an.[17] One of Shami Damulla's many disciples was Shaykh Ziyovuddinxon ibn Eshon Boboxon(ov) (1908–1982), who, ironically, would serve as SADUM's chief *mufti* from 1957 to 1982. From the 1950s onward, SADUM propagated purism and brought Salafi religious literature to Uzbekistan through official Islamic exchanges with Libya, Syria, Jordan, and Egypt. This phenomenon inadvertently allowed the ideas of political Islam to spread.[18] As in Tajikistan, given the fluid boundaries between "registered" and "unregistered" *ulama*, these ideas diffused to *ulama* outside SADUM as well.[19]

Another puritanical movement emerged indigenously and was particularly strong in the widespread Ferghana Valley *hujras* that offered clandestine Islamic study, to carry on the deep pre-Soviet institution of *madrasa* education.[20] Abdulhakim Qori Marg'iloni (also known as Hakimjon Qori, b. 1896) was an Uzbek reformist who spent years in hiding during Stalin's persecution, but then led one of the most influential *hujras* in the Ferghana Valley. He advocated a return to the Salaf (the first Muslims and companions of the Prophet) and to the "pure" teachings of the Qur'an.[21] Abdulhakim Qori had reportedly collected not

[15] Edward Lazzerini, "Volga Tatars in Central Asia, 18th–20th Centuries," in *Central Asia in Historical Perspective*, ed. Beatrice Manz (Boulder, CO: Westview Press, 1994), 82–100; Paolo Sartori, "Towards a History of the Muslims' Soviet Union: A View from Central Asia," *Die Welt des Islams* 50 (2010): 315–34.

[16] The followers of Ibn al-Wahhab sought to return to practices of seventh-century Islam. The Soviet KGB used the term "Wahhabism" to target those they considered extremists, and this practice has continued through the present. Ashirbek Muminov, "Fundamentalist Challenges to Local Islamic Traditions in Soviet and Post-Soviet Central Asia," in *Empire, Islam, and Politics in Central Asia*, ed. Uyama Tomohiko (Sapporo, Japan: Slavic Research Centre, 2007), 253–58; Muminov, Gafurov, and Shigabdinov, "Islamic Education in Soviet and Post-Soviet Uzbekistan"; Bakhtiar Babadzhanov, "Islam in Uzbekistan: From the Struggle for 'Religious Purity' to Political Activism," in *Central Asia: A Gathering Storm?*, ed. Boris Rumer (London: M. E. Sharpe, 2002), 307.

[17] Muminov, "Fundamentalist Challenges," 253–55.

[18] Interview with Shaykh Muhammad Sodiq Muhammad Yusuf, former *mufti*, Tashkent, Uzbekistan, January 2003.

[19] Interview with Haji Akbar Turajonzoda, Dushanbe, Tajikistan, December 2011.

[20] Naumkin, *Radical Islam*; Muminov, "Fundamentalist Challenges," 258–59.

[21] BBCUzbek.com, "Taniqli ulamo, marhum Abdul Hakim Qori ota Vosiyevning 1992 yili BBC bilan suhbati," YouTube, March 13, 2011, https://www.youtube.com/watch?v=RxctgfHF5RQ.

only Ibn Taymiyyah's work but also the founding twentieth-century works of political Islam written by Mawdudi and Qutb. Many of these works were brought to Tashkent by Arab exchange students, and from there to the underground libraries of Ferghana Valley religious scholars.[22] Abdulhakim Qori taught numerous students, some of whom had joined his *hujra* after splitting with the renowned scholar Domulla Hindustoniy, because of his political quietism under Soviet rule.[23]

These puritanical reformist ideas, which scholars in the twentieth century have referred to as Salafism, became particularly influential across the Uzbek Ferghana Valley through *hujra* networks and a legacy of long-standing resistance to Bolshevism and atheism. Like the parallel Nahzat movement in Tajikistan, these young revivalist imams also called themselves the Mujaddidiya (the Renewers), suggesting the influence of Sirhindi as well (see Chapter 5). In the 1970s and 1980s, they developed networks spreading a political theology of Islam.[24] They included, most notably, Rahmatulloh Qori Alloma (1950–1981), Abduvali Qori Mirzoyev (1950–1995?), and Obidxon Qori Nazarov (1958–).[25] These young mullahs rejected any *mazhab* (school); they only followed the Qur'an, *hadith*, and *sunna* of the Prophet Muhammad.[26] They rejected Sufism and "folk Islam," which they wrongly portrayed as the product of the Soviet destruction of pure Islam. They wanted to expunge "the time of atheism, or drunkenness, when no one could talk about religion except in a *hujra* secretly," and reverse the communist secularization of society and state.[27] More pointedly, they accused the *qadimist* (conservative, traditionalist) Hanafi *ulama* of cooperating with the communist regime and allowing Soviet-era "innovations" to desecrate Islam.[28]

Domla Hindustoniy and other Hanafi traditionalists, who accepted Central Asian Sufism, pejoratively referred to these reformers as "Wahhabis" and claimed they were tainted by the "foreign" ideas of Muhammad ibn Abd al-Wahhab (d. 1791). Al-Wahhab was the puritanical Hanbali theologian of eighteenth-century

[22] Bakhtiyar Babajanov, A. Muminov, and A. von Kügelgen, *Disputy musul'manskikh religioznykh avtoritetov v Tsentral'noi Azii v XX veke* (Almaty: Daik-Press, 2007), 45–46.

[23] Martha Brill Olcott, *Whirlwind of Jihad* (Washington, D.C.: Carnegie Endowment for International Peace, 2012), 102–3.

[24] Babadzhanov, "Islam in Uzbekistan," 299–332; Bakhtyar Babadjanov, "The Economic and Religious History of a Kolkhoz Village: Khojawot," in Dudoignon and Noack, *Allah's Kolkhozes*, 258–60.

[25] Bakhtiyar Babadjanov and Muzaffar Kamilov, "Muhammadjan Hindustani (1892–1989) and the Beginning of the 'Great Schism' among the Muslims of Uzbekistan," in *Islam in Politics in Russia and Central Asia: Early Eighteenth to Late Twentieth Centuries*, ed. Stéphane Dudoignon and Komatsu Hisao (London: Kegan-Paul, 2001), 195–219; Muminov, "Fundamentalist Challenges."

[26] Allen J. Frank and Jahangir Mamatov, eds., *Uzbek Islamic Debates: Texts, Translations, and Commentary* (Springfield, VA: Dunwoody Press, 2006), ix, 129, 149–50.

[27] Interview with Gulom, registered imam, n.p., 2005.

[28] Babajanov, Muminov, and von Kügelgen, *Disputy musul'manskikh religioznykh avtoritetov*.

Arabia and ideologue of the Wahhabi movement, whose ideas about the pure, nearly utopian golden age of Islam became the basis of rule in modern Saudi Arabia. Al-Wahhab, in turn, had been ideologically inspired by Ibn Taymiyyah.[29] According to SADUM's *mufti* Muhammad Sodiq Muhammad Yusuf, the strident arguments between the "young mullahs" and Hindustani ultimately culminated in a "great schism" in the religious field between political quietists and activists.[30]

Rahmatulloh Qori's Ideology: *Musulmonobod* and Jihad

The most notable figure to emerge from the purist Ferghana Valley *hujras* was Rahmatulloh Alloma, known as Rahmatulloh Qori (1950–1981).[31] Uzbek scholars note that he penned a tract titled *Musulmonobod* in the late 1970s. In this work, he went beyond political theology to articulate an Islamist ideology, or blueprint for the state. It entailed several core ideas; the term itself, *Musulmonobod*, referred to Central Asia and the Muslim world as a single, unified territory of Islam. Here, *shariat* would rule relations between people, who would all believe in Allah, and the real *ulama* (not SADUM) would rule society.[32]

Rahmatulloh Qori reportedly died in a car accident in 1981, at age thirty-one, although some Uzbeks speculate the KGB was responsible. Whatever the truth, his death was convenient for the government, and even forty years later Uzbek Islamists still blamed the Communist Party and viewed him as a martyr. In 2021, an Islamist propaganda video traced subsequent Uzbek Islamist opposition leaders and scholars, each of whom it glorified, to Rahmatulloh Qori.[33] In the short term, in contrast to the Tajik republic, where the clandestine Nahzat group survived and spread in the 1970s, the neophyte Mujaddidiya network in the Uzbek republic lost its figurehead at a key moment. Nonetheless, ongoing repression and reactionary dissemination of Rahmatulloh Qori's ideas contributed to a renewal of underground Islamist growth in the late 1980s. The Soviet invasion of Afghanistan and the jihadi efforts of the mujahidin captured the imagination of the Uzbek *hujras*, as they did in the Tajik republic.

Rahmatulloh Qori's followers saw the mujahidin's anti-Soviet jihad as an example for themselves, and they brazenly denounced Hindustoniy for his political quietism and opposition to militancy. In the 1980s, Hindustoniy addressed a letter to certain unnamed young mullahs. In it, he debated his challengers,

29 Abou El Fadl, *The Great Theft*, 75–80.
30 Interview with former *mufti* Muhammad Sodiq Muhammad Yusuf.
31 Ashirbek Muminov, *Rodoslovnoe drevo Mukhtara Auezova* (Almaty: Zhibek Zholy, 2011).
32 Abduvakhitov, "Islamic Revivalism," 79–100.
33 "Раббоний Узбек Уламолар, Узбекча Нашида билан. (Тушларимда курсайдим бир бор яна)," Al Buhoriy channel, YouTube, January 21, 2021, https://www.youtube.com/watch?v=WOWM1XH-ihQ.

comparing them to Dukchi Eshon, the leader of a failed 1898 anti-Russian jihad in Andijon region of the Ferghana Valley. Hindustoniy wrote, "You blindly proclaim jihad. . . . Do not become like Dukchi Eshon, the cause of your own annihilation, and that of others who are guilty of nothing! God commands '. . . do not with your own hands cast yourself into ruination' (Qur'an 2:195). Therefore, first prepare your weapons against your enemy!"[34] Hindustoniy sympathized with their anger at the USSR's atheism, but he also made the classical theological distinction between greater and lesser jihad: "I, praise be to Allah, have also waged 'jihad of the tongue.' And for this I have been deprived of my freedom many times."[35] Hindustoniy decried his challengers for foolhardiness, for advocating "the murder of those who pray, the confiscation of people's property, the murder of women and children. Is this truly jihad? . . . No! Not by any means!"[36] Hindustoniy's interlocutors, the "young mullahs" of Uzbekistan, had "accuse[d] [him] of . . . having friendly relations with the state" and denounced him as an "unbeliever," a scathing accusation in the Muslim community; after praising the state for reopening mosques, Hindustoniy "cursed" Rahmatulloh Qori and beseeched the others to reject his path.[37] Discussion of jihad was probably rare, but the Soviet-Afghan War was shifting Muslim debate in Uzbekistan, as it had in Tajikistan.

The Political Theology of Abduvali Qori and Obidxon Qori

The Mujaddidiya became particularly popular in the Ferghana Valley, especially in Namangan and Andijon. One of the most prominent of these imams was Abduvali Qori, considered to be the "heir to [Rahmatullo Qori's] ideas."[38] Born in 1950, Abduvali Qori came of age in the late 1960s and 1970s in Andijon, one of the most strictly observant areas of Uzbekistan. He studied in the *hujra* of Abdulhakim Qori, and later worked as Rahmatulloh Qori's assistant.[39] In 1989, as *perestroika* began opening associational space, the

[34] The text of Hindustoniy is printed as an appendix to Bakhtiyar Babadjanov and Muzaffar Kamilov, "Muhammadjân Hindûstânî (1892–1989) and the Beginning of the Great Schism among the Muslims of Uzbekistan," in *Islam in Politics in Russia and Central Asia (Early Eighteenth to Late 20th Centuries)*, ed. Stéphane A. Dudoignon and Hisao Komatsu (London: Kegan Paul, 2001), 210–19.

[35] Babadzhanov and Komilov, "Muhammadjan Hindustani," 214.

[36] Babadzhanov and Komilov, "Muhammadjan Hindustani," 216.

[37] Babadzhanov and Komilov, "Muhammadjan Hindustani," 218.

[38] Abduvakhitov, "Islamic Revivalism"; Abdujabbar Abduvakhitov, "The Jadid Movement and Its Impact on Contemporary Central Asia," in *Central Asia: Its Strategic Importance and Future Prospects*, ed. Hafeez Malik (New York: St. Martin's Press, 1994), 74.

[39] Olcott, *Whirlwind of Jihad*, 103.

charismatic thirty-nine-year-old Abduvali Qori became imam of Andijon's main mosque.[40] Another of these young reformers was Obidxon Qori; from Namangan, he had studied under both Rahmatulloh Qori and Abduvali Qori. Obidxon Qori would become imam of Tashkent's To'xtaboy Mosque, which extended his growing religious and political influence. Although they themselves did not engage directly in politics, their independent stance on religious issues, well-known opposition to communism and secularism, and occasional public critiques—first of the USSR's communist dictatorship, and subsequently, of President Karimov's tightening grip on independent Uzbekistan—attracted those inclined to political activism. Both Abduvali Qori and Obidxon Qori recorded hundreds of sermons in the 1980s and early 1990s on cassettes or videotapes.[41] The sermons offer an important glimpse into the ideas and messages they were spreading at that time. As throughout the Ferghana Valley, they particularly emphasized the need to emulate Arab Islamic practice, by which they specifically meant Saudi, Salafist interpretations of Islam, coming directly from the holy centers of the Islamic world, Mecca and Medina. They viewed Saudi practice and teachings as pure and the epitome of true Islam, what Uzbeks had been denied throughout the Soviet era.[42] Their lectures focused on Salafi themes of puritanical reform and renewal, societal morality, and opposition to "polytheism."

Abduvali Qori and Obidxon Qori called Muslims to return to the time of the early caliphs, before "innovations," "superstitions," and Soviet practices had appeared and corrupted Islam. They declared local shrine pilgrimages that had been common for centuries to be un-Islamic. Sufi customs, the imams proclaimed, were "illicit" and "varieties of polytheism."[43] They simultaneously blamed other religions for spreading polytheism: "The Messenger of Allah (peace be upon him) cursed those who committed that deed. May Allah's curse be upon the Jews and the Christians, for they have taken their prophets' graves as places of worship."[44] Abduvali Qori also declared Soviet-era marriage practices "illicit" because they allowed Muslims to marry "polytheists"—meaning "Christians and Jews."[45] His sermon was a strike at Karimov, who was married to a Christian. Abduvali Qori and Obidxon Qori did not demand the conversion or expulsion of non-Muslims living in Central Asia. Yet both strongly opposed the Christian conversion of Muslims. Obidxon Qori proclaimed any convert away from Islam

[40] Personal communication with resident of Osh, Kyrgyzstan, who attended Abduvali Qori's mosque, July 2004.

[41] Many of these audiocassettes of sermons were made available thanks to the archive of David Tyson. Some were later collected in the primary source volume: Frank and Mamatov, ed., *Uzbek Islamic Debates*. Transcribed sermons and documents are in Uzbek, Russian, and English. Followers later posted many of these grainy videotapes on YouTube.

[42] Interview with Tyson.

[43] Abduvali Qori, lecture 55, in *Uzbek Islamic Debates*, 74.

[44] Abduvali Qori, lecture 55, in *Uzbek Islamic Debates*, 78.

[45] Abduvali Qori, lecture 30, in *Uzbek Islamic Debates*, 51.

to be guilty of rejecting both his faith and ancestors.[46] They did not condemn apostates to death, but Obidxon Qori declared that "Muslims have inhabited these lands since distant antiquity," and "if [missionary books] falls into our hands we have to seize them, burn them and destroy them. There's no other way. May God the Exalted grant us devotion and guidance."[47]

The sermons of these imams were laced with implicit criticism of communist rule, because it had supplanted *shariat*. Abduvali Qori argued that the Qur'an was unchanging for all times: "God (may He be praised and exalted) made the Holy Qur'an and the *shariat* for humanity until Judgement Day. Saying that the rules of the Qur'an do not apply to the present and are obsolete is polytheism, brothers."[48] In another sermon, he emphasized that monotheism requires the belief that "the holy Qur'an is the law and canon . . . promulgating the law, is the right of Allah Himself. . . . Attributing a single partner to Him is polytheism."[49] Such words challenged communist ideology, law, secularism, and Hanafi Islam; seventh-century *shariat* applied unchanged to the modern state. In another lecture, Abduvali Qori directly blamed the USSR for "ignorance of the fundamentally correct *hadith* of Islam. . . . This came about as a result of the murder and liquidation of wonderful scholars . . . these martyred scholars of Islam." He blamed the USSR for "introducing lies and fabrications into Islam," saying that the "enemies of Islam were always portraying Islam as something bad."[50]

The imams condemned both Soviet and post-Soviet cultural and political practices: "[H]anging pictures on the wall, placing statues in parliament . . . doing all these things gradually led people into idolatry."[51] Abduvali Qori castigated the Soviet regime because "the intention of the inveterate enemies of Islam was to slaughter and liquidate in a short time every one of the most eminent individuals in the country . . . the finest masters in the field of Islamic law. . . . This prevented the common people from observing true Islam"; instead they were misled and learned to follow "phony Islam."[52]

In sharp contrast to the IRPT, these imams advocated only the *umma*—no nation or country, no modern ethnonational categories that divided Muslims. They demanded Muslim unity: "Allah created every nation . . . Uzbeks, Arabs, Tajiks, Kyrgyz, Turks, whatever, English, Russians, Jews."[53] Such ideas were a direct criticism of the state's emerging nationalism in the early post-Soviet period.

[46] Obidxon Qori, lecture 10, in *Uzbek Islamic Debates*, 172.
[47] Obidxon Qori, lecture 28, in *Uzbek Islamic Debates*, 220.
[48] Abduvali Qori, lecture 55, in *Uzbek Islamic Debates*, 79.
[49] Abduvali Qori, lecture 30, in *Uzbek Islamic Debates*, 42, my italics.
[50] Abduvali Qori, lecture 36, in *Uzbek Islamic Debates*, 92.
[51] Abduvali Qori, lecture 30, in *Uzbek Islamic Debates*, 39.
[52] Abduvali Qori, lecture 39, in *Uzbek Islamic Debates*, 91.
[53] Obidxon Qori, lecture 23, in *Uzbek Islamic Debates*, 186.

The themes of Obidxon Qori's sermons included fear of Allah and Judgment Day, the Islamic requirement of wearing hijab, and the lack of job opportunities for Muslims in Moscow. He praised a poet whose verse condemned "Godless atheist infidels,"[54] and he blended religion and politics in a call for justice: "May Allah give justice to us all. . . . Allah help us against our enemy; defeat those who want to defeat the faith with Your mercy and power."[55] In another sermon, titled "On Deceivers," Obidxon Qori criticized "those who in the past became a Red person, or Red Muslim,"[56] a reference to Muslims who had joined the Communist Party, or the "Red mullahs" and "Red teahouses" that were under communist control. Obidxon Qori condemned "the ones with authority today, the army they control today," as those perpetrating religious oppression: "All of it will be gathered up, brought together, and placed on the field of Judgment Day. There, maybe all of their soldiers, all of their police. . . . Their jails, their dungeons, their threats, their weapons, their bombs, their guns and whatever else. Allah the Exalted will gather it up on the plain of Judgment Day. Allah says, 'Now you're going to Hell. . . . *They* will submit to questioning then [Qur'an 37:26]."[57] Without mentioning them by name, Obidxon Qori's words were a trenchant condemnation of all communists. He dismissed Marx and Lenin as "lackeys of Satan."[58] In late 1991, Abduvali Qori likewise openly condemned the communist and ex-communist leadership of Uzbekistan as "Jews and atheists," "the enemies of Islam."[59] Obidxon Qori compared communism to slavery: "[I]t [communism] enslaves the world for itself. . . . We practiced socialism in half the world. . . . [Socialism] attempt[ed] to own the world. . . . [Human] nature, bad character, the satanic nature, the satanic soul, is like that."[60] He compared the communist destruction of Islam to the devastation wrought by the Mongol invasion. By contrast, he declined to criticize the Taliban's killings; he declared that critical news of the Taliban was spread by "immoral Muslims" and "non-Muslim circles"—no doubt a reference to Karimov's regime, Russia, and the West.[61]

Obidxon Qori voiced sharp criticism of the post-Soviet Karimov government as well. He challenged state restrictions on performing *namaz* and the ban on the hijab. Denouncing "half naked" women in "satanic dress," he contrasted them with the virtuous "who cover . . . with the black hijab."[62] He declared that "Allah

[54] Obidxon Qori, lecture 17, in *Uzbek Islamic Debates*, 121.
[55] Obidxon Qori, lecture 17, in *Uzbek Islamic Debates*, 125.
[56] Obidxon Qori, lecture 23, in *Uzbek Islamic Debates*, 185.
[57] Obidxon Qori, lecture 23, in *Uzbek Islamic Debates*, 184–85, my italics.
[58] Obidxon Qori, lecture 23, in *Uzbek Islamic Debates*, 199.
[59] Frank and Mamatov, *Uzbek Islamic Debates*, xv.
[60] Obidxon Qori, lecture 12, in *Uzbek Islamic Debates*, 180.
[61] Obidxon Qori, lecture 25, in *Uzbek Islamic Debates*, 206.
[62] Obidxon Qori, lecture 24, in *Uzbek Islamic Debates*, 196.

has ordered the hijab," so if the "earthly boss" opposes it, "he is a scoundrel, an infidel."[63] He further declared that in Uzbekistan, the struggle to wear hijab was also a "jihad."[64]

Obidxon Qori returned often to discussion of a threat to Muslims, making implicit references to Rahmatulloh Qori's death and Abduvali Qori's disappearance in 1995; many devout believers attributed both to the secret police. Obidxon Qori proclaimed: "If the faithful are together . . . there's no one who can make them disappear. . . . Allah the Exalted reassured the faithful Muslims, saying, 'When all the people of the world assemble and say, we're going to attack the Muslims,' no one will have the strength."[65] Obidxon Qori continued: "The present time is an era in which the affairs of Muslims are difficult. . . . Infidels, hypocrites . . . are looking to dig up dirt on them. Muslims need to be careful, vigilant."[66] He stressed the need for Muslim unity against all those attacking Muslim communities; he even blamed the bloody interethnic pogroms of 1989–90 in Parkent and Osh on "people who are trying to divide Muslims" for "political ends."[67]

In short, these imams revealed their antisecular and anticommunist political views to their followers, albeit sometimes obliquely. Their popularity, charisma, and implicit political discussions caused the Uzbek authorities to fear them and their potential for organizing an Islamist opposition. At least some of these imams' adherents would turn to direct activism.

The Outcome: First-Wave Uzbek Islamist Mobilization

Like its Tajik counterpart, Uzbek Islamism grew from underground ideas and religious entrepreneurs, who harbored long grievances against the USSR for repression and exclusion of observant Muslims and became activists in the growing space of *glasnost* and *perestroika*. As waves of protest engulfed the USSR, Islamist entrepreneurs used mosque networks to mobilize demonstrators. Two Islamist organizations were particularly notable: Adolat and its militia, Islom Lashkarlari (the Armies of Islam), and the Islamic Revival Party of Uzbekistan and its armed wing, called Tavba (Repentance).

63 Obidxon Qori, lecture 24, in *Uzbek Islamic Debates*, 195–96.
64 Obidxon Qori, lecture 24, in *Uzbek Islamic Debates*, 199–200.
65 Obidxon Qori, lecture 27, in *Uzbek Islamic Debates*, 212.
66 Obidxon Qori, lecture 27, in *Uzbek Islamic Debates*, 213.
67 Obidxon Qori, lecture 27, in *Uzbek Islamic Debates*, 213.

Adolat and Islom Lashkarlari

Adolat and Islom Lashkarlari emerged sometime between 1988 and 1990, in the turbulent context of the Ferghana Valley, as long-simmering dissatisfaction turned to protest. These Islamist organizations were conceived in *hujras* of the Ferghana Valley, where young mullahs and their followers had begun confronting SADUM's imams and local government officials to take control of local mosques.[68] In 1989, mullahs from Andijon and Namangan organized their communities in demonstrations demanding the replacement of the quietist *mufti* of SADUM. Gorbachev agreed to the appointment of Muhammad Sodiq Muhammad Yusuf as the new *mufti*. The latter, an esteemed theologian from Andijon, strategically allied with *perestroika* reformers and was thereby able to advance Islamic revival. SADUM began to return more mosques to local communities. Ironically, the *mufti*'s steps brought these activists into open contention with the state. Some mosques were taken over by activist imams who opposed the state. In Kokand, for example, a struggle for the central Friday mosque ensued; young members accused the older candidate for imam of committing innovations (*bid'ah*), and selected an imam who was both puritanical and anti-Soviet.[69] This process unfolded across the Valley, as formerly SADUM-controlled mosques were soon led by independent imams. Often, nonstate imams simply set up shop in reopened mosques with no appointed imam, given the sudden shortage of state-trained religious personnel.

In some mosques, puritanism became the basis of Islamism. As had the "young mullahs" of Kokand, some new imams quickly voiced opposition against the Soviet regime. In one prominent case, Imam Abdulahat (Barnoyev) took over the Atovalixon To'ra Mosque in Namangan.[70] Another follower of Rahmatulloh Qori and Abduvali Qori, Imam Abdulahat turned ideas into political activism.[71] His mosque became a rallying point for opposition Islam.[72] Young male members of his mosque formed martial arts clubs to train.[73] The central Friday Gumbaz mosque in Namangan and the Mullah Kirgiz *madrasa* also attracted militant youth and became centers of the nascent IRPU and Adolat.[74]

[68] Olcott, *Whirlwind of Jihad.*

[69] Nasriddin-damulla Toychiyev, "Alamli Dil Nidosi," in Babajanov, Muminov, and Kügelgen, *Disputy musul'manskikh religioznykh avtoritetov*, 180.

[70] Frank and Mamatov, *Uzbek Islamic Debates*, xv.

[71] Abdujabbor Abduvohidov, *Uzbekistan: Center of Confrontation between Traditional and Extremist Islam in Central Asia* (Washington, D.C.: Nixon Center, July 16, 2003).

[72] Olcott, *Whirlwind of Jihad.*

[73] Abdujabbor Abduvohidov, "Independent Uzbekistan: A Muslim Community in Development," in *The Politics of Religion in Russia and the New States of Eurasia*, ed. Michael Bordeaux (Armonk, NY: M. E. Sharpe, 1995), 298.

[74] Abduvohidov, "Uzbekistan: Center of Confrontation."

Adolat quickly gained a following among the population of Namangan and Andijon, both in urban centers and the villages. Adolat's members were Salafi revivalists turned activist. Most prominent among them was the young and energetic Tohir Yo'ldosh, a fiery, self-proclaimed religious leader and a disciple of Abduvali Qori and Obidxon Qori. Not one to be complacent, much less take orders, Yo'ldosh soon emerged as Adolat's leader. According to Tyson, a scholar who attended Adolat gatherings in Namangan region as a graduate student, Yo'ldosh was "a thinker." He was committed to establishing an "ideal" of "pure Arab Islam" to replace *jahiliyya*, a term (meaning the period of ignorance and barbarism before Islam) that he frequently used to characterize the Soviet era.[75] Yo'ldosh saw Muslims in Uzbekistan as unenlightened due to communist erasure of their Islamic knowledge and past. Whether or not Yo'ldosh had directly encountered similar ideas in the writings of Sayyid Qutb is unclear, but his preaching echoed the radical Muslim Brotherhood thinker's call for action to reverse such a despicable state of affairs. Yo'ldosh rejected the traditional Uzbek Hanafi-Sufi synthesis. Although he spoke no Arabic and had no direct Arab contacts at the time, he clearly idealized and sought to emulate Saudi purists, not the Muslim Brotherhood, the Iranians, or the Afghans. Adolat propagated Islamist demands, including the precedence of *shariat* and an Islamic state, without specifying what that would entail. At the time, notably, Adolat members focused all their animosity and effort on opposition to communism, to the USSR; they had no hate for America, and were even curious about Americans, given their support for the Afghan mujahidin.[76]

As opposed to the Nahzat's decade of preparation, Yo'ldosh and his comrade-in-arms Jumaboy Hojiyev (more commonly known as Juma Namangoniy) moved directly into political activism. Namangoniy, more the activist than the philosopher, had been deployed as a paratrooper in the Red Army in Afghanistan in 1987, where he was an eyewitness to the USSR's war on Muslims, as many in Namangan viewed it.[77] Adolat mobilized about two thousand adherents, who pledged loyalty not only to Adolat but also personally to Yo'ldosh. That number reportedly increased to eight thousand by 1991.[78] Sympathizers across the Ferghana Valley were even more numerous.

In August 1991, as crime erupted during the collapse of the USSR, Adolat formed a vigilante militia from its martial arts clubs.[79] Calling themselves

[75] Interview with Tyson.

[76] Interview with Tyson.

[77] Orozbek Moldaliev, "An Incongruous War in the Valley of Poison: The Religious Conflict in Southern Kyrgyzstan," *Central Asia and the Caucasus* 1 (2000): 11–20; Ahmed Rashid. "They're Only Sleeping: Why Militant Islamicists in Central Asia Aren't Going to Go Away," *Annals of Terrorism*, January 2002, https://www.newyorker.com/magazine/2002/01/14/theyre-only-sleeping.

[78] Olcott, *Whirlwind of Jihad*, 240.

[79] Communication with businessman from Kokand, Tashkent, Uzbekistan, January 2005.

Islom Lashkarlari, they began to patrol the streets of Namangan and Andijon and to enforce *shariat* law.[80] Initially, the group was respected for creating order in what had become a lawless area; it even cooperated with local authorities in Namangan.[81] The movement raided hotels looking for prostitutes, insisted upon a strict dress code for men and women, enforced the hijab, banned music, and monitored public morality. They punished violators by flogging thieves, warning unveiled women, and harassing people who missed prayer services. They publicly slapped a Russian woman for dressing immodestly, to the shock of Uzbek passersby; such an action broke traditional norms of Uzbek politeness and respect for other religious and cultural groups.[82]

In September 1991, following the resignation of communist hard-liners in Moscow, Uzbekistan became an independent state. But its communist leadership under Islom Karimov clung to power, leading Yo'ldosh to mobilize popular protests. Yo'ldosh demanded the creation of an Islamic center in Namangan in place of the Communist Party headquarters, as well as the creation of an Islamic state in Uzbekistan.[83] Some twenty-five thousand Muslims gathered in a mosque in Namangan calling for the Party to be banned, along with any successor organizations, for its property be nationalized, and for improved living standards. They also declared their support for the IRPT against communist rule in Tajikistan, suggesting that they were closely following the IRPT's mobilization strategy.[84] Local activists of Birlik (Unity), an Uzbek nationalist organization and independence movement that had formed during the Gorbachev years, joined in support of Adolat's demands; the two organizations shared a nationalist, anticommunist ideology.

By December 1991, with their demands unmet and President Karimov a candidate in the first post-Soviet presidential election, Adolat activists escalated their strategy. Islom Lashkarlari seized the former Communist Party IsPolKom building, the regional government for Namangan *oblast*. Yo'ldosh insisted that Karimov personally meet with his followers, and further, demanded his resignation. Karimov conceded to visiting Namangan. Yol'dosh organized a large demonstration in Namangan's central square, demanding Karimov face them.[85] The throng grew from five hundred to fifty thousand.[86] On his third day in

[80] Alec Rasizade, "Dictators, Islamists, Big Powers and Ordinary People: The New 'Great Game' in Central Asia," *International Politics and Society Online*, 2002, http://library.fes.de/pdf-files/ipg/ipg-2002-3/artrasizade.pdf.

[81] Interview with Namangan informants, Namangan, Uzbekistan.

[82] Interview with Tyson.

[83] Abduvohidov, "Independent Uzbekistan," 297; Babadjanov, "Economic and Religious History," 246–47.

[84] "Muslims Rally Against Communists in Namangan," *Moscow INTERFAX*, September 28, 1991, *Daily Report. Soviet Union*, FBIS-SOV-91-189, September 30, 1991. The IRPT protests had escalated in September 1991, as discussed in Chapter 5.

[85] Interview with journalist, Namangan, Uzbekistan, July 2003.

[86] Interview with journalist, Namangan, July 2003.

Image 8.1 Adolat leader Tohir Yo'ldosh (standing) challenges President Islom Karimov (seated), Namangan, 1991
Source: Screenshot of Video Posted on YouTube

Namangan, Karimov finally emerged from closed meetings to address the agitated crowd.[87] Yo'ldosh pacified his supporters by reciting a verse from the Qur'an and insisting that the president kneel (see Image 8.1). The all-male audience loudly responded, "Allahu Akbar" (God is Great). A gifted orator, Yo'ldosh spoke with force and passion about Karimov's consistent refusal to meet with the Uzbek people.[88] The much older, dour Karimov sat hunched, awaiting his turn, as Yo'ldosh elaborated his demands: change the Constitution to recognize Islam as the state religion, give *shariat* legal precedence, swear the oath of office on the Qur'an, declare an Islamic state in Uzbekistan, establish gender-segregated schools, and turn the Communist House of Education into a place for religious groups to convene.[89] After brushing aside Karimov's repeated attempts to speak, he at last passed the president the microphone. In a rambling response Karimov insisted that Yo'ldosh's demands were anticonstitutional. At one point, Yo'ldosh again grabbed the microphone, forcing the president to listen.[90] Karimov, humiliated, backed down. Yo'ldosh insisted that the president of Uzbekistan have *Islamic* authority. A visibly agitated Karimov responded, "No such authority can be given. Only if it is stated in the constitution." Equivocating, he

[87] Interview with journalist, Namangan, June 2004.
[88] "Каримов Наманганда (1991)," Turkiston TV, YouTube, August 20, 2011, https://www.youtube.com/watch?v=xwVS8CQg2s4.
[89] Abduvohidov, "Independent Uzbekistan," 279.
[90] Interview with journalist, Namangan, Uzbekistan, June 2004.

continued, "[W]e are going to make a new constitution. . . . We have to have them [the legislature] write that specific phrase."[91] He implied that he would accede to parliament's will. Ultimately, Karimov's only concession was to swear his oath of office on the Qur'an.

The moment was defining. Some believe the incident indelibly shaped Karimov's view of independent Islam and that he returned to Tashkent determined to crush the Islamists.[92]

The demonstrators meanwhile proved unappeased by these meager concessions. Karimov's victory, in what appeared to be a fixed election, triggered further unrest. In early 1992, Adolat and its Islamist allies continued to control the Namangan Communist Party building, took hostages, and declared Islamic law for Namangan. This time, Karimov responded with force. Police surrounded the building while the activists performed *namaz*, arresting large numbers. Over the next year, the sharp drop in mosque attendance reflected the fact that many young men had fled, possibly about three thousand, some becoming *muhajir*s (immigrants to a new land, as in the Prophet Muhammad's time) as they brought their wives and children with them to join Yo'ldosh and Namangoniy across the border. They set up camps in the Tavildara Valley of Tajikistan, an Islamist stronghold, and fought alongside the IRPT in its war against Tajikistan's regime.[93] They subsequently fled to Afghanistan with the IRPT and UTO in late 1992 and 1993.

In the assessment of a Namangan resident who was sympathetic to Adolat, "Had Karimov sat and talked with them, they would not have become terrorists. . . . No one even knew Juma Namangoniy then. He was just an ordinary person. . . . But Karimov needs terrorists."[94] Those words proved true: for twenty-five years after the Namangan showdown, Karimov used the specter of "Islamic extremism" and "terrorism" to justify his ever-escalating brutality.

Islamic Revival Party of Uzbekistan

Loosely connected to Adolat was another Islamist group, which emerged as a political party, much like the IRPT. At the 1990 congress of the All-Union Islamic Revival Party (AUIRP) in Russia (see Chapter 5), Uzbeks were heavily in attendance.[95] Led by Imam Abdulla Uta, Uzbek activists attempted to organize and register a party branch inside the Uzbek republic. Denied permission, the

91 "Каримов Наманганда," Turkiston TV.

92 Interview with journalist, Namangan, Uzbekistan, July 1997; communication with Uzbek NGO representative, Tashkent, Uzbekistan, January 2003.

93 Interview with Tyson; interview with Michael Croissant, retired CIA officer, July 2022.

94 Interview with anonymous respondent, Namangan 2004.

95 Interview with former AUIRP member Davlat Usmon, who was also an IRPT activist and deputy prime minister, Dushanbe, Tajikistan, November 2010.

Uzbek party met underground. Sympathizers came from both Tashkent and the Ferghana Valley, and information about its agenda was distributed furtively through neighborhood *mahallas*. Some estimated membership at about fifty thousand in 1991.[96] Though that number is probably exaggerated, the IRPU likely drew on supporters of Adolat and other newly emergent Islamist groups.

Despite Karimov's claim that the IRPU was "Wahhabi," its program—a variant of the AUIRP's from which it had emerged—was neither puritanical nor revolutionary. Its main demands concerned Islamic rights and revival. The party pledged to achieve these by encouraging obedience to the Qur'an and *hadith*, creating a publishing house, extolling Islam in the media, reopening *madrasas*, and rejecting scientific atheism. They demanded a return to pre-Soviet institutions like the *waqf* and the creation of Islamic charities. They sought to strengthen the family "according to the principles of Islam," a vision which promoted a conservative role for women. The IRPU aimed to "fight, through understanding and persuasion, national and racial discrimination, crime, alcoholism, and other things forbidden by *shariat*." It wanted to develop relations with the Muslim world and "equal relations with representatives of other religions."[97] Finally, it advocated "principles of an Islamic economy," a commitment to food distribution according to *shariat*, and, like the Muslim Brotherhood, a promise "to solve the problems of people according to the holy Qur'an and *hadith*."[98] The party platform endorsed cooperation with democratic parties.[99] In short, the program was primarily about de-secularization rather than enforcing an Islamic state. However, the IRPU was fragmented over ideology and strategy, which led to one network forming in Tashkent, another in Kokand, and another in Andijon and Namangan. Some members had been followers of Rahmatulloh Qori, and the party leader, Imam Abdullah, had been a student of Abduvali Qori; that wing of the party was puritanical and antidemocratic, while the other wing, like the IRPT, was more open to parliamentary politics and coalition building with democrats and nationalists, like Birlik.[100]

Despite lacking legal registration, the Islamist party organized protests in Uzbekistan in the summer of 1991. At one meeting planned in Kokand just after the August 1991 coup, the IRPU demanded the release of its members as well

[96] A. Khalmukhamedov, "Islamskyi factor v Uzbekistane," *Svobodnaia mysl'* 4 (1998): 54; "Text of Islamic Renaissance Party of Uzbekistan, Programme," in *Political Organization in Central Asia and Azerbaijan: Sources and Documents*, ed. Vladimir Babak, Demian Vaisman, and Aryeh Wasserman (London: Frank Cass Publishers, 2004), 386.

[97] "IRPU programme," in *Political Organization in Central Asia and Azerbaijan: Sources and Documents*, ed. Vladimir Babak, Demian Vaisman, and Ayreh Wasseman (London: Frank Cass, 2004), 387.

[98] "IRPU programme," 387; Abduvakhitov, "Islamic Revivalism," 96–97.

[99] "IRPU programme," 387; Abduvakhitiov, "Islamic Revivalism," 84, 96.

[100] Interview with Birlik member, Namangan, Uzbekistan, June 2004. Frank and Mamatov, *Uzbek Islamic Debates*, xv.

as other opposition activists held as political prisoners; it claimed that Karimov had used the coup as a pretext to engage in a widespread arrest of its members.[101] The party also formed a vigilante group, Tavba, which operated in Namangan to enforce *shariat*.[102] As intra-Muslim contestation over advocating political Islam ensued, the new *mufti*, Muhammad Sodiq Muhammad Yusuf, spoke publicly against the Islamic party.[103]

The state barred the IRPU from competing in the 1991 presidential election. In spring 1992, Karimov again turned his ire on the party, arresting most activists in several waves. In late 1992, Imam Abdulla mysteriously vanished, very likely abducted by Karimov's security services.[104] His disappearance triggered the flight of other members and precluded the emergence of a strong Islamist party.

Late Soviet and early post-Soviet Uzbekistan paralleled the Tajik case in many ways. Brutal Soviet repression had made Islam a major grievance for some, while marginal increases in associational space had fostered the dissemination of Islamist ideas and writings within *hujra*s of the Ferghana Valley from the late 1970s onward. The elimination of the key religious entrepreneurs, however, beginning with Rahmatullo Qori, stalled the Islamist movement's emergence. It reappeared under new leaders—Yo'ldosh, Namangoniy, and Imam Uta, who were directly supported by Imam Barnoyev and inspired by Abduvali Qori and Obidxon Qori. Yet, those entrepreneurs were arrested, exiled, or "disappeared." Meanwhile, *mufti* Muhammad Sodiq Muhammad Yusuf, although critical of the government and actively pushing Islamic revivalism, chose a different path from Qozikalon Turajonzoda; he did not back the Islamists' protests and political demands. With the elimination of these entrepreneurial leaders, between 1992 and 1998 very little Islamist activity occurred inside Uzbekistan.

The democratic-nationalist opposition, Birlik and Erk, was also crushed, and Karimov quickly consolidated power. However, the roots of a more radical Islamist movement had been planted. Islamist exiles were regrouping in Tajikistan and Afghanistan.

Assessing the Relative Success of First-Wave Islamist Mobilization

Karimov's decisive crackdown was critical to rapid demobilization of Islamism in 1992. Before then, however, Uzbek Islamists proved to be moderately

[101] "Protest Against 'Communist Dictatorship' Planned," *Moscow INTERFAX*, August 29, 1991, *Daily Report, Soviet Union*, FBIS-SOV-91-169, August 30, 1991.

[102] Interview with Birlik member; Olcott, *Whirlwind of Jihad*.

[103] Abduvohidov, "Independent Uzbekistan," 297–98.

[104] Human Rights Watch, "Creating Enemies," 21.

successful in mobilization, albeit arguably much less so than their contemporary, the IRPT. I turn now to the three factors that facilitate high mobilization: sacred authority, networks, and ideational adaptation. The Uzbek movement gradually constructed sacred authority and drew on localized networks, but failed at broader networking and ideational adaptation.

The Uzbek Islamist movement had up to eight thousand Adolat members and thousands more IRPU members. They had mobilized twenty-five thousand to fifty thousand protesters in regular challenges to the state between September 1991 and April 1992. Data from the early 1990s, when public opinion surveys faced less state intervention, revealed a strong base of popular support for political Islam.[105] One survey question in January 1992, before the crackdown drove the Islamist movement to flee the country, asked respondents how much "confidence" they had "in the Islamic Party"; 57 percent responded that they "have confidence in the Islamic Party."[106] In subsequent polls, 57 percent (1993) and 51 percent (1994) of Uzbek respondents agreed that "in Islam one can find the answer to many of Uzbekistan's problems." Thus, there was significant popular support for an Islamic party and the idea that Islam should have a role in the function and governance of the state. Such support was a substantial feat in Uzbekistan's suffocating political environment—arguably far more repressive than Tajikistan's. In March 1993 only 19 percent had confidence in the Islamic Party, and in 1994 only 1 percent did.[107] Rising fear following the government's elimination of Adolat and the IRPU in mid-1992 explains this rapid fall in reported support for an Islamic party. Beyond Karimov, however, several other factors explain the weaker foundation of Adolat and the IRPU.

First, the movement struggled for sacred authority. The premature death of Rahmatulloh Qori had stopped the movement from building its sacred authority and underground networking. Yo'ldosh, while a bold self-proclaimed mullah, was young and lacked substantial authority in 1989. He had relatively little religious training, even in *hujras*. He had challenged religious elders in the Ferghana Valley, as well as in SADUM's establishment.

Abduvali Qori and Obidxon Qori, among others, did lend significant authority to the Islamist movement. Their mosques were widely attended, and their sermons were broadly distributed. However, Abduvali Qori "was disappeared," while Obidxon Qori was forced to hide underground and later flee Uzbekistan. Their disappearances undercut their ability to mobilize, but also triggered

[105] Arustan Joldasov and Nancy Lubin, "Central Asians Take Stock: Part II, 1993 and 2007," Report, The National Council for Eurasian and East European Research, Seattle, Washington, 2009.

[106] The survey item did not specify the IRPU, but rather, intentionally left it vague. Some respondents may have expressly supported the IRPU, while others may have expressed support for an unspecified Islamic party.

[107] Steven Grant, "Faith in Central Asia: Kazakhstan, Uzbekistan, and Islam," Opinion Analysis, M-95-31, U.S. Information Agency, Washington, D.C., 1995.

animosity toward the government. The public prominence of such religious leaders in the 1980s and 1990s was striking. For example, Abduvali Qori, who was given the honorific title "Shaykh" because of his great learning, was the focus of dozens of YouTube videos. One of the earliest available, dated 1986, showed the young, bearded imam confidently speaking into a microphone from the head table at a gathering of male elders. The video then cut to footage from 1994, when the shaykh addressed a packed group of men, apparently gathered for a funeral; he occupied a position of honor within the company.[108] The video caption simply read, "Mujaddid,"[109] but had 88,964 views in just one of its many postings. A 1990 speech by the young Shaykh Abduvali Qori, addressing those who appeared to be older members of the *ulama*, had 31,708 views less than two years after being posted, despite its poor sound quality. Some videos had tens of thousands of hits, such as one posted October 13, 2010, with 137,720 views.[110] Another titled "Shaykh Abduvali Qori, ALLOH yo'lida shahid bo'lishlik" (To become a martyr for the sake of Allah) had 70,764 views.[111] Yet another, apparently filmed in Abduvali Qori's mosque in 1994 and posted on December 15, 2010, had 148,916 hits in just a few years. In a March 1995 video, Abduvali Qori's voice resonated before a mosque crowded with men of all ages, spilling out into the courtyard and street.[112] Small children were visible too, listening attentively to the imam's words. Published online on January 21, 2014, the hour-long video had nearly 110,000 views in six years.[113] This cursory glance at the imam's online profile strongly suggests that he wielded high sacred authority before his disappearance in 1995. Moreover, his arrest made him a martyr to the evolving Uzbek Islamist movement, as the next chapter will demonstrate.

Likewise, videos of Obidxon Qori's sermons were posted on Salafist websites and YouTube and were still being watched globally twenty-five years after he was forced into hiding; videos had thousands and even tens of thousands of hits, also presumably by ethnic Uzbeks, since Uzbek was the language of his sermons. The popularity of these videos, despite the risk entailed in accessing Islamic materials from within Uzbekistan, underscores the high authority of both Shaykh Abduvali Qori and Obidxon Qori.

[108] "шайх Абдували қори 1986," YouTube, October 16, 2015, https://www.youtube.com/watch?v=792Iym3w-S8.

[109] "шайх Абдували қори."

[110] "шайх Абдували қори."

[111] "Shayh Abduvali Qori, ALLOH yo'lida shahid bo'lishlik," YouTube, April 17, 2017, https://www.youtube.com/watch?v=1Tus8G865lM. The 1994 video was later posted, removed, and reposted many times on YouTube.

[112] "Abduvali Qori Andijoni 1995, ahli islom sodiqlar," YouTube, January 21, 2014, https://www.youtube.com/watch?v=YvG8n5zPqrg.

[113] "Abduvali Qori Andijoni 1995."

Image 8.2 The IMU's martyr, Shaykh Abduvali Qori: "Teacher, in the name of Allah, I love you."
Source: Screenshot, YouTube Video

Nonetheless, these mullahs lacked the other religious resources wielded by the IRPT. Whereas the IRPT had the national backing of the Tajik *qozikalon*, Adolat lacked support from the Uzbek *mufti* and other Islamic leaders in Uzbekistan, most of whom avoided politics. The young mullahs' influence therefore remained regionally limited to the Ferghana Valley with some adherents in Tashkent. Yo'ldosh's stunning confrontation with Karimov, blatantly humiliating the elder statesman on video in December 1991, in defiance of Uzbek culture, rallied a fringe of young men. Yet, that defining moment also alienated mainstream Uzbek Muslims by revealing Yo'ldosh's utter disrespect for elders.[114] It defined him as too radical, too extreme for most.

Second, the Islamist movement drew on local networks—extensive friendship, kinship, sports, mosque, village, and *mahalla* networks—in Namangan and Andijon. Such networks were dense and often overlapping. While both traditional and newer urban networks were critical to the dissemination of religious knowledge for many decades, these networks were localized; they lacked both transcommunal and national ties.[115] The Islamist movement's influence therefore remained limited. No phenomenon equivalent in size or trauma to the forced migrations in Tajikistan had created networks that spanned regions of the country.

[114] Interview with Tyson. According to Tyson, the videocassette was widely distributed underground.
[115] Babadjanov, "Economic and Religious History," 258.

Third, Adolat, the IRPU, and their allies in part focused on ideas rooted in the Uzbek experience and context: reviving Islam, ending repression of Islamic practice, and creating more space for Muslim prayer and practice inside public buildings. Their moderate political demands—bringing Islam into politics in some way, as in the oath of office, creating Islamic banking (without interest), and ending corruption—also resonated, particularly in the Ferghana Valley. However, the puritanical views of the Mujaddidiya and Adolat, and their implementation by Yo'ldosh's *shariat* militia, were not widely endorsed throughout Uzbekistan. Whether in the more European and secularized Tashkent, or even in Andijon, where the head *mufti* and the traditional Hanafi *ulama* were still influential, there was strong skepticism about imposing *shariat* and engaging in political activism. While some support for specific *shariat* laws and punishments existed in Namangan *oblast*, there was little support elsewhere.[116]

Sacred authority and local networks were certainly important in mobilizing the first wave of Islamism in Uzbekistan, especially when facing the formidable Karimov regime; however, in order to create a more durable and mass-based movement, Islamists needed broader networks as well, beyond their own origins. Moreover, while Adolat's criticism of the regime was trenchant, it never adapted its Salafist ideas to the mainstream Islamic norms and practices that characterized most of Uzbekistan in 1990.

Conditions Breeding Second-Wave Islamism: Repeating the Past

Marginal Associational Space Allows Ideational Diffusion

Despite Karimov's success in disbanding the Islamist movement by late 1992, the collapse of the USSR de facto increased associational space inside Uzbekistan. Trade and travel opened up. Religious ideas spread as businessmen, who were often missionaries as well, came from the United Arab Emirates, Saudi Arabia, and Turkey, where communities of Uzbek émigrés had settled.[117] According to one informant, "after 1989, until about 1992 or even 1995, Uzbeks from Saudi Arabia came back and taught, donated books, and financed mosques."[118] In 1993, the government expelled two thousand foreigners, who reportedly included at least "forty-four Islamic emissaries."[119] By 1997, Arab money had

[116] Collins, "Political Role of Clans."
[117] Bayram Balcı, *Islam in Central Asia and the Caucasus since the Fall of the Soviet Union* (Oxford: Oxford University Press, 2018).
[118] Interview with journalist, Namangan, Uzbekistan, June 2004.
[119] *Daily Report, Uzbekistan*, FBIS-Sov-93-196, September 28, 1993, 45.

financed one of the largest mosques in Tashkent, and dozens of smaller ones in other towns, according to many local residents.[120] Religious education abroad skyrocketed.[121] Some imams reported that after independence, local government officials had even paid to send youth abroad, to study in Egypt at Al-Azhar University.[122] Multiple respondents reported knowing young men who went to Egypt, Kuwait, Turkey, or Pakistan to study. Foreign sponsors gave scholarships to Uzbek students for engineering studies in Arab countries, but when the youth arrived at their destination, they found that they were enrolled in religious instruction.[123] The University of Medina, among others, indoctrinated students with Salafism. One could also travel to Kyrgyzstan on a daily basis to study in Arab-financed *madrasas*.[124] Muhammad Sodiq Muhammad Yusuf admitted that foreign Muslim charities regularly paid religious students' expenses, and that for much of the 1990s this sector was minimally regulated.[125]

For a time, Karimov's pursuit of national and cultural legitimacy also increased space for religion and wove Uzbekistan's religious revival into the new nationalism.[126] OMI (the Muslim Board of Uzbekistan, which replaced SADUM after independence) legalized eleven *madrasas*, including two for women, and the Tashkent Islamic Institute. Yet each had small enrollments. In 1999, the government opened the Tashkent Islamic University, where administrators emphasized the deep interconnection between national and religious identity, among other state-approved Islamic themes.[127] The rector wrote, "Uzbekistan is building a society containing a thousand years of spiritual-moral development . . . with a restored Islamic culture."[128] The state celebrated Imam al-Buxoriy, a revered compiler of the *hadith*, who was a son of Bukhara in the tenth century. It refurbished the Sufi shrine of Bahouddin Naqshbandi in Bukhara for tourism, and for use in government propaganda.[129] State historians rewrote the history of Central Asian Sufism, excluding instances of its political opposition. They revived the once-purged Jadids as part of the post-Soviet Uzbek state's emphasis on modern, national, and strictly apolitical Islam. By co-opting Islam, Karimov sought both to

[120] Interview with *mufti*, Tashkent, Uzbekistan, n.d.

[121] Balcı, *Islam in Central Asia and the Caucasus.*

[122] Interview with imam, mosque in Samarqand *oblast*, Uzbekistan, June 2004.

[123] David Abramson, "Foreign Religious Education and the Central Asian Islamic Revival," Report. Central Asia Caucasus Institute-Silk Road Studies Program. Washington, D.C., March 2010, 32.

[124] Personal communication with NGO expert from Osh, Kyrgyzstan, November 2014; interview with students and teachers in a Jalalabad *madrasa*, Jalalabad, Kyrgyzstan, June 2004.

[125] Interview with Muhammad Sodiq Muhammad Yusuf, Tashkent, Uzbekistan, January 2003.

[126] Laura Adams, *The Spectacular State: Culture and National Identity in Uzbekistan* (Durham, NC: Duke University Press, 2010).

[127] Interviews with administrators and teachers, Tashkent Islamic University, Tashkent, Uzbekistan, May 2004.

[128] Rector Karamatov, *Toshkent Islom Universitesi* (Tashkent: Islamic University, 2000), 10.

[129] Interview with Islamic studies expert, Tashkent, Uzbekistan, January 2005.

increase his legitimacy and to tightly manage the Islamic revival, much as Stalin had done during World War II.

In this brief and narrow civic space, some religious leaders worked to reinvigorate Islam, and the state only partially controlled the realm of religious ideas.[130] Karimov's regime was still focused on eliminating what it perceived to be bigger threats: Birlik and Erk.

Renewed Religious Repression: Exterminating Independent Islam, 1993–97

Within a few years, however, the regime tightened its grip on both state Islam and independent Islam. By 1993, the government had forced the independent-minded *mufti* into exile, and most mosques became strictly controlled.

As we have seen, members of the IRPU, Adolat, and their militias had been arrested, gone underground, or fled the country by late 1992, yet detentions nonetheless increased. In 1993, Umarkhon Buzruhon(ov), for example, the prominent imam of Namangan's Friday mosque, was convicted of financial crimes and sentenced to multiple prison terms. According to Memorial Human Rights Center, a renowned human rights organization established during *perestroika*, "he was one of the first victims of the campaign against political Islam."[131] The state replaced him with a young, compliant imam, who claimed, "I have no interest in or knowledge about political matters."[132] Most religious prisoners had been activists in Kokand, Marg'ilon, and Andijon—the heart of the Ferghana Valley.[133] Muhammadjon Nizomboyev of Namangan, convicted of verbally supporting Yo'ldosh, served ten years in prison. Repeatedly tortured, he contracted a severe form of tuberculosis before being freed in 2002.[134] Yo'ldosh's three brothers were imprisoned on various charges, including terrorism; one was released only in 2018, twenty-three years later.[135]

As political and religious conditions continued to deteriorate, Karimov began to cast his net wider, imprisoning more "independent" Muslims in 1995–96. Abduvali Qori's popularity and occasional outspokenness on political issues made him a target. His home was burned down and his library of religious books

[130] Interview with expert, Institute of Strategic and Regional Studies under the President of Uzbekistan, Tashkent, Uzbekistan, November 2004.

[131] Memorial, "Uzbekistan: Obzor sobytii v oblasti prav cheloveka za noiabr' 2002 goda," Moscow, December 10, 2002.

[132] Interview with imam, Namangan, Uzbekistan, June 1998.

[133] Human Rights Watch, "Creating Enemies," 21–22.

[134] Memorial, "Uzbekistan."

[135] "Brother of Late IMU Chief Says He's Out of Prison after 23 Years," *Radio Free Europe/Radio Liberty*, January 11, 2018, https://www.rferl.org/a/islamic-movement-of-uzbekistan-yuldoshev/28969382.html.

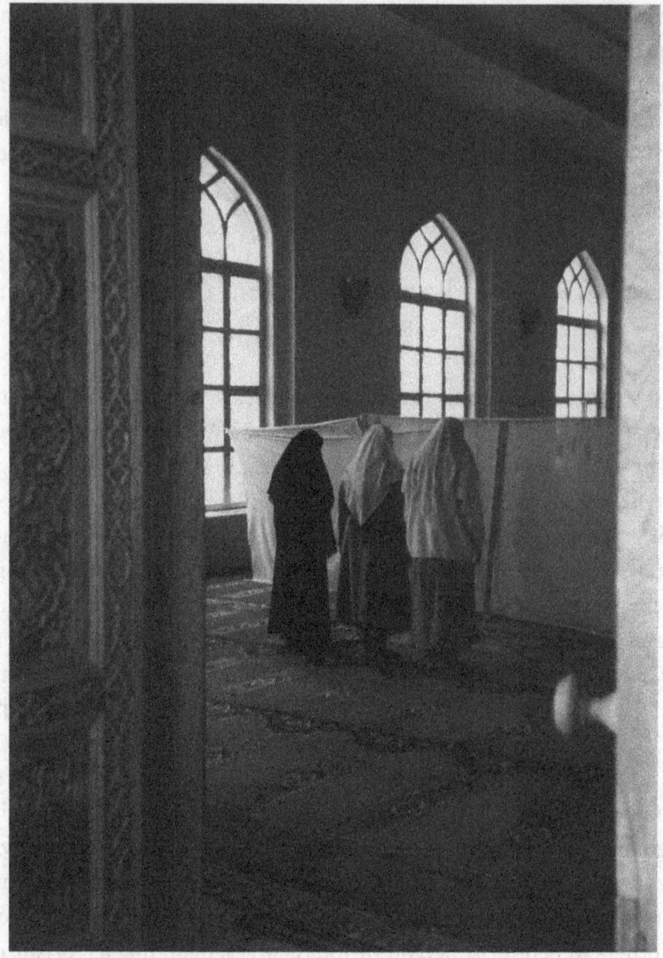

Image 8.3 Women visit a mosque in Bukhara
Source: Author's photo collection

was destroyed. His supporters believed the National Security Service (known by the acronym MXX, formerly the KGB), was intimidating him.[136] On August 29, 1995, Abduvali Qori "disappeared" as he and his student checked in for a flight leaving Tashkent airport; they planned to attend the World Islamic Symposium. Human rights groups believe that security agents seized the imam.[137] The activist website Muslim Uzbekistan condemned Karimov: "May Allah punish those

[136] "It Has Been Six Years since Shaykh Abduvali Qori," posted by Uzbek activist website, Muslim Uzbekistan, 2001, http://Muslimuzbekistan.com (website now defunct).

[137] Interview with human rights activist, Andijon, Uzbekistan, July 2003.

kuffar [infidels] and *munafiqs* [hypocrites] who are fighting against the Shaykh and other Muslims."[138] Abduvali Qori's followers believe he and his student were tortured to death, martyred.

Karimov's government also increasingly restricted Muslim practice and dress, and came into more direct conflict with Obidxon Qori. The imam openly voiced opposition to government pressure on Muslims to stop the call to prayer: "If Allah wants it, we must perform it."[139] He lambasted the government's new regulations that prevented women from praying at the mosque or in public.[140] He preached that "the [head] scarf is a religious obligation commanded by Allah, and a human right. These are women's rights." He added that those who obstructed women from wearing it, including "Lenin, Marx, and Satan," were "infidels."[141] He demanded, "When will we give women liberty? To say a woman is half naked is not to say she's free"; by contrast, he promised, "[W]e'll give women freedom to wear the [hijab]."[142] He denounced the government's Human Rights Ombudsman as a sham,[143] and boldly demanded a government apology to Muslims: "They [the government] acted against the faith. They betrayed the faith. . . . Harassing so many women, girls, old men, and kids, they shamed themselves before the whole world. . . . [L]et them apologize."[144] While not an activist, when mosque attendees asked him for news about Tohir Yo'ldosh, the imam responded, "Tohirjon is our deputy. Praise Allah, [he] is alive and well. The enemies of the faith became his enemies. They did many evil deeds against him. However, Allah the exalted saved our brother Tohirjon from their evil deeds, praise Allah. They [the secret police] went and planted hashish in his pockets, but the bullets in their scheme did not find their target. . . . There were roadblocks on the road, and he didn't fall into the hands of the dogs."[145] Notably, he had affectionately referred to Tohir Yo'ldosh as "Tohirjon" (dear Tohir) while castigating the regime as "dogs." Obidxon Qori was soon removed from his prominent position as imam of the To'xtaboy Mosque. By the mid-1990s, he was forced into hiding to avoid arrest and his followers were persecuted.

The Uzbek state's repression of independent Islam steadily expanded. By the mid-1990s, the residents of the Ferghana Valley lived with constant surveillance, arbitrary arrests, harassment, and interference with mosque attendance. Many of those identified as independent Muslims were threatened at work or interrogated. And inside prisons, "believer" inmates faced harsher treatment.[146]

138 "It Has Been Six Years since Shaykh Abduvali Qori."
139 Obidxon Qori, lecture 28, in *Uzbek Islamic Debates*, 218–19.
140 Obidxon Qori, lecture 28, in *Uzbek Islamic Debates*, 219.
141 Obidxon Qori, lecture 24, in *Uzbek Islamic Debates*, 197–99.
142 Obidxon Qori, lecture 27, in *Uzbek Islamic Debates*, 214.
143 Obidxon Qori, lecture 24, in *Uzbek Islamic Debates*, 198.
144 Obidxon Qori, lecture 25, in *Uzbek Islamic Debates*, 208.
145 Obidxon Qori, lecture 25, in *Uzbek Islamic Debates*, 207.
146 Human Rights Watch, "Creating Enemies," 12; Bukharbayeva, *Vanishing Generation*.

The Outcome: Second-Wave Islamism Begins

Hizb ut-Tahrir al-Islami

The earliest of the second-wave Islamist groups to appear was HTI. Unlike its predecessors in Uzbekistan, HTI was founded in Palestine (see Chapter 6 for background), as a transnational Islamist party. It established a regional organization in Uzbekistan in the mid-1990s. By the late 1990s and early 2000s, it was growing rapidly. Ongoing repression of Islam, together with marginal increases in associational space and a new and attractively simple political theology, incentivized HTI's emergence and mobilization.

According to HTI ideologist Dr. Mohamad Malkawi, HTI realized in the 1990s that "there was a bleeding wound in Uzbekistan. . . . Islam [had] stayed [in Central Asia] despite all the atrocities and oppressions" from the Mongols, the Russians, the Soviets, and Karimov.[147] Consequently, HTI sent Islamic missionaries and benefactors of mosques and religious schools to Uzbekistan,[148] promising to address the grievances of Muslims, and to do so without violence. HTI's message was simple: the tyrannical regimes of Karimov and Rahmon had to be overthrown and replaced with a caliphate.

Initially, HTI found little support.[149] In the mid-1990s, foreigners were greeted with suspicion; associating with them was risky.[150] But the organization spread through clandestine cells across the Ferghana Valley, which was undergoing harsh times following Adolat's failed Islamist movement there.[151] HTI also spread to Qashqadaryo, Tashkent, and other areas initially under less surveillance.

One Uzbek human rights activist stated that "in its early years people were wary of HTI," but by the early 2000s "the population was helping them." HTI likely had many thousands of followers at its peak in Uzbekistan around 2003, as Karimov began imprisoning hundreds to thousands.[152] Estimates range from

[147] Mohammad Malkawi, Hizb ut-Tahrir Netherlands, "A Talk on the Muslims in Uzbekistan," May 10, 2015, http://www.khilafah.com/muslims-in-uzbekistan-by-dr-mohammad-malkawi/.

[148] Interview with Omurzak Mamayusupov, head of the State Committee on Religious Affairs, Bishkek, Kyrgyzstan, August 2004.

[149] Alisher Khamidov, "Hizb-ut-Tahrir and the Challenges for Central Asian Security," Working paper, Brookings Institution, Washington, D.C., May 2002.

[150] Collins, "Political Role of Clans," 171–90.

[151] Interviews with human rights activists, Tashkent, Andijon, Namangan, and Ferghana, Uzbekistan, January 2005.

[152] Estimates in this section are based on various independent sources with an on-the-ground presence and knowledge of regions, neighborhoods, and villages where HTI has activists and significant support. Similar assessments come from International Crisis Group, "Radical Islam in Central Asia: Responding to Hizb ut-Tahrir," Asia Report No. 58 (Osh/Brussels: ICG, June 30, 2003), 17; personal communications with journalists in Uzbekistan, Tajikistan, and Kyrgyzstan, 2003–2007; Farangis Najibullah, "Central Asia: Hizb ut-Tahrir Gains Support From Women," *Radio Free Europe/*

five thousand to sixty thousand HTI followers in Uzbekistan, though reasonable estimates hover around ten thousand members. Data on arrests also sheds light on HTI's mobilization as well as its durability and popular support. Uzbekistan engaged in widespread arrests of alleged HTI members from about 1998 to 2005. As many as 4,700 to 6,500 HTI members were in prison on charges of extremism and terrorism in 2004. Another 257 convictions, mostly of HTI adherents, took place in 2005 and 2006, following the Andijon protests.[153] Those alleged to be HTI constituted the majority of political and religious prisoners in Uzbekistan, who numbered some thirteen thousand by 2015.[154]

HTI's activism in Uzbekistan consisted mainly of the clandestine distribution of its literature to induce ideological change; members disbursed leaflets in courtyards and on doorsteps during the night. They recruited through small, secretive cells. Only occasionally did HTI reach a broader audience. There was a mass, open distribution of HTI leaflets in the Uzbek city of Qarshi in November 2002.[155] HTI also fomented small protests against the regimes, mostly as family members mobilized in defense of those arrested for HTI membership. Journalists reported HTI-related protests in Tashkent and Andijon and in Surxondaryo *oblast*.[156] In August 2001, 423 women from the Ferghana Valley signed an appeal to President Karimov to release their husbands and relatives who had been arrested on charges of HTI membership, denied amnesty, and treated more brutally because they were "religious prisoners."[157] In the late 1990s and early 2000s, it was possible to obtain multiple HTI leaflets in Central Asia, but by the mid-2000s leaflets were either no longer distributed or recipients discarded them immediately because of fear. HTI's international offices posted online propaganda and Uzbek-language news about Karimov's dictatorship that state media would not print.

Escalating repression and total closure of associational space led to HTI's demise. By late 2005, HTI had mostly demobilized inside Uzbekistan, and its activity had shifted to Kyrgyzstan. Moreover, HTI's radical push for a caliphate and

Radio Liberty, July 11, 2007, https://www.rferl.org/a/1077570.html. The latest comprehensive estimates are found in Karagiannis, *Political Islam in Central Asia*.

153 U.S. Department of State, Bureau of Democracy, Human Rights, and Labor, "Country Report: Uzbekistan," March 8, 2006, https://2009-2017.state.gov/j/drl/rls/hrrpt/2005/61684.htm

154 Interviews with Mikhail Ardzinov, director, Independent Human Rights Organization of Uzbekistan (IHROU), Tashkent, Uzbekistan, January 2003; Abdusalim Ergashev, IHROU, Andijon, Uzbekistan, January 2003; Freedom House country representatives, Tashkent, Uzbekistan, January 2003 and November 2004.

155 Memorial, "Uzbekistan."

156 "Religious Discontent Evident in the Ferghana Valley," *EurasiaNet*, January 17, 2007, https://www.refworld.org/docid/46cc31e3c.html; International Crisis Group, "Radical Islam," 23; interview with Rajab Mirzo, journalist and activist, Dushanbe, Tajikistan, August 2005; interview with journalist, Ferghana, Uzbekistan, June 2004.

157 IWPR, "Uzbek Women Plead for Religious Prisoners," August 12, 2001.

the absence of endorsement by Uzbek religious authority figures limited its potential. Comparing HTI with Adolat, for example, reveals its lack of any local, Uzbek sacred authority. Furthermore, its cells used kin and friendship networks but lacked the type of transcommunal bonds that the IRPT had. Most of all, HTI's overwhelming focus on the caliphate found little resonance, even though its denunciations of Karimov drew some interest (Chapter 12 assesses HTI's appeal).

Ongoing Religious Repression Sets the Stage for Violent Radicalization

Repression again escalated in the late 1990s and continued through Karimov's death in 2016. Repression triggered contention, which led to more repression and greater radicalization, especially of Uzbek Islamists who managed to escape to Afghanistan.

In November and December 1997, several Namangan policemen and two others were assassinated and their severed heads posted on a gate. The government blamed Islamists, both Adolat's militia leader Juma Namangoniy and HTI. Throughout 1998, the security services waged a brutal crackdown, reportedly detaining thousands in Namangan and across the Ferghana Valley. The government began targeting all "independent Islam," including any unregistered Muslim believer, teacher, cleric, and organization.[158] Reports circulated that security services rounded up entire villages, especially any bearded men, on charges of "Wahhabism."[159] After forced confessions, believers were subjected to "show trials."[160] Defendants appearing beaten and drugged were paraded before the court and forced to admit to being either Wahhabi or an HTI party member.[161]

In 1998, Uzbekistan passed a new, harsh law on religion.[162] Legislation and extralegal repression steadily returned to Soviet-era policies. Each mosque community seeking legal registration had to demonstrate that it had one hundred members, but applications were risky; officials demanded the identities and

[158] Interview with journalists, Andijon, Uzbekistan, January 2003, June 2004.

[159] Interview with human rights activists, Tashkent, Uzbekistan, June 2004, January 2005; interview with political and human rights officers, U.S. Embassy, Tashkent, Uzbekistan, August 1998 and January 2003.

[160] UN Commission on Human Rights, Report of the Special Rapporteur on Torture and Other Cruel, Inhuman or Degrading Treatment or Punishment, December 23, 2003, E/CN.4/2004/56, https://www.refworld.org/docid/45377acc0.html.

[161] Interview with human rights activists, Namangan, Andijon, and Tashkent, Uzbekistan, January 2005.

[162] The Law of the Republic of Uzbekistan on Freedom of Worship and Religious Organizations, May 1, 1998, found at CIS – Legislation, https://cis-legislation.com/document.fwx?rgn=822.

addresses of mosque members. The state closed 80 to 85 percent of the estimated four thousand to five thousand functioning mosques. By late 1998, only seven hundred were legally registered.[163] Pretexts such as "inadequate plumbing" justified converting mosques into warehouses, as in the 1930s. For a growing population (then about thirty-two million, over 90 percent Muslim), this amounted to about one mosque per sixteen thousand to eighteen thousand Muslims. For some perspective, in Egypt under Mubarak's dictatorship, over ninety-three thousand mosques functioned in 2006, or one mosque for every one thousand inhabitants.[164]

As during Soviet times, repression was most severe in areas where religious practice was high and mosques numerous, especially in the Ferghana Valley.[165] For instance, in Namangan *oblast*, with over two million residents, 971 mosques were functioning before the 1998 law. Afterward, only 180 remained. One local businessman bitterly complained that in Namangan they had one mosque for thirty thousand people.[166] In the Ferghana Valley city of Marg'ilon, there had been 360 mosques before 1917, but only two worked during the Soviet era. Only thirty-six mosques had legally functioned there in the 1990s—for 180,000 Muslims. After 1999, ten of them were closed. Of those still open, most were there "in building only," due to fear of gathering.[167] In Samarqand, there were only two or three functioning mosques; most had once again become "mere museums."[168] The MXX required the *mahalla* committee to make a list of all who went to mosque,[169] turning the community organization into an instrument of state surveillance and intimidation.[170] Plainclothes police videotaped those who attended. Only elders could pray without fear. Raids of unregistered mosques were constant, resulting in arrests, detention, and confiscation of religious materials. The policy struck a major blow to communal life and religious practice. By preventing prayer gathering, Karimov hoped to diminish the authority of religious leaders and the possibility of networking.

In a further blow to faith that harkened back to the Soviet period, the 1998 law prohibited "private teaching of religious principles."[171] Those caught teaching

163 Bruce Pannier, "Uzbekistan: Mufti Integrates Secular and Religious Life," *Radio Free Europe/Radio Liberty*, October 7, 1998, https://www.rferl.org/a/islamic-movement-of-uzbekistan-yuldoshev/28969382.html.

164 Masoud, *Counting Islam*, 33.

165 Interview with Tyson.

166 Interview with businessman, Namangan, Uzbekistan, June 2004.

167 Oral history with imam #2, Marg'ilon, Uzbekistan, November 2004.

168 Communication with mosque attendee, Samarqand, Uzbekistan, April 2005.

169 Interview with journalist, Namangan, Uzbekistan, July 2004.

170 Communication with Uzbekistani experts, 2004, 2005, 2012 and 2014; Human Rights Watch, "From House to House: Abuses by Màhalla Committees," *Human Rights Watch* 15, no. 7 (September 2003), https://www.hrw.org/reports/2003/uzbekistan0903/9.htm.

171 "The Law of the Republic of Uzbekistan on Freedom of Worship and Religious Organizations," May 1, 1998, found at CIS – Legislation, https://cis-legislation.com/document.fwx?rgn=822.

religion privately or possessing unapproved religious literature were prosecuted. Youth under age eighteen were barred from attending mosque, a move that effectively made it impossible for minors to receive any religious instruction. Scores of women in hijab were expelled from universities and schools. Men in Islamic dress or with beards were accused of allegiance to dissident imams, Wahhabis, or HTI. State officials compelled imams throughout the Ferghana Valley to denounce Arab or Pakistani head and body coverings as "Wahhabi."[172]

Seeking to eliminate foreign religious influence, the law banned the *da'wat*, and required state approval of all religious literature. Reading religious literature and performing *namaz* were confined to houses of worship. Ordinary people often complained that OMI was corrupt and filled with MXX agents. It even limited hajis to 4,500 per year, despite the 25,000-person quota allowed for Uzbekistan.[173] As in Soviet times, imams' Friday sermons became propaganda tools for the state.[174] Karimov's photograph and the flag of Uzbekistan adorned every mosque, from Samarqand to Urganch, Namangan to Tashkent.

Violations of the law on religion became criminal offenses. Sentences involved high fines; repeat violations were crippling, sometimes three hundred times the minimum monthly wage. Those charged with "extremism" were given up to twenty-year sentences.[175] The total number of arrests and sentencings remains unknown. Local human rights activists who had followed the pattern of arrests since the beginning of the campaign put the number between 6,500 and 7,000. Estimates reached 8,000 in 2001.[176] HTI alone claimed that 4,000 of its members had been arrested.[177] Some of the detainees served long sentences in hard labor camps, where conditions were reminiscent of the Stalinist Gulag.[178] Many were incarcerated in the notorious Jasliq Prison, notorious for its dehumanizing conditions, including sexual abuse, intentional tuberculosis exposure, and systematic torture of religious and political prisoners.[179] In a few cases, the MXX returned the bloodied bodies of young men to their families. In most cases,

[172] Human Rights Watch, "Uzbekistan: Human Rights Developments," *World Report 1999* (Human Rights Watch, 1999), https://www.hrw.org/legacy/worldreport99/europe/uzbekistan2.html.

[173] Igor Rotar, "Uzbekistan: Religious Freedom Survey April 2005," *Forum 18*, April 20, 2005, http://www.forum18.org/Archive.php?article_id=546.

[174] Communication with Uzbekistan expert, Tashkent, Uzbekistan, August 2004.

[175] Human Rights Watch, "From House to House"; interview with human rights activists, Tashkent and Ferghana Valley, Uzbekistan, January 2005.

[176] Memorial Human Rights Center and the Information Center for Human Rights in Central Asia, "List of People Arrested and Tried in Uzbekistan for Political and Religious Reasons, December 1997–August 2001," Report (Moscow: Memorial, October 2001).

[177] Human Rights Watch, "Creating Enemies," 1.

[178] Елена Рябинина, "Гулаг имени Каримова. Воспоминания узбекского зэка," *Ferghana.ru*, October 30, 2007, www.ferghana.ru/article.php?id=5439.

[179] Personal communication with Uzbek human rights activist, November 2014; Bukharbayeva, *Vanishing Generation.*

people simply disappeared into prison for years. Religious repression had returned to levels not seen since the 1930s.

In this chapter, I have told the story of the birth and death of first-wave Islamism in Uzbekistan, and of the renewed repression that would generate a second wave. As in Tajikistan, the first wave of Uzbek Islamist opposition was rooted in Soviet religious repression and exclusion dating to the early Bolshevik era and continuing throughout the 1980s. Repression politicized Islamic identity, especially in Uzbekistan's Ferghana Valley, motivating activists to challenge the state once marginal increases in associational space allowed *hujra*s to form and religious students to network, share their anger, and discuss ideas about justice. That space also allowed both indigenous Salafism and Islamist ideologies from abroad to spread and inspire the young mullahs of the Ferghana Valley to articulate sharp political critiques of communism, Karimov, and secularism.[180] Consequently, religious entrepreneurs, most prominently Tohir Yo'ldosh of Adolat, began advocating for an Islamic state, making bold demands of the regime, and even forming *shariat* militias.

This first Islamist movement was a fractured and neophyte opposition, but it shook the credibility of the regime. It was bolstered by the sacred authority of a handful of esteemed religious leaders, such as Abduvali Qori, and by strong local networks. Some of Adolat's ideas were congruent with local concerns, such as repression of the hijab, mosque closures, and anticommunism. The Adolat movement thus achieved a moderate level of mass mobilization—not insignificant given the regime surveillance under which it operated. Nonetheless, the movement lacked broader, transcommunal networks. In contrast to the IRPT, the Uzbek movement did not have the head *mufti*'s national network and resources behind it. Nor did it alter its puritanical agenda to appeal to mainstream Hanafi-Sufi norms which characterized much of Uzbekistan, especially outside the Ferghana Valley. When Karimov decisively cracked down, the movement demobilized or fled.

Yet, Karimov's oppression failed to resolve the confrontation between Islamists and the state. Instead, the mid- to late 1990s repeated the conditions that had led to the first wave. Religious repression escalated, while limited associational space could not stop the flow of transnational Islamist ideas. HTI entered Uzbekistan through clandestine cells, whose activists inspired local religious entrepreneurs to network underground. HTI's success was limited, but Karimov responded brutally to independent Islam in the late

[180] Bakhtyar Babadjanov and Sharifjon Islamov, "The 'Enlighteners' of Koni-Zar: Islamic Reform in a Cotton Kolkhoz," in Dudoignon and Noack, *Allah's Kolkhozes*, 286–87.

1990s. This spurred Uzbek Islamist entrepreneurs who had gone into exile in Afghanistan—namely, Adolat's survivors—to further radicalize, inspired by the militant political theology and ideology of al-Qaeda. Chapter 9 turns to their story: the IMU's mobilization inside Afghanistan. Unlike Adolat and HTI, the IMU would last for nearly two decades, with decidedly negative consequences for Uzbekistan, the United States and its policy in Afghanistan, and regional stability.

9
Making Extremists
The Uzbek Jihad Moves to Afghanistan

> We are dissatisfied about many things. There is no justice. The ruler must be just or there will be no peace.
>
> —*Otincha*, Namangan, 2005

> The government is completely against the people. . . . People only want a just and normal life. . . . Religion is oppressed, like in Soviet times.
>
> —MXX official, Tashkent, 2005

The widely renowned *Mufti* Muhammad Sodiq Muhammad Yusuf frequently emphasized that "justice is a core value in Islam."[1] Yet in Uzbekistan there was no justice, as he knew well. He was under surveillance even as I spoke with him. The *otincha* (female religious teacher) and the MXX official quoted above were less cautious than the *mufti* in stating the obvious. Both had no doubt seen the state exercise horrendous brutality against ordinary Muslims. The absence of justice was the defining feature of life for Muslims in Karimov's Uzbekistan. Religious repression, coupled with political oppression and corruption, have violated the principle of justice on a daily basis and fed support for radical Islamism, including violence.

In the previous chapter, we saw that the post-Soviet Uzbek state crushed the first wave of Islamism in the early 1990s. Karimov then decimated HTI and the potential for a second wave to crest inside Uzbekistan. For the next two decades, the Karimov government projected itself as a success story of strong counterterrorism prevailing over Islamist extremism.[2] In reality, Uzbek émigrés in Afghanistan were becoming violent extremists. The angry youth who had formed Adolat almost a decade earlier were still driven to establish an Islamic state, but now they intended to do so through militant jihad. Adolat's core was reborn as

[1] Interview with Muhammad Sodiq Muhammad Yusuf.

[2] There are strong parallels with the PRC's "counterterrorist" war against the Uyghurs and its "self-fulfilling prophecy." Sean Roberts, *The War on the Uyghurs: China's Internal Campaign against a Muslim Minority* (Princeton, NJ: Princeton University Press, 2020).

Politicizing Islam in Central Asia. Kathleen Collins, Oxford University Press. © Oxford University Press 2023.
DOI: 10.1093/oso/9780197685068.003.0010

the O'zbekiston Islomiy Harakati (Islamic Movement of Uzbekistan, IMU). Over time, the organization would shift from national to transnational jihadist goals and tactics under the influence of al-Qaeda. The IMU never seriously threatened Karimov's grasp on power, but it did become a security threat to the Afghani and Pakistani governments and to U.S. and NATO forces in Afghanistan.

In this chapter, I trace the causes and dynamics of the IMU's emergence, rise, and fall over almost twenty years. The IMU's trajectory illuminates my core argument: that Karimov's religious repression and torture of Muslims was the fundamental driver of Islamist opposition. The latter intermixed with radical religious entrepreneurs and ideologies; the outcome was a militant jihadist movement. With the associational space to network inside the Taliban's Afghanistan, the IMU mobilized and fought for nearly two decades. Second, I demonstrate that despite the obstacles to growth and survival in a war zone, the IMU continued attracting recruits by constructing sacred authority, building new networks, and adapting its ideology over time. In fact, the proximity of Afghanistan's failed state, with its haven for other Islamists and its opportunities for accessing weapons, funding, and training, actually fostered the IMU's growth and durability. While the IRPT had benefited from the aid of Massoud's forces, the IMU would benefit from the Taliban's shelter. Unlike the IRPT, whose leaders had rejected radicalism and opted for a return to peace, the IMU accepted al-Qaeda's extreme ideology and financing.

Conditions Breeding Second-Wave Emergence and Mobilization

Associational Space in Afghanistan

After being driven out of Uzbekistan and subsequently failing to win the civil war in Tajikistan, Uzbek Islamist exiles had taken shelter in Afghanistan. Afghanistan was not only a failed state, providing the conditions for militant groups to thrive; by the mid-1990s, Afghanistan was under the control of the Taliban, a radical Islamist movement that sympathized with the IMU and allowed it the space to grow. Led by Mullah Omar, the Taliban had been created in 1994 and swept to power with assistance from Pakistan's government, particularly from its military and Inter-Services Intelligence agency.[3] Saudi money further armed and financed the Taliban's victory.[4] The movement was fueled by thousands of youth who had

[3] Ali Ahmad Jalali, *A Military History of Afghanistan* (Lawrence: University of Kansas Press, 2017), 439; Peter Tomsen, *The Wars of Afghanistan* (New York: Public Affairs, 2011), 531–38, 547.
[4] Tomsen, *The Wars of Afghanistan*, 535.

grown up as Soviet-Afghan War refugees in puritanical Deobandi *madrasas* along the Afghanistan-Pakistan border and who had learned little more than a radical interpretation of Islam and the duty of militant jihad.[5] Thousands of Pakistani fighters joined their military campaign to win Afghanistan. The Taliban took Kabul in 1996, and by 1997 they were attacking the last holdout against them, in the northern Badakhshan region of Afghanistan, on the Tajik-Afghan border. It was the Taliban's advance that had spurred the IRPT and its allies to end the Tajik Civil War and return to Tajikistan (Chapter 5). For the next few years, the Taliban controlled about 97 percent of Afghanistan's territory, including the regions where Uzbekistani militants were regrouping.

Also growing in influence in Afghanistan, sheltered by the Taliban, were the Afghan Arabs, thousands of foreign fighters who had participated in the 1980s anti-Soviet jihad, inspired by the thought of Abdallah Azzam and Salafi jihadism.[6] These fighters had either stayed on after the Soviets pulled out or had returned in the 1990s to regroup. Prominent among the Afghan Arabs were the Saudi radical financier Osama Bin Laden and the Egyptian Islamic Jihad leader, Ayman al-Zawahiri. By 1996, al-Qaeda was building a base inside Afghanistan for its transnational jihad,[7] and it would offer new opportunities for Uzbek exiles. In short, Taliban Afghanistan offered Uzbek Islamists a safe haven to grow, train, and attract financing.

Religious Repression and Closing Associational Space in Uzbekistan

Meanwhile, inside Karimov's Uzbekistan, religious repression had turned to all-out state terror after a spate of killings in Namangan, in December 1997. Those targeted were policemen and others who represented the government; one of the murdered policemen was reportedly beheaded.[8] According to Human Rights Watch, the notorious Ministry of Internal Affairs arrested over a thousand in Namangan and Andijon alone within just a few days. In 1998, a wave of arrests of

[5] Ahmed Rashid, *The Taliban: Militant Islam, Oil, and Fundamentalism in Afghanistan* (New Haven, CT: Yale University Press, 2002); Alex Strick van Linschoten and Felix Kuehn, *The Taliban Reader: War, Islam, and Politics* (Oxford: Oxford University Press, 2018).

[6] Hegghammer, *The Caravan*, Chapter 1.

[7] Anne Stenersen, *Al-Qaida in Afghanistan* (Cambridge, UK: Cambridge University Press, 2017); Michael Scheuer, *Osama Bin Laden* (New York: Oxford University Press, 2011); Lawrence Wright, *The Looming Tower: Al-Qaeda and the Road to 9/11* (New York: Knopf Doubleday Publishing Group, 2007).

[8] Vitali Ponomaryev, "Unprecedented Security Measures in Uzbekistan: Religious Fanatics Are Accused of Brutal Murders in Namangan Province," *Nezavisimaia gazeta*, no. 2, January 14, 1998, reprinted in *Current Digest of the Russian Press* 50, no. 2 (February 11, 1998).

Image 9.1 Warning poster, hung at a mosque in Khiva, showing alleged extremists
Source: Author's photo collection

alleged Islamists swept across the Ferghana Valley, then Tashkent, and on to remote Khorezm. Some were released, others imprisoned after show trials.[9]

State terror in turn generated more violence. On February 16, 1999, six car bombs ripped through several Uzbek government buildings and a motorcade in an apparent attack on President Karimov's regime. Sixteen people were killed and about 120 were injured, but Karimov was unharmed.[10] Government representatives alternately blamed "Wahhabis," former Adolat leaders living in Afghanistan, HTI, and Akromiya, a religious business association in the Ferghana Valley. Of these, only HTI constituted a political opposition within Uzbekistan, but it eschewed violence. Karimov ordered a sweep of all alleged opposition, including thousands who merely attended independent mosques and prayer groups. "Terrorist wanted" signs with the faces of the alleged perpetrators were posted in police stations, mosques, bakeries, and universities.[11] Thousands were arrested for nothing more than having a beard.

[9] Multiple communications with U.S. Embassy personnel, Tashkent, Uzbekistan; Human Rights Watch, "Republic of Uzbekistan: Crackdown in the Farghona Valley," May 1998, https://www.hrw.org/legacy/reports98/uzbekistan/, 10, 4, 2.

[10] Bruce Pannier, "Ten Years after Terror's Arrival in Central Asia," *Radio Free Europe/Radio Liberty*, February 16, 2009. On Karimov's tyranny, see David Lewis, *The Temptations of Tyranny in Central Asia* (London: Hurst & Co., 2008).

[11] Communications with Uzbek informants, Tashkent, Uzbekistan.

There has been much speculation about the actual perpetrators of the February 16 attack. Counterterrorism experts generally accepted it as the work of terrorists and blamed the IMU, which they knew to be operating already in Afghanistan. Given the size of the bomb blasts and complexity of the operation, the perpetrators may have received external assistance.[12] By contrast, an Uzbek human rights group, some scholars, and journalists advanced theories that the bombings were either planted by the Uzbek security forces to create a justification for a crackdown, or that the event was an inside coup attempt. While such theories are plausible, no evidence emerged to support them.

Former Adolat leader Tohir Yo'ldosh, writing from Afghanistan, sent a letter to "Uzbekistani exiles and mujahidin brothers in Chechnya" in which he criticized the bombings as reckless and unsanctioned by his leadership of the IMU, as yet a relatively unknown organization internationally.[13] Yo'ldosh put responsibility for the attack on a group of Uzbek exiles who had been living in Afghanistan and had then gone to Chechnya to fight. Chechen jihadists had assistance from the Saudi jihadi leader Khattab, born Samir Salih Abdallah al-Suwaylim. Khattab was a veteran Afghan Arab with close ties to al-Qaeda but more interested in local jihads than in fighting the United States.[14] After aiding the jihad in Tajikistan, Khattab had attracted a number of Arab and Central Asian exiles in Afghanistan, including some Uzbek citizens, to wage jihad in Chechnya during the 1994–96 war.[15] Yo'ldosh notably did not deny the rightness of jihad against Karimov. He stated, "[W]e acknowledge that these acts were in conformity with Islamic law," but he criticized the attackers' insufficient preparation as leading to huge losses. Indicating that there had been a split over how soon to attack Karimov, he added, "[T]he Islamic Movement of Uzbekistan will absolutely not accept the blame that has been levied against us for 'delaying' jihad."[16] He declared that the IMU would "without any doubt begin the armed struggle . . . to reestablish the Islamic caliphate," but he urged patience to wait for the right "time and place."[17] However the operation unfolded, Karimov's oppressive policies before the attack undoubtedly sowed the seeds of militant extremism, and his continuing brutality against independent Muslims would escalate militant opposition over time.

[12] Interviews with Michael Croissant, retired CIA officer, July 2022; interview with David Tyson, retired CIA officer, July 2022.

[13] "A Letter on Jihad from the Commander of the Islamic Movement of Uzbekistan to all of the Uzbekistani Exiles and Mujahidin Brothers in Chechnya." The letter was later published in the IMU periodical issued in Afghanistan, *Islom Ummati*, No. 2 (July 5, 1999), which was republished in *Uzbek Islamic Debates*, 421.

[14] Byman, *Road Warriors*, 93.

[15] Byman, *Road Warriors*, 81–88.

[16] "Letter on Jihad," 421.

[17] "Letter on Jihad," 422.

Islamist Ideology and Religious Entrepreneurship in Afghanistan

Religious repression motivated the Islamists, and radical political theologies shaped their ideology and strategy. Having abducted Abduvali Qori Mirzoyev and driven Obidxon Qori Nazarov into hiding, the Uzbek regime had thwarted any potential role they might have had in the evolution of an Islamist movement within Uzbekistan. Yet, the imams' voices continued through Yo'ldosh, once their student, who promised to create an Islamic state.

Inside Afghanistan, Yo'ldosh became closely associated with Shaykh Zubayr Abdurrohim o'g'li, a religious scholar from the Uzbek émigré community in Arabia, who would provide the IMU religious leadership. The shaykh claimed descent from the pre-Soviet rulers of Bukhara and boasted a Saudi Islamic education.[18] With goals and methods that were already more radical than Adolat's in 1992, the IMU's ideology continued evolving, becoming more extreme throughout the 1990s, and especially after 9/11.

While Yo'ldosh initially denied connections to and influence from foreign jihadists,[19] his statements and lectures revealed a turn to the militant jihadist ideology of the Taliban and al-Qaeda. The Taliban, under whom the Uzbek exiles were sheltered after the movement took Kabul in 1996, advocated militant jihad to establish a puritanical Deobandi Islamic emirate for Afghanistan. A similar ideology, Salafi jihadism, had come to Afghanistan during the Soviet-Afghan War (1979–89). Its roots lay in the Egyptian Muslim Brotherhood's Sayyid Qutb, whose work *Milestones* argued that militant jihad was necessary against apostate rulers; jihad was "obligatory" for all, a pillar of Islam.[20] More concretely, another follower of the Muslim Brotherhood, the Palestinian Shaykh Abdallah Azzam, was a writer, itinerant Islamist ideologue, and "'alim-mujahid"—the jihadist Islamic scholar who played a defining role in the Afghan Arab fighter movement.[21] In two tracts that had global significance, *In Defense of Muslim Lands: The Most Important of Individual Duties* (1985) and *Join the Caravan* (1987), Azzam called on all able-bodied Muslim men to wage jihad in Afghanistan, even if their family or government opposed it.[22] Assassinated in Peshawar, Pakistan, in 1989, Azzam's legacy would continue throughout the region, carried on by al-Qaeda and then the IMU, among others. Ayman al-Zawahiri, who joined Bin Laden in the 1990s and eventually became al-Qaeda's leader, further radicalized jihad;

[18] Michael Feldholm, "From the Ferghana Valley to Waziristan and Beyond," Monterey Institute for International Studies, Islam, Islamism and Politics in Eurasia Report No. 22, August 25, 2010, 8.

[19] "Interview with Tohir 'Foruq,'" in *Uzbek Islamic Debates*, 437.

[20] Qutb, *Milestones*, 53–76.

[21] Hegghammer, *The Caravan*, 328.

[22] Hegghammer, *The Caravan*, 289–90, 300.

he argued that civilian casualties, even Muslim civilian casualties, were permissible.[23] Becoming al-Qaeda's ideologist, he propagated religious justifications of suicide bombing. All these ideologues broke from mainstream jihad theory, which for centuries had emphasized spiritual over militant jihad and justified the latter primarily in self-defense.

Likewise, in Yo'ldosh's lessons, speeches, and interviews, his discussion of jihad became almost exclusively militant: "We know that our devotion is not terrorism, but rather is the devotion of jihad, which is a *farz* (religious duty) in Islam."[24] Yo'ldosh praised his Uzbek martyrs who had fought in the "Afghan jihad," supporting the Taliban even before the U.S. war in Afghanistan: "It is the wish of every one of us to become such martyrs in the future."[25] The theme of martyrdom became more salient over time.

Afghan Arab jihadists—Khattab, members of al-Qaeda, and others—were also actively seeking influence with Central Asians. They considered Central Asia key to both regional and global jihad. They saw Uzbek Islamists, like the Tajik Islamists in the early 1990s, as a means to this goal.[26] Following the success of the mujahidin and the end of the Soviet-Afghan War, al-Qaeda had formed inside Afghanistan. It grew under Taliban rule and trained Central Asian and Chechen militants in its camps in the 1990s.[27] In one jihadist tract titled "The Muslims in Central Asia and the Upcoming Battle of Islam," author Umar 'Abd-al-Hakim praised the continuation of "armed jihad in many areas of the Muslim world," and focused explicitly on Central Asia.[28] Identified only as an Afghan Arab fighter, 'Abd-al-Hakim argued, "The downfall of the Soviet Union in Afghanistan and the materialization of the serious jihad movements, unleashed new crusade campaigns under what they call 'The New World Order.' "[29] He argued that "jihad in this region [Central Asia] has an importance, rather, a priority, over all of the other arenas." He referred to a prophecy that said "the people of Islam . . . will have a gathering and strength in Khorasan," where they will be victorious first.[30] 'Abd-al-Hakim wrote, "Signs of hope for the prophesies of jihad began moving in Central

[23] Gilles Kepel and Jean-Pierre Milelli, eds., *Al Qaeda in Its Own Words* (Cambridge, MA: Harvard University Press, 2008), 147–236.

[24] "Interview with Tohir 'Foruq,'" 440. He uses the Uzbek "*farz*," meaning religious duty or obligation.

[25] "Interview with Tohir 'Foruq,'" 439.

[26] Ahmed Rashid, *Descent into Chaos* (New York: Viking 2008), 69.

[27] Stenersen, *Al-Qaida in Afghanistan*, 50–51; Scheuer, *Osama Bin Laden*, 73.

[28] 'Umar 'Abd-al-Hakim, "Muslims in Central Asia and the Upcoming Battle of Islam," 1999, Harmony database, AFGP-2002-002871, Combating Terrorism Center at West Point, https://ctc.usma.edu/harmony-program/the-muslims-in-central-asia-and-the-upcoming-battle-of-islam-original-language-2/, 28.

[29] 'Umar 'Abd-al-Hakim, "Upcoming Battle," 28.

[30] 'Umar 'Abd-al-Hakim, "Upcoming Battle," 24.

Asia from Tajikistan to Uzbekistan to East Turkestan and to some other territories."[31] He pragmatically argued that the presence of former Soviet military equipment and stockpiles were "booties that are waiting . . . [and] will provide us with what is needed to start jihad."[32] He extolled an unnamed shaykh—possibly Abduvali Qori—for "accepting martyrdom" after helping to revive Salafi Islam in *hujra*s across Central Asia. And he celebrated the "birth of jihad" that led to Uzbek jihadists' plans to kill President Karimov in the February 1999 bombings, whom he denounced for the arrests and executions of Muslims that followed.

A letter from Bin Laden to the Taliban emir Mullah Omar more explicitly discussed the Afghan jihad alongside the "continuing jihad" in post-Soviet Central Asia: "Following the Russians' departure, the country was subjected to great calamity. . . . [T]he Islamic republics were looking towards supporting their Muslim brothers in Afghanistan. . . . We ask Allah . . . to support His religion and our brothers in Bukhara, Samarqand, Termiz and other Muslim countries."[33] Bin Laden elaborated on concrete cooperation and strategic goals: "Previously, with the grace of Allah, we were successful in cooperating with our brothers in Tajikistan in various fields, including training. We were able to train a good number of them, arm them, and deliver them to Tajikistan. Moreover, Allah facilitated us in delivering weapons and ammunition to them. We pray that Allah grants us all victory. We need to cooperate together to continue this matter, especially jihad, [so] the efforts of Russians and their Americans allies [in Central Asia] will be scattered."[34] The letter indicated that al-Qaeda had aided the Islamist opposition groups that had rejected the 1997 Tajik peace accord. Bin Laden saw allying with Uzbek militants as a potential pathway to both expanding the jihad and obtaining resources: "The region [Central Asia] is rich with significant scientific experience in conventional and non-conventional military industries, which will have a greater role in future Jihad against the enemies of Islam."[35] Bin Laden had long had his sights on materials for weapons of mass destruction (WMD) left behind in Uzbekistan in the wake of the USSR's collapse.[36]

31 'Umar 'Abd-al-Hakim, "Upcoming Battle," 29.

32 'Umar 'Abd-al-Hakim, "Upcoming Battle," 24.

33 "Letter to Mullah Muhammed `Umar from Bin Laden," Document No. AFGP-2002-600321, Translation Date: June 5, 2002, Combating Terrorism Center at West Point, Harmony Program Database, https://ctc.usma.edu/.../Letter-to-Mullah-Mohammed-Omar-from-bin-Laden-Translation.

34 Document No. AFGP-2002-600321.

35 Document No. AFGP-2002-600321.

36 Scheuer, "Central Asia in Al-Qaeda's Vision," 7.

The Outcome: Second-Wave Uzbek Islamist Mobilization

The convergence of these three factors—Karimov's escalating religious repression, Afghanistan's safe harbor, and the radical ideologies taken up by the entrepreneurial Yo'ldosh—led to the establishment of the IMU and its nearly twenty-year jihad.

The IMU's Emergence and Early Mobilization, 1996–2001

Yo'ldosh and Juma Namangoniy had already shown their extreme puritanism and their proclivity for violence when they created a vigilante *shariat* militia to enforce religious dress and behavior in Namangan in 1990–92. After fleeing Uzbekistan in the 1992–93 crackdown, Yo'ldosh and his followers fought for several years in the Tajik Civil War on the side of the Islamic Revival Party of Tajikistan against the secular authoritarian government. Yo'ldosh and Namangoniy had become the religio-political and military leaders, respectively, of an Uzbek Islamist militia, first in Tajikistan and then in Afghanistan. Having opposed the deal that finally ended the Tajik war without achieving an Islamic state, and unable to return to Uzbekistan, they remained in Afghanistan. They received both payment and training through their developing relationships with the Taliban and al-Qaeda.[37] During the mid-1990s, under the protection of their Taliban hosts, the exiled remnants of Adolat regrouped in Kabul to form the IMU, with the aim of seizing power from Karimov and establishing an Islamic state. They trained, recruited, and planned their jihad.

Their funding sources remain obscure, but most likely came from the narcotics trade[38] and al-Qaeda payments for assistance in fighting the Northern Alliance and running rudimentary training camps, which taught basic military skills and attempted to develop poisons.[39] They had camps in the north, near Mazar-i-Sharif, and in Takhar and Badakhshan. In Kabul, they kept offices for the leadership and a "jail" for vetting those who arrived from Uzbekistan seeking to join them. Uzbek *muhajirs* fleeing Karimov came throughout the 1990s, but they were first interrogated to prevent penetration of the group by either Uzbek or Russian intelligence; both were constant threats.[40]

[37] Rohan Gunaratna and Anders Nielsen, "Al Qaeda in the Tribal Areas of Pakistan and Beyond," *Studies in Conflict and Terrorism* 31 (2008): 775–807.

[38] UNODC, "Money Laundering and Related Issues in Uzbekistan," GPML Central Asia Briefing No.2, May 24, 2002, www.unodc.org/documents/archive/imolin/Uzbekpro.pdf, 6–7.

[39] Interview with Tyson, July 2022.

[40] Interview with Tyson, July 2022.

In August 1999, just six months after the February Tashkent bombings, Yo'ldosh openly declared jihad on the government of Uzbekistan. His statement merged a militant Salafi jihadist ideology with his Uzbekistani nationalist objective. Opening with the "sword verses" of the Qur'an, it declared: "'And fight them until there is no more *fitna* and the religion is all for Allah' (Al-Anfal: 39). The emir of the Islamic Movement of Uzbekistan, Mohammad Tohir Foruq[41] has announced the start of the jihad against the tyrannical government of Uzbekistan and the puppet Islam Karimov and his henchmen." Claiming the support of religious scholars, it made five key points:

1. "[The IMU has] . . . clear evidence of the obligation of Jihad against the infidels, as well as to liberate the land and the people."
2. "[The] primary objective for this declaration of Jihad is the establishment of an Islamic state with the application of the *shariat*, founded upon the Qur'an and the Noble Prophetic *Sunna*."
3. "The goals of . . . jihad are: the defense of our religion of Islam in our land against those who oppose Islam; the defense of the Muslims in our land from those who humiliate them and spill their blood; the defense of the Islamic scholars and Muslim youth who are being assassinated, imprisoned, and tortured in extreme manners—with no rights given them at all . . . who number some 5,000 in prison . . . and to reopen the thousands of mosques and Islamic schools that have been closed by the evil government."
4. "The Mujahidin of the Islamic Movement, after their experience in warfare, have completed their training and are ready to establish the blessed Jihad."
5. "The Islamic Movement warns the Uzbek government . . . and tourists . . . lest they be struck down by the Mujahidin."[42]

The IMU declared that it would, "by the will of Allah, make Jihad" until it achieved its aim of "removing . . . the ruling government and Karimov . . . unconditionally, before the country enters into a state of war and destruction of the land and the people."[43] The IMU's religious leader, Shaykh Zubayr Abdurrohim o'g'li, signed the declaration on August 25, 1999. It announced the IMU's jihad to the world.

The declaration revealed that the IMU's political theology directly shaped its political goals. Couched in holy scripture, it asked, "What is the matter

[41] Around 1997, Yo'ldosh began using the name "Mohammad Tohir Foruq" to enhance his sacred authority.

[42] "IMU Declaration of Jihad," in Ahmed Rashid, *Jihad: The Rise of Militant Islam in Central Asia* (New Haven, CT: Yale University Press, 2002), 247–49.

[43] "IMU Declaration of Jihad," 247–49.

with you, that you do not fight in the way of Allah and the weak and oppressed amongst men, women, and children?" (An Nisaa:75). In subsequent statements, Yo'ldosh contrasted his vision with Karimov's Uzbekistan, "atheists who have deified for themselves satanic and bestial feelings" led by "a modern-day Pharaoh . . . preaching democratic rule."[44] He juxtaposed the Islamic state with the usury, brothels, and sodomites of Western democracy. He promised that an Islamic state would eradicate injustices: "From the head of state to the ordinary worker and farmer, a society that is able to completely fulfill the precepts of Islam will be healthier than unbelief, tyranny, injustice, conspiracy, treason, violence, usury, bribery, vulgarity, and all the other qualities that are alien to human character."[45]

Yo'ldosh's rhetoric contrasted justice and injustice, belief and unbelief. He offered no concrete plan, but he provided a vision and meaning for those willing to risk everything for the jihad. Following Qutb and al-Zawahiri, IMU literature declared, "It is also a religious obligation for Muslims to overthrow the infidels' political system in order to fully implement Islamic law, and to establish Islamic authority!"[46] Yet there were few specifics: "As for building an Islamic state, that is an issue we will discuss later. First our intent is to settle accounts with the tyrants and take them before *shariat* courts."[47] Yo'ldosh claimed that "83 percent of the population of Uzbekistan is Muslim. They [the Muslims] have a thousand-year history. The atheist group that appeared over seventy to eighty years ago is the new group. Living in conformity with Islamic law is the wish of every Muslim."[48] Atheist oppression shaped his intent to establish *shariat*. He announced that the IMU would "reestablish the Islamic caliphate . . . [through] this blessed jihad."[49] Even the caliphate's boundaries remained unclear, however; sometimes Yo'ldosh referenced Uzbekistan alone; at other times he included the Ferghana Valley or all of Central Asia.

Early IMU statements and publications also revolved around Karimov's religious persecution. Yo'ldosh declared, "We want to overthrow tyranny. It is our movement's main goal in declaring jihad . . . against the corruption and injustice taking place in our country. Our main goal is to free the hundreds of thousands of Muslims in our country from prison, and for that reason, we are offering our lives."[50] He repeatedly claimed that "thousands of Muslims are

[44] "An interview with the Commander of the Islamic Movement of Uzbekistan Muhammad Tohir 'Foruq,'" *Islom Ummati*, No. 2 (July 5, 1999), in *Uzbek Islamic Debates*, 418.

[45] "Interview with Muhammad Tohir 'Foruq,'" 418.

[46] Zubayr Abdurrohim o'g'li, "Comment," *Islom Ummati*, No. 2 (1999), in *Uzbek Islamic Debates*, 413.

[47] "Interview with Tohir 'Foruq,'" 439.

[48] "Interview with Tohir 'Foruq,'" 438.

[49] "Letter on Jihad," 422.

[50] "Interview with Tohir 'Foruq,'" 439.

being thrown into the dungeons by the tyrannical infidel regime."[51] Referring to the February bombings, Yo'ldosh said, "Total repression began after February 1999," but he also emphasized that the IMU's roots lay "in Stalin's repression of Muslim scholars." He denounced Karimov as the successor to the communist "Red Empire,"[52] telling the world, "The Karimov regime, not us, *they* are the terrorists."[53]

A poem in an IMU journal published in Afghanistan in July 1999 encapsulated the group's religious grievances:

> Greetings, people of Turkestan, greetings, people in dungeons,
> Innocent and oppressed people suffering tyranny,
> Don't say the refugees are weak and asleep,
> When Allah wishes it, millions will sacrifice themselves.
> Turkestan remains a prisoner
> Please Allah show mercy and make Turkestan happy.[54]

Likewise, in a commentary on the political situation in Uzbekistan, another IMU religious leader, Zubayr Abdurrohim o'g'li, wrote:

> The infidels are using their wealth to block [people] from Allah's path. . . . [T]he world's Muslims are in a state of oppression. . . . The enemies of Islam are committing savage deeds in Uzbekistan. They are torturing Muslims to keep them from their faith. They are electrocuting them, putting hot coals on their bodies, keeping them in root cellars, putting them in vacuum chambers, inflicting torture on their privates, and locking up four people where there is space for only one. They pick up someone by his arms and legs and throw him to the floor and then they document it by saying, "He died of an illness."[55]

After lambasting prison conditions and abuses, Zubayr condemned the "tragedy" of "millions of Muslims in Uzbekistan" who could not know their religion.[56] He concluded with a series of verses from the Qur'an, about Allah's light and eternal paradise for those who suffer and follow Allah's true path.[57] Despite seven years in exile, Yo'ldosh committed to changing Uzbekistan by bringing "jihad to its conclusion."[58]

51 "Letter on Jihad," 421.
52 "Interview with Tohir 'Foruq,'" 436.
53 "Interview with Tohir 'Foruq,'" 435, my italics.
54 The author of the poem is unknown, but the work comes from a volume titled *Musaddosati Mahmudiyya, Islom Ummati*, No. 2 (July 5, 1999), in *Uzbek Islamic Debates*, 426.
55 Zubayr, "Comment," 414.
56 Zubayr, "Comment," 414.
57 Zubayr, "Comment," 415.
58 "Interview with Tohir 'Foruq,'" 435.

Early Attacks

The IMU's declaration of its existence and jihad took place together with its first militant strikes into Kyrgyzstan and Uzbekistan. The Uzbek and Kyrgyz governments have long exaggerated the IMU's strength, but in 1999–2000 the threat it posed was real.

The declaration of jihad explained the IMU's rationale for attacking not only Uzbekistan but Kyrgyzstan as well: because President Askar Akayev had returned Uzbek refugees to Karmiov to be tortured, he too was a target. More pragmatically, access to Uzbekistan was easiest via southern Kyrgyzstan, already known to the IMU because of its involvement in the narcotrade from Afghanistan to Kyrgyzstan.

In August 1999, the IMU launched its jihad with guerrilla incursions from Afghanistan into the post-Soviet states. Passing through Tajikistan—they were believed to have once again set up a base camp in the Tavildara, a Tajik Islamist stronghold—they entered the Ferghana Valley of Kyrgyzstan, demanding passage to Uzbekistan. When Kyrgyzstan's government refused, the IMU took control of several villages near Batken and seized hostages, including some Japanese geologists. Reports indicated that numerous locals had joined them, perhaps because of generous payments for food and shelter. According to one former IMU member, Batken's destitute residents shared a belief that an Islamic government would solve their problems.[59] According to veteran journalist Bruce Pannier, Kyrgyzstan's neophyte military, including many poorly trained conscripts wearing sweatpants and sandals in place of uniforms, failed to repel the band of militants. (Kyrgyzstani officials had been claiming since 1994 that their "military needed uniforms, not training," from its partnership with NATO.)[60] Kyrgyzstan first bribed the IMU to leave (reportedly giving it $50,000), but then requested military support from Uzbekistan, which struck the villages with warplanes, killing civilians. The IMU returned in greater numbers within a few weeks and maintained a holdout in the mountainous border region, this time countered by an elite Kyrgyzstani military unit. Fighting continued until late October, when winter made the rugged mountain passage impossible.[61] Despite their small numbers, the IMU killed some fifty Kyrgyzstani soldiers and civilians. Its perceived success also attracted new recruits. They released the hostages for a lucrative ransom, according to U.S. government sources. IMU forces in

[59] Sultan Jumagulov, "Captured Senior IMU Official Talks to IWPR about His Experiences in the Guerrilla Movement," IMU Insight, *Institute for War and Peace Reporting*, February 21, 2005, https://iwpr.net/global-voices/kyrgyzstan-imu-insight.

[60] Communication with Janysh, Ministry of Foreign Affairs, Bishkek, Kyrgyzstan, June 2002.

[61] Bruce Pannier, "The Summer of 1999 and the IMU in Kyrgyzstan," *Radio Free Europe/Radio Liberty*, September 24, 2019, https://www.rferl.org/a/the-summer-of-1999-and-the-imu-in-kyrgyzstan/30180837.html.

Afghanistan grew; estimates claimed between seven hundred and more than several thousand militants.

In August 2000, a second IMU attack on southern Kyrgyzstan began, making its way into southeastern Uzbekistan as well, with about one hundred fighters. En route, the IMU kidnapped three American climbers in the Pamir-Alai mountain range, probably planning to ransom them. Ultimately, after several weeks of clashes, taking more lives than during nearly three months of fighting in 1999, the Uzbekistani and Kyrgyzstani military forces drove the IMU back into Tajikistan, where they had a base in Tavildara.[62] The Uzbek government mined the borders to prevent further incursions. Tajikistan's government then sought to expel them and ultimately made a deal with Yo'ldosh to airlift the IMU fighters to northern Afghanistan.[63]

Following the attacks, Yo'ldosh praised the progress of the "mujahidin since their declaration of jihad," claiming that thirty enemy soldiers were killed and that the IMU had successfully destroyed military vehicles and seized arms. He eulogized their "mujahidin brothers" who "were martyred."[64] He further boasted that because of their campaign, three hundred Uzbeks imprisoned for religious beliefs had been released.

In the meantime, the movement sought to grow and solidify its base in Afghanistan. An IMU document from July 2001 urged Uzbeks to "seek safety for themselves, their religion, and their honor, after the persecution of the Karimov regime against anyone who tries to return to his Muslim identity." It praised the Taliban's Islamic Emirate of Afghanistan for providing shelter, but also noted that IMU leaders would have to provide a longer-term solution for "all persecuted Muslims." The document laid out its plan for a base camp in Afghanistan to accommodate a growing number of recruits coming with their families. Called "the 'Bukhari' Camp for Immigrants Beyond the River," the anticipated base would house 250 existing IMU families and accommodate a thousand families in the future.[65] It was to be organized around *shariat* principles, complete with twelve neighborhood mosques (one for every eighty-five families) and one large central mosque. It planned construction of a hospital, Islamic schools, an electric power generator, and even sports facilities. Estimated costs approached $2.5 million. The IMU emphasized Allah's rewards for those "who believed, migrated

[62] Bruce Pannier, "Central Asia: Conflict with Islamic Militants Widens," *Radio Free Europe/Radio Liberty*, August 8, 2000, https://www.rferl.org/a/1094573.html.

[63] Interviews with Croissant and Tyson, July 2022.

[64] "Interview with Tohir 'Foruq.'"

[65] "Islamic Movement of Uzbekistan (IMU) Letter Detailing the Establishment of the IMU's Bukhari Camp," Document Number: AFGP-2002-000489, Combating Terrorism Center at West Point, Harmony Program Database, https://ctc.westpoint.edu/harmony-program/afgp-2002-000489/.

and struggled in the cause of Allah (Al-Anfal:74)," and anticipated that the camp facilities would convince more Uzbeks to join the movement, despite the risks.[66]

In 2001, Shaykh Zubayr published a work, titled "Hijra Will Continue." It included interviews and testimonies with some rank-and-file members about their path from Karimov's Uzbekistan to Afghanistan. His goal was to remind Muslims that they had a duty to make a pledge to the caliphate and to convince potential recruits that the IMU would care for them. Zubayr compared recruits to the early Muslims who made the *hijra* (holy migration) to establish a Muslim community under the Prophet.[67] The accounts he included revealed how young men might join radical movements. For example, one account detailed the arrests of seventeen villagers and their subsequent lengthy imprisonment, which triggered the migration of multiple families that could no longer tolerate police surveillance and charges of extremism merely for "perform[ing] *namaz*." So they went to Gharm, Tajikistan, where a mujahid recruiter was based, and then to the IMU in Afghanistan. In another account, a young man left Uzbekistan because both his family and the state were preventing him from performing *namaz*. The MXX raided his *hujra*, torturing many. He had heard of Juma Namangoniy and Tohirjon Yo'ldosh, and with help from his "master," he made his way to Tajikistan and then Afghanistan. He declared that he had "made the *hijra*"; his goal was to flee "the *kuffar* (infidels)" and get to the "Receptacle of Islam." When he finally crossed the Tajik-Afghan border, after narrowly escaping Russian border guards, he claimed that the Taliban saved him and united him with the IMU.[68]

In a third account, an Uzbek migrant identified as Abdulmajid recalled how he had turned away from sin and had come to believe in Allah and the resurrection. He and his brother decided, "[E]ven one more day of our lives under *kuffar* rule became too much for us." His brother suggested making the *hijra*: "Your wife cannot go outside wearing the hijab. You cannot grow a beard. If you serve in the path of Islam, they will call you a terrorist and extremist! This is the land of the *kuffar*. If it continues in this way, you will be imprisoned! See how many Muslims spit blood in prisons. Now *hijra* has become a *fard al-Ayn* (obligation). One should go to a Muslim state." Later that year, his brother "made the *hijra* to Chechnya to fight against the *kuffar*." Abdulmajid and his family subsequently made their way to the IMU in Afghanistan, which by then included *muhajirs* (migrants) from across Central Asia and beyond.[69] With satisfaction,

66 "Islamic Movement of Uzbekistan (IMU) Letter."

67 Zubayr Abdurrohim o'g'li, "Hijrah* Will Continue," posted as "Four Personal Accounts of Islamic Movement of Uzbekistan Members' Migration to Afghanistan," Combating Terrorism Center at West Point, Harmony Program Database, Document No. AFGP-2002-601123, 5, https://ctc.westpoint.edu/harmony-program/four-personal-accounts-of-islamic-movement-of-uzbekistan-members-migration-to-afghanistan-original-language/.

68 Zubayr, "Hijrah* Will Continue," 8, 43, 37, 43–52.

69 Zubayr, "Hijrah* Will Continue," 55–56, 64.

he described living under *shariat* law. These accounts were no doubt IMU propaganda, but the common motivations, rooted in the reality of Uzbek life, were plausible: religious repression and the need for a just Islamic government.

The IMU's Evolution, 2001–16

The IMU never again waged major incursions into the territory of Uzbekistan. The U.S. war in Afghanistan intervened and changed the course of events. Nonetheless, Karimov's ongoing persecution still motivated Uzbek Islamism, even as the Taliban and al-Qaeda would significantly affect the IMU's evolution. A cycle of Islamist-state contention and radicalization continued for more than fifteen years, and the IMU and its offshoots were central players.

Uzbek Religious Repression in the 2000s

State surveillance of independent Muslims became increasingly pervasive throughout Uzbekistan. Through the Shanghai Cooperation Agreement (SCO), Russian and Chinese security services aided the Uzbek MXX in counterterrorism.[70] For example, in 2002 Russian authorities extradited Mannapjon Rahmatullayev, who had been working as an imam in Russia for seven years. Wanted by the Uzbek authorities for making the hajj without governmental permission in 1992, the imam was charged with "infringing on the constitutional order of the Republic of Uzbekistan."[71] Arrests sometimes triggered demonstrations and more abuses. The MXX threatened the wives of alleged extremists with rape. Human rights defenders, like Yelena Urlayeva, were beaten, incarcerated, or sentenced to psychiatric hospitals for forced injections of psychotropic drugs.[72] Another human rights activist, who met with victims and families of Andijonis charged with Wahhabism, remarked that the only thing that kept him out of prison was the U.S. Embassy. Show trials were used to legitimize the state and sow fear of "Islamic extremists" among the population.[73] A journalist and former democratic activist declared, "We've returned to 1937," the year of Stalin's Great Terror.[74] Even a government-appointed imam revealed

[70] Kathleen Collins, "Economic and Security Regionalism among Patrimonial Authoritarian Regimes: The Case of Central Asia," *Europe-Asia Studies* 61, no. 2 (2009): 251–83.
[71] Memorial, "Uzbekistan: Obzor sobytii v oblasti prav cheloveka za noiabr' 2002 goda," Moscow, December 10, 2002.
[72] Memorial, "Uzbekistan."
[73] Interview with human rights activist, Namangan, Uzbekistan, January 2005.
[74] Interview with journalist, Namangan, Uzbekistan, June 2004.

that he believed "the government itself" was fabricating terrorism to justify repression, while "our lives get worse and worse."[75]

The government's persecution of independent Muslims spiraled into mass violence in the Ferghana Valley city of Andijon in May 2005. Members of Akromiya—an unregistered Muslim organization formed around the spiritual leader Akrom Yo'ldosh in the mid-1990s—were on trial, charged with religious extremism. For years, Akromists had pursued prayer and religious study, reading Yo'ldosh's text, *Imonga yo'l* (The Path to Faith). *The Path* was not oppositional in the vein of the Mujaddidiya's teachings, much less overtly Islamist.[76] Akromiya's members, calling themselves "the brothers" (Birodarlar), became popular locally; their *jamaat* (community) formed a Muslim business league that supported Andijonis with Islamic, interest-free loans.[77] They provided decent jobs, employing some two thousand people.[78] Uzbeks in southern Kyrgyzstan were Akromiya followers as well.[79] The Uzbek authorities, long suspicious of the group's leader, harassed and arrested him several times. In the purges following the 1999 Tashkent bombings, Yo'ldosh received a seventeen-year sentence. He died in prison.

In 2004, the state arrested twenty-three Akromiya members, all successful Andijoni businessmen, on charges of religious extremism. The trial proceeded on thin evidence from January through May 2005. The accused awaited judgment while relatives, friends, and their business network organized increasingly large but peaceful demonstrations, attracting some two thousand protesters at first, and up to fifteen thousand by May.[80] The government initially appeared uncharacteristically irresolute about cracking down; protests had been taking place in other cities as well, but the regime had restrained itself from mass arrests, probably in order to maintain its improved post-9/11 relationship with the United States.

Protesters' demands ranged from freeing the Akromiya members to addressing broader economic problems and establishing justice. The government exacerbated the escalating conflict by seizing the main Andijon mosque.[81] One of the accused, Tursun Nazarov, testified, "We were good businessmen,

[75] Interview with Gulom, *mahalla* mosque imam, Uzbekistan, 2005.

[76] Sarah Kendzior, "Poetry of Witness: Uzbek Identity and the Response to Andijon," *Central Asian Survey* 26 (2007): 317–34.

[77] Babadjanov and Kamilov observed the development of this "purely local group" well before 2004–5 ("Muhammadjan Hindustani," 205).

[78] Matluba Azamatova, "Controversial Trial Triggered Uzbek Violence," *Institute for War and Peace Reporting*, November 20, 2005.

[79] Interviews with journalists, Osh Media Center, Osh, Kyrgyzstan, August 2004, June 2005.

[80] International Crisis Group, "Uzbekistan: The Andijon Uprising," Briefing 38, Europe and Central Asia, May 25, 2005, https://www.crisisgroup.org/europe-central-asia/central-asia/uzbekistan/uzbekistan-andijon-uprising.

[81] Rashid, *Descent*, 343–46.

paid our taxes on time and gave people jobs. It's clear that someone was not too pleased about this, so we were put in jail. But if we are sentenced, our families will not just sit twiddling their thumbs. . . . People will lose faith in justice."[82] Tension built while the verdict was pending. One Akromiya supporter declared, "If the sentence is unjust, we will be forced to act."[83]

The events culminated in an armed uprising, followed by a government massacre and cover-up. The precise trigger, turn of events, and numbers killed will probably never be known, but journalist Bagila Bukharbayeva has provided an extraordinary eyewitness account that uncovers part of the tragedy.[84] On May 13, 2005, Qobuljon Parpiyev and Bahrom Shakirov, both of whom had previously been jailed due to their association with Akromiya's leader, led an armed uprising. They claimed to represent an "association of businessmen" numbering twenty-five thousand members,[85] aiming to free the businessmen and force the state to recognize their rights. Parpiyev told Bukharbayeva, " 'If they kill us, let it be. Why live like this? Why live if you have no rights?' "[86] According to some reports, the violence erupted when the Akromists attacked a police station, whereas others reported that the group raided a military weapons storage facility.[87] They subsequently broke into the prison holding the accused Akromists, released up to five hundred prisoners, and then seized the central Andijon government building.[88] Bukharbayeva points out that they took hostages, including police, and partial video footage of the protest on the town's central Bobur Square appears to confirm this.[89] Some report that thirty to forty rebels carrying small arms set fire to two theaters and destroyed cars on Bobur Square.[90] The video footage shows that most of the thousands of protesters had no weapon; however, some of the leaders were armed.[91] The protesters are heard shouting both "Allahu Akbar" and "Ozodlik" (Freedom).[92] According to journalists, the government sent in armored personnel carriers and dozens of security forces, both police and soldiers. Youth hurled rocks at the military vehicles. From available evidence it is not clear who fired first, what the military's orders were, or whether there

82 Azamatova, "Controversial Trial."
83 Azamatova, "Controversial Trial."
84 Bagila Bukharbayeva, *The Vanishing Generation: Faith and Uprising in Modern Uzbekistan* (Bloomington: Indiana University Press, 2019); Human Rights Watch, "Bullets Were Falling Like Rain: The Andijon Massacre, May 13, 2005," http://hrw.org/reports/2005/uzbekistan0605/.
85 Bukharbayeva, *Vanishing Generation*, 150–51.
86 Bukharbayeva, *Vanishing Generation*, 134.
87 Martha Olcott and Marina Barnett, "The Andijon Uprising, Akramiya and Akram Yuldashev," Carnegie Endowment for International Peace, June 22, 2006.
88 International Crisis Group, "Uzbekistan."
89 Bukharbayeva, *Vanishing Generation*, 132–35.
90 Olcott and Barnett, "The Andijon Uprising."
91 Video footage of the protest was provided to me by the U.S. government source, June 2006.
92 Olcott and Barnett, "The Andijon Uprising," 2006.

were orders to fire on unarmed protesters. In a partial audio recording of the beginning of the violence, sporadic small arms fire was heard, suggesting the possibility that either skittish soldiers fired their rifles without orders, or that the Akromists used their weapons.[93] Yet, according to Bukharbayeva, soon thereafter, the security forces systematically mowed down men, women, and children, even those who raised white flags.[94]

Andijon's Bobur Square became Uzbekistan's Tiananmen Square; most viewed it as a massacre. Human rights advocates, journalists, and the International Crisis Group estimated that government forces killed 700 to 1,000 civilians, mostly unarmed.[95] Some locals claimed up to 1,500 had perished. One city pathologist reported seeing five hundred bodies laid out for identification in one school alone, but Karimov declared that only nine had died.[96] The government later announced that 187—all terrorists—had been killed. The deceased were buried quickly, without Islamic rituals, in mass graves; verification of the dead was impossible. According to the Memorial Human Rights Centre (known as Memorial), over three hundred people were subsequently arrested and sentenced in Andijon, allegedly for Akromiya membership.[97] The regime's cover-up and hostile reaction to Western calls for an investigation fueled suspicion of what lay behind its secrecy.

Some analysts, echoing the Uzbek government, justified the state's use of lethal violence[98] as a necessary response to "Islamic terrorism" and an "insurgency." As noted, some Akromists did engage in violence to take over government facilities, and they did take hostages. Their actions in some ways paralleled Tohir Yo'ldosh's seizure of the Communist Party building in Namangan in 1991. Yet, the protesters' endgame was unclear.[99] The few dozen armed assailants of the prison were clearly insufficient in number to overpower the state. The government could have reasserted control without mass killing of hundreds of unarmed participants, who were there in a justifiable demonstration, seeking their rights.[100] Consequently, on November 14, 2005, the EU imposed a visa ban on twelve Uzbek officials thought to

[93] Interview with Croissant.

[94] Galima Bukharbayeva, "No Requiem for the Dead," *Institute for War and Peace Reporting*, May 16, 2005; Bukharbayeva, *Vanishing Generation*, 135–40.

[95] International Crisis Group, "Uzbekistan.".

[96] Bukharbayeva, "No Requiem."

[97] Vitaly Ponomaryev, *Politicheskie repressii v Uzbekistane v 2009–10 godakh* (Memorial: Moscow, 2011), 54.

[98] Shirin Akiner, "Violence in Andijon, 13 May 2005: An Independent Assessment," Silk Road Paper, Johns Hopkins-SAIS, 2005.

[99] Video footage of Andijon.

[100] Interview with expert, International Crisis Group, Osh, Kyrgyzstan, August 2005.

be directly involved in the slaughter, including Interior Minister Zakirjon Almatov, Defense Minister Kadyr Gulamov, and the head of the National Security Service, Rustam Inoyatov.[101]

Scores of Uzbeks who had fled to Kyrgyzstan during and after the violence struggled over whether to return home; the secret police were threatening their relatives.[102] According to Memorial's data, after the Andijon tragedy, repression was even "higher than in its previous peak period. . . . [T]here is a repressive mechanism at work that fabricates collective cases in which grave charges are leveled at dozens of defendants, based on nothing more than informal Islamic teaching, religious debates, or communication between acquaintances."[103] During 2009–10, no fewer than 868 people were tried for political extremism, and the "blacklist" of tens of thousands of Uzbeks was still growing.[104] The government claimed to have unearthed extremism and terrorism among alleged members of HTI, Wahhabis, IMU, and Akromists.[105] It hunted down followers of Said Nursi (1876–1960), a Turkish Islamic scholar who founded the antisecular but nonviolent Nur movement. The number of religious prisoners in what was widely known as the "Uzbek Gulag" escalated.

The Uzbek regime also hunted down dissidents abroad, seeking to silence their ideas and eliminate their sacred authority. One of Tohir Yo'ldosh's early sympathizers, Imam Obidxon Qori, escaped Uzbekistan, then fled Kazakhstan under threat from the MXX. He received asylum in Sweden. However, even there, his widespread sacred authority so worried Karimov that the Uzbek government orchestrated an assassination attempt in 2012.[106] The plot failed, but incapacitated Obidxon Qori.

The legacy of martyred Uzbek religious scholars survived. Uzbek imams and opposition websites continued their online sermons and accusations against Karimov's regime. It was in this context that the IMU rebounded after 9/11, despite its initial heavy losses.

[101] European Union, "Council Common Position 2005/792/CFSP of 14 November 2005 concerning restrictive measures against Uzbekistan," *Official Journal of the European Union*, November 16, 2005, https://www.sipri.org/sites/default/files/2016-03/2005-792-CFSP.pdf.

[102] Personal communication with Uzbekistani expert, Washington, D.C., November 2012.

[103] Interview with Vitaly Ponomaryev, "Uzbek Government Repression Feeds Instability," *Institute for War and Peace Reporting*, March 24, 2011, https://iwpr.net/global-voices/uzbek-government-repression-feeds-instability.

[104] Ponomaryev, *Politicheskie repressii*, 4, 54.

[105] Ponomaryev, *Politicheskie repressii*, 51.

[106] RFE/RL Uzbek Service, "Prominent Uzbek Cleric in Critical Condition after Sweden Shooting," *Radio Free Europe/Radio Liberty*, February 22, 2012, https://www.rferl.org/a/exiled_uzbek_cleric_survives_attack/24493065.html.

The IMU after 9/11

In the 1990s, neither Adolat nor the IMU had been anti-American; the United States was not the target. In fact, the first generation of Uzbek Islamists, and especially those who had fought in the Soviet-Afghan War, considered the United States an ally; they were well aware of American aid to the anti-Soviet mujahidin.[107] Following 9/11, although Karimov's repression still motivated the IMU, the U.S. invasion of Afghanistan in 2001 and the IMU's close relationship with al-Qaeda changed Tohir Yo'ldosh's focus; he took on al-Qaeda's jihad.

The U.S. government, at Uzbekistan's urging, had already placed the IMU on its terrorist list in 2000.[108] Consequently, once Operation Enduring Freedom began, the U.S.-led NATO mission attacked the IMU together with the Taliban and al-Qaeda. Estimated at 2,500 militants, the IMU fought together with hundreds of Tajiks, Uyghurs, and other former Soviet Muslims in northern Afghanistan against the United States and its Afghan allies, the Northern Alliance.[109]

U.S. strikes, however, together with General Abdul Rashid Dostum of the Northern Alliance, decimated the IMU shortly after the war began. As early as November 2001, the IMU was fighting alongside al-Qaeda near Mazar-i-Sharif. IMU leader Juma Namanganiy was killed in a U.S. airstrike on November 18. IMU members were prevalent among a group of four hundred al-Qaeda prisoners—all foreign fighters—held captive at Dostum's Qala-i Jangi fort in northern Afghanistan. Two CIA officers, Mike Spann and David Tyson, the latter a fluent Uzbek and Dari speaker, were the only Americans at the fort. They were questioning prisoners, trying to glean information about al-Qaeda, when a deadly uprising broke out.[110] Prisoners attacked the Americans and overwhelmed Spann, who became the first American casualty of the U.S. war in Afghanistan. The Qala-i Jangi violence, which took six days to quell, was an early indication of al-Qaeda's strength in Afghanistan, bolstered by the IMU.

The U.S. invasion solidified the IMU–al-Qaeda relationship, which had previously been tense due to their divergent goals; before 9/11 the IMU was still primarily focused on Karimov and an Uzbek Islamic state, not al-Qaeda's global jihad. Al-Qaeda saw Central Asians as lesser Muslims, as insufficiently pure, and even as "cannon-fodder" in its larger agenda.[111] But Yo'ldosh's forces proved to be well-trained, well-equipped, and critical to al-Qaeda during Operation Anaconda, a U.S. operation to root out enemy forces in eastern Afghanistan, in

107 Interview with Tyson.

108 Interview with former official in the Ministry of Foreign Affairs, Tashkent, Uzbekistan, July 2002.

109 Rashid, *Descent*, 81.

110 Toby Harnden, *First Casualty: The Untold Story of the CIA Mission to Avenge 9/11* (Boston: Little, Brown, 2021), 174–235; interview with Croissant.

111 Interviews with Croissant and Tyson.

March 2002.[112] When the NATO coalition and the Northern Alliance toppled the Taliban regime in 2001, surviving IMU fighters retreated into tribal areas of Pakistan with the Taliban and al-Qaeda.[113] Some were reportedly airlifted there by Pakistan's Inter-Services Intelligence agency.[114]

In 2002, the U.S. government signed a "strategic partnership" with President Karimov.[115] The agreement committed the United States to attacking the IMU and providing military and counterterrorism equipment to Uzbekistan in exchange for using Uzbekistan's Karshi-Khanabad Air Base (known as K2) in the war effort.[116] Consequently, the IMU continued to be a major U.S. target. Safe harbor in Pakistan's Federally Administered Tribal Areas (FATA), outside of central government control, allowed the IMU to regroup beyond American or Uzbekistani reach. It formed bases in North and later South Waziristan, two large FATA districts, where the Afghan Taliban, al-Qaeda, and Tehrik-i-Taliban Pakistan (TTP, a subset of the Pakistani Taliban, known to be its largest and deadliest militant faction), as well as other foreign fighters, were also operating.[117] Whereas earlier, much of the IMU's income came from the opium trade and kidnappings,[118] its finances were subsequently tied to their association with al-Qaeda, the Afghan Taliban, and TTP, for whom they ran training camps and subcontracted on operations.[119] Maintaining close ties with these factions was necessary to regroup in Pakistan.

From the FATA, it appears the IMU opened up multiple fronts in its pursuit of a caliphate. In 2006, Yo'ldosh made threats against not only Karimov but also several presidents of Muslim states in Eurasia.[120] Bombings, often improvised explosive devices (IEDs) as in Afghanistan, occurred in Andijon (Uzbekistan), Dushanbe (Tajikistan), and Osh (Kyrgyzstan).[121] The IMU plotted but failed to

[112] Interviews with Croissant and Tyson; Bill Roggio, "Islamic Movement of Uzbekistan Leader Thought Killed in August Strike in South Waziristan," *FDD's Long War Journal*, October 2, 2009.

[113] Interview with Damon Mehl, former analyst, U.S. Department of Defense, Washington, D.C., August 2018.

[114] Rashid, *Descent*, 164.

[115] Alexander Cooley, *Base Politics* (Ithaca, NY: Cornell University Press, 2008), 223–26.

[116] Interview with John Herbst, U.S. Ambassador to Uzbekistan, Tashkent, Uzbekistan, June 2003.

[117] Interview with Mehl; Gunaratna and Nielsen, "Al Qaeda in the Tribal Areas," 778.

[118] Mariya Omelicheva and Larry Markowitz, *Webs of Corruption: Trafficking and Terrorism in Central Asia* (New York: Columbia University Press, 2019), 93.

[119] Interview with Mehl; Australian Government, "Australian National Security, Islamic Movement of Uzbekistan," March 3, 2018, https://www.nationalsecurity.gov.au/what-australia-is-doing-subsite/Pages/islamic-movement-of-uzbekistan.aspx.

[120] Roger McDermott, "IMU Issues New Threat to Central Asian Leaders," *Eurasia Daily Monitor*, September 2006, https://jamestown.org/program/imu-issues-new-threat-to-central-asian-leaders/.

[121] Data from U.S. National Counterterrorism Center, in Thomas Sanderson, Daniel Kimmage, and David Gordon, "From the Ferghana Valley to South Waziristan," Center for Strategic and International Studies, March 25, 2010, https://www.csis.org/analysis/ferghana-valley-south-waziristan.

bomb both a hotel and the U.S. Embassy in Kyrgyzstan in May 2003.[122] Yet, according to the UN Security Council, the IMU successfully orchestrated deadly explosions every year from 2002 to 2004 in Bishkek and Osh, killing both civilians and a police officer.[123] There were also small-scale border attacks on all three states between 2006 and 2015, involving both trained assailants and IEDs. Given the absence of state media coverage, these attacks were unlikely to have been fabricated by Karimov. Some analysts believe the IMU was involved in the prison break and uprising in Andijon in May 2005, although evidence is lacking.[124] However, several significant prison breaks in Tajikistan—in 2006, 2010, and 2016—did involve the IMU or its offshoots as contractors for al-Qaeda or the Taliban. Throughout this period, IMU fighters crossed the Afghan-Tajik border. The former UTO militia leader, Mullah Abdullo, after rejecting the 1997 Tajik peace accord, had remained in Afghanistan and come under the IMU's and al-Qaeda's direction. He was reportedly sent back to Tajikistan to become "al-Qaeda's man" there; his three hundred fighters had killed about a hundred Tajik forces by early 2011.[125]

Despite such incidents, the goal of overthrowing Karimov seemed far off. The post-9/11 war between the West and al-Qaeda and the Taliban had irrevocably drawn in the IMU, reorienting its goals.

The IMU Targets ISAF and the Pakistani and Afghani Governments

By the mid-2000s, the IMU had clearly shifted from fighting its Karimov-centered "near jihad" to the "far jihad," much as other militant Islamists had done as a result of the Soviet-Afghan War.[126] Working with the Pakistani Taliban, the IMU's target was now the United States and its allies. Multiple U.S. Department of Defense (DoD) reports of U.S. military engagement in Afghanistan detail the IMU striking at U.S. and International Security Assistance Force (ISAF)

[122] Interview with U.S. embassy staff, Bishkek, Kyrgyzstan, May 2005; Lionel Beehner, "Documenting Andijon," Council on Foreign Relations, June 26, 2006, https://www.cfr.org/backgrounder/documenting-andijan.

[123] UN Security Council, "Islamic Movement of Uzbekistan," April 7, 2011, https://www.un.org/securitycouncil/sanctions/1267/aq_sanctions_list/summaries/entity/islamic-movement-of-uzbekistan.

[124] Rashid, *Descent*, 344.

[125] Roggio, "Islamic Movement of Uzbekistan Leader Thought Killed"; Bruce Pannier, "An Extremist Link between Tajikistan, Waziristan," *Radio Free Europe/Radio Liberty*, January 27, 2011, https://www.rferl.org/a/tajikistan_waziristan_extremists/2289634.html; Alexandr Shushtov, "Mullo Abdullo Reported Dead in Tajikistan," *Strategic Culture*, April 26, 2011.

[126] Fawaz Gerges, *The Far Enemy: Why Jihad Went Global* (New York: Cambridge University Press, 2005).

forces and the Afghan National Army, as well as at the Pakistani government for its cooperation with ISAF.[127] Consequently, the IMU also became a central U.S. target. U.S. drone strikes and missions sought to seize or kill senior IMU commanders in both Afghanistan and Pakistan. A U.S. drone strike killed the Pakistani Taliban leader Baitullah Mehsud, Yo'ldosh's longtime ally and host in FATA, on August 5, 2009. A few weeks later, Pakistani security officials and Radio Liberty reported that Yo'ldosh had died in South Waziristan in late August 2009; he was most likely killed by a U.S. drone strike.[128] The IMU's spokesman denied the claim, however, declaring, "Glory to Allah, our Emir is alive and well."[129] Although shaken by the blow, far from dissolving the IMU, Yo'ldosh's death gave it a martyr. So too did other combat losses. The organization's website regularly featured multiple *shahids*. Their names and biographical information suggested most were Uzbekistanis.[130] Their numbers included a younger generation of émigrés as well as those born in the 1990s to Uzbek exiles in Afghanistan; they became known as "Afghan-Uzbeks."[131]

The IMU's announcement of Yo'ldosh's death a year later in 2010 was accompanied by a message from its new leader, Usmon Odil. He declared that the IMU would continue fierce fighting in Afghanistan and Pakistan and against the "infidel governments" of Central Asia by the "the path of jihad."[132] The IMU's "mujahidin," he promised, would "drive out the enemies of Islam from our shrines and lands that they occupied, to bring the oppressed Muslims to Islam's joyful life."[133] Moreover, the IMU's propaganda and actions seemed ever more influenced by al-Qaeda's radical strategy; al-Zawahiri had boldly contended that martyrdom and suicide were necessary in jihad. It was with this ideological and strategic shift that the IMU continued to fight the U.S.-Afghani-Pakistani alliance. In 2011, *Mufti* Abu Zar al-Burmi, a prominent IMU spiritual leader, met with Pakistani *ulama*, publicly praised suicide bombers who attacked the Pakistani government, and called more to join their ranks.[134] The IMU did not urge attackers to avoid civilian or Muslim casualties; rather, they justified

[127] Jeremy Binnie and Joanna Wright, "The Evolving Role of Uzbek-Led Fighters in Afghanistan and Pakistan," *CTC Sentinel* 2, no. 8 (August 2009).

[128] Abubakar Siddique, "Sources Claim IMU Militant Leader Yuldash Killed," *Radio Free Europe/Radio Liberty*, October 2, 2009, https://www.rferl.org/a/Pakistani_Agents_Say_IMU_Leader_Militant_Killed/1841609.html.

[129] Dilbegim Mavlonius, "Information about the Death of IMU Leader Tahir Yuldash Is Refuted Once Again," *Radio Azattyq*, October 4, 2009, azattyq.org.

[130] Interview with Mehl.

[131] Interview with Tyson.

[132] Bruce Pannier, "IMU Announces Longtime Leader Dead, Names Successor," *Radio Free Europe/Radio Liberty*, August 17, 2010, https://www.rferl.org/a/IMU_Announces_Longtime_Leader_Dead_Names_Successor/2130382.html.

[133] Pannier, "IMU Announces."

[134] "Uzbekistan al-Qaeda Affiliate Pushes Attacks against Pakistan," *IPT News*, August 30, 2011, http://www.investigativeproject.org/3135/uzbeksitan-al-qaeda-affiliate-pushes-attacks.

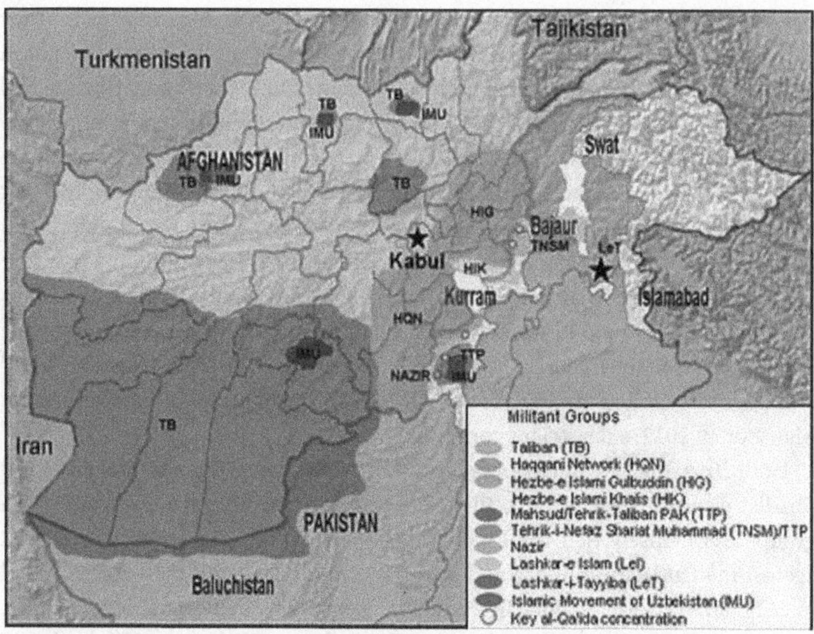

Map 9.1 Location of IMU and insurgent operations in Afghanistan, 2010
Source: United States Army, Center for Lessons Learned, 2010, https://en.m.wikipedia.org/wiki/File:Insurgent_Regions_in_Afghanistan_and_Pakistan.jpg

such deaths by adopting the Salafi jihadist idea of *takfir* (excommunicating or declaring a Muslim an apostate).[135]

The IMU became an influential force in northern Afghanistan. Some eight to ten years after nearly being decimated, it was no longer hiding in Pakistan. It waged attacks in Balkh, Taloqan, Kunduz, Badakhshan, Takhar, Baglan, Sar i-Pul, Samangan, and Wardak provinces. It became particularly influential in non-Pashtun-governed areas. In Takhar, for example, a senior IMU commander was known as the "shadow governor" of the province.[136] The IMU's militant capabilities also strengthened. According to DoD reports, the IMU frequently orchestrated IED attacks. It trained the IED experts who designed attacks in Baglan, Kunduz, and elsewhere. An IMU militant known by the religious honorific Qori Asrar planned IED attacks targeting Afghani and Pakistani government officials as well as ISAF forces.[137] The IMU ran both basic training

[135] U.S. Department of Defense, Report, September 19, 2011 (no longer available), http://archive.defense.gov/news.

[136] Bill Roggio, "Uzbek Terror Commander Serving as Taliban Shadow Governor Killed by US Special Forces," *FDD's Long War Journal*, September 2, 2010.

[137] U.S. Department of Defense, Report, January 10, 2013 (no longer available), http://archive.defense.gov/news.

camps and suicide training camps in Sar i-Pul and Samangan provinces.[138] They instructed jihadi recruits in military tactics as well as a radical interpretation of the Qur'an.[139] They began using female suicide bombers,[140] a tactic they had likely learned from Chechens. Some IMU suicide missions hit major targets, including Pakistani government compounds and ISAF military installations. One senior IMU leader known as Shakrullah orchestrated a suicide bombing that killed forty-one Afghans.[141] Multiple successful attacks were coordinated with the Taliban, including one in May 2010 in which about forty militants struck at Bagram Air Base, the largest U.S. military base in Afghanistan. An IMU commander claimed in a propaganda video that "twenty martyrdom-seekers" were among the assailants; they included IMU fighters together with other jihadis.[142] Although the United States killed the IMU's chief military commander, Abbas Mansoor, in 2012, such strikes continued.

Until 2014, the IMU also operated closely with other foreign fighter and local jihadist groups, most prominently, the TPP and the Haqqani network; both groups were closely tied to al-Qaeda. While the TTP was primarily directed against the Pakistani military and government, the Haqqani network, founded by Afghan warlord Jalaluddin Haqqani, a veteran of the anti-Soviet jihad, was known for its sophisticated and high-profile attacks on the U.S. and coalition forces.[143] From their mutual sanctuary in South Waziristan,[144] TTP, the Haqqani group, and the IMU collaborated and sometimes waged joint attacks. IMU expertise in prison breaks led to the April 2012 collaboration with TTP to besiege the Bannu Prison in Pakistan. They reportedly freed 384 prisoners, including a few dozen Islamists. An IMU propaganda video featured the attack later that year.[145] In May 2013, they killed the police chief in Quetta, Pakistan. They attacked the governor's compound in Panjshir province, Afghanistan. The TTP and IMU together attacked Jinnah International Airport in Karachi on

[138] Australian Government, "Australian National Security, Islamic Movement of Uzbekistan"; Bill Roggio, "Taliban Overruns Another District in Northern Afghanistan," *FDD's Long War Journal*, July 28, 2015; Bill Roggio, "ISAF Captures IMU Leader Who Ran Terror Camps in Afghan North," *Long War Journal*, March 22, 2011.

[139] Interview with Mehl.

[140] U.S. Department of Defense, Daily Report, May 2011, (no longer available), http://archive.defense.gov/news.

[141] U.S. Department of Defense, Daily Report, November 30, 2012, (no longer available), http://archive.defense.gov/news.

[142] Bill Roggio, "IMU claims 2010 attack on Bagram Airbase was executed 'in coordination and cooperation with other jihadi groups,'" *FDD's Long War Journal*, October 19, 2011.

[143] Interview with Mehl.

[144] Damon Mehl, "The Islamic Movement of Uzbekistan Opens a Door to the Islamic State," *CTC Sentinel* 8, no. 6 (June 2015): 11–14.

[145] SITE, "IMU Video Focuses on Bannu Prison Break," accessed July 18, 2018, https://news.siteintelgroup.com/Jihadist-News/imu-video-focuses-on-bannu-prison-break.html.

Image 9.2 Propaganda video of IMU suicide assault team
Source: FDD's Long War Journal, https://www.longwarjournal.org/archives/2014/06/imu_involved_in_suic.php

June 8, 2014,[146] providing the ten-man assault team, all of whom were prepared for suicide.[147] Twenty-four victims and all the militants died.[148] According to analyst Damon Mehl, throughout this period, the IMU was neither a peripheral player nor on the decline, but a resilient organization essential to many such collaborations against ISAF and the Afghani and Pakistani governments.[149]

Coming under assault from the Pakistan military offensive into the tribal regions, the IMU reestablished a base in Afghanistan in 2015,[150] where it proved itself capable of magnifying the terrorist problem in both Afghanistan and Pakistan. It engaged in racketeering, kidnapping, and hostage-taking to generate funds, bolster its image, and induce fear. For example, in February 2015, IMU militants kidnapped thirty Afghans from a bus, beheaded one of the hostages on video, and demanded the release of IMU members from an Afghan jail.[151] Following the example of ISIS, they then used the video for propaganda purposes.

By 2014, the IMU had survived the death of its top leadership and multiple migrations to new safe havens and had revived its fighting force. As military

[146] Anne Stenersen, "The Islamic Movement of Uzbekistan's Role in Attacks in Pakistan," *CTC Sentinel* 7, no. (July 2014); Australian Government, "Australian National Security, Islamic Movement of Uzbekistan."

[147] The TTP had struck several other hard targets: Mehran Naval Base in 2011 and the Minhas Airbase and Peshawar Airbase in 2012. IMU may have participated in those attacks.

[148] Stenersen, "Islamic Movement."

[149] Interview with Mehl.

[150] Interview with Mehl.

[151] "Afghanistan Kidnap Video: Hostage Beheaded 'by Uzbek Gunmen,'" *BBC*, April 7, 2015, https://www.bbc.com/news/world-asia-32200835.

analyst Anne Stenersen observed, although the IMU did not present a significant threat to the stability of the Uzbek, Afghan, or Pakistani states, the jihadist group played an important role in "recruiting and training suicide squads," and its attack capabilities were increasingly sophisticated.[152] Residents of northern Afghanistan reported in late 2015 that Uzbeks and Tajiks were still coming across the border to join the IMU.[153]

Following al-Qaeda, the IMU initiated operations in the West as well. In 2012, the U.S. Treasury imposed sanctions on Qori Ayyub Bashir, a terrorist financier who facilitated travel for IMU recruits and moved funds from Europe and Turkey to the IMU. Multitalented, Bashir had also led an IMU militia in attacks on ISAF in Afghanistan's Kunduz and Takhar provinces.[154] Some of his operatives went to the United States to wage jihad. One was Ulug'bek Qodirov, who was sentenced to nearly sixteen years in prison by a court in Alabama in July 2012, after pleading guilty to making a threat to kill the president of the United States and to illegal possession of a firearm.[155] Another IMU operative, Fazliddin Qurbonov, was charged in both Idaho and Utah in 2013 for conspiring to provide material support to the IMU and for distributing information on making explosives and WMD. According to the court, "Qurbonov . . . procured bomb-making materials in the interest of perpetrating a terrorist attack on American soil."[156] Qurbonov considered military bases in Idaho and Texas as possible attack sites. In 2017, while serving his sentence, Qurbonov attempted to behead a prison warden.[157]

Internal Weaknesses

The IMU's global reach, however, remained limited, as its core in Afghanistan began to fracture shortly after 9/11. Factionalism had existed from the

152 Stenersen, "Islamic Movement."

153 Bruce Pannier, "The Islamic Movement of Uzbekistan Comes Unraveled," *Radio Free Europe/Radio Liberty*, November 28, 2015, https://www.rferl.org/a/qishloq-ovozi-islamic-movement-uzbekistan-fractured/27395160.html.

154 U.S. Department of the Treasury, "Treasury Imposes Sanctions on Pakistan-Based Terrorist Facilitators," October 17, 2012, http://www.treasury.gov/press-center/press-releases/Pages/tg1739.aspx.

155 "Uzbek National Sentenced to Nearly 16 Years in Prison for Threatening to Kill the President and Providing Material Support to Terrorism, The United States Attorney's Office," Press Release, Northern District of Alabama, July 13, 2012, https://www.justice.gov/archive/usao/aln/News/July%202012/July%2013,%202012%20Uzbek.html.

156 U.S. Department of Justice, "Federal Jury Convicts Kurbanov on Terrorism Charges," August 12, 2015, https://www.justice.gov/opa/pr/federal-jury-convicts-kurbanov-terrorism-charges.

157 "Indictment: Boise Man Serving Terrorism Sentence Tried to Kill Prison Warden," *KTVB*, May 26, 2017, https://www.ktvb.com/article/mobile/news/crime/indictment-boise-man-serving-terrorism-sentence-tried-to-kill-prison-warden/443012947.

organization's beginnings. As more broadly in Uzbek culture, regional rivalry existed between those IMU members coming from the Ferghana Valley (especially Namangan) and other regions. The IMU's ethnic Uzbek core from Namangan, led by Yo'ldosh and Namangoniy, determined the organization's ideology, set its goals and agenda, and ran the internal security and intelligence structures. Those from other regions, such as the IMU's Khorezm faction, were less trusted by the leadership and occupied a lower place in the rank and file. Yo'ldosh's hotheaded nature and leadership style became more tyrannical over time. Yo'ldosh obsessively controlled the group and opposed dissent. He regularly treated dissenters as "spies," and incarcerated them in the "IMU prison." Those who fled risked being hunted down in Afghanistan or Pakistan since they could not return to Uzbekistan.[158] Over time, these internal dynamics would weaken morale and loyalty and eventually foster the IMU's decline. But first, we turn to the strategies that fostered the IMU's relative success, despite the odds, for about two decades.

Explaining the IMU's Relative Success in Mobilizing

Scholars have often dismissed the IMU as a tiny fringe group, not to be taken seriously. Certainly, one must be cautious about overestimating such groups. Nonetheless, as we have seen, the IMU was an organization to be taken seriously. At its height, the IMU roughly paralleled al-Qaeda, which was estimated at three thousand to four thousand members just before 9/11.[159] The IMU was small by comparison with the IRPT and made far less progress in achieving its political goals in Uzbekistan or globally. Still, the IMU recruited moderate numbers for a militant Islamist group and sustained itself for nearly two decades, from 1998 through 2015. The organization did so despite being exiled in a war zone, where it could offer minimal material incentives. Recruits continued to join, even as dozens were killed by the Afghan National Army, the Pakistan Army, and ISAF.[160] Journalists and local experts estimate that several thousand Uzbeks, including families, had fled Uzbekistan with Yo'ldosh and Adolat in the 1990s. Seven years later, sources estimated that up to eight hundred IMU members fought in its initial attacks launched in the late summers of 1999 and 2000. Another thousand fought together with the Taliban against Ahmad Shah

[158] Interview with Tyson.
[159] Gunaratna and Nielsen, "Al-Qaeda in the Tribal Areas," 778.
[160] Interview with Mehl.

Massoud at Taloqan in 2000.[161] In the summer of 2001, just before the United States entered Afghanistan, the IMU was about twenty-five hundred strong.[162]

Despite massive losses in 2002 due to the initial U.S. strikes after 9/11, as we have seen, the IMU regrouped. The DoD believed in June 2002 that about 3,500 foreign fighters had taken refuge in South Waziristan,[163] of whom 500 to 600 were IMU members. There they rebounded. In 2007, Saylab Mas'ud, a journalist based in North Waziristan, put the number of Uzbek militia in the area at 2,000 to 2,500.[164] By 2009, DoD and other journalists estimated that the IMU again included 2,500 to 5,000 fighters.[165] Taking into account combat deaths and attrition following the Pakistani Army assault on safe havens in Waziristan and the escalation of U.S. drone strikes, the DoD believed that IMU numbers had dropped to as low as 1,200 in 2010.[166] Returning to Afghanistan again allowed growth. In late 2013, after years of clashes with ISAF and Afghan forces, some intelligence assessments estimated that there were still about 3,000 IMU members total, including 2,000 fighters in Pakistan, 700 fighters in Afghanistan, 140 military advisers and trainers, "and an undisclosed number active elsewhere, including in Central Asia, the Caucuses, Iran and Syria."[167] Given their prominence in training Afghani Taliban and in waging attacks throughout this period, these numbers seem plausible. After the split with ISIS, a mere 200 to 300 remained as IMU in 2016.[168]

From the late 1990s onward, the IMU invested heavily in three mobilization strategies. It constructed sacred authority and established new networks outside Uzbekistan. However, its ideological propaganda emphasizing Salafi jihadism, as we shall see in the next chapter, was too extreme and distant from Uzbekistani norms and everyday concerns to garner widespread support at home.

[161] David Witter, "Uzbek Militancy in Pakistan's Tribal Regions," Report, Institute for the Study of War, January 27, 2011; Rashid, *Descent*, 17.

[162] Rashid, *Descent*, 80–81; Yossef Bodansky, *Chechen Jihad: Al-Qaeda's Training Ground* (London: Harper, 2009).

[163] Rashid, *Descent*, 268.

[164] Daniel Kimmage, "Has the IMU Reached the End of the Line," *Radio Free Europe/Radio Liberty*, March 30, 2007, http://www.rferl.org/content/article/1075600.html.

[165] Roggio, "Islamic Movement of Uzbekistan Leader Thought Killed"; Kimmage, "Has the IMU Reached the End of the Line"; Rashid, *Descent*, 347.

[166] Sanderson, Kimmage, and Gordon, "From the Ferghana Valley to South Waziristan," 12.

[167] Australian Government, "Australian National Security, Islamic Movement of Uzbekistan."

[168] U.S. State Department, "Country Reports on Terrorism 2016—Foreign Terrorist Organizations: Islamic Movement of Uzbekistan (IMU)," July 19, 2017, https://www.state.gov/reports/country-reports-on-terrorism-2016/.

Image 9.3 Propaganda video of IMU leader Shaykh Muhammad Tohir Foruq Yo'ldosh in Afghanistan
Source: YouTube screenshot

Constructing Sacred Authority

The IMU had initially lacked sacred authority. Most Uzbek Muslims rejected the IMU's rhetoric, goals, and theological claims, and those of Salafi jihadism broadly. The esteemed former *mufti* Muhammad Sodiq Muhammad Yusuf contended that the IMU's "extremist interpretation" of the Qur'an, Islamic law, and Islamic history was based on a weak understanding of theology.[169] To counter the mainstream Uzbek *ulama*, who disparaged him, Yo'ldosh invested in his image as a spiritual, political, and military leader. His sermons were in Uzbek, but he often recited verses from the Qur'an in Arabic. He gave lessons discussing passages from the *hadith*. He co-opted the renowned Shaykh Abduvali Qori as the IMU's martyred spiritual leader, and he portrayed himself as the shaykh's successor. Yo'ldosh in the 2000s looked strikingly different from the young Tohirjon who had formed Adolat during *perestroika*. In propaganda videos, he often sat in the position of a religious teacher, Qur'an open, lecturing to his followers. Alternatively, he appeared as the jihadi leader, Kalashnikov in hand and dark beard flowing, like the iconic image of Bin Laden in 1980s Afghanistan.

[169] Interview with Muhammad Sodiq Muhammad Yusuf, Tashkent, Uzbekistan, 2003; interviews with Uzbek imams.

Yo'ldosh assumed the name "Muhammad Tohir Foruq," invoking greater sacred authority with the name of the Prophet. "Foruq" means "the one who distinguishes between right and wrong." By the early 2000s, a series of IMU propaganda videos depicted Yo'ldosh as a great leader, fulfilling the will of Allah. One such video was titled "A Grand Trade—If You Give Your Life to Allah, You'll Get Paradise." Another celebrated his early life studying Islam in the clandestine *hujras* in Uzbekistan. Yo'ldosh portrayed the IMU as purists and true followers of the Qur'an, *sunna*, and *hadith* of al-Buxoriy, as the "people of the *sunna* and society." Like al-Qaeda, he ignored the greater, inner jihad and failed to address the correct conditions for the lesser, militant jihad.[170]

In one of Yo'ldosh's lectures, posted on an IMU website, the self-proclaimed Islamic scholar-mujahid gave an "address to the *umma*" regarding "the hypocrites."[171] In his teaching on the *Sura al-Fath* (the Victory), Yo'ldosh referred to the battle of Hudaybiyyah, a turning point during which the Prophet Muhammad was victorious and "hypocrites" were punished. Yo'ldosh decreed that any Muslim who avoids fighting the jihad, who "remains behind" to stay in "warm conditions," is "like a hypocrite" and will be punished by Allah. Yo'ldosh glorified the IMU's time in Tajikistan and Afghanistan. He boasted it was their *hijra*, resembling the Prophet Muhammad's own *hijra* to Medina: "[I]n Tajikistan, Allah gave us strength and power to turn into a political-military organization. . . . We don't feel sorry for those of our own killed in Tajikistan."[172] It was preparation for the jihad against Karimov.

Over time, the IMU adopted and posted (in Uzbek translation) extensive religious writings to demonstrate its theological legitimacy. Using images, music, and symbols, videography carefully crafted a transnational Salafi jihadist message. Images of Mecca drew the viewer in, and then shifted to footage of IMU soldiers clad in Pakistani or Afghani dress, weapons slung over their shoulders, marching through the mountains of Afghanistan, accompanied by religious chants, known as *nasheeds*, songs praising Allah and glorifying jihad. This genre of music is shared by jihadists globally. Like al-Qaeda's online videos, black flags were held or positioned behind the speaker to invoke the supposedly black battle flag of the Prophet Muhammad. The IMU's flag inscribed the *shahada* and resembled those flags of al-Qaeda or other Salafi jihadi terrorist groups. Other IMU banners read, "There is no duty but to Allah."

[170] Raymond Ibrahim, ed., *The Al-Qaeda Reader: Essential Texts of Osama Bin Laden's Terrorist Organization* (New York: Broadway Books, 2007).

[171] Tohir Yuldashev bilan suhbat, 2 (of a 7-part series), no date, Jundarulloh.com, accessed November 11, 2011 (link now defunct).

[172] Tohir Yuldashev bilan suhbat, 2.

All this solidified Yo'ldosh's image as a jihadi leader endowed with sacred authority. He thus not only appealed to radicalized Central Asians, but also bolstered IMU credentials among Arab and Pakistani Salafi jihadist sponsors.

Ideological Adaptation for Ordinary Uzbeks

In its early years, IMU ideology and recruiting propaganda emphasized the common persecution of Uzbek Muslims and the brutality of Karimov. The seven-part IMU video series titled *O'zbekiston Islomiy harakati Afg'onistonda* (The IMU in Afghanistan) and similar pieces received thousands of views on YouTube. Each "history" drew parallels between the IMU and the Companions of the Prophet, emphasizing the persecution of Muslims inside Uzbekistan and the necessity of *hijra*. Other videos investigated the probable abduction and torture in 1995 of Shaykh Abduvali Qori, whose sermons were an inspiration for Adolat and the IMU. One video, titled "Chained Killer," recorded partial footage of the IMU's interrogation of an MXX agent. The agent, the video claimed, admitted that Abduvali Qori had been in MXX custody since "disappearing" in 1995. IMU web postings and propaganda claimed the imam as its own martyr.[173] Comments posted in response to the video revealed that it effectively stoked anger at the Uzbek government.

Ideological Adaptation for Radical Financiers

For several years, the IMU's websites (furqon.com, jundarrahmon.com, jundarulloh.com) delivered its message to potential followers.[174] The IMU propaganda department posted videos, lectures, and jihadi texts on the websites. The sheer volume and variety of the online propaganda was striking. The IMU posted books, pamphlets, poetry, and videos in Uzbek or Arabic, and sometimes in Russian and Kazakh. Jundullah Studio, the IMU media center based in Pakistan, produced and posted videos on IMU websites and often on YouTube. Given the risk in accessing them from inside Uzbekistan, where they were blocked, it is surprising that a significant number of viewers did open them. Some videos targeted Karimov. For example, they disseminated information about the 2005 Andijon massacre, an issue that fueled rage at the Uzbek regime. However, the propaganda overall revealed how the IMU's association with the Taliban and al-Qaeda had reshaped its ideology and its mission.

[173] Studio Jundullah, "Zanjirband killer qissasi 1-qism," dated August 12, 2011, www.jundurrahmon.com (link now defunct); reposting available at: https://archive.org/details/ZanjirbandKillerQissasi1-qism,. Abduvali Qori's photo and links to his sermons were previously posted on www.jundurrahmon.com.

[174] The IMU's websites have been defunct since about 2016. However, Furqon Media produced IMU videos that occasionally appeared on Russian social media.

From Nation to *Umma* and Caliphate

In contrast to its earlier ideas, by the 2000s, like al-Qaeda, the IMU claimed it had an Islamic duty to create a new caliphate. This became its primary political goal. Yo'ldosh declared, "After the 9/11 events in the U.S., all the Islamist factions gathered in Afghanistan to establish an Islamic state . . . Arab and non-Arab. Our goal was to reestablish the caliphate, but . . . all the Christians, Jews, Communists, atheists, unbelievers, and hypocrites joined to fight against us."[175] The solution to Muslim political problems was a new caliph: "Now there is no leadership for the whole *umma*. . . . The *umma* must find a head. . . . The purpose of all efforts is to establish a caliphate."[176]

In his "Message to the *Umma*" (all Muslims, not just Uzbeks), Yo'ldosh unequivocally shifted from pursuing an Islamic state in Uzbekistan to pursuing a transnational caliphate. Reflecting key elements of transnational Salafi jihadism, he spoke of Islamic *hukumat* (governance), the unity of Muslims, and the individual duty of militant, global jihad:

> The Prophet Muhammad [peace be upon him], and the caliphs were trying to establish the will of Allah on earth because everything belongs to him and everything should be in accord with his command. All of our efforts are aimed at establishing his commands, and his governance, and that's why we are continuing the jihad against the *kuffar*. We're responding to Allah's order . . . on a big, global scale. . . . All humanity is divided into two camps. We are the group which follows the Qur'an and *Sunna*, which follows *tawhid* [unity in the oneness of Allah]. . . . We won't be soldiers of regional *murtadd* [bad/apostate Muslim leaders]. . . . We'll only be soldiers of Allah [*JundAllah*].[177]

Yo'ldosh used the Prophet's own life—the example of the Battle of Uhud—as proof that all men must fight jihad to accomplish this goal "in Afghanistan, in Africa, in Andalusia, and in the Uzbek and Tajik homeland, Bukhara. . . . Conquering all these lands, we [Muslims] should have one state, one flag, the Islamic state, the Islamic caliphate."[178]

The pursuit of the caliphate was linked to his emphasis on a unified Muslim *umma* and opposition to nationalism, a historical phenomenon that, Yo'ldosh said, had undermined the caliphate in the nineteenth and twentieth centuries. Postings to the IMU website reflected its transnational membership, a sign of its shift to the *umma* over the Uzbek nation. In 2011, for example, the IMU claimed

175 "IMU tarixining videosi, Jundurrahmondan, Muhammad Tohir Foruq, Muqaddas tijorat, 1," no date, accessed November 13, 2011, Jundarulloh.com (link now defunct).
176 "Ummatga," no date, accessed November 11, 2011, Jundarulloh.com (link now defunct).
177 "Ummatga."
178 "Ummatga."

eighty-seven martyrs had died in its ranks that year alone (including both combat and suicide missions). Among them were sixty-four Afghan nationals, ten Tajiks, six Kyrgyz, four Uzbeks, and one each from Tatarstan, Germany, and Pakistan.[179] Yo'ldosh merged the concerns of repressed Uzbek Muslims with all Muslims in addressing the *umma*: "In the history of Islam, there were many incidents when Communists and Russians would invade, and Jews occupied Palestine, but there has never been such a bleak day for Muslims before now, when true believers are tortured, put under psychological and physical hardships. That's why for all Muslim men jihad is a religious duty, regardless of race, language . . . to stop this assault on Muslims."[180] Although the IMU was initially an Uzbek movement, Yo'ldosh eventually condemned the idea of "nation," saying that "the British, Italian, and Spanish empires, the USSR, Germany, America, and now Russia . . . had no fear of Allah" and therefore collapsed.[181] He lambasted regionalism: those who say "I'm from Tashkent, Namangan, Andijon—these are traps of Satan and his soldiers. . . . It is ignorance to be divided into states and regions." He blamed "the *kuffar*," who seek to divide and rule Muslims.[182] Yo'ldosh even denounced the nationalist opposition to Karimov: "If we preach righteousness and want to create an Islamic society then you have to get rid of all these divisions. . . . Nationalists such as Birlik, Erk, they do not use the flag of Islam. . . . [L]et them know that if they die as nationalists, they will go to hellfire. . . . If they act not for faith, but for other causes, they'll end up in hellfire.[183]

From Purist Revivalism to Global Jihad

In contrast to Adolat, which had advocated purism but not violent jihad, the IMU had adopted a Salafi jihadist ideology.[184] IMU website postings featured statements by its spiritual leaders; the message was clear, radical, and violent. One lengthy treatise was titled *Jihad Lovers' Attractions to the Battleground*. Published in South Waziristan and translated into Uzbek, it justified militant jihad using passages from the Qur'an and *hadith* and it emphasized a mujahid's reward in heaven. The websites featured "questions," "*fatwa*s," and "news" from the jihadists' perspective—all meant to draw in recruits.

Early IMU propaganda had referred chiefly to jihad in Uzbekistan or Khorasan broadly. After 9/11, however, Yo'ldosh's video-recorded lectures

179 Damon Mehl, presentation and personal database, shared with me, August 2018.

180 "Ummatga."

181 "Millatchilar emasmiz." This series of radio lessons was posted on the IMU website, accessed November 14, 2011, www.jundurrahmon.biz//radio/ (link now defunct); available at https://archive.org/details/juma_dasturi_101-110/juma_110.mp3.

182 "Millatchilar emasmiz."

183 "Millatchilar emasmiz."

184 Henri Lauzière, *The Making of Salafism: Islamic Reform in the Twentieth Century* (New York: Columbia University Press, 2016); Shiraz Maher, *Salafi-Jihadism: The History of an Idea* (Oxford: Oxford University Press, 2016).

became explicit about the global jihad against Russia and the U.S.-led NATO coalition in Afghanistan. For example, one video replayed the collapse of the World Trade Center towers, reminding viewers that President George W. Bush had divided the world: "either with or against the U.S."[185] Yo'ldosh declared that because of the United States, "we got together, united to defend our Islamic state.... Our mujahidin of the IMU were among the first to sacrifice their lives. Hundreds and hundreds were killed."[186] The video was accompanied by *ayats* (verses) about sacrifice and reward.

IMU media shifted to focusing on the goals of its host, the Taliban, and ally, al-Qaeda, particularly the war with the *kuffar*. Their message involved a radical retelling and reinterpretation of Islamic history, Islamic *shariat* and jihad, and passages from the Qur'an and the *hadith*, to give their political agenda a theological basis. In one video, Yo'ldosh emphasized that Chechens, Tajiks, and Uzbeks were all fighting their common enemy in a civilizational conflict: "Now we're fighting all enemies of Islam on a global scale. All of humanity is divided into two camps: the Muslims and the Judeo-Christian world, or believers and unbelievers. And we, the IMU, were firmly holding the flag of *tawhid*. First, we said we want to fight with Karimov, but now we fight with all the *kuffar*, with the Jews and Christians, on a global scale."[187] The U.S. war in Afghanistan globalized the IMU's ideas. On its websites, video clips shifted between pictures of IMU soldiers training or fighting in Tajikistan and Afghanistan and clips of U.S. air strikes; the narrator called the listener to "come defend your people" by jihad.[188] The "fighting with our own enemies on a local scale," he declared, is "finished."[189] In typical videos, as Yo'ldosh spoke, images of Karimov with U.S. Secretary of Defense Donald Rumsfeld appeared, followed by U.S. military planes at Uzbekistan's K2 base. The "blood-sucking Karimov," Yo'ldosh continued, is but a "small goal."[190] Later images showed U.S. drone strikes and an American soldier shooting at the Qur'an. Videos stoked hatred of the United States and glorified the Uzbek mujahidin as belonging to a long history of fighters for Islam.[191]

[185] "IMU tarixining videosi, Jundurrahmondan, Muhammad Tohir Foruq, Muqaddas tijorat, 1."

[186] "IMU tarixining videosi, Jundurrahmondan, Muhammad Tohir Foruq, Muqaddas tijorat, 2," no date, accessed November 13, 2011, Jundarulloh.com (link now defunct).

[187] "IMU tarixining videosi, Jundurrahmondan, Muhammad Tohir Foruq, Muqaddas tijorat, 2."

[188] A seven-part series featuring clips from fighting in Afghanistan was posted on its site: "O`zbekiston Islomiy harakati Afgonistonda7-qism," July 12, 2011, Studio Jundullah (link now defunct), but available at: https://archive.org/details/OzbekistonIslomiyHarakatiAfgonistonda7-qism; "Ty bilan suhbat," pt. 2 of 7, no date, accessed November 14, 2011, Jundarulloh.com (link now defunct).

[189] "IMU tarixining videosi, Jundurrahmondan, Muhammad Tohir Foruq, Muqaddas tijorat, 2."

[190] "IMU tarixining videosi, Jundurrahmondan, Muhammad Tohir Foruq, Muqaddas tijorat, 2."

[191] "Uzbek Mujahidin," Jundullah Productions, November 14, 2005, available at https://archive.org/details/uzbek-mujahideen.

The IMU adapted its message to recruit Pakistanis as well. Its websites posted extensive Urdu literature with titles such as *What Is Going on in FATA, Pakistan?* and *The Tasks of the Mujahid*. These too stressed the glory of *hijra*, but this time across the Afghani-Pakistani border. Extensive Arabic and Urdu Islamic texts, translated into Uzbek, were linked.

It is hard to know how effective such videos were, but they did have hundreds to thousands of hits. After the websites became inaccessible, either cut off by the security services or because the IMU operation in Pakistan was disrupted, propaganda continued to be posted on YouTube. It too was eventually removed. Given its investment, the IMU must have valued its online profile.

Building Networks

A third IMU strategy involved expanding its networks. The movement had originated in networks of kin, friends, mosques, martial arts groups, and villages from the Ferghana Valley—supporters of Adolat and the IRPU.[192] The IMU then recruited Uzbeks fleeing Karimov. It drew supporters from connections in Namangan and Andijon. The IMU used rural religious ties and even former collective farm networks to recruit in the Ferghana Valley. In the village of Koni-Zar, for example, an unregistered imam, Bahodir Mamajonov, had established an underground Islamic society and preached a return to true Islam and *shariat* as the solution to political and economic problems.[193] Yo'ldosh's recruiters drew support there in the 1990s, when the IMU fought in the Tajik Civil War. Later, Mamajonov and twelve more Koni-Zar families left together to join the IMU's jihad as mujahids.[194] By the 2010s, however, the flow of exiles was slowing. Few dared to undertake the journey, and Yo'ldosh's ties to its Uzbek home grew weaker.[195]

Yet, the IMU also mobilized human and financial resources transnationally. It had networks of supporters in the Caucasus and Arab states. In 2011, the U.S. Treasury Department listed Fazal Rahim as a specially designated terrorist.[196] An Uzbek, Rahim had been raising and transferring money from Gulf-based donors to the IMU in Pakistan. In 2012, Treasury listed Qari Ayyub Bashir—the "head of finance" for the IMU as well as a member of the IMU *shura* (council)—as a terrorist; for years, he had provided financial and logistical support for IMU operations in both Pakistan and Afghanistan, and had fundraised from

[192] Sanderson, Kimmage, and Gordon, "From the Ferghana Valley to South Waziristan."

[193] Bakhtiyar Babadjanov and Sharifjon Islamov, "The 'Enlighteners' of Koni-Zar: Islamic Reform in a Cotton Kolkhoz," in *Allah's Kolkhozes*, ed. Stéphane Dudoignon and Christian Noack (Berlin: Klaus Schwarz Verlag, 2014), 265–86.

[194] Babadjanov and Islamov, "The 'Enlighteners,'" 270.

[195] Interview with Tyson.

[196] UN Security Council, "Fazal Rahim," March 6, 2012, https://www.un.org/securitycouncil/sanctions/1267/aq_sanctions_list/summaries/individual/fazal-rahim.

Turkey and Europe.[197] In September 2016, a dual Dutch-Turkish citizen living in Germany, İrfan Demirtaş, pleaded guilty on charges of materially supporting and fundraising for the IMU. The IMU's transnational links, through Demirtaş alone, extended from Afghanistan through Turkey, Jordan, the Netherlands, and France.[198] Demirtaş likely recruited both financiers and migrant laborers as recruits.

Although the majority of the IMU's cadre was still ethnic Uzbek, born in Uzbekistan, difficulty recruiting at home inside Karimov's powerful surveillance state meant that it had to rebuild its membership elsewhere after suffering heavy losses from U.S. strikes in Afghanistan. Over time, the IMU incorporated ethnic Uzbeks from Kyrgyzstan, Tajikistan, and Kazakhstan. It successfully recruited a new cadre from among the ethnic Uzbek population of northern Afghanistan,[199] some of whom had previously fought for the Taliban but were discontent with that group's Pashtun dominance.[200] Other former Soviet Muslims who fled to Afghanistan due to oppression at home—Kazakhs, Uyghurs, and Dagestanis—signed on as well. The IMU became a transnational jihadist organization tied to the Afghan Taliban, TTP, Haqqani network, and al-Qaeda.

The IJU Is Formed

The first major breaks within the IMU took place in March 2002, inside Pakistan's tribal areas and not long after the U.S. invasion of Afghanistan. Najmiddin Jalolov and Mansur Suhayl (born Suhayl Buranov) split from the IMU to establish the Islomiy Jihod Ittifoqi (Islamic Jihad Union, IJU).[201] Representing a younger generation of fighters and those discontent with Yo'ldosh's suffocating control and wholesale adoption of al-Qaeda's jihad, the IJU returned to focusing on the overthrow of the government of Uzbekistan.[202]

A small group, the IJU sought global attention to launch its jihad. Between March 28 and April 1, 2004, it orchestrated several terrorist acts inside Uzbekistan that killed at least forty-seven people. In the first suicide attack in Central Asia, a woman suicide bomber, a medical student, targeted police at Tashkent's Chorsu bazaar; she defied the stereotype of Central Asian Islamists as being poor, rural

[197] U.S. Department of the Treasury, "Treasury Imposes Sanctions on Pakistan-Based Terrorist Facilitators," October 17, 2012, https://home.treasury.gov/news/press-releases/tg1739.

[198] U.S. Department of Justice, "Defendant Pleads Guilty to Providing Material Support to Islamic Movement of Uzbekistan," September 15, 2016, https://www.justice.gov/usao-dc/pr/defendant-pleads-guilty-providing-material-support-islamic-movement-uzbekistan.

[199] Interview with Damon Mehl, Washington, D.C., November 2018.

[200] Interview with Tyson.

[201] Guido Steinberg, *German Jihad: On the Internationalization of Islamist Terrorism* (New York: Columbia University Press, 2013), 59–67, 79.

[202] Interview with Tyson.

men. More attackers targeted police in several other bombings in Tashkent, while explosives also detonated in Bukhara. Thirty-three IJU militants died.[203] A wave of arrests in the spring culminated in show trials in July 2004. On July 30, three more coordinated suicide bombings shook Tashkent, striking the U.S. and Israeli embassies and the General Procurator's Office and killing two.[204] In statements on internet jihadi websites, the IJU claimed credit, reasserted its goal of overthrowing the Uzbek government, declared its support for Muslims in Palestine, Iraq, and Afghanistan as part of a global insurgency, and called for martyrdom attacks to continue.[205] Although conspiracy theories again claimed that the bombings had been orchestrated by the MXX, U.S. Embassy personnel who observed the trials were convinced that the perpetrators were in fact radicalized Islamists.[206]

In May 2005, the IJU issued a statement supporting the armed attacks on Uzbek police and military personnel in Andijon, Uzbekistan, but without claiming responsibility for the prison break. On May 26, 2009, the IJU orchestrated two coordinated attacks on Uzbek police. In one strike, well-armed assailants fired rocket-propelled grenades at a police station in Khanabad, near the former U.S. military base, killing one. A few hours later, a suicide bomber detonated an IED in Andijon city, killing himself and one policeman and wounding three civilians. The IJU claimed responsibility for these attacks, saying in an online video that their goal "was to raise the Word of Allah over the land and to take vengeance for the oppressed Muslims."[207] The mujahidin, it said, were well-prepared for jihad and "these [attacks] are the beginning of our serious actions against the dictatorial-Zionist regime of Karimov."[208]

Despite its initial focus on Uzbekistan, the IJU was also shaped by the U.S. war in Afghanistan and its base and connections with al-Qaeda inside North Waziristan. Thus the IJU refocused its jihad against the United States and attracted operatives transnationally. The group's most daring plot, meant to be a "second 9/11," was orchestrated by its "Sauerland cell" in Germany; the plot targeted the U.S. Ramstein Air Base and Frankfurt Airport, among other targets.[209] German authorities disrupted the plot in September 2007 and

203 U.S. Department of State, Country Reports on Terrorism 2017—Foreign Terrorist Organizations: Islamic Jihad Union, September 19, 2018, https://www.state.gov/reports/country-reports-on-terrorism-2017/.

204 UN Security Council, "Islamic Jihad Group," January 18, 2018, https://www.un.org/securitycouncil/sanctions/1267/aq_sanctions_list/summaries/entity/islamic-jihad-group.

205 U.S. State Department, "Country Reports on Terrorism," April 28, 2006, http://www.state.gov/s/ct/rls/crt/2005/65275.htm.

206 Conversations with U.S. State Department representatives, Tashkent, Uzbekistan, June 2004, and Washington, D.C., July 2006.

207 Ponomaryev, *Politicheskie repressii*, 21.

208 Ponomaryev, *Politicheskie repressii*, 21.

209 Steinberg, *German Jihad*, 76–79; Simone Kaiser, Marcel Rosenbach, and Holger Stark, "Operation Alberich: How the CIA Helped Germany Foil Terror Plot," *Spiegel Online*, May 21, 2015

detained three IJU operatives, including two German citizens.[210] The attacks utilized al-Qaeda–like tactics, emphasizing mass casualties,[211] and the UN Security Council reported that IJU leaders had direct links to al-Qaeda.[212]

Limited in Europe, however, the IJU turned back to the Afghanistan-Pakistan region, where it again collaborated with the Taliban, the Haqqani network, and al-Qaeda against ISAF. The IJU orchestrated the airport attack in Khost, Afghanistan, in 2008 and multiple vehicle-born IED attacks in 2008–9.[213] Although not as regular a participant in such strikes as the IMU, the IJU boasted skilled fighters. It joined the September 2015 Taliban siege of Kunduz, which killed thirteen Afghan police and wounded some 848 civilians.[214] In 2015, the IJU renewed its pledge to the Taliban under Mullah Mansour. In 2021, the IJU was still active, albeit very small.

Explaining the IJU's Low Mobilization

In contrast to the IMU, the IJU began as a small splinter organization. Most fighters came from among those discontented with the IMU, especially Russian speakers, who were not among the IMU's elite core. Unable to network inside Uzbekistan, the IJU did find some new recruits, often Turks and Europeans, over time. Although durable for about fifteen years, the IJU never grew above two hundred fighters.[215]

The IJU's ideological messaging mimicked the IMU's, but less prolifically. It conveyed its message mainly through postings on its website, Sodiqlar.com, pitched both to an Uzbek audience and to a broader Muslim jihadist audience. The site appealed emotionally by emphasizing the persecution of Muslims in *nasheeds*. The lyrics of "Song for Mama," cried:

> Another Muslim is jailed,
> Just because he is Muslim. . . .
> Despite all his difficulties he did not succumb to the enemies of Allah. . . .

(2007), https://www.spiegel.de/international/germany/operation-alberich-how-the-cia-helped-germany-foil-terror-plot-a-504837.html.

[210] U.S. State Department, "Country Reports on Terrorism," 2011, https://2009-2017.state.gov/j/ct/rls/crt/2010/170264.htm.

[211] Gunaratna and Nielsen, "Al Qaeda in the Tribal Areas," 784.

[212] United Nations Security Council, "Islamic Jihad Group," January 18, 2018, https://www.un.org/securitycouncil/sanctions/1267/aq_sanctions_list/summaries/entity/islamic-jihad-group.

[213] Binnie and Wright, "Evolving Role of Uzbek-Led Fighters," 4–5; Steinberg, *German Jihad*.

[214] U.S. State Department, "Country Reports on Terrorism," 2016, https://2009-2017.state.gov/documents/organization/170479.pdf.

[215] U.S. State Department, "Country Reports on Terrorism, Uzbekistan," 2016.

> The one behind bars has saddened eyes.
> He was gasping from all the torture. . . .
> We hope for victory.[216]

There were frequent references to the "place of no return," Jasliq prison for alleged "religious extremists," where prisoners reportedly often died of horrendous torture and intentional exposure to tuberculosis. The site was devoted to posting stories, such as those of Uzbek women suffering the loss of loved ones or police harassing innocents.

Sodiqlar.com also posted news and longer analytical articles, explaining global events pertinent to the Muslim world and emphasizing its victimization by the West. Videos displayed footage of NATO bombing campaigns, explaining that "these little children are the victims of NATO and the U.S." The IJU clearly sought to induce Central Asians to identify with the global *umma*.

The website's utopian message proclaimed militant jihad as the answer to all Muslim persecution. Fighters were heroic soldiers of Allah. They scaled the Afghan terrain to the mournful lyrics of jihadi music. A video released in 2016 demonstrated the IJU was still fighting independently, while the IMU had merged into ISIS-K. Videos glorified militants attacking U.S. and Afghan military bases and fighters training in North Waziristan, Pakistan. They praised jihadi "martyrs."[217] Emotionally evocative, the site appealed to angry young men searching for justice and glory. It also demonstrated the IJU's credentials to potential financiers.

Second, in an attempt to build its sacred authority, the IJU site posted religious and political books, theological questions and answers, and *fatwa*s on various subjects—attempting to root the IJU's agenda in Islamic doctrine. One *fatwa* even declared that Christian crucifixes should not be worn, appealing to widespread anger at Christian missionaries in Central Asia. Other topics included a *tafsir* (exegesis) on jihad and "suicide actions" by Ustoz Abdushukur Samarqandiy (a religious ideologue from Samarqand, Uzbekistan). The cleric misrepresented the classical understanding of just war and supported the IJU's broader violence. Such extreme *fatwa*s would be echoed by ISIS and al-Qaeda, but few Uzbeks would accept the little-known imam's decrees as authoritative.[218]

Third, developing new networks inside Uzbekistan, beginning in the 2000s, proved difficult given government surveillance. The IJU therefore turned to multiethnic, transnational recruiting, competing with the IMU; however, the IJU

[216] The above paragraph refers to the postings on the main webpage, http://www.sodiqlar.com, accessed November 15, 2011, accessed December 2011 (link now defunct).
[217] Caleb Weiss, "UN: Islamic Jihad Union Operates in Syria," *FDD's Long War Journal*, July 31, 2019.
[218] Information posted on www.sodiqlar.com.

primarily posted in Russian, and sometimes in Kazakh or Arabic, suggesting a broader target audience. Some of its recruits were not Central Asians. The IJU attracted a network in Germany, including Turkish and Afghan migrants to Germany, and some German-born recruits.[219] The IJU's international networking in Europe, run by a Syrian and a German recruiter, sustained it, but recruits were too few for large-scale mobilization.

ISIS Triggers the IMU's Decline

A far more serious rupture within the IMU occurred in 2014, with the rise of ISIS and the Syrian jihad. After over a decade of close cooperation with the Taliban, the IMU's emir Usmon G'oziy openly criticized Mullah Omar and announced, "On behalf of members of our Islamic Movement, I herewith announce to the world that we are siding with the Islamic Caliphate [ISIS]."[220] The IMU took an oath of allegiance to Islamic State leader Abu Bakr al-Baghdadi on July 31, 2015. Standing in front of the Islamic State's flag, G'oziy declared, "From now on we are not just a movement, we are a state. . . . Thank the Lord, following the Almighty's will we have pledged our allegiance [*bay'ah*] to the Caliphate that has bowed to Islam. . . And we are now part of it."[221] IMU fighters would now be called fighters from the Islamic State in Khorasan province (ISIS-K). G'oziy's 2015 statement was posted by the IMU's Furqon TV in a video showing IMU militants attacking Afghan army posts. The message was clear: former IMU, now ISIS-K members, would continue waging jihad in both Afghanistan and Syria.[222]

The IMU's turn away from the Taliban and al-Qaeda to pledging support to ISIS was a dramatic move but reflected several long-term problems, beginning with distrust caused by the Taliban's secrecy about Mullah Omar's death.[223] Further, Uzbekistan had joined the coalition against ISIS in 2015. The revived U.S.-Uzbek government relationship paved the way for an IMU-ISIS allegiance against this new threat. Numerous TPP fighters, IMU allies, had also defected and joined ISIS-K in 2014. Perhaps most important, the Islamic State from 2014

[219] Office of the Coordinator for Counterterrorism, "Germany," in "Country Reports: Europe and Eurasia Overview," April 30, 2009, https://2009-2017.state.gov/j/ct/rls/crt/2008/122432.htm; Office of the Coordinator for Counterterrorism, "Germany," in "Country Reports: Europe and Eurasia Overview," August 18, 2011, https://2009-2017.state.gov/j/ct/rls/crt/2010/170256.htm; Steinberg, *German Jihad*.

[220] Edward Lemon, "IMU Pledges Allegiance to Islamic State," August 1, 2015, http://www.eurasianet.org/node/74471.

[221] Merhat Sharipzhan, "IMU Declares It Is Now Part of the Islamic State," *Radio Free Europe/Radio Liberty*, August 6, 2015, https://gandhara.rferl.org/a/afghanistan-imu-alliance-islamic-state/27175460.html.

[222] Lemon, "IMU Pledges."

[223] Interview with Mehl.

until early 2017 represented an almost unstoppable force for Islamists against their oppressors. By contrast, the IMU had battled for almost two decades with no progress in establishing a state, in either Uzbekistan or Afghanistan.

With the IMU's declaration of allegiance to ISIS, it merged into the forces of the ISIS-K, which had been established by factions of the Afghan Taliban and the TTP between late 2014 and January 2015.[224] IMU militia leader Hikmatulloh Qori became a senior ISIS-K commander in northern Afghanistan,[225] reflecting the IMU's central role within the new movement, especially in Zabul and Faryab provinces. As ISIS-K, the Uzbek militia continued to draw Uzbeks to its ranks. Although attacks within Uzbekistan had been few, on September 28, 2015, assailants threw Molotov cocktails at the U.S. Embassy in Tashkent. Some sources believe the IMU wing of ISIS-K perpetrated that attack, but such claims remain unverified. Under ISIS-K leadership, Uzbek fighters continued to perpetrate IED, vehicle-born IED, and suicide bomber attacks against the Afghan National Army and ISAF. Yet, the Taliban saw ISIS-K as a rival and the IMU as betraying them. In a fierce battle in December 2015 in Zabul province, the Taliban reportedly killed up to 90 percent—at least several thousand—of G'oziy's fighters there. No more than three hundred remained.[226] Even with these heavy losses, both the IMU and ISIS-K were still a threat to Afghan security forces.[227]

The IMU's End or Rebirth?

In the years following the IMU-Taliban split, the organization's fate was uncertain. Within ISIS-K, the IMU had no independent existence.[228] In mid-2016, part of the IMU reemerged after breaking with ISIS-K. In a sharp, public rebuke of the Islamic State, the IMU claimed that "several al-Qaeda and other Salafi ideologues . . . believe Abu Bakr al Baghdadi 'is not a caliph of Muslims but only an Emir of the "Islamic State" group.'"[229] The IMU's spiritual leader Abu Dher al Barmi denounced ISIS-K, stating, "[A]fter a year, I learned of many evil deeds within this group, such as their killing the Muslims on charges that lack evidence,

224 Antonio Giustozzi, *The Islamic State in Khorasan: Afghanistan, Pakistan, and the New Central Asian Jihad* (London: Hurst, 2018), 127–31.

225 Bill Roggio, "US Military Kills Senior Islamic State Commander in Afghan North," *FDD's Long War Journal*, April 9, 2018.

226 Australian Government, "Australian National Security, Islamic Movement of Uzbekistan."

227 U.S. Department of Defense, Press Briefing by Brigadier General Cleveland via teleconference from Afghanistan, April 14, 2016, https://www.defense.gov/News/Transcripts/Transcript/Article/721738/department-of-defense-press-briefing-by-general-cleveland-via-teleconference-fr/.

228 Interview with Mehl.

229 Bill Roggio and Caleb Weiss, "Islamic Movement of Uzbekistan Faction Emerges after Group's Collapse," *FDD's Long War Journal*, June 14, 2016.

and their issuing of *fatwas* against those who did not join their group. . . . After their *fatwa* was issued in Khorasan in which they infidel-branded the Taliban, who have waged jihad for nearly forty years against the Russians, the Americans, and their agents, it pained my heart!"[230] The statement revealed deep discontent with ISIS-K's goals and strategy. Probably no more than a few hundred remained, but these IMU members once again pledged themselves to fight jihad on the side of the Taliban and al-Qaeda.

U.S. military operations in Afghanistan were on the wane by 2016, as President Donald Trump steadily decreased troop numbers, especially after signing an agreement with the Taliban in February 2020. Even so, the IMU did not regain its former strength. With the August 2021 fall of Kabul, however, the remnants of the IMU and IJU, like al-Qaeda, again had safe harbor under the Taliban regime.

The second wave of Uzbekistani Islamism emerged from conditions similar to those of the first wave. Karimov's ruthless religious repression was the primary motivation; he had succeeded in making extremists. Although virtually no space to network existed within Uzbekistan, Afghanistan in the 1990s and 2000s provided that space. Afghanistan also introduced Uzbek emigres to both al-Qaeda's Salafi jihadist ideology and the Deobandi Taliban's jihadist path to an Islamic state. Uzbek religious entrepreneurs formed radical groups that continually adapted to the challenges of survival and operation in Central Asia for almost two decades. Although it remained relatively small in size, the IMU proved resilient and destructive, particularly as it turned its jihad against the United States and its allies in the war in Afghanistan.

Despite the odds, the IMU's strategy achieved significant mobilization, in numbers and durability. It initially centered its ideology on Karimov's torture of Muslims and on the duty to wage jihad to correct injustice. The IMU crafted sacred authority from Adolat's martyred imam, while Yo'ldosh transformed himself into a religious leader. Sacred authority facilitated both recruiting and sponsorship. Recruiting was challenging once ties to the homeland withered, but Afghanistan and Pakistan proved fertile ground for networking among exiles from the USSR and its successor states. The IJU, by contrast, faced difficulty networking, could not hone its message, and, like HTI, had no revered religious figurehead; consequently, its numbers remained extremely limited, albeit still deadly.

[230] Bill Roggio, "Former IMU Cleric Latest to Denounce Islamic State," *FDD's Long War Journal*, August 30, 2016. "Forty years" was an exaggeration that portrayed the Taliban as having fought the Soviet Union.

When the IMU focused on national concerns, its message resonated with Uzbeks. But the IMU's shift to al-Qaeda's jihad against the United States, in pursuit of a global caliphate by violent means, traded its Uzbek support base for a transnational jihadist one to attract such financiers. Yet, as the next chapter will argue through an analysis of focus groups, Salafi jihadist ideas had limited appeal among Muslims in Uzbekistan.

10
Society and Islamist Ideas in Uzbekistan

> Everyone wants justice. They completely blame our government for the absence of justice.
>
> —Imam, Qarshi, 2005

> A Muslim court would be just.
>
> —Student, Andijon, 2005

> An Islamic state would give the people "freedom of religion."
>
> —Accountant, Namangan, 2005

> I read this book and remember one thing in particular. It was in the beginning in the sura "Baqara." There it's written that there is no compulsion in religion, regarding accepting Islam. Everything must be done on the basis of kindness and free-will.
>
> —Businessman, Bukhara, 2005

> [Suicide bombers] have no spiritual riches. They have no civilization. They're terrorists.
>
> —University student, Urganch, 2005

These respondents were among hundreds who expressed their views about Islam and politics in focus groups and interviews throughout Uzbekistan.[1] Most shared certain core ideas, values, and opinions. Performing *namaz* was more central to their lives than twenty to twenty-five years earlier, during Soviet times. Anger at government injustice—from the police and the courts to the president—was palpable. Their views on better governance differed, and most were circumspect, but many believed that Islam could bring justice to a broken polity through Islamic courts. Yet very few sought an Islamic state, much less a global caliphate. Few endorsed violent change.

Previous chapters discussed President Karimov's brutality in repressing not only political Islam but *any* independent Islam. We have also seen that a range of Uzbek Islamist actors emerged; they were more radical in their goals and extreme

[1] See the appendix for details on focus groups and interviews.

Politicizing Islam in Central Asia. Kathleen Collins, Oxford University Press. © Oxford University Press 2023.
DOI: 10.1093/oso/9780197685068.003.0011

in their means than the IRPT. By the late 1990s and 2000s, there were no moderate, mainstream Islamists in Uzbekistan. Did ordinary Muslims see these movements as the solution to Karimov's regime? Here I examine the discourse of participants in thirty-two Uzbekistani focus groups and responses from fifty-four semi-structured interviews. I identify views of the majority, those of the minority, and areas where views were fluid and changing. For most, the issues they discussed—from Islamic education to corruption—were salient, everyday matters.

I demonstrate that inside Uzbekistan, the typical views and norms of those identifying as practicing Muslims were moderate; on a spectrum of views about religious education, women's roles, politics, and courts, most could not be described as liberal or secular, but only a minority were puritanical. Few supported radical ideas—either antisystemic or violent.[2] Since Uzbekistan's independence, only radical Islamists—some violent and some nonviolent radicals—had emerged there, and their ideas generally fell on fallow ground, thereby severely limiting the societal support that such groups might obtain.

After briefly recapping the core ideology and messages of Islamists seeking support in Uzbekistan in the 1990s and 2000s, I explore respondents' discourse about a range of issues central to Islamist messaging. These issues include Islamic revival, correct forms of practice and education, repression of Islam, justice and injustice, religious minorities, the meaning of jihad, and the legitimacy of suicide bombing. As in Chapter 7, I present the group discussions holistically to understand the broad set of concerns people faced and the views they held. I further present regional variations. Finally, I analyze communal elites' views about HTI since this was the only Islamist group active inside Uzbekistan in the 2000s. Respondents were less willing to speak about the IMU, and probably had less knowledge or experience of that movement.

Core Islamist Ideas

In Chapters 8 and 9, we encountered various Islamist groups, each propagating differing ideas with the hope of gaining and shaping a social base of support. In 1990–92, Adolat centered its messages on the evils of Soviet communism, its atheism and oppression of Islam, and the need for Islamic revival and education. Adolat also espoused puritanical ideas about Islamic praxis, such as enforcing the hijab and condemning *urf-adat* (customary practices) as idolatry. It denounced missionaries and was intolerant of Jews and Christians, whom it branded as *kuffar*. It advocated *shariat* to replace Soviet law, and the establishment of a vaguely defined Islamic state. Adolat demanded radical, antisystemic

[2] See Chapter 1 for definitions of "mainstream/moderate" and "radical" Islamist ideas.

change—establishment of a purist Islamic state—but not through radical means or militant jihad. In 1992, Adolat had called Karimov to do so through constitutional change.

The IMU, springing from the remains of Adolat, focused its messaging on post-Soviet religious repression, injustice, and torture in Karimov's Uzbekistan. It inveighed against Uzbek regionalism and nationalism. By the 2000s, the IMU was overtly espousing a caliphate and transnational Salafi jihadist ideas that it encountered through its relationship with al-Qaeda in Afghanistan and Pakistan. Martyrdom and suicide bombing became central to its message and means. Other militant groups including Uzbeks (the IJU, KTJ, KIB, ISIS, and ISIS-K)[3] also centered their propaganda on creating either an Islamic state or a caliphate through militant jihad. They too glorified suicide bombing and martyrdom. Whether the IMU or KTJ, their jihad was no longer just aimed at deposing Karimov, but at the West as well.

HTI propagated several similarly extreme Islamist ideas, namely anti-Semitism, total rejection of democracy, and reestablishment of the caliphate. HTI's ideology also emphasized transnational Muslim issues, starting with the Palestinians' victimization, as well as the plight of Afghans, Iraqis, and Syrians. Rather than focus on puritanical interpretations of Muslim practices, HTI's messages centered on repression of Muslims' right to wear the hijab or have a beard and attend mosque. Unlike the IMU, HTI emphasized nonviolent political change. Moreover, HTI adapted its message to Uzbekistan, focusing relentlessly on Karimov—his regime's corruption and injustice and his repression of Muslims. In contrast to Tajikistan, in Uzbekistan no movement propagated mainstream, moderate views about Islam and politics. The IRPU might have evolved into a moderate Islamist party like the IRPT, but it was decisively destroyed in 1992.

Profiles of Focus Groups from Uzbekistan

Accustomed to state oppression, respondents in Uzbekistan were often more guarded than elsewhere; hence, I limited the questions accordingly. In the earlier round of focus groups (2005), most of which took place before the Andijon massacre, participants were more open in discussing frustrations, oppression, and religious issues than in the later round (2013), even though it took place well after Andijon. Since in Uzbekistan no Islamist party or movement was legal, I did not seek to probe their views about such groups. Yet, most respondents opened up about their grievances, Muslim identity, and some ideas of governance.

[3] ISIS, KTJ, KIB, and ISIS-K will be discussed in connection with the Syrian jihad in Chapter 14.

The group discussions presented in this chapter represent the range of views I encountered and indicate some regional differences. In Bukhara, Urganch, and Tashkent, the discussions typically expressed moderate and sometimes liberal or even secular ideas. By contrast, at least some focus groups in the Ferghana Valley of Uzbekistan (Namangan, Andijon, Marg'ilon, and Ferghana) revealed very mixed and occasionally some radical ideas, reflecting in part the long-standing religious repression they had faced, together with the spread of puritanical political theologies there. Groups in many areas revealed extreme frustration with injustice and some proclivity to seeking a solution in *shariat*. Examining the overall discourse in typical groups reveals how respondents connect religion and politics. Their discourse demonstrates the limited effect of radical groups, such as the IMU's call to jihad or even HTI's advocacy of the caliphate, in shaping the opinions and preferences of ordinary Uzbeks.

Mainstream Views about Islam and Politics

Most respondents voiced opposition to a secular society and political system, but not support for an Islamic state. Some respondents articulated their preference for bringing some *shariat* into state law. But most conceived of Islamization as state support of Islamic education, revival of a national Islamic identity, and an end to religious repression, injustice, and corruption. Curiously, these were all ideas that moderate Islamists such as the IRPT articulated, but no Islamist party in Uzbekistan has been able to legally voice such issues.

Women, Bazaar Traders/Small Entrepreneurs, Twenty to Twenty-nine Years Old, Tashkent, 2005

A group of women in Tashkent, young traders and mothers,[4] identified as practicing Muslims but were not strictly devout. They had little interest in religious education or politics. They favored many rights for women. They were clearly not extremists, but they openly criticized the state's oppression of Islam. They viewed the "Wahhabi trials" as egregious. One woman's brother supported those on trial with profits from his store. "My brother and others give loans and credit to those people . . . so they can live better. He says to not give them money is wrong." Another advocated almsgiving: "Sometimes it's necessary to help schools or hospitals." To her, this was simple Muslim charity. But Gul'nora warned her of the political repercussions of such generosity: "They [the security services] can grab your parents. Better to be careful." Another woman recounted how the MXX had killed her neighbor's son simply for going to a mosque: "Mavluda.

[4] UZ-FG#4.

She had four sons. One son joined an extremist group; he even took another name. Then, after February 16 [the 1999 bombings], they [the MXX] took this woman's other three sons and they never returned. And the mother doesn't know what happened to them." Yet another woman in the group recounted how her neighbor was "walking to the mosque. Along the road, they snatched him and arrested him. He died [in MXX custody]. . . . He died a *shahid.* I don't know who brought [back] the body. In the *mahalla*, they said he died a *shahid.*" Their discourse starkly revealed that repression of Islam had spread beyond the Ferghana Valley and affected the lives of ordinary Tashkentis.

These respondents were neither puritanical nor Islamist, but they sympathized with those who were caught in the vortex of Karimov's counterextremism agenda. Their anger at the regime was unambiguous. Their group discussion took place in mid-2005, and their conversation was clearly a denunciation of the Andijon massacre, which had recently taken place. Several declared the state media coverage of the violence was "all lies." Jalol said, "They [Akromiya] were not extremists, just some sort of movement." Nilufar added, "They gave people loans and credit." Their conversation revealed their sympathy at the plight of the protesters:

LOLA: They just stood up to protest!

GUL'CHERA: They were simple people.

NIGORA: A grandpa—with a beard, wearing a *cho'pon* [Uzbek traditional robe] and *do'ppi* [national hat]—was only crying "Give us bread."

SAYORA: Karimov is covering it up and saying they are terrorists, not the Uzbek people. But the people are hungry. Indeed [in Andijon] there are those who haven't received their salary for three or four months.

LOBAR: It was not because of religious beliefs.

NAZIRA: The government doesn't give information. It's all lies! They hide information!

NOILA: A lot of people perished there.

Nilufar cut off the dialogue, saying nervously, "Talking about it is scary and dangerous." Although fearful to speak out in public, the participants were clearly enraged at the brutal repression and the subsequent cover-up.

The women held vague political views, unsure of what to demand. They opposed Karimov, but they rejected democracy altogether. "Full democracy is not for Uzbeks," said Nazira. "We have our own system," Dilorom explained. "Democracy does not have a place here." Another went further, saying, "It's necessary to have an Islamic state." Some favored the idea of a religious party. Their views and discussion seemed mixed and uncertain, typical responses in a situation where no good option was apparent. Islam seemed a possible solution to them, but they had no clear idea about how its principles could be translated into governance. They opposed democracy but did not envision an Iranian or Saudi state, much less a caliphate.

They rejected violence. Most feared Islamist movements would bring war, as in Tajikistan and Afghanistan. They turned to discussing jihad, both theologically and in concrete examples familiar to them. Nigora called jihadists and suicide bombers "bloodthirsty"; they were not *shahids* because "in *Musulmonobod* [a Muslim land or state], killing other people isn't allowed." Most of the women dismissed the Taliban as "bloodthirsty," and considered its "jihad against the United States" to be unjust. They dismissed such groups as using Islam as a veneer for their acts. Nasiba explained her criticism of militants who claimed to wage jihad: "Islam does not condone suicide." They either opposed or doubted the very existence of Osama Bin Laden. Some called him a U.S. agent. Feruza, however, interjected, "Bin Laden was fighting for Islam." Her comment was unusual in Uzbekistan, where most did not condone 9/11 or any example of suicide bombing.

Men, White-Collar (Some Unemployed), Thirty-five to Forty-five Years Old, Tashkent, 2013

Soviet-educated generations, especially those with higher degrees and white-collar jobs, are often assumed to be secular, especially in Tashkent. Yet, some such men[5] had become more religious over time and supported an Islamic revival in Uzbekistan. They donated to the mosque, fasted, and performed *namaz* "because it's Allah's will." Both for themselves and their children, they sought a religious education outside the state, where they would have "good teachers," but "not extremists," they emphasized, to show that they were not "Wahhabis." Some youth, they explained, went to the Ferghana Valley to study in *hujras*, to get a serious religious education, not with "state imams" in Tashkent. Still, the respondents were not purists; they celebrated Navruz and observed *urf-adat*, as most Uzbeks had for centuries.

Their religious views grounded their moderate political views that eschewed antisystemic change and were inclusive of non-Muslims. Tohir said, "Some Arab states have adopted certain laws of *shariat* and live by them. But if we say we'll do the same, we won't have time to change everything. We need to look again at the whole state. Changing our conditions so sharply isn't possible." Muhammad added, "In 1917, we had a revolution, and everyone knows what sort of life we had after that . . . Soviet life . . . drunkenness and so forth. So, after independence, all this religion is so that we develop again along that path that we had from ancient times." He too urged caution in changing the law. Hayriddin said, "There,

[5] UZ-FG#32.

in Arab countries, more people are believers. . . . Maybe only later we can reach the level of the Arabs." Tohir in the meantime emphasized that they "need to respect everyone," all religions, not just Islam. The men went on to discuss the religious repression of the 1930s, the starvation of the early Soviet era, and growth in religious possibilities since 1991. After blaming communism for many evils, however, they had little positive to say of their own government. Tohir explained, "[Karimov's] People's Democratic Party was previously the Communist Party. It just changed its name."

They discussed democracy; most viewed it favorably. As Hayriddin said, "In democracy you can defend your interests." Farhod said simply, "It's freedom." Muhammad elaborated that democracy would mean "freedom of belief and freedom of speech." Husain declared with conviction, "In Western democracy, there is justice." Tohir stressed that they wanted "real democracy," not the "anarchy they have in Kyrgyzstan." He continued, "In other Muslim countries they have democracy. There are religious parties. I think it's good." Several others agreed with him. Their idea of democracy, however, was not liberal; for instance, they wanted to ban blasphemy. Hayriddin said, "Not one nation has the right to ridicule and draw cartoons of the religion and traditions of another nation. It is necessary to punish this." They also held conservative ideas about women; for example, they agreed that women should work only in limited areas such as teaching, not as political leaders, and not as the head of a *mahalla* committee; that was "contrary to our tradition." They supported legalizing polygyny, another idea typically propagated by those favorable to Islamic law. Overall, they did not want "an Islamic state"; instead, they wanted both "democracy" and the state "to support" Islam, especially religious marriage and education. Tohir even suggested a new Muslim "state organization like the Soviet Pioneers, to teach values of right and wrong."

When they turned to discussing political conflict, the men opposed any violence. Mirhamid declared, "No one has the right to give away his own life and to take away the lives of others! We oppose this!" They all condemned the very idea of *shahid*s and martyrdom. At the same time, some of them refused to accept the government line about Islamist "extremists." They believed HTI was being wrongly persecuted. Tohir said, "In several countries—European countries, I can't recall which—Hizb ut-Tahrir is recognized [legally] as a party. . . . I don't know its goals so I can't really say anything good or bad about it." Hayriddin agreed: "Nowadays we have very little information about them. . . . [W]e only heard about them on television. . . . You can't meet anyone in the group. So, like Tohir said, we can't say anything good or bad about it." In sum, the men held complex views; they were judiciously skeptical of the government and its persecution of religion, alleged extremists, and democratic rights. Some of them leaned in favor of a blend of Islamic law with democracy, but held markedly illiberal views about women and blasphemy. Yet they eschewed violence, so would very likely have rejected the call of the IMU.

Men, White-Collar, Forty to Forty-nine Years Old, Marg'ilon, Ferghana Oblast, 2005

Views favorable to integrating Islam and governance in some ways—without supporting extremism—were common outside Tashkent as well. In a reputedly puritanical town in the Ferghana Valley, men with white-collar jobs and a Soviet-era university education[6] discussed the central role of religion during Soviet times and since independence. Abduvohid said, "There were a lot of forbidden things. If you were a member of the CPSU [Communist Party of the Soviet Union], they watched your every step. You were forbidden to go to the mosque and pray. They'd throw you out." Ulug'bek recalled, "Then it was forbidden to go to a funeral. I remember in Soviet times, when I was in Tashkent, a professor couldn't go to the funeral of his mother. Now it's different." But Olim pointed out that "then it was the KGB. . . . now it's the MXX. If you perform *namaz* often, it will be bad for you." Nonetheless, they praised the growth of religiosity in their community, especially among the youth. They wanted the state to provide religious education in school. "The more the better," said Abduvohid. "A few hours a week," said others. Like many who sought Islamic revival, they also approved of the hijab, without seeking to force it on women. Yet, they were highly intolerant of converts from Islam. Shukrullo exclaimed, "God willing, we have none here!" Abduvohid insisted, "In Marg'ilon there will never be any." Their views may have been influenced by their proclivity for Arab-trained imams. "They are better" and "have stronger knowledge than what is taught in Uzbekistan," To'lqin and Ulug'bek asserted. Nonetheless, their discourse about the legal system they desired revealed moderate views overall:

SOLIHJON: We are all Uzbek, Muslim. So [Uzbekistan] should be a Muslim state.

ABDUVOHID: Of course, it must be Muslim.

TOLIB: But the court should not be Muslim because it's already been a long time since we had such laws. Nowadays we can't amputate someone's hand or leg for theft.

ULUG'BEK: When we talk about *shariat* law, it seems to me it's more just. Only an educated person can understand that. In earlier days, according to *shariat* there were three judges. If one judge could not resolve the problem it would go to the second, then the third. They tried to follow books and writings and judge each situation well, and come to a just decision. Today only one individual makes every decision.

[6] UZ-FG#6.

SHUKRULLO: But if you think it [the decision] is unfair [today, in the secular court] you can go to the *oblast* court.

Clearly most did not want the *shariat* legal system of premodern Uzbekistan. But when asked about democracy, few responded. According to Ulug'bek, "We have a Muslim democracy and it's growing." "We need a *democratic* democracy," replied Shukrullo. There was silence, but everyone seconded him when he added, "We would like our government to be just." They did not call for a caliphate as the answer. And consistent with their other views, they condemned violent jihadists and suicide bombing as "a sin." They claimed that such problems would be resolved by "improving upbringing of children" and by "improving life conditions."

Men, Small Business Owners/Entrepreneurs, Twenty-five to Thirty-five Years Old, Ferghana City, 2013

In another Ferghana Valley focus group, the young businessmen were devout.[7] They all supported their mosque through *hashar*. They advocated a strong Islamic revival but also believed that *urf-adat*'s traditional practices "were inseparable" from *O'zbekchilik* and Islam; in contrast to Salafists, Xurshidbek claimed, "It's wrong to separate them." Performing *namaz* and performing *nikoh* were obligatory, despite the law. They emphasized conservative dress and "opposed miniskirts" and "Tashkent values," saying, "The Ferghana Valley is different." Although fearful of discussing politics, several agreed that "the government should preserve our values" rather than allowing television to corrupt the youth. Although they initially avoided criticizing the government, they clearly opposed religious restrictions. They explained, "Those in government can't participate in the mosque, because of their work." They said that the state even controlled the sermons in mosques and compelled imams to use weekly lectures to call on people to pay for gas or to labor harder to collect cotton. Mosque closures had increased as well. Yusuf pointed out, "Our own Andijonis, the respected Muhammad Sodiq Muhammad Yusuf is recognized and known in the whole world," but he had been stripped of his students. In fact, the state had severely restricted his religious activity, they observed. "Why aren't we allowed to study [Islam]?" one angrily asked.

Some expressed ideas typical of many Islamists; they suggested that all Muslims should unite "against nationalism" and intra-Muslim divisions. About half also believed religious law was needed. Under *shariat*, participants argued, fear of the state and God would be stronger, as in Saudi Arabia. Religious law, said Murod, would "prevent women from turning bad" and allow polygyny,

[7] UZ-FG#28.

according to a literalist interpretation of *shariat*. If there were strong religious laws, there would be less crime, argued some. However, Ulug'bek said that a state like Saudi Arabia was "not possible for Uzbekistan" because it had a "non-Muslim population of Russians" and the *shariat*'s strict *hudud* penalties applied under an Islamic state were "too harsh." Several debated this view, noting that "in Arabia people don't steal because they have a strong faith, and they fear losing [heaven]." Hakimjon and Oybek claimed that many would vote for religious parties, but others asserted that such parties would not succeed because there were not enough mosques and *madrasa*s to support them; that is, due to state closures of religious institutions, people would fear voting for them. They concurred that jihad should be an inward struggle only, and that suicide bombers were merely "kamikazes." Respondents hurried to close off further discussion, saying, "Let's not talk politics." In sum, like the group from Marg'ilon, they preferred some law by *shariat* but were opposed to most radical Islamist ideas, especially the caliphate and violence.

Men, University Students, Eighteen to Twenty-five Years Old, Namangan, 2005

Both outsiders and Uzbekistanis often have assumed Namangan and the Ferghana Valley to be politically "radical." My findings were mixed, and of course, responses there may have been tinged with more fear than elsewhere. One group of middle-aged, well-educated men was puritanical in its religious views, though the men held contradictory and inconclusive political ideas.

Yet at least two other groups in Namangan and one in Ferghana revealed moderate views about both religion and politics. One of them was a group of male university students who were being educated in the post-Soviet era.[8] The men regularly fasted and sometimes attended mosque. Skeptical of state imams, one of the male students claimed, "We have very strong *domla*s (religious teachers) and they know the Qur'an from beginning to end." Their views about women were mixed, both conservative and liberal. The male students wanted leaders to "call more women to Islamic dress," but insisted wearing the hijab should be "by choice." Yet their conservative views about piety and women were not radical.

The male students offered no comment on communism, but they blamed Karimov's government for the growth of radicalism. Isroil said, "Hizb ut-Tahrir uses our difficulties, the difficulties of the transitional period. People blame the government." Abdulla added, "They influence youth with material incentives. They give out their books to people, which they bring in from abroad. One such Hizb ut-Tahrir book was published specifically for Uzbekistan and its situation. They say they want to change the government." Shuhrat claimed, "They

[8] UZ-FG#10.

want to raise up their own political system." All the men disapproved. Husayn said, "It's not possible [to do so] without force." The men all agreed that HTI, the IRPU, and Adolat were "religious groups with religious goals." However, Xurshid stressed that their friends and neighbors did not support such ideas: "When Juma Namangoniy came to the city he said that he would put thirteen demands before the president, including women wear the *paranji*, only men work[ing], and many others. But these laws aren't suitable for our laws." Shuhrat argued that they needed democracy, not an Islamic state. A student of philosophy and history because, he explained, political science was banned, he described democracy by referencing Aristotle's *Politics*. He then added, echoing Churchill, that despite its problems, "democracy is better than any other system." Most of the students agreed, though some also wanted a more Muslim-style democracy. Muhiddin and others said, "Islam should play a leading role" in society and state, but no one specified how, except to say that they wanted a "Muslim court." They debated whether the West or Arabs had better governance and "no state interference" in religion. In short, some of them appeared to favor greater religious freedom and Islamic influence on politics, but not the radical Islamist ideas of Adolat or the IMU.

Women, Housewives and Blue-Collar, Thirty to Thirty-nine Years Old, Namangan, 2005

Another Namangan group consisted of women, all housewives; they had no more than a high school education, which they had completed between 1988 and 1991, at the end of the Soviet era and during the time of Islamist opposition in Namangan.[9] They identified strongly with Islam and had been learning their faith since childhood. They fasted. Most had studied Islam with "our *otins* (female religious teachers)," illegally. But now, all were afraid of independent religious study. The women had some liberal ideas, though; they believed they should be allowed to do any type of work. They spoke of their lack of rights, religiously, in marriage and divorce, which took place according to Islamic ritual in Namangan. Ra'no complained, "We have no choice." Salomat said, "We have to put up with it." All opposed religious pressure to wear the hijab. And they expressed fear in wearing it. Ra'no associated it with HTI membership. Sohiba said, "We have a good *mahalla*. No one wears the hijab." They all approved of the Islamic revival of a national Uzbek form and did not seek to purge national impurities. They were relatively tolerant of Jews and Christians. Matluba sympathetically observed that Jews had "left in the early 1990s because of discrimination against them." They opposed conversion from Islam, but even when describing a neighbor's adoption

[9] UZ-FG#11.

of Christianity, Farida remembered that "no one called him *kafir*." Bashorat tolerantly added, "Everyone has their own religion."

Like most Uzbeks, the women bitterly complained about corruption, the lack of work, and "not enough money for food." They articulated no clear view of the state that they preferred, but they expected Uzbekistan to go the way of Kyrgyzstan, that is, instability due to popular frustration and protests over corrupt government.

Women, White-Collar, Thirty-five to Forty-five Years Old, Ferghana City, 2013

Another group of ten women from the Ferghana region, in their late teens and early twenties when the USSR collapsed,[10] held similarly mainstream views. They had benefited from Soviet policies that had liberated women; they were well-educated, and some worked in white-collar jobs as accountants, teachers, doctors, and librarians. They criticized the puritanical messages about Islam that men received in the local mosques; imams were preaching polygyny and allowed *taloq* (divorce)—both of which they saw as abusive of women's rights.[11] They lived by Islamic values but were not purists; they also followed national traditions, *urf-adat*. As Dilnoza insisted, "Our religious values are nationalized. In each Uzbek family, in our mentality, from childhood onwards, fasting and *Eid* become national traditions." On some issues they were strictly observant; Muhayyo claimed, "Weddings are now always conducted according to Islamic religious traditions. When a *domla* comes and he reads *ayat*s separately to men and separately to women. It's good this is now done; for example, we don't drink [alcohol] at weddings. There are no scandals. It's all done peacefully and beautifully."

The women believed Islamic revival and education were necessary for Uzbeks. At first, some proclaimed that the government provided such education in Tashkent's Islamic Institute. Yet, many later admitted that they had studied Islam and Arabic "in secret, with an *otincha*," in the 2000s, just as others had done during Soviet times. Sevara said that "studying openly was not possible." Even though many of them had parents who had once been in the Communist Party, their fathers, husbands, and sons, and about 80 percent of men in their *mahalla* after independence, attended mosque in spite of government pressure not to pray. They wanted their daughters to wear the hijab, fast, and perform *namaz*. Some expressed skepticism of the state-appointed imam in the registered

[10] UZ-FG#26.

[11] Most Islamic jurists agree that a man has the right to divorce his wife, but the woman has that right only in extremely limited circumstances. Jurists differ about the legality of a man being permitted to marry up to four wives. Polygyny is banned in Central Asia, but allowed in Islamic states.

mosque. In the *mahalla*, parents instead sent their children to a religious teacher to take private Islamic lessons "in his home," just "as in the past." Most of them wanted a state that would support Islamic education. Like many participants in other groups, they envisaged Saudi Arabia as a place of pure Islam and the ideal religious education.

Without talking about Karimov, they indicated that state oppression was increasing. Zarifaxon, for example, said, "The possibility of studying in a group with an *otincha* is being destroyed." Like the men in Termiz, these women noted that many new mosques had been built with local sponsorship after independence, but that too had ended. Gulchehra said, "In the past five years they were stopped," and Muhayyo added, "They [the police] destroyed the old ones." Others noted that some remained closed. Iroda added, "One is now turned into a 'rehabilitation center for mothers and children.'" Aziza said, "One mosque in our *mahalla* was closed last year. The other was left."

The women were clearly dissatisfied with state repression, but they generally opposed seeking an Islamic state and adopting the *hudud* penalties for theft. Yet, they also said, "Imams, *domla*s, and *eshon*s should take part in adopting laws." Islam was a necessary part of law, because in their view, democracy meant blasphemy against Islam and immorality on television.

However, they disparaged existing Uzbek Islamists. Whether expressing personal knowledge or repeating state propaganda, they criticized those they called "Wahhabis"—including HTI and Akromiya; they "have different names, but one goal, power." Others claimed that HTI wanted "to take power into their own hands" and "destroy the peace." Dilorom insisted that they all "wanted to kill people." Iroda decried jihad as "the murder of others." Despite opposition to violence, all were vociferously anti-American. Umida even said, "America itself organized 9/11." Overall, they had no clear political preference. They were not inclined to support radical Islamism, but were certainly not secular democrats.

Men, Ethnic Tajik, Wealthy Entrepreneurs, Thirty-five to Fifty-five Years Old, Bukhara, 2005

In Bukhara, a region of the country considered less observant than the Ferghana Valley since the Soviet era, participants were ethnic Tajik men, prosperous entrepreneurs[12] who had learned their Islamic faith from childhood but had become more devout since 1991. They all kept the fast and performed *namaz* when possible; they even debated how to keep the fast correctly. Rustam and Islombek wanted the government to provide more religious education and Islamic television programming to counter Western values and dress. They were traditional in their practice of Islam, but not purists; they incorporated Sufi practices and

[12] UZ-FG#16.

accepted the teachings of Shaykh Naqshbandi. Their views on women and Jews were relatively liberal. They deplored converts, but they agreed that conversion to another religion was "their choice."

Unlike many participants in other groups, they openly sympathized with HTI and Wahhabis, whom they saw as "young people who were deceived" or simply "misled" by radical leaders. As Kamriddin said, "They [HTI] just wanted an Islamic education," which was not possible in Uzbekistan. He told of a neighbor who had been detained after studying in Turkey and accused of being an extremist, an HTI member. Such repression invoked some support for political Islam.

While not espousing an Islamic state or caliphate, they expressed one of the most common justifications for some state law by *shariat*; they believed, said Ziyodulla, that "there will be less corruption in a country where the laws are Islamic." The problem, as Ahmad said, was that "corruption . . . is the very first of problems for raising our children!" Ulug'bek agreed: "Corruption has a huge negative effect on the upbringing of youth . . . [and] will be less in a country where the laws are Muslim." Others connected corruption to drinking and prostitution. Sirojiddin, Islombek, and Anvar agreed, and Islombek criticized the existing system of law. They came to the consensus that "Muslim courts would be more just, because then people would have to answer for their actions before all the community." They did not specify how such a system might come about. Some participants expressed sympathy for certain militant jihadis—against the United States in Iraq and against the Russians in Chechnya—but they rejected terrorism, and no one wanted violence in Uzbekistan. Ahmad reminded the group, paraphrasing a *sura* of the Qur'an, "There is no force or violence in religion."

Mixed Views about Islam and Politics

Many groups of respondents exhibited mixed views—often some puritanical religious interpretations, intolerance of religious minorities, and some preferences for Islamic law, together with a desire for democracy and a rejection of violence. A preference for adopting *shariat* so as to punish corruption was not uncommon in the 2000s.

Men, Blue-Collar, Thirty-five to Forty-five Years Old, Termiz, 2013

In Termiz, on the Uzbek-Afghan border, a group of men who worked in construction[13] held mostly moderate views on religion and political issues. The men affirmed their religiosity and had practiced at least some of the pillars of

[13] UZ-FG#29.

Islam, together with the Uzbek rituals of *urf-adat,* since childhood. They were about twenty years old when the USSR ended; they recalled the Soviet system as a time of "totalitarianism," as Odil said. Yusuf observed, "We were blind then." Bahriddin remembered they were forcibly "taught that Lenin is God." Yet, most recalled being able to learn Islam at home, secretly, but most had forgotten *namaz*, said Shokir. He had studied with his uncle and was now teaching his children the same way. There was "no active repression" in their youth. They and their families, at least, had not experienced it personally. They all approved of the post-Soviet revival of Islam. Some mosques, they said, had been built by *hashar* or sponsored by businessmen. They emphasized the importance of the mosque and *namaz*, and then dared, cautiously, to complain that so many had been closed and that youth were "no longer allowed." They did not mention why.

Yusuf said, and others agreed, that their most important value was "Muslimness." They identified themselves as both Sufi and Sunni and emphasized that "pilgrimages to shrines" were "important for having strength in life, and for spiritual cleansing." Saints' shrines, they said, such as that of the Sufi shrine to Ahmad Yassaviy in Turkiston, were better attended than mosques. Sufis were "faith-healers" whom people visited for cures. They also held the view that "women should be covered," but the "hijab is not necessary because it might cause women to join radical movements." But they simultaneously were very traditionalist; they claimed that "men are superior to women," who should stay at home and stay out of many jobs. Many of the men also believed polygyny should be legal.

Some puritanical views, fostered by their imam, existed within their community. Although favorable to Jews, they strongly opposed Christian missionaries and converts. Hamid recounted, approvingly, that when he was at *juma-namaz*, the Uzbek imam told the men in attendance that one family in a nearby village had converted to Christianity: "The imam said, 'In the constitution it's written that everyone can choose their own religion. How do you feel about this?' . . . They [those at prayer] went outside and began to talk, and said it was necessary to expel them [the Christians]. Their neighbors also thought so." The men laughed, and Bahriddin joked, "They put them [the converts] on the right path!" Hamid continued, "If he'd lived in this village, the *oqsoqol* would have expelled him already, not left him in peace." Most of the others similarly criticized converts. Their intolerance extended to blasphemy too; European cartoon caricatures of the Prophet "were absolutely unacceptable," they said, and should not be treated as democratic freedom of speech.

Yet, when the discussion turned to other issues of law, the men rejected radical Islamist ideas. Hamid said, "Nowhere in the Qur'an is it said that one must throw stones or cut off the hand of a thief. Our ancestors only did so because they couldn't put anyone in prison." They agreed that an Islamic state would not be suitable. Some even said, possibly to demonstrate that they were loyal citizens, "Hizb ut-Tahrir should be shot" for mixing in politics. When asked about religious restrictions, Tol'qin insisted, "I can perform *namaz* anywhere. No one grabs my hand and stops me. No one forbids it. Probably, it's freedom." Yet, most refused to discuss democracy. Bahriddin commented briefly, "It hasn't yet developed here." Ziyodulla said, "For us freedom is better."

The group strongly condemned militant ideas of jihad and suicide bombing as "irrational" and "wrong." They agreed that the bombers "only use Islam as a mask" for their political ends. They noted that numerous locals had left for Afghanistan, without explaining why. The implication was that they were aware of individuals who had emigrated because they believed they would have a better life in Afghanistan with the IMU.

Women, University Students, Eighteen to Twenty-five Years Old, Ferghana City, 2013

Women university students from the Ferghana Valley[14] also voiced a mix of views, some moderate and sometimes radical-leaning views about Islam and politics. They favored religious revival and described the strict religious character of their town. No alcohol was sold, and everyone fasted and performed *namaz*. They gave *zakat* as often as possible. They recounted that one wealthy businessman from Andijon had built a road and a maternity home. Another had built a huge mosque in Andijon. None of this, they said, was possible under Soviet repression, when their elders had studied in *hujra*s and prayed at home.

However, they described pervasive state control, including security services watching the mosques and barring children and youth from entry for prayer or study. Religious freedom, said Yulduz, had initially increased after independence, but then places of prayer were closed "because of extremism," the government's legal justification for shuttering independent Islam and intimidating the population. Practice, they said, had subsequently declined because of widespread fear. In Marg'ilon, only one mosque was left open. According to Shahlo, as in the Soviet era, "Now mosques aren't even called mosques. But written above the entrance is a sign: 'House of Spirituality and Cultural Activities.'" Xursanoy added, "It means it's [a building] for forming cultured, spiritual people," not specifically for Islamic worship. "The mosque can't teach any more. Such places are now closed." Many of the women had learned Islamic practices from an *otincha* or relative, books, or by reading the *hadith*; such study at home was illegal. They described the constant fear and trouble with the government for wearing the hijab; they were "not admitted to school because of wearing it." Despite such pressure, many of them continued to do so. In fact, Mashura criticized her "friend [who] took off her

[14] UZ-FG#27.

hijab and committed a sin in order to be admitted to the Polytechnical Institute." Such government repression clearly angered them. They wanted the government to support Islamic revival and to allow broad Islamic education and dress.

The women's strict emphasis on Islamic purity extended to negative views of other religions, which they portrayed as polytheistic, just as Salafi imams often did. Most of the women were highly anti-Semitic. Nigora and others repeated various stereotypes, for example, "Jews worship statues and don't recognize Allah." Therefore, they said that Marg'ilonis were hostile to converts, although they seemed unaware that Jewish proselytism was nonexistent in Uzbekistan. They were decidedly unfavorable to Christians as well. Yulduz believed that all other religions "bow to statues," which indicated worship of other gods, in her view; by contrast, she emphasized their monotheism: "We believe in one Allah." The women also sharply distinguished among Muslims. They insisted that "Arabs follow classical [Islam]," as opposed to many Uzbeks, who had adopted incorrect practices (*bid'ah*), sullied by the Soviet era. Their purist theological views were similar to those advocated in the early 1990s by Imam Abduvali Qori.

The young women held mixed political views. Much like proponents of mainstream Islamist ideas (such as the IRPT, with which they had no experience), they favored a greater role for Islam in public life and adopting some *shariat* as law. They claimed to oppose the idea of an Islamic state or caliphate. Like many mainstream Islamists, they were also skeptical of Western democratic styles of government and secular law. As one woman said, "We need religion—for culture, for morality, for order, humanity, and customs." While most claimed that religion should "not mix in politics," they agreed with San'at, who said, "It would be better [for Uzbekistan] if religion and politics were equal, better for our rights. . . . Now [secular] politics are always first." Mashhura argued that even without an Islamic state, some laws needed to be harsher, so "adopting *shariat* laws . . . would be correct." For example, they pointed out that some problems would be ameliorated if there were a Muslim influence on society through law; they specifically mentioned laws on adultery, alcoholism, and blasphemy. San'at said, "It's necessary to introduce punishments which cause people to have fear. . . . [T]oo much freedom—freedom to burn books, to burn the Qur'an—is sick." One woman specifically said that it would be good to "have a religious country like Saudi Arabia so that we could use religion in the constitution." Such comments suggested that they favored strict Saudi-style law and the *hudud* penalties.

Most of the women expressly condemned Akromiya, HTI, and all Islamist parties. They claimed not to understand the term "jihad," but they all condemned suicide bombing, which they had heard about through state media. We cannot possibly know what their full political views were, as they clearly feared speaking more openly. One of them even abruptly cut the conversation short, saying, "We don't want to talk politics . . . [or] against the constitution." Nonetheless, they clearly shared ideas about law, society, and education in accord with mainstream and even some radical-leaning Islamists. Their beliefs, views, and experiences had made them open to some Islamist messages, while they opposed the use of violence.

Women, Students, Twenty to Twenty-five Years Old, Tashkent, 2005

A group of women university students in Tashkent[15] revealed extreme anger at the government and an inclination toward some elements of radical Islamic governance, but strong opposition to violent forms of radicalism.

The women were devout, but like most Uzbeks, they considered Sufi practices to be intrinsic to Islam. Nigora mentioned visiting the shrine of Ahmad Yassaviy. They blended such practices with puritanical ideas and favorability to legal restrictions on women. Oydina stressed a woman's obligation to wear the hijab. While Kamila believed higher education for women was important, Shahnoza considered both work and any political role for women to be against Islam. Some argued that Islam demanded that women be obedient to both their husbands and government.

Overall, Islam's revival in Uzbekistan was important to them, and not merely to learn their national culture; they bought and studied Islamic books of theology sold near the mosques, and they informally studied the Qur'an and Arabic, privately, with an *otincha*. They all criticized government imams, and in doing so revealed their negativity toward state control of religion; Shahnoza claimed, "They do not work for us, but just receive a salary from the state." Fotima and Kamila agreed it was better not to trust state imams.

Politically, they expressed anger against Karimov's regime, but also uncertainty. Iroda condemned the "injustice" of the state in which they lived. Nigora lambasted the "role of nepotism and connections" in government. Oydina added, "Now you don't need to study. Just pay something [to do well in school]." Teachers, Kamila explained, "don't get salaries for two to three months." Shahnoza dared to say, "Especially in most of the security services, people are so corrupt now. They claim to be Muslim but engage in dirty business. It's true that they [the security services] go unpunished. But Allah sees everything. . . . [W]e need some sort of democracy . . . and second, we need laws that defend our rights. Not the sort where you buy a lawyer, pay him a lot of money so he fixes everything with the prosecutor's office." Although young, they knew well that money and connections, not justice, ruled the courts. They clearly perceived the absence of any rule of law and the oppression of the president, the police, and the security services.

15 UZ-FG#19.

The women all sympathized with the protests in Andijon. They boldly discussed the massacre and criticized the president directly. One woman cried with indignation, "Karimov hides it [the killing]. He says they are all terrorists! But the people in Andijon haven't received a salary for three to four months! What should they live on?" The protests, Iroda agreed, "were because of destitution." "The Uzbek government doesn't recognize our suffering," Aziza sympathized. "They just play music everywhere on TV," said Shahnoza, referring to the endless government media coverage of national festivals and the continual television ads displaying bazaars replete with mountains of grapes, apricots, and all varieties of meat and *non*. "But they don't show the Andijon events." Oydina added, "Why do they lie? People live terribly everywhere, not just in Andijon! In all regions. Everywhere it's the same." Another added that the government "hides information from us," and several agreed that it did so because Karimov wanted to create "fear."

Because of oppression, corruption, and injustice, the women claimed that they "needed a Muslim government" or perhaps "Muslim democracy." Aziza went further, arguing in favor of the *hudud* penalties. She said, in Islamic states, "they cut off the hand of a thief. You see everything, and fear such a harsh punishment so no one repeats that crime. There would, maybe, be justice." At that point, Shahnoza, who had previously advocated for democracy, said, "In a Muslim court there are three witnesses to verify the evidence, so a Muslim court is probably more just [than a secular one]." Oydina added, "In a Muslim state there is no crime, so there is no one to put on trial." The women suggested that in Saudi Arabia, the law and courts were better. They also disparaged the immorality in Western-style democracies, which "do not suit us." Despite being open in criticizing the Uzbek government, and despite seeing Islamic courts as a solution, they did not support HTI's vision of a caliphate, much less the IMU's. Fotima offered the example of her neighbor's path to alleged radicalism: "He came from a very religiously devout family.... They never even drank.... He joined HTI. Is it good he sacrificed himself for Islam? Is it good to blow oneself up in the name of Islam?" She apparently assumed that either rumors or state propaganda accusing HTI of violence, and her neighbor of being an HTI member, were true. More generally, the women opposed killing as a sin against Islam:

SHAHNOZA: In the Qur'an it is written you can't even kill a soul that Allah has made!

EL'NORA: What *shahids*! They kill people! They sin!

OYDINA: They are killing innocents.

IRODA: There is no such thing in Islam!

KAMILA: Even if they [the Russians] are *kuffar*, they are still people.... [I]n Islam there is no such thing [as killing unbelievers].

Like those in many other groups, the women drew a sharp line against the use of violence or suicide bombing to kill non-Muslims, even in wars they considered justifiable—defensive wars, such as in Afghanistan and Iraq. Thus, while their views about governance were favorable toward certain Islamist ideas, such as adopting the *hudud* laws, they were unwilling to support any Islamist group associated with violence.

Radical-Leaning Views

Those who expressed some radical-leaning views were a small minority. In only one group did the majority of participants express a preference for an exclusivist Islamic state. A handful of participants voiced such a view in just seven other groups. No participant in any group expressed support for a caliphate—the clarion call of radical Islamists like the IMU and HTI. Some participants did, however, voice extreme views on adopting *shariat* as law and restricting minority rights. Two groups of young, post-Soviet-generation men in the Ferghana Valley expressed such views.

Men, University Students, Eighteen to Twenty-two Years Old, Andijon, 2005

A group of male college students—studying law, economics, and agricultural sciences—gathered in Andijon, in the Ferghana Valley.[16] They expressed religious and political views similar to those of the Adolat movement.

The young men described their *mahallas* as becoming more religious since independence and explained that they, like many in their city, prayed five times a day. They also fasted and gave *zakat* "as much as possible," given their limited finances. They studied Islam with an imam or teacher in a *hujra* in defiance of state law, admitted Shuhrat. They listened in particular to one highly respected imam who spoke many languages. They said that "the people" paid the expenses of their religious leaders, who were "independent" imams with high sacred authority in the region. The young men added that "Arab imams" and those trained in Arabia were better than Uzbek imams because they spoke Arabic freely, read the Qur'an in Arabic, and had a pure Islamic education.

When describing their Uzbek national traditions, they complained about nepotism, money, connections, and bribery, as "Uzbek" vices, and again voiced a preference for living like "real" Muslims, in Arabia. Uzbeks were "at least better," Jasur believed, "than Kyrgyz and Kazakhs," who were "not real Muslims" at all because they had adopted "European ways." The Arab puritanical influence on

[16] UZ-FG#22.

them was strong; like many Ferghana Valley Uzbeks, the Andijonis opposed all alcohol and tobacco use, in contrast to common Central Asian practices since the Soviet era. Shuhrat declared, "Those who smoke have a weak will." They even proposed "stopping the sale of alcohol and cigarettes." The young men criticized "foreign customs." Ahror said that "foreign films have a negative influence on religious and spiritual values and national traditions." They even linked foreigners to prostitution. They were intolerant of other religions. Jews and Christians, they believed, were "the cause of prostitution and narcotics." Yahyo said, "Other religions have a negative influence and lead our girls to remove their veils." Another added, "They cause them to dress European." Ahror declared, "In Tashkent when you drive, you think you've landed in America." Yahyo agreed: "In Tashkent, they don't even know what fasting is. In our *mahalla*, everyone, young and old, fasts." Zuhriddin claimed that other religions "are atheist." He included among them Jews and Christians, who are respected by most Muslims as "People of the Book." Ahror said, "All evils come from them [Jews]." Others called Jews "a threat" and declared they were "cannibals" who "eat children." They were particularly aggrieved by Christian missionaries and converts: "It [conversion] is a sin, a betrayal of our religion." Conversion was unthinkable, "not even possible." Jasur and Shuhrat exclaimed, "[Conversion] never happens in the Ferghana Valley," in contrast to Tashkent. Furqat's view was more extreme: "All the enemies of Muslims are followers of other religions." Their intolerant views reflected the teachings of Salafist imams in the Ferghana Valley since the late Soviet era, as well as Islamist ideas propagated first by Adolat and later by HTI.

Their view of the state was influenced by narratives about the USSR from their elders. The men decried Soviet oppression of Islam. Murodjon said, "In the Soviet times, they shot you or sent you to the Gulag for messing in politics if you had Muslim values." Zuhriddin said that the Communist Party "forbade Muslims to pray in the mosques, fast and observe our national traditions. Muslims didn't have Russian values."

Yet, they wavered about the precise role of Islam in politics. Many responses were vague and circumspect, possibly due to fear of challenging the secular regime, but nonetheless most approved of Islamic influence on the state, law, and courts. Some said a "Muslim state" would be better than what they had, but they were not clear about what that entailed. Shuhrat, for example, praised their town for being "completely Muslim in fulfilling the laws of *shariat* everywhere," but he added, "The state should be in the middle, not too Muslim and not too far from Islam." Zuhriddin responded, "[Adopting] a Muslim state should be decided during a session of parliament." And a third added, cautiously, "It depends on the president. If he agrees to it [adopting *shariat*] . . . maybe there would be elections and a referendum on it." They appeared to believe an Islamic state would be better for them, but they feared to endorse it openly.

A few disagreed with the majority. Jasur said, "We don't need a state based on the Qur'an. We respect it and fulfill what's written in the Qur'an, but democracy should be based on the republic's constitution. . . . We need a religious and constitutional democracy." However, others replied, "In a Muslim country there is less corruption" and "Almost no corruption exists there." Furqat explained, "In Muslim countries, if you take bribes, you are put in prison and you suffer various punishments. So, in Muslim countries there is very little bribery. In other countries it exists widely, a lot. In these countries, if a person is caught with a bribe, he can escape a punishment by paying a bribe." Consequently, they preferred a "religious democracy." Others simply decried Uzbekistan as a "state where the government is rich and the people are poor." Ahror said, "We should have a government where there is no corruption," but declined to say what state that would be.

When discussing the courts and law, the young men were more specific. Zuhriddin declared that "a Muslim court is more just. It would uphold the laws of the Qur'an . . . and the guilty would go to prison for the appropriate sentencing." Furqat added, "There [in an Islamic court], even a small violation is punished. Here, the court does nothing to those who have money. They can do anything without being sentenced in court." Only one student, Afzal, countered that "in Germany, all the laws are strict," implying that an Islamic court was not necessary for the law to work.

Despite such views, the students voiced strong opposition to HTI. Yahyo said, "If HTI comes to power, it will be like Afghanistan: war, violence, everywhere lack of peace, narcotics." However, Jasur contrasted HTI with the IRPU, which was banned and then destroyed in 1992: "The Islamic Revival Party has many positive sides, they only do good. I only know about this one. But HTI is a bad party." Yahyo agreed that "the Islamic Party has never participated in elections, but it *should* be able to participate in elections, so that the people know their plan and opinions." Another claimed, "The Islamic Party doesn't try to take power." The men had clearly heard about the IRPU, even though its leaders had been in prison, underground, or in exile for over a decade.

Despite their political views, the young men were not overtly militant. Jasur said, "When war happens, the state doesn't develop." Nevertheless, most did express sympathy for various militant jihads—in Palestine, Chechnya, and Iraq—to "defend the religion" of Islam. Murodjon said "blood for blood and life for life" was necessary in Palestine. Others said the Palestinians were only defending their land and their religion. The men sympathized with the Chechens fighting Russia and the Iraqis waging suicide attacks on the United States. They called suicide bombers *shahids*, a sign of respect. Such *shahids* were acting justly "in extreme circumstances," said Jasur. Yahyo and others believed that these *shahids* needed either "to avenge their families and close friends" or to use the money "to support their families." These respondents were hardly Salafi jihadists, but they were influenced by puritanical interpretations of Islam, and also by injustice and repression.

Men, Blue-Collar Workers, Twenty to Twenty-nine Years Old, Marg'ilon, Ferghana Oblast, 2005

A group of poorly educated blue-collar workers and small entrepreneurs from Marg'ilon,[17] also in the Ferghana Valley, held views similar to those of the Andijoni students. The workers were also strictly religious. They were highly critical of alcohol use, smoking, and those who did not observe Islamic rules on fasting and daily *namaz*. They too idealized "Arabs" as both "living under pure Islam" and having "better imams." Many of the men wanted Uzbek women to "wear the *paranji* and sit at home, as in Saudi Arabia." According to Erkin, "Men and women are not equal; women must be lower than men." He justified his view religiously. Possibly influenced by the ideas of Salafist imams like Abuvali Qori, the men were highly intolerant of Jews and converts. They agreed with Azizbek, who declared, "Jews are the ancient enemies of Muslims."

A few of them recalled *perestroika* and the greater religious freedom that had existed "in 1988–89," when independent mosques in their region had begun to flourish. Like others in the Ferghana Valley, they too complained about the "decline of religious freedom" since the mid-1990s. The men were also bitter about corrupt and repressive governance, which they described as "strong and long-standing clannism." "Corruption," they said, was everywhere. Their political frustration, together with their puritanical religious views, led them to advocate "the Saudi model" of Islamic governance. They too favored adopting the *hudud* penalties of *shariat* through "Muslim courts, [which] are just." Elyorjon said, "Take, for example, the simple case of theft, cutting off the hand of a thief. Fear of losing a hand makes people think before stealing. It's an example, every time you see someone on the street without a hand." Most believed that such laws would be good for Uzbekistan. Only a few argued for a more mainstream, pluralist "Muslim democracy."

The workers did not express support for any particular Uzbek Islamist movement, and they probably had no connection to any Islamist group. Notably, they did articulate respect for the IRPT, which at the time was propagating an Islamic democratic agenda in Tajikistan. No doubt they knew that the Islamic party once active in Uzbekistan, popular in their own region in the early 1990s, had been destroyed.

But most held more extreme views than the IRPT or IRPU. Atypical of Uzbek participants, the Marg'iloni men expressed sympathy not only for violent jihad

17 UZ-FG#5.

but also for suicide bombing, albeit only "in a desperate situation" or when there was "no other way out." They discussed bombers in Palestine, Chechnya, Iraq, and even close to home, in Tashkent in 2004, calling them "desperate" youth with no other options. Even more unusual was this comment from Ikromjon: "If the [Palestinians] call us we will go to fight on their side." Another, possibly referring to Uzbekistan, said, "Look what happens. The husbands are arrested. Their wives remain. The husbands don't ask for pardon and aren't released from prison. Their wives remain with two or three children. If she's on a true path of Allah, then she could become a *shahid*." From their puritanical religious views to their sympathy for Salafi jihadist forms of violence, their opinions were congruent with ideas advocated by radical Islamists.

Although their views on violence were uncommon, as Chapter 14 discusses, when ISIS propagated such ideas and stoked such anger a few years later, thousands of Central Asians joined.

Secular Views about Governance

Those favoring secular governance were also a minority. In only three focus groups did most participants voice a preference for a "secular" state that would separate religion and politics. A handful of respondents in other groups also favored wholly secular politics. Given that voicing a preference for "secular" governance was the safe response in Karimov's Uzbekistan, it is striking that so few articulated such preferences. "Secular" respondents—those opposed to a religious role in politics but not personally irreligious—specified that they wanted secular laws and courts, as opposed to *shariat* law and Islamic courts. They were divided among those with a preference for Soviet-style authoritarian secularism, for secular democracy (which they generally assumed to be a Western system in which religion had no influence on democratic law and politics), or for what many called the "Russian model" of the 2000s.

Some Tashkent entrepreneurs expressed secular views about the state.[18] Not very devout, they had not experienced religious repression and expressed little awareness of it. They feared a Muslim state, which Nazira described as "a state where all the laws are based on the Qur'an, like Afghanistan and the Arab states." Although such views were less common outside of Tashkent, in Urganch small businessmen also favored a secular political system.[19] They were deeply concerned about corruption, but they did not see Islamic courts as the solution. O'tkir worried that "if the courts become Islamic, it will turn the country

18 UZ-FG#23.
19 UZ-FG#13.

backwards to old laws," not suitable to the modern world. Dilshod added, "There will be no democracy in an Islamic court! Those *qazis* (Islamic judges) will only defend the rights of the rich." The men favored a secular democracy. Qudrat said, "Allah is in the soul," so there is no need for *shariat* as law. Dilshod affirmed that "freedom is better than that [Islamic law]." As in Tajikistan, secular and liberal democratic views were a minority among participants.

Societal Elites and the Limits of Support for Radical Islamism

Societal elites were far from uniform in their views, but most were either directly or implicitly critical of Karimov's dictatorship. All appeared troubled by the lack of fairness, equality, and justice in Uzbekistan, and some were sympathetic to Islamic political solutions, but not violence.

One strictly observant *oqsoqol* in Marg'ilon declared his preference for democracy, which he described as "fairness" and "equality before the law." He said, "I must repeat: The law should be the same for everyone."[20] Most societal elites, given a choice, preferred a more Muslim society and politics than what they had lived under all their lives. To them, Muslim politics did not mean strict, literalist *shariat* enforced by the state. For example, in Shahrixon, a town in the Ferghana Valley, one *mahalla* leader said, "In religious countries, there is less bribery. There is more justice." But when asked whether the Uzbek secular court system should become Islamic, he responded, "Islam says that you need to chop off your hand for theft. Such a sentence was passed in accordance with that time. It doesn't suit us now."[21] A very devout and influential local journalist from Qashqadaryo said, "A Muslim court can sentence the offender to various corporal punishments. I don't approve of this. It creates fear in society. . . . To correct a person, you can find other forms of reeducation—such as arrest or a fine."[22]

Others cast doubt on secular law as appropriate for Uzbekistan because, as many pointed out, the country is predominantly Muslim. One respondent said, "Ask ordinary people what the constitution is. Many know what it is, but don't know what is written in it. Ask them what *shariat* is. Everyone will know what it is and explain its meaning."[23] Tashpulat, a businessman among the new middle class and a mosque donor, stated, "It seems to me that everything should be religious" in order for the state to be just.[24] A *mahalla* leader from Namangan,

[20] Interview with *oqsoqol*, Marg'ilon, Uzbekistan, 2005.
[21] Interview with *mahalla* leader, Shahrixon, Uzbekistan, 2005.
[22] Interview with journalist, Qashqadaryo, Uzbekistan, 2005.
[23] Interview with businessman #2, Tashkent, Uzbekistan, 2005.
[24] Interview with businessman #1, Namangan, Uzbekistan, 2005.

despite the fact that such leaders were supposed to report to the state, believed, "The state must be fair. Where there is justice, there is no bribery and crime. If the state is Muslim and has its own laws, then the court will be Muslim and it will be fair."[25] When considering a preferable form of governance, an *oqsoqol* in Qashqadaryo contrasted democracy in the West and East: "They have more freedom than we do . . . [but] Muslim democracy is better. We still have certain boundaries, but they do not."[26] A state-appointed imam was more cautious when discussing *shariat* and courts: "I think our government courts are just . . . but they don't correct the criminals, who continue to carry out crimes."[27]

Some informal social leaders did favor both a Muslim legal system and strict *shariat* penalties. A businessman from Urganch, who had helped finance a mosque, said:

> A Muslim state is more just, because, firstly, [the people] are afraid of Allah; besides, a Muslim . . . will always be a supporter of justice. Nowadays there are many people who deceive each other, and borrow money and do not give it back. In Islam, this should not and does not exist. The fair side is the one that does the will of Allah. The intended religious punishment is carried out in front of the people. Other criminals, seeing this, are frightened. And in our country, they are punished and judged in closed trials, and no one sees. They do not receive a life lesson. As a result, the crime rate rises. Therefore, I think that it is necessary to punish criminals in public, openly.[28]

A minority of interview respondents openly endorsed the *hudud* penalties under *shariat* courts because they would force the person to remember his crime and be "a lesson" to society. Another businessman said:

> We can't call our country Muslim because it does not fulfill the requirements of the Islamic religion. If we want to create an Islamic state, then we must eradicate a lot of negative events in our society. For example, according to *shariat* law, one is strictly punished for a proven crime. Having proven theft, they cut off the hand even if the person has a high position in society, because before Allah everyone is equal. . . . If this punishment is given to just one person, then other people will be afraid to commit such a crime. But in our society, criminals are sent to jail, but after they are freed, they continue to commit theft and other crimes. If we cut off his hand, he will not be able to steal again.[29]

25 Interview with *mahalla* leader, Namangan, Uzbekistan, 2005.
26 Interview with *oqsoqol*, Qashqadaryo, Uzbekistan, 2005.
27 Interview with official religious leader, Urganch, Uzbekistan, 2005.
28 Interview with businessman #1, Urganch, Uzbekistan, 2005.
29 Interview with businessman #2, Tashkent, Uzbekistan, 2005.

The common theme behind support for *shariat* courts was "justice," and anger at injustice and corruption. Societal elites widely viewed Islamic courts as just, and they knew well that their secular courts were not just. One social leader said, "A Muslim court is more just than a non-Muslim one. Because in a Muslim court they punish based on a real crime, not on a lie [fabricated charges]."[30] In the words of another: "If those who are judges have an Islamic upbringing, then the court will be just. Because they can distinguish the dirty from the pure *shariat.*"[31] A Tashkent businessman argued, "A Muslim court [would be] more just. If one thinks about it, all the laws of the state and prosecutor [would be] taken from the *shariat*."[32] Others, especially in the Ferghana Valley, implicitly tied law and courts to a Muslim state: "If a state is Muslim and has its own laws, then the court will also be Muslim and also just."[33]

Discussing the IMU or other violent groups was dangerous, but societal elites did offer perspectives on HTI. Views were occasionally sympathetic to those who joined, but still overwhelmingly negative about the caliphate. The vast majority of local-level societal elites—including registered and unregistered religious leaders and teachers, *mahalla* leaders, journalists, women's leaders, *otincha*s, and local government officials—opposed HTI and thus limited its impact. Some perhaps feared expressing support, but most genuinely rejected the movement. One state imam in Namangan said, "HTI is outside of Islam."[34] He did not even recognize it as Muslim. Many called HTI members "terrorists" and insisted that they used violence. Multiple others said HTI members had been "hypnotized" and become "zombies," or that HTI was a creation of Saudi Arabia or perhaps the CIA, a plot to sow division among Muslims.[35] Such statements often reflected government characterizations of the organization, but may also have been expressed genuine opprobrium.

Other societal elites disagreed with HTI's goals but sympathized with its members. Over and over, these individuals pointed to the absence of "justice" as the driving cause behind HTI's attraction. A Tashkent imam said, "Youth join because they lack knowledge of true Islam. HTI calls them to the wrong path . . . [but] the government violates our rights. . . . A just government must be Islamic."[36] In Qashqadaryo, a *mahalla* leader for women explained, "[HTI] youth are just expressing their dissatisfaction with the current government. They say it will be better once they establish a caliphate. But a caliphate is not possible today. . . . There will be bloodshed. It's better to do it in a peaceful way."[37]

[30] Interview with *otincha*, Ferghana, Uzbekistan, 2005.
[31] Interview with informal *mahalla* leader, Tashkent, Uzbekistan, 2005.
[32] Interview with businessman #1, Tashkent, Uzbekistan, 2005.
[33] Interview with informal *mahalla* leader, Namangan, Uzbekistan, 2005.
[34] Interview with imam, Namangan, Uzbekistan, 2006.
[35] Interview with ethnic Uzbek journalist, Osh, Kyrgyzstan, 2006.
[36] Interview with imam, Tashkent, Uzbekistan, 2005.
[37] Interview with informal *mahalla* leader, Qashqadaryo, Uzbekistan, 2005.

Like many focus group participants, societal elites suggested that people had joined HTI because of "corruption," "necessity," or "deprivation," but later they realized such groups could neither eradicate those problems nor create a caliphate. G'ayrat, a successful Tashkent businessman, explained that Islamic movements could improve life. He too had once held "optimistic expectations about [HTI] . . . but now," he believed such parties "were divisive. . . . In Islam it's a sin to create a party using Islam's name. There is one Islam, and it does not need any sort of party to fight for the state. . . . Youth who join [HTI] have been duped. They've seen a fake Islam. It's their attempt to recognize—to give an [important] place to—religion." While HTI was not a political solution, he said, "The laws of the state are against the people. . . . They are worse than corruption. . . . Our life each day becomes worse and worse. . . . It's necessary to change everything. . . . If people little by little come to religion, if they are all believers and if the bulk of the population wants it, then in these conditions, you can and must create a Muslim state. But if not, there will be conflict, war."[38] His words were strikingly similar to those of the eminent Islamic leader Haji Akbar Turajonzoda in Tajikistan. By contrast, Xayrulla, a Namangani businessman, approved of Islamic parties. He argued that "if Islamic parties are created, they should participate in elections, but now they don't have that right." Nonetheless, he declared his opposition to HTI, because he believed that "it's violent."[39] Hayrulla would have preferred a mainstream party like the IRPT.

Some religious leaders and teachers also spoke against HTI and the IMU, but nonetheless expressed a desire for an Islamic party. For example, a mullah from Bukhara said, guardedly, that he opposed HTI for being subversive, but added, "If there were Islamic parties that were not radical, they could participate in elections."[40] One religious teacher insisted that HTI was "a religious movement, not just terrorists," as the government claimed. He noted that a "great deal of religious literature" had circulated after 1991 in the "euphoria" after many years of a "vacuum of religion." He explained that those participating in religious movements had been calling people who did not perform *namaz* to become real Muslims. They urged women to cover their heads, and he approved of this. However, he disagreed when "they branded someone as a *kafir*. There's no right to call anyone a *kafir*." He observed that in the 2000s, religiosity among youth had again declined because "[members of] HTI and other religious sects . . . were put in prison. . . . Yes, they broke the law, so they had to serve a punishment, but still."[41] He did not finish his thought. He explained that he personally knew many

[38] Interview with businessman #2, Tashkent, Uzbekistan, 2005.
[39] Interview with businessman #1, Namangan, Uzbekistan, 2005.
[40] Interview with mullah, Bukhara, Uzbekistan, 2005.
[41] Interview with unregistered religious teacher/*mahalla* leader, Qarshi, Uzbekistan, 2005.

HTI members and did not consider them "terrorists," but he appeared afraid to directly criticize the government.

Surprisingly, even government officials were sometimes understanding of HTI's motives. One representative of the Liberal Democratic Party of Uzbekistan—a pro-Karimov party, despite its name—empathetically commented that young people joined HTI "because it's interesting. . . . They get lessons, turn their lives around. . . . Religion gives strength to a person. . . . They are just seeking peace. Then they get trapped."[42] She claimed to have suggested to the regional governor that people be provided government-supervised religious education to counter youth interest in HTI. A member of another pro-Karimov party, Fidokorlar, explained why HTI had been very popular in Urganch: "People had no hope of solutions to their problems from the government. . . . Of course, they are angry."[43] He agreed that some elements of *shariat* were needed in the law, but that HTI had no real program. He added that most HTI adherents had been arrested or fled.

Even some sympathizers did not believe that HTI could possibly achieve its ends without violence, and for them, this made the party unattractive. An *otincha* from Qashqadaryo, like many respondents along the Tajik border, where people were often strictly observant, favored the "Arab form" of government. She expressed a desire for all law by *shariat*. She too insisted that HTI only wanted a religious state. She explained HTI's appeal this way: "[HTI's] rules are drawn from the Qur'an and they have their prayers. For example, you love Islam, and Islam means submission to Allah. Some read the Qur'an but don't understand its meaning. . . .They read some passage from the Qur'an and accept it as an ideology. That's how they read the Qur'an and *hadith*. . . . Then they argue with you. They call you to this path, and in the end explain that it's an ideology, that our ruler must be Islamic, and our country must be an Islamic country. If you go to this path [they say], you will establish Islam." Sympathetic to HTI's goals, she claimed, simply and openly, "Under Islam . . . your children will live well, and you can't argue with this opinion." Yet she added, "I oppose bombs, [and] all violence," and she indicated that for HTI, violence would be necessary: "In the time of the Prophet (peace be upon him), there were also wars. . . . There will be compulsion. There will be bloodshed."[44] Although favorable to HTI's ideas in theory, she opposed radical means of achieving them. Some, however, were sympathetic to those who wanted to use violence. Another women's leader explained that jihad and bloodshed were wrong, but "our system is run by the police. They first

42 Interview with LDPU party activist, Qashqadaryo, Uzbekistan, 2005.
43 Interview with Fidokorlar party activist, Urganch, Uzbekistan, 2005.
44 Interview with *otincha*, Qashqadaryo, Uzbekistan, 2005.

beat you up and then murder you. Because of that, those who will rise up against the government's politics will do so with weapons."[45]

As had ordinary Uzbeks in the focus groups, most societal elites exhibited both a reluctance to discuss the IMU and IJU and also genuine disapproval of militant movements. However, a handful of societal elites did approve militant defense of Islam. One imam explained the concept of jihad in traditional Islamic thought: " 'Jihad' can be used in the event that any people or other religion wants to destroy our religion, subjugate our people, conquer our Motherland! In this case, a 'jihad' can be declared, in which men and women must take part in order to protect their home, their homeland. However, nowadays there are emerging trends that declare all sorts of 'jihad.' . . . A person who replied, '*Alhamdulillah* (all praise and thanks belong to Allah), I am a Muslim,' is prohibited from waging 'jihad' with a sword. First of all, we must declare 'jihad' against our passions."[46] A mosque donor, by contrast, voiced a radical, exclusively militant view of jihad: "In my opinion, jihad is war. . . . [I]f America or Russia begins to wage war with someone—the [response] is a jihad in the glory of such a goal [for Islam]. For example, Iraq, Afghanistan, Yugoslavia were necessary jihads and they are equally a jihad. All take place thanks to this goal. . . . Sacrificing oneself [martyrdom] is also jihad. What's been happening in our country—the explosions and antigovernmental acts—it is jihad connected with the changes in our society."[47] His comments on the jihad against the Uzbek government, presumably the 1999 and 2004 bombings, and his characterization of such acts as sacrifice suggest sympathy with that path. An unregistered mullah said more directly, "It is necessary to wage jihad . . . necessary to spread Islam. . . . Jihad has been this way since the Prophet's time."[48] Such views were expressed by a small minority, but as Chapter 14 will discuss, even a handful of local leaders fostering militancy among their followers or community would play a significant role in mobilizing fighters for Syria. As we have seen, most societal leaders rejected Islamist radicalism, whether HTI's nonviolent radicalism or the IMU's jihadist path.

Listening to both ordinary people and societal elites has demonstrated that, by the 2000s, most Uzbeks' views about politics and religion were neither Soviet nor secular. Nor were they radically Islamist. Instead, as in Tajikistan—across region, gender, occupation, and age—the majority wanted a larger role for Islam in society, the public sphere, and even law and politics. Ordinary Uzbeks considered being Muslim integral to their identity and daily life. They widely endorsed

[45] Interview with *mahalla* leader, Qashqadaryo, Uzbekistan, 2005.
[46] Interview with imam, Bukhara, Uzbekistan, 2005.
[47] Interview with businessman #1, Qashqadaryo, Uzbekistan, 2005.
[48] Interview with unregistered mullah, Qarshi, Uzbekistan, 2005.

nationally rooted Islamic revivalism. They hoped for the spread of state-sponsored Islamic education, freedom to build mosques and *madrasas*, and the right to wear the hijab, gather for prayer, and study Islam with elders. Religious repression was a concern for the majority in Uzbekistan. Likewise, standing up to the corruption and injustice of the government, especially the police and courts, and solving these problems through bringing *shariat*, of some form, into the legal system and state, were ideas that resonated. Opposition to secularism—to the antireligious policy of the USSR and the Karimov regime, and even to secular democracy—was widespread. Uzbeks, much like Tajiks, typically associated secularism with immorality, Western influence, and repressive and corrupt governance. Focus groups revealed such views to be common not only in strictly observant regions of the Ferghana Valley but increasingly in Tashkent, Urganch, and other regions not previously known for strict piety.

Most were afraid of advocating for an Islamic party or of speaking critically about the government. It was still the time of Karimov. Yet, the desire of many Uzbeks for a more Muslim society and polity was clear. Various forms of Muslim politics and civil Islam would likely have flourished in Uzbekistan in the 1990s and 2000s if the government had relented on religious repression and opened space to religious actors. It is also likely that the ideas of mainstream Islamist parties—such as the IRPT—might well have resonated inside Uzbekistan.

By contrast, the various extremist ideas propagated by HTI, the IMU, and IJU—whether intolerance of Jews and Christians, adopting a total Islamic state or caliphate, or using militant jihad to achieve such ends—found little support. Suicide bombing was widely and vociferously condemned by nearly all. As we will see in Chapter 14, however, by 2014 ISIS, KIB, and KTJ would draw on anger at Karimov and desire for justice, motivating it with new, emotionally charged propaganda promising a better life under the caliphate in Syria.

PART V

KYRGYZSTAN

Civil Islam and Emergent Islamists

11
Religious Liberalization and Civil Islam in Kyrgyzstan

> During the time of the Union we had no possibility for following Islam, but after we separated from the Union, we became an independent state and a lot changed. Kyrgyz began to build mosques; the Muslim faith became free. Since 1991 a lot has changed.
>
> —Maksat, Kyrgyz businessman, Bishkek, 2007

> Now we have religious freedom.
>
> —Meerim and Baktigul, *madrasa* students, Naryn, 2013

> Now our state is Muslim. . . . We have many mosques in the city, and a lot of people perform namaz, everything, all customs are done according to Islamic shariat. . . . [F]or us democracy is good. . . . The local authorities respect the mosque and the mullah.
>
> —Sodiq, Uzbek mullah, Batken, 2005

About a decade after the Soviet collapse, as a student living in the Russified center of Kyrgyzstan's capital city, Bishkek, I asked a Kyrgyz friend to take me to visit one of the new mosques I had heard about.[1] After a lengthy quest on the outskirts of Bishkek, we came upon one such building. Its cheaply constructed silver dome bore a crescent moon; no minaret had yet been erected. The space looked like it would seat only about a hundred men. It was closed, with no caretaker in sight. My friend apologized and said, "There just aren't many mosques here." Bishkek, and northern Kyrgyzstan more broadly, were still considered by many locals "not very religious." Politicians and local experts believed that Islam would never be politicized there because the Kyrgyz were "not so Muslim," which meant they were less scripturally observant than Uzbek or Tajik Muslims. Ethnic Kyrgyz have long been characterized by Soviet scholars, their own political leaders, and

[1] In this and subsequent chapters, I use "Kyrgyzstan," the commonly accepted post-Soviet name for the former Kyrgyz SSR. "Kyrgyz" refers to ethnic Kyrgyz, and "Kyrgyzstani" refers to any citizen of Kyrgyzstan (which includes a substantial ethnic Uzbek minority, especially in the southern regions).

Politicizing Islam in Central Asia. Kathleen Collins, Oxford University Press. © Oxford University Press 2023.
DOI: 10.1093/oso/9780197685068.003.0012

Westerners as "nomads" who are "superficially" Islamic.[2] "Go to the south [of Kyrgyzstan].[3] There you'll find Uzbeks, real Muslims," my Bishkek friends said.

I flew to Osh, a three-thousand-year-old city in the south. It was separated from Bishkek by formidable mountains. Culturally, it seemed like another world. My companion and I strolled to the central mosque, where the imam invited me for tea and grapes after thousands of Friday worshipers, young and old, left. The imam recounted the history of the mosque, emphasizing that despite the travails of the previous decades, they now had religious freedom. There, a stricter form of Islam was visible—in conservative female dress, the prevalence of mosques, and the call to prayer—but it was not puritanical. Both my Kyrgyz and Uzbek hosts brought me to Takhti Sulayman, the most visited shrine in Kyrgyzstan, where pilgrims left offerings and prayed for health or fertility. Locals had long called it a "second Mecca." They went there during the Soviet era, when making the hajj was impossible. Since independence, Kyrgyzstan had been re-Islamized, most rapidly in the south, where thousands of mosques were either reopened or newly built—in Osh, Kara-Suu, Jalalabat, and Batken, all in the Ferghana Valley (not far from the border and Uzbekistan's cities of Andijon and Namangan).[4] Local inhabitants shared mosque-centered practices with neighboring Uzbeks in Uzbekistan. Nonetheless, Islam there remained focused on piety, not politics, for many years.[5]

No Islamist movement emerged in Kyrgyzstan during the first decade of independence, when religious freedom was high, even though wide associational space had facilitated the spread of various Islamist ideas. Unlike Uzbekistan and Tajikistan, religious revival did not breed Islamism in Kyrgyzstan as the USSR collapsed or even later in the 1990s.

In this chapter, I explain the conditions—religious freedom and associational space—that prevailed from 1990 through about 2005. Then I examine Islamic revivalism—a surge in piety and practice—that gradually increased from about 1990 on. I argue that, in contrast to Tajikistan and Uzbekistan, Islamic revival took place in Kyrgyzstan *without* the emergence of an Islamist movement in this period. I contend that a consequence of the coexistence of religious liberalization and revival was the continued growth of "civil Islam" and everyday Muslim politics; actors and movements challenged secularism but without demanding an Islamist political order.[6]

[2] Interview with Professor Iskander Ormon uluu, Yiman Fondu, Bishkek, Kyrgyzstan, June 2019.

[3] The Ferghana Valley regions of Kyrgyzstan include the urban centers and surrounding regions around Osh, Kara-Suu, Jalalabat, and Batken.

[4] Omurzak Mamayusupov, Kanatbek Murzakhalilov, and Kanybek Mamataliyev, *O Monitoringe Deiatel'nosti Gosudarstvennykh Organov v Realizatsii Religioznykh Prav i Svobod* (Osh: Goskommissiia PKR po Delam Religii, 2004), 423–24.

[5] Liu, *Under Solomon's Throne.*

[6] Hefner, *Civil Islam.*

Religious Liberalization Undercuts Islamist Emergence

From the late 1980s through 2004, Kyrgyzstan's government created wide associational space and full religious freedom. Although the same political theologies spreading in Uzbekistan and Tajikistan had drawn the attention of certain Muslim leaders in Kyrgyzstan, no Islamist movement emerged; most Kyrgyzstanis were content with the religious freedoms and inclusion they enjoyed.

Great Associational Space and Religious Freedom

During the Soviet era, the Kyrgyz republic had experienced less religious repression and, consequently, less contention over Islam, thanks to Soviet stereotyping of the recently "nomadic" Kyrgyz as "superficially" Muslim. Since Brezhnev, few had experienced repression of religion in Kyrgyzstan, in sharp contrast to Tajikistan and Uzbekistan. As one deputy *mufti* said, "The Party did not bother us . . . but for seventy years we had moved far away from Islam."[7] Even in the south, said one imam, "we had freedom [to pray], and there were no arrests of Islamic spiritual leaders then . . . so the mosques were not an 'opposition.'"[8] The Ferghana Valley town of Kara-Suu was, like Osh and Jalalabat, heavily ethnic Uzbek and home to a major bazaar and trading center. Uzbek religious leaders in southern Kyrgyzstan, much like their kin across the border, often remembered and passed on narratives of Soviet religious repression. According to the widely renowned Imam Alauddin Mansur of Kara-Suu, "Our elders lived in a communist country. . . . [I]n Soviet times atheism shone . . . it was truly like that. Then, the followers of atheism destroyed real religious scholars, the *ulama*, many religious activists were destroyed, they shot the real teachers of Muslimhood. It was really that way. It's been passed on to us." He continued, remembering the Stalinist era, "Stalin wanted to destroy religion . . . he was against Allah." Yet, Mansur proudly claimed, "religion—Islam survived, Muslimhood was saved. Religion could not be destroyed . . . and thanks to our great elders, the followers of Islam, our religion was preserved."[9] Moreover, in Kyrgyzstan, in contrast to Tajikistan and Uzbekistan, said the imam, repression had receded by the 1970s and 1980s: "One could read the Qur'an, and the state wasn't in the mood to try to influence or pressure such people."[10] He recalled no arrests of religious actors. Memories of more distant repression in the 1930s were placated by greater freedom for Islam.

[7] Interview with deputy *mufti*, Bishkek, Kyrgyzstan, August 2010.
[8] Interview with Imam Orozov, Jalalabat, Kyrgyzstan, November 2010.
[9] Interview with Imam Alauddin Mansur, Kara-Suu, Kyrgyzstan, November 2010.
[10] Interview with Imam Mansur.

That view continued to influence state religious policy during the late 1980s and after independence.[11] Unlike elsewhere in Central Asia, associational space in Kyrgyzstan continued to increase dramatically from the late *perestroika* era through the 1990s. In part, this was due to the more liberal ideology and governance of President Askar Akayev, elected with Gorbachev's support in 1990. By the early 1990s, Kyrgyzstan had liberalized the press, civil society, education, travel, the electoral and party system, and many aspects of the economy. Although never a liberal democracy, Kyrgyzstan in the 1990s was relatively pluralist.[12]

Akayev's government, however, soon became extremely corrupt through insider privatization and state capture by clan factions loyal to the president. Democratization stalled. Electoral manipulation kept Akayev and other incumbents in power, despite popular frustration with clan politics, bribery and extortion, economic decline, and inequality.[13] By 2000, Akayev's cronies had effectively hollowed out the formal institutions of democracy.[14] Despite this, in Akayev's Kyrgyzstan, far greater de facto and de jure associational space existed than in neighboring states. I argue that the absence of religious repression precluded the politicization of religious identity in Kyrgyzstan. Democratization and ethnonationalism, not Islam, were the frames used by protesters during *perestroika* and throughout the 1990s to challenge the regime.

Under Akayev in the first decade of independence, religion was free. *Namaz*, the hajj, mosque construction, and Islamic weddings, dress, and education—all became suddenly and widely possible. The government neither blocked nor controlled Islamic revival. The renamed Spiritual Administration of the Muslims of Kyrgyzstan (SAMK) became independent of both SADUM and the new Kyrgyzstani state. Initially, SAMK was also inclusive of ethnic Uzbeks, an important factor in preventing the rise of a more puritanical Uzbek ethnoreligious opposition inside Kyrgyzstan.

According to Imam Mansur, in the late Soviet years "there were no Islamic organizations. . . . Then there was only one goal, to worship Allah. . . . There were no Sufi brotherhoods. Mullahs did not carry out any antistate activities. Their opposition to the state ended with passing on religious knowledge to simple people . . . teaching them to say prayers, fear Allah, and study *suras* of the Qur'an and the rules of *namaz*. That was their work. . . . It was not opposition to government policy. . . . Thanks to Allah there was no Islamic opposition.

[11] Interview with staff, SCRA, Bishkek, Kyrgyzstan, January 2002; conversations with government officials, Ministry of Foreign Affairs, 1997–2002; interview with Ambassador Kadyr Toktolgulov, Embassy of the Kyrgyz Republic to the United States, Washington, D.C., November 2018.

[12] Collins, *Clan Politics*, 177–88.

[13] Interview with democracy activist, Sardar Bagishbekov, Bishkek, Kyrgyzstan, August 2004; Erica Marat, *The Tulip Revolution: Kyrgyzstan One Year After* (Washington, D.C.: Jamestown Foundation, 2006).

[14] Collins, "The Logic of Clan Politics."

Who needs it?"[15] Imam Mansur followed the example of the "greatly respected Domla Hindustoniy," who "did not get into politics." Mansur expressed satisfaction that religion had become largely free under Gorbachev, and in the early 1990s he was able to distribute fifty thousand copies of his Uzbek translation of the Qur'an. "Akayev was not atheist. He didn't do anything against religion. He gave freedom to Muslims."[16] Other imams shared this view. An ethnic Uzbek imam in Osh emphatically stated that under Akayev's government, "freedom of religion in our country has been a great achievement for us. There is no ban on the part of the government. There is no supervision."[17] Another Uzbek imam in the southern city of Batken said, "Our state is Muslim. Our President Askar Akayev is also a Muslim, and does not interfere with the development of religion. . . . Mosques are being built; everyone is doing things so that we can practice our religion. . . . Everything is fine."[18] A prominent Uzbek businessman who sharply criticized government corruption under Akayev nonetheless praised the country's religious freedom: "In contrast to the past, the government seriously opened all roads for religion. A believer can freely perform *namaz*, and no one will bother him."[19] Data on religious activity in the south during this time supports their view. In 2004, nearly 70 percent (807 of 1,185) of registered mosques and twenty-eight of forty-three *madrasas*, were located in the south, which had about 50 percent of the population and most of the ethnic Uzbek minority.[20]

Although the transnational Islamist party Hizb ut-Tahrir al-Islami (HTI) crossed into Osh and Kara-Suu, fleeing Uzbekistan between 2000 and 2005, the Akayev government at first ignored it and then invited it to compete legally in elections. Only when HTI rejected the offer, demanding its anticonstitutional goals, did Kyrgyzstan ban the group.[21] Still, the State Committee on National Security and police rarely imprisoned HTI members before Akayev left office. Most were released after paying a small fine or bribe.[22]

In sum, following a somewhat less repressive Soviet experience, the Akayev era brought religious liberty and set the stage for a pluralist religious revival, most of which was apolitical and all of which was nonviolent.

[15] Interview with Imam Mansur.

[16] Interview with Imam Mansur.

[17] Interview with imam, Osh, Kyrgyzstan, July 2005.

[18] Interview with imam, Batken, Kyrgyzstan, 2005.

[19] Interview with ethnic Uzbek businessman, Osh, Kyrgyzstan, 2005.

[20] Mamayusupov, Murzakhalilov, and Mamataliyev, *O Monitoringe Deiatel'nosti*, 423–26.

[21] Interview with SCRA director Omurzak Mamayusupov August 2004; interview with O. Moldaliyev, state adviser, Bishkek, Kyrgyzstan, June 2004, June 2019.

[22] Interviews with journalists, Osh, Kyrgyzstan, May 2004 and August 2005; International Crisis Group, "Radical Islam in Central Asia: Responding to Hizb ut-Tahrir," *Asia Report* No. 58, June 30, 2003, 37–39.

Image 11.1 *Juma namaz* at Imam Sulaiman-Too Mosque in Osh
Source: https://rus.azattyk.org/a/kyrgyzstan_mosques/25070424.html

Political Theology and Islamist Ideology Spread, but Potential Religious Entrepreneurs Don't Mobilize

Contrary to popular perception, in the 1990s Kyrgyzstan did have religious leaders and activists—potential entrepreneurs—who were influenced by the ideas driving Islamist movements in Uzbekistan. Since the Uzbek-Kyrgyz republic border was only nominal before 1991, many residents of Kyrgyzstan simply traveled across the border to Uzbekistani *hujras*.[23] Ideas thus spread easily from one community to the next. Although *hujras* were less common in Kyrgyzstan, they did exist during the Brezhnev years.[24] They mostly attracted the ethnic Uzbek community of the south. Many of those Kyrgyzstani Uzbeks studying in such underground networks would have been exposed to the same writings of Qutb and Mawdudi that were gaining traction in Andijon and Namangan. Some conservative ethnic Kyrgyz studied in the *hujras* as well, such as Abdusatar Majitov, who was elected *mufti* in 1996.

[23] Interview with Moldaliyev, Bishkek, Kyrgyzstan, June 2019.

[24] Interview with Sodiqjon Kamoluddin, former *mufti*, director of International Center for Islamic Cooperation, Osh, Kyrgyzstan, June 2005; interview with Ormon uluu; interview with resident who attended *hujra* in the 1980s, Osh, Kyrgyzstan, June 2018.

Religious entrepreneurs with the potential to mobilize these ideas also existed. One such individual was Sodiqjon Qori Kamoluddin (b. 1950). Kamoluddin came from Kara-Suu and an Uzbek family of *ulama* prominent in the Ferghana Valley.[25] His grandfather, Domla Habibulloh Qori, a well-known theologian of the Kokand Khanate, had passed on knowledge to his grandsons, who had few other opportunities for Islamic education. Sodiqjon Qori's path of study resembled that of the Tajik Qazi Akbar Turajonzoda and the Uzbek *mufti* Muhammad Sodiq Muhammad Yusuf. Both were officially educated in Bukhara and Tashkent but also studied in *hujra*s with the purist Mujaddidiya and abroad. Sodiqjon Qori studied in Libya and Jordan. He was appointed the imam of the central Osh mosque (1977–86), one of the most influential in the republic in the late Soviet era. He became the chief *qazi* of Muslims of the Kyrgyz SSR (1987–90) and was subsequently the first head *mufti* of independent Kyrgyzstan.

Influenced by the purist scholars who trained him, Sodiqjon Qori espoused a Salafi or rigidly purist interpretation of Islamic teaching, rooted in the Qur'an and *sunna*; Salafism was a revivalist movement that sought to return to the practice of Islam at the time of the Prophet and his early followers. The *mufti* sought to eradicate Soviet impurities and false local traditions. He opposed both Soviet and Western variants of secularism and sought a prominent role for Islam in the family, society, public sphere, and law. Unlike other Mujaddidiya, however, he did not brand non-Muslims as *kuffar* (infidels) or use *takfir* (excommunication) to stigmatize impious Muslims.[26] Sodiqjon Qori expressed approval of the Saudi religious and state model, but his Salafist religious views did not dictate his political choices. Like Haji Turajonzoda, he did not eschew politics. He was even a candidate for the republic's Supreme Soviet in the *perestroika*-era election in 1990.[27]

As an ethnic Uzbek, Sodiqjon Qori maintained good relations with President Akayev, whom he credited with liberalizing Islam. Akayev's policy allowed Sodiqjon Qori to found his own *madrasa*, import religious books from Saudi Arabia, and encourage Arab funding of religious revival.[28] He opened up educational connections with Arab states. He established a foundation in Osh, the International Center for Islamic Cooperation, with a restaurant serving halal food.[29] Under Sodiqjon Qori's direction, mosques and *madrasa*s began to open and operate even before independence. In 1990, in Osh *oblast* alone, there existed

[25] N. U. Kurbanova, *Islam v obshchestvenno-politicheskoi zhizni Kyrgyzstana* (Bishkek: Altyn Print, 2009), 65.

[26] Interview with Ormon uluu; interview with Mamatbek Myrzabayev, Bishkek, Kyrgyzstan, June 2019.

[27] Kurbanova, *Islam v obshchestvenno-politicheskoi zhizni*, 65.

[28] Interview with former *mufti* and Director of International Center for Islamic Cooperation, Sodiqjon Kamoluddin, Osh, Kyrgyzstan, July 2005.

[29] Interview with Sodiqjon Kamoluddin.

more than two hundred unregistered Muslim societies, with over three hundred religious employees. According to Nazira Kurbanova, these associations had influence in local-level government.[30]

Sodiqjon Qori also credited Akayev with maintaining stability, preventing a resurgence of the anti-Uzbek violence that had devastated Osh in 1990, and granting broader religious freedom than had existed in the previous seventy years. In the context of Kyrgyzstan's independence, the ethnic Kyrgyz *ulama*, which had long been a minimal presence in the *muftiyat*, sought to gain control of SAMK and its financial opportunities and shape Islam in Kyrgyzstan. Sodiqjon Qori was replaced by an ethnic Kyrgyz *mufti*.[31] Still, he presented no political challenge to Akayev; he recognized that the position of Uzbeks in Kyrgyzstan—religiously, economically, and politically—was far superior to that in Uzbekistan. Even after his removal from SAMK, the imam was able to run his educational and spiritual foundation and projects. Sodiqjon Qori's decision subsequently to refrain from politics met approval from many in the ethnic Uzbek religious community, who contrasted their freedom to practice Islam with the total oppression a few miles away in Karimov's Uzbekistan.[32]

Another potential entrepreneur in the 1980s and 1990s was Sodiqjon Qori's brother, Imam Muhammad Rafiq Kamoluddin (known as Rafiq Qori). He too had studied Islam in the *hujra*s of Hindustani, Hakimjon Qori, and Abduvali Qori (luminaries of Tajikistan's and Uzbekistan's independent Islam; see Chapters 5 and 8). According to his assistant, "despite the USSR's religious repression, Rafiq and his brother Sodiqjon desired to become scholars of Islam."[33] Perhaps because of his anti-Sufi, purist beliefs, SADUM appointed the young Rafiq Qori as *imam-khatib* of the As-Saraxsi Mosque in Kara-Suu in 1983. His former assistant told me that because of Soviet repression of Islam, only twenty to thirty men then performed Friday *namaz* at the mosque. Rafiq Qori studied and taught in a *hujra*, which was always threatened by the KGB.[34] He nonetheless became a respected teacher and religious authority among the predominantly Uzbek-speaking population. Widely known as "the people's imam,"[35] he had followers in Osh, Jalalabat, and Batken provinces as well. Over ten thousand worshipers attended Rafiq Qori's mosque on Fridays. After independence in 1991, they often included Uzbek citizens, who crossed the border when possible

[30] Kurbanova, *Islam v obshchestvenno-politicheskoi zhizni*, 66.

[31] Aurelie Biard, "Power, Original Islam and the Reactivization of a Religious Utopia in Kara-Suu, Kyrgyzstan," in *Being Muslim in Central Asia*, ed. Marlène Laurelle (Leiden: Brill, 2018), 110–29.

[32] Interview with imam, Osh Buxori Mosque, Osh, Kyrgyzstan, July 2005.

[33] Interview with mosque assistant to Rafiq Qori and Rashod Qori, Kara-Suu, Kyrgyzstan, June 2013.

[34] Interview with mosque assistant to Rafiq Qori.

[35] Nurbek Bekmurzaev, "Independent Islam in Central Asia: Reasons behind Independent Islamic Leaders' Resistance towards State Control of Religion in Kyrgyzstan," M.A. thesis, OSCE Academy, Bishkek, 2014.

so that they could worship freely. Rafiq Qori's son claimed that over the next decade he regularly attracted at least twenty thousand followers in Kyrgyzstan.

Rafiq Qori was particularly influenced by the renowned and controversial Imam Abduvali Qori, who lived just across the Kyrgyz-Uzbek border in Andijon, Uzbekistan. Abduvali Qori, whom we met in Chapter 8, would become Rafiq's brother-in-law and spiritual mentor. Following Abduvali, Rafiq split with traditional Hanafi Islam's acceptance of custom, tradition, and certain Soviet practices. He too advocated puritanical ideas against *shirk* (polytheism). In one sermon, Rafiq Qori condemned the International Women's Day celebration, saying, "Soviet Russia came with the socialist system and when communists took over Central Asia, March 8th was a day to burn *paranji*s. It's the day when Muslim women were told . . . 'Show your faces, eyebrows, breasts, necks! Open up!' . . . [Y]our faith burns off and you become a *kafir*. . . . A Muslim man, who has faith . . . protects the hijab.' "[36]

As religious conditions in the Kyrgyz republic improved in the 1980s and 1990s, Rafiq Qori led an Islamic revival in the south, and like his brother, he was a candidate in the Kara-Suu city council election during *perestroika*.[37] In doing so, he rejected what some local scholars have called the "classical Salafism" of his brother and the Mujaddidiya, in several ways.[38] While they focused on theological purism, Rafiq espoused a political theology, criticizing Hanafi Islam's accommodation of the secular state and political quietism, even when the government neither interfered with nor repressed Islam. He openly denounced the Soviet state, and later the democratic state, declaring that both contradicted *shariat*.[39] Rafiq Qori sought religio-political solutions to immorality and injustice in Kyrgyzstan. He was *potentially* a religious entrepreneur, but he did not politically act on his ideas.

Akayev's inclusive treatment of ethnic Uzbeks and the religious freedom of the 1990s led Rafiq Qori, like his brother, to avoid directly challenging Kyrgyzstan's government. They both rejected the path of the IRPT and the IMU. Even when HTI's ideas about the caliphate began spreading, neither brother endorsed the party, criticizing HTI's deviation from "pure Islam."[40] Although openly sympathetic to HTI, Rafiq Qori refused membership. Despite their political leanings, these imams did not engage in religious entrepreneurship; they did not contest power through Islamist party or movement formation.

[36] "Rafiq Qori—8 mart baytami," YouTube, October 11, 2016, https://www.youtube.com/watch?v=QV7rrNkroGM.

[37] Kurbanova, *Islam v obshchestvenno-politicheskoi zhizni*, 65.

[38] Interview with Iskender Ormon uluu; interview with Mamatbek Myrzabayev, Bishkek, Kyrgyzstan, May 2019.

[39] Interview with Mamatbek Myrzabayev; Bekmurzaev, "Independent Islam."

[40] Interview with Sodiqjon Kamoluddin, former *mufti* and director of the International Center for Islamic Cooperation.

As for HTI itself, the movement's ideas and entrepreneurs entered Kyrgyzstan in the late 1990s and early 2000s.[41] Their advocacy of a new caliphate spread through activists and propaganda coming from Uzbekistan's Ferghana Valley. HTI hoped for support among ethnic Uzbeks, such as Rafiq Qori. And yet, these ideas gained little ground for several years.

The Outcome: Islamic Revival without Islamism

A notable consequence of Kyrgyzstan's liberal religious policy was the vibrant proliferation of Islamic teachers, missionaries, mosques, and piety. A widespread and peaceful Islamic revival, characterized by both new and traditional religious forms, foreign and domestic, distinguished Kyrgyzstan from its neighbors.[42] The growth of Islamic identification and belief, practices, institutions, and education all reflected growing Islamization. According to one national survey in 1996, just five years after the USSR's collapse, 55 percent of ethnic Kyrgyz and 87 percent of ethnic Uzbeks in Kyrgyzstan self-identified as Muslim.[43] Those considering themselves Muslim "believers" rose from 93 to 98 percent in national surveys I conducted in 2006 and 2010.[44] Moreover, respondents did not merely claim to be Muslim; in my 2010 national survey, 44 percent of Kyrgyz self-identified as "deeply a believer," as did 81 percent of Uzbek citizens of Kyrgyzstan.[45] Respondents professed that Islamic practices had increased significantly as well—from mosque attendance to fasting and studying the Qur'an.

While the difference between Uzbeks and Kyrgyz was still noticeable, by the late 2000s observance was not primarily in the heavily Uzbek south but was widespread across regions, ethnic groups, and generations. The revival of the 1990s continued, driven by personal interest in Muslim identity, friendship networks among youth, and the strong influence of imams and missionaries, many of whom had come from abroad and then trained local missionaries to bring the *da'wat* (call to Islam). By the 2010s, there were dozens of mosques in Bishkek, and signs of strictly observant religiosity were visible in most places. One needed only to travel half a mile from the government White House to the central mosque to find up to ten thousand men gathered for Friday prayer,

[41] Chapter 9 discusses HTI's prior emergence in Uzbekistan.

[42] Balcı, *Islam in Central Asia*; Emil Nasritdinov, "Spiritual Nomadism and Central Asian Tablighi Travelers," *Ab Imperio*, no. 2 (2012): 145–167.

[43] IFES survey, cited in Eric McGlinchey, "Islamic Revivalism and State Failure in Kyrgyzstan," *Problems of Post-Communism*, May–June 2009.

[44] Collins, Kyrgyzstan national surveys, conducted in 2006 (n = 1100) and 2010 (n = 1200), data in author's possession; Barbara Junisbai, Azamat Junisbai, and Baurzhan Zhussupov, "Two Countries, Five Years: Islam in Kazakhstan and Kyrgyzstan through the Lens of Public Opinion Surveys," in *Being Muslim in Central Asia*, ed. Marlène Laurelle (Leiden: Brill, 2018), 38–61.

[45] Collins, Kyrgyzstan survey, 2010.

so many that the surrounding streets were regularly closed to accommodate the overflow. When I perused the nearby bookstalls, full of religious literature printed in Saudi Arabia, Kuwait, and Pakistan, passersby often invited me to lessons, explaining that they could teach me the "last and true religion." One was Abdulahad, an Islamic missionary (referred to in Kyrgyzstan as a *da'watchi*) who had joined Tablighi Jamaat. He took me to the nearby teahouse to talk about the "correct path of life." Such *da'watchi*s were numerous and influential.

A few miles away, in one of Bishkek's largest outdoor markets, a dried fruit trader named Cholpon invited me to join a women's study group, which met in an unmarked house nearby. It was unregistered, but the government did not crack down on such schools in the north. Attendees included teenage girls, young medical students, mothers with infants, and grandmothers who had migrated to Bishkek from the mountain villages of Naryn *oblast*. Over a hundred women packed into a large room on Saturdays, in sweltering summer heat, with barely space to breathe; on weekdays, only a few dozen came, as many were obligated to work. The teacher, an ethnic Kyrgyz-Tatar woman, was a former labor migrant to Russia. There, she had become acquainted with an Islamic *domla* who convinced her to become "a real Muslim." For over ten years she had been preaching a puritanical interpretation of Islam, influenced by Egyptian and Saudi texts she had received from her son, who had studied in Cairo and then Medina. Such study had formerly been highly unusual in northern Kyrgyzstan, but by the 2000s these semi-legal house schools existed by the hundreds.

Nor did the women who attended them remain at the margins of society. Women in hijab—some colorful and excessively fashionable, some dark and severe—could be seen dining, shopping, and working throughout Bishkek, where hijab shops did a prosperous business. These women strolled among their secular counterparts, who donned tight miniskirts and low-cut blouses. Even on Bishkek's central Moskovskaya Street, where many shopped for European products, a luxury women's Muslim boutique displayed photos of attractive Arab models in hijab, currying the approval of wealthy Kyrgyz women. Even "Miss Kyrgyzstan" publicly encouraged other young women to express their beauty in a moral, Islamic fashion.[46] A tense, but stable multiculturalism had emerged as Kyrgyzstanis continually debated among themselves—in families, villages, universities, and politics—what kind of Muslim they should be and what role Islam should play in education and the public sphere.

Meanwhile, in the heavily Uzbek south, some elements of the more strictly observant Islamic culture had also become increasingly conservative in dress and

[46] Will Worley, "'My faith is irrelevant': Former Beauty Queen Defends Decision to Wear Hijab," *Independent*, October 5, 2016, https://www.independent.co.uk/news/people/aikol-alikzhanova-hijab-beauty-queen-kyrgyzstan-miss-world-islam-muslim-a7345651.html.

practice, as Arab donations to mosques, *madrasas*, and NGOs had proliferated.[47] Throughout the bustling streets of Osh, young men commonly wore beards, and the central mosque was overflowing on Fridays. Women wore everything from black *chadors* to colorful local headscarves. Wandering through the labyrinthine bazaar, I encountered shop after shop of young women selling the new hijab styles; some students enrolled in Osh State University instructed me on the proper way to wear the Muslim headscarf. At a crowded new upscale Osh restaurant, men and women were overwhelmingly segregated. My three female companions, university students already in hijab, debated among themselves whether it was necessary to cover their entire face and hands, as did those belonging to a new puritanical group, Yakin Inkar. An offshoot of Tablighi Jamaat that formed its own movement around 2014 and quickly gained followers, Yakin Inkar was even more puritanical in its religious interpretation. Yakin Inkar sought to follow the path of Muslim life in the seventh century, which it interpreted as segregating women from men and enforcing the *paranji*.

Religious revival was also reflected in observance of the pillars of Islam. In 1990, only 40 individuals from the entire USSR had made the hajj. In 1991, 350 went from Kyrgyzstan alone. By 2003, that figure was 3,000.[48] Soon thereafter, about 4,500 Kyrgyzstanis went every year. Thousands more applications were turned down because Saudi Arabia's quota for Kyrgyzstan was full.[49]

Fasting during Ramadan became another widespread symbol of re-Islamization, even in Bishkek. In 2019, in contrast to a decade earlier, Kyrgyz friends invited me to dine only after sundown during Ramadan. Fasting was observed by 37 percent of Kyrgyz and 57 percent of Uzbeks in 2010. *Namaz* was also widespread; 24 percent of Kyrgyz and 50 percent of Uzbeks regularly performed *namaz*.[50] On *Eid-al-Fitr*, as many as fifteen thousand men and boys gathered to pray in Bishkek's old central square. Most walked there, and the streets of Bishkek were a flood of men, some in typical Western dress, others in the flowing *shalwar kameez* of Pakistan or the "short pants worn by Salafis," as some disapproving locals called them. Mosque attendance—which is expected of Muslim men on Friday—had been abysmally low throughout the USSR due to fear of punishment, but now 40 percent of Kyrgyzstani Muslim men attended once a month or more, and 26 percent attended at least weekly.[51]

The institutional basis of Islam grew exponentially. More mosques than schools had been built in Kyrgyzstan since 1991. According to one Kyrgyz

[47] Kadyr Malikov, "Muslim Community in Kyrgyzstan: Social Activity and the Present Stage," Report, Social Research Center, American University of Central Asia, Bishkek, 2010.

[48] Interview with staff, SCRA, Bishkek, Kyrgyzstan, May 2005.

[49] Interview with Kanatbek Murzakhalilov, deputy director, State Committee on Religious Affairs, Bishkek, Kyrgyzstan, May 2007.

[50] Collins, Kyrgyzstan national survey, 2010.

[51] Collins, Kyrgyzstan national survey, 2010.

NGO director, in his village of five thousand in Osh province, there were now five mosques but only one school and one kindergarten for an overwhelmingly young population.[52] Overall, the number of legally registered mosques increased from 39 in 1991 to almost 1,000 a decade later; by the end of the Akayev era, they numbered 1,598.[53] Unlike in Uzbekistan and Tajikistan, many mosques were entirely new.[54]

Performing *namaz* and attending mosque had been relatively uncommon in Kyrgyzstan even before the Soviet era, when few mosques had existed among the nomads. Moreover, proficiency in Arabic had been almost nonexistent, so few knew how to pray or attend mosque. Yet weekly sermons now took place in Uzbek, Kyrgyz, and even Russian, so that mosque-goers could choose an imam preaching in a language they could follow. Growing attendance reflected trust; Eric McGlinchey's study found that confidence in the mosque was higher than in state institutions.[55]

Meanwhile, cultural practices and civic life became increasingly strict and Islamic. Consumption of alcohol and intermingling of the sexes became less common at weddings. Many women still wore European-style gowns, but, as Julie McBrien has argued, participants valued the ceremony as an opportunity to learn about Islam from the officiating imam.[56] Marva TV, founded in 2004 by a prominent conservative Muslim leader, pushed for more traditional roles for women, even underage marriage, to prevent prostitution and immorality. Ayan TV, broadcasting since 2015, advocated living by *shariat*. A halal meat shop opened up on the avenue formerly named after the Russian tsarist military commander General Mikhail Vasilyevich Frunze. Halal taxi drivers banned customers who drank or smoked and required moral conduct with women in their cabs. EkoIslamikBank, an Islamic banking firm, began lending to *shariat*-compliant firms.

Religious education also became widespread. Focus group participants reported that they had learned *namaz* from grandparents, friends, books, websites, or even Instagram.[57] Islamic knowledge grew as religious publications

[52] Interview with Keneshbek Sainazarov, Search for Common Ground, Washington, D.C., November 2018.

[53] Omurzak Mamayusupov, Kanatbek Murzahalilov, Kanybek Mamataliev, et al., *Islam v Kyrgyzstane: Tendentsii Razvitiia* (Osh: Goskommissiia PKR po Delam Religii, 2004), 356.

[54] Interview with staff, SCRA, Bishkek, Kyrgyzstan, January 2003.

[55] McGlinchey, "Islamic Revivalism"; Collins survey, 2010.

[56] Julie McBrien, "Listening to the Wedding Speaker: Discussing Religion and Culture in Southern Kyrgyzstan," *Central Asian Survey* 25, no. 3 (2006): 41–57.

[57] See also Emil Nasritdinov, Zarina Urmanbetova, Kanatbek Murzakhalilov, and Mametbek Myrzabaev, "Vulnerability and Resilience of Young People in Kyrgyzstan to Radicalization, Violence and Extremism: Analysis across Five Domains," Central Asia Program, Paper no. 213, Institute for European, Russian, and Eurasian Studies, The George Washington University, Washington, D.C., January 2019.

proliferated; Kyrgyz and Russian translations of works by scholars in Saudi Arabia, Turkey, and Tatarstan were sold widely. Kyrgyz scholars also published religious texts.[58] The topics ranged from instructions on performing *namaz* to explanations of the names of Allah. Many larger volumes dealt with the *shariat* or the foundations of Islam, such as *200 Questions for Believing in Islam* and *The Call*, both Arab works translated into Russian and printed inside Russia. Beginning in the early 1990s, the presence of such literature had steadily increased; it was sold cheaply outside of mosques, in kiosks, at bazaars, and in specialty bookstores.

Self-education was supplemented by formal and informal instruction. The State Commission on Religious Affairs (SCRA) registered 243 Islamic missionaries from Egypt, Pakistan, and elsewhere in 1996–99; many more preached unregistered.[59] There were thirty-seven registered *madrasa*s in 2004, and sixty-seven in 2013.[60] *Madrasa* enrollments increased substantially to over 3,300 students annually.[61] In Bishkek alone there were also dozens of unregistered "house *madrasas*" which anyone could attend. Religious training abroad surged as well; thousands studied in Turkey, Egypt, Kuwait, Saudi Arabia, Pakistan, Bangladesh, Malaysia, and elsewhere, where religious donors or governments sponsored their education.[62] Many returned as imams. The state kept few data on these exchanges for two decades.[63]

Local religious activists also spread *da'wat,* traveling throughout the country, even to remote mountain villages.[64] Interviews suggest that their numbers were high. I frequently saw *da'watchi*s congregating around rented buses outside the central mosque. In the mid-2000s, although only 248 were registered, SCRA believed that there were about 2,000 *da'watchi*s proselytizing Islam.[65] Many mullahs, teachers, and ordinary Muslims pursued *da'wat* unofficially.[66] SAMK and SCRA did not require certification before registration for well over a decade.[67] By 2015, 2,500 imams were registered.

[58] Interview with Jamal Frontbek kyzy, director, Mutakallim, Bishkek, Kyrgyzstan, July 2010.

[59] Interview with imam, Jalalabat, Kyrgyzstan, July 2010; interview with *madrasa* students, Jalalabat, Kyrgyzstan, 2005.

[60] Mamaiusupov et al., *Islam v Kyrgyzstane*; interview with SRCA officials, Bishkek, Kyrgyzstan, 2013.

[61] Interview with staff, SCRA, Bishkek, Kyrgyzstan, November 2010.

[62] Author conversations with first secretary, Embassy of Turkey, Bishkek, Kyrgyzstan, 1995; author interview with member, Adep Bashaty, Bishkek, Kyrgyzstan, 2013; David Abramson, "Foreign Religious Education and the Central Asian Islamic Revival," Central Asia Caucasus Institute-Silk Road Studies Program, Washington, D.C., March 2010.

[63] Interview with Kanatbek Murzakhalilov SCRA, May 2013.

[64] Interview with administrative personnel, SAMK (still known as the *muftiyat*), Bishkek, Kyrgyzstan, June 2013; conversations with *da'watchi*s, Bishkek, near main mosque, June 2013, May 2019.

[65] Interview with Kanatbek Murzakhalilov and researchers, SCRA, Bishkek, Kyrgyzstan, May 2013.

[66] Interview with Jazgulya, assistant to the *mufti* of Kyrgyzstan, Bishkek, Kyrgyzstan, May 2007.

[67] Interview with Haji Lugmar, deputy *mufti* of Kyrgyzstan, Bishkek, Kyrgyzstan, May 2007.

Foreign education opportunities were also available within Kyrgyzstan. In 1992, the Turkish Fethullah Gülen movement established private religious schools in Kyrgyzstan that still operate widely; they emphasized education without corruption, religiously grounded morality, and humanism, but followed the secular state curriculum.[68] A more conservative Gülenist trend was the Nursi movement, which, its adherents boasted, "was active in preserving Islam against Atatürk, Marx, and Darwin." Smaller and facing more suspicion from the government, this sect gathered merely to read books and listen to teachers. "The most active [students] are the youth . . . many nationalities, but mostly Kyrgyz," according to Aliya, a female adherent.[69] Some attendees, like her, also studied in registered *madrasa*s. Meanwhile, the Turkish Diyanet Foundation developed the Faculty of Theology at Osh University in the 1990s. Its teachers criticized Sufi practices such as shrine visitation; they claimed that the pilgrimage to Takhti Sulayman was un-Islamic, the result of "Shamanist influence."[70] Turkish influence was political too; Turkey built Bishkek's grandiose new Imam Sarakhsi Mosque, which opened for worship in 2018 with room for twenty thousand worshipers. It far exceeded the old central mosque in capacity and beauty. President Erdoğan of Turkey called the mosque "a symbol of unity and solidarity . . . of one *umma*."[71]

Tablighi Jamaat, a global Islamic revivalist movement from South Asia, was even more influential[72] in gaining followers across Kyrgyzstan in the 1990s and 2000s. Its mission was to re-Islamize post-Soviet Central Asians, especially in Kyrgyzstan, where secularization had been particularly strong. One Tablighi Jamaat *da'watchi* lamented:

> In the USSR people became atheist and didn't know Allah. The communists gave everything for free to win them over, and the Communist Party acted as Allah. His prophet was Lenin. . . . Kyrgyz accepted the USSR because faith was weak. For example, in one village of fifty homes, half did not pray already. Then the NKVD and KGB carried out purges in the whole region. Many fled. . . . Those who remained became communists. . . . The Basmachi in the Ferghana Valley wanted to preserve Islam, so the Soviets called them "bandits." . . . My grandfather, a Tatar imam, nearly died of hunger. The USSR began to use schools and modernization, the railroad, to control us. . . . Our

[68] Communications with students, Bishkek, Kyrgyzstan, May 2013; communications with graduates of Sebat school, Bishkek, Kyrgyzstan, January 2010, May 2013, June 2019. For an excellent discussion, see: Balcı, *Islam in Central Asia*, 53–65.

[69] Interview with Aliya, Nursi adherent, Bishkek, Kyrgyzstan, August 2015.

[70] Interview with P. Pınarbaşı, teacher, Osh Theological Institute, Osh, July 2005.

[71] "Bishkek Republic Central Imam Sarakhsi Mosque Opened to Worship with Prayers," Diyanet, November 14, 2018, https://www.diyanet.gov.tr/en-US/Content/PrintDetail/11921.

[72] Barbara Metcalf, "Travelers' Tales in the Tablighi Jamaat," *Annals of the American Academy of Political and Social Science* 588, no. 1 (July 2003): 136–48.

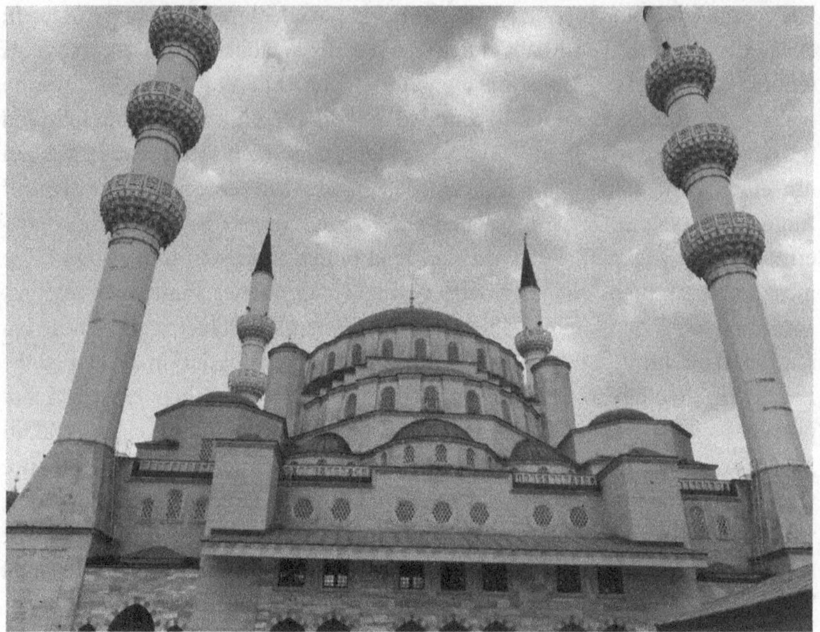

Image 11.2 Imam Sarakhsi Mosque in Bishkek, Kyrgyzstan
Source: Author's photo collection

> republic suffered terribly! . . . Even in the 1970s–1980s we lived as if in a "camp." But the propaganda on the TV said we're the very best country, everything in the USSR is good. People agreed to Russian technology, TV, clothes, streets, and it changed the psychology of the people. The new generation became one hundred percent like Europeans, totally atheist, drinking alcohol, narcotics, free marriages. People didn't know who Muhammad was. In Osh, Jalalabat, and Batken, there was also little faith, but they were less atheist than the north, few mixed marriages. No one fasted. . . . It was communist ideology, but in their souls, Allah was still there.[73]

He related the Soviet collapse to Afghanistan and Islam: "Muslims didn't want to shoot Muslims in the Afghan war, but the USSR sent a whole Muslim battalion. . . . Allah took away the USSR." He did not pitch global Islamism. Instead, he appealed to the Kyrgyz experience of repression and loss. He said that the renowned Kyrgyz author "Chyngyz Aitmatov talked about the soul. People have searched for their roots, religious roots. Our *aksakals* (male elder; literally, a white beard) began to send their grandsons to study Islam, and it quickly

[73] Interview with Tablighi Jamaat elder and religious scholar, Bishkek, Kyrgyzstan, June 2018.

spread among the Kyrgyz. Now they too are proselytizing Islam." The *da'watchi*'s knowledge of Islam and recollection of the Soviet era were deeper than most. As a respected elder, he articulated a narrative of Muslim suffering to persuade Kyrgyzstanis to return to Islam.

Tablighi Jamaat's program initially appeared at odds with Kyrgyz Islam. It advocated dress modeled on traditional Pakistani-style clothing for men, and for women, the hijab—plain and conservative, sometimes black. This was immediately noticeable both in the villages and in cities.[74] Young men grew long beards, atypical and even culturally offensive in Kyrgyz and Uzbek society, where a beard was the sign of a respected elder, an *aksakal*. Tablighi Jamaat's theology emphasized knowing the Qur'an and *sunna*; the group's scripturalist focus seemed alienating to ethnic Kyrgyz.[75] Yet, it successfully spread its message of leaving behind Soviet customs and becoming better Muslims. It also adapted to the Kyrgyz context; it rejected both the theological purism and political implications of some Salafist groups. Its members did not condemn shrine visitation and other customary practices, as long as they joined in Qur'an reading.[76] Its door-to-door *da'wat* worked well with a populace unaccustomed to mosque attendance or *madrasas*. Its ideas were passed on through oral teaching, similar to Kyrgyz oral tradition.[77] Additionally, its ideology attracted those lacking rigorous, scripture-based Islamic knowledge, particularly ethnic Kyrgyz in the north. Ethnic Kyrgyz often viewed Tablighi Jamaat as bringing them "real Islam."[78] They appreciated its focus on the simple life, being a good Muslim. As one member, Ali, said, "Most other Islamic groups have the goal of creating an Islamic state. But Tablighi Jamaat's goal is to help people, to direct them to the right path."[79] By one estimate, in the 2010s the organization had up to 100,000 members in Kyrgyzstan; many analysts concur that Tablighi Jamaat had become the most popular movement in the country.[80]

[74] Interview with Mukaram Toktogulova, professor, American University of Central Asia, Bishkek, Kyrgyzstan, May 2013.

[75] Emil Nasritdinov, "Translocality and the Folding of Post-Soviet Urban Space in Bishkek," in *Mobilities, Boundaries, and Travelling Ideas: Rethinking Translocality Beyond Central Asia and the Caucasus*, ed. Manja Stephan-Emmrich and Philipp Schröder (Cambridge, UK: Open Book Publishers, 2018), 319–48.

[76] Mukaram Toktogulova, "The Localization of the Transnational Tablighi Jama'at Network in Kyrgyzstan," in *Islam, Society, and Politics in Central Asia*, ed. Pauline Jones (Pittsburgh, PA: University of Pittsburgh Press, 2017), 223–42.

[77] Nasritdinov, "Spiritual Nomadism and Central Asian Tablighi Travelers."

[78] Interview with Emil Nasritdinov, American University of Central Asia, Bishkek, Kyrgyzstan, May 2013, December 2018; interview with Tablighi Jamaat adherent, Bishkek, Kyrgyzstan, June 2013; interview with Mukaram Toktogulova, AUCU, Bishkek, Kyrgyzstan, May 2013.

[79] Interview with Ali, Tablighi Jamaat adherent, Osh, Kyrgyzstan, August 2015.

[80] Igor Rotar, "Pakistani Islamic missionary group establishes a strong presence in Central Asia," *Eurasianet*, July 23, 2007, https://www.refworld.org/docid/46a883eca.html; Nasritdinov, "Spiritual Nomadism and Central Asian Tablighi Travelers."

Tablighi Jamaat took no public political positions and sought to avoid even the appearance of having a political agenda or of creating a political movement. Its members claimed only to desire freedom of religion and to teach Islam. Yet, it still raised suspicion among secularists because it was wholly outside of government control and its appearance was jarring to many Kyrgyz raised during the Soviet era or to those favoring Westernization.

Another trend within the Islamic revival was largely Arab, reflecting the influence of Al-Azhar University in Cairo, as well as that of Saudi Arabia, Kuwait, and Jordan. Those associated with this trend considered themselves "pure" and "orthodox" in belief, dress, and practice; some were Salafist. Many Arabs provided money for mosque-building after 1991, and some offered Islamic education to Kyrgyzstani students.[81] The teacher of the women's *madrasa* (mentioned earlier) adopted a curriculum based on her son's Egyptian and Saudi texts, which she claimed emphasized purism. She also focused on teaching the correct role for Muslim women—being a mother and obedient wife—rather than participating in the labor force and stated that "women do not need secular knowledge, only Islamic [knowledge]." Women in this *madrasa* were taught to wear a dark and plain hijab; bright clothes shamefully attracted notice. Red, I was told, was "the color of the devil" and "forbidden"; the clothing of most Kyrgyz women was similarly "sinful." Although proclaiming herself Hanafi, not Salafi, the teacher condemned many Kyrgyz practices as un-Islamic; "pilgrimages to Suleyman and Turkistan [we]re great sins," and visiting springs was heresy, she said, since "the only holy water is in Mecca." Kyrgyz "*Eid* celebrations are wrong," she said, as are "their memorials for the dead and crying loudly at funerals." The *madrasa*'s ideas about other religions were likewise more akin to Salafist views than to Hanafi and Sufi views typical of Central Asia. The *madrasa* teachers branded Christians and Jews as *kafir* and the "cause of all evils."[82] Notably, the central Kyrgyzstan Islamic University (formerly a smaller institute) in Bishkek under the *muftiyat* taught many of the same strict and puritanical ideas and interpretations of Islam in the mid-2000s, in contrast to the national syncretism of Sufism and Hanafi Islam espoused previously. Students at the institute, many of whom came from northern, mountainous regions of Kyrgyzstan such as Naryn, where nomadic and Sufi practices once were the norm, now idealized "Islam in Arabia." They also strongly identified with Arab political issues, such as Palestine. Many expressed stridently anti-American views, shaped especially by their understanding of U.S. support for Israel and the war in Iraq.[83]

[81] Interview with Rector Asan Sulaimanovich Ormushev, Nongovernmental Oriental University, named after Mahmud Kashkari-Barskani, Bishkek, Kyrgyzstan, May 2007. The university received funding from Kuwait.

[82] Interview with teacher, women's mosque, Bishkek, Kyrgyzstan, June 2018.

[83] Interview with women's *madrasa* teacher, and interview with a group of women students, Kyrgyzstan Islamic University, Bishkek, Kyrgyzstan, May 2010.

While secular elites often exaggerate the phenomenon of "Arab money," a foreign, puritanical trend evidently existed; dozens of such *madrasas* had organized around Bishkek alone. Kuwaiti and Egyptian donors and organizations giving moral guidance comprised other elements of this conservative Islamic movement. Its activists sought to Islamize society and to bring Islam back into the public square.

Outcome: Civil Islamic Activism without Islamism

Kyrgyzstan's liberalization of religion, and its broader associational space, effectively "deprivatized" Islam; that is, it allowed Islam back into the public sphere, after nearly seventy years of totally secular public space.[84] It also led to the growth of Islamic activism—not Islamism—a revivalist trend that continued through the 2000s. Although Islamic activists are often associated with Salafism and a mission to re-create the caliphate or Islamic state, the Kyrgyzstani case suggests that when Islam is not repressed and politicized by state policy—as in Kyrgyzstan's north throughout most of its post-Soviet independence, and in the south before 2005—many religious actors reject Islamism. Instead, in a society in which Islam is no longer forcibly kept out of the public square, religious actors may advocate what Robert Hefner calls "civil Islam."[85] Islam was no longer shuttered behind one's apartment walls or inside one's family plot, and Muslim believers, NGOs, and leaders could make their views known on many public and political issues. Kyrgyzstan was following, in some respects, on a much smaller scale, the path of Indonesia (without legalizing an Islamic party); Islam had a place in civic discourse and behavior. Civil Islam in Kyrgyzstan has often worked to the advantage of Kyrgyzstani society and the state by aiding in women's education and caring for the poor. Still, civil Islam's vocal presence in the public square often unnerved secular elites. A decade into independence, the hijab, religious education, and marriage law all became points of heated debate between secularists and religious conservatives.

Within the sphere of civil Islam, one of the most notable religious leaders to challenge the secular-religious divide was Jamal Frontbek kyzy, who in 2000 had founded Mutakallim (Arabic, for "knowledge") as a "progressive" and Islamic women's organization. Frontbek kyzy's experience of being told to remove her veil at an airport passport control had triggered her civic and political activism. Mutakallim offered a striking contrast to the many more conservative Islamic

[84] Casanova, *Public Religions*, 211.
[85] Hefner, *Civil Islam*.

groups to emerge in the post-Soviet era, such as Yakin Inkar.[86] Mutakallim also challenged the patriarchal religious conservatism of Hanafi Central Asian Islam, which taught women subservience in the private sphere. Mutakallim's message and activism exhibited a distinctive Muslim modernity. Its "primary goal was the spread of Islam among women," a religious agenda, but it also "sought to elevate Muslim women's rights . . . through education, aid to women and charity."[87] Mutakallim offered women an Islamic education to counter patriarchy, underage marriage, and domestic abuse. It provided women knowledge of their constitutional rights and religious knowledge so that they could assert their rights under *shariat*. The group began offering free Arabic study, aided by Kuwait, and published a monthly religious newspaper. It provided care for women's health issues, charity for the indigent, and religious books for students.[88]

Frontbek kyzy also sought to make the hijab mainstream in Kyrgyzstan by Islamizing Kyrgyz society, where Russian norms for women had prevailed since Soviet times. She pressed the government to end the pressure to become "modern" and "European." Having won the legal right for Muslim women to wear the hijab in passport photos, Mutakallim became a legal defender of girls across the country who were evicted from schools and universities and of women who were wrongly denied work because they veiled. In a very public demonstration of their movement, Mutakallim organized a "bicycle march" of five hundred women in hijab, en route to donate blood. They sought to dispel stereotypes of the hijab as antimodern and extremist.

Frontbek kyzy developed friendly relations with the state because she publicly accepted the Constitution and legislative framework on religion, preached against extremism and violence, and actively developed projects to circumvent women's radicalization, which was growing after 2011. Mutakallim encouraged women's education and participation in society, unlike both traditionalists and Salafists. There were limits to Mutakallim's "modernity," however; it opposed Christian proselytism and Christian burial in Muslim cemeteries. It also opposed secularism. Frontbek kyzy said, "I don't like the word 'secularism.' Because of it many women suffer. Under a secular government the state has no religion." Nonetheless, Mutakallim accepted secular parties and elections. In the October 2020 parliamentary election, it organized a campaign against vote-buying. Unlike other Muslim leaders, Frontbek kyzy endorsed democracy: "Let the country be democratic, but at the same time respect the citizens and freedom to practice one's belief."[89]

[86] Interview with Salafi adherents, Osh, May 2013, June 2019, and Bishkek, Kyrgyzstan, June 2018 and June 2019.

[87] Interview with Jamal Frontbek kyzy.

[88] Interview with Jamal Frontbek kyzy.

[89] Interview with Jamal Frontbek kyzy.

Other Islamic organizations and teachers also held political views shaped by their religious beliefs and education, views that sometimes led them to engage in Muslim politics and spark debate about Islam's public role. The Islamic charity named after Imam Bakyt worked in the educational sector, hoping to bring to Kyrgyzstan purist norms about women's segregation and the need for *shariat* as law. In 2010, in the context of the constitutional debate, Imam Bakyt wholly rejected the document because it designated Kyrgyzstan as "secular." The organization's representative said, "America is secular, religious and democratic. . . . But in Kyrgyzstan, in Osh and Jalalabat and everywhere in the government we have corruption. It comes from one thing. In Kyrgyzstan there is no religion. . . . Religion teaches morality."[90]

SAMK officials took a similar position. One deputy imam said, "We in Kyrgyzstan are constantly in decline [politically and economically]. I'm not calling you to perform *namaz* or fast, but let's talk about morals, values, behavior. If we will become closer to the Qur'an and Allah, do what Allah asks, then the country will develop. . . . Otherwise, there will be a cataclysm. . . . We have a spiritual, moral crisis."[91] He went on, "We need a democracy, but not like the West's."[92] Another civic organization, the Social and Progressive Fund Adep Bashaty, founded by Kyrgyzstani graduates of Egyptian universities and funded by Kyrgyz businessmen, sought to spread Salafist values and law.[93] One activist, having studied in Saudi Arabia and Egypt, advocated proper female dress and behavior to improve society.[94] Another demanded, "Why shouldn't religion influence state law? I know that in some Arab states, religion directly affects their laws. For example, the laws on divorce and marriage all are taken from religious laws. . . . It's not a caliphate. A caliphate is something else. Laws made by man will inevitably have mistakes."[95] A renowned theologian, Kadyr Malikov, countered, "We can talk about a secular state's [problems] . . . but it's too early to talk about an Islamic republic. . . . We are not ready for that . . . to accept *shariat* norms."[96]

Since independence, some younger ethnic Kyrgyz imams also advocated a more activist role for Islam in public life, law, and politics. One in particular, Shaykh Chubak ajy Jalilov (chief *mufti* in 2010–12), gained a wide following by promoting Islamic values in the public sphere. Although not an Islamist, his deep

[90] Interview with Iman Bakyt NGO, Bishkek, Kyrgyzstan, May 2013.
[91] Interview with deputy *mufti*, Bishkek, Kyrgyzstan, August 2010.
[92] Interview with deputy *mufti*.
[93] Malikov, "Muslim Community in Kyrgyzstan"; Yanti Holzchen, "Religious Education and Cultural Change: The Case of Madrasas in Northern Kyrgyzstan," in *Approaching Ritual Economy*, ed. Roland Hardenberg (Tubingen: University of Tubingen Press, 2017), 105–34.
[94] Interview with activist, Adep Bashaty, Bishkek, Kyrgyzstan, June 2013.
[95] Interview with activist, Adep Bashaty, Osh, Kyrgyzstan, August 2010.
[96] Kadyr Malikov, "Rostu religioznykh radikal'nikh organizatsii mozhet protivodeiststvovat' tol'ko rost religioznogo samosoznaniia," Bishkek, Kyrgyzstan, October 20, 2010, n.p., courtesy of the author.

Islamic knowledge and calls for Islamic rights led him to become embroiled in several conflicts with the government. As *mufti*, Chubak ajy justified certain Islamist ideas, such as the adoption of some *shariat* as law. He lobbied for a parliamentary bill to change the Labor Code to allow a two-hour work break on Fridays so that Muslims could perform *juma namaz*; secular elites staunchly blocked the bill. He responded by threatening to refuse *janaza* (funeral rites) for deputies who opposed the *shariat*-based legislation. Deputies and members of government accused him of illegally violating secularism.[97] The highly publicized rift led Kadyr Malikov to again intervene: "The position expressed by Chubak ajy Jalilov was a purely private, civic point of view and does not violate the constitutional norm on freedom of expression. Unfortunately, we are faced with an extremely radical and even aggressive idea of secularism in an atheistic context. In a democratic, secular state, the laws of the country must also take into account the rights of the believing part of the population to perform rituals on Friday or Sunday. Where are the equal civil rights of believers?"[98] Malikov and Chubak ajy represented a view similar to that of Haji Turajonzoda and the Islamic Revival Party of Tajikistan, that radical secularism should not block the rights of believers in a democracy. They denied that public expression of religion was a threat to democracy. After resigning as *mufti*, the shaykh remained a prominent public figure. He continued to preach via YouTube, Facebook, and television. Just one video, a lecture on morality and women's sins, had over eighty-two thousand views in just over two years.[99]

Although conceding that democracy was necessary, the former *mufti* was also openly critical of it, particularly the immorality of Western films, sexual norms, media, and social practices that had become widespread since independence. He vociferously opposed the LGBTQ movement and supported legislation to ban it. He fomented controversy by taking a second wife extralegally, announcing it, and calling on other men to practice polygyny to aid widows and poor women.[100] He was challenging the secular nature of democracy, and secularists responded angrily. For example, Aziza Abdurasulova, head of the prominent human rights organization Kylym Shamy, pronounced that Chubak ajy Jalilov "has knowingly broken the law and is encouraging citizens to do the same. . . . Kylym Shamy will file an official statement to the Bishkek prosecutor's office."[101]

[97] Interview with Kanatbek Murzakhalilov, SCRA, Bishkek, Kyrgyzstan, May 2013.

[98] Kadyr Malikov, "Conflict between Jalilov and Akayev Must Be Settled," *Radio Azattyq*, June 10, 2016.

[99] #Насаат_Медиа #жашоодогу_суроолор #Сунна_маселеси, "Чоң күнөөлөр 2-сабак СУРОО-ЖООП. Аялзатына сабак," Шейх Чубак ажы, YouTube, October 29, 2017, https://www.youtube.com/watch?v=V_fxBx-Q35U.

[100] Interview with Dr. Elvira Ilibezova, El-Pikr Center for Public Opinion, Bishkek, Kyrgyzstan, June 2019.

[101] Sherie Ryder and Maruf Sydykov, "'My First Wife Is Upset a Little': Kyrgyz Scholar on Polygamy," *BBC Monitoring*, November 28, 2017.

Supporters meanwhile praised the former *mufti* on blogs and Facebook, claiming that Kyrgyzstan was finally moving toward *shariat*. Despite, or because of, such controversies, Chubak ajy continued to be one of the most respected imams in Kyrgyzstan. He weighed in on other public debates, including the 2016 presidential election, and sparked accusations from the secular elite that he was violating the separation of religion and state.[102]

Despite his call for a more public Islam and some law according to *shariat*, Chubak ajy was not extremist. He supported Kyrgyz statehood, not a transnational caliphate. He wore the Kyrgyz *kolpak* (national felt hat) and displayed Kyrgyzstan's flag in his office. He used his Facebook page to praise the secular Kyrgyz novelist and Nobel laureate, Chyngyz Aitmatov, as "a great Turkic writer." He supported secular education as well as Islamic study, and asked Arabs to spend less money on building mosques and more on building schools. He posted links to Hanafi Islamic literature and lessons on the Qur'an and rejected the Salafism of the former *mufti*, Sodiqjon Qori, and his brother, Rafiq Qori. He advocated for moral politics under democracy, which he claimed was the "closest system to Islam," despite its problems. His views were illiberal, but he rejected an Islamic state, a utopian caliphate, and militant jihad.

Neither Frontbek kyzy nor Chubak ajy founded a movement or party to contest political power, but they were critical voices leading the return of public Islam in post-Soviet Kyrgyzstan. They lobbied on behalf of the religious population before the secular state. Other, smaller Islamic groups and movements similarly promoted civil Islam, not Islamism. Gülenist teachers and graduates extolled the virtues of democracy and emphasized personal, *shariat*-grounded morality as a way to eliminate corruption.[103] Their modernist outlook emphasized secular education for men and women.[104] Nursi followers also criticized corruption and current political conditions, but they sought a less liberal democracy through religious restrictions on blasphemy. They advocated legal polygyny and a more traditional Islamic role for women. One Nursi adherent declared, "Democracy already exists in Islam. . . . I agree and disagree with a secular constitution. If we will live by *shariat* it will be better. Look, we say that there is democracy in Kyrgyzstan, but in reality, there is none. . . . We have no results from our government. What did [President] Akayev or [his successor, President] Bakiyev do? A strongly believing person wouldn't have led that way. . . . I think there should be an Islamic party. Turkey is a good model. The president and prime minister

[102] Uran Botobekov, "Kyrgyzstan's Self-Defeating Conflict with Moderate Islam," *The Diplomat*, June 22, 2016.

[103] Interviews with Gülenist teachers, Bishkek and Osh, Kyrgyzstan, May 2013, Bishkek, May 2019, Osh, Kyrgyzstan, June 2019.

[104] Interview with Nurlan Kudaiberdiev, director of Sapat Educational Network, Bishkek, Kyrgyzstan, May 2019.

are Muslims."[105] He was clearly disaffected with the existing government and preferred a more Islamic system, but unsure what that would entail—*shariat* or possibly a Muslim-style democracy in which an Islamic party and more moral Muslim politicians governed. Both Gülenists and Nursi adherents claimed their *da'wat* was a "struggle with atheism," and they rejected political activism, but they nonetheless held political preferences for more religious governance.[106]

Tablighi Jamaat was an even more prominent example of a religious movement that neither directly engaged in political debate nor founded a political movement to contest power, but nevertheless prompted Kyrgyzstanis to question the proper role of Islam in civic life. Tablighi Jamaat adherents were tolerant of other religions and sects and expressed support for democracy in principle because it "respected Islam" and "was not in contradiction to Islam." Tablighi Jamaat articulated no public position on government. Yet, members privately expressed a preference for a legal system that integrated *shariat* in some way. Aziza said, "We don't need a caliphate. [Democracy] is necessary, but it would be good if some elements of democracy were founded on Muslim *shariat*." She believed that "*shariat* courts would be more just" than the current system. "If there were religious leaders who could influence the government, then it would be different. If laws were reworked on the basis of *shariat*, then a person would fear Allah and not break them. Now no one fears the law."[107] Her deep piety affected her political views. Ali, also a Tablighi Jamaat follower, similarly said, "We need democracy, but both Muslims and non-Muslims in government must respect Islam. The laws of *shariat* are more just. If the existing courts were just then we wouldn't need *shariat* courts. We don't need a caliphate. The most important thing is a just president. Now there is no justice."[108] Nasibakhon explained her desire for Muslim democracy, different from the current system: "Democracy is freedom in all spheres. Yes, we need democracy, but Kyrgyzstan needs a Muslim democracy—let people wear Muslim dress, let them develop themselves freely in all spheres, let them have Muslim courts, which would be more just, and some laws on the basis of *shariat*—like marriage, divorce, women, and homosexuality."[109] Asadullah said, "Religion and state must be separate, and we don't get into the affairs of government and political power, but it's important that . . . a good government put people on the right path," not a caliphate, but democracy with limits on blasphemy, and the full right to wear hijab; "adhering to the law," he said, should be "follow[ing] the *shariat*."[110] Other members expressed

[105] Interview with A, student at Islamic University and Nursi adherent, Bishkek, Kyrgyzstan, July 2012.
[106] Interview with Nursi adherent, Bishkek, Kyrgyzstan, August 2015.
[107] Interview with Aziza, Tablighi Jamaat adherent, Osh, Kyrgyzstan, August 2015.
[108] Interview with Ali, Tablighi Jamaat adherent, Osh, Kyrgyzstan, August 2015.
[109] Interview with Nasibakhon, Tablighi Jamaat adherent, Osh, Kyrgyzstan, August 2015.
[110] Interview with Asadulla, Tablighi Jamaat adherent, Osh, Kyrgyzstan, August 2015.

criticism of the West's sexual mores, "phony Islam," and the U.S. role in Iraq and Syria. They branded Chechen and Kurdish Islamists as "terrorists," but also deplored the "genocide" of those ethnic groups, which they blamed on the West. Their views were often informed not only by their piety but by their knowledge of world politics.

Over time, Tablighi Jamaat gained influence in the *muftiyat*. The head of the *da'watchi* department emphasized the movement's important role in re-Islamizing society, and the *mufti* himself (2018–20) was believed to be a Tablighi Jamaat follower. While key individuals within the *muftiyat* may, therefore, have increasingly acted in accordance with Tablighi Jamaat's principles and objectives, it maintained its practice of "not mixing in politics."[111] Given the legal impossibility of any religious party competing for Kyrgyzstan's parliament, some Tablighi Jamaat members favored Ata Meken (Reform Party) in October 2020. They joined the protest against corruption and vote-buying. They saw democracy and religious freedom as prerequisites of a more just and moral society and state.

Thus, although a wide range of indigenous and foreign Islamic activists offered strident critiques of Kyrgyzstan's political system, religious revival did not trigger Islamism. Pious Muslims, Islamic leaders, and missionary movements continued along a path of civil Islam; they sought to make society and democratic government more moral through Islamic education, engagement, and norms.

Kyrgyzstan has shown us that a regime's liberalization of religion can lead to widespread and long-lasting Islamic revival, but without the emergence of Islamism. Religious repression is the crucial factor in politicizing Islam, and from the 1980s through the early 2000s in Kyrgyzstan—both north and south—the *perestroika*-era and post-Soviet government under Akayev rolled back repression of Islam, which had never been as brutal as elsewhere in Central Asia.

Full-fledged religious freedom lasted about fifteen years. Despite democratic backsliding in this period, associational space remained far greater than in Tajikistan or Uzbekistan. Indeed, *potential* religious entrepreneurs openly preached among the south's ethnic Uzbek population; they had studied in the same *hujras* and had been influenced by the same political theologies as had religious entrepreneurs in Tajikistan and Uzbekistan. They could have followed the path of either the IRPT or Adolat, but they chose not to do so. Although they did not approve of democracy or secular governance, they cautiously accepted broad

[111] Interview with Talant, Tablighi Jamaat adherent, Islamic scholar, Bishkek, Kyrgyzstan, June 2019.

Islamic freedoms rather than pursuing antisystemic change. Religious liberalization precluded an Islamist movement.

Some have assumed that this absence of Islamist politics was due to Kyrgyzstan's low religiosity, or "superficial" Islam, but I have shown, to the contrary, that Kyrgyzstan experienced a vibrant Islamic revival throughout the country from 1990 onward. Many new Islamic groups, such as Tablighi Jamaat, stayed outside of politics, but other religious adherents became activists and regularly engaged in public debate about Islamic issues, much as Evangelical Christian leaders do in the United States. Kyrgyzstan's public square became less secular; frequent legal struggles pitted secularists against Muslim activists who accepted democracy but also pushed for some *shariat*-based laws within a more just, more Muslim, and less liberal system. But this was the normal process of Muslim politics, or any religious politics. Kyrgyzstan's civil Islam was compatible with democracy.

However, this period of revival and civil Islam did not last. Chapter 12 will show that as religious repression returned after 2005 and particularly targeted Uzbeks, these same ideas and leaders would foster Islamist emergence and mobilization.

12
Emergent Islamism in Kyrgyzstan

> We should realize that there is no hope for the Kyrgyz establishment and for democrat politicians. . . . This government system based on unbelief will not change, no matter how many times the government changes, the *umma*'s hopes will remain vain and we will return to humiliation every time!
>
> —Media Office of Hizb ut-Tahrir, Kyrgyzstan July 5, 2018

Under President Akayev, Kyrgyzstanis had celebrated their ability to openly practice Islam. I frequently asked *aksakal*s, businessmen, cab drivers, and traders at the bazaar what was better—if anything—about independence. A common response was "religious freedom." But conditions shifted after Akayev's ouster, as President Kurmanbek Bakiyev (2005–10) consolidated power. New national legislation curtailed the religious rights of all but was implemented primarily in the south. Some imams close to the border of Uzbekistan claimed that they were being surveilled by both Uzbek and Kyrgyz security services. Following Uzbekistan's lead, increasing religious repression, cloaked under counterterrorism but with the intention of destroying any internal political opposition, targeted the ethnic Uzbek minority. However, associational space was still sufficient to allow the dissemination of political theologies, both local and from abroad. While Kyrgyzstani religious leaders still stopped short of organizing an Islamist opposition, foreign entrepreneurs found increasingly fertile ground.

The call of Hizb ut-Tahrir al-Islami, the transnational pro-caliphate party, had fallen largely on deaf ears in 1999 when it first sought adherents in Kyrgyzstan. By the mid- to late 2000s, however, HTI's message resonated with more and more Muslims. Even those who did not support its radical ideology and agenda had come to reject democracy as a Western sham. In Osh and Jalalabat, I had tea with HTI activists, educated men and women who professed faith in the caliphate and disdain for the corrupt, repressive secularism of Kyrgyzstan's regime.

In this chapter, I examine the conditions fostering Islamist emergence, namely, targeted religious repression that began under Bakiyev, together with the diffusion of Islamist ideologies by new religious entrepreneurs. I then explore two paths that followed: contention between the state and the ethnic

Politicizing Islam in Central Asia. Kathleen Collins, Oxford University Press. © Oxford University Press 2023.
DOI: 10.1093/oso/9780197685068.003.0013

Uzbek community, and the growth of HTI-Kyrgyzstan.[1] Finally, I explore the strategies HTI used to achieve moderate success in mobilizing membership inside Kyrgyzstan: drawing on local imams' sacred authority and on ethnic Uzbek networks facilitated HTI's growth, as did its ideational adaptation to Kyrgyzstani concerns.

Conditions Fostering Islamist Emergence

Authoritarian Return and Rising Religious Repression, 2004–10

In its second decade of independence, Kyrgyzstan saw a marked deterioration of political freedom.[2] Injustice proliferated. Popular anger rose. In the spring of 2005, months of protest against corruption, electoral fraud, and clan-based politics culminated in the Tulip Revolution that ousted Akayev's government.[3] Peaceful protesters gave way to angry mobs that stormed Kyrgyzstan's White House. Pro-democracy activists and civil society claim that their democratic revolution was "stolen" or "hijacked" by former regime elites who gained power through elections.[4] Akayev's successor, President Bakiyev, quickly began consolidating a new authoritarian system. Over the next few years, he proved to be far less tolerant of protest, free speech, and opposition parties, more reliant on Kyrgyzstan's state security service, the State Committee on National Security (GKNB), and even more corrupt than Akayev had been.[5] Bakyiev was also increasingly oppressive of Islam and the Uzbek ethnic minority.

The government had already banned HTI in 2003 as ideologically extremist and a threat to national security.[6] However, arrests had been few under Akayev. HTI operated relatively openly with little problem. Bakiyev, by contrast, launched "a war on terror," despite the fact that in Kyrgyzstan, the only known Islamist terror activity had originated from Islamic Movement of Uzbekistan militants seeking a passage to Uzbekistan in 1999 and 2000. Regional concerns of "spillover" from Afghanistan, and a shared desire to eliminate any internal opposition under the guise of "anti-extremism," caused Russia, China, and Uzbekistan,

[1] Chapter 9 discusses HTI's prior emergence in Uzbekistan.

[2] Lewis, *The Temptations of Tyranny in Central Asia*; Marat, *The Tulip Revolution: Kyrgyzstan One Year After*; Johan Engvall, *The State as an Investment Market* (Pittsburgh, PA: University of Pittsburgh Press, 2016); Collins, *Clan Politics*, 222–49.

[3] Interview with activist, Citizens Against Corruption, NGO, Osh, Kyrgyzstan, July 2005.

[4] Interview with Tolekan Ismailova, human rights defender, Citizens Against Corruption, Bishkek, Kyrgyzstan, March 2011.

[5] Kathleen Collins, "Kyrgyzstan's Latest Revolution," *Journal of Democracy* 22, no. 3 (July 2011): 150–64.

[6] International Crisis Group, "Radical Islam in Central Asia: Responding to Hizb ut-Tahrir," *Asia Report*, no. 58, June 30, 2003.

Image 12.1 Imam Rafiq Qori (seated in the center), Kara-Suu
Source: YouTube screenshot

through the Shanghai Cooperation Organization, to pressure Kyrgyzstan to do the same.[7]

Kyrgyz authorities began to view any Muslim who expressed antiregime political views as a threat.[8] Bakiyev's Law on Countering Extremist Activity of August 2005 was used to repress Islamic activism; the law defined extremism as including everything from hooliganism and "affronts to national dignity" to terrorism.[9] Bakiyev and his successors specifically targeted ethnic Uzbeks of southern Kyrgyzstan, whose more conservative and Salafist-leaning mosques operated independently of the *muftiyat* and state and attracted the regime's scrutiny. Escalated oppression took the form of a crackdown on HTI and extremists.[10] In August 2006, the GKNB killed Rafiq Qori, the prominent ethnic Uzbek imam in Kara-Suu, in a security raid, claiming he was part of an IMU militant group in Kyrgyzstan. The killing sent shockwaves through the Uzbek Muslim community and triggered intense anger and large protests against the regime.

On October 1, 2008, state security services blocked a religious gathering from celebrating *Eid-al-Fitr* in Nookat, a heavily ethnic Uzbek and Tajik town in southern Kyrgyzstan. Muslim community organizers were accustomed to holding large, open prayers in the town stadium, then sharing

[7] Kathleen Collins, "Economic and Security Regionalism among Patrimonial Authoritarian Regimes: The Case of Central Asia," *Europe-Asia Studies* 61, no. 2 (March 2009): 249–81.

[8] Interview with representative, SCRA, Bishkek, Kyrgyzstan, August 2009.

[9] Mariya Omelicheva, "Ethnic Dimension of Religions Extremism and Terrorism in Central Asia," *International Political Science Review* 31, no. 2 (2010): 167–86.

[10] Communication with Dr. Alisher Khamidov, Washington, D.C., October 2020.

palov (a traditional meal) and distributing meat to the community.[11] But this time the GKNB and police closed the stadium. When locals protested, the security services dispersed the gathering, sparking a riot of several hundred young men. The GKNB arrested and tortured dozens of participants, demanding they turn in the names of "extremists," including HTI members. Thirty-two were sentenced to prison, some for nineteen to twenty years; the oldest man convicted was fifty years old, while the youngest was just seventeen.[12]

The regime's brutality was seared in the minds of locals after the Nookat crackdown. Some participants were quite vocal against the injustice of Bakiyev's secular governance; one Nookat resident said:

> I'm opposed to the idea that religious leaders should not influence the state. Muslim leaders must have influence on state and government. Do you see how secular laws have worked? No! If only a religious leader came to power, then the state would achieve a normal level [of existence]. Democracy is necessary but only if it is an Islamic democracy. We need to adopt laws based on *shariat*. . . . The current legal system does not work. Now is the time of the rich. . . . [T]he laws don't exist for them. Laws are written only for poor people. . . . I think the best form of government is based on *shariat*. Religious leaders have never done what our rulers do. Our rulers destroy the country.[13]

The Nookat protests had revealed the strength of local Muslim organizations and communal leaders, and their intense dissatisfaction with corrupt, unjust, secular politics and law.[14] The consequence of the state's attack was a reification of the divide between the religiously observant population and the secular state. Even with new elections on the horizon, another Nookat protester insisted, "A new government will be like the past ones. It's just more elections. . . . I have no hope in it." He claimed, as many religious inhabitants of Kyrgyzstan did, that "in some countries, such as Morocco, things are better. Only after the laws of *shariat* become the foundation, only then we will have order and justice in our country." He believed that "Arabic countries' governments

[11] Alisher Khamidov, "The Lessons of the Nookat Events: Central Government, Local Officials and Religious Protests in Kyrgyzstan," *Central Asia Survey* 32, no. 2 (June 2013): 148–60.

[12] Vitalii Ponomaryev, "Kyrgyzstan: Narusheniia prav cheloveka v sviazi s delom o 'Nookatskih sobytiiakh,'" Human Rights Center "Memorial," January 27, 2009, https://memohrc.org/ru/reports/kyrgyzstan-narusheniya-prav-cheloveka-v-svyazi-s-delom-o-nookatskih-sobytiyah; communication with Tolekan Ismailova, human rights defender, Bir Duino and Citizens Against Corruption, March 2010.

[13] Interview with Zafar, participant in Nookat demonstration, Nookat, Kyrgyzstan, July 2010.

[14] Khamidov, "The Lessons of the Nookat Events."

are good. There the laws work for the simple people and not against them. It's a good example for us all."[15] Consequently, some in the community joined HTI.[16]

Conditions for religious freedom further declined with the adoption of a new law regulating religion on December 30, 2008.[17] Following the example set by other regional post-Soviet nations, this Kyrgyz law imposed strict rules on the registration of mosques, *madrasa*s, and religious organizations. Whereas previously one could register a religious organization with only ten members, under this new law the state required two hundred signatures and addresses.[18] The law also prohibited private religious instruction, banned religious activity and organizations in schools and universities, and limited study abroad. The unsanctioned distribution of religious materials and proselytizing were now illegal. The law introduced vague limits on religious organizations' right to property, which threatened the interests of various imams who ran prosperous businesses to support their mosques and patronage networks. Some unregistered *madrasa*s were closed, including the puritanical school I had visited in Jalalabat (see Chapter 11). Muslim activists and communities from across the religious spectrum were outraged by the law's renewed attack on education and worship.

Bakiyev's new law hit conservatively dressed, mosque-going Muslims the hardest, especially Uzbeks.[19] Few new mosques would be registered, and some in the south were closed. In heavily Uzbek Jalalabat, Spravedlivost' (Justice), a human rights organization, claimed that it received roughly a thousand appeals for help each year, many related to violations of ethnic and religious rights.[20] By contrast, those practicing Islam through less puritanical customs, such as Sufi saint veneration, elaborate funerals, or tomb visitation—common in the north—were less affected. Bakiyev also began using the GKNB for the regular surveillance of suspect imams.[21]

[15] Interview with Alimjan, participant in Nookat demonstration, Nookat, Kyrgyzstan, July 2010.

[16] Aurelia Biard, "Power, 'Original' Islam."

[17] Interview with U.S. Embassy staff, Bishkek, Kyrgyzstan, May 2013; interview with Dr. Alisher Khamidov, Bishkek, Kyrgyzstan, October 2015.

[18] For an overview of the "Law on Freedom of Religion and Religious Organizations in the Kyrgyz Republic, December 31, 2008, see: "Freedom of Religion and Belief in the Kyrgyz Republic: Overview of the Legislation and Practice" (Bishkek: Open Viewpoint Public Foundation, 2011), http://www.osce.org/bishkek/93786; Dmitry Kabak, *Freedom of Religion: On the Implementation of the Rights of Believers in Kyrgyzstan* (Bishkek: Open Viewpoint Public Foundation, 2015), https://www.osce.org/files/f/documents/7/2/187536.pdf.

[19] Interview with Professor Emil Nasritdinov, American University of Central Asia, Washington, D.C., December 2018.

[20] Interview with activist, Spravedlivost', Jalalabat, Kyrgyzstan, January 2011.

[21] Interview with former government official, Bishkek, Kyrgyzstan, May 2013.

The "Democratic Revolution" and Its Aftermath: A Tale of Two Kyrgyzstans

In 2010, more protests—mostly led by Bishkek-based secular civil society organizations, opposition parties, and urban intellectuals demanding democracy—quickly led to Bakiyev's ouster and again brought some liberalization to Kyrgyzstan.[22] An interim government, led by Acting President Roza Otunbayeva and backed by democratic civil society, initiated a series of reforms, which included the reduction of presidential authority and the reestablishment of parliamentary powers, greater press freedom, and more economic liberty. Mosques became liberalized again; at least 1,720 were legally registered at the end of 2010.[23] A new, more parliamentary constitution passed by referendum in June 2010, although marred by violence against ethnic Uzbeks in the south. The constitution protected religion from state control, but some wanted to go further and advocated for removing the term "secular." Others argued Kyrgyzstan needed greater "freedom of religion," not "freedom from religion"—what they considered to be a lingering communist-era mentality. They wanted Muslim organizations and mosques to be able to operate widely and freely, not simply an individual right to "freedom of conscience."[24] However strident, this debate barely made headway in the parliament. A secular democratic elite, suspicious of Islamic revivalism, dominated the constitution-drafting process,[25] leaving many devout Muslims excluded and disappointed in a system they believed would preclude justice.[26] Nonetheless, renewed democratization improved religious conditions in the north as repression eased.

In the south, by contrast, the 2010 revolution brought immeasurable suffering. Ethnic Uzbek citizens of Kyrgyzstan became pawns in the intra-Kyrgyz political upheaval.[27] On June 10–14, horrific pogroms erupted in which Kyrgyz mobs reportedly attacked the Uzbek population of Osh; the event was reminiscent of interethnic violence there in 1990.[28] The violence resulted in the deaths

[22] Interviews with Roza Otunbayeva, former president of Kyrgyzstan, and with Tolekan Ismailova, Bishkek, Kyrgyzstan, June 2013.
[23] Interview with staff, SCRA, Bishkek, Kyrgyzstan, November 2010.
[24] Interview with former Kyrgyzstani government official, presidential administration, Bishkek, Kyrgyzstan, May 2013.
[25] Interview with former Kyrgyzstani government official.
[26] Interview with Islamic university student, Bishkek, Kyrgyzstan, June 2013; interview with Islamic NGO activist, Bishkek, Kyrgyzstan, June 2013; interview with *muftiyat* worker, Bishkek, Kyrgyzstan, May 2013.
[27] Kathleen Collins, "After the Kyrgyz Spring: Challenges to Democratic Deepening," *Brown Journal of World Affairs* 19, no. 1 (Winter 2012): 21–44.
[28] Human Rights Watch, "'We Live in Constant Fear,'" September 17, 2018, https://www.hrw.org/report/2018/09/18/we-live-constant-fear/possession-extremist-material-kyrgyzstan, 11.

of an estimated 426 persons, about three-fourths of whom were ethnic Uzbeks.[29] Credible reports suggested that the overwhelmingly ethnic Kyrgyz police and military had stood by, effectively supporting Kyrgyz attackers, and that the ethnonationalist Osh mayor, Melis Myrzakmatov, had intended to drive Uzbek citizens of Kyrgyzstan out of Osh.[30] In one case investigated by Human Rights Watch, an ethnic Uzbek woman reported that "on June 11, a mob invaded her home and beat and burned her as they tried to get her to reveal her son's whereabouts. She refused, but as she watched, helpless, the men entered and then torched an adjacent building where the son was taking shelter, burning him to death."[31] Thousands of Uzbeks lost their homes and businesses. Many fled to the border of Uzbekistan seeking protection, but they were refused entry by President Karimov.

In the investigations that followed, angry mobs and local officials threatened and even beat journalists and human rights activists. The state pinned blame on Azimjon Askarov, a prominent ethnic Uzbek human rights activist; he was found guilty of killing a police officer and inciting interethnic hatred and sentenced to life in prison. Human rights defenders denounced the accusation as preposterous; they believed Askarov was targeted because he had defended ethnic Uzbeks from police abuse.[32]

The 2010 revolution led to increased religious repression and exclusion of ethnic Uzbeks as local security services, police, and officials circulated the narrative that Islamist extremists had used Uzbek citizens to foment the pogroms. Political, economic, and religious threats to Uzbeks continued.[33] The coupling of ethnic and religious persecution of Uzbeks set the stage for radicalization.[34]

Otunbayeva's successor, Almazbek Atambayev, won a competitive election in October 2011 and pledged to continue reforms. Ignoring the ongoing crisis in the south, where the central government had little power, he focused on the north,[35] where political opportunity again increased and religious repression declined. Islam was even becoming a source of political legitimation. Political candidates hung billboards with photos of them praying with Islamic leaders.

[29] Human Rights Watch, "Distorted Justice: Kyrgyzstan's Flawed Investigations and Trials on the 2010 Violence," June 8, 2011, https://www.hrw.org/report/2011/06/08/distorted-justice/kyrgyzstans-flawed-investigations-and-trials-2010-violence.

[30] Human Rights Watch, "The Need for International Action in Southern Kyrgyzstan: Testimony for the Tom Lantos Human Rights Commission," July 1, 2010, https://www.hrw.org/news/2010/07/01/need-international-action-southern-kyrgyzstan.

[31] Human Rights Watch, "Kyrgyzstan: New Evidence Emerges on Brutality of Attacks," June 25, 2010, https://www.hrw.org/news/2010/06/25/kyrgyzstan-new-evidence-emerges-brutality-attacks.

[32] Interview with Ismailova.

[33] Interview with Bir Duino, human rights activists, Bishkek, Kyrgyzstan, May 2013, May and June 2019; interview with sociologist, Bishkek, Kyrgyzstan June 2019; interview with activists, Osh, Kyrgyzstan, June 2018.

[34] Omelicheva, "Ethnic Dimension."

[35] Collins, "After the Kyrgyz Spring."

Table 12.1 Registered Mosques and Muslim Population, 2015

Country	Number of Registered Mosques*	Muslim Population of each state (est.)	Mosques/1 million Muslims
Kyrgyzstan	2,669	5,146,000	518
Uzbekistan	2,065	28,500,000	72.1
Tajikistan	3,930	7,742,000	507

*El'mira Nogoybayeva, et al., *Central Asia: A Space for "Silk Democracy": Islam and State* (Almaty: Friedrich Ebert Stiftung, 2017), 8, https://centralasiaprogram.org/wp-content/uploads/2017/11/Islam-and-the-state.pdf.

In 2011, amid controversy with secularists, parliamentarians opened a prayer room. State officials touted the high number of Kyrgyzstanis making the hajj.[36] In contrast to Bakiyev's regime, President Atambayev's government registered another 488 mosques between 2011 and 2015.[37] Even more mosques, plus about 1,000 prayer rooms, functioned without any registration. The density of mosques in Kyrgyzstan exceeded that of its once more religiously strict neighbors, as seen in Table 12.1.

Despite the renewed liberalization in the north following Bakiyev's ouster, the 1990s' broad freedom of religious practice did not return. The State Commission for Religious Affairs (SCRA) reestablished greater control over Islam.[38] It supported Hanafi Islam and the central *muftiyat* despite the institution's low credibility as a consequence of corruption and sex scandals.[39] The SCRA banned Ahmadi Muslims and harassed alleged Salafis, as well as HTI, accusing them of "religious fanaticism and extremism."[40] The GKNB engaged in regular surveillance and intimidation of imams and demanded reports from the *muftiyat*. *Mufti* Chubak ajy Jalilov was removed, in part because he was advocating the adoption of certain laws in accord with *shariat*.

Many state elites remained committed to a secularism that entailed the strict omission of religion from the political sphere. They became increasingly

[36] Interview with Emil Kaptagayev, President's Councilor on Religious Affairs, Bishkek, Kyrgyzstan, May 2013.

[37] El'mira Nogoybayeva, et al., *Central Asia: A Space for "Silk Democracy,"* in *Islam and State* (Friedrich Ebert Stiftung: Almaty, 2017), https://centralasiaprogram.org/wp-content/uploads/2017/11/Islam-and-the-state.pdf, 8.

[38] Kathleen Collins, "Christian Repression and Survival in Post-Soviet Central Asia," in *Under Caesar's Sword*, ed. Daniel Philpott and Timothy Shah (Cambridge: Cambridge University Press, 2018), 162–98.

[39] Interview with Kyrgyzstani government official, Bishkek, Kyrgyzstan, May 2013. Within the state, there were power struggles over control of this lucrative sector. SAMK, the SCRA, and the executive branch all sought to control the hajj business.

[40] Mushfig Bayram, "Ahmadis 'Must Not Worship Together,'" *Forum 18*, July 17, 2014.

suspicious of any public religious presence.[41] Elites created cultural battles that mirrored debates in the West between the secular left and Christian right in the United States, or over the hijab in Turkey and Europe. President Atambayev stirred opposition with his public criticism of women wearing the hijab, even while he praised women in miniskirts; the latter, he claimed, would not become suicide bombers.[42] The state urged women to adopt "national" Kyrgyz dress. Controversy erupted as officials demanded that women uncover for their passport photos. Meanwhile, traditional mullahs sought to teach a Kyrgyz variant of Hanafi Islam in schools to counteract both Western secularism and what they called "radical" Islam being spread by foreigners.

The SCRA repeatedly debated whether or not to ban Tablighi Jamaat, as had Russia and the other Central Asian states.[43] Russia and Uzbekistan continued pressuring Kyrgyzstan to ban the South Asian Islamic revivalist movement as "extremist." Kadyr Malikov, a leading member of Kyrgyzstan's Council of Ulama, argued against a ban, pointing out that the movement was then apolitical, whereas such state action could politicize it.[44] His position won the debate and only softer restrictions were adopted, such as requiring all legally registered clerics to pass exams "to prove their theological credentials and reliability."[45] In practice, the government still only lightly enforced the laws on religion and extremism in the north.

By contrast, in the south, ethnic Uzbeks—and increasingly Uyghurs as well—in Osh, Kara-Suu, Aravon, Batken, and Jalalabat faced ongoing threats. State security services claimed that religious groups were fomenting instability. Osh acted almost as an independent government for several years, defying the president's liberalizing reforms. There, the 2012 amendments to the religion law were more restrictive, criminalizing unregistered religious activity. Registration of religious communities was extremely difficult, and some fines for unregistered activity amounted to about eighteen months' average salary.[46] Mere possession of written materials, videos, or online information deemed "extremist" by the SCRA was made a criminal offense. Article 299-2 of the religion law was used liberally; 252 people were convicted on charges of extremism between 2013 and 2015.[47] Since Bakiyev's time, and even more so after the 2010 pogroms, ethnic

[41] Interview with Kyrgyzstan government official, Washington, D.C., November 2018.

[42] BBC, "Kyrgyzstan President: Women in Miniskirts Don't Become Suicide Bombers," August 13, 2016, *BBC*, https://www.bbc.com/news/blogs-trending-36846249.

[43] Interview with staff, SCRA, Bishkek, Kyrgyzstan, October 2010; interview with Abdulatif Jumabayev, SCRA, Bishkek, Kyrgyzstan, May 2013.

[44] Interview with Jumabayev; interview with Nasritdinov, December 2018.

[45] Interview with Jumabayev, SCRA, May 2013.

[46] Ministry of Justice, "Кыргыз Республикасындагы Дин Тутуу Эркиндиги Жана Диний Уюмдары Жөнүндө," 2012, available at http://cbd.minjust.gov.kg/act/view/ky-kg/202498/30?cl=ky-kg.

[47] Interview with Colin Cram, second secretary, U.S. Embassy, Bishkek, Kyrgyzstan, June 2019.

Uzbeks comprised the majority of those charged and imprisoned, according to human rights activists and journalists.[48] Indeed, the GKNB chief for Osh explicitly targeted Uzbeks for detention. Declaring them "extremist" and reviving Soviet tactics, he "over-fulfilled his quota" of arrests to advance his career.[49] Local police and security services perpetrated vicious, extrajudicial human rights abuses against such alleged extremists. In 2013, the UN Committee on Torture was "seriously concerned at numerous, consistent and credible reports [of] the use of forced confessions as evidence in courts" in Osh region.[50] In the first half of 2019, 171 allegations of torture were registered, according to government statistics; again, most victims were ethnic Uzbek citizens.[51]

The number of designated, illegal "extremist" organizations rose to over twenty groups, mostly Islamic, but some apolitical fundamentalists were included as well.[52] Yakin Inkar was banned as an extremist organization in 2017 because its members sought to live as in the time of the Prophet Muhammad; the group rejected state schools, modern dress, and technology. It considered Kyrgyzstan's constitution incompatible with *shariat*, even though it did not advance a political agenda or perpetrate violence.[53] In 2022, it was still attracting thousands of followers as an underground group claiming to follow pure Islam.

Associational Space, Islamist Ideologies, and Entrepreneurs

Despite the return to heavy-handed authoritarianism and religious repression under Bakiyev, and the vacillations of the regime's policy from 2010 onward, associational space continued. It was adequate to allow the flow of Islamist ideas, even in areas under surveillance. Although declining, space was also sufficient to allow some entrepreneurship to continue, even if illegal.

It would be an oversimplification to claim that the north and south have taken two mutually exclusive paths in Kyrgyzstan, but notable differences in Muslim-state relations did emerge in about 2005. In the north, Islamist ideologies and entrepreneurs were minimal; instead, many forms of the vibrant Muslim activism that had emerged under Akayev continued in the still open religious environment. Civil Islam, exemplified by Mutakallim, thrived.

[48] Interview with representatives of: Bir Duino, Bishkek, Kyrgyzstan, June 2019; and Voice of Freedom, "Azimjan Askarov: a Story of a Human Rights Defender," October 2, 2014, https://www.civicsolidarity.org/article/1012/azimjan-askarov-story-human-rights-defender.

[49] Interview with Nasritdinov, December 2018.

[50] UN Committee Against Torture, "Concluding Observations on the Second Periodic Report of Kyrgyzstan," Report, December 20, 2013.

[51] Voice of Freedom, cited in Human Rights Watch, "World Report 2020: Kyrgyzstan, Events of 2019," http://www.hrw.org/world-reprot/2020/country-chapters/kyrgyzstan#.

[52] Interviews with SCRA, and with U.S. Embassy staff, Bishkek, Kyrgyzstan.

[53] Interview with Cram; interview with Rasul, International Alert, Bishkek, Kyrgyzstan, June 2019.

By contrast, as the oppression of Islam and Uzbeks returned under Bakiyev, previously quietist imams—discussed in Chapter 11—began openly propagating alternative political theologies in the south. They stopped just short of becoming entrepreneurs and laying out an Islamist ideology or founding movements. However, they were at the center of rising contention between Islam and the state. Meanwhile, other religio-political activists did engage in direct entrepreneurship, spreading the foreign ideology of HTI across the border from Uzbekistan (see Chapter 9). Those ideas resulted in HTI's mobilization inside Kyrgyzstan.

The Outcome: Two Trends in Emergent Islamism

Beginning with Bakiyev, there were two trends in emergent Islamism: first, Uzbek imams' contention with the state in the south, and second, the concurrent growth of HTI's transnational underground party.

Contention between the State and Salafist Uzbek Imams

Kara-Suu, in southern Kyrgyzstan, was home to the mosque of Imam Rafiq Qori, which became the epicenter of Islamic contention with the state. Kara-Suu also became known as the "HTI capital of Central Asia" in the mid-2000s.[54] Throughout the 1990s, the Uzbek imam Rafiq Qori had remained a quietist Salafi when religious freedom in Kyrgyzstan was high. By the mid-2000s, however, his sermons were responding both to the Karimov regime's crackdown on Islam and to growing repression in Kyrgyzstan. He was inspired by his two Uzbekistani brothers-in-law: Abduvali Qori, whom Karimov had "disappeared," and Muhammad Qori, who had died in an Uzbek prison serving his fourth sentence.[55] A widely popular imam in the Ferghana Valley, Rafiq Qori preached about both their killings and carried on their ideas, vociferously pronouncing Islam's central role in politics and law, and becoming a thorn in the side of both the Uzbek and Kyrgyz governments. The political context was charged, as ethnic exclusion and religious oppression continued to rise. Karimov's suppression of the uprising and massacre of protesters in Andijon, Uzbekistan, in May 2005, had sent several hundred Uzbeks fleeing to the nearby Kyrgyz-Uzbek border. Kyrgyzstan's failure to protect the refugees further angered Uzbeks of the south. Some residents of Kyrgyzstan's Kara-Suu wanted to ally with Uzbekistanis just

[54] Interview with journalists, Osh Media Center, Osh and Kara-Suu, Kyrgyzstan, May 2005; Emmanuel Karagiannis, *Political Islam in Central Asia: The Challenge of Hizb ut-Tahrir* (London: Taylor & Francis, 2010).

[55] Bekmurzaev, "Independent Islam in Central Asia."

on the other side of the border. "It was horrible. Those people [Uzbekistan's government and security forces] have no soul," said one Uzbek TV journalist in Osh. "There were no religious fanatics there [in Andijon]. They are Muslims and no one can tell us we can't practice our faith."[56] The Uzbek MXX "came across the border" in the following months, threatening not only refugees but also Uzbek journalists and companies and pressuring the Kyrgyz government to drive them out of business.[57] In the meantime, many came to believe that Bakiyev had replaced democratization with "the principle of clan appointments; almost half of the budget went to his family members and close friends. Only the label changed."[58]

As these larger events unfolded, HTI gained traction among Uzbeks in Kyrgyzstan. So too did Imam Rafiq Qori's prominence rise. He had opposed communism, but he also rejected democracy, pointing to its failure in Kyrgyzstan. Most important, he boldly challenged political secularism: "Religion is politics itself, brothers. These fools, who want to rule the world, are separating religion from the state. Fourteen hundred years ago Allah sent politics to the whole world through the Prophet Muhammad. . . . *La ilaha ilallah* [There is no God but Allah] is the greatest politics on earth. . . . No one can make a judgment but Allah. This is politics. Preachers are the greatest politicians . . . imams, *khatib*s, *mufti*s, *qazi*s. But to change [Allah's] politics to his servant's politics is treason." Rafiq Qori claimed that the USSR and independent Kyrgyzstan had collapsed because they had formed wrongful constitutions. He preached the Salafist view that the constitution "is God's authority, politics." To rectify the state's injustices, he urged Kyrgyzstanis to "do what *shariat* law tells us, not what our feelings, intelligence, or power tell us."[59]

In advocating his religio-political program, Rafiq Qori implicitly contrasted a utopian, divinely guided caliphate with the corrupt Kyrgyz rulers it would replace: "A caliph will divide all the wealth to everyone, everywhere. . . . The caliph will take public money only to the degree that he needs—no more." The caliphate, he taught, united Muslims and prevented oppression by nonbelievers: "*Kuffar* [nonbelievers] want to divide us, and they are succeeding. The Caliphate disappeared not more than one hundred years ago. . . . After the Caliphate was gone, a million Muslims were dead. If the caliph were alive, Muslims would unite on his word to oppose repression."[60]

56 Interview with journalist, Mezon TV, Osh, Kyrgyzstan, July 2005.
57 Interview with journalist, OSH TV, Osh, Kyrgyzstan, July 2005.
58 Interview with local expert, Osh, Kyrgyzstan, June 2013.
59 Muhammad Rafiq Qori, "Islomiy Siyosat va Halifalik Nima," YouTube, April 26, 2011, https://www.youtube.com/watch?v=HepTXqMB5vE. It had almost forty thousand views on this link from April 2011 through August 2018, and was reposted elsewhere multiple times.
60 Rafiq Qori, "Islomiy Siyosat va Halifalik Nima."

Rafiq Qori also advocated the rightness of militant jihad, in principle, according to classical Islamic theory. He explained, "If a caliph declares jihad, it will be an obligation for everyone. Every Muslim will stand up. The infidel fears this. . . . Infidels don't want Muslims to be united. Even leaders of all the Muslim countries don't want this. If there is a Caliphate, they would lose their titles as kings; there wouldn't be presidential titles." Urging global Muslim unity, a challenge to secular nation-states like Kyrgyzstan and Uzbekistan, he said, "The Prophet, peace be upon him, said, 'If anyone stands up for nationalism and dies for it, he will stand under that flag in hell.' Nationalism is forbidden. The Prophet, peace be upon him, said 'Whoever calls for nationalism is not on my side.' "[61]

Contention with Bakiyev's regime increased as the imam openly welcomed HTI into his mosque. Rafiq Qori insisted he had neither joined the party nor permitted it to recruit within the mosque, but he also defended HTI: "I am not a member of Hizb ut-Tahrir. . . . But I do not support the view that Hizb ut-Tahrir members are terrorists, enemies of the government, or enemies of the people. . . . They are Muslims! . . .They want Islam and serve Islam."[62] He had also boldly allowed *Vovchiks* ("Wahhabis," a derogatory label equated with terrorism) to enter his mosque.[63] The imam's tacit support for HTI and open endorsement of Salafist ideas, in addition to his criticism of both Uzbek and Kyrgyz secular governance, made him an enemy of those regimes.

The situation erupted on August 6, 2006, when the Kyrgyzstani and Uzbekistani security services pursued Imam Rafiq's car and engaged its occupants in a shootout, killing the imam. The Kyrgyz government claimed that the imam belonged to the IMU and that multiple IMU members were with him.[64] Outrage and mass protests followed in Kara-Suu. Thousands of men attended Rafiq Qori's funeral, and mourners carried his body to the cemetery, with supporters chanting, "Allahu Akbar!" (God is great!) and "Shahid!" (Martyr!).[65] The imam's son, Rashod Qori, insisted that his father had become a *shahid* by dying in the service of Islam. HTI blamed the Kyrgyz government for Rafiq Qori's murder, claiming, "Bakiyev [was] openly against Islam, even prohibiting holding public Muslim celebrations for *Eid-al-Fitr* and *Eid-al-Adha* and brazenly killing Imam Muhammad Rafiq Kamolov of As-Saraxsi Mosque at Kara-Suu."[66]

61 Rafiq Qori, "Islomiy Siyosat va Halifalik Nima."

62 Bruce Pannier, "Kyrgyzstan: Imam Extends Welcome to Hizb ut-Tahrir," *Radio Free Europe/Radio Liberty*, May 12, 2006, https://www.rferl.org/a/1068353.html.

63 Journalist interviews and conversations with residents, Osh, Kyrgyzstan, June 2018; conversation with mosque attendant, Kara-Suu, Kyrgyzstan, May 2006.

64 Gulnoza Saidazimova, "Prominent Imam Killed in Security Raid," *Radio Free Europe/Radio Liberty*, August 7, 2006, https://www.rferl.org/a/1070381.html.

65 Gulnoza Saidazimova, "Family, Followers Reject Terrorist Claims against Slain Cleric," *Radio Free Europe/Radio Liberty*, August 8, 2006, https://www.rferl.org/a/1070412.html.

66 Media Office of Hizb ut Tahrir in Kyrgyzstan, "Kyrgyz Authorities Killed Another Muslim," August 11, 2014, http://www.hizb-ut-tahrir.info/en/index.php/press-releases/kyrgyzstan/5442.html.

Rashod Qori assumed the leadership of his father's mosque and continued to draw between four thousand and five thousand followers on Fridays.[67] Like his father, he was widely respected for being in touch with the people's grievances and was a charismatic speaker with a broad following.[68] Young and savvy, Rashod Qori developed a wide online base as well. Many of his sermons—in the mosque or at community gatherings and life-cycle rituals—were recorded and posted. His lectures—lessons on how to pray, lending and borrowing money without interest, *halal* and *haram* behavior, proper dress for women, and Muslim unity—implicitly challenged the regime's politics. One video of the sermon titled "Alloh rozi bo'sin" (Let It Please Allah) had over 172,000 views on YouTube in just over two years. Rashod Qori spoke in a casual but eloquent manner, seated among men in the communal teahouse. He recited verses from the Qur'an, then called for the unity of "all Muslims . . . Tajik, Arab, Kyrgyz, Uzbek . . . one people of Allah."[69] He contrasted Muslim unity with the *kafir*.

In replacing his father, Rashod Qori stepped into a highly contentious situation. His community was irate over the murder of its leader and continued surveillance by intelligence services. Early in his tenure as imam (2006–14), the harsh new Law on Religion took effect, casting him and like-minded Muslims as a threat to secularism.

Like his father, Rashod Qori believed Islam was imbued with a political theology of justice and moral law, although neither father nor son articulated any Islamist ideology. Nor did either form an Islamist movement. In the context of the 2008 law, the 2010 violence, and the subsequent political exclusion, religious repression, and human rights abuses against Muslim communities, the sacred authority of Rashod Qori grew. Rather than either disavow or endorse all political action, he cautiously called people to turn to *shariat* to know when to act politically. For example, he criticized the Tunisian government as "tyrannical," but argued that the 2011 protests were at the wrong time: "After this Arab Spring, so many people died. . . . It is highly recommended that one implement every *shariat* law exactly on time. Not doing so is forbidden. Jihad is also like this. To do jihad at the right time is obligatory and whoever doesn't do so or starts jihad at the wrong time also does a forbidden thing."[70] Activism was not wrong but required strategic implementation and Islamic leadership.

Yet Rashod Qori's words notably implied sympathy for those going to fight in Syria and minimized the death toll among Kyrgyzstani fighters: "Now, wherever

[67] Interview with mosque representative, Kara-Suu, Kyrgyzstan, August 2010.

[68] Interview with members of Yiman Fondu, Bishkek, Kyrgyzstan, June 2019.

[69] "Rashod Qori (Allah rozi bo'sin)—Maruza," YouTube, June 27, 2016, https://www.youtube.com/watch?v=Ulnqjokm7i8.

[70] Rafiq Qori, "Islomiy Siyosat va Halifalik Nima." The video had over 62,000 views on one YouTube channel. Posted on another YouTube channel, it had 59,000. By contrast, his video lecture on drinking beer, posted about the same time, had only 19,000 views.

you [look], government officials trumpet that so many people went to Syria, saying that thirteen people died and so on. . . . But we get word that two hundred fifty people die in Russia every year [as migrant laborers, who encountered discrimination and abuse]. They don't tell people this. . . . The enemies of Islam benefit from this, not Muslims. What's my aim in recounting these things? In every situation we must be connected to the *shariat*."[71]

Much like his father, Rashod Qori made the case for the historical importance of the caliphate in a sermon recorded in 2014. His core message was that the caliphate was a good form of political governance that had "existed for thirteen hundred years." He urged all Muslims and their societies to pray for the return of the caliphate and to try to live under it. As he finished speaking, his listeners expressed agreement, saying loudly, "Allahu Akbar." Within a few years, over 100,000 had watched the video clip posted on YouTube.[72] He called neither for violence to establish the caliphate nor for jihad in Kyrgyzstan or elsewhere. Yet within Kyrgyzstan's secular authoritarian system, his ideas were considered close to HTI's, antisystemic and radical.

Rashod Qori was arrested on February 9, 2015, and on October 7, 2015, an Osh court found him guilty of "inciting religious discord" and "possessing and distributing extremist materials"; he was given ten years in a penal colony.[73] The prosecutor charged the imam for merely stating that "the caliphate will be reborn and Muslims must live, hoping for it, and pray to Allah for it"; that no Muslim can say there is no caliphate; and that "we need to follow a man who will create the caliphate—it is a requirement for us."[74] The prosecutor claimed, based on "expert testimony," that these statements encouraged the violent, anticonstitutional creation of the caliphate; he also claimed that the imam's use of the term *kafir* had offended the dignity of believers of other religions, and that he had incited interethnic hatred.[75] An initial investigation by the human rights organization Memorial assessed the charges and expert testimony as lacking a basis in concrete facts.[76]

Denying the charges, Rashod Qori declared that the remarks in question had taken place during one sermon in which many attendees asked him to explain the caliphate, the Syrian conflict, and the Islamic State (ISIS). He declared, "[T]he

71 Rafiq Qori, "Islomiy Siyosat va Halifalik Nima."

72 "Rashod Qori aka Halifalik xaqida (kesilgan)," YouTube, July 2014, accessed August 10, 2019, https://www.youtube.com/watch?v=wytCkhX2-NM (link now defunct).

73 Global Freedom of Expression, Columbia University, "The Prosecutor General of Osh City vs. Rashod Kamalov," https://globalfreedomofexpression.columbia.edu/cases/case-of-imam-rashod-kamalov/.

74 Global Freedom of Expression, "The Prosecutor General of Osh City vs. Rashod Kamalov."

75 Global Freedom of Expression, "The Prosecutor General of Osh City vs. Rashod Kamalov."

76 Vitaly Ponomaryev, "Zakliuchenie spetsialista," no. 103/15, July 20, 2015, provided to Ferghan.ru by Pravozashchitnyi tsentr "Memorial," *Fergana News*, August 2015, https://fergananews.com/news/photos/2015/08/kamalov.pdf.

caliphate is a Qur'anic term defined in various Islamic religious texts." He claimed he had "differentiated between the canonic caliphate and the pseudo-caliphate of ISIS," that his statements "did not stray from accepted Islamic dogma," and that they were not "extremist."[77] Rashod Qori denied telling youth to travel to Syria to wage jihad: "I did not urge anyone to take to streets or overthrow the government." However, his views, like his father's, were complicated. By advocating "the concept of [the] caliphate [which] is found in the Qur'an and *hadith*,"[78] the imam was indirectly challenging the Kyrgyz state and secularism. Although he was only exercising religious freedom through free speech, the government now treated this as criminal.

The government's guilty verdict elevated Rashod Qori's sacred authority, much as Rafiq Qori's killing had made him a martyr. Protests erupted. His followers may even have grown in number, as tens of thousands viewed his arrest and his sermons online between 2015 and 2021.[79] One Uzbek-language video of him answering questions inside a barred cage during his trial drew almost one million views in the five years after being posted (December 2015–December 2020).[80] By the fall of 2018, Rashod Qori's sermon on the caliphate had over 105,000 hits. The 899 "likes" were accompanied by comments praising the imam as "pleasing to Allah" and as an excellent teacher. One man wrote, "God-willing, Islam will win." Others simply expressed enthusiasm for the imam's sermon, writing: "Takbir!," "God-willing!," or "Allahu Akbar!" Although the original video of Rashod Qori's sermon was removed, a clip was reposted by multiple different accounts, under different titles. One such reposting in April 2019, apparently by a user called "Arabicuz," inserted a written introduction of Rashod Qori by Abu Bakr al-Baghdadi, the caliph of ISIS (until his death in October 2019).[81] The posting appeared to be an attempt to give Rashod Qori ISIS's endorsement, but this version had just over two thousand views.

Neither Rashod Qori nor his father had overtly called for a caliphate or explicitly endorsed HTI, though they provided symbolic support and safe harbor. Given their widespread sacred authority in their community, and in the south broadly, these imams' statements that the caliphate was the solution to injustice clearly resonated. HTI shared those ideas. So too would Salafi jihadists, who by 2013 were recruiting from their mosque and the surrounding districts.

[77] Shakhrukh Saipov, "Kyrgyz Court Hands Five-Year Sentence to Imam Prominent in South," *Ferghana News*, October 12, 2015, http://enews.fergananews.com/articles/2945.

[78] Saipov, "Kyrgyz Court."

[79] A video of Rashod Qori's arrest and sentencing, posted in February 2015, had almost 460,000 viewers in the subsequent four years: https://www.youtube.com/watch?v=rIxrLCfYn4A.

[80] Фергана информагентство, "Рашот Камалов в зале судебного заседания," YouTube, December 2, 2015, https://www.youtube.com/watch?v=ox_aWF8wXtc.

[81] "Roshod qori Xalifalik haqida," YouTube, April 19, 2019, https://www.youtube.com/watch?v=lfPYrXrAK7c&t=7s, and https://www.youtube.com/@arabicuz5889/videos.

HTI's Emergence and Mobilization in Central Asia

Driven by ideology and carried by transnational religious entrepreneurs, HTI entered Central Asia in the 1990s, facilitated by the new associational space granted by the Soviet collapse. There, HTI found local supporters motivated by the wave of post-Soviet religious repression and injustice. Its core mission in Central Asia was the overthrow of the region's secular regimes in favor of a caliphate.[82]

HTI's transnational activists had initially landed in Uzbekistan. With mass arrests and virtually no associational space, the movement's focus shifted, according to Kyrgyzstani officials and journalists, to southern Kyrgyzstan from 1998 to 2000. It first operated in Uzbek-populated areas, where it launched its anti-Karimov propaganda.[83] Ethnic Uzbek communities in Kyrgyzstan, particularly in Osh, Kara-Suu, Jalalabat, and Batken,[84] often had sympathy for and kinship ties with repressed Uzbekistanis, some of whom braved the precarious border checks to pray in Rafiq Qori's Kara-Suu mosque.[85] Within a few years of oppression under Bakiyev, both ethnic Uzbeks and ethnic Kyrgyz in Kyrgyzstan began to join HTI.[86] Kyrgyz villages in the northern Issyk-Kul region—not a strictly observant Islamic area, historically—also became "HTI converts."[87]

HTI activism focused on implementing the first two stages of its ideological program, which was primarily political rather than religious. HTI began with "culturing," its term for recruiting a core group of believers, its activists. It developed clandestine cells of activists who became educated in the organization's literature, but cell members knew little about the broader organization. The structure facilitated its growth underground and ability to evade state security services in Uzbekistan; in Kyrgyzstan members were more open until the 2010s. HTI next engaged in *da'wat* to the "Central Asian Muslim *umma*" broadly, to change society's beliefs.[88] They did so primarily by disseminating leaflets. As HTI's spokesman described these initial stages, "[The party] calls everyone. . . . [I]t wakes Muslims up. . . . It's a political and ideological struggle."[89] The "third stage"—establishing the caliphate—was vague; they specified neither the means nor a timeline.

[82] Karagiannis, *Political Islam.*

[83] Communications with journalists, Osh, Kyrgyzstan, January 2003 and Jalalabat, Kyrgyzstan, July 2004.

[84] Interview with journalist, Osh, Kyrgyzstan, May 2005.

[85] Interview with journalist, Osh, Kyrgyzstan, May 2005; Pannier, "Kyrgyzstan: Imam Extends Welcome to Hizb u-Tahrir."

[86] Interview with HTI members, Jalalabat, Kyrgyzstan, June 2007.

[87] Interviews with journalists, Bishkek, Kyrgyzstan, May 2007, June 2013; McGlinchey, "Islamic Revivalism," 20–21.

[88] Interview with HTI regional representative, Osh, Kyrgyzstan, May 2005.

[89] Interview with HTI spokesman, Kyrgyzstan, Jalalabat, Kyrgyzstan, August 2005.

The group refrained from mass public action, in large part due to the near certainty of arrest anywhere besides Kyrgyzstan. According to one Uzbekistani journalist who followed HTI in the Ferghana Valley region for years, "HTI just offers leaflets."[90] But other journalists reported that HTI protests had occurred in Osh, Jalalabat, and Kara-Suu, in addition to several in Uzbekistan and Tajikistan.[91] HTI became particularly active in Jalalabat just after the Aksy crisis in March 2002, when police had killed at least five protesters, among hundreds demanding the release of a jailed opposition politician. Bakiyev, then prime minister, was implicated in directing the police to shoot into the crowd. The subsequent arrest of an HTI activist in Jalalabat province sparked riots in August 2002. Mobs attacked the Kyrgyz police, who fired on them, wounding one.[92] In early 2005, HTI mobilized in larger numbers, calling for an election boycott.[93] In August 2006, HTI joined the protests following Rafiq Qori's killing. An HTI spokesman called the murder an "extrajudicial killing."[94] HTI also participated in the 2008 Nookat protests. Within a few years, contention between HTI and the Kyrgyzstani state was escalating. Associational space remained due to the weakness of Kyrgyz authoritarianism, but HTI shifted underground as the GKNB increased surveillance. Nevertheless, with a nonviolent strategy for establishing the caliphate, HTI did not move toward armed confrontation with the regime. Most independent analysts, journalists, and even some officials claimed there was no credible evidence of HTI turning to violence.[95]

HTI's Moderate Success in Mobilizing

Given its clandestine organization, it is difficult to assess the number of HTI's adherents, much less of nonmember supporters or sympathizers. HTI's Kyrgyzstan and Uzbekistan representatives claimed thousands to tens of thousands of members, but such public statements were likely aimed at

[90] Interview with journalist, Ferghana city, Uzbekistan, May 2004.

[91] "Religious Discontent Evident in the Ferghana Valley," *Eurasianet*, January 17, 2007, https://reliefweb.int/report/kyrgyzstan/religious-discontent-evident-fergana-valley; International Crisis Group, "Radical Islam in Central Asia," 23; interview with Rajab Mirzo, journalist, Dushanbe, Tajikistan, August 2005; interview with journalist, Ferghana city, Uzbekistan, June 2004.

[92] Alisher Khamidov, "Countering the Call: The U.S., Hizb-ut-Tahrir, and Religious Extremism in Central Asia," Report, Brookings Institution, Washington, D.C., June 2003.

[93] Gulnoza Saidazimova, "Kyrgyzstan: Hizb ut-Tahrir Rallies in South, Urges Election Boycott," *Radio Free Europe/Radio Liberty*, http://www.rferl.org/featuresarticle/2005/2/2FF7FDEF-DAE8-4323-8F61-346A404F3EE9.html.

[94] Alisher Khamidov and Alisher Saipov, "Antiterrorism Crackdown Fuels Discontent in Kyrgyzstan," *Eurasianet*, August 8, 2006, https://eurasianet.org/anti-terrorism-crackdown-fuels-discontent-in-southern-kyrgyzstan.

[95] Interview with official, Ministry of Internal Affairs (police), Namangan, Uzbekistan, 2005; interview with U.S. government official, U.S. Department of State, Washington, D.C., July 2018.

demonstrating strength to attract recruits.[96] While the data are imperfect, we can identify several trends in HTI's mobilization in Central Asia. First, membership numbers appeared to be increasing from the late 1990s through about 2010. Interviews with local experts and journalists in 2002–3 put membership at about ten thousand total in Central Asia: roughly five thousand in Uzbekistan, several thousand each in Tajikistan and Kyrgyzstan, and a few dozen to a few hundred in Kazakhstan.[97] Around 2009–10, Emmanuel Karagiannis's study of HTI in Central Asia estimated membership to be twenty-four thousand, likely the peak.[98] Second, HTI spread in Uzbekistan from the late 1990s until 2004, then declined.[99] HTI's growth in Tajikistan probably peaked at about five thousand by 2003, and subsequently declined. By contrast, in Kyrgyzstan HTI grew from a few hundred in the early 2000s to eight thousand in 2009, and reports of its recruiting continued.[100]

My interviews with HTI members, local journalists, and human rights activists suggest that the organization spread territorially, from southern to northern Kyrgyzstan, in the 2000s. Islamic scholar and former *mufti* Sodiqjon Kamoluddin believed that HTI was growing over time in Kyrgyzstan,[101] while waning in Uzbekistan. While in 2006, 7.8 percent of respondents in my national survey in Kyrgyzstan reported a positive view of HTI, in 2010 almost no one responded to the question, most likely out of fear. Given significantly increased repression of the organization, it had gone underground.[102] HTI's mobilization across Central Asia was limited but remarkable, given government campaigns to portray the group as both extremist and terrorist.[103] For a time, the banned party arguably had more support than many secular parties.[104] In Kyrgyzstan, HTI built a wider and more durable movement than elsewhere, which warrants explanation.

[96] Interview with HTI press spokesman, Jalalabat, Kyrgyzstan, August 2005.

[97] International Crisis Group, "Radical Islam"; Collins, "Ideas, Networks, and Islamist Movements."

[98] See Karagiannis' in-depth study of HTI, *Political Islam in Central Asia.*

[99] International Crisis Group, "Radical Islam."

[100] International Crisis Group, "Women and Radicalisation in Kyrgyzstan," *Europe & Central Asia Report*, no. 176, September 3, 2009, https://www.crisisgroup.org/europe-central-asia/central-asia/kyrgyzstan/women-and-radicalisation-kyrgyzstan.

[101] Interview with Sodiqjon Kamoluddin, former *mufti*, Osh, Kyrgyzstan, July 2005.

[102] Collins, Kyrgyzstan National Surveys, 2006, 2010 (data in author's possession).

[103] Kurbonali Mukhabbanov, "Religiozno-oppozitsionnye gruppy v Tadjikistane: Hizb ut-Tahrir," in *Religioznyi Ekstremizm v Tsentral'noi Azii: problemy i perspektivy*, ed. OSCE (Dushanbe: Sharq, 2002), 73–90.

[104] HTI's membership also very likely surpassed that of the secular democratic parties in Tajikistan (each numbered one thousand to three thousand in the early 2000s). None of these parties was able to mobilize protests in multiple instances of rigged parliamentary elections. Among opposition parties, only the IRPT surpassed HTI in numbers of supporters.

Growing Local and Transcommunal Networks

HTI has long operated underground through highly secretive networks of cells (*halka* or *doira*) that demand great trust among their members. HTI first spread in Uzbekistan's Ferghana Valley, then spread to ethnic Uzbek networks of the Ferghana Valley regions of Kyrgyzstan and Tajikistan. All were politically and economically excluded, religiously conservative minority communities.[105] The Uzbek community, highly concentrated in the mostly urban *mahallas* of Kara-Suu, Osh, Jalalabat, and Batken, provided the basis for particularly strong networks in Kyrgyzstan.[106] There were also kin connections between ethnic Uzbeks on each side of the Kyrgyz-Uzbek state border. Given that families had lived in the same village or neighborhood for generations, such ties were dense, characterized by personalism and confidence and by distrust of the Kyrgyz-dominated state.

Many HTI members interviewed in Kyrgyzstan cited a *da'watchi* as responsible for introducing them to HTI's ideas;[107] they operated freely throughout the country and were able to reach ethnic Kyrgyz in rural or mountainous areas. Once an existing communal network was penetrated by an HTI adherent, HTI's preference for trusted circles ensured the spread of the organization within a limited geographical area, whether in Uzbekistan or Kyrgyzstan. According to one local report, from January to August 2000, 237 people joined HTI from the small Ferghana Valley town of Marg'ilon, Uzbekistan.[108] Likewise, in Kyrgyzstan's Ferghana Valley, according to local journalists, HTI spread through particular *mahallas*.[109] Political refugees from Uzbekistan comprised another network through which HTI recruited.[110]

Due to less repression in Kyrgyzstan than elsewhere, cells were larger, including up to ten members. When a respected village elder or prominent businessman became a member, others in his circle sometimes joined. Members reported being recruited through friends and were linked by local village, student, mosque, and *gap* (male discussion circle) networks.[111] These networks also

[105] Igor Grebenshikov, "The Hizb-ut-Tahrir through the Eyes of Kyrgyz Journalists," Media Insight Central Asia, January 2002, https://www.cimera.org/en/publications/ind_mica.htm; Omelicheva, "Ethnic Dimension."

[106] Interview with journalist, Osh, Kyrgyzstan, July 2005.

[107] Interviews with HTI members, Osh, Jalalabat, Kara-Suu, Issyk-Kul, Kyrgyzstan, 2004, 2005, 2007, 2010, 2013.

[108] "Uzland," October 7, 2000, accessed June 30, 2010, http://www.khalifah.com (link now defunct). Marg'ilon was known as one of the most conservative—arguably puritanical—cities in the Ferghana Valley in the Soviet and early post-Soviet era. Its population was about 150,000 in 2000. Women widely veiled according to Islamic norms; alcohol was not sold.

[109] Interview with Almaz, journalist, Osh Media Research Center, Osh, Kyrgyzstan, June 2007.

[110] Interview with Baktygul, journalist, Osh Media Research Center, Osh, Kyrgyzstan, June 2007.

[111] Collins, "Ideas, Networks, and Islamist Movements."

helped to avoid the association of HTI with a particular clan or region, in contrast to most corrupt political elites. Like Akromiya in Uzbekistan, HTI offered collective leadership and self-help to members, as well as work opportunities.[112] They would "discuss everything, from religion to politics, corruption, prostitution, and financial issues."[113] They often distributed meat and *palov* to the community on Muslim holidays.

Even incarcerated HTI members developed networks.[114] True believers—not unlike Tajikistan's Mullah Sayid Nuri—used prison to disseminate their message among a vulnerable and angry population. The combination of inhuman treatment and incarceration in appalling conditions, even for petty crimes, with lax, corruptible prison guards meant that both mafias and charismatic extremists had growing influence within the prisons.[115]

Drawing on Local Imams' Sacred Authority

We have seen that sacred authority was critical to both the IRPT's and IMU's mobilization. By contrast, HTI struggled for such authority in Tajikistan and Uzbekistan. Its Palestinian figurehead and its spokespeople in the United Kingdom had no connection to Central Asia. Most Uzbeks and Tajiks were suspicious of foreign missionaries.[116] HTI attempted, but ultimately failed, to establish its own mosque connections in Uzbekistan and Tajikistan in the 1990s.[117] Moreover, Haji Akbar Turajonzoda, Muhammad Sodiq Muhammad Yusuf, and Muhiddin Kabiri denounced HTI's message.[118] Mainstream Hanafi imams portrayed HTI as a conspiratorial organization created by the West and Israel. For example, one imam from Namangan derided the organization as "foreign to Islam."[119]

In Kyrgyzstan, however, HTI built some sacred authority. Local activists took on the role of *da'watchi*. HTI gained legitimacy by sharply criticizing the *mufti* of Kyrgyzstan for his inadequate Islamic knowledge.[120] The organization had the

112 Interview with group of male and female HTI members, Jalalabat, Kyrgyzstan, August 2004.

113 Interview with Almaz.

114 Interview with HTI spokesman; interview with Sardar Bagyshbekov, democracy activist, Bishkek, Kyrgyzstan, August 2004; interview with Mus Sever, Freedom House representative, Tashkent, Uzbekistan, November 2004.

115 Interview with Penal Reform International representative, Bishkek, Kyrgyzstan, June 2018.

116 Kathleen Collins, "The Political Role of Clans in Central Asia," *Comparative Politics* 35, no. 2 (January 2003): 171–90.

117 Interview with journalist, Uzbekistan, March 2005.

118 Interview with Haji Turajonzoda; interview with Muhammad Sodiq Muhammad Yusuf; interview with Muhiddin Kabiri; interview with Sodiqjon Kamoluddin.

119 Interview with imam, Namangan, Uzbekistan, November 2004.

120 Saniia Sagnayeva, "Religiozno-oppozitsionnye gruppy v Kyrgyzstane: Hizb ut-Tahrir," in *Religioznyi Ekstremizm v Tsentral'noi Azii: problemy i perspektivy*, ed. OSCE (Dushanbe: Sharq, 2002), 69.

greatest success recruiting where it had the protection and even tacit support of the renowned imams Rafiq Qori and his son Rashod Qori, discussed earlier in this chapter. Both welcomed HTI into their mosque, lambasted government repression of the party, and preached about justice under the caliphate, according to *shariat*—messages similar to those espoused by HTI. Although they denied endorsing the movement, these imams' broad sacred authority in the Ferghana Valley region, particularly among ethnic Uzbeks and more strictly observant Kyrgyz, and their similar ideas very likely facilitated the party's growth. In the north, however, the *muftiyat* worked actively against HTI. The deputy *mufti* of Kyrgyzstan widely criticized the organization: "They said they'd create the caliphate in twenty years, then fifty, then one hundred fifty. But they haven't created one road of the caliphate yet, not one district or city. . . . Respected Muslims, open your eyes."[121]

Partial Ideational Adaptation

Given its Middle Eastern roots and focus on Palestine and a global caliphate, HTI initially appeared inconsistent with the Islamic norms and concerns of most Central Asians. Yet over time, it skillfully adapted much of its message to meet local issues in Central Asia. It focused on several key areas: religious oppression and injustice; corruption; Western, Russian, and Chinese colonialism; a caliphate for Central Asia; and nonviolent methods.

Such adaptation was essential in Kyrgyzstan, where the caliphate was little known. In 2006, just 10.5 percent of Muslim survey respondents in Kyrgyzstan agreed that "Muslims should live in a caliphate"; the rate was similar in a 2010 survey (10.02 percent).[122] Few Kyrgyzstanis had interest in the Palestinian conflict either. HTI therefore localized its ideas by making injustice its primary focus. It laid bare the oppression of Muslims across Central Asia, particularly in neighboring Uzbekistan. One leaflet claimed that "the unsustainability and injustice of the existing system . . . far removed from the flawless Islamic system," caused all problems.[123] Leaflets graphically exposed the torture of Muslims.[124] One claimed, "Karimov has closed thousands of mosques, which are God's houses. . . . They have not stopped conducting mass arrests of thousands upon thousands of Muslims who preach Islam. More than 4,000 members of HTI have

[121] Interview with deputy *mufti*, Bishkek, Kyrgyzstan, August 2010.
[122] Collins, Kyrgyzstan national surveys, 2006, 2010.
[123] Hizb ut-Tahrir Uzbekistan, "The Political and Economic Situation in Uzbekistan: Problems and Solutions," February 7, 2003, printed as Leaflet #1, in *Uzbek Islamic Debates*, 248.
[124] Much like the IMU, HTI turned to using safer online publication in order to disseminate its ideas and news about Karimov.

been tormented, and given long prison sentences."[125] An online leaflet dated May 2005 accused "the tyrant" Karimov of giving the order "to kill all those in the main square in Andijon, whether they were elderly, women, children, or youth, without discrimination." HTI exaggerated the death toll to seven thousand, over seven times the consensus among human rights groups. The leaflet pointed to HTI's role in bringing justice: "The pure blood of the Muslims, which the butcher of Andijon spilt, will not be in vain. Hizb ut-Tahrir will never forget that . . . the return of the Caliphate will be realized by the will of Allah, the most glorified, the most high. Then there will be a just and severe retribution for the butcher of Andijon that will scare those who stand behind him."[126]

In September 2013, HTI posted a video titled "The Real Face of Karimov, When Will the Criminal Regime End?" on YouTube. The video, which quickly had over three million views, detailed the plight of two HTI followers from Kara-Suu and Andijon; it claimed the middle-aged men were being tortured in detention. The video discussed other HTI members, including women, who were also on trial in 2013. It blamed the "Jew Karimov" for violating their "physical rights." The video wove in discussion of Uzbekistan's participation in the "war on terror," showing photos of Karimov with Donald Rumsfeld, prison, barbed wire, and weeping Muslim women.[127] Another leaflet detailed the case of Hamid, who served three terms in prison, including one in Uzbekistan's Jaslik Prison, notorious as the "place of no return" due to the systemic torture of its religious prisoners.[128] Hamid's family was informed that he had died of a heart attack.[129] Other publications called on members of the security services to turn against Rustam Inoyatov, the brutal chief of the MXX, and against Karimov himself, "head of the *kafir*." HTI glorified those dying in the prisons: "Hundreds of [our] *shabaab* [youth] have been martyred."[130] It described the state's murder of Salah Kadhim Dinov from Andijon, whose family was forced to bury him quickly so none would witness the crime. These messages resonated with ethnic Uzbeks living in Kyrgyzstan. In 2006, a few months after the Andijon massacre,

[125] Hizb ut-Tahrir Uzbekistan, "What Doctrine Is the President of Uzbekistan Karimov Imposing on Muslims?" Leaflet #4, in *Uzbek Islamic Debates*, 276.

[126] HTI, "This Is How the Butcher of Andijon Executed His Crimes," May 21, 2005, http://www.hizb-ut-tahrir.org/index.php/EN/nshow/155/.

[127] Hizb ut-Tahrir, "The Real Face of Karimov, When Will the Criminal Regime End?" HTIvideo.info, September 2013, accessed August 1, 2018, http://www.youtube.com/watch?v=HDt18_Q91QY (link now defunct).

[128] Bukharbayeva, *Vanishing Generation*, 78–79.

[129] HTI Uzbekistan, "The Regime of the Butcher Karimov Continues to Murder Members of Hizb ut-Tahrir!," April 12, 2013, http://www.hizb-ut-tahrir.org/index.php/EN/wshow/1601.

[130] HTI, "Some of the Crimes of Karimov, the President of Uzbekistan, and His Thugs and How the United States and the European Union Deals with Him," January 31, 2012, http://www.hizb-ut-tahrir.info/en/index.php/leaflet/uzbekistan/1175.HTIml.

17 percent of respondents in Kyrgyzstan "agreed" or "completely agreed" with HTI's call to overthrow Karimov in Uzbekistan.[131]

With the counterterrorism law, Rafiq Qori's killing, and the 2008 law on religion, HTI's focus on religious oppression became even more salient in Kyrgyzstan. Its branch there condemned both Bakiyev's authoritarian and Atambayev's purportedly democratic regime: "Bakiyev was openly against Islam, even prohibiting holding public Muslim celebrations for *Eid-al-Fitr* and *Eid-al-Adha*, and even brazenly killing Imam Muhammad Rafiq Kamalov of As-Saraxsi Mosque at Kara-Suu. The current president Atambayev participates in *namaz*. . . . His every second word is 'Allah,' but at the same time he fights against blameless Muslim women."[132] Numerous leaflets condemned the security forces for killing both ethnic Uzbek and Kyrgyz Muslims. Another "state crime," the HTI Kyrgyzstan leaflet charged, was the "ruthless murder of our brother Kadyrali Raimzhanavich Kulmirzayev," sentenced to eight years for allegedly inciting ethnic and religious hatred, during which he was subjected to "prolonged inhumane torture." It continued: "Our brother Kadyraly became a *shahid* by the will of Allah, on the 9th of August 2014. . . . More than three thousand Muslims from all parts of Kyrgyzstan came to take part in the *janaza namaz*."[133] HTI bluntly accused the Kyrgyzstani state of "murder[ing] Muslims." In fact, it further claimed "the government plans to use the security forces to control all the imams . . . to change *shariat* laws to fit secular life. . . . They select imams who cooperate with the government. . . . Imams dedicated to Islam will all be removed."[134] In their view, Rafiq Qori's death was part of this broader scheme.

HTI was even spreading in northern regions, such as Issyk-Kul, where Islam had never been strictly observed and was not typically targeted by the new counterterrorism measures.[135] In the north, HTI spread in part by playing to society's growing resentment against conversion to Christianity; its leaflets blamed Christians and Russians for oppressing Muslims.[136]

HTI further localized its message by focusing on government corruption and attacking injustice in the border region of the Ferghana Valley, where family members, traders, and even mosque communities were divided by predatory visa regulations. HTI pinned such hardships on "capitalist democracy" and secularism, as well as the lack of currency convertibility, long a problem for the vast majority of Uzbeks.[137] In a critique of Kyrgyzstan's government, HTI wrote,

[131] Collins, Kyrgyzstan national survey, 2006.

[132] HTI Kyrgyzstan, press release, "Kyrgyz Authorities Killed Another Muslim," August 11, 2014, http://www.hizb-ut-tahrir.info/en/index.php/press-releases/kyrgyzstan/5442.HTIml.

[133] HTI Kyrgyzstan, "Kyrgyz Authorities Killed Another Muslim."

[134] "Imams of Kyrgyzstan Will Be Retested," *Turkiston*, September 28, 2018, http://en.turkiston.biz/2018/09/26/imams-of-kyrgyzstan-will-be-re-attested/ (link now defunct).

[135] Interview with official, Ministry of Internal Affairs, Issyk-Kul, Kyrgyzstan, 2005.

[136] Interview with official, Ministry of Internal Affairs, Issyk-Kul.

[137] HTI Leaflet, "The Political and Economic Situation in Uzbekistan," 248.

"[P]ower is in the hands of corrupt capitalists and nationalists who threaten the *umma*. . . . Because of their insatiable greed, millions of our citizens leave home and family, and [are] forced to wander the world in search of work."[138] HTI blamed the massive migrant labor problem on the Western, democratic, capitalist system adopted in Kyrgyzstan's constitution. Its media office alleged that "the [Kyrgyz] government is trying to cover up the current debauched climate. . . . The people's wealth is still being robbed!"[139] Leaflets similarly attacked Tajik president Rahmon for corrupt "clannish rule." Other leaflets criticized police abuse, unjust taxes, and restrictions on bazaar traders—issues that had triggered protests in Uzbekistan.[140] The theme of injustice was multifaceted: HTI offered manifold examples from the lives of ordinary Central Asians.

Its emphasis on Islam as a just alternative to flawed, corrupted democracy resonated widely, especially in Kyrgyzstan, where many had lost faith in democracy after two decades of its failures.[141] Propaganda called Muslims to reject "moderate Islam" and to boycott democratic elections "conducted on *kufr* principles."[142] Similar leaflets sought to delegitimize the IRPT's support for democracy in Tajikistan.[143] Another common HTI message in Central Asia, adapted from its global online messaging, was the revitalization of Islamic values in opposition to the West. Yet, whereas in the Middle East anti-Semitism was central to its agenda, HTI's literature in Kyrgyzstan more commonly denounced Christian missionaries; it claimed the West had sent them to threaten Islam. Leaflets and online materials also blamed Kyrgyzstan's societal degradation—including prostitution and drugs—on secularism, democracy, and Western influence.

One 2013 leaflet condemned the United States and European Union for removing sanctions and pretending that Uzbekistan was "moving towards improving conditions of human rights": "[B]e wary of . . . the *kafir* hypocritical states, because they pretend to be interested in humanitarian matters."[144] HTI accused "the colonial *kafir* West" of appointing "puppet tyrants in the *umma* of Islam." It likened Karimov to "allies" of the West, among whom HTI included Egyptian President Hosni Mubarak, Libyan President Muammar Qaddafi, and

[138] HTI Kyrgyzstan, "Crashing the System of State Control of Kyrgyzstan," January 31, 2017, http://www.hizb-ut-tahrir.info/en/index.php/press-releases/kyrgyzstan/12376.HTIml.

[139] HTI Kyrgyzstan, "New Government of Kyrgyzstan Continues Solving Corruption Cases of Previous Establishment," July 5, 2018, http://www.hizb-ut-tahrir.info/en/index.php/press-releases/kyrgyzstan/15691.HTIml; HTI Kyrgyzstan, "At a Time the Kyrgyz Government Seeks to Prevent Corruption Its Corruptors Loot the People with the Thieves!," January 15, 2015, http://www.hizb-ut-tahrir.info/en/index.php/press-releases/kyrgyzstan/6777.HTIml.

[140] HTI paper leaflets, Uzbekistan, provided by RFE/RL journalist, October 2002.

[141] Khamidov, "Countering the Call."

[142] HTI Kyrgyzstan, "The Islamic Climate in the Country Created by Muslims—Isn't It a Gift from Allah That Ulema Must Protect?," August 17, 2017, http://www.hizb-ut-tahrir.info/en/index.php/press-releases/kyrgyzstan/13851.HTIml; interview with Almaz.

[143] Mukhabbanov, "Religiozno-oppozitsionnye gruppy v Tadjikistane: Hizb ut-Tahrir," 79.

[144] HTI, "Some of the Crimes of Karimov."

Syrian President Bashar al-Assad.[145] Its website posted articles blaming the West for the demise of the caliphate. The language throughout the site referred to the "Muslim *umma*," "Islamic lands," and "Islamic peoples," of which Central Asia was a core part. It emphasized other common enemies of Islam as well: Russia and China. Those states' repression of Muslims under the rhetoric of counter-terrorism, which had accelerated under the regional initiatives of the Shanghai Cooperation Organization (SCO), was central to HTI's locally adapted literature.[146] HTI condemned the China's intelligence-sharing for facilitating the arrests of its members in Kyrgyzstan.[147] Postings reminded Central Asian citizens of China's "repression of the Turkistoni *ulama*," accusing the country of planning to colonize Kyrgyzstan and destroy Islam, as it was doing among the Uyghurs of East Turkestan.[148] Appealing to Kyrgyz workers, one leaflet recounted a Chinese boss beating a Kyrgyz factory employee and called for uniting against the "dirty infidels" of China who took their land.[149] HTI's Kyrgyzstan office reported less about Russia than China, but did periodically report that Kyrgyz HTI members who had migrated to Russia to spread *da'wat* were being persecuted there.

Core to HTI's ideology and strategy was its emphasis on nonviolent means for establishing the caliphate.[150] The party declared that it worked only through "peaceful" means. According to Tursunbai Bakir Uluu, an HTI sympathizer and Kyrgyzstan's human rights ombudsman for many years, HTI activists had claimed, "We can only create the caliphate through propaganda. . . . We hate the IMU! They use guns!"[151] This message resonated powerfully in Central Asia, where most feared the bloodshed of civil war.[152] All were acutely aware of the ongoing war in Afghanistan and the Tajik Civil War. They shunned the thought of "brother killing brother," as one Kyrgyz *aksakal* from the Ferghana Valley told me. HTI's ideational commitment to nonviolence helped drive its growth.

However, after almost a decade of disseminating the idea of a nonviolent path to the caliphate, HTI's ideology in Central Asia was evolving, drawing on the widespread Muslim disapproval of U.S. policy in Afghanistan and Iraq. Local and global leaflets praised jihad in Afghanistan, Iraq, and Chechnya, while mocking the American failure in Afghanistan and berating the U.S.-Pakistan alliance.

145 HTI leaflet, April 13, 2013, on hizbutahrir.org (link defunct).

146 On the SCO's "security regionalism," see Collins, "Economic and Security Regionalism," 251–83.

147 HTI Kyrgyzstan, "The States of the Shanghai Cooperation Organization Conspire Together to Combat Hizb ut-Tahrir," July 12, 2014, http://www.hizb-ut-tahrir.info/en/index.php/press-releases/kyrgyzstan/5160.HTIml.

148 HTI Kyrgyzstan, "China Is Gradually Colonizing Kyrgyzstan," August 6, 2018, http://www.khilafah.com/china-gradually-colonizes-kyrgyzstan/.

149 HTI Kyrgyzstan, "China Is Gradually Colonizing Kyrgyzstan."

150 OSCE, unpublished memo, courtesy of OSCE representative, Dushanbe, July 2002.

151 Interview with Tursunbai Bakir Uluu, Bishkek, Kyrgyzstan, January 2003.

152 Khamidov, "Countering the Call."

From 2011 on, HTI's online posting about Syria clearly sanctioned militant jihad in that specific context. One of HTI's most direct calls for justice suggested that violence against brutal authorities who repressed Islam was more broadly justified: "By the will of Allah, the Khalifah State [ISIS] is knocking at the doors. On this day . . . the oppressors will answer. . . . When the Messenger of Allah Muhammad conquered Mecca, he ordered the killing of those who fought violently against Islam. We call on the authorities and members of the security agencies to avoid this fate."[153]

This statement illustrates a puzzling contradiction: HTI claimed to oppose using violence to overthrow existing regimes, but it supported militancy once a caliphate was established. HTI's leadership reminded Muslims that Syria was "the heartland of the Abode of Islam."[154] The brutality of the Syrian crisis had radicalized HTI. A U.K.-based activist wrote, "The Muslim *umma* must call upon their armies to liberate Bilad al-Sham [the province of Syria; the Levant] and to re-establish the Caliphate. . . . It is unequivocal that the people of al-Sham require a military incursion . . . by our own Muslim armies . . . to liberate the Muslims from their oppression by establishing a new political leadership under the shade of Islam."[155] Articles posted for "Muslims of Turkestan" also suggested growing approval of violence. One accused the West of waging "unjust, brutal, and global wars against Islam and Muslims."[156] The piece ended with a passage from the Qur'an (3:12, 13), about the Battle of Badr, between the army of believers and unbelievers.[157] It reminded readers that "Allah helps believers."

HTI never directly endorsed ISIS, but its verbal support of jihad against the Assad regime suggested that it recognized the proclamation of a new caliphate in Syria and Iraq. By about 2013, reports of HTI's activity inside Kyrgyzstan had declined. At the same time, Kyrgyzstanis were beginning to go to Syria to fight with the transnational foreign fighter movement, as Chapter 14 will explore. It is not clear whether HTI's messaging influenced this flow, but around the globe, tens of thousands of Muslims were expressing belief in the caliphate and the legitimacy of violent jihad because of the stunning success of ISIS.

153 HTI Kyrgyzstan, "Kyrgyz Authorities Killed Another Muslim."

154 HTI, "Dr. Abdul Wahid's Open Letter to the Muslim Community about the Continuing Repression in Syria," March 1, 2012, http://www.hizb.org.uk/viewpoint/dr-abdul-wahids-open-letter-to-the-muslim-community-about-the-continuing-repression-in-syria/.

155 HTI Editor, "Top 10 Responses to the Syrian Crisis," Hizb ut-Tahrir Britain, December 29, 2016, http://www.hizb.org.uk/viewpoint/top-10-responses-to-the-syrian-crisis/.

156 The HTI site links to the journal *Al'-Wai* (in Russian, Uzbek, and Kyrgyz), including the article: "Ислам—это религия Аллаха," no. 381, n.d. http://al-wayi.org/archive/225-381/2413-Islam-eto-religiya-allakha, 5.

157 "Ислам," 8.

Wavering Repression Continues under Jeenbekov, 2018–20

As we have seen, since the early 2000s, Kyrgyzstan's state has repeatedly wavered in its religious policy. Over time, political rights and associational space have fluctuated as well, from liberalization in the early Akayev years to Bakiyev's authoritarian return, followed by Atambayev's renewed democratization in the north, even as local elites escalated repression in the south. In 2017, Atambayev's term in office ended and President Sooronbay Jeenbekov was elected in a competitive vote. His victory initially appeared positive for religious freedom; he drew on Islam symbolically to build popular support, and his rhetoric was more conducive to a public role for Islam. Tablighi Jamaat became less concerned about being banned since Jeenbekov's brother and the new *mufti* were reportedly members.[158] However, Jeenbekov's government and the legislature made no attempt to reverse Bakiyev's harsh law on religion. Harassment and arrests of Yakin Inkar members and other alleged "Salafis" increased.[159]

More broadly, by 2018 democratization was in reversal once again as Jeenbekov consolidated greater executive control and increased surveillance of any democratic opposition. His administration and parliament became riddled with corruption and criminal elements. HTI continued to issue leaflets lambasting democracy as criminal governance. The most significant problems for Muslim believers, as before, persisted in ethnic Uzbek areas, where officials often arrested Uzbeks under false pretenses, either for extortion or to fulfill quotas. A 2019 directive required all sermons to be delivered in the Kyrgyz or Russian language, another blow to Uzbek believers. Kyrgyzstan's Supreme Court again upheld the life sentence given to the ethnic Uzbek human rights defender Azimjon Askarov; he died in July 2020, after a decade of torture and denial of medical treatment.[160] Destroyed Uzbek homes were not rebuilt. Myrzakmatov, the Osh mayor who had overseen the pogroms, remained unpunished. The convergence of ethnic and religious exclusion, and the branding of Kyrgyzstani Uzbeks as extremists, continued unabated.

The return of state-sponsored religious repression under Bakiyev partially reversed the course of Islam's peaceful and democratic integration into Kyrgyzstan's public sphere. The state's targeting of certain ethnic Uzbek religious activists and believers, through legislation and extralegal means, politicized Islamic identity. Increased ethnic, political, and economic exclusion of Uzbeks,

158 Interview with Tablighi Jamaat members, Bishkek, Kyrgyzstan, May 2018.
159 Interview with Cram.
160 Interviews with Tolekan Ismailova and human rights activists, Bir Duino-Kyrgyzstan, Bishkek, Kyrgyzstan, March 2013, June 2017, May 2019.

especially surrounding the 2010 pogroms, intertwined with religious repression. Uzbek religious leaders in Kyrgyzstan shifted from political quietism to openly preaching the justice of a caliphate, even though they stopped short of founding an Islamist movement, much less espousing violence.

These conditions fostered HTI's expansion into Kyrgyzstan, where associational space was still considerably greater than elsewhere in Central Asia. HTI had some success for over a decade. Like the IRPT, it accessed local and transcommunal networks, including ethnic Uzbek *mahallas* and Kyrgyz *da'watchi* connections. Although HTI had initially struggled for authority in both Uzbekistan and Tajikistan, inside Kyrgyzstan the tacit endorsement of the renowned imams Rafiq Qori and Rashod Qori bestowed some sacred authority on the party, despite its lack of religious training. Just as important, HTI partially localized its propaganda by emphasizing the injustices faced by Kyrgyzstan's ethnic Uzbeks and all Muslims persecuted inside Karimov's Uzbekistan. Significantly, until 2013 HTI stressed the creation of a Central Asian caliphate, not a global one, through nonviolence. By turning to focus groups and interviews with ordinary Kyrgyzstanis as well as HTI recruits, the next chapter will demonstrate that these ideas gained traction over time. Nonetheless, focus groups also reveal that HTI's opposition to nation-states, radical anti-Semitism, and rejection of democracy alienated most Kyrgyz respondents and limited HTI's influence.

13

Society and Islamist Ideas in Kyrgyzstan

The police and courts have no conscience. They show no justice.

—Entrepreneur, Kara-Suu, 2007

Muslim democracy is better than Western democracy, because it will be without injustice. It's necessary to completely destroy corruption.

—Businesswoman, Osh, 2007

We are not ready for a caliphate.

—Trader, Jalalabat, 2007

In Kyrgyzstan, as in Tajikistan and Uzbekistan, societal ideas and norms placed limits on the spread of Islamism. Most ordinary Kyrgyzstanis, as well as those with social and sacred authority—mullahs, imams, and community leaders—emphasized mainstream interpretations of Islam's role in politics; that is, they were moderate, not antisystemic and not revolutionary. They generally opposed violent interpretations of jihad. Yet, consistent with the mainstream views of a devout public, they sought a greater role for Islam in education and the public square. Some also approved a role for Islam in politics, law, and the state. Participants and societal elites generally disapproved of Islamist movements, whether Hizb ut-Tahrir, the IMU, or other militant groups.

Consistent with the findings of Chapters 11 and 12, focus group discourse revealed greater politicization of Islam among ordinary Kyrgyzstanis[1] during President Bakiyev's rule than previously, under President Akayev. Under Bakiyev, religious repression and injustice escalated and angered ordinary people, especially ethnic Uzbeks. Kyrgyzstani respondents also revealed the influence of Islamic missionaries, both foreign and local, who had introduced more puritanical and more political interpretations of Islam than were common throughout the country in the Soviet and early post-Soviet eras.

[1] "Kyrgyzstani" refers to any citizen of Kyrgyzstan. Within Kyrgyzstan, there are two major ethnic groups: Kyrgyz and Uzbeks. Focus groups were separated along ethnic lines because of episodes of interethnic conflict between Kyrgyz and Uzbeks. Each group's ethnicity is noted.

Politicizing Islam in Central Asia. Kathleen Collins, Oxford University Press. © Oxford University Press 2023.
DOI: 10.1093/oso/9780197685068.003.0014

Overall, their discourse suggests that injustice and religious repression made some Islamist ideas attractive. Yet, respondents' discourse also revealed that in Kyrgyzstan, as elsewhere, not all Islamist ideologies and movements resonated; HTI's partial ideational adaptation—its focus on Central Asia's political injustice and corruption—aided in its recruiting. Still, only a minority of respondents had come to approve of an Islamic state or to view a caliphate and Islamic courts as more just than their own secular system. Like the business owners and small traders quoted above, however, most simply sought justice, not radicalism. To the extent that Kyrgyzstani respondents favored a greater Islamic influence on politics, their views were closer to those of Mutakallim, Tablighi Jamaat, and the former *mufti*, Chubak ajy Jalilov—manifestations of Muslim politics and "civil Islam." They espoused de-secularization and creation of a more Muslim society and polity in accord with *shariat*.

After briefly recounting the core ideas of those Islamists and religious activists in Kyrgyzstan seeking to influence societal opinion, I turn to the discourse of twenty-five focus groups and fifty interview respondents. I recount representative views about specific issues related to Islam and politics and central to Islamist messaging: Islamic revival and education, repression of Islam, injustice, corruption, law and courts, religious minorities, jihad, and suicide bombing. Within this discussion, I compare typical group discussions from the north and south of the country to assess differences due to regional variation in religious liberalization/repression and the spread of political theology. I also compare responses over time to uncover the effect of increased repression from 2005 to 2010. Next, given that Kyrgyzstan was the one Central Asian country where HTI members were relatively unafraid to meet and speak, I present their own words to better understand why they found the party appealing. Finally, I turn to the views expressed by societal elites who were influential in shaping public attitudes.

Core Ideas of Islamists Recruiting in Kyrgyzstan

By the early 2000s, Kyrgyzstanis were exposed to varying political theologies and Islamist ideas. HTI was propagating a nonviolent but nonetheless radical ideology of the caliphate; HTI's ideology was anti-Western, antidemocratic, anti-Christian, and anti-Semitic. HTI's propaganda also prominently addressed the repression of Muslims, corruption, injustice under democracy, the Karimov regime's torture, and abuses Uzbeks suffered in both Uzbekistan and Kyrgyzstan. Despite its nonviolent strategy within Central Asia, HTI actively propagated support for militant jihad against Americans in Iraq and Afghanistan, and it praised jihad against the Bashar al-Assad regime in Syria.

Meanwhile, various puritanical Islamic leaders such as Rafiq Qori had propagated purist, Arab-style practices as the true Islam. While they did not directly endorse any political system, these religious authorities denounced democracy as un-Islamic and idealized the historical caliphate. At least one young mullah, the future leader of Katibat al-Tawhid wal Jihad (KTJ), would also propagate the ideas of al-Qaeda in southern Kyrgyzstan after his return from study in Syria. By 2012, he was advocating the caliphate as the solution to injustice and preaching the duty of militant jihad (Chapter 14). By contrast, Mutakallim, Tablighi Jamaat, and Chubak ajy Jalilov represented variants of "Muslim politics" and "civil Islam" (Chapter 11); each advocated a public role for Islam. While not Islamist, they openly espoused de-secularization—creating a more Muslim polity in accord with *shariat*.

Profiles of Focus Groups from Kyrgyzstan

Exploring the discourse of ordinary Kyrgyzstanis (including both ethnic Kyrgyz and Uzbeks; northern and southern; and various age groups, education levels, and occupations) enables us to better understand the appeal and limits of Islamist ideas in the 2000s, a few years before the Syrian Civil War erupted.[2]

Focus group discussions elicited a range of views about Islam's role in politics. As elsewhere, no group or even individual expressed either wholly liberal or entirely radical opinions. Respondents' views were often multifaceted, uncertain, and fluid, and were shaped by evolving political conditions as well as the influence of family and friends, or even the opinions voiced by others in the group.[3] Yet, the discussions uncovered notable regional and temporal differences in Kyrgyzstan.

Mainstream Ideas about Islam and Politics in the South

While southern Kyrgyzstan (Osh, Jalalabat, and Batken *oblasts*) was more strictly pious than northern Kyrgyzstan, most ethnic Kyrgyz and Uzbeks in the south held moderate, mainstream views on the range of issues discussed. Members of those groups were primarily concerned about corruption and injustice, and less so about religious repression, which they had generally not experienced as of 2005.

[2] For a discussion of the focus group methodology and specific details of the groups, see the appendix.

[3] All names used are pseudonyms.

Women, Ethnic Kyrgyz, University Students, Twenty to Twenty-three Years Old, Osh, 2005

A group of young women in Osh, all ethnic Kyrgyz university students,[4] openly expressed their strict piety, belief in following both Muslim and national "traditions," and satisfaction that "Islam was becom[ing] stronger and more influential than before." "Religion is blooming!" announced Aziza. They stressed the importance of prayer and conservative, modest dress (though not the hijab) as a way of demonstrating their piety, but they also emphasized the importance of women's political rights. They opposed the common practice of "excluding the Muslim religion from their [state-run] education." They held tolerant views of Christians and Jews and their right to worship in Kyrgyzstan, but they also sharply opposed conversions.

The women believed democracy was the best system for them because it gave them "freedom of speech and freedom of religion." While they preferred learning from Arab-educated imams, as Aziza said, "in our country we should not be like people in Muslim countries such as Saudi Arabia." They distinguished their traditions from literalist Saudi religious practice and they rejected the Saudi model of an Islamic state. They did, however, agree that Muslim courts would be more just than their own, secular ones. Visibly angry at corruption, Tazagul said, "Even teachers want bribes!" They agreed with Dinara, who said that protesters "want to establish justice." They mostly leaned in favor of a democratic government for Kyrgyzstan, but one that was Muslim, not secular.

Their views on political Islam were mixed and nuanced. They opposed HTI, yet they also stressed that HTI was peaceful and distinctly different from the IMU—contrary to government claims. One declared, "Juma Namangoniy [the IMU's cofounder] causes conflicts and does terrorist acts. . . . It's not right," said Gul'zira. While they supported punishing "Wahhabis . . . [with] life in prison," they were divided over whether Islamic parties should be legal. Some thought such parties could be effective. Kanikei stated hopefully, "We are moving towards Muslimhood [a Muslim state]."

Women, Ethnic Kyrgyz, White-Collar, Twenty to Twenty-nine Years Old, Jalalabat, 2005

A group of well-educated ethnic Kyrgyz women from Jalalabat[5] heartily supported the religious revival, even praising the "many women now wearing the *paranji*"—they used the term for the pre-Soviet dark, full hijab, a version of which was again worn by some women in Kyrgyzstan, especially in the south. The group participants, in their late twenties, boasted, "Now, every young person

4 KY-FG#6.
5 KY-FG#4.

knows the Qur'an, children perform *namaz* in school, [and] the rich build mosques." They approved of the Islamic revivalism underway for nearly fifteen years. They claimed "always" to have high respect for the authority of imams. They also expressed a preference for foreign-educated imams, not because they were Salafis but because they "had more knowledge." Unlike Salafis, they expressed tolerance of non-Muslims.

The women also wanted to see growing Islamic influence on the state. They agreed that the Kyrgyz state "should be Muslim," culturally and politically. Mairam argued that "a Muslim state fits us" and "Muslim states are more just." They approved of mullahs serving in parliament because they claimed people needed a place for prayer at work. They expected that elected mullahs would allow prayer rooms in parliament. Controversy over legalizing rooms for performing *namaz* had continued in Kyrgyzstan's parliament for years. When Kyrgyzstan became a democracy, said Gulmira, "it gave everyone the right to choose their own religion," but the "deputies make promises, then forget about us as soon as the election is over." She thought mullahs in government might be better.

Beyond freedom of religion, however, they saw democracy as failing to care for people. They demanded "justice," not democracy. All of them, despite not being able to explain *shariat* or how it would become law, wanted "Muslim courts," which they claimed "are just." "We have no justice [currently]," they unanimously agreed.

The women believed that a Muslim state would be good for them. As Bermet explained, "corruption is not connected with religion" and "whoever demands to be free, demands justice." They agreed that Kyrgyzstan "should be a Muslim state . . . because the majority are Muslim," but it was not clear what this would entail. The women associated a "Muslim state"—not Iranian- or Saudi-style—with a government that would reduce corruption, especially in the courts. Jazgul worried that "corruption could be a cause of conflict, because it prevents Kyrgyzstan's development more than anything." Aselia, a teacher, qualified the discussion of a Muslim state. She expressed a desire for "Muslim democracy." Others were unsure. They denounced post-Soviet governments, including Kyrgyzstan, as "unjust." They expressed disgust at the police killings in Aksy. The event had sparked outrage across Kyrgyzstan. Despite their anger at the government, the women decidedly rejected HTI; they did, however, reveal that within their community, "many people had joined HTI's ranks," people who were likewise enraged at injustice.

The women did not condone radical Islamists' use of violence. Their views on jihad were complex. On the one hand, they did not categorically oppose militancy because they believed that "jihad is a war on the *kafir*" and was sometimes necessary.[6] They also believed that most non-Muslim countries were enemies.

[6] Participants sometimes used the term *kafir* (*kofir* in Uzbek) in the singular to refer to infidels.

And yet, they opposed militant jihad except in self-defense, when invaded by "a *kafir* country." They also categorically opposed suicide bombing. Like the preceding group, these women were conservative in their desire for moral politics; they wanted religious influence on politics, but they did not favor radical solutions or radical means.

Men, Ethnic Kyrgyz, Small Business Owners, Forty to Forty-nine Years Old, Jalalabat, 2007

One group of businessmen in Jalalabat, raised and educated in the Soviet era,[7] praised the growth of piety in their *mahalla*: "It has increased about 60 percent." Aibek said, "I think every person must believe in Allah. In my circle, everyone has become more religious. More and more people perform *namaz*. The number of people who fast has increased too." They agreed that religious education and piety were "important to society," but they were tolerant of those Muslims who could not fulfill all Islamic norms. They themselves followed *urf-adat*. They had little respect for local imams; they preferred foreign ones, but they also worried that "youth are being sponsored and stirred up" by religious agitators. Ismail said, "Now, more believing Muslims wear long Arab clothes. I heard the sermon of a shaykh from the Emirates . . . speak about this . . . but in the religious books it's not written that you have to dress that way. But now youth are wearing beards and long clothes."

They themselves had not experienced religious repression and they blamed Karimov's injustice in Uzbekistan for causing HTI to emerge among ethnic Uzbeks: "His government is not just." They were also extremely dissatisfied with "widespread corruption" in Kyrgyzstan. Nuriddin said, "First of all, the old system of corruption has continued. . . . The government doesn't defend our interests." Satarbek added, "In our country, a big source of corruption is clan ties. Even in the labor market everyone tries to put their relatives and kin into jobs." Kairat remarked, "To get a job or be elected deputy, it's family ties, what clan you are from, and whether you are from the north or south."

Still, their religious views and political experiences did not lead to radicalism. Satarbek said, "I'm Muslim, but I'm opposed to making the state Muslim. . . . The state must have a law for freedom of religion and for the people." Others agreed. Kubanych explained, "I'm not against Islam, but I am against forcing it." Nuridin said, "We must study many cultures of different states, European and Asian. . . . We need Russian education. We can preserve our national traditions and Muslim values in family laws," which he implied would be informal moral guidelines, not legislation. All the men opposed adopting *shariat* as state law, and they opposed using Muslim courts. They even opposed allowing religious leaders to influence

[7] KY-FG#22.

the state. Their views on jihad were similarly moderate; they believed that jihad should be limited to the defense of Islam and the homeland.

But in one significant area—religious liberty—they diverged. They were not merely intolerant of Jews, Christian missionaries, and converts; they wanted to ban those groups by law. Moreover, they did not endorse secularism or liberal democracy. They all agreed that Kyrgyzstan "needed its own form of government." They supported having democratic parties, including an Islamic party. Aibek believed that "if a Muslim party is responsible, it must participate in elections." Satarbek and others agreed: "If they exhibit the positive side of Islam [promoting morality and ending corruption], then such [Islamic] parties must participate."

Mainstream Ideas about Islam and Politics in the North

The religious situation in the 2000s was extremely fluid, even in the north. While northern respondents had once been neither strictly pious nor supportive of a political role for religion, many increasingly favored a new, stricter form of Islam as well as a public role for Islam; they supported Islam's influence on politics.

Women, Ethnic Uzbek and Dungan, White-Collar, Thirty to Thirty-nine Years Old, Bishkek, 2005

An ethnically mixed group of women in Bishkek, educated and employed in white-collar jobs and belonging to the *perestroika* generation,[8] expressed moderate views. In contrast to many similarly well-educated Kyrgyz women, they had learned Islamic religious values from their parents in the 1970s and 1980s. They supported religious revivalism, fasted more than in the past, and performed *namaz*. They believed that important differences distinguished Muslim believers from nonbelievers, but held unanimously favorable opinions of Jews. Only a minority of the group, however, was tolerant of Christian missionaries and converts. Whereas Jews did not proselytize, "new Christians" were actively seeking converts from Islam. The women approved of growing mosque attendance and supported the mosques' distribution of food aid. They turned to local mullahs for marriage matters, Qur'an study, and conflict resolution. They wanted the government to provide "more books on Islam and religious programs on TV." They wanted their children to have an Islamic education. They preferred local mullahs and spiritual healers. They wanted Islam to be taught "in a state school" because foreign teachers were too literalist and strict in interpretation.

The women decried the state itself as corrupt and unjust:

[8] KY-FG#14.

MAVLIUDA: We need just government, just power.
YULDUZ: The government doesn't defend our interests.
ZUHRA: They don't even listen to us.
LEYLA: Corruption grows right here among us. And the political powers so far don't stop grabbing all the wealth for themselves.

Gulchera suggested that "a Muslim court would be more just because in religious countries they punish theft severely." Saniya noted that "a Muslim court will better fulfill the laws. People will fear Allah." Their understanding of *shariat* law was both vague and moderate; they did not advocate adopting the *hudud* penalties but did assume that some religious laws would have a positive influence. They opposed "radicals" and they believed that "all" Islamic parties and movements were "fanatics." They wanted some form of democracy. Not naïve, they agreed with Alfiya, who said: "We only have democracy on paper. They [the government] can imprison you for free speech. But in the West, it's different." Suffering injustice had led them to prefer a democracy influenced by Islamic values.

Women, Ethnic Kyrgyz, White-Collar, Thirty to Thirty-nine Years Old, Bishkek, 2007

One group of Bishkek women was highly educated, held white-collar jobs, and was also very pious.[9] Its members claimed that everyone in their community had become more observant in recent years. Religious values, they said, "were extremely important," and they worried about the influence of corruption and Western secularism. They believed the *muftiyat* to be corrupt and were more impressed with imams who had studied in Arabia, Turkey, or Pakistan. "It's a fact that an imam who has studied abroad is immediately more respected in the eyes of society," said Venera. Sharipa and Zamira agreed: "They know a lot more."

These women wanted more justice and morality in society and politics. They believed that "corruption doesn't just exist. It's the cause of everything." Another added, "Corruption plagues everything and everyone. Because of corruption we [the country] don't develop." One claimed, "Corruption now [under Bakiyev's government] is worse than in Akayev's government." Others agreed: "It's not at all better." Asked whether the government was just, Zamira scoffed, "Seriously?" Another declared, "There's not one sphere where power is not abused by those working in their positions." Gulnora complained that "money and connections decide everything." Asel agreed: "Because of corruption, young people don't stay in business." Janara declared that "the courts and police are sold. They are not just." Another added, "I think in our country, you can buy any policeman, and

[9] KY-FG#17.

judge." Venera stated that "the only areas that are just and honest are things that aren't profitable." All agreed: "Corruption is everywhere, but . . . nowhere is there any justice." Speaking approvingly of popular protests against Bakiyev, Sharipa said, "The protesters' goal is justice." These women too simply wanted justice.

They hoped and expected that a Muslim form of democracy would bring justice. They argued that *shariat* should play some role in law and the state. They sought some mix between what they called "Muslim" and "Western democracy." "We should have our own sort of democracy. Why copy the West? Western democracy has its bad side," said Zamira, "but a totally Muslim [state] is also not correct." Gulnara explained, "Democracy comes from the Greeks. It means people power. . . . We don't have democracy . . . but democracy should fit our particularities, not have a set Western standard."

They unanimously rejected not only Bakiyev's corrupt authoritarianism but also the democratic parties that existed, parties widely known for corruption. "There are no just people in the government," said Sharipa. Yet, when they debated alternatives and whether the state "should be Muslim," about half disagreed, saying it was not possible due to the immorality of Kyrgyzstan's officials. Others, like Venera, said that "it would be better to have a Muslim state. It would be good if all Kyrgyzstanis were Muslim. It would unite the state and eliminate problems like alcoholism and prostitution."

At the same time, most of the women held liberal views regarding women's rights. They supported wearing the hijab by choice, but not by law. Among them, only Gulbadam wanted polygyny to be legal. The respondents were also tolerant and inclusivist toward Jews, whom they did not perceive as a threat. They did not consider the Palestinians' problems to be about religion, and the conflict was of little concern to them. On the other hand, several of the women wanted legal restrictions on Christian proselytization. They debated whether religious freedom was more important than preventing conversions. They also sought to outlaw blasphemy. They believed that both conversions and blasphemy were violating Islam within their own community and that the state had a duty to prevent such offenses; however, many participants also emphasized "noncompulsion" in Islam, that is, a normative Islamic teaching that belief in Islam cannot be forced upon an individual.

While the women were informed of events in the broader Muslim world, they did not simply rally with the Muslim *umma*, as radical Islamists hoped society would do. The women expressed strong criticism of the United States and the West, but they also opposed the use of jihad in Iraq, Afghanistan, and Chechnya. They condemned terrorism and suicide bombing. "Osama Bin Laden," said Zamira, "was cruel. There were probably not only Americans in the towers." They did not believe innocents should die in a political conflict. Terrorists and jihadis were "not *shahids*," they agreed. In fact, they opposed "violence in any circumstances," agreeing with Gudam that "in the Qur'an it's forbidden to kill or commit suicide." Such categorically nonviolent views were a minority, as we shall see in other groups.

Mixed Views about Islam and Politics in the South

During the Bakiyev era, focus groups revealed that the situation in the south was becoming oppressive and Islam more politicized.

Men, Ethnic Kyrgyz, Small Business Owners, Twenty to Twenty-nine Years Old, Kara-Suu, 2007

In Kara-Suu, a group of ethnic Kyrgyz men[10] proudly spoke of the Islamic revival in their community. Kaldar claimed that "the mosques are so crowded, you need to pray outside the doorway." It was not only Uzbeks but ethnic Kyrgyz attending. Emil added, "Many youth have become religious nowadays." All preferred foreign missionaries to local imams, and several mentioned their interaction with Egyptian missionaries and foreign funding for the mosques and social programs. Perhaps as a result, their views on practice were puritanical; echoing Salafist teachings, they spoke of the need "to cleanse incorrect traditions, such as expensive weddings and the many rituals that Kyrgyz observe after funerals." The men sought purification and eradication of "national" Islamic traditions. However, they were liberal regarding women. They believed the hijab "should be a [woman's] choice," and that women should be allowed to enter politics.

They were stridently anti-Semitic, calling Jews "our enemy." According to Batir, "There is a threat to Muslimhood. . . . Jews direct all the terrorists. . . . They are trying to destroy religion among Muslims." Such views were atypical in Central Asia, where religious differences had been minimized in the Soviet era and different faith communities had coexisted for centuries. Batir went on to accuse Jews of suicide terrorism, claiming it was their idea "because in Islam there is no suicide." Unusually extreme, these men wanted to ban not only Christian missionaries and conversion, but also Judaism and Christianity in Kyrgyzstan.

The businessmen sought to "follow our Islamic law and religion" and "not democracy and capitalism." They wanted Islamic banking and clean courts, and lambasted government corruption. Ilhom declared, "The police work only for bribes. Every single driver has to pay off the police." Others claimed that the courts, procurator, and police were all corrupt. "Nowadays the politics of our people and our country aren't just," added Kubanych. But they opposed imams playing a role in politics.

10 KY-FG#24.

Some of them opposed all parties, including Islamic parties, as corrupt and responsible for "dividing Muslims." They were conflicted about the proper relationship between Islam and the state. They generally rejected the adoption of *shariat* as law and the idea of the caliphate. Shamsi worried, "If there's a caliphate, then all law will be by *shariat*, and that's not necessary for us, since we live in a democratic state. Politics and religion should be separate." Jirgal, on the other hand, was open to living under a caliphate: "Right now the caliphate is not suitable for us. A democratic system should decide all problems. But if an Islamic state were to come about, then the caliphate would resolve everything." He seemed confused about what exactly a democracy, Islamic state, and caliphate entailed. Most suggested following the models of Turkey, Egypt, or Malaysia—just "not Karimov . . . for in Uzbekistan the country is rich, and the people are poor." Most opposed the Russian political system and that of the United States. These men claimed to have faith that the government would improve if it incorporated elements of Islam within democracy. Given their desire to restrict religious freedom for minorities and free speech through blasphemy laws, their preferred government was decidedly illiberal.

Unlike many Uzbeks in Kara-Suu, who were sympathetic to HTI, these Kyrgyz men viewed the organization with hostility. Kubanych claimed, "HTI spreads propaganda about jihad and suicide. They want to create *shariat* in the Ferghana Valley . . . and teach people that it's necessary to kill." As we have seen, such allegations were false and probably reflected either hearsay or government propaganda about a group they had not actually encountered but feared anyway. The men consistently voiced opposition to all suicide bombing and terrorism, but not to militant, especially defensive, jihad. Batir said, "Jihad is the means to fight for the faith, for Islam, thanks to the prophet Muhammad, peace be upon him. It's a war for justice." Kaldar and Emil held the more mainstream view that "in a jihad you have to defend the faith, Muslimhood."

Women, Ethnic Uzbek, Small Business Owners/Traders, Thirty to Thirty-nine Years Old, Kara-Suu, 2007

Focus group discourse revealed that within Kara-Suu especially, as in the south more generally, greater politicization of Islam was taking place, especially as a result of Bakiyev's policies. Many were followers of Salafi imams, as discussed in Chapter 12. Consequently, they felt more religiously as well as ethnically oppressed. A group of ethnic Uzbek women in Kara-Suu[11] all considered themselves to have been born Muslim. Unlike many Kyrgyz, they did not see themselves as suddenly learning about Islam a decade after the USSR's collapse. Although educated under Soviet "scientific atheism," they had developed a particular interest

[11] KY-FG#23.

in studying the Qur'an and learning to perform *namaz* as teenagers in the 1980s. One woman had studied with a local *otincha* as a youth. Another had turned to Islam after being prohibited from entering the university, which even then expected parents to pay bribes for their children to be admitted. A third had been raised Muslim but began performing daily *namaz* only following the outreach of Arab-taught missionaries in the 1990s.

The women subscribed to purist Islamic practices. They eschewed the elaborate weddings and traditional national rituals typical of Uzbek and Kyrgyz Muslims in Kyrgyzstan. They were extremely intolerant of religious minorities. Unlike most Kyrgyzstanis, these women from Kara-Suu wanted Kyrgyzstan to ban Judaism, some Christian sects, and all Christian missionaries and to prohibit conversion from Islam to another religion. They justified this by agreeing that "Jews were against the Prophet Muhammad, peace be upon him," and "wanted to destroy him." They agreed that the way the young, especially women, dressed in European styles revealed that "our values are being destroyed." They had been exposed to more than a decade of missionaries, Salafist teaching, and ideas emanating from the Kara-Suu mosque of Rafiq Qori, known for encouraging Arab practices and Salafism.

The women claimed to prefer Muslim laws but were forced to live under secular ones. They were convinced that "if laws were based on the *shariat* there would be no corruption." Gulnara insisted, "The state must save the purity of our religion. Our religion is necessary to lead the people, but in Kyrgyzstan religion is forbidden to interfere with political matters." They complained that they could not even participate in Muslim student groups, much less form an Islamic party, since both were banned by the secular system. Furthermore, they blamed the secular government for declining Islamic values; they saw the government as a threat to Islam. Nazira thought life would improve if "Bakiyev would pray five times a day."

The women saw the secular system as horribly corrupt. Gulya elaborated, "The government 'bosses,' the rich people, can have big expensive weddings. If you try to get higher education, nowadays those people who have money can study. But if you don't have money but are smart and knowledgeable, you can't study. . . . None of the government 'bosses' thinks about this or tries to resolve the problems of simple people. No deputies have a conscience. They only line their pockets and build big houses. . . . That's all." Aygul complained that "corruption is everywhere." Gulnara seconded the point: "Police and the courts have no conscience. They show no justice. . . . In an Islamic state there is justice." The group unanimously supported adopting Muslim courts based on *shariat* in place of the system that existed "because there is no justice anywhere." Like the renowned Uzbek imam in her district, Rafiq Qori, Dina declared, "There is justice in Islam."

The women viewed democratic opposition parties in Kyrgyzstan overwhelmingly negatively. They associated democracy with the existing corruption and political conflict. Dina and others said that democracy is "too free. . . . We don't need democracy." Tamara declared, "Democracy is destroying peace!" They praised the UAE and Turkey as effective Muslim states. Yet, as they debated governance, most wanted only a limited role for religion. Aysalkin said, "We don't want an imam in place of the president." Gulnara mostly concurred: "Culture and education should be Islamic. The law and courts should be separate from religion. But laws should be based on religion." Begimay said, "Religion must not interfere with political issues." Dina countered, "If the laws are based on *shariat*, there is no corruption. First the state must preserve the purity of our religion. Our religion is necessary to lead the people." Two others argued about the caliphate:

NAZIRA: Maybe it's my Soviet upbringing, but I have a negative view of the caliphate. I like the Turkish form of government [the AKP].

GULYA: What's bad about it? For example, in the [United] Arab Emirates there's a caliphate. I like that form of government.

NAZIRA: So, a person comes along and says, "I'm caliph and my word is law." How can I follow him?

GULYA: It's only because of the Soviet political system that our understanding of the caliphate is not correct. One can either have a government like the caliphate, or what we have now. It's necessary to learn justice.

NAZIRA: So, you think religion should be the law of Kyrgyzstan?

GULYA: Yes, of course.

Some opposed but others voiced sympathy for HTI. The latter group asserted that young, unemployed people joined HTI and other Islamic movements for understandable reasons. Gulnara said, "We get only negative information about it [HTI]. [The government and media] blame them whenever there is war and conflict. But if they [would] spread Islam and all its laws, then people would support them." Gulya declared, "If it's nonviolent and if they have a positive ideology, and will fight crime, narco-business and corruption, honestly, we will support it; if they only spread propaganda about killing, then I'm opposed. . . . [B]ut if they bring justice, and bring people to a good life, then we should support them." All the women favored gradually legalizing Islamic parties.

Unlike radicals, they shunned violence. Even Gulya, the participant who was most strongly supportive of establishing the caliphate, condemned terrorism and suicide bombing: "It's absolutely incorrect. Those people are psychologically not normal, they're religious fanatics." All were sympathetic to the Palestinians and

Afghans who used such violence against Israel and the United States. America, they agreed, was an invader and had wrongly seized Iraq and Afghanistan. Yet, they opposed violence.

In short, this group had come to support puritanical and intolerant interpretation of Islam. Some of them also sought to adopt all law by *shariat* and live under the caliphate. However, support for Islamism was largely driven by frustration with corruption and injustice, as well as Bakiyev's targeting of observant Uzbeks for "counterterrorist" surveillance and arrest, policies which would escalate from 2008 onward.

Mixed Views about Islam and Politics in the North

In northern Kyrgyzstan, even among ethnic Kyrgyz, views had become less secular over time. Views were also less moderate during the Bakiyev years, as anger at government oppression and corruption increased.

Men, Ethnic Kyrgyz, Small Business Owners, Thirty to Thirty-nine Years Old, Bishkek, 2007

In Bishkek, a group of entrepreneurs,[12] part of the transitional generation educated during the late Soviet and early post-Soviet years, also expressed mixed views. They advocated Islamic revival and education. They had studied Islam from a *da'watchi,* in a *madrasa*, or from grandparents and friends. They were strictly observant, but not puritanical.

They debated Islam's correct political role. Some claimed that religion "should have no role in politics" and that politics "should be decided by elected leaders." Others admitted that they were unsure. Azamat offered, "Now we have a Western democracy, but it would be better if we used some Muslim principles in our own government." Tolkunbek declared, "Justice is a religious, Islamic value . . . but in Kyrgyzstan we have no justice. Everything is about money." On the corruption of the secular system, they agreed:

BERDIBEK: The police and courts are not just.
MAKSAT: There is no justice in any sphere of government.
BAKYT: Corruption is a critical problem for ordinary people.
ALMAZ: Yes, [it's a problem] not only for me, but for the country.

[12] KY-FG#16.

Maksat suggested that "there would be less corruption in a religious state, [where there is] law by *shariat*." Another countered, "We have many imams and mullahs, but corruption is very apparent among them too. Those people became religious leaders because they had money [paid bribes]." Others reasoned that the secular courts were extremely corrupt; therefore, "the courts should be based on religion" and "some *shariat* . . . because justice is a religious value." They believed that "religious leaders" or "the *mufti* should take part in deciding on political problems." All agreed with Bakyt: "The most important values are Islam, honesty, and justice."

Most claimed to favor democracy, but they were decidedly illiberal. Several suggested a democracy suited for Kyrgyz Muslims. For example, some of them wanted the state to ban not only Christian missionaries who had become active in Kyrgyzstan, but also any existing Christian churches and Jewish temples. One disagreed: "Non-Muslims are not a threat. There is one God for all." Most held negative views of secular democratic parties: "They work badly—they are all promises." In the minority was Maksat, who wanted "a constitution based on the Qur'an" and all law by *shariat*. Azamat more cautiously reasoned, "A caliphate would be good, but it's not realistic."

The men agreed with Bakyt's view that "Islamic parties can probably decrease corruption." They held varied views of existing Islamist movements. Some mentioned that Tursunbai Bakir-uluu, who had challenged Bakiyev in the presidential election and who was a supporter of legalizing HTI, was one of the few good Muslim politicians. Yet they claimed to oppose HTI because it "duped" its followers. Throughout the discussion, the men were also highly critical of religious repression in Uzbekistan.

Although they all claimed to oppose violence, in a rare show of sympathy for militant Islam, Almaz declared, "Maybe Juma Namangoniy would be a better leader than Karimov!" Azamat strongly concurred. Although not Uzbek themselves, they had sympathy for the Uzbeks' plight.

Radical-Leaning Views in the South

No groups expressed exclusively radical views consistent with HTI's ideology, much less Salafi jihadism. A few years into Bakiyev's rule, however, several groups were amenable to some ideas propagated by radical Islamists—including restrictive Salafi views about the rights of women and religious minorities, apostasy, blasphemy, and the *hudud* penalties. Some voiced support for militant jihad. Verbal opinions are far removed from actual participation in a movement, of course. But the decline of inclusive and mainstream views and the growth of radical-leaning views were notable.

Women, Ethnic Uzbek, White-Collar and Housewives, Forty to Forty-nine Years Old, Osh, 2007

A group of ethnic Uzbek women from Osh, highly educated and urban,[13] were strictly pious; they followed the five pillars, wore hijab, studied the Qur'an with an *otincha*. They believed that the mosque should help needy families. They claimed to interact frequently with their imam, for whom they had great respect. Beyond such piety, they held certain Islamist ideas: that there should be restrictions on women's work and that women should be punished for infidelity and immoral behavior. They were intolerant of non-Muslims and agreed that "Judaism should not be legal because it violates our religion." They supported Nigora's view that "missionaries should be illegal because they are a threat to Islam."

Politically, they leaned radical, in part due to frustration with their government. Minura complained, "There is not one sector in Kyrgyzstan which is not corrupt." Nigora agreed: "Of course Kyrgyzstan should be a Muslim state, because almost everyone knows the Qur'an and performs *namaz*. . . . But it won't happen immediately. It demands time. Maybe in ten years." Others concurred. Shahista said hopefully, "Maybe in ten years our children will live in a Muslim state." Nigora asserted, "Everything in the state must be Muslim, all laws, courts, education." Shahista partially disagreed: "Education shouldn't be Islamic because women according to *shariat* have to stay at home." The others argued with her, claiming that according to Islam, everyone "must be educated in Islam and other forms of knowledge." Asked what sort of laws they should have, the women responded, "Islamic laws." The consensus was that "religious leaders must influence political leaders." Nigora elaborated: "If we have an Islamic state, religious leaders will have influence on the decisions of political leaders, but if it's not an Islamic state, then there must be some elements of Islam in the state. . . . Democracy must be more Muslim. A Muslim democracy is better because it allows us to study Islam and follow Islam's advice." They were very frustrated with corruption and government, and so their views on law shared some radical Islamist ideas. All laws, said Nurjamal, "should be Islamic laws." Nigora endorsed the *hudud* penalties: "Muslim courts will be more just than secular ones because they are very harsh. Someone who has had one hand cut off will not want to lose the other." They all believed that the UAE and Saudi Arabia had less corruption and were good models for Kyrgyzstan. Another example of their illiberal views emerged in a discussion of the Danish cartoon caricatures of the Prophet Muhammed. Minura said, "They don't have the right to draw those. Those people who responded with violence and [creating] disorder were right to do so." Nigora declared, "[Europeans] call it free speech but they are wrong."

[13] KY-FG#19.

Like many Salafis, who in theory opposed all parties, most of the women agreed with Nigora that "in Islam, elections are forbidden." Only one speculated that "Islamic parties could improve life." Most simply supported the goal of establishing "an Islamic state," which they could not define, "over time." Despite their opposition to parties in general, some approvingly mentioned the party leader Tursunbai Bakri-uluu. Like other groups, they supported him because he's "known as [a member of] HTI."

Questioned about suicide bombing and martyrdom, the women were divided. Shahista said, "In Islam it's never allowed to use this method because Allah created life and He alone must take it away." They agreed jihad was necessary for Kyrgyzstanis, but only in defense, "when they [non-Muslims] destroy our women and threaten our religion. A person does not have the right to take another life." Only Nigora again voiced a more radical view. She expressed sympathy for al-Qaeda: "I think, if we blame America for the jihad, probably there are reasons. Probably this jihad of his [Bin Laden's] is a just jihad."

Radical-Leaning Views in the North

Men, Ethnic Uzbek/Uyghur, Migrants/Blue-Collar, Twenty to Twenty-nine Years Old, Bishkek, 2007

A group of young men who had worked in a variety of blue-collar jobs as manual and migrant laborers[14] also exhibited certain radical-leaning views. Although raised Muslim, they had become more pious as migrants. In Bishkek they had met Muslim missionaries who educated them more deeply in their faith. They tended toward purism and were highly critical of those who did not strictly abide by Islam's rules. They described themselves as Sunnis who follow only the Qur'an, no sect or school of Islam. They were critical of "those in their forties and fifties [the Soviet generation] who are atheist. . . . The young follow *shariat*." Tahir distinguished between "real Muslims who believe purely in Allah" and "follow all the rules completely," as opposed to "non-Muslims, who drink, run around, and don't believe in Allah." Azat said, "Allah gave us the Qur'an and *sunna*. . . . We must follow all the pillars. A pure Muslim will live by these rules."

Furthermore, they agreed that "Muslims must never change their religion." Extremely intolerant, they wanted to ban Jews because, said Tohir, "Jews are people who have always hated Islam." Il'hom complained that many Christian sects "have a negative influence on our religion, our mentality." "Many people convert . . . because they say Islam has done nothing for us," Rasul reported. Most

[14] KY-FG#25.

wanted to ban conversion. Avaz agreed: "Yes, their effect on our life is extremely negative." They claimed converts sold the faith for money and would go to hell. It is difficult to know if such views were common five, ten, or twenty years earlier. Such views did likely reflect both the contentious rise in Christian missionaries entering the region and the spread of both Arab-trained imams and Islamist ideologies in the 2000s. Consistent with their purist leanings, these men wanted religious education in Kyrgyzstan to follow Saudi Arabia.

Despite not having experienced religious persecution themselves, the men repeated a narrative of Soviet repression of Islam. Avaz explained, "In the USSR years, religion was forbidden. *Oqsoqol*s often say that they had to perform *namaz* in the fields. They couldn't freely go to the mosque to perform *namaz* like we do now. They forbade burials by Muslim rites. People fulfilled rituals secretly." Azat pointed out, "Back then it was the ideology. All religion was repressed." They complained that, despite nominal religious freedom, they were forbidden to organize Muslim groups at school. They criticized the Kyrgyz state "for defending Islamic values only in documents . . . not in reality," and they opposed negative Western influences, which they viewed as immoral and "barbarian."

Most of their complaints were against corruption in government. Avaz declared, "On Judgment Day, the corrupt kings and presidents will go to hell for all the money they have stolen from the people." Islam would somehow be a solution. Ilhom declared that "corruption would be less in a Muslim country." Azat agreed: "Take [Saudi] Arabia. There the level of corruption is much lower than in secular states." While Iskender thought a "Muslim democracy" might work, most of the men supported Avaz's view: "Islam and democracy are not compatible. Democracy is freedom of speech, but in Islam you must live by *shariat*. . . . Democracy is chaos." The men concurred that a system with "a Muslim court would be better" and that religious leaders "must sit in [parliament]."

They envisioned the ideal state as "a just Islamic one." Every one of them agreed that "all laws and rules for society and the state must be according to *shariat*." When asked to specify what type of state they preferred, the men responded by posing a radical change of government:

ISKENDER: A caliphate—all laws of *shariat*.
AVAZ: A caliphate. It's kingship.
AZAT: Yes [a caliphate].
IL'HOM: An Islamic state. The caliph is like a president. A caliphate would be the best form of governance.

They sought to live by the Qur'an "as the constitution." Such a law, they offered, would uphold Islam and legalize the *paranji*, hijab, and polygyny, for "family laws must be Muslim." "All culture and courts must be according to the Qur'an," said others. Avaz explained the appropriateness of stoning a wife for adultery. The others would adopt strict penalties for theft and corruption, uphold Islamic values, and prevent the blasphemy that took place in Europe. "Muslims think that freedom of speech is not right," said Rasul. They became quiet when asked about HTI, with whom their ideas closely aligned, but then voiced agreement with Iskender, who said, "If it's possible, please, let's create an Islamic state without violence." Il'hom added, "It [an Islamic state] would be very good, if it's done without violence."

The men disagreed about jihad. Most explained that "jihad is war against *kafir*" and for the "defense of one's family, country, and values." Only Azat totally opposed this interpretation: "No, jihad is not war, but a struggle on the path to Allah. It doesn't mean 'go kill people for the faith.'" Even among those who agreed that jihad was "war with weapons," only one espoused offensive jihad, as opposed to the more mainstream legitimation of defensive war. Yet, the men also strongly condemned suicide bombing, including the 9/11 attacks on the United States.

Overall, the group revealed that some radical ideas had also circulated in the north, as in the south. The men's direct declaration of support for a caliphate and *shariat* as state law was highly unusual for focus group participants or interview respondents, as were their extreme views on Jews and Christians. These ideas were associated with anger at Bakiyev's unjust rule and the influence of puritanical Islamist teaching.

Secular Political Views

Very few groups supported secular governance, especially in the south. Only a minority of respondents, including some pious Muslims, rejected all Islamist ideas and all Islamic influence on the state. They emphasized religious freedom but rejected religious influence on the law and state. In the north especially, a preference for secular governance was common in the early 2000s.[15]

Women, Ethnic Kyrgyz, University Students, Twenty to Twenty-three Years Old, Bishkek, 2005

A group of women university students in Bishkek,[16] despite being believers, fasting, and following many rules of Islam, supported "freedom of the people"

[15] Collins and Owen, "Islamic Religiosity."
[16] KY-FG#12.

and "Western . . . secular democracy." "*Shariat* is a rule we are supposed to follow," said Rahat; however, none condoned religious influence in law or state. Ainura summed up their attitude: "The mullah should sit in the mosque and mind his own business. There is nothing for him to do in political affairs." Some thought that any party, including HTI, had a constitutional right to participate in politics, but they opposed any religious law. Other women, less-educated traders from Issyk-Kul, also favored secularism. One asked, "Why is a Muslim state necessary for us? We have a multiethnic population. It will immediately bring conflict." Another worried that "when the state becomes Muslim the rights of women will be harmed." For women in northern Kyrgyzstan, accustomed to secular rights, this was a common concern. A third portrayed Islamic law in extreme terms: "In the past, in Muslim courts, they knocked [the accused] senseless with stones and lashed them." Her perception was inaccurate but revealed a fear among those with secular political preferences.

Men, Ethnic Kyrgyz, Agricultural Workers/Blue-Collar/Traders, Twenty to Twenty-nine Years Old, Batken, 2005

In Batken, a group of Tajik men, poor and little-educated,[17] defied the stereotype that those with few economic prospects joined Islamist movements. They were pious Muslims. They appreciated their freedom to study Islam and attend mosque but were skeptical of hypocritical religious authority and all Islamist groups. Toktosun said, "You need to do what the mullah says, not what he does." They overwhelmingly claimed HTI youth were "hypnotized." They decried the anti-Christian and anti-Semitic rhetoric of radical Islamists and calls for war against non-Muslims. Kambar said, "Nonbelievers are people too." Abdurashid explained, "In order for the state to develop well, it's necessary to be secular. . . . [F]or example, if everyone is religious and prays five times a day, who will work?" Salim added, "I think Muslim parties . . . should not take part [in politics]. . . . They haven't shown their positive side." They favored democracy: "Democracy gave us the possibility to build mosques and practice our religion in the mosques. . . . There is no need to mix religion and state." They uniformly opposed the United States and its role in Kyrgyzstan and Central Asia. Samad said, "America is an enemy country for Muslim states." Abdurashid said, "America should play a just role." They believed the United States was seizing Muslim land. Nonetheless, consistent with their other liberal views, the men opposed violence. Nemat said, "It's forbidden to cause bloodshed. It's necessary to solve everything in a civilized and educated manner."

[17] KY-FG#2.

Support for HTI—What HTI's Followers Say

Kyrgyzstan was the only Central Asian country where some HTI activists would speak directly and openly. They complained about the lack of justice and about religious oppression. An older respondent, Tair, viewed HTI's message in religious, rather than political, terms: "Justice is necessary, but for there to be justice, there must be faith in every house and people must live in faith," that is, according to Islam. He was attuned to events in Uzbekistan as well and was angered that "innocents died in Andijon" and that no one had been held accountable.[18] Erkin, a forty-two-year-old Kyrgyz member of HTI, was motivated to join by religious injustice: "There is no justice, not in Kyrgyzstan and not in Uzbekistan! They only talk about democracy. There is nothing Muslim in their actions. . . . They oppress Muslims even more now than during Soviet times—although they talk about freedom of religion. It's because of this that we should become an Islamic state!"[19]

"We want justice" was the common demand of HTI members. The religious dimension of HTI's plan for justice—spreading *da'wat*—was essential. An HTI supporter in Issyk-Kul echoed HTI's solution: "In Muslimhood there is justice. Their [HTI's] goal is to improve our life. They seek to change conditions. . . . Their method is only words [not violence]. . . . Islam must spread from the heart."[20] According to Aziz, the idea of the caliphate as justice addressed the widespread desire of HTI members to "live in a just and fair society. Nowadays there is no justice. . . . But the caliphate existed for fourteen centuries. It was a just system." Several HTI women claimed they joined because "everything the [current] government does is against justice."[21] "There is no justice," responded both Adina, a thirty-five-year-old housewife with only a secondary school education, and Sevara, a twenty-eight-year-old economist. Alisher linked the lack of justice to secularism: "There are already many atheists and they treat us believers badly. People do not think about higher questions. Everyone only lives for the present day. In Kyrgyzstan, there is no justice. The situation is bad."[22] Shukhrat exclaimed, "Where there is no justice, evil things happen . . . like here. Every person demands justice!"[23] Erjan explained that even after the 2010 democratic transition, things were no less corrupt. Atambayev's regime was unjust: "Like Akayev's and Bakiyev's, if you have money, you have rights, but if not, you have

[18] Interview with Tair, HTI member, Osh, Kyrgyzstan, October 2007.
[19] Interview with Erkin, HTI member, Osh, Kyrgyzstan, October 2007.
[20] Interview with Azamat, HTI supporter, Issyk-Kul, Kyrgyzstan, July 2011.
[21] Interview with HTI women members, Jalalabat, Kyrgyzstan, August 2004.
[22] Interview with Alisher, HTI member, Osh, Kyrgyzstan, October 2007.
[23] Interview with Shukhrat, HTI member, Osh, Kyrgyzstan, October 2007.

no justice."[24] The absence of justice was a core grievance of, and often the central motivation for, those activists; HTI was the answer.

Like HTI's propaganda, its members tied injustice to political corruption and non-Muslim government. According to Alisher, an ethnic Uzbek from southern Kyrgyzstan, "there is no justice because corruption is everywhere. Without money, you can't do anything. Everyone deceives everyone else. Who is a friend and who is an enemy . . . you can't tell."[25] A woman from southern Kyrgyzstan who had joined HTI said, "There is justice, but only a little [justice] in Kyrgyzstan. And there's none in Uzbekistan. Even in Kyrgyzstan, people are ready to strangle each other for a piece of bread. . . . So, when you think about it, there is no justice in Kyrgyzstan either!" She was fed up with the government: "It's always a conflict for the 'chair' [political boss]. Everyone only thinks about his own profit."[26] An ethnic Uzbek, she believed HTI's political solution was to corrupt infidel regimes. Gulnara, formerly a teacher but now a young mother and housewife, said the solution was through HTI: "Our goal is to establish one caliphate in Central Asia."[27] Her words reflected HTI's adaptation to Central Asia—espousing a regional caliphate, not a Middle Eastern one. She and her husband, both Uzbeks from southern Kyrgyzstan, believed in the utopian solution HTI offered.

The idea of Islamic values and *shariat* as the remedy to a range of societal ills resonated widely. Most HTI members claimed that drunkenness, sexual looseness and prostitution, drug use, and AIDS were the consequences of a corrupt state that, as Adina said, "lacks Islamic law."[28] Erkin laid blame on "people [who] don't accept the Qur'an's laws."[29] Azamat joined HTI because "the government does nothing" about the moral crisis.[30] Thanks to *da'watchis*, he said, people were becoming more Islamic. In a caliphate "there would be no drunkenness."[31] Sanjar, in Issyk-Kul, joined for the same reasons: the moral decline of society and corruption. He explained that it's not HTI but "corruption and . . . the government itself that causes conflict."[32]

Other HTI ideas, however, were less salient. HTI members were divided about Jews; not all were anti-Semitic. "Let them alone and we will mind our own business," said Erkin; however, he did believe Jews and Christians should have no rights in a caliphate. Alisher declared, "America is ruled by

24 Interview with Erjan, HTI member, Bishkek, Kyrgyzstan, May 2013.
25 Interview with Alisher.
26 Interview with Cholpon, HTI, Osh, Kyrgyzstan, October 2007.
27 Interview with Gulnara, HTI, Osh, Kyrgyzstan, October 2007.
28 Interview with Adina, HTI member, Osh, Kyrgyzstan, October 2007.
29 Interview with Erkin.
30 Interview with Azamat.
31 Interview with Erkin.
32 Interview with Sanjar, HTI member, Issyk-Kul, Kyrgyzstan, 2005.

Jews and everyone knows it. Because of this, America creates wars and division in Central Asia and other places. . . . It does a lot of evil. . . . Christians and Jews are *kafir*. . . . The true religion is Islam. I'm not sure, but I think that under a caliphate, when they live among Muslims, they will not be legally allowed to have churches and synagogues."[33] Yet others urged tolerance. "Pure religious people, even Baptists, are not a threat. . . . It's their right to choose," said Sanjar.[34] As in the focus groups, only a minority considered the Palestinian-Israeli conflict to be an issue of concern for Muslims in Central Asia.

HTI members in Kyrgyzstan almost uniformly emphasized their opposition to any violent jihad. Tair, an unemployed villager with an incomplete secondary education, insisted, "The most important jihad is inner. . . . The Prophet said that the biggest enemy is not a war or a conflict with someone, it is a jihad against yourself and faults. . . . This is the most important and difficult question. . . . They will never lose their way to the Almighty Allah."[35] Some declared, "No military jihad is right. . . . It's not in Islam."[36] Cholpon believed that "jihad by violence is not moral, not conscionable."[37] Most HTI members in Kyrgyzstan staunchly opposed suicide bombing as well. Adina unequivocally stated, "Suicide is a great sin and it contradicts the *shariat*. I think that one may only be called a *shahid* if one dies doing good for other people."[38] Erkin also condemned suicide bombing: "Suicide bombing is not right. There is no such thing in Islam. It's a great sin."[39] Shukhrat opposed any violence, "even if they attack your country."[40]

Despite the prevailing position against violence, a small minority of HTI members did justify violent jihad against Israel and against the United States in Afghanistan and Iraq. Especially since the U.S. invasion of Iraq, they viewed the United States as an invader and those wars as defensive jihads. One HTI respondent went so far as to justify suicide attacks as "right, because they are fighting for the honor of the Muslim religion."[41] As noted above, HTI's nonviolent ideology certainly resonated, more so than the violent messages of other jihadists in the region. And yet, a creeping shift toward approving violence was evident.

33 Interview with Alisher.
34 Interview with Sanjar.
35 Interview with Tair.
36 Interview with Erkin.
37 Interview with Cholpon.
38 Interview with Adina.
39 Interview with Erkin.
40 Interview with Shukhrat.
41 Interview with Gulnara.

Societal Elites and the Limits of Support for HTI and Radicalism

As in Tajikistan and Uzbekistan, communal leaders in Kyrgyzstan were influential among ordinary Muslims, and many such individuals actively undermined Islamist messages and their potential for mobilization. Under Akayev's era of religious liberalization, most interview respondents, even the more rigidly pious Uzbeks, did not support Islamism, even HTI's nonviolent Islamism. According to one Uzbek imam in Osh, "Glory to Allah, we have no prohibitions on religion. We have many mosques, and more and more people have begun to perform *namaz* and keep the fast."[42] Many leaders, in both north and south, staunchly opposed HTI. Another Uzbek mullah in Osh said, "HTI's goal is to divide people"; he and many others claimed that youth "sold themselves" to it "for money."[43] In Batken, an imam condemned both the IMU and HTI, alleging incorrectly that "the IMU and HTI are the same party." He added, "They steal children."[44] He sought to instill fear of joining those organizations.

However, injustice would make some open to Islamist messages. A journalist in Issyk-Kul, where HTI had started recruiting ethnic Kyrgyz, said, "I oppose HTI [because] it cannot create a Muslim state without force, [but] we cannot say that we live under a just government."[45] While opposing HTI, many recognized that injustice was a fundamental problem.

Some societal elites were sympathetic to HTI. A wealthy and pious businessman who sponsored construction of a Uyghur mosque explained HTI this way: "Youth are devoted to their values and ideas. HTI shows them the path to a bright future." He supported legalizing Islamic parties; however, he himself believed that "freedom of speech" and "Western democracy" were better. He complained about the current corruption of elections: "The candidate [here] bought more voters. So, he got elected and became a parliamentary deputy. This is the root of conflict."[46] An ethnic Dungan businessman and sponsor of a mosque said, "As far as I know, HTI youth have a goal—to create a more honest, just society. Such [Islamic] parties call for more justice. Youth and the population would support this. Of course, I don't prefer using physical force. Ideological influence is necessary."[47] He was skeptical of the prospect of democracy achieving justice.

42 Interview with Uzbek imam, Osh, Kyrgyzstan, 2005.

43 Interview with unregistered Uzbek mullah, Osh, Kyrgyzstan, 2005; interview with unregistered Kyrgyz mullah, Batken, Kyrgyzstan, 2005.

44 Interview with Uzbek imam assistant, Batken, Kyrgyzstan, 2005.

45 Interview with Kyrgyz journalist, Issyk-Kul, Kyrgyzstan, 2005.

46 Interview with Uyghur businessman, Bishkek, Kyrgyzstan, 2005.

47 Interview with Dungan businessman, Bishkek, Kyrgyzstan, 2005.

In southern Kyrgyzstan, Uzbek communal leaders were often far more sympathetic to HTI. An Uzbek imam from Osh emphasized the party's religious motivation: "HTI thinks that Muslims today have very little religious freedom . . . so their main goal is to take power."[48] One Osh imam just wanted to live in a "Muslim state . . . with no corruption"; he explained that "youth join HTI because they lack religious education. HTI attracts people who know nothing. . . . Allah knows, even if they promise [an Islamic state], they can't do anything. It's not possible to create an Islamic state without violence."[49] But he went on to say that there should be legal Muslim parties that participate in elections. A businessman in Jalalabat region who had helped to build a mosque likewise said, "If an Islamic state is created, one hundred percent, then it will be possible [for the government to be just]. But Hizb ut-Tahrir cannot create [an Islamic state], because the [existing] state is opposed to it." Even a police official in Osh said that HTI was society's response to "injustice" and "the government." He further admitted that "there are no people in the security organs who are truly working for citizens."[50] A consequence of these conditions was the popularity of HTI. One religious teacher confirmed that HTI was popular in his mostly ethnic Uzbek community: "Yes, many young people join the ranks of Hizb ut-Tahrir. This party considers itself a party of *azattyk* [freedom]. It wants to create an Islamic state. By promoting this, it attracts young people. At the same time, it gives them money. . . . They want all people, all countries to be united into an Islamic state. They gather people into their ranks under these slogans."[51]

Many religious leaders and societal elites supported the creation of Islamic courts to address corruption and injustice. One religious teacher said, "The Muslim court is more just, since Muslims are judged according to the Qur'an. They condemn a person, assessing the severity of the act he has committed. This judgment is fair."[52] An imam from Batken, also ethnic Uzbek, said, "A Muslim court is fairer. It is based on Islam and religion." An Uzbek woman *da'watchi* from Osh cautiously agreed: "Maybe an Islamic court is more just. If everything is done according to the Qur'an, then everything will be fair, since the person who fears Allah will endure a just punishment."[53] An ethnic Kyrgyz imam in Osh said, "In Arabia, they have no crime. No one drinks. In Pakistan, they don't sell alcohol. In Arabia during time for *namaz*, everyone goes and they leave shops open and no one steals. Because they fear Allah. . . . In Muslim courts, they don't give bribes. Or pay money to get out of jail. . . . Now there is no justice. There could perhaps

[48] Interview with Uzbek imam, Osh, Kyrgyzstan, 2005.
[49] Interview with Kyrgyz imam, Osh, Kyrgyzstan, 2005.
[50] Interview with ethnic Kyrgyz official, Ministry of Internal Affairs, Osh, Kyrgyzstan, 2005.
[51] Interview with Uzbek imam assistant, Batken, Kyrgyzstan, 2005.
[52] Interview with Uzbek imam assistant, Batken.
[53] Interview with Uzbek *da'watchi*, Osh, Kyrgyzstan, 2005.

be [justice] on the basis of the Islamic religion."[54] Even in the north, some Kyrgyz imams had begun to argue for adopting Islamic courts. An imam in Issyk-Kul argued that Islamic courts and "judgment by *shariat* . . . as in Muslim countries" would be better.[55] These ideas from HTI's propaganda, it seemed, resonated.

Even if sympathetic to the idea of an Islamic party or state, religious leaders generally supported only defensive war. One imam explained, "Jihad is a fight for justice. Jihad is when Muslims express their dissatisfaction when other countries threaten their religion. If they attack and want to take away our religion, we can declare jihad."[56] An influential Uzbek mosque donor spoke out against *any* militant version of jihad, and even against nonviolent radicalism, explaining, "Jihad existed at the time of our prophet Muhammad, peace be upon him. Nowadays there are adherents of jihad, such as the Wahhabi parties. I do not support them. They want to create their own Islamic state under the banner of Islam, but we will not agree to this. There are many Arab countries and they also do not accept Hizb ut-Tahrir, as far as I know." The real jihad, he explained, "means, to fight against myself, I should not do anything bad, steal, or take from anyone."[57] A Batken imam, one of the few to express radical views concerning both Jews and jihad, said, "Jihad means that if . . . the fight is against the infidels, then . . . it is necessary to stand strong and then the *kafir* will not be able to defeat us."[58] He referred to Jews as "kafir" but condemned suicide bombers, saying, "This is just bloodshed, and will not lead to anything good."[59] Even in the south, there was opposition to violence, if not to Islamic governance. One Osh imam, commenting on Chechen suicide bombers, said, "It's wrong. What they are doing is a sin," even if Russia had attacked Chechnya. A *mahalla* leader from Batken emphasized the wrongs perpetrated by Russia against the Chechens, by Israel against the Palestinians, and by the United States in Afghanistan and Iraq, but said, "It's better to resolve things peacefully." Moreover, he asserted that there were financial motives, not religious ones: "*Shahid*s are just doing it for money."[60] Another religious leader also strongly condemned those who "fight jihad and blow themselves up." He said, "They are not [real] *shahids*."[61]

Whether university students, poorly educated laborers, white-collar professionals, or migrant workers, ordinary Kyrgyzstanis revealed common political and

54 Interview with unregistered Kyrgyz religious leader, Osh, Kyrgyzstan, 2005.
55 Interview with Kyrgyz imam, Issyk-Kul, Kyrgyzstan, 2005.
56 Interview with Kyrgyz imam, Issyk-Kul, Kyrgyzstan, 2005.
57 Interview with Uzbek businessman, mosque donor, Osh, Kyrgyzstan, 2005.
58 Interview with Uzbek imam, Baken, Kyrgyzstan, 2005.
59 Interview with Uzbek imam assistant, Batken, Kyrgyzstan, 2005.
60 Interview with Kyrgyz *aksakal*, *mahalla* leader, Batken, Kyrgyzstan, 2005.
61 Interview with Uzbek imam assistant, Batken, 2005.

economic frustrations in their discussions: desire for justice, and for freedom of Islamic belief, practice, and education. Most Kyrgyzstanis—regardless of education or class, gender, or region—were believers, and for many, their beliefs and values influenced their political ideas about the society and state in which they hoped to live. In this respect, whether ethnic Kyrgyz or ethnic Uzbek, northern or southern, many Kyrgyzstani group participants voiced opinions strikingly similar to those of the Tajikistanis and Uzbekistanis discussed in Chapters 7 and 10.

The Kyrgyzstani respondents' political preferences were hardly uniform, however, and they were influenced by the type of religious authority or teaching they had encountered. Those who idealized "Arabia" or "Arab Islam" as true and pure often held more puritanical interpretations of *shariat* and less tolerant views of religious minorities. Their views paralleled the views of those in the Ferghana Valley of Uzbekistan. They were also more likely to see Islam as a political and social solution to widespread problems and to advocate a greater role for *shariat* in law, sometimes including extreme interpretations of the *hudud* penalties by the state. In short, the ideas advocated by missionaries and respected imams were shaping public opinion in the context of failed democracy and growing corruption and repression. By contrast, those educated in the Soviet era, who were believers but not strictly observant, not followers of new Islamic missionaries, and more likely to practice national Kyrgyz traditions, were often skeptical of any role for Islam in political life.

Comparing groups across the north and south and over time revealed the effect of growing religious repression. In earlier focus groups during the late Akayev era, most ethnic Uzbeks of Kyrgyzstan appeared satisfied with their religious freedom, and held moderate views about the role of Islam in politics and law. Certain ideas congruent with puritanical imams and radical Islamist propaganda—such as banning Christian missionaries and converts, adopting all law by *shariat*, and limited sympathy for militant jihad—became more common in the south in the context of growing religious, ethnic, and political repression under Bakiyev. During this time, radical ideas about rejecting democracy and establishing the caliphate, as well as religious intolerance, began spreading in the north as well. Focus groups revealed that many Kyrgyzstanis became not only dissatisfied with their government but also skeptical of democracy. If they supported democracy, they often envisioned a less liberal, more Muslim style of democracy.

Yet, Kyrgyzstani respondents also exhibited a hesitancy to support or trust HTI, the most prominent Islamist movement operating inside Kyrgyzstan. HTI had a growing but still limited appeal in the mid-2000s. Although some of its ideas did resonate—particularly its focus on corruption, injustice, and repression in both Kyrgyzstan and Uzbekistan—its core ideology had not changed and was too extreme for most Kyrgyzstanis. Most respondents rejected HTI's transnational goal of establishing the caliphate. More radical Islamist ideas, violent jihad to pursue an Islamic state, were unacceptable to the overwhelming majority of Kyrgyzstanis. Yet, a small minority was sympathetic to such ideas. As Chapter 14 will address, the evocative ideological propaganda and skillful recruiting of KTJ and ISIS would mobilize some Kyrgyzstanis to fight in Syria.

PART VI

FROM CENTRAL ASIA TO SYRIA

Transnational Salafi Jihadists

14
Central Asians Join the Syrian Jihad

Izzat yo'li jihoddir! [Jihad is the way of honor!].
—Abu Saloh, posted on YouTube, October 17, 2017

On July 29, 2018, several Western cyclists were making their way through Tajikistan on a trip around the globe. They had most recently been biking through the Pamirs, exchanging gestures of kindness with locals, while taking in the beauty of the rugged terrain. The trip ended tragically when five young Tajik men rammed them with a car, then attacked them with an axe and knives. They killed two Americans and two Europeans. Tajik government security services soon apprehended the attackers, killing four of them. Two days later, ISIS's Amaq News Agency released a previously recorded video of the perpetrators pledging allegiance to the Islamic State in Iraq and Syria before an ISIS flag.[1] The deadly attack was one of the most gruesome, but hardly the only, violent attacks perpetrated by Central Asian Islamists since ISIS emerged. According to Human Rights Watch, Central Asian nationals were implicated "in at least seven attacks by extremist armed groups, including ISIS, between 2016 and July 2018."[2] Human Rights Watch found that at least 117 people were killed and more than 360 were injured in those attacks.

Rather than withering beneath state repression, Central Asian Islamism had become even more radicalized and transnational, ultimately sending adherents to Syria and motivating attacks within their own borders. This latest, third wave of Islamism across Central Asia drew its recruits not only from Uzbekistan and Tajikistan but also from Kyrgyzstan, Kazakhstan, and Turkmenistan.[3]

[1] The Islamic State is alternately called ISIL (the Islamic State in Iraq and the Levant) and is also sometimes referred to by its Arabic-language acronym, Da'esh.

[2] Human Rights Watch, "'We Live in Constant Fear': Possession of Extremist Material in Kyrgyzstan," September 17, 2018, https://www.hrw.org/report/2018/09/18/we-live-constant-fear/possession-extremist-material-kyrgyzstan.

[3] For example, residents of Aktau in western Kazakhstan reported unprecedented extremist propaganda in their town, and journalists have documented a surge of ISIS recruits from central Kazakhstan; both regions had long been considered relatively secular and Westernized. Author's conversations with residents of Aktau, and with a *Radio Free Europe/Radio Liberty* journalist in Washington, D.C., November 2018.

Politicizing Islam in Central Asia. Kathleen Collins, Oxford University Press. © Oxford University Press 2023.
DOI: 10.1093/oso/9780197685068.003.0015

Mobilizing well over five thousand Central Asians to fight for a caliphate in Syria and Iraq was a striking feat in societies that forty years earlier had virtually no connection to Islamism, the Middle East, or the idea of the caliphate. The number of Central Asian foreign fighters exceeded the numbers of Muslim foreign fighters joining jihads in Bosnia (1992–95), Chechnya (1994–2009), and Somalia (1991–present), and even those joining the Sunni insurgency in Iraq (2003 to approximately 2009).[4] Central Asian numbers in Syria were roughly equal to low-end estimates of Arab foreign fighters in Afghanistan in 1979–92—the largest Muslim foreign fighter movement prior to Syria.[5] In military effectiveness, the Central Asians surpassed the Afghan-Arab movement. Unlike the Saudis in the anti-Soviet jihad, who reputedly had few military skills, the Uzbeks and Tajiks in Syria were respected as experienced and fierce fighters. According to one Iraqi military officer, Uzbeks were reputed to be "the most outstanding combat groups" waging jihad against Bashar al-Assad.[6] They had fought through the Russian carpet-bombing of Idlib and were still holding territory in 2022, over four years after ISIS's caliphate fell.

That Central Asians would join this fight was not a foregone conclusion. Yet as early as 2011, some religious entrepreneurs left for Syria to form militias and fight in a new, great jihad against Assad and his Russian-backed, secular dictatorship. Within the overall foreign fighter movement in Syria, some Central Asians formed groups fighting under al-Qaeda's front in Syria (i.e., KTJ, KIB, and various Russian-speaking groups), while others joined ISIS directly. This chapter lays out the three common factors leading to the emergence of two major groups: Katibat al-Tawhid wal Jihad (KTJ), which fought with al-Qaeda; and, collectively, Central Asians in ISIS. First, injustice and religious repression both at home and in Syria motivated opposition. Second, entrepreneurs propagated a new, caliphate-centered ideology. Third, the closure of associational space at home pushed Islamists to move abroad, to a terrain where they anticipated success. Next, I examine the strategies these groups used in mobilizing. Whether under al-Qaeda or ISIS these groups achieved some success through new network formation, but KTJ arguably did more to build sacred authority. Both only partially adapted their ideational propaganda to Central Asians' concerns.

[4] Thomas Hegghammer, "The Rise of Muslim Foreign Fighters, Islam and the Globalization of Jihad," *International Security* 35, no. 2 (Winter 2010–11): 61. Hegghammer's data set of Muslim foreign fighters ends in 2009–10.

[5] Hegghammer, "The Rise of Muslim Foreign Fighters," 61.

[6] Mohamed Mostafa, "Officer: Uzbeks, Uyghurs among Remaining Foreign Militants in Mosul's Old City," *Iraqi News* (Manama, Bahrain), April 24, 2017.

The Third Wave: Transnational Salafi Jihadism

Foreign fighters began heading to Syria and Iraq in 2011–12. The United States had just withdrawn from Iraq, leaving the country vulnerable to the remaining elements of al-Qaeda and other jihadist organizations. By 2013–14, ISIS had become a major Islamist fighting force, first taking territory inside Iraq.[7] Al-Qaeda was again growing there as well. Across the border, inside Syria, what had begun as an anti-Assad and pro-democracy protest movement during the Arab Spring in 2011 spiraled into a brutal civil war, drawing in more than forty Islamist groups by 2012. Most of them were not Syrian, but transnational Sunni, Salafi jihadist fighters. With the internet and social media facilitating awareness of Assad's barbaric conduct, including the use of chemical weapons on women and children, popular outrage among Muslims across the world had erupted.[8] The war triggered this new form of transnational jihadism, and the foreign fighter influx catapulted ISIS to its initial success, allowing it to wrest control of a territory larger than Great Britain from the Syrian and Iraqi states.[9] In June 2014, just five months after President Barack Obama dismissed it as a mere "JV team," ISIS took Mosul. This was a devastating blow; the United States had defeated the Iraqi insurgency only in Iraq's second largest city, after significant casualties, between 2004 and 2008. With the United States gone, a mere thousand ISIS fighters defeated thirty thousand Iraqi government troops—a stunning victory that spurred tens of thousands from around the globe to join ISIS and other groups in this new great jihad.[10] By 2015, the overall number of foreign fighters in Syria and Iraq was far higher than estimates of Afghan Arabs fighting in Afghanistan in the 1980s, at the height of the Afghan jihad against the Soviets.

Previous chapters have demonstrated that there is no sweeping, mass support for Islamist radicalism, of a militant or nonmilitant form, in Central Asia. Central Asian governments' claims of an escalating ISIS threat from within rang hollow, given their long history of exaggerating threats to justify political crackdowns, appease Russia, and appeal for U.S. support. Furthermore, given the enormous risk associated with militant group participation—whether inside a conflict zone such as Syria or under the repressive regimes in Central Asia—it is surprising that anyone would join such movements. Whether the Egyptian Islamic Jihad,

[7] Richard Barrett, "Beyond the Caliphate: Foreign Fighters and the Threat of Returnees," Report, The Soufan Center, New York, October 2017; Joby Warrick, *Black Flags: The Rise of ISIS* (New York: Anchor Books, 2015); Michael Weiss and Hassan, *ISIS: Inside the Army of Terror* (New York: Regan Arts, 2016).

[8] Peter Neumann, "Foreign Fighter Total in Syria/Iraq Now Exceeds 20,000; Surpasses Afghanistan Conflict in the 1980s," *ICSR Insights*, Report, Department of War Studies, King's College, London, January 26, 2015.

[9] Charles Lister, *The Syrian Jihad: Al-Qaeda, the Islamic State and the Evolution of an Insurgency* (Oxford: Oxford University Press, 2015).

[10] Weiss and Hassan, *ISIS*, xi.

the Islamic Movement of Uzbekistan, or al-Qaeda itself, militant Islamist groups have operated with relatively few active recruits, as the risk in joining is simply too high.

By 2015, Islamism appeared to have failed in Central Asia. There, the IRPT and HTI were largely defeated. Renewed government crackdowns, combined with Islamists' inability to effect change and maintain relevance in such repressive conditions, undermined their societal influence, and even more so the prospects of their political success. Inside Afghanistan, the IMU and IJU were also struggling to survive. Despite these challenges, some strands of Central Asian Islamism, like global jihadism, continued evolving along an increasingly extreme trajectory. The third wave of Central Asian Islamists has been explicitly antidemocratic and intent on establishing a caliphate through violence—including suicide bombing of civilian targets. This third wave reflected the ideology of transnational Salafi jihadism, which, over the past two decades, has fostered extreme violence around the globe. Since the Syrian Civil War erupted, Salafi jihadism has inspired tens of thousands of Muslim foreign fighters to flood to Iraq and Syria. A handful of Central Asian radicals operated underground within their home states, but far more turned to open radicalism by joining jihadist groups in the Middle East, under the banners of al-Qaeda or ISIS. Videos of Central Asian battalions—Uzbek, Tajik, and Kyrgyz, and even some Turkmen and Kazakh—appeared online and urged viewers to join fellow Muslims there.

These militants remain unlikely to overthrow any of the Central Asian regimes. Nonetheless, these third-wave jihadists have inflicted significant damage. They have waged multiple deadly (if small-scale) terrorist attacks, from Dushanbe to Moscow, Stockholm, and New York. In concert with al-Qaeda and ISIS, they have proven themselves to be highly skilled and somewhat successful in combating Syrian, Russian, and Afghan forces and in waging terror attacks in Afghanistan. More broadly, they offered Central Asians an alternative means of opposition to their repressive and corrupt regimes and a vision for justice through a caliphate abroad.

Precise data on any foreign fighters, especially citizens of authoritarian states, are difficult to obtain. Journalists provided some evidence of some Central Asian sympathy for and participation in the Syrian jihad. In 2014, for example, a local resident informed the BBC that an ISIS flag had been hoisted outside a school in Yangiyo'l, a town in the Tashkent region, in an act of extraordinary defiance against the Uzbek regime. Another report claimed that ISIS flags had been draped over a Tashkent bridge.[11] Imam Rashod Qori openly stated that mosque attendees in southern Kyrgyzstan were asking many questions about ISIS's caliphate. Journalists detailed the stories of individuals, including young women,

[11] Communication with Uzbekistani sociologist, Tashkent, Uzbekistan, May 2016.

who left Kyrgyzstan and Kazakhstan for Syria.[12] Kyrgyz security services similarly have been releasing data since 2015 on hundreds of Kyrgyz who fought there.[13] When U.S. troops liberated ISIS-controlled territory, the Pentagon obtained records of hundreds of Central Asian and other Russian-speaking women residing in ISIS "guesthouses."[14] The IRPT's Chairman Muhiddin Kabiri warned in 2016 that over two thousand Tajiks had gone to Syria to join ISIS and that former IRPT members who had fled the Tajik state's oppression were joining the flow. Although precise numbers are uncertain, even using conservative estimates, more Central Asians were fighting in Syria and Iraq than had fought for the IMU at its height.

Expert databases on foreign fighter flows compiled by international organizations and NGOs working in the region offer the most reliable estimates. The data suggest that at least 40 percent of ISIS's total fighting force was foreign.[15] The number of foreign fighters in Syria and Iraq grew from under 1,000 in 2011 to more than 8,500 in 2013, about 18,000 in 2014, and roughly 31,500 by late 2015.[16] At its height, before a U.S./NATO-led counteroffensive made significant progress, the Pentagon estimated that ISIS included about 33,000 foreign fighters.[17] Similarly, the International Centre for Counter-Terrorism (ICCT) in The Hague found that "foreign recruits from 104 countries [had] been drawn into the conflict in Syria and Iraq alone, notwithstanding the absence of ethnocultural links of many fighters to Syria and the Arab world."[18] ICCT estimated total foreign fighters at more than 40,000, coming from more than 110 countries, at the peak.[19]

The actual number of Central Asians involved in this foreign fighter movement—including ISIS- and al-Qaeda–linked groups—remains contested.[20]

[12] Dilara Isa, "'Джихадисты из Казыгурта' угрожают Назарбаеву," *Radio Azattyk*, March 30, 2016, https://rus.azattyq.org/a/kazygurt-jikhadisty-ugrozy-nazarbaevu/27643406.html.

[13] "Сириядагы урушка катышкан кыргызстандыктар 600дөн ашты," *Radio Azattyk*, August 3, 2016, https://www.azattyk.org/a/27897290.html.

[14] Daniel Milton and Biran Dodwell, "Jihadi Brides? Examining a Female Guesthouse Registry from the Islamic State's Caliphate," *CTC Sentinel* 11, no. 5 (May 2018): 20, https://ctc.westpoint.edu/jihadi-brides-examining-female-guesthouse-registry-islamic-states-caliphate/.

[15] Alex Schmid, "Foreign (Terrorist) Fighter Estimates: Conceptual and Data Issues," ICCT Policy Brief, International Centre for Counter-Terrorism, The Hague, October 2015, 1.

[16] Neumann, "Foreign Fighter Total in Syria/Iraq Now Exceeds 20,000." See also U.S. Congress Homeland Security Committee, *Final Report of the Task Force on Combating Terrorist and Foreign Fighter Travel*, Report, Washington, D.C., September 2015; Cameron Glenn, "ISIS Losses by the Numbers," Report, Woodrow Wilson International Center for Scholars, Washington, D.C., March 25, 2016; Schmid, "Foreign (Terrorist) Fighter Estimates," 1.

[17] Jeff Seldin, "Far from Dead: Tens of Thousands of IS Fighters Linger in Iraq, Syria," *Voice of America*, August 14, 2018, https://www.voanews.com/a/far-from-dead-tens-of-thousands-of-is-fighters-linger-in-iraq-syria/4527452.html.

[18] Schmid, "Foreign (Terrorist) Fighter Estimates," 1.

[19] Schmid, "Foreign (Terrorist) Fighter Estimates," 1.

[20] Abdujalil Abdurasulov, "Central Asians Respond to the Lure of the Islamic State," *BBC News* (Almaty), June 2, 2015; International Crisis Group, "Syria Calling: Radicalisation in Central Asia,"

Some independent research centers have generated realistic approximations based on compilations of media reports and both independent and government estimates. While imperfect, these data are the best available and give some sense, comparatively, of the numbers of fighters from individual countries. The International Centre for the Study of Radicalisation and Political Violence (ICSR) indicated in 2013 that only small numbers from Central Asia had become foreign fighters in Syria and Iraq; most came from Kyrgyzstan and Kazakhstan (estimates ranging from 23 to 180), with fewer than a dozen each from Uzbekistan, Tajikistan, and Turkmenistan.[21] The number of foreign fighters from the former Soviet states increased rapidly. By January 2015, just six months after ISIS's capture of Mosul, ICSR estimated the total number of citizens from Central Asia fighting to be 1,400, and the total from the former Soviet region to be 2,900.[22] This included 500 Uzbekistani citizens,[23] although it is unclear from the data set whether they left directly from Uzbekistan or were already living abroad (e.g., as migrant laborers in Russia, religious students in Turkey, or foreign fighters in Afghanistan).

According to The Soufan Center's data, from June 2014 to 2018 "estimates suggest a near-300 percent increase in known fighters."[24] Soufan's 2015 approximations put recruits from the former Soviet republics at 4,700. By May 2016, Uzbekistan had provided an estimated 1,500 fighters. As of February 2017, Central Asians joining the jihad in Syria and Iraq had increased to some 5,000 in total.[25] Those figures may still be underreporting Central Asians, since many fighters arriving via Russia were registered as "Russian residents."[26] As seen in Table 14.1, within the region estimates of foreign fighters were greatest

Europe & Central Asia, Briefing No. 72, Brussels, January 20, 2015, https://www.crisisgroup.org/europe-central-asia/central-asia/syria-calling-radicalisation-central-asia.

[21] Neumann, "Foreign Fighter Total in Syria/Iraq Now Exceeds 20,000."

[22] Neumann, "Foreign Fighter Total in Syria/Iraq Now Exceeds 20,000."

[23] The estimates for Central Asian foreign fighters (not just ISIS), especially for Uzbeks, were higher in the Soufan Center's data, which put the total at about two thousand from Central Asia, roughly the same. *Radio Free Europe/Radio Liberty* (RFE/RL) put the figure at about one thousand in November 2014. See Neumann, "Foreign Fighter Total in Syria/Iraq Now Exceeds 20,000"; Bruce Pannier, "State, Religion, and Radicalism in Central Asia," *Qishloq Ovozi, Radio Free Europe/Radio Liberty*, November 24, 2014, https://www.rferl.org/a/central-asia-islam/26707668.html.

[24] "Countries Don't Want Their Foreign Fighters Back," *Intelbrief*, The Soufan Center, New York, July 23, 2018, 4.

[25] Barrett, "Beyond the Caliphate," 12.

[26] The Combating Terrorism Center (CTC) database of available ISIS records—which CTC emphasizes is not comprehensive or necessarily representative—includes 4,018 files, with citizenship information on 3,244 individuals. See Brian Dodwell, Daniel Milton, and Don Rassler, "The Caliphate's Global Workforce: An Inside Look at the Islamic State's Foreign Fighter Paper Trail," CTC at West Point, April 18, 2016, https://ctc.westpoint.edu/the-caliphates-global-workforce-an-inside-look-at-the-islamic-states-foreign-fighter-paper-trail/, 8–11; Neumann, "Foreign Fighter Total in Syria/Iraq Now Exceeds 20,000"; "Countries Don't Want Their Foreign Fighters Back."

Table 14.1 Foreign Fighters Joining Sunni Militant Islamist Organizations in Syria and Iraq

State	Total Number of Fighters as of January 2015[a]	Fighters per Million Muslim Citizens[b]	Total Number of Fighters, 2016–17[b,c]	Fighters per Million Muslim Citizens[b]
Afghanistan	50	1.5	n/a	n/a
Algeria	200	5.1	170	4.3
Azerbaijan	104–206	11.2–22.2	>900	96.8
Egypt	360	4.3	~ 600	7.2
Jordan	1,500	166.7	~ 3,000	333.3
Kazakhstan[d]	250	20.3	>500	40.7
Kyrgyzstan	**100**	**18.5**	**>500–580[e]**	**92.6–107.4**
Libya	600	96.7	600	96.7
Pakistan	500	2.6	>650	3.4
Russia	800–1,500	47.0–88.2	3,417	201.0
Saudi Arabia	1,500–2,500	75–125	3,244	162.2
Tajikistan	**190**	**22.9**	**>1,300[f] (+ 308/ 2,651)**	**156.6 (193.7/ 476.0)**
Turkmenistan	360	73.5	>400	81.6
Tunisia	1,500–3,000	135.1–270.3	2,926	263.6
Turkey	600	7.7	1,500	19.3
Uzbekistan	**500**	**18.9**	**>1,500**	**56.6**

[a] According to ICSR, all figures were "conflict totals." As of January 2015, ICSR estimated that between 5 and 10 percent of the foreigners had died, and a further 10 to 30 percent had left the conflict zone, returning home or stopped in transit countries. As a result, the number of foreigners remaining on the ground in Syria and Iraq at the time was "likely to be significantly less than the figures provided." However, all reports indicated that very few Central Asians had left Syria or Iraq before 2019. See Neumann, "Foreign Fighter Total in Syria/Iraq Now Exceeds 20,000."

[b] Fighter numbers in columns 3 and 5 are per million Muslim citizens. Population data are from the United Nations Department of Economic and Social Affairs, Population Division, "World Population Prospects 2019," https://population.un.org/wpp.

[c] Fighter totals are from Richard Barrett, "Beyond the Caliphate: Foreign Fighters and the Threat of Returnees," Report, The Soufan Center, New York, October 2017.

[d] ISIS included citizens from across Central Asia. Data suggest that growing numbers of Kazakhstanis and Turkmenistanis were among them. Religious repression and corruption in Turkmenistan was high and repression and corruption in Kazakhstan were increasing, thus making the movement and its networks and propaganda appealing to some Kazakhstanis and Turkmenistanis as well.

[e] In June 2019, independent analysts and Kyrgyz government officials were credibly putting this figure at about 580.

[f] Tajikistan data for 2016–17 provide additional estimates (in parentheses) of Tajikistani fighter recruits stopped in Turkey and arrested or returned to Tajikistan before reaching Syria. Data on those stopped or returned are not available for other Central Asian states.

Table 14.2 Foreign Fighters in Syria and Iraq by Region, 2017

Former Soviet Republics	8,717
Middle East	7,054
Western Europe	5,778
The Maghreb	5,356
South Asia and Southeast Asia	1,568
Balkans	845
North America	444

Source: Richard Barrett, "Beyond the Caliphate: Foreign Fighters and the Threat of Returnees," Report, The Soufan Center, New York, October 2017.

from Russia (3,417), then Uzbekistan (> 1,500), followed by Tajikistan (1,300–2,700), Azerbaijan (> 900), Kyrgyzstan (500–600), Kazakhstan (> 500), and Turkmenistan (> 400). This phenomenon was unimaginable only a decade earlier.

To facilitate comparison across countries, Table 14.1 presents both total estimates from 2015 and 2016–17 as well as fighters per million Muslim citizens of each country, and the change over time. By 2017, Uzbek fighters numbered more than 1,500 (56 per million Muslims).[27] In spite of its distance from the Middle East, Uzbekistan was the source of higher numbers per million Muslim citizens than multiple Arab states or Turkey, and far higher numbers than Afghanistan, Pakistan, or Egypt, although it was well below the rate of major recruiting source states like Tunisia, France, and Jordan. For Kyrgyzstan, the rate of recruits increased from 2017–19, with 93–107 per million Muslim citizens. For Tajikistan, 2017 estimates of fighters per million ranged from 194 to 476, putting it among the highest contributors.

It is striking that by 2017 the former Soviet states were providing the largest regional contingent of foreign fighters going to Syria and Iraq.[28] (See Table 14.2.) Of total global foreign fighters in Syria and Iraq in January 2015, about 9 percent came from Russia and Central Asia. In 2016–17, that figure had increased to about 27 to 31 percent. While the data show that many other nationalities left during or shortly after the U.S. campaign against ISIS

27 Barrett, "Beyond the Caliphate," 12–13.
28 Barrett, "Beyond the Caliphate."

began, very few Central Asians returned home until 2019, when Kyrgyzstan repatriated a few dozen.[29]

One might have expected that fighters would be killed off and recruitment numbers would decline once ISIS began losing the war against the U.S.-led coalition. Even in 2018, as the movement declined, both the Pentagon and the United Nations believed that ISIS still had between 28,600 and 31,600 fighters, despite the huge losses.[30] The foreign fighter contingent, including battalions of hundreds to thousands of Central Asians, was still strong. Additionally, according to a 2018 UN report, "the Al-Nusra Front for the People of the Levant (ANF) remain[ed] one of the strongest and largest al-Qaeda affiliates globally . . . commanding between 7,000 and 11,000 fighters, including several thousand foreign terrorist fighters."[31] ANF's main power base was in Idlib Province in northwestern Syria, bordering Turkey. Many of its fighters were also Central Asians.

By March 2018, according to the U.S. government, ISIS had lost 98 percent of the territory it had once controlled.[32] Thousands of Central Asians remained in Syria, some of them in deconfliction zones in the Idlib-Aleppo region. Others were reportedly returning to Afghanistan to continue fighting jihad there with the Islamic State of Khorasan Province (known as ISIS-Khorasan or ISIS-K), a regional branch that ISIS had formed in late 2014 to extend its caliphate to south Central Asia. Extremely few Tajiks, Uzbeks, and Kyrgyz had returned home, in contrast to returnee rates from other states (some numbering 30 to 50 percent). The Central Asian fighting force remained formidable for several more years.

Explaining the Emergence of Central Asian Foreign Fighters

This third wave of Central Asian Islamism actually included multiple militant groups, some fighting under ISIS and others affiliated with ANF, al-Qaeda's front there. One of the first Uzbek groups in Syria, based in the Aleppo region, was Seyfuddin Uzbek Jamaat (SUJ), commanded by the Uzbek Abu Husayn. It began fighting for the ANF in 2014. SUJ maintained ties to the IMU, which U.S. intelligence officials believed to be training fighters and aiding them in traveling

[29] Interview with U.S. Embassy personnel, Bishkek, Kyrgyzstan, June 2019; interviews with representatives of two international organizations, Bishkek, Kyrgyzstan, June 2019.

[30] Seldin, "Far from Dead."

[31] UN Security Council, "Twenty-first Report of the Analytical Support and Sanctions Monitoring Team Submitted Pursuant to Resolution 2368 (2017) concerning ISIL (Da'esh), Al-Qaida and Associated Individuals and Entities," S/2018/14/Rev.1*, February 27, 2018, 8.

[32] "Islamic State and the Crisis in Iraq and Syria in Maps," *BBC News*, March 28, 2018, https://www.bbc.com/news/world-middle-east-27838034.

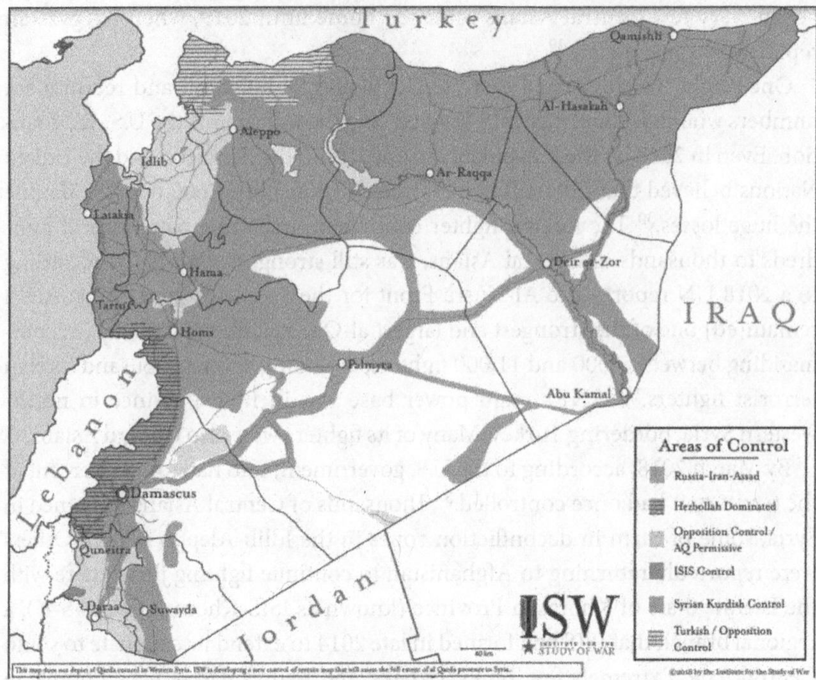

Map 14.1 Location and control of Central Asian al-Qaeda–linked fighters in Syria, March 2018

Source: Institute for the Study of War, "Syria Control of Terrain Map," March 22, 2018, https://www.understandingwar.org/backgrounder/syria-control-terrain-map-march-2018.

to Syria to fight with al-Qaeda–affiliated militias there.[33] Ethnic Uzbeks became prominent in the ranks of groups fighting under ANF (later reorganized under Hay'at Tahrir al Sham, HTS). According to one Iraqi military officer, Uzbeks were reputed to be "the most outstanding combat groups,"[34] with the best-trained fighting forces, in large part because many had experience in Afghanistan. SUJ was followed by at least three other groups of Central Asians—KTJ, KIB, and Central Asian battalions within ISIS.

The IMU and IJU's direct ties to al-Qaeda in Afghanistan facilitated the movement of some fighters from the Afghan battlefield to join al-Nusra. In November 2013, the IMU Facebook page reportedly posted praise for an al-Nusra–affiliated

[33] Bill Roggio, "Uzbek Commands Group within the Al Nusrah Front," *FDD's Long War Journal*, April 25, 2014; Bill Roggio, "IMU Praises Slain Syrian Islamist Brigade commander," *FDD's Long War Journal*, November 20, 2013.

[34] Mostafa, "Officer: Uzbeks, Uyghurs among Remaining Foreign Militants."

commander, a "martyr" in Syria:[35] "We are in one battle, for those whom we fight in Tajikistan, Afghanistan, and Pakistan are unjust tyrants like Bashar al-Assad. . . . [Y]our martyr is our martyr, your wounded is our wounded, and your victory is our victory and a victory for the *umma* and the religion."[36] The IMU's 2015 pledge to ISIS facilitated the movement of more fighters. Others arrived directly from Tajikistan, Kyrgyzstan, or Kazakhstan. Still others had been migrant laborers in Turkey or Russia.

As with the previous Islamist waves, religious repression, ideology and entrepreneurs, and associational space together fostered the emergence of this third wave. The groups comprising Central Asian foreign fighters were motivated by religious oppression and injustice. At home, conditions had steadily worsened. The massacre in Andijon, the swelling of the "Uzbek Gulag" for "religious terrorists," ethnic pogroms against Uzbeks in Osh, and the banning of the IRPT all demonstrated that Central Asian states were perpetrating violence against independent Muslims. The grotesque slaughter of Syrians by the Assad regime was another factor. Many Central Asians following social media coverage increasingly identified with the Syrians' plight.

Not only ISIS and al-Qaeda, but also Central Asian religious entrepreneurs, following Abdallah Azzam, propagated the idea of an individual Muslim duty (*fard al-Ayn*) to fight a militant jihad for Islam on foreign territory. One Uzbek émigré, Imam Abdulloh Buhoriy, who had relocated from the Ferghana Valley to Istanbul, made such an argument to Uzbeks. Like the émigré Imam Obidxon Qori, Abdulloh Buhoriy had been a follower of Imam Abduvali Qori in the early 1990s and had fled Uzbekistan. In exile in Istanbul for twelve years, he developed a network of mosques where he preached against Karimov. After 2011, Imam Abdulloh began advocating a Qu'ranic duty to wage jihad in Syria, preaching in one video that had nearly twenty thousand views, "Jihad in Syria was a blessing for the whole Islamic world. . . . 'Fighting has been made obligatory' upon you 'believers,' though you dislike it. . . . If you make jihad you will get your reward, and be powerful and victorious. *Kuffar* will not be able to do atrocities. . . . If you say there is no jihad in this era, you deny so many *ayat*s and *hadith*s. You can't deny or try to stop jihad. It's like denying *namaz*."[37] The imam had a strong following among the 150,000 Central Asian migrant laborers and asylum-seekers in Turkey, mostly ethnic Uzbek.[38] In December 2014, he was assassinated. Online videos posted after his death and propaganda from HTI treated him as

[35] Roggio, "Uzbek Commands Group"; Roggio, "IMU Praises Slain Syrian."
[36] IMU Facebook page, cited in Roggio, "IMU Praises Slain Syrian."
[37] Shaykh Abdulloh Buhoriy, "Jihod Haqida [About Jihad]," YouTube, August 15, 2013, https://www.youtube.com/watch?v=2zRYJm_9BVc.
[38] "Russian Suspect Nabbed in Uzbek Preacher's Murder," *Daily Sabah*, December 3, 2014, https://www.dailysabah.com/turkey/2014/12/13/russian-suspect-nabbed-in-uzbek-preachers-murder.

a "martyr" and blamed Karimov and Putin for his killing.[39] Inspired by his martyrdom, and by other such ideologues, Central Asians began seeing themselves as part of a common jihad. The foreign fighter movement's transcendence from local or national to transnational ideas and goals distinguished this wave from earlier ones.

Associational space within Uzbekistan and Tajikistan was minimal, but it did exist online and among migrant laborers living in Russia and Turkey. Under Kyrgyzstan's new regime as of mid-2010, space was increasing there again. Finally, the movement's novel use of social media and apps such as Telegram distinguished this latest wave of Islamism both in providing associational space and in giving a platform to religious entrepreneurs. That space facilitated the diffusion of radical ideology and the creation of transnational networks.

Evaluating and Explaining the Level of Mobilization to Syria

As shown in Tables 14.1 and 14.2, the foreign fighter numbers from Central Asia were relatively high in comparison with other countries and regions. Any assessment of mobilization and durability must also be in comparison with similar fighter movements or other opposition movements within the Central Asian context, where any opposition mobilization has been nearly impossible. As discussed above, the number of Central Asians fighting in Syria between 2015 and 2018 was over 5,000. These combatants did not outnumber peak HTI members across Central Asia, much less IRPT supporters. But the Central Asian foreign fighter movement compared favorably to other militant Islamist movements. Central Asian fighters in Syria outnumbered the IMU and far outpaced groups such as the IJU and Jamoati Ansorulloh (JA). Estimates of Arab Afghans in 1979–92 ranged from 5,000 to 20,000. The Bosnian and Chechen foreign movements—each of which attracted some Central Asians—were no more than 1,000–2,000 and 200–300, respectively. Even during the U.S. war in Iraq, Sunni foreign fighters numbered about 4,000–5,000.[40]

Another dimension of Islamist success is durability, which entails discipline, ideological commitment, and organization in the face of state oppression. Central Asians proved a more durable force than fighters from many other countries. Rather than dissolving and going home with the defeat and collapse of ISIS's caliphate in Syria and Iraq in 2017, in early 2022 many Central Asians

[39] Hizb ut-Tahrir Britain, "Uzbekistan: Imam Abdullah Bukhari—May Allah Have Mercy on Him—Assassinated in Istanbul," December 25, 2014, https://www.hizb.org.uk/dawah/national-dawah/uzbekistan-imam-abdullah-bukhari-may-allah-have-mercy-on-him-assassinated-in-istanbul/.

[40] Hegghammer, "The Rise of Muslim Foreign Fighters," 61.

either continued fighting with al-Qaeda in Syria or joined ISIS-K in Afghanistan. The sustained mobilization of several thousand fighters in a violent conflict zone calls for examination.

Analysis of the two most prominent groups—KTJ (under al-Qaeda) and Central Asians in ISIS—reveals the salience and effectiveness of the three mobilizational strategies I have discussed throughout this book: *sacred authority*, *ideational adaptation to the targeted audience*, and *transcommunal networking*.

Katibat al-Tawhid wal Jihad

KTJ's Emergence

KTJ, the Battalion of Monotheism and Jihad, was founded by Sirojiddin Muxtorov, an ethnic Uzbek Uyghur born in southern Kyrgyzstan. Muxtorov went to Syria in 2011, not long after the civil war started, and joined other Uzbek fighters already there; most of them were former IJU and IMU militants. In 2013, by some accounts, he organized KTJ as an independent group under the al-Nusra Front of al-Qaeda. According to other reports, Muxtorov assumed that position by virtue of his fighting and leadership skills.

KTJ is a microcosm of this book's argument about the combined role of repression, associational space, ideas, and religious entrepreneurs in fostering Islamist emergence and mobilization. Muxtorov's path to Syria began in the Kara-Suu district of the Ferghana Valley, where he was exposed to Salafist political theology. As a young man, he had religious training, reportedly guided by Imam Rashod Qori, son of the slain imam Rafiq Qori, whose mosque he attended until about 2010 (see Chapter 12). Muxtorov's political radicalization was linked to the religious and ethnic oppression of Kyrgyzstani Uzbeks that had begun around 2006, under President Bakiyev's counterterrorism campaign.

In the mid-2000s, at about age twenty, Muxtorov sought a more purist religious education and began studying theology in Syria at the Islamic University of Al-Fatah al-Islamiya.[41] During his time there, Muxtorov reportedly "became an ideological supporter of al-Qaeda, deeply immersing [himself] in the theological works of Islamic scholars and founders of the radical current of Salafism and Wahhabism," namely, Taqi al-Din Ahmad Ibn Taymiyyah (1263–1328) and Muhammad Ibn Abd al-Wahhab (1703–1792).[42] Returning to Kyrgyzstan, Muxtorov became an assistant imam at a small mosque in the vicinity of Kara-Suu. Muxtorov would have experienced the escalating surveillance and threats

[41] Uran Botobekov, "*Katibat al-Tawhid wal Jihad*: A Faithful Follower of Al-Qaeda from Central Asia," *Modern Diplomacy*, April 27, 2018, https://moderndiplomacy.eu/2018/04/27/katibat-al-tawhid-wal-jihad-a-faithful-follower-of-al-qaeda-from-central-asia/.

[42] Botobekov, "*Katibat al-Tawhid wal Jihad*."

Image 14.1 KTJ battalion training in Syria
Source: Screenshot, www.tavhidvajihod.com, www.longwarjournal.org/archives/2016/04/uzbek-al-qaeda-battalion-trains-commandos-in-aleppo.php.

against Imam Rashod Qori by the new, purportedly "democratic" government after 2010. After the Syrian war broke out, Muxtorov returned to Syria to fight. He assumed the nom de guerre Abu Saloh al Uzbeki.

Although primarily ethnic Uzbek, KTJ's militia also drew Uyghurs and various Russian speakers from Central Asia.[43] Many KTJ members came from the Ferghana Valley of southern Kyrgyzstan, adherents who typically had not fought in Afghanistan with the IMU or IJU. They totaled up to a thousand fighters. In 2015, KTJ joined the ANF, al-Qaeda's official branch in Syria, and made an oath of loyalty to al-Qaeda's leader, Ayman al-Zawahiri.[44] KTJ fought within the ANF for several years, playing an important role in the Idlib offensive in 2015 and in breaking Assad's siege of Aleppo in 2016. KTJ operated alongside Junud al Sham, a militia led by the Chechen leader Muslim Shishani, formerly of the Islamic Caucasus Emirate. KTJ also cooperated with the Syrian wing of the Turkistan Islamic Party, which was largely Uyghur. KTJ reportedly ran at least

[43] Caleb Weiss, "Uzbek Group Pledges Allegiance to Al-Nusrah Front," *FDD's Long War Journal*, September 30, 2015, https://www.longwarjournal.org/archives/2015/09/uzbek-group-pledges-allegiance-to-al-nusrah-front.php.

[44] "Узбекские боевики примкнули к «Аль-Каиде» в борьбе против России," *Radio Ozodlik*, November 3, 2015, https://www.ozodlik.org/a/27342533.html.

two training camps in Syria; in a video it released, its fighters honed the skills of new "commandos" (see Image 14.1).[45]

Abu Saloh remained KTJ's militant and spiritual leader, its emir, despite Russian airstrikes targeting him and killing his wife and son in 2018.[46] Moreover, while pursuing the caliphate, KTJ established *shariat* law and governance in the areas it controlled.

KTJ's Jihad in Syria and Beyond

Notably, throughout this period KTJ pursued interests beyond Syria as well. Abu Saloh orchestrated attacks inside Kyrgyzstan. In 2015, he was tied to at least two attacks on Ahmadiyya Muslims in southern Kyrgyzstan, killing a former teacher. Police arrested two citizens of Uzbekistan and four Kyrgyzstanis. The attackers reportedly claimed that Abu Saloh, who had once been the assistant imam of their village, had inspired their actions because of his puritanical opposition to the Ahmadiyya Muslim community; Abu Saloh and other Salafis deemed them apostates. The Kyrgyz government also blamed Abu Saloh's KTJ for the terrorist strike on the Chinese Embassy in Kyrgyzstan in August 2016; copying al-Qaeda's modus operandi, a suicide attacker rammed the embassy gate with a car containing an IED. Kyrgyzstan's State Committee on National Security (GKNB) identified the driver as twenty-one-year-old Zoir Halilov, an ethnic Uyghur with a Tajik passport. Halilov, a member of the East Turkistan Islamic Movement (also known as the Turkistan Islamic Party), reportedly had YouTube videos and audio recordings of Abu Saloh on his phone. Terrorism expert Uran Botobekov identified one video message from al-Qaeda's al-Zawahiri, titled "Turkestan: Patience and Then Victory," praising "Turkestan Islamic Party fighters for their commitment to conducting jihad all over the world"; he called on "warriors of Islam to be ready to conduct holy war against the atheistic Chinese regime, [and] to liberate [the] western province of Xinjiang from Communist occupants."[47] The incident suggested that the East Turkistan Islamic Movement and KTJ, both active and cooperating in Syria and both followers of al-Qaeda, were collaborating in bringing jihad back to Central Asia and Xinjiang.

Abu Saloh's organization proved itself able to mobilize radicals elsewhere in the former Soviet region. Another reported plot, thwarted by Russia, targeted the 2016 Russian May Day parade. In 2017, at Abu Saloh's bidding, Akbarjon Jalilov allegedly detonated a suicide bomb on a subway car in St. Petersburg,

[45] Caleb Weiss, "Uzbek al Qaeda Battalion Trains 'Commandos' in Aleppo," *FDD's Long War Journal*, April 20, 2016.

[46] Uran Botobekov, "Uzbek's *Katibat al-Tawhid wal Jihad* Changed Its Leader," *Modern Diplomacy*, April 19, 2019, https://moderndiplomacy.eu/2019/04/19/uzbeks-katibat-al-tawhid-wal-jihad-changed-its-leader/.

[47] Uran Botobekov, "Al-Qaeda, the Turkestan Islamic Party, and the Bishkek Chinese Embassy Bombing," *The Diplomat*, September 29, 2016.

killing sixteen and injuring more than sixty others, on a day when President Putin was visiting the city.[48] Jalilov, a twenty-two-year-old ethnic Uzbek born in Kyrgyzstan, held Russian citizenship, but his family lived in Kyrgyzstan's Ferghana Valley. Russian authorities reportedly found another IED that same day, also with Jalilov's DNA. They accused a second Kyrgyzstani-born Russian citizen, Abror Azimov, of training Jalilov. According to Russia's Federal Security Service, Abu Saloh gave the attack directive virtually. KTJ was seeking a transnational reach.[49] Such attacks increased as ISIS and al-Qaeda lost territory inside Syria and Iraq after spring 2017.[50]

The Decline of KTJ?

Three years after the fall of ISIS, the Syrian government was closer to winning the war against the remaining jihadists. Factionalism and disagreement over the future of the jihad—whether to be national or transnational in focus—led to KTJ's decline, much as had happened in the IMU. In early 2019, Abu Saloh reaffirmed KTJ's *bay'ah* (oath) to al-Zawahiri. He distributed a video of the pledge ceremony on Telegram. His speech aimed to motivate followers to continue the jihad in close connection with al-Qaeda. HTS was primarily focused on Syria, but inside KTJ some wanted to return to their roots in Central Asia, while Abu Saloh wanted to pursue transnational jihad. In early 2020, Abu Saloh and about fifty of his battalion left KTJ and HTS's umbrella organization. They joined Jabhat Ansar al Din, a group more closely aligned with al-Qaeda's and their own global jihadist ideology.[51] Both leaders were apprehended and arrested by HTS in June 2020 in a move that shook the Central Asian foreign fighter community.[52] In 2021, however, Abu Saloh was reportedly released but under tight HTS control. His YouTube channel continued to post his sermons, which were still getting thousands to tens of thousands of hits in 2021–22. Whether or not he was alive and free remained unclear, given that most postings used still images and audio, not video.

[48] "Members of *Katibat al-Tawhid wal Jihad* Terrorist Group Detained in Uzbekistan," *Interfax*, February 19, 2020, https://interfax.com/newsroom/top-stories/17519/.

[49] Oved Lobel, "Is Al-Qaeda's Syrian Affiliate Adopting Islamic State Tactics in Russia?," *New Arab*, July 4, 2017. The Russian government provided no public evidence of these claims.

[50] R. Kim Cragin and Ari Weil, "Virtual Planners in the Arsenal of Islamic State External Operations," *Orbis* 62, no. 2 (Spring 2018): 294–312.

[51] Uran Botobekov, "Top Jihadist Leader Suffers for Loyalty to Al-Qaeda," *Modern Diplomacy*, July 10, 2020, https://moderndiplomacy.eu/2020/07/10/top-uzbek-jihadist-leader-suffers-for-loyalty-to-al-qaeda/.

[52] Caleb Weiss, "Jihadist Group Confirms Arrest of Uzbek Commander," *FDD's Long War Journal*, June 18, 2020.

Nonetheless, KTJ continued. In 2021 it was still fighting in Idlib. Its new emir, Abdul Aziz Uzbeki, a native of the Ferghana Valley of Uzbekistan, was deeply experienced. He had previously fought with the IMU against President Karimov in the 1990s, and then with the Islamic Jihad Union in Afghanistan for almost twenty years.[53] While he lacked Abu Saloh's charisma, a new religious leader was appointed to deliver Friday sermons and religious propaganda. With the U.S. withdrawal from Afghanistan, there was speculation that some KTJ members returned to the Afghan theater, where al-Qaeda was again operating under the Taliban's protection. Others, however, continued in Syria, posting occasional propaganda from Idlib. Both Uzbekistan's and Kyrgyzstan's police and security services claimed that several recruiters for the Syrian jihad, identified as citizens of neighboring states, were apprehended inside Kyrgyzstan in 2021 and 2022. Between March 2020 and May 2022, one Kyrgyzstani resident of Osh, the same region from which many KTJ militants had originated, transferred two million rubles (about US$34,000) to KTJ in Syria.[54] A number of other Kyrgyzstanis were also implicated in the collection of funds for Syria.

In June 2022, Abu Saloh posted a new video in which he declared, "I'm in need of your support to establish the *shariat* of Allah. You will be questioned about sitting idle. . . . Some of the *kufr* media is spreading news that . . . 'mujahidin are losing in Sham.' Don't believe it, brothers! Praise to Allah, we mujahidin are present in Sham and we continue our jihad. And we will never lay down our arms *Insha'allah* until we conquer Palestine."[55] Nonetheless, threatened by the Assad regime, the Central Asian governments, and internal jihadi factionalism, KTJ's future was uncertain.

Explaining KTJ's Moderate Success at Mobilization

Given the significant political control and surveillance inside Kyrgyzstan and Uzbekistan, the harsh repercussions of participating in any Islamist movement, and the high risks of fighting in Syria, mobilizing up to one thousand supporters and sustaining a group of that size for at least seven years despite heavy loss of territory and life since 2016–17 was itself a notable phenomenon.

[53] UN Security Council, "Twenty-fifth Report of the Analytical Support and Sanctions Monitoring Team Submitted Pursuant to Resolution 2368 (2017) concerning ISIL (Da'esh), Al-Qaida and Associated Individuals and Entities," S/2020/53, January 20, 2020, 15.

[54] Yuri Kopytin, "Osh Resident Transfers over 2 Million Rubles to Militants in Syria," *24.KG*, July 1, 2022, https://24.kg/english/238736_Osh_resident_transfers_over_2_million_rubles_to_militants_in_Syria/.

[55] "Abu Saloh," YouTube, June 9, 2022, accessed June 20, 2022, https://www.bing.com/videos/search?q=youtube+abu+saloh&&view=detail&mid=0B823DED9AF37E57AAAC0B823DED9AF37E57AAAC&rvsmid=BCAEC91FB32082F994C0BCAEC91FB32082F994C0&FORM=VDMCNR (link now defunct).

Building Networks for Recruiting Militants

KTJ effectively utilized four networks to recruit. First, it drew on religious ties through Abu Saloh's former mosque connections. The mosques and neighboring villages and *mahallas* of highly politicized Uzbek imams had become Hizb ut-Tahrir's recruiting sites in the early 2000s (see Chapter 12). By 2013, the same regions had become targets for transnational recruiters, including both ISIS and al-Qaeda–linked groups such as KTJ.

Second, KTJ targeted the ethnic network of persecuted Uzbek minorities in southern Kyrgyzstan, an especially vulnerable population since the pogroms against Uzbeks of the 2010s. Kyrgyzstan's government data—supported by credible news reports and YouTube videos posted by fighters in the Uzbek language—suggested that about 90 percent of recruits from Kyrgyzstan were ethnic Uzbeks. The phenomenon was due to neither their ethnicity nor to Islam. Rather, the coupling of politically charged persecution and religious repression among the more religiously observant Uzbek population of southern Kyrgyzstan had motivated Islamist emergence there,[56] while tapping into close ethnic, neighborhood, kin, and friendship networks among that population provided a means of recruitment and mobilization.[57] KTJ's propaganda leaflets were disseminated in the predominantly Uzbek and heavily oppressed regions of Central Asia: Jizzax, Ferghana, and Namangan in Uzbekistan; Chimkent and Qyzylorda in Kazakhstan; and Osh, O'zgen, Nookat, Jalalabat, and Aravan in Kyrgyzstan.[58] A study by *Radio Free Europe/Radio Liberty* found that Aravan and its surrounding districts—only about twenty miles from Kara-Suu, Abu Saloh's hometown and the site of Imam Rashod Qori's Salafist mosque—sourced fully 33 percent of the several hundred Kyrgyzstani foreign fighters in Syria.[59] Both Kara-Suu and Aravan are located roughly twenty miles from Andijon, the site of the Akromiya uprising and Uzbek government massacre of protesters in 2005 (see Chapter 9). Thousands had fled from Andijon to Kara-Suu after the massacre. Radical networks consequently had an ample basis for development there. These small towns had become "hot spots" of Islamist opposition.[60]

Central Asian labor migrants in Russia provided a third network for KTJ. Kyrgyzstani migrants were particularly attracted to KTJ; the southern—Jalalabat, Batken, and Osh provinces—had the most migrants. They came from

[56] Mariya Omelicheva, "Ethnic Dimension of Religions Extremism and Terrorism in Central Asia, *International Political Science Review* 31, no. 2 (June 4, 2010): 167–86.

[57] Interview with Emil Nasritdinov, American University of Central Asia, Washington, D.C., December 2018.

[58] Uran Botobekov, "New Ideological Tactics of Al-Qaeda to Revive Its Power," *Modern Diplomacy*, March 13, 2018, https://moderndiplomacy.eu/2018/03/13/new-ideological-tactics-of-al-qaeda-to-revive-its-power/.

[59] Interview with Muhammad Tahir, journalist, *Radio Free Europe/Radio Liberty*, Washington, D.C., November 2018.

[60] Interview with Tahir.

Image 14.2 From "The Hijra"
Source: YouTube screenshot

Abu Saloh's home region, which also had the largest concentrations of ethnic Uzbek and Tajik minorities within Kyrgyzstan.[61]

Fourth, KTJ effectively used videos and social media to network and recruit.[62] Abu Saloh had his own Telegram and YouTube channels, and dozens of followers reposted his messages and propaganda. Embedded in descriptions of the videos were actionable messages to the viewer, often with ways to make contact with the organization. For example, posted inside one video, "The Hijra," was the line, "Get in touch with us through https://telegram.me/muhojir. Our official website is: https://telegram.me/abusalohbot" (Image 14.2).[63] The image

[61] Eurasian Development Bank and United Nations Development Program Regional Bureau for Europe and the Commonwealth of Independent States, "Labor Migration, Remittances, and Human Development in Central Asia," Report, *Central Asia Human Development Series* (2015), 19, https://www.undp.org/sites/g/files/zskgke326/files/migration/eurasia/c92b245a761853edd6ab095b3f1f8229d655ecce1479c5b2922edabde64052ea.pdf.

[62] Interview with counterterrorism officer, Kyrgyzstani Ministry of Internal Affairs, Osh, Kyrgyzstan, June 6, 2019.

[63] "Abu Saloh—Hijrat," (Abu Saloh—The Hijra), YouTube, January 2018, https://www.youtube.com/watch?v=_AdkVfumUnA.

Image 14.3 Abu Saloh, leader of Katibat al-Tawhid wal Jihad
Source: Screenshot, https://www.longwarjournal.org/archives/2020/06/hayat-tahrir-al-sham-reportedly-arrests-uzbek-jihadist-leader.php.

evoked a mysterious but enticing path for those following the Prophet's example of making the *hijra*.

Abu Saloh's Telegram channel was reportedly widely used. Videos often also provided an email address or directions to other links on WhatsApp or Vkontakte. Others instantly sent a message on Telegram to anyone who "liked" them. Social media technology and virtual networking made recruitment possible, especially among migrants who had freer access to such apps outside of Uzbekistan and Tajikistan, even when surveillance made in-person recruiting from mosques or neighborhoods impossible. Such technology made transcommunal networking far easier than for earlier waves of Islamists.

Building Sacred Authority

In joining the fight against Assad's regime, Abu Saloh had gained sacred authority by becoming a defender of Islam in a holy jihad, one that most Muslims in Kyrgyzstan and elsewhere deemed justified. Yet Abu Saloh also invested in building his spiritual credentials, which appear to have been a factor in KTJ's ability to recruit. Although recent, his mosque, ethnic, and local ties to prominent Salafist imams in the Ferghana Valley like Rashod Qori bolstered KTJ's efforts to cultivate sacred authority among Central Asians. His online propaganda displayed his young movement as possessing spiritual knowledge and legitimacy. Abu Saloh gave sermons and lessons, or made propaganda statements, sometimes sitting in front of shelves of religious books, sometimes standing with a Kalashnikov in military fatigues (Image 14.3).

He assumed the title *ustoz*. He had studied Islamic law both in Syria and with Salafist imams in Kyrgyzstan's Ferghana Valley. Among younger Central Asians, an Islamic degree from the Middle East was prestigious. Abu Saloh gave the appearance—at least to those less deeply educated in the Hanafi tradition—of being knowledgeable and teaching true Islam. He often used Arabic when reciting passages from the Qur'an in his sermons—dozens of which were posted on KTJ's website and YouTube—to solidify his image as a religious authority. Much like Tohir Yo'ldosh, the young Abu Saloh portrayed himself as a pure young mullah who had rejected the corrupt older generation.

The transition to a new KTJ leader in April 2019 proved difficult and again highlighted the importance of constructing sacred authority. KTJ's statement announcing its new emir read, "Our Shaykh Abdul Aziz Hafizullah . . . devoted his life to Allah, has many years of experience on the path of the jihad and deep knowledge of [Islamic] science." The statement called members of the group to strict obedience. It cited the Qur'an: "O you who have believed, obey Allah and obey the Messenger and those in authority among you."[64] KTJ clearly realized that establishing sacred authority was critical to keeping the group united in the jihad.

However, KTJ faced competition from other figures in Central Asia holding spiritual authority and seeking to undermine the flow to Syria. Independent and influential religious leaders in Kyrgyzstan, such as the theologian Kadyr Malikov and the former *mufti* Chubak ajy Jalilov (see Chapter 12), denounced the ideas of extremists and militants in Syria and elsewhere.[65] Kyrgyz *ulama* frequently used YouTube to counter militancy; in one video, for example, titled "A Refutation," the Kyrgyz imam Abdug'ani Domla urged gratitude for religious freedom in Kyrgyzstan and directly challenged KTJ's message, declaring, "Muslims in Kyrgyzstan have no business fighting jihad in Syria."[66] In 2021–22, various new "independent" imams in Uzbekistan—most likely with backing from the government—were denouncing Abu Saloh and KTJ in their own YouTube sermons.

Yet, jihadists benefited from popular distrust of the Muslim hierarchies. In Uzbekistan and Tajikistan they were often a voice for the regime's propaganda, and in Kyrgyzstan they were notoriously corrupt. Focus groups revealed that among youth, imams educated outside the country usually possessed greater authority than the official *ulama*. Other interpretations of Islam, including

[64] Botobekov, "Uzbek's *Katibat al-Tawhid wal Jihad* Changed Its Leader."

[65] Interview with Asel Abdyramanova, Search for Common Ground, Bishkek, Kyrgyzstan, June 2019; interview with Elvira Ilibezova, director, El-Pikr Center for Public Opinion, Bishkek, Kyrgyzstan, June 2019.

[66] "Raddiya," (A Refutation), YouTube.com, September 6, 2017, accessed October 12, 2018, https://www.youtube.com/watch?v=ybYiYJ5QgHQ, republished February 19, 2019, accessed June 24, 2019 (link now defunct).

Salafism, had consequently gained ground.[67] It was widely known that Imam Rashod Qori in southern Kyrgyzstan was sympathetic to the idea of the caliphate and the Syrian jihad, even though he openly endorsed neither ISIS nor militancy.

Ideational Congruence and Dissonance

KTJ invested in extensive propaganda and technology to spread its ideas, build sympathy, and recruit. Its propaganda was primarily in the Uzbek language but occasionally in Uyghur. As of September 2019, more than seventy-six videos of Abu Saloh's popular sermons existed on YouTube. Most ranged from one to three minutes long and reported from 1,000 to 135,000 hits. Although many were subsequently removed, at least sixteen new ones were posted in 2019, and a dozen more from 2021 through mid-2022, even as other groups were leaving Syria. The videos were accessible without going to a specific website that could be easily blocked. According to one Kyrgyzstani expert who interviewed dozens of later returnees from Syria, many youths who joined KTJ had been motivated by the emotional images and ideological rhetoric of jihad in such videos.[68]

As argued in previous chapters, one key to broader mobilization is adapting global Islamist ideas to local contexts. KTJ's core ideas aligned with the Salafi jihadist principles of al-Qaeda.[69] The righteousness, necessity, and individual duty of waging both offensive and defensive jihad, the virtues of martyrdom, and condemnation of the *kafir* pervaded most of Abu Saloh's videos.[70] Yet transnational political issues and Salafist jihadist ideology did not resonate with most Central Asians. KTJ, therefore, also localized its radical message, mixing a focus on jihad and the caliphate with issues salient in Central Asia, especially among Uzbekistanis and Kyrgyzstanis, its target audience.

Local issues repeatedly surfaced in the videos. In discussing religious repression, Abu Saloh criticized phony clerics or "palace imams" who "do not admit that the war in Syria is a war for our religion."[71] This was clearly a reference to Central Asia's government-appointed imams who preached against the Syrian jihad. *Hutba* videos (filmed sermons) sought to draw in viewers by simply discussing basic religious themes of interest in Kyrgyzstan: *tawhid* (monotheism), the

[67] Bayram Balci, *Islam in Central Asia and the Caucasus since the Fall of the Soviet Union* (Oxford: Oxford University Press, 2019).

[68] Interview with Mametbek Myrzabaev, director, Research Institute for Islamic Studies, Bishkek, Kyrgyzstan, June 2019.

[69] Botobekov, "Katibat al-Tawhid wal Jihad."

[70] "Устоз Абу Салох Хафизахуллох, Шахид'лик фазилатлари 1-дарс," (Honored Teacher Abu Saloh Hafizahulloh, The Virtues of Martyrdom, Lesson 1), YouTube, October 4, 2018, https://www.youtube.com/watch?v=UEQt6ouJonY&t=23s.

[71] "Устоз Абу Салох Хафизахуллох: Сирияда Нега Уруш Бўляпди," (The Teacher Abu Saloh Hafizullah: Why There Is a War in Syria), YouTube.com, December 22, 2016, accessed September 1, 2018, https://www.youtube.com/watch?v=Nda446zh2sA (link now defunct); this video received almost forty thousand hits before being removed.

rules of the *sunna*, pride, who is obliged to give *zakat*, understanding the soul, miracles, and, the "path of salvation." Abu Saloh espoused a more tolerant, less puritanical version of Islamic practice than most Salafis. For example, in one widely watched video, he appealed to the audience by explaining that Allah does not look at "our beards or weapons in our hands, but at our souls."[72] He focused on internal attempts to be a pure Muslim with a strong faith. This interpretation of Islam resonated more widely.

Many videos deliberately mixed religious teaching and politics. Some discussed family life under the caliphate, featuring children living in a land where their parents could raise them according to *shariat*. Videos encouraged women to participate as well, by becoming jihadi brides. This familial message resonated. In Nookat, Kyrgyzstan, for example, police reported that dozens of families had left the town for Syria under the delusion that their family would have a better life there.[73]

Abu Saloh also attempted to make the West's policies in the Middle East and elsewhere a concern for Central Asians. In his 2015 declaration of loyalty to al-Qaeda, he blamed "the American-Russian alliance against Muslims,"[74] an odd claim given the sharp decline in U.S.-Russian relations, but to many Central Asians the United States and Russia were both Western powers that had waged war on Muslims in Chechnya, Syria, Iraq, and Afghanistan.

Arguably, KTJ's messages would have found little purchase twenty-five years earlier, especially in then religiously liberal Kyrgyzstan. But given the corruption, injustice, and religious oppression of the post-Soviet regimes, these ideas were met with some enthusiasm. For example, one theme that pervaded several of Abu Saloh's online sermons was Muslim women's right to wear the hijab: "The government authorities jail those who defend the religion . . . [make] it a crime to wear a beard or hijab. They call us enemies and prevent Muslims from fighting jihad."[75] Those words resonated in Uzbekistan, and to some extent in southern Kyrgyzstan.

A constant theme of KTJ propaganda was defending Islam through militant jihad. Abu Saloh taught, "Some people say now is not the time of jihad. No, we will fight jihad! We will fight to defend our religion, to prevent our enemies from burning our

[72] "Abu Saloh, 'U kunda najot topguvchilar,'" (Abu Saloh, "On That Day They Will Find Salvation"), *VK.com*, September 23, 2015, https://vk.com/video271523988_171596680.

[73] "Kyrgyz Cop Turns Filmmaker in Fight with IS," *Radio Free Europe/Radio Liberty*, January 19, 2016, https://www.rferl.org/a/kyrgyzstan-cop-extremism/27496211.html.

[74] Global Security, "Katibat al-Tawhid wal Jihad (Uzbek)," February 2020, https://www.globalsecurity.org/military/world/para/ktj.htm.

[75] "Abu Saloh, 'Agar aytsalar aytgin 2,'" (Abu Saloh, "If They Say So, Tell Them, 2"), YouTube, October 18, 2017, accessed November 4, 2018, https://www.youtube.com/watch?v=MUZjG2GnlMc (link now defunct); the original was removed but the video was reposted on February 8, 2020 (with the seven other parts in the lecture series) on the YouTube channel USTOZLAR DAVATLARI, https://www.youtube.com/watch?v=faP_bIBMd3c.

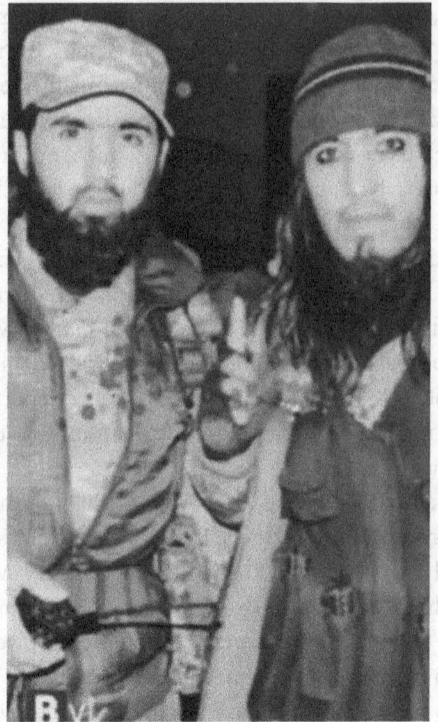

Image 14.4 Abu Saloh—"Are You Afraid to Go to Jihad?"
Source: YouTube screenshot

Qur'an, from attacking us. When they see our might, they will think twice."[76] Like other transnational jihadist groups, KTJ explained and justified jihad as an individual obligation to defend all Muslims, not just one's own nation. Abu Saloh called upon *all* Muslims to fight Islam's enemies in Syria: "Infidels compete with each other in making caricatures of the Prophet, in mocking Islam, and in killing Muslims. . . . In Syria, young children are being killed by the chemical bombs. Who is going to help them?"[77] Abu Saloh emphasized jihad's roots in the time of the Prophet: "Do not be afraid, look at the example of the Companions of the Prophet. . . . We can be brave like them because we have the same God, same Prophet, and same religion."[78] In another video, Abu Saloh discussed the Prophet Muhammad's death as a

[76] "Abu Saloh, 'Agar aytsalar aytgin 2.' "

[77] "Абу Салоҳ - Аллоҳни динига ансор болинглар!," (Abu Saloh - Be supporters of Allah's religion!), YouTube, Reposted May 9, 2022, https://www.youtube.com/watch?v=ge_9WYuQNoE.

[78] "JIHODGA chiqishdan qo'rqasizmi?؟ Sahobalarday shijoatliymiz," (Are You Afraid to Go to Jihad? We Are as Brave as the Companions), YouTube, May 22, 2017, accessed October 30, 2018, https://www.youtube.com/watch?v=az6aI-F9bZc (link now defunct).

martyr: "Jihad was fought by other prophets and jihad will be fought until the Day of Judgment. Nonbelievers killed the prophets before, and they wanted to kill our Prophet Muhammad. Our Prophet died a *shahid*. . . . Of course, the deaths of our commanders, scholars, and mujahidin are a great calamity, but it's also a test for us."[79] The message of defensive jihad against the assault on Islam also resonated, in contrast to messages simply advocating aggressive violence.

The language of jihad featured prominently in most propaganda, and in some it pushed well beyond the norms of jihad that most Central Asians accepted (see Chapters 7, 10, and 13). One video, simply titled "Abu Saloh, Usman" went up in January 2017 and was viewed almost 136,000 times in the eighteen months before it was removed. In it, Abu Saloh preached the virtues of jihad and of becoming a mujahid.[80] He took on the Western narrative that he and others in Syria were terrorists. More than five hundred individuals, apparently mostly Central Asians (since the responses were overwhelmingly in Uzbek or Russian), responded to the video online. The majority who commented were positive, although some were skeptical. One person queried, "Who would go to someone else's jihad?" Another insisted that Islam does not need to be spread "with a gun."[81] In a video posted a few months later, titled "Are You Afraid to Go to Jihad?" (Image 14.4) Abu Saloh again called on Muslims to fight. It was viewed more than twenty-six thousand times before being removed and prompted almost two hundred online comments. Again, many were directly supportive of Abu Saloh. One viewer wrote, "Let God be pleased. Abu Saloh is a believer." Another commented, "O Allah, allow me to help the mujahidin."[82] Abu Saloh directly challenged those who rejected militant jihad: "The true meaning of [jihad] is to fight in the battlefield. . . . Jihad can be understood as having four forms—a struggle against greed, the devil, the infidel, and the *munafiq* [hypocrite Muslims]. But the most important one is jihad against infidels because you can get all the rewards from other forms in just that one." He continued, "The objective of jihad is to elevate the religion of Allah and to eliminate polytheism and *fitna* [disorder]."[83]

Abu Saloh linked the need for jihad to oppression of Islam in Central Asia and elsewhere: "Nowadays Muslims face lots of hardships. Women are forced to remove the hijab. Having a beard is a crime now. Some Muslims say there is no need for jihad now. Who will defend Muslims in Palestine, Myanmar, Syria if

[79] "Абу Салоҳ, Нусрат йўли 1," (Abu Saloh, Path to Victory 1), YouTube, September 3, 2018, accessed November 1, 2018, https://www.youtube.com/watch?v=gcsUIzeZuW4 (link now defunct).

[80] "Абу Солох, Усман," (Abu Saloh, Usman), YouTube, January 8, 2017, accessed September 12, 2018, https://www.youtube.com/watch?v=1LBtYYqz3QA (link now defunct).

[81] "Абу Солох, Усман."

[82] "JIHODGA chiqishdan qo'rqasizmi?"

[83] "Абу Салоҳ, Жанг фиқҳи 1," (Abu Saloh, Fiqh of Jihad, 1), YouTube, August 26, 2018, accessed November 1, 2018, https://www.youtube.com/watch?v=3QQ3MfqiSp4 (link now defunct). This video had almost 400 views as of November 2018 and 3,310 as of August 2019.

Image 14.5 Abu Saloh—"Jihad is the Way of Honor!"
Source: YouTube screenshot

there is no need for jihad?"[84] Forced unveiling and forced shaving of beards were themes that perpetually resonated.

Some video images portrayed the caliphate with KTJ as idyllic, the reward for jihad. One "lesson" was accompanied only by the image of a smooth road leading to the light and a beautiful terrain (Image 14.5) and the words "Jihad is the way of honor!"[85] Moreover, KTJ added intensely emotive propaganda to lure young male Central Asian labor migrants living in Moscow and other difficult locations. Far from reality, Syria was shown as a place leading to the beauty of paradise; in the video "Abu Saloh—Hurlar haqida" (Abu Saloh—About the Virgin Servants from Paradise) he claimed that jihad in Syria will lead to freedom, as opposed to the dirty life that migrants endured and that so many indigent Central Asians lived at home, where corruption and injustice prevented one from flourishing (Image 14.6).[86] Abu Saloh

[84] "Abu Saloh—Izzat yo'li," (Abu Saloh—the Way of Honor), YouTube, March 12, 2022, https://www.youtube.com/watch?v=i-BrK-tx6Uk.
[85] "Abu Saloh—Izzat yo'li."
[86] Abu Saloh, "Hurlar haqida" (About the Houris [virgin servants from paradise]), YouTube, March 18, 2017, https://www.youtube.com/watch?v=OvLz3X45N0g&t=1s.

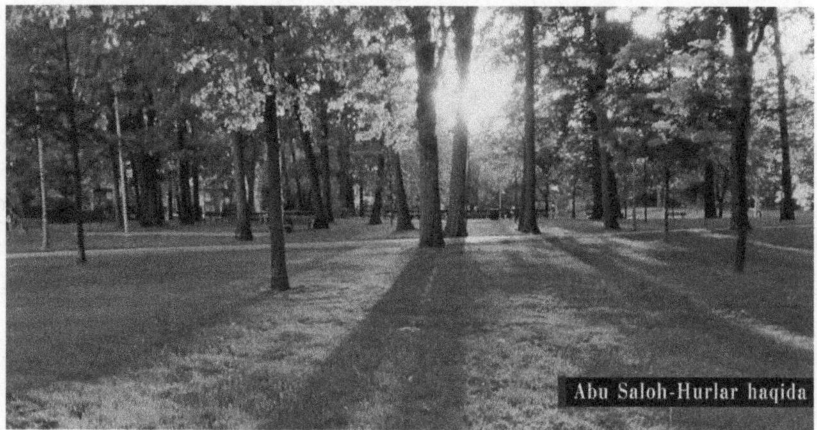

Image 14.6 Abu Saloh—"About the Virgin Servants"
Source: YouTube screenshot

promised not only brides in Syria but also virgins in paradise. The 2017 video received more than seventeen thousand views even after the Syrian jihad was in decline.

As was evident in surveys and focus groups, suicide bombing was overwhelmingly opposed across Central Asia, but many did respect martyrdom.[87] In one video, Abu Saloh discussed the virtue of martyrdom and the *shahid*'s rewards. Posted in November 2019, it received over three hundred hits in just six days on YouTube, before being removed. It was reposted and had nearly sixty thousand hits by mid-2022. The video portrayed a smiling and peacefully dying *shahid* in the arms of another jihadi. Again, a Telegram address to contact the movement was posted within the video (see Image 14.7).[88]

Breaking from al-Qaeda's and ISIS's practices, Abu Saloh urged caution in treatment of non-Muslims in jihad. That caution likely resonated with Kyrgyzstani Muslims, who had long lived side by side—and generally peacefully—with non-Muslims. In a video titled "Unjust Blood," Abu Saloh taught that Islamic *fiqh* forbids killing some people: "During the times of [the Prophet], one Muslim killed a non-Muslim without justification, and Allah sent a warning not to harm innocent people."[89] He cautioned that "one needs to be careful in calling someone '*kafir*.' "[90] Such statements echoed mainstream Hanafi

[87] Collins, Kyrgyzstan national survey, 2010 (in author's possession).

[88] "Шахиднинг мукофоти Абу Салох хафизахуллох," (The Martyr's Reward—Abu Saloh, hafizahulloh), YouTube, November 19, 2019, https://www.youtube.com/watch?v=aMw4A9LggUE.

[89] "Abu Saloh, 'Nohaq qon va Takfir,'" (Abu Saloh, "Unjust Killing and Takfir"), YouTube, August 30, 2018, accessed September 14, 2018, https://www.youtube.com/watch?v=49Rn_q6G1eA (link now defunct).

[90] "Abu Saloh, 'Nohaq qon va Takfir.'"

Image 14.7 Abu Saloh—"The Shahid's Reward"
Source: YouTube screenshot

Islam, which respected "People of the Book" and opposed ISIS's executions of non-Muslims.

Abu Saloh echoed al-Qaeda's view of jihad but tried to draw in Central Asians. He sought to evoke their rage: "People will be punished for ignoring the evil befalling al-Sham. Some Muslims say it is *fitna* in Syria, and not to send them money, but that is wrong—it is jihad, not *fitna*."[91] In one video watched nearly forty thousand times, he explained, "The war in Idlib is a defensive war. After the Ottoman caliphate was destroyed, all our wars are defensive ones. Aggression and attack are happening against Muslims. Our sisters and young children are being killed. . . . The people of Sham are defending themselves against the oppression of the *kuffar*. . . . Islam commands that we fight back against oppression."[92] He portrayed the war in Syria as "a war for the religion."[93] He directly countered

[91] "Abu Saloh, 'jihod haqida,'" (Abu Saloh, "About Jihad"), YouTube, April 5, 2018, https://www.youtube.com/watch?v=YV_Xu47foY0.

[92] "Abu Saloh—Mahmud Abdulmo'min," (Abu Saloh—Mahmud Abdulomin), You Tube, December 20, 2020, https://www.youtube.com/watch?v=d3mHSCzggx0.

[93] "Abu Saloh—Bizning jangimiz Allohni shariatini oliy qilish uchundir," (Abu Saloh—Our Battle Is to Make Allah's Shariat Supreme), YouTube, January 6, 2022, https://www.youtube.com/watch?v=AKQsafqZqMc.

the "palace imams" who mouthed the Uzbek government's claim that it was not jihad and attempted to undermine his message.

Despite its emphasis on jihad, KTJ's rhetoric resonated with some Central Asians' hopes for an ideal state for Muslims. Abu Saloh's sermons and videos promoted joining such a state in Syria, even as he also mentioned returning home to Central Asia. His videos depicted the beauty of life in a Muslim state with idyllic images meant to contrast sharply with the poverty of Kyrgyz and Uzbek villages—which lacked running water and heat—and with the squalid ghettos of Moscow and other cities where Central Asian labor migrants lived.

In sum, KTJ emotionally appealed to Muslim identity, and its persistent rhetoric about oppression and injustice within Central Asia, not just in Syria, broadened its appeal, even among Central Asians not inclined to favor the radicalism of either a caliphate or violent jihad. More so than other groups, KTJ delivered a compelling message that wove together Central Asian and Middle Eastern concerns. Still, KTJ's Salafi jihadist goals and methods did not reflect most Central Asians' traditional understandings of Islam and preference for their own nation-state. Its ideational appeal, therefore, remained limited.

ISIS's Emergence and Mobilization: From Iraq and Syria to Central Asia

ISIS, the most notoriously violent Salafi jihadist organization of the modern era, stunned the world with its meteoric rise in 2013–14. The emergence of ISIS was in part the tragic, unintended consequence of the 2003 U.S. invasion of Iraq, which had rapidly defeated Saddam Hussein but then unleashed the bloodlust of Abu Musab al-Zarqawi, the leader of al-Qaeda in Iraq (AQI) from 2004 to 2006.[94] Al-Zarqawi was a Salafi jihadist whose ideology of "monotheism and jihad" was so extreme and use of suicide bombings against Shia and civilians so rampant that even al-Qaeda Central attempted to rein him in.[95] Al-Zarqawi fomented a sectarian civil war that continued several years after his death in 2006 and claimed the lives of over 100,000 civilians by 2011. Although the United States had quelled most of the violence by 2009, the abrupt and total U.S. withdrawal in 2010–11, before a stable and inclusive regime was in place, opened space for a radical Islamist resurgence.[96]

[94] Gerges, *ISIS: A History*; Warrick, *Black Flags*, 182–86.

[95] "Zawahiri's Letter to Zarqawi," July 5, 2005, Combating Terrorism Center at West Point, Harmony Database, https://ctc.usma.edu/harmony-program/zawahiris-letter-to-zarqawi-original-language-2/.

[96] Hassan and Weiss, *ISIS*, 93–96.

The onset of the Syrian Civil War in 2011 gave AQI the opportunity to spawn a new jihadist operation in Syria. Disagreements over leadership and strategy led the group to break from al-Qaeda Central and rename itself in 2013 the Islamic State of Iraq and Syria. By 2014, ISIS leader Abu Bakr al-Baghdadi had declared a new caliphate. The group's military advances in 2013–14 led, as we have seen, to the spectacular growth of its fighting force, including tens of thousands of foreign fighters. ISIS conquered a vast swath of territory (40 percent of Iraq and 30 percent of Syria) that enabled it to control, at its peak in 2015, some ten million people. Its extreme ideology surpassed even that of AQI. ISIS summarily condemned all Muslims who did not follow it; it had adopted the radical doctrine of *takfir* (the pronouncement of someone as *kafir*, or no longer Muslim) and slaughtered Christians, Jews, and Yazidis in its genocidal path. Its conquests triggered a refugee flow of millions out of Syria and Iraq; about six million more were internally displaced in areas conquered by ISIS.[97]

Why and how did Central Asians choose to join ISIS—an Arab-created, extreme jihadist transnational movement? The origins of Central Asian foreign fighters for ISIS in Syria and Iraq are complex. Some came from the ranks of IMU fighters in Afghanistan or Pakistan. Other ISIS recruits came from those areas of Kyrgyzstan and Tajikistan where ethnic Uzbek minorities had long been excluded, politically and economically.[98] As shown in Tables 14.1 and 14.2, the number of recruits from Central Asia and Russia—a figure that likely included Central Asian migrants—was particularly high. In addition to the quantitative estimates presented in Tables 14.1 and 14.2, multiple videos posted on ISIS sites showed Central Asians living and fighting in Syria and Iraq and calling for jihad.[99]

Other evidence revealed that Central Asian women joined ISIS. Among U.S. Defense Department documents retrieved from Syria were ISIS records from one largely Russian-speaking guesthouse for jihadi wives. A registry of guesthouse occupants listed women from Dagestan (two hundred), Tajikistan (seventy-three), Azerbaijan (sixty-one), Kyrgyzstan (fifty-three), Chechnya (fifty), Uzbekistan (forty-four), Kazakhstan (thirty-four), Kabardino-Balkaria (ten), and Ingushetia (seven)—all Muslim-majority former Soviet regions. Tajikistani and Kyrgyzstani women were among the largest national groups. "The contingent of women in the log books from Central Asia [wa]s comparatively larger than almost all other sub-regional groups," indicating that there was not only a notable Central Asian fighter presence but that they brought families with them

97 "Islamic State and the Crisis in Iraq and Syria in Maps," *BBC News*.
98 Interview with U.S. government analyst, Washington, D.C., August 2018.
99 Isa, "'Джихадисты из Казыгурта' угрожают Назарбаеву."

or married women who had traveled there alone; they intended to make the caliphate their home.[100] Reports put women from Central Asia and Russia in the third largest group of women in ISIS, after those from Iraq and Syria and then other Middle Eastern countries; Central Asian government officials put their number at more than a thousand by 2015.[101] Several Central Asian women even became high-ranking leaders of the al-Khansaa Brigade, ISIS's female moral police force.[102] Many of these women had received a secular education in the post-Soviet system yet became Islamists.

ISIS's Relative Success at Mobilization in Central Asia

Given the difficult conditions, ISIS did attract a fair number of recruits, most likely several thousand across Central Asia, mostly from Tajikistan. It used strategies similar to KTJ's.

Building Networks for Recruiting Militants

First, ISIS used networks of all kinds to invest heavily in the spread of its ideas in the former Soviet states. It disseminated its message in multiple languages, especially Russian, Tajik, and Uzbek, and on multiple social media platforms—through Odnoklassniki, Vkontakte, Telegram, and other outlets that Central Asians could access, if not at home, then at least when working in Russia. Twitter was once a favorite networking tool, but by 2016 it had purged most ISIS postings. Telegram, however, continued to be used widely.

A study of more than one million ISIS propaganda postings on the internet found that the Russian-language site Mail.ru was one of ISIS's more frequently used platforms.[103] Postings on mail.ru increased threefold between 2015 and 2017, and the domain ranked sixth and seventh in those years in a frequency analysis of domains associated with ISIS propaganda URLs. According to Flashpoint, a business risk intelligence firm specializing in dark web threats, "from an information warfare perspective . . . the efficacy of [ISIS]'s propaganda program requires access to multiple target audiences."[104] The growing use of

[100] Milton and Dodwell, "Jihadi Brides?," 10–12.

[101] Jack Moore, "Hundreds of ISIS Women from America, Europe, Asia Will Be Expelled from Iraq, Along with Their Children," *Newsweek*, September 19, 2017.

[102] Uran Botobekov, "The Central Asian Women on the Frontline of Jihad," *The Diplomat*, January 10, 2017, https://thediplomat.com/2017/01/the-central-asian-women-on-the-frontline-of-jihad/.

[103] Ken Wolfe, "An Analysis of Islamic State Propaganda Distribution," Report, *Flashpoint* (2019), 3–5.

[104] Wolfe, "An Analysis of Islamic State Propaganda."

mail.ru revealed ISIS's investment in Russian-speaking audiences—decisive in targeting Central Asians, especially those working as migrant laborers in Russia.

Furat Media, ISIS's Russian-language media wing, assiduously spread Russian-language propaganda across the former Soviet republics. Islom Atabiyev, better known as Abu Jihad, produced large numbers of such videos for ISIS. A Russian national, he was sanctioned by the U.S. Treasury Department in August 2015, which "considered [him] to be the main Russian-speaking ideologue of [IS] IS . . . popular among jihadists in the post-Soviet region."[105] Another Furat media expert was a Tajik national from Dushanbe known as Abu Daoud Tojiki. Abu Daoud became known for producing extensive propaganda about Tajiks in ISIS. Furat frequently distributed martyrdom videos of Tajiks who had died as *shahid*s in Syria.[106]

As with al-Qaeda–linked groups, both virtual and actual networks played a major role in ISIS's ability to mobilize in high-risk conditions.[107] In May 2015, Col. Gulmurod Halimov left his position as a lieutenant-colonel and commander of the Tajik Interior Ministry's Special Purpose Police Unit (known as OMON) and joined ISIS. Halimov's prominent position made his online propaganda videos an effective recruiting tool.[108] The following year, another 1,000 to 1,300 Tajiks went to Syria. Other recruiters operated in Tajikistan, albeit on a smaller scale. The small Tajik town of Norak became known for its network of ISIS supporters, including twenty-six-year-old Anushervon Asimov, believed to have recruited about a hundred individuals to join ISIS before being killed in Syria in 2016. Another was Abu Usama Noraki (born Tojiddin Nazarov). Tajik authorities claim he launched a campaign to brainwash young Tajiks to join ISIS. Noraki reportedly recruited thirty men from one village alone. Tajik authorities detained another twenty alleged militants in Norak before they left for Syria. Two other ISIS recruits, Asliddin and Jafar Yusupov, were brothers from Norak; they became infamous in 2018 for killing the four Western cyclists mentioned at the start of this chapter.[109]

Similarly, several villages and towns from northern Kyrgyzstan have been major recruiting networks.[110] Some of those who went from Kyrgyzstan to join

[105] Aleksandre Kvakhadze, "Abu Jihad: A Brief Profile of Islamic State's Russian Propaganda Master," *Jamestown Foundation: Militant Leadership Monitor* 9, no. 7 (July 2018).

[106] Joanna Paraszczuk, "Have Tajik IS Militants Faked Their Own 'Martyrdoms'?," *Radio Free Europe/Radio Liberty*, July 1, 2015, https://www.rferl.org/a/islamic-state-tajikistan-tracking-/27104720.html.

[107] "Tajik Court Issues First Verdict for ISIL Recruitment," *Asia-Plus*, July 6, 2015, https://asiaplustj.info/en/news/tajikistan/laworder/20150706/tajik-court-issues-first-verdict-isil-recruitment.

[108] Interview with Mehl.

[109] Farangis Najibullah and Mumin Ahmadi, "Deserted Streets, Anxious Parents: The Tajik Town That Spawned the Cyclists Attack," *Radio Free Europe/Radio Liberty*, November 4, 2018.

[110] Interview with U.S. government analyst, August 2018; interview with Tahir, November 2018; interview with Colin Cram, second secretary, U.S. Embassy, Bishkek, Kyrgyzstan, June 2019.

ISIS in 2015 or 2016 were then sent back to their native village to recruit more fighters. The Ferghana Valley region of Batken, where the IMU recruited in 1999–2000, was one such site. Surveillance inside Kyrgyzstan was lower than in neighboring republics, and flights from there to Turkey were easy. From Turkey, recruits crossed into Syria.[111] Another network existed for forging Kyrgyzstani passports.[112]

As opposed to KTJ, which relied largely on Uzbek kinship, ethnic, village, and mosque connections in the Ferghana Valley, the major path to ISIS was from migrant networks in Russia or Turkey, where several million Tajik, Uzbek, and Kyrgyz migrants worked as of 2018. Kabiri, whose Islamic party had actively worked with Tajik migrants in Russia, Turkey, and Europe for years, stated that, "over 90 percent of those [Tajiks] who joined ISIS were labor migrants."[113] Many migrant workers labored and lived in degrading conditions, without traditional religious networks or family elders to influence them.[114] These young men were more vulnerable to new and radical ideas of Islamism. Tajik scholar Hafiz Boboyorov concluded that the combination of having experienced an Islamic revival without the moderating influence of national Tajik customs, while also experiencing discrimination in Russia, made these migrant workers ideal targets for recruiters.[115]

Struggling for Sacred Authority

Unlike the IRPT or even KTJ, which were led by indigenous leaders with high sacred authority, ISIS had minimal authority within Central Asia. Its leader, Abu Bakr al-Baghdadi, was little known in the region. Even Central Asian leaders with Salafist leanings, such as Imam Rashod Qori, condemned ISIS.

Yet, ISIS recruits often challenged government imams, who lacked legitimacy. That struggle for sacred authority was exemplified in a war of words between one government-appointed mullah, Haji Mirzo Ibronov, and an ISIS recruit, Nusrat Nazarov. In a pro-ISIS video in May 2014 on the Russian social networking platform Odnoklassniki, Nazarov directly challenged Ibronov, who had dissuaded Tajiks from fighting jihad. Nazarov accused the state-appointed mullah of serving the Tajik government, not Islam. Nazarov demanded, "How

111 "ISIS Recruiter Detained in Kyrgyzstan," *24.KG*, August 20, 2021; "Two Foreigners-Recruiters Detained in Bishkek," *24.KG*, July 27, 2021.

112 "The Guardian: ISIL Members Buy Kyrgyz Passports to Leave Syria," *24.KG*, February 4, 2022.

113 "Current Political, Social and Economic Challenges in Tajikistan: An Interview with Muhiddin Kabiri," conducted by Sebastien Peyrouse, CAP Paper, No. 257 (Washington, D.C.: Central Asia Program, May 2021), 11.

114 Communications with Uzbek and Tajik mosque attendees, Moscow, Russia and Istanbul, Turkey; interview with U.S. Department of State official, Washington, D.C., December 2018.

115 "IS Targeting Unemployed Tajik Youth and Labor Migrants, Study Finds," *Radio Free Europe/Radio Liberty*, February 24, 2015, https://www.rferl.org/a/islamic-state-unemployed-tajik-youths-migrants/26866182.html.

can you say there is no jihad here? Children are being killed here. . . . You say you are the government's mullah . . . the government which is against Allah's laws."[116] Nazarov soon became known as a successful militant recruiter with a network based in southern Tajikistan.

Colonel Halimov's defection from the Tajik OMON to ISIS was a major boon for the Islamic State. A high-level individual, straight from the innards of the Tajik power structures, Halimov was a rare recruit. In a stunning YouTube video posted in May 2015, he pledged his allegiance to the Islamic State, unequivocally declared that he was motivated by the Tajik government's religious persecution and extensive torture of Muslims, and promised bloodshed to create Islamic law: "Listen, you dogs, the president [Rahmon] and ministers, you don't know how many of the guys here, our brothers, are waiting to return to Tajikistan to revive *shariat* law. . . . We are coming to you with slaughter, *Insha'allah*." Halimov added threats to Russia and the United States as well: "We will come to your cities, to your homes, and we will kill you."[117] Given his stature and insider knowledge of the Tajik regime, his words imparted great authority to ISIS. For Tajiks, Halimov became a symbol of strength. He demonstrated that one could make a transition from secular to sacred. In doing so, he began to build sacred authority for the Islamic State. Moreover, his training—by the Tajik and Russian special forces and at a course in the United States—allowed him to discredit all those governments. His skills also led him to quickly rise to become minister of war for ISIS. By September 2016, Halimov was second-in-command of ISIS forces, answering directly to al-Baghdadi.

Ideational Congruence and Dissonance

Ideological outreach and virtual associational space proved critical for ISIS in disseminating its message—including news of repression and atrocities in Syria, the ideology of radical Salafi jihadism, and its "success" in establishing a caliphate for all Muslims. This propaganda enabled ISIS's substantial mobilization of foreign fighters.[118] As noted already, ISIS extensively used social media platforms, as well as secure messaging apps (especially Telegram and Zello), to recruit a transnational following. Despite the dissonance between its core ideas and Central Asian norms about Islam, ISIS at least partially adapted to various

[116] Farangis Najibullah, "Tajik Mullah's Remarks on Jihad Spark War of Words," *Radio Free Europe/Radio Liberty*, Tajik Service, May 27, 2014, https://www.rferl.org/a/tajikistan-syria-war-words/25400717.html.

[117] The video text is quoted in Andrew Roth, "Police Commander From Tajikistan Appears in ISIS Video," *New York Times*, May 29, 2015. The May 2015 video link is no longer available. Andrew Kramer, "Tajik Police Commander, Trained in U.S., Appears to Rise in Islamic State Ranks," *New York Times*, November 10, 2016; "US Confirms Training Tajik Ex-Police Commander Who Joined ISIS," *Radio Free Europe/Radio Liberty*, May 30, 2015, https://www.rferl.org/a/tajikistan-is/27045624.html.

[118] Barrett, "Beyond the Caliphate."

Image 14.8 Tajik Colonel Gulmurod Halimov in ISIS video
Source: YouTube screenshot, https://rus.ozodi.org/a/27042528.html.

local target audiences, using Russian, Uzbek, Kyrgyz, Uyghur, and other languages to spread regionally salient messages.

ISIS propaganda focused on several key themes, much like KTJ. First was the oppression of Muslims under unjust religious and political conditions—especially of Syrian Muslims under the heavy hand of Assad. ISIS propaganda melded this message into a discussion of Russian and Western support for both Syria and secular dictators in Central Asia. ISIS promised the caliphate would bring justice and restore the rights and security of Muslims within and beyond Syria. This was not just idle rhetoric. No other Islamist movement in the previous century had come so close to re-creating the caliphate's territory.

As with KTJ and the IMU before it, ISIS's positioning of an Islamist polity as a remedy to injustice and repression resonated with many Central Asians. Colonel Halimov's video blatantly revealed how oppression of believers motivated recruits. He had denounced the Tajik government for crimes perpetrated by the police and security services against Muslims and Islam. Much like Abu Saloh, Halimov threatened to bring jihad to Russia and Tajikistan.[119] Although Tajik authorities quickly blocked the video on YouTube, it went viral through social media.

A second central ISIS theme was the glorification of jihad and martyrdom. While not an idea typically resonant among Central Asians, multiple martyrdom videos about Tajiks who died fighting in the ranks of ISIS bolstered its legitimacy

[119] "Tajik OMON Commander Wanted for Treason," *Radio Free Europe/Radio Liberty*, June 5, 2015, https://www.rferl.org/a/tajikistan-police-commander-islamic-state-treason/27051207.html.

and further spread its radical message among Tajiks at home.[120] One study found that Tajiks actually topped the list of those becoming suicide bombers in Syria. Between December 2015 and late November 2016, twenty-seven Tajik citizens had perpetrated suicide attacks, constituting 11.3 percent of total suicide attacks by foreign fighters in this period. Citizens of Saudi Arabia and Morocco, despite much larger Muslim populations, accounted for seventeen each (9.1 percent).[121] Whether they were ideologically motivated to suicide bombing, used as cannon fodder for ISIS, or faking martyrdom to protect their family back home, as one journalist suggested, is unclear.

ISIS's appeals were not limited to Tajikistan. Not to be outdone by al-Qaeda affiliate KTJ, ISIS released its first video targeting Kyrgyzstanis in 2015.[122] The nine-and-a-half-minute film by Furat Media featured a Kyrgyzstani militant, speaking Kyrgyz and pitching ISIS's core message: make the *hijra* to the caliphate and wage jihad, one's duty to Allah. In many ways, the video echoed Abu Saloh's messages. It also included anti-Semitic and anti-Christian rhetoric: "Today, the Jews and Christians of the entire world and their henchmen have united and are . . . oppressing Muslims. They are banning us from wearing beards."[123] According to the young, bearded speaker, Muslim men must wear beards to distinguish themselves from Jews and Christians. Standing in front of ISIS's black flag, he declared that all Muslims are one and that everything comes from Allah, thanks to Allah. He spoke of law by *shariat* and condemned democracy as government "for the *kufr*."[124] Such ideas found an audience among those angry at corruption and oppression across Central Asia and disillusioned with the promise of secular democracy.[125]

ISIS released Russian-language videos—geared toward Kyrgyz, Kazakhs, Dagestanis, and Chechens—highlighting the benefits of bringing one's entire family to the caliphate to partake in jihad. This emphasis on family was appealing to Central Asians, among whom kinship networks have remained critical. In an ISIS video titled "Message from the Heart to the Land of Kazakhstan," several Russian-speaking Kazakh fighters called on their brethren to leave "Kafiristan"—Kazakhstan was the land of the infidel—and live "in the land of the caliphate," to raise their children "according to *shariat*."[126] From 2013 to 2018, more than

[120] Paraszczuk, "Have Tajik IS Militants Faked Their Own 'Martyrdoms'?"

[121] Charlie Winter, "War by Suicide: A Statistical Analysis of the Islamic State's Martyrdom Industry," Report, ICCT, The Hague, February 27, 2017, 21–22.

[122] Joanna Paraszczuk, "How to Recruit Militants and Influence People: IS's First Ever Kyrgyz Recruitment Video," *Radio Free Europe/Radio Liberty*, July 27, 2015, https://www.rferl.org/a/islamic-state-kyrgyz-recruitment-video/27155247.html.

[123] Paraszczuk, "How to Recruit Militants."

[124] The video in Kyrgyz by the al-Furāt Media Center was posted as "A New Video Message from the Islamic State: Message to Our People in Kyrgyzstan" on the website Jihadology.net on July 25, 2015.

[125] Collins and Owen, "Islamic Religiosity and Regime Preferences."

[126] Isa, "'Jihadists from Kazygurt' Threaten Nazarbayev."

fifty-five ISIS "family videos" showed Central Asian children as heroes who migrated with their parents and joined the ISIS youth fighters, called "Cubs of the Caliphate."[127]

In August 2016, more than fifteen ISIS video and audio clips promoted "violence and the brutal killing of prisoners and civilians."[128] ISIS's rhetoric and use of violence in general—from beheadings and mass executions to the extermination of Jews and Christians—was repulsive to most Central Asians. While many Central Asians supported the concept of defensive jihad, they did so under very limited conditions. The vast majority of Tajik and other focus group respondents, even those supporting either mainstream Islamist ideas or sympathetic to a caliphate, had condemned suicide bombing as un-Islamic (see Chapters 7, 10, and 13). Focus groups did reveal that anti-Semitism and resentment against Christian missionaries existed, but such sentiments did not engender support for the interconfessional violence that characterized ISIS's genocidal rule. Just as important, apart from Colonel Halimov's video, ISIS propaganda did not highlight the everyday political concerns of Central Asians, who demanded a more Islamic society and state at home. ISIS only localized some of its ideas; its radical ideology of the caliphate and unrestrained violence limited its appeal in Central Asia. Its draw, mainly for Tajiks, lay more in the networks it established and inspiration from Halimov than in support for its radical ideology. Nonetheless, that across the region several thousand did join revealed that Central Asian norms against violence and radicalism were breaking down, particularly among the younger post-Soviet generation.

ISIS's Shift to Afghanistan and Central Asia

From 2017 onward, ISIS was clearly in decline, mainly due to sustained military strikes from the West's coalition. According to a senior UN official, by August 2018 the total number of ISIS fighters in Syria and Iraq had dropped to as low as twenty thousand.[129] Of these, several thousand were Central Asians. Estimates of Tajik foreign fighters remaining with ISIS in 2018 ranged from nine hundred to two thousand.[130] About 80 percent of Kazakh citizens in Syria had been

[127] "Over 10,000 Citizens of Uzbekistan, Kyrgyzstan, Tajikistan, and Kazakhstan Fought for ISIS: Reports," *EurAsian Times*, December 19, 2018; Uran Botobekov, "Central Asian Children Cast as ISIS Executioners," *The Diplomat*, September 20, 2016.

[128] Botobekov, "Central Asian Children."

[129] Bethan McKernan, "Up to 30,000 ISIS Fighters Remain in Iraq and Syria, Says UN," *The Independent*, August 15, 2018.

[130] Interview with U.S. Department of State official, Washington, D.C., December 2018; Damon Mehl, "Converging Factors Signal Increasing Terror Threat to Tajikistan," *CTC Sentinel* 11, no. 10 (November 2018): 25–30; Edward Lemon, presentation at Helsinki Commission, "Mosque and State in Central Asia: Can Religious Freedom Coexist with Government Regulation of Islam?," Washington, D.C., December 17, 2018.

killed,[131] as had more than three hundred Tajik citizens.[132] The death toll among Uzbekistanis and Kyrgyzstanis was much lower.[133] By 2021, few Central Asian fighters had returned home under "amnesty" and "reintegration" programs offered by the Tajik and Uzbek governments. The prospects for going home were too risky.

Instead, as ISIS numbers declined in Syria and Iraq, some Central Asian fighters joined ISIS-Khorasan. ISIS-K had originated around a Pakistani militant core—ex-TTP, among others—who were frustrated with the Taliban and hoped to achieve an Islamic state more quickly by joining ISIS.[134] That group had established a base in Afghanistan's Nangarhar Province in October 2014 and publicly announced itself as ISIS-K in early 2015. At its height in 2016, various sources estimated that ISIS-K had from three thousand to six thousand militants.[135] In December 2017, U.S. Army Gen. (Ret.) Stanley McChrystal warned that ISIS-K already controlled parts of Afghanistan; other U.S. military assessments concluded that ISIS-K had many foreign fighters, including Central Asians.[136] ISIS-K spread especially during the peace negotiations between the United States and the Taliban in 2019–20. Although Taliban attacks on U.S. forces were declining, ISIS-K's continued, destabilizing numerous regions. In January 2019, U.S. Army Ranger Sgt. Cameron Meddock was fatally wounded by ISIS-K militants in a battle in Badghis Province, a once-stable region in northwest Afghanistan. ISIS-K was gaining a foothold there, as elsewhere, and escalating strikes during the U.S. drawdown.[137] Notably, according to the Afghan Ministry of Defense, many of the ISIS-K militants in Badghis and elsewhere were not Afghans, but foreign fighters.[138]

As Damon Mehl, a former senior analyst with the U.S. Department of Defense, argued, the relocation of Central Asian ISIS fighters from Syria and

[131] "80% казахстанцев, отправившихся воевать в Сирию и Ирак, уже погибли, заявляют эксперты," *Zakon.kz*, November 3, 2014, https://www.zakon.kz/4664942-80-kazakhstancev-otpravivshikhsja.html.

[132] Joanna Paraszczuk, "Why Are All the Russian, Central Asian Militants Vanishing from Social Networks?" *Radio Free Europe/Radio Liberty*, November 5, 2015, https://www.rferl.org/a/russian-central-asian-militants-vanish-social-networks/27347535.html.

[133] Botobekov, "Central Asian Women on the Frontline of Jihad."

[134] Antonio Giustozzi, *The Islamic State in Khorasan: Afghanistan, Pakistan, and the New Central Asian Jihad* (London: Hurst, 2018).

[135] "Afghanistan: Who Are Islamic State Khorasan Province Militants?," *BBC News*, October 11, 2021, https://www.bbc.com/news/world-asia-58333533; "Explainer: ISIS-Khorasan in Afghanistan," Wilson Center, August 27, 2021, https://www.wilsoncenter.org/article/explainer-isis-khorasan-afghanistan.

[136] Kosh Sadat and Stanley McChrystal, "Staying the Course in Afghanistan: How to Fight the Longest War," *Foreign Affairs*, November/December 2017.

[137] Kyle Rempfer, "An Army Ranger Wounded in Northwest Afghanistan on Sunday Has Died," *Army Times*, January 18, 2019.

[138] "10 ISIS-K Militants Killed, 16 Foreign Fighters Arrested, Badghis Province," *Khaama Press*, January 13, 2019, https://www.khaama.com/10-isis-k-militants-killed-16-foreign-fighters-arrested-in-badghis-province-03104/.

Iraq posed a serious threat to Afghanistan.[139] Afghanistan was a logical destination for Central Asians, given that some 750 Central Asian nationals (mostly Uzbeks, Tajiks, and Kyrgyz) were already fighting there under ISIS-K.[140] Hundreds of these were ethnic Uzbek former IMU fighters, who had defected from the Taliban to join ISIS-K in 2014–15. ISIS also had support among some Tajik fighters; JA reportedly began collaborating with ISIS-K in early 2017.[141] JA remained in Afghanistan, difficult to access, and sheltered from easy capture by the Afghan government, NATO forces, or the Tajik government.[142] JA and the ex-IMU offered Tajiks and Uzbek fighting in Syria and Iraq easy integration, should they migrate to Afghanistan.[143]

Several ISIS-K strikes involving Tajik citizens have taken place inside Afghanistan. In one devastating attack, on March 8, 2017, two militants used a suicide bomb and waged a gun assault for several hours on a military hospital in Kabul. The ISIS Amaq News Agency released names of the attackers; they included two Tajik nationals. At least forty-nine people were killed and scores were injured. Another attack on a Shia memorial ceremony in Afghanistan in March 2020 killed or wounded dozens with rockets and other small arms. In statements and with a photo disseminated by Amaq, the Islamic State claimed responsibility, identifying two jihadist perpetrators, a Tajikistani using the nom de guerre Ahmad al-Tajiki and another Tajik migrant, named Abdurahmon al-Muhojir; both militants had fought in Syria and then migrated to Afghanistan.[144]

Furthermore, the Afghan-Tajik border was vulnerable to ISIS-K.[145] Inadequate security to monitor the rough terrain combined with an easily bribed border force made the frontier relatively porous. While it was difficult to return and reintegrate into a village without being arrested, returning to border regions was possible. Moreover, Colonel Halimov had promised that he would bring jihad back to his homeland—a statement not lost on Tajik authorities. Despite multiple Russian and Iraqi reports of his death, several sources indicated that Halimov was still alive.[146] According to Mehl, two sources, "a Tajik opposition leader and an Afghan intelligence official," reported in 2018 that Halimov had migrated to Afghanistan, "where he was making preparations to enter and fight

[139] Mehl, "Converging Factors," 25.

[140] UN Security Council, "Twenty-second Report of the Analytical Support and Sanctions Monitoring Team Submitted Pursuant to Resolution 2368 (2017) concerning ISIL (Da'esh), Al-Qaida and Associated Individuals and Entities," S/2018/705, July 27, 2018, 17.

[141] Giustozzi, *The Islamic State in Khorasan*, 156; interview with Mehl; Mehl, "Converging Factors."

[142] Interview with official, U.S. Department of State, Washington, D.C., December 2018.

[143] Mehl, "Converging Factors," 26–27.

[144] Thomas Joscelyn, "Islamic State Claims Two Recent Attacks in Kabul," *FDD's Long War Journal*, March 7, 2020.

[145] Interview with Mehl.

[146] "Tajik Islamic State Commander Moves to Afghanistan," *BBC Monitoring Newsfile*, September 14, 2018.

in Tajikistan," as he had vowed to do.[147] As of 2022, the UN Security Council still designated Halimov a wanted terrorist. Increased ISIS-K as well as Taliban activity reported in Kunduz and Badakhshan provinces, close to the border of Tajikistan, posed a definite threat to Tajik stability.[148]

The deteriorating situation in Afghanistan threatened Central Asia's states. In early November 2019, about twenty Central Asian militants, allegedly ISIS-K members, crossed from Kunduz, Afghanistan, into Tajikistan. From there, they struck a Tajikistan-Afghanistan border checkpoint, killing seventeen, including fifteen militants and two Tajik security forces, in one of the larger firefights on the border in a decade. ISIS did not claim responsibility for that failed attack,[149] but it did claim responsibility that same month for killing ten Tajik border guards in a more successful assault on a security checkpoint on the Uzbek-Tajik border. In another propaganda video the perpetrators pledged allegiance to the newly appointed ISIS caliph, Abu Ibrahim al-Hashimi al-Qurayshi.[150]

Another threat from ISIS emerged from its 2018 directive, ordering its followers to "stay in place" and launch attacks at home rather than go to Syria. Investigation of the 2018 murder of the Western cyclists in Tajikistan revealed that some of the Tajik attackers were "virtual" ISIS members, directed by ISIS via social media and encrypted apps.[151] The path of Husayn Abdusamadov, the leader of the attack and its sole survivor, was revealing. He had once been a rising student in Dushanbe, where he had graduated from the prestigious Presidential Lyceum in 2002.[152] Although he had begun university studies, he quit after becoming inspired by the young radical cleric Imam Qori Nosir, who had renounced IRPT membership because the party had rejected militancy and an Islamic state. For a time, Abdusamadov drifted from job to job, in and out of the country, sometimes doing migrant labor work in Russia, and traveling in the Middle East. According to journalist Rukmini Callimachi, who spent seven years covering ISIS and interviewed Abdusamadov from prison in 2019, the latter recounted how he had gone to Syria with Qori Nosir to join ISIS. He fought with ISIS in the battle for Tal Afar in 2017, and was later directed to organize an attack in Europe. When visa problems prevented his entry, he was dispatched

147 Mehl, "Converging Factors," 28.

148 Interview with Mehl.

149 Bruce Pannier, "Reported Attack in Tajikistan Could Have Broad Implications for Central Asia," *Radio Free Europe/Radio Liberty*, November 6, 2019, https://www.rferl.org/a/reported-attack-in-tajikistan-could-have-broad-implications-for-central-asia/30256653.html.

150 Reuters Staff, "Islamic State Claims Tajik-Uzbek Border Attack," *Reuters*, November 8, 2019, https://www.reuters.com/article/us-tajikistan-attacks/islamic-state-claims-tajik-uzbek-border-attack-idUSKBN1XI29W.

151 Cragin and Weil, "Virtual Planners."

152 "From 'Presidential Lyceum' to Jihadist Drifter," *Radio Free Europe/Radio Liberty*, August 15, 2018, https://www.rferl.org/a/tajik-cyclists-attack-abdusamadov-terrorist-ringleader/29435946.html.

home to strike in place for ISIS, targeting "non-believers."[153] He worked in contact with another prolific Tajik ISIS recruiter hailing from his home region, Abu Usama Noraki, known for active online video propaganda and messaging. Abu Usama had brought in two of the group's attackers, while Abdusamadov himself had drawn in the others. All had been labor migrants in Russia. After contacting Qori Nosir, still in Syria, about their opportunity to strike the cyclists, Abdusamadov received the directive to attack via the mobile app Zello. An ISIS spokesman later declared that more attacks in Tajikistan would be forthcoming, while from prison Abdusamadov maintained his pledge to ISIS and expressed no remorse.[154]

Prison riots in Central Asia have also been tied to ISIS. In November 2018, one such uprising killed fifty inmates at the high-security facility in Khujand, Tajikistan, where those sentenced as Islamists had been incarcerated. ISIS again claimed responsibility. Prison breaks had occurred in the same location before and were previously attributed to the IMU (see Chapter 9). Another prison uprising took place in Vahdat, in May 2019. Journalists were unable to verify the details, but Tajikistan's Interior Ministry claimed that the riot involved seventeen ISIS members, including Halimov's son, who had been incarcerated there in 2017 for attempting to go to Syria. Prisoners took hostages, set a fire, and killed three prison guards, allowing some ISIS prisoners to escape. During the uprising, ISIS prisoners killed IRPT members also incarcerated there, another indication of ISIS's radicalism.[155]

Some ISIS plots were foiled. For example, in early November 2018, Tajik authorities claimed that they had apprehended twelve suspects in a plot against a school in Tajikistan. The suspects were also implicated in a thwarted plot against the Dushanbe location of the Russian 201st Military Base in Tajikistan, which at the time hosted the largest contingent of Russian troops outside of Russia.[156] Tajik officials charged that the perpetrators were "recruited" online and had taken an oath of allegiance to ISIS;[157] U.S. government experts believed these reports to be credible.[158]

[153] See Rukmini Callimachi's interview with Abdusamadov, "When ISIS Killed Cyclists on their Journey Around the World," *New York Times*, June 21, 2019, https://www.nytimes.com/2019/06/21/the-weekly/isis-bike-attack-tajikistan.html; Thomas Joscelyn, "Assailants in Tajikistan Swore Allegiance to Baghdadi before Attack," *FDD's Long War Journal*, July 31, 2018.

[154] Mehl, "Converging Factors," 28–29; Rukmini Callimachi, interview with Abdusamadov.

[155] "Tajikistan Prison Riot Kills Prominent Opposition Members," *Al Jazeera*, May 21, 2019, https://www.aljazeera.com/news/2019/5/21/tajikistan-prison-riot-kills-prominent-opposition-members; "Tajik Opposition Members among 32 Killed in Prison Riot," *Radio Free Europe/Radio Liberty*, May 20, 2019, https://www.rferl.org/a/29951879.html.

[156] "After Denial, Tajik Security Service Confirms the Report about Plot to Attack Russian Military Base," *Asia-Plus*, Dushanbe, Tajikistan, November 14, 2018.

[157] Ashley Scarfo, "Terror Threat Turns Inward on Central Asia," *Jamestown Foundation: Terrorism Monitor* 16, no. 23, December 3, 2018.

[158] Interview with U.S. Department of State official, December 2018; interview with Mehl, November 2018.

Kyrgyzstan also saw signs of instability. Initially, those targeted by Kyrgyzstan's anti-extremist crackdown were primarily alleged HTI supporters, and government claims were highly suspect. The head of the GKNB, for example, announced in 2011 that there were 1,279 known "terrorists" in Kyrgyzstan, mostly HTI. In October 2016, the Ministry of Internal Affairs had a much longer "extremist watch list" of 4,154 individuals. Kyrgyzstan's security services claimed in 2018 to be uncovering ISIS cell members or sympathizers on a weekly basis; this too seemed incredible.[159] The arrests were particularly focused on the south, among ethnic Uzbeks. The security services' pernicious antiminority bias and the desire to "over-fulfill arrest quotas" obscured the extent of actual ISIS activity.[160] Human Rights Watch and local rights defenders claimed that the government put mostly ethnic Uzbek and Uyghur minorities on its watch list. Many such arrests may have been fabricated, but even so, they were likely to breed more opposition to Kyrgyzstan's regime, as in the case of KTJ's emergence.

Kyrgyzstan did experience a rise of confirmed ISIS-backed incidents, according to local and international experts. On November 26, 2015, two assailants in Bishkek stabbed Kadyr Malikov, the mainstream Hanafi theologian and government adviser on religion. A staunch opponent of religious extremism, Malikov had been extremely vocal in criticizing ISIS and Salafi jihadism; he had received threats from ISIS supporters before the attack.[161] In 2016, the Turkish government extradited the would-be killer, a Kyrgyzstani citizen who was en route to Syria.[162] Death threats against Malikov persisted.[163]

Returning ISIS prisoners posed both legal challenges and a potential security threat for Kyrgyzstan and the region. According to a Kyrgyz security services official, twenty children had returned from Syria in 2016 and "were held criminally responsible," in accord with articles of the Criminal Code of Kyrgyzstan banning mercenary behavior and participation in armed conflicts or military actions.[164] Their incarceration probably deterred actual fighters from returning. The long-term implications remained unknown for Kyrgyzstani children and youth born or raised in Syria and Iraq, who returned with their parents only to be prosecuted and jailed as extremists. As of September 2021, in addition to an unknown number of fighters, 109 Kyrgyzstani women and their 271 children were

[159] Human Rights Watch, "We Live in Constant Fear," 19–20; interview with representatives of the human rights movement Bir Duino-Kyrgyzstan, Bishkek, Kyrgyzstan, June 2018.

[160] Interview with Emil Nasritdinov, December 2018.

[161] Interview with Bir Duino-Kyrgyzstan.

[162] "Second Suspect of Attack on Kadyr Malikov Detained in Turkey," *24.kg*, March 6, 2017, https://24.kg/english/46566_Second_suspect_of_attack_on_Kadyr_Malikov_detained_in_Turkey/ ; "Islamist Jailed for Life over Attack on Kyrgyz Theologian," *Radio Free Europe/Radio Liberty*, June 9, 2016, https://www.rferl.org/a/kyrgyzstan-theologian-attack-islamist/27788276.html.

[163] Interview with Nasritdinov, December 2018.

[164] Botobekov, "Central Asian Children."

being held in three prison camps in Syria.[165] The government of Kyrgyzstan was not moving to repatriate them.

Reports of ISIS threats inside Uzbekistan, by contrast, have been few. The Uzbek government claimed to be dealing with ISIS returnees humanely, even as it also claimed to be increasing religious freedom. Yet in April 2022, Uzbekistan was the target of the first ISIS rocket attack on a Central Asian state. From the Afghan-Uzbek border, across the Amu Darya, ISIS-K launched ten Katyusha rockets on Uzbek forces deployed in the city of Termiz.[166] The attack, eight months after the U.S. withdrawal from Afghanistan, solidified fears that ISIS-K was expanding in the region.

For those Central Asians neither killed nor in custody, remaining in Syria or Iraq may ultimately prove impossible, given the steady advance of Assad's regime. So too returning home seemed unlikely if they wanted to avoid incarceration. As will be discussed in Chapter 15, in 2020, the UN Security Council reported evidence that some militants were relocating to Afghanistan.[167] Should they follow the path of Uzbek IMU émigrés to Afghanistan since the early 1990s, they would become the next generation of regional and transnational jihadists.

Central Asians in ISIS Attack the West

A handful of ISIS-radicalized Central Asians figured prominently in attacks in the United States, Europe, Turkey, and Russia as well. Central Asian supporters of ISIS were following ISIS recommendations regarding vehicular attacks, the use of knives, and targeting civilians in crowded shopping or tourist areas. The media impact was high, projecting strength even as ISIS lost its Syrian base. While sometimes treated as "lone wolf" attacks, evidence revealed online coordination between ISIS and the attackers.

An attack on Istanbul's Atatürk Airport on June 28, 2016, exemplified this phenomenon. Three suicide bombers opened fire, then detonated explosives, killing forty-six people and injuring about 240. Turkish authorities identified the attackers as ISIS members; they included a Dagestani Russian citizen, an

[165] Darya Podolskaya, "MP Asks Authorities to Take Women and Children out of Camps in Syria," *24.kg*, September 12, 2021, https://24.kg/english/207241_MP_asks_authorities_to_take_women_and_children_out_of_camps_in_Syria/.

[166] "Islamic State Khorasan Claims Rocket Attack on Uzbekistan," *Voice of America*, April 18, 2022, https://www.voanews.com/a/islamic-state-khorasan-claims-rocket-attack-on-uzbekistan-/6534866.html.

[167] UN Security Council, "Eleventh Report of the Analytical Support and Sanctions Monitoring Team Submitted Pursuant to Resolution 2501 (2019) concerning the Taliban and Other Associated Individuals and Entities Constituting a Threat to the Peace, Stability and Security of Afghanistan," S/2020/415, May 27, 2020, 20–21.

Uzbekistani, and a Kyrgyzstani.[168] Experts believe it was orchestrated by Ahmed Chatayev, a Russian citizen of Chechen ethnicity who became an ISIS recruiter.[169] Another attack in Turkey took place in the early hours of New Year's Day 2017 at Istanbul's Reina nightclub. According to Turkish authorities, ethnic Uzbeks aligned with ISIS perpetrated this strike, which killed thirty-nine and wounded more than seventy. When one of the three attackers, Muhammad Xurosoniy (born Abduqodir Masharipov), was captured, Turkish authorities uncovered an ISIS cell that was highly trained and well-financed and living across several districts of Istanbul. The network included Central Asian and Caucasian recruits to ISIS, multiple Uzbeks, and ethnic Chechens, Dagestanis, Kyrgyz, Tajiks, Turkmen, and Uyghurs—all from former Soviet Muslim republics. According to news reports, a senior ISIS operative in Raqqa, Syria, used Telegram to direct Xurosoniy.[170]

Yet another attack involving an Uzbek took place in Stockholm on April 7, 2017. Rahmat Oqilov, inspired by the 2016 Bastille Day assault in Nice, France, plowed a truck into pedestrians in a crowded shopping district. He killed five. Oqilov came from Samarqand, Uzbekistan. He had sought asylum in Sweden but had been denied. He claimed during his trial that he had aimed to force Sweden to stop fighting ISIS.[171] Evidence presented at the trial revealed that he had used WhatsApp, Telegram, Viber, Facebook, and Zello to discuss martyrdom in radical chat rooms and had used fifty-three SIM cards to download execution videos and thousands of jihadi photos.[172] On the eve of his attack, Oqilov had sworn allegiance to ISIS.

At least one foiled plot involved daring attempts on the U.S. military in Europe. In April 2020, five Tajiks, allegedly ISIS affiliates, were arrested as they planned attacks on U.S. military facilities in Germany. Some were known to be training in martial arts clubs in Europe.[173]

Central Asians attempted several ISIS attacks inside the United States as well. In August 2014, two Uzbekistani citizens and one Kazakhstani citizen

[168] Fatma Bülbül, "Istanbul Airport Suicide Bombers Revealed as Foreigners," *Anadolu Agency*, June 30, 2016; "Istanbul Airport Attackers 'Russian, Uzbek and Kyrgyz,'" *BBC News*, June 30, 2016, https://www.bbc.com/news/world-europe-36670576; "Death Toll Rises to 46 in 2016 Istanbul Airport Attack," *Hürriyet Daily News*, October 23, 2017.

[169] "Istanbul Airport Attack: 30 Charged Including Foreigners," *BBC News*, July 5, 2016, https://www.bbc.com/news/world-europe-36712557.

[170] Ahmet S. Yayla, "The Reina Nightclub Attack and the Islamic State Threat to Turkey," *CTC Sentinel* 10, no. 3 (March 2017): 9–16.

[171] Christina Anderson, "Uzbek Asylum Seeker Gets Life in Prison for Deadly Truck Attack in Sweden," *New York Times*, June 7, 2018.

[172] "Stockholm Truck Attacker Found Guilty of 5 Counts of Murder, Gets Life," *CBC News*, June 7, 2018, https://www.cbc.ca/news/world/uzbek-man-convicted-stockholm-truck-attack-1.4695424.

[173] UN Security Council, "Twenty-seventh Report of the Analytical Support and Sanctions Monitoring Team Submitted Pursuant to Resolution 2368 (2017) concerning ISIL (Da'esh), Al-Qaida and Associated Individuals and Entities," S/2021/68, February 3, 2021, 13.

were arrested for plotting to kill President Obama. U.S. Justice Department documents noted that two of them had verbally pledged loyalty to ISIS. One of the operatives, Abdurasul Hasan Jo'raboyev, had communicated with an ISIS media website editor that month. In his message, he claimed to be "in the land of infidels" and declared, "[B]ecause he is an enemy of Allah, I will execute Obama."[174] Jo'raboyev and his co-conspirator, a Kazakh citizen living in Brooklyn, were also plotting to kill police officers, to join the military and kill U.S. soldiers, and to plant a bomb on Coney Island.[175] They were arrested purchasing tickets to fly to Turkey, from where they planned to cross the border to Syria, to join ISIS. The third man sentenced, an Uzbekistani citizen living illegally in the United States, provided material aid. They were not the only ones to attempt to aid ISIS. In September 2019, Dilhayot Kasimov was convicted in New York for conspiring and attempting to provide material aid to ISIS. In June 2022, Kasimov's three affiliates were convicted on related charges and were awaiting sentencing.[176]

The October 31, 2017, attack in New York City proved more deadly. It followed the same low-tech vehicular plot recommended in an ISIS publication and used successfully in Europe. Sherali Saipov, a twenty-nine-year-old Uzbek national living in the United States, drove a rented truck into a crowd in Lower Manhattan, killing eight and injuring eleven. Saipov was allegedly inspired by viewing Islamic State videos, including a message in which al-Baghdadi had urged Muslims in the United States to respond to Muslims being killed in U.S. airstrikes in Iraq.[177] After being arrested, Saipov brazenly requested that an ISIS flag be placed in his hospital room.[178] A green-card holder in the United States since 2010, he appeared to have been radicalized by online ISIS propaganda—videos and pictures, hundreds of which were found on his phone—and by personal ties to another Uzbek citizen with terrorist connections.[179]

Russia, too, became a target of ISIS, especially since President Putin began a military campaign to bolster Assad's regime in September 2015. Most ISIS plots against Russia involved its own citizens, primarily Chechens and Dagestanis.

[174] *United States of America v. Abdurasul Hasanovich Juraboev, also known as "Abdulloh Ibn Hasan," Akhror Said Akhmetov, and Abror Habibov*, U.S. District Court, Eastern District of New York, February 24, 2015, http://www.justice.gov/file/344761/download.

[175] U.S. Department of Justice, Office of Public Affairs, "Uzbek Citizen Sentenced to 15 Years for Conspiring to Provide Material Support to Terrorists," news release, October 27, 2017.

[176] "U.S. Court Sentences Uzbek Citizen to 15 Years in Prison for Supporting Islamic State," *Radio Free Europe/Radio Liberty*, June 4, 2022, https://www.rferl.org/a/uzbek-kasimov-isis-sentenced-terrorist/31883416.html.

[177] Göktuğ Sönmez, "Violent Extremism among Central Asians: The Istanbul, St. Petersburg, Stockholm, and New York City Attacks," *CTC Sentinel* 10, no. 11 (December 2017): 14–18.

[178] Julia Ioffe, "Why Does Uzbekistan Export So Many Terrorists?," *The Atlantic*, November 1, 2017.

[179] Sönmez, "Violent Extremism among Central Asians."

Yet several attacks were orchestrated by Central Asians, allegedly recruited by Russian-speaking ISIS agents. Russian authorities further claimed that ISIS followers from Kyrgyzstan, Uzbekistan, and Tajikistan were plotting mass assaults in Russia modeled on the Bataclan theater and other strikes in Paris in 2015 that had killed 130 people.[180]

Such incidents comprise a minuscule fraction of Central Asians traveling to, living in, or seeking asylum in the West. However, these plots demonstrated that ISIS, as well as al-Qaeda, had inspired a gruesome turn among some radicalized Central Asians. Given ISIS's decline in Syria and Iraq and the difficulties both of returning to Central Asia and of staying home and operating under high surveillance and repression, Central Asians in ISIS were likely to continue striking abroad.

The third wave of Central Asian Islamists was far too extreme to appeal to most Muslims in the region. A transnational and militant movement to create a caliphate in a region far from home hardly seemed likely to garner broad support in Central Asia, where prevailing norms abhorred violence and the harsh application of *shariat*, and where most barely understood the idea of the caliphate. In addition, the very emergence of ISIS in Syria and Iraq had spurred a widespread state crackdown on independent Islam and more surveillance across Central Asia, increasing fear of any political or religious activity. Islamist activism and recruiting at home were almost totally repressed. By all indicators, the foreign fighter movement had little chance of success in drafting Central Asians.

It is thus all the more remarkable that a third wave of Islamism did take off, cresting between 2015 and 2017 as a significant component of the overall Islamist fighter movement in Syria and Iraq. It also proved to be durable, surviving from 2013 through at least 2021 and outlasting many other foreign fighters who went to the jihad and left by 2017. And it was militarily effective, both within al-Qaeda's front in Idlib and Aleppo as well as within ISIS. Many fighters who left Syria appeared to continue the jihad, joining Central Asians allied with either ISIS-K or al-Qaeda in Afghanistan.

Despite significant differences from earlier waves of Islamism—namely its extreme Salafi jihadist and transnational nature—this militant third wave was also born of secular authoritarianism, brutal repression of Islam, and widespread injustice, both at home and in Syria. Associational space to organize and mobilize at home was nearly impossible, but this wave of fighters found space to do so in

180 Brian Glyn Williams and Robert Troy Souza, "The Islamic State Threat to the 2018 FIFA World Cup," *CTC Sentinel* 11, no. 5 (May 2018): 6.

Syria and Iraq, repeating a pattern Hegghammer has observed in Saudi Arabia and across the Middle East; those repressed at home went abroad.[181]

As in previous waves, ideology and entrepreneurs also played a critical role. KTJ's leaders, the Tajiks in ISIS, and others fighting in Syria and Iraq were inspired by the idea of the caliphate and by the radical jihadist ideology of al-Qaeda and ISIS. Having seen the failure of nonviolent Islamism at home in the killing of Rafiq Qori and jailing of HTI members, and angry at the West's role in Afghanistan and Iraq, these new entrepreneurs were eager to turn to violent jihad. In many ways, the foreign fighter wave was an extension of the second wave, when the Uzbek Islamist opposition and some Tajik Islamists had accepted the radical ideologies and strategies of al-Qaeda to survive.

We have seen yet again the strategies that made some Islamist movements relatively successful, despite the odds against gaining followers in unspeakably high-risk conditions for mobilizing. As of 2022, KTJ was still fighting in Syria. It mobilized by consciously investing in sacred authority, drawing on ties to popular imams in southern Kyrgyzstan as well as Abu Saloh's own Islamic credentials and rhetoric. ISIS lacked such sacred authority; its leader, al-Baghdadi, was relatively unknown in Central Asia. ISIS compensated by networking through sympathetic Central Asian imams living in Iran or Turkey and by manipulating the spectacular transformation of Gulmurod Halimov from OMON colonel to ISIS commander.

Second, KTJ and ISIS both effectively used networks—within Kyrgyzstan, Russia, and Turkey, and especially among migrant laborers. Social media significantly facilitated transcommunal networking. However, social media had limits; it reached a segment of youth prone to take risks, but not the broader and deeper networks that the IRPT and Haji Turajonzoda had mobilized in the 1990s.

Third, KTJ and ISIS waged striking propaganda campaigns to spread their radical ideology of the caliphate and jihad. In doing so, they manipulated Central Asians' emotions—inspiring anger, empathy, a desire for honor in fighting jihad and accepting martyrdom, machismo, and adventurism. Spread through social media, these images and messages played on the passions of youth. Furthermore, Abu Saloh and Colonel Halimov skillfully blended support for the caliphate in Syria with promises of rectifying injustice at home. Still, their ideology did not resonate with the broader Muslim audience in Central Asia and inevitably limited their growth; most still held to mainstream Central Asian norms of Islam, favoring local and national Islam, moderate Sufi and Hanafi interpretations of *shariat* and governance, and opposition to most violence.

Nonetheless, the rapid emergence and growth of *any* support for transnational, radically militant Islamism suggests that among youth, long-standing Central

[181] Hegghammer, *The Caravan*, 493–94.

Asian norms were weakening. According to one government representative, formerly a journalist from southern Kyrgyzstan, too many negative trends in the post-Soviet era—the decline and corruption of secular education, the corrupt Islamic hierarchy and unjust government, the absence of parents due to migrant work, and collapsing communities, in addition to ongoing religious repression—have led to the decline of traditional Islam and the social institutions that upheld it.[182] In this context, the continual influx of emotionally charged, Salafi jihadist ideologies claiming to bring Islamic justice portend ill for the future of Central Asia. Such ideas have already fostered militancy and extremism, leading youth from Aravan to Aleppo.

[182] Interview with Kyrgyzstani government official, Osh, Kyrgyzstan, June 2019.

15

From Central Asia to Afghanistan, Syria, and Beyond

> I hope that you write this down so that people will know what is happening to us.
>
> —Nargiza, university student, Uzbekistan

Nargiza wanted me to write this book. She lived and studied in Tashkent but hailed from the Ferghana Valley, where her family had lived through the Andijon massacre. She courageously recounted neighbors disappearing because they had attended mosque or religious lessons. She spoke of how her mother worried every time Nargiza left her apartment, lest the same happen to her. She told of her family's everyday misery and of the fear that overshadowed their lives. She wanted me to tell her story, and Uzbekistan's story.

Listening to Nargiza, like the many others whose experiences I have recounted throughout this book, gives us insight into understanding Islamism's causes and the often tragic consequences for ordinary Muslims living through the ongoing conflict between Islamists and the state. When we look at the Central Asian trajectories today, over a century since the Bolshevik Revolution imposed an atheist regime on Central Asia and thirty years since the region's independence, we find that religion is still the source of significant contention.

After returning to my core arguments about the factors that drove three waves of Islamism in Central Asia and the strategies that proved more successful in facilitating high-risk mobilization, this chapter will consider whether or not those same conditions have changed. The picture is mixed: marginally improved but still uncertain in Uzbekistan, worsening in Kyrgyzstan, and significantly darkening in Tajikistan. In particular, I focus on the implications of the Taliban's return to power in Afghanistan for the future of Central Asian Islamists. Finally, I briefly consider how the insights of this book help us understand Islamism in secular authoritarian cases beyond Central Asia.

Politicizing Islam in Central Asia. Kathleen Collins, Oxford University Press. © Oxford University Press 2023.
DOI: 10.1093/oso/9780197685068.003.0016

Explaining Islamist Emergence in Central Asia

Muslims are not born Islamists, much less violent extremists. Religious repression and ideologies drive Islamist emergence. This may be a very straightforward claim, but scholars, journalists, and policymakers seldom consider repression in their analysis, and most dismiss the role of religious ideology.

I have shown that in the Soviet and post-Soviet Central Asian cases, state repression was the first step in politicizing Islam. When authorities tightly controlled, banned, or punished Islamic practice and imprisoned revered religious leaders, the observance of faith itself became a political act. Indeed, the oppression of Islam by secular authoritarian states has been the common, unifying factor that all Central Asian Islamists have pointed to—in interviews, in their writings, and in propaganda videos. The injustice of state repression—from the hijab ban and the confiscation of religious books and cell phones storing one's Qur'an, to the desecration or bulldozing of mosques, to the disappearance of imams and torture of religious prisoners—is the core grievance that has motivated Central Asian Islamists. When Sayid Abdullohi Nuri formed the Nahzat and Haji Akbar Turajonzoda chose to support the IRPT, they did so because they sought to rectify the injustices of Stalin's "Red Terror" that had decimated Islam.[1] When Uzbeks and Tajiks protested, fought, and struggled against the communist and postcommunist regimes—whether in the Ferghana Valley in the 1920s, in Dushanbe and Namangan as the USSR collapsed, in Andijon during the Akromiya trial, in Kara-Suu when Rafiq Qori was killed, or throughout the Afghanistan conflict and Syrian jihad—they did so in large part because unjust and brutal regimes had oppressed Islam, which was at the core of their identity and way of life. As one Tajik respondent, an IRPT supporter, said, "Islam flows in our blood." Politicization of Islam was a direct result of actions taken by regimes hostile to religion.

Islamist emergence began in Central Asia as the "young mullahs" prominent in the chapters of this book debated new religious ideologies as solutions to injustice. The works circulating in the underground *hujras* of the late Brezhnev era—Islamist tracts such as *Milestones*—inspired these religious entrepreneurs. Armed with powerful new ideas about justice under *shariat* and an Islamic state, and learning from the models of the Muslim Brotherhood, the Jamaat-i Islami, the Iranian Revolution, the Afghan mujahidin—and later, the Taliban, al-Qaeda, and ISIS—Central Asian religious entrepreneurs embarked on the high-risk endeavor of forming covert Islamist movements. Each time, their long-term goals were to establish justice by Islamizing society and state.

[1] Interview with Haji Akbar Turajonzoda, Dushanbe, Tajikistan, December 2011.

By the 1980s, as *glasnost* and *perestroika* opened associational space, the first wave of Islamism was moving to challenge Soviet power in the Tajik and Uzbek republics. The IRPT and Adolat were the leading Islamist organizations until 1993; both the IRPT and the remnants of Adolat would ultimately take refuge in Afghanistan as the Tajik and Uzbek governments cracked down. In the late 1990s and 2000s, in independent Tajikistan and Uzbekistan, renewed religious repression again generated Islamist opposition. This second wave of Islamism again reflected the multivocal nature and differentiated paths of political Islam. It included the extremist but nonmilitant movement HTI and increasingly radical Salafi jihadists: the IMU, IJU, and JA. The IRPT, now defining itself as both Islamic and democratic, reemerged as well; it expanded as a legal and more inclusive party and defender of Muslim human rights after the civil war's end. This pattern repeated itself even in Kyrgyzstan, where religious repression had begun much later than elsewhere, and was more targeted; there, HTI's nonviolent party grew slowly in response. By the 2010s, Central Asians angry at religious and political injustice, despairing of any change at home, and ideologically and emotionally motivated by the propaganda of ISIS and KTJ, joined the transnational foreign fighter movement in Syria and Iraq.

As we have followed each Islamist wave's trajectory, along the way we have also seen the fallacy of state arguments about the perils of religious liberalization. Dictators often claim that controlling religion is necessary to prevent violent Islamist extremism. An investigation of Kyrgyzstan in the 1990s, however, challenges their argument. In contrast to Uzbekistan's and Tajikistan's oppression, Kyrgyzstan's liberalization in the 1990s revealed that religious freedom can deter Islamist emergence and instead foster the development of civil Islam. For over a decade, President Askar Akayev's government allowed a flourishing of religion. No strong state or security apparatus was monitoring, shaping, or controlling Islam. Associational space—civic, religious, and to some extent political—was wide, even for the more religious Uzbek minority. The same ideas that had invigorated religious entrepreneurs in Uzbekistan's Ferghana Valley and in central Tajikistan were also readily accessible to the imams and *hujra* students of the Kyrgyz republic's Ferghana Valley. In fact, since many of the region's inhabitants were also ethnic Uzbeks, they had themselves studied in the Uzbek republic's *hujra*s before the USSR's collapse. Yet in Akayev's Kyrgyzstan, these imams had set aside their political theology and agreed to live within an imperfect democratic system.

Instead, Islam in Kyrgyzstan revived in the 1990s; much of the country became far more observant—even puritanical—than it was during the Soviet era. However, instead of Islamist mobilization, Kyrgyzstan experienced the growth of both Muslim politics—public, peaceful debate over the proper role of Islam in society and law—and civil Islam. Multiple civic Islamic organizations engaged in the ordinary and important work of developing democratic society, encouraging voting and nonviolent protest, while actively working against extremism. Neither faithful Muslim leaders nor parliamentary deputies who dabbled in Muslim politics to gain votes sought to overthrow Kyrgyzstan's secular nation-state. Instead, they called for Islamizing society and for allowing Islamic leaders and *shariat* to influence limited areas of law, through parliament. They were not liberal democrats; their ideas cut against the grain of some individual rights enshrined in liberal democracies, but they accepted democracy as better than Islamism's alternatives.

Islamism began to spread in Kyrgyzstan only after Akayev's liberalization ended, with President Kurmanbek Bakiyev's adoption of a severely restrictive law on religion and the repression of ethnic Uzbek citizens, alleged to be extremist because of their strict observance and outspoken imams. Government violence against Kyrgyzstan's Uzbeks in the name of countering extremism actually created some extremists. Again, as in decades before, the politicization of Islam stemmed from religious oppression.

While the Kyrgyz path has shown that civil Islam can exist, the Tajik case has demonstrated that Islamist parties can and have played by democratic rules. The IRPT confirms that multiple variants of Islamism exist, evolve over time, and can come to endorse an Islamic form of parliamentarism—what some call "Muslim democracy."[2] Exemplifying this path, the IRPT shifted from its youthful underground days advocating a purist Islamic society and vague notions of an Islamic state to espousing democracy, elections, and human rights. At the same time, the IRPT still staunchly opposed secularization of society, public space, and governance, and advocated a wider political role for Islam, including *shariat*'s influence, through parliament, on state law. They opposed certain individual rights widespread in the West and critiqued liberal democracy. But whatever its liberal shortcomings, the IRPT—and not the government—abided by democratic rules. For almost two decades, from 1997 through 2015, it pursued a peaceful, electoral path to representation, despite President Imomali Rahmon's return to brutal dictatorship.

Explaining Mobilizational Success and the Limits of Islamism

The second core argument of this book is that Muslim society often limits the spread and sometimes the character of Islamism. Islamists' willingness and capacity to use the three strategies I have outlined—building sacred authority,

[2] Nasr, "The Rise of 'Muslim Democracy.'"

using local and transcommunal networks, and ideational adaptation—shape their relative success in gaining and sustaining followers.

Some of the Islamist organizations we have encountered were bolstered by long-standing sacred authority. The IRPT benefited from the many decades that Ustod Nuri and Ustod Himmatzoda spent studying and teaching Islam in the underground *hujra*s of Tajikistan. The party also gained substantially from its alliance with Qozikalon Turajonzoda, his Sufi lineage, and his connections with esteemed Sufi *eshon*s. Adolat was propelled by the prominence of Ferghana Valley imams such as Shaykh Abduvali Qori. The IMU's Tohir Yo'ldosh and KTJ's Abu Saloh attempted to build sacred authority through their roots in puritanical *hujra*s in the Ferghana Valley, and later by portraying themselves as young mullahs teaching the Qur'an to their militia members in Afghanistan and Syria. Both leaders invested heavily in online propaganda videos to bolster their religious authority before potential followers and funders. ISIS and HTI, both wholly foreign organizations with enigmatic leaders, had far greater difficulty. In contrast to other organizations, their leaders lacked the sacred authority Central Asian religious entrepreneurs could leverage by claiming to have defied the Soviet regime.

Network-building was also essential in reaching and mobilizing communities, especially under authoritarianism. The IRPT drew on multiple networks, from mosque congregations and Sufi connections to its regional ties and communities of forced migrants. After the war, IRPT leader Muhiddin Kabiri established new student networks. Inside Soviet Uzbekistan, Adolat used its regional base in the long-repressed mosque communities of the Ferghana Valley, while the IMU and IJU were dependent on a much narrower network of émigrés. HTI networked among oppressed and excluded ethnic and religious groups. KTJ and ISIS each built online networks and recruited among labor migrants from Central Asia to Russia, Turkey, and Europe. Apart from the IRPT, however, none had sufficiently extensive networks within its home country to mobilize a mass social following.

We have also seen that more successful Islamists adapted their ideas to the population they targeted. The IRPT gained support over time by accepting national Islamic norms and emphasizing gradual Islamization and by rejecting puritanism, an exclusivist Islamic state, and jihadist violence. The party focused its message on defending Muslims' religious freedom, bringing justice, and ending corruption. Its vision of democracy was limited to a "Muslim-style" democracy, not a fully liberal and secular model, and many Tajiks welcomed these ideas.

Groups other than the IRPT generally failed to adapt their ideas about Islam and the state to local norms. Focus group discourse and interviews revealed that radical Islamist ideas—puritanical interpretations of *shariat*, calls for an exclusivist Islamic state or caliphate, and militancy beyond defensive jihad—were alien to Central Asian interpretations of Islam. Throughout this study we have seen that most ordinary Muslims rejected the Salafi jihadist ideas of the IMU, al-Qaeda, and ISIS. They repeatedly condemned suicide bombing as "un-Islamic" and "barbaric" actions committed by those who were "insane" or "animals" and who "could not be buried according to Islam." Those few who were open to a caliphate believed that it would bring justice and end the abuses against Islam. While Adolat initially had a strong, if regionally based, following, the IMU's militant and increasingly transnational focus lost its base inside Uzbekistan but resonated among exiles in Afghanistan and Pakistan.

KTJ and ISIS offer two examples of movements that overcame the norm against violence, at least among some of the younger generation, who were inflamed by injustice and had access to extensive social media propaganda. Both KTJ and ISIS skillfully adapted their emotive propaganda to their audience, promising a righteous caliphate in Syria *and* justice back home in Dushanbe or Tashkent. They promised glory in martyrdom, while pitching the message that women and children can live safely in Syria. They each wove together impassioned appeals about saving gassed Syrian children with references to Uzbek or Tajik victims of torture. They portrayed Russia's Putin, Tajikistan's Rahmon, Syria's Assad, and the U.S. government as unified oppressors of Muslims everywhere. They thus magnified anger and desire for righteousness through militancy. They declared that every Muslim had a duty to wage jihad and cloaked their message in religious language and symbolism.

This radicalization under the aegis of al-Qaeda and ISIS has proved deadly but limited. Indeed, we must remember that Central Asians themselves—ordinary business owners, housewives, students, and laborers—have curtailed the growth and potential of these movements. Nonetheless, the third wave, the foreign fighter movement, has been unspeakably destructive in Syria, Iraq, and Afghanistan, and threatening to Central Asian states and the West. The continued evolution of Islamism in Central Asia will in large part depend on the direction of state policy toward its Muslim citizens.

Current Political Trajectories and Implications for Islamism

Uzbekistan: Reform or Retrenchment?

Uzbekistan has changed far more than the other Central Asian states in recent years. After the death of its nearly thirty-year dictator, Islom Karimov, Uzbekistan seemed markedly improved in numerous ways. President Shavkat Mirziyoyev has been authoritarian, but less driven to eliminate independent religion and civic life than his predecessor. Borders and travel once again became relatively open. A few online bloggers and media dared to report on controversial issues.

After taking office, Mirziyoyev vowed to reform the national security agency, whose practices he rightly compared with those of the NKVD during Stalin's Great Terror of 1937–38. The notorious Jasliq Prison—a symbol of torture—was closed. Mirziyoyev dismissed the infamous National Security Service head, Rustam Inoyatov, who had run the secret police for nearly twenty-three years.[3] Although he was not prosecuted, five other agency officials were charged with torture and sentenced to fourteen to eighteen years in prison. Society began to breathe again.

From 2017 through 2020, religion became more liberalized. Many forms of everyday religious activity became possible and even normal for the first time in decades. Persecution of independent Muslims eased. The "blacklist" of suspected Islamists reportedly shrank. The government released some prisoners of conscience and journalists after nearly two decades of incarceration. Those in prison for "religious extremism" were less likely to have their term extended. The government eased surveillance of mosques and enforcement of the ban on wearing a hijab. The government claimed that 1,500 religious prisoners were released, although specific names were hard to obtain. In 2018, the U.S. State Department's Commission on International Religious Freedom removed Uzbekistan's previous designation as a Country of Particular Concern, marking it as one of the world's worst violators of religious freedom, to recognize change and urge further reform.[4] Albeit still staunchly secular, the state began to prominently use interactions with Islamic leaders to improve its image and legitimize its goals.

Sensing greater associational space, Uzbekistan's society began to revive. For several years, the everyday elements of Muslim life—*mahalla* mullahs reading prayers at weddings and funerals, mosque communities engaging in charity, public religious celebrations, religious dress—increased. Religious leaders focused on mundane social issues, such as relations between family members, deeds considered *halal* or *haram*, the role of women in society, and marriage. A few Muslim leaders also began loudly voicing their views on social issues, in mosques, the public square, and online. Arguably a nascent civil Islam was emerging,[5] one that did not propose creating an alternative state, much less militant jihad. In fact, numerous imams spoke out against KTJ and ISIS.

[3] In 2018, Mirziyoyev also symbolically changed the agency name to the Davlat Xavfsizlik Xizmati (State Security Service).

[4] Communication with Robin Schulman, South and Central Asia Team, Office of International Religious Freedom, U.S. Department of State, Washington, D.C., December 2018; U.S. Department of State, "Uzbekistan 2018 Report on International Religious Freedom," https://www.state.gov/wp-content/uploads/2019/05/UZBEKISTAN-2018-INTERNATIONAL-RELIGIOUS-FREEDOM-REPORT.pdf.

[5] Sebastien Peyrouse, "Engaging with Muslim Civil Society in Central Asia," Report, U.S. Institute of Peace, Washington, D.C., December 2021.

Yet, as in Kyrgyzstan, newly vocal religious elites were often notably illiberal. Strict sexual mores and strident criticism of homosexuality and other behaviors they deemed Western constituted one salient theme of new Muslim preaching. For example, the chief imam of Tashkent's Mirzo Yusuf Mosque, Rahmatulloh Saifutdinov, stirred controversy when he denounced certain television programs as harmful to the nation, suggesting that they gave rise to impure thoughts.[6] Imams advocating a return to strict Muslim values became prominent, in part because they condoned intolerance of sexual minorities.[7] The growing popularity of many religious actors since 2017 reawakened the political elite's deep-seated suspicion of Islam and shook the government's commitment to liberalizing religion.

By 2021, the new era of openness already appeared to have stalled. In July 2021, Mirziyoyev signed the Law on Freedom of Conscience and Religious Organizations, which relaxed some religious registration requirements but still defied most recommendations from the UN Special Rapporteur for Freedom of Religion and Belief and the UN Human Rights Committee. The law again banned unregistered religious education, meeting to pray outside registered places of worship, proselytization, and the production, import, and distribution of religious materials.[8] The Criminal Code's definition of extremism remained excessively broad and open to abuses. For example, the Ministry of Internal Affairs' Anti-Terrorism and Extremism Directorate imposed fines on the news organizations Kun.uz and Azon.uz and individual journalists for allegedly possessing and publishing religious material.[9] Imams' sermons were again closely monitored, and some imams were dismissed, although not imprisoned, for deviating from the state line. Over 1,500 students were recalled from religious study abroad. While some forms of a headscarf were legally permitted, school and university officials frequently evicted young women for wearing the hijab. The police sporadically detained and forcibly shaved bearded men.[10]

[6] "Имом: `Турк сериалларидаги актёрларга ҳавас қилган аёллардан гейлар туғилади,'" BBCUZBEK.COM, March 7, 2018, https://www.youtube.com/watch?v=kQwBcJ1FWAw.

[7] Agnieszka Pikulicka-Wilczewska, "Islam Has an Online Revival in Uzbekistan," *Foreign Policy*, April 22, 2021, https://foreignpolicy.com/2021/04/22/uzbekistan-online-religious-revival-islam-radicalism/.

[8] U.S. Department of State, "Uzbekistan 2021 Report on International Religious Freedom," June 2, 2022, https://www.state.gov/reports/2021-report-on-international-religious-freedom/uzbekistan/.

[9] Committee to Protect Journalists, "Uzbek News Websites Kun.uz and Azon.uz Fined for Allegedly Publishing 'Religious Material' Without Approval," June 24, 2021, https://cpj.org/2021/06/uzbek-news-websites-kun-uz-and-azon-uz-fined-for-allegedly-publishing-religious-material-without-approval/.

[10] Steve Swerdlow, "Annual Report on Uzbekistan, 2021: Uzbekistan's Religious and Political Prisoners: Addressing a Legacy of Repression," United States Commission on International Religious Freedom (USCIRF), https://www.uscirf.gov/sites/default/files/2021-10/2021%20Uzbekistan%20Report_0.pdf.

In mid-2022, the Uzbek government claimed that five thousand prisoners had been freed as a result of Mirziyoyev's pardons.[11] Yet, journalists reported that those released were not cleared of charges and thus had difficulty finding employment. Meanwhile, the Uzbek government continued to incarcerate over 2,200 religious prisoners[12]—"more than the entire population of religious prisoners in all the former Soviet states combined and one of the largest in the world."[13] Prison beatings and torture have reportedly continued. There have been hundreds of new detentions of alleged HTI members, and arrests of some charged with seeking to join ISIS or KTJ. The resurgence of the Taliban provided Mirziyoyev with a justification for curtailing religious freedom and resuming broad counterextremism policies.

One must ask whether the state's nascent, and then reversed, liberalization of its treatment of Islamic practice may backfire over time, leading to another wave of Islamism. Although previous Islamist waves have largely subsided, some religious entrepreneurs have attempted to recruit in increased associational space, and online networking further facilitates this. Renewed state repression is likely to foster their appeal, especially since the ideology of Islamism continues.

Abu Saloh and other online jihadi propagandists have continued targeting Uzbeks. One 2021 propaganda video told a chilling narrative of religious repression through a genealogy of Uzbek Islamism, flashing images of revered Islamic leaders to the audio of a *nasheed* (religious song), titled "If I Could See You in My Dreams One More Time." Posted on both YouTube and Telegram, the video began with Hakimjon Qori, described as the greatest religious scholar of his time and responsible for training a thousand students under Soviet rule, including Abduvali Qori, Obidxon Qori, and Tohir Yo'ldosh. The video walked the viewer through its "history" of the luminaries of the "Uzbek *ulama*"—or more precisely, all the leading figures in the Uzbek Islamist movements discussed in this book. The video included Rahmatulloh Alloma Qori, believed to have been killed by the KGB forty years earlier. The Salafi imam Rafiq Qori, slain in 2006 by the security services, appeared. Rashod Qori's image stood behind bars, reminding viewers that he still languished in a Kyrgyz prison. The video tied these figures to the religio-political ideologues Shaykh Samarqandiy and Imam Abdulloh Buhoriy, who was assassinated in Istanbul; both imams had urged Uzbeks to wage jihad in Afghanistan and Syria. The "Uzbek *ulama*" and jihadist leaders were portrayed as if belonging to one lineage, from the IMU's Tohir Foruq Yo'ldosh, Juma Namangoniy, and Usmon G'oziy, to KIB's Salohiddin al-Uzbeki, and finally KTJ's Abu Saloh. The video's last image brought the faces of all these

[11] Communication with USCIRF representative, July 2022.

[12] "USCIRF Releases Report on Religious Freedom in Uzbekistan," September 2, 2022, https://www.uscirf.gov/release-statements/uscirf-releases-report-religious-freedom-uzbekistan.

[13] "USCIRF Releases Report on Religious Freedom in Uzbekistan."

Image 15.1 "One more friend of mine became a *shahid*"
Source: YouTube screenshot

esteemed Islamic scholars and jihadists together, as the *nasheed*'s lyrics continued: "One more friend of mine became a *shahid*. . . . I saw him in my dreams" (see Image 15.1).[14] While mournful, the video left the impression of a movement that had yet to crest, one that carried on and gained strength even though—or perhaps because—most of its leaders had been martyred.

Kyrgyzstan's Ongoing Political and Religious Turmoil

In contrast to Uzbekistan, Kyrgyzstanis have generally experienced greater religious liberalization and less violent Islamism since independence. The political turmoil of fall 2020 brought another new dictator to power, with President Sadyr Japarov solidifying his mafia-backed rule in sham elections in January 2021. His new regime has proven to be as corrupt as its predecessors'.[15] Despite ushering in a new authoritarianism, Japarov has not curtailed civil Islam, which has remained legal and active at the time of this writing. Tablighi Jamaat has continued to flourish across Kyrgyzstan while being banned elsewhere across the region. Positive legislative changes in 2019, which had led to a decline in arrests for religious extremism, have not been reversed. Many Kyrgyz politicians have come to view Islam as a source of political legitimacy. With the decline of ISIS,

[14] "Раббоний Узбек Уламолар, Узбекча Нашида билан (Тушларимда курсайдим бир бор яна)," [Godly Persons of the Uzbek *Ulama*, with an Uzbek *Nasheed* (If I Could See You in My Dreams One More Time)], Al Buhoriy Channel, YouTube, January 21, 2021, https://www.youtube.com/watch?v=WOWM1XH-ihQ.

[15] Personal communications with Kyrgyzstanis, Bishkek, Kyrgyzstan, January, March 2022.

radical Islamist ideas have lost some of the sway they once had, although reports of nonviolent HTI activity have continued.

Yet, in southern Kyrgyzstan, the ethnic Uzbek population still lives in fear. Mosques with purist imams who articulate any political message are watched, branded as Salafi, and risk extremism charges. Even in 2022 there have been multiple reports of Abu Saloh's propaganda being disseminated and of financial transfers to militants. It is plausible that KTJ, as it continues fighting in Syria, is still recruiting. And yet, there are still troubling reports of arrests made to fulfill security agencies' quotas for putting away extremists, especially among the ethnic Uzbek minority. Chinese pressure to surveil the Uyghur population has become a pretext for harassing observant Muslims and invoking counterterrorism measures. Although religious policy overall has remained unchanged, its informal application in the south continues to be oppressive. Over time, greater curtailing of religious freedom in deteriorating political conditions could again incite Islamist opposition.

Tajikistan's Ongoing Assault on Independent Islam

In Tajikistan, unmitigated religious and political repression has continued. The situation in 2022 was reminiscent of Uzbekistan under President Karimov. The U.S. State Department has again designated Tajikistan a Country of Particular Concern due to its egregious violations of religious freedom.[16]

Since shuttering the IRPT, President Imomali Rahmon has only further consolidated his nearly three-decades-long grip on power. He brazenly rigged the 2020 election and changed the Constitution. Over two hundred IRPT leaders and activists were still imprisoned seven years later, and reports of their torture and of inhumane prison conditions have continued.[17] Opposition figures who relocated to Russia or Turkey faced threats and extradition. Some have been assassinated. Prosecutions of alleged extremists continued to rise. The Tajik prosecutor-general stated that Tajikistan recorded 1,029 extremism- and terrorism-related crimes in 2019, a 30 percent increase over 2018. In 2021, the government opened 214 probes against alleged Salafi followers, in addition to criminal cases against 395 Tajik nationals who were charged with links to foreign terrorist organizations or with fighting for terrorist groups abroad.[18] According

[16] U.S. Department of State, "Report on International Religious Freedom: Tajikistan," 2016–2021, https://www.state.gov/reports/2021-report-on-international-religious-freedom/tajikistan/.

[17] IRPT Supreme Board, "IRPT Appeal to International Organizations: IRPT Members' Lives in Danger," Nahzat.org, October 5, 2021, https://en.nahzat.org/irpt-appeal-to-international-organizations-irpt-members-lives-in-danger/.

[18] RFE/RL's Tajik Service, "After Clampdown on 'Muslim Brotherhood,' Tajikistan Goes After Alleged Salafiya Members," *Radio Free Europe/Radio Liberty*, June 16, 2021, https://www.rferl.org/a/tajikistan-musllm-brotherhood-clampdown-salafiya-islamic-renaissance-rahmon/31311621.html.

to human rights activists, the government used torture to extract confessions of terrorism from dozens of detained Salafis and those accused of being Muslim Brotherhood members. Legal changes in 2020 increased fines and sentences for independent religious activity deemed "extremist."

The threat of "religious extremism" has undeniably been exaggerated by Central Asian state leaders to justify oppressing any political opposition and to gain Western aid. Nonetheless, militant radicalism associated with ISIS has existed in Tajikistan and on its Afghan frontier, and has worsened since the Taliban retook control of Afghanistan in August 2021. As Rahmon has persecuted all other forms of opposition, militancy has become the only outlet for Islamists. The IRPT's beleaguered leader, Kabiri, has continued calling for international pressure on Rahmon's regime, repeatedly warning that its policies were breeding radicals. Before its 2015 closure, most in opposition to the regime had supported the IRPT; since 2015, with no alternative to Rahmon, thousands instead became foreign fighters. Even IRPT members themselves have defected to extremist groups, at first to HTI, but more recently to ISIS and ISIS-K. Angry youth increasingly saw the IRPT's nonviolent opposition as futile.[19]

Although the flow of Tajiks to ISIS declined after the fall of the caliphate in 2017, we have seen that Tajiks directed by ISIS successfully struck multiple targets at home and abroad, including Westerners. Extremist ideas urging violence have spread despite government attempts to block them. In one case, a Tajik self-taught imam who migrated to Russia and then the West posted dozens of YouTube videos between 2019 and 2021. His lectures decried Soviet, Russian, and Tajik government brutality against Islam and Muslims. He urged Tajiks to "gather weapons and be prepared for battle" against Rahmon's "weak, apostate, selfish, greedy, infidel" government. He promised, "If a jihad and a battle is waged in Tajikistan in order to establish the honor of Islam and run an Islamic regime, the whole region would walk with us." He called Tajik men to take up their "duty," "be honorable," and defend Islam.[20] He praised Tajik insurgents fighting with the Taliban as they retook Afghanistan in 2021 and assured his audience that life was better under Taliban rule. These incendiary messages were reaching thousands of viewers.

While he only spread ideas from afar, some Tajiks did fight alongside the Taliban in 2021, helping them retake territory as the United States drew down its forces; one group of Tajiks carried out a slaughter of Afghan government troops, beheading some, in Maymay district in November 2020.[21] With the Taliban

[19] Communication with Muhiddin Kabiri, Chairman, IRPT, December 2022.

[20] "Be Ready for the Big Battle," YouTube, posted by Abdussalam Adina-Zada, February 2, 2021 (link now defunct).

[21] RFE/RL, "Dushanbe Reinforces Border after Tajik Militants Appear in Video Fighting in Afghanistan," *Radio Free Europe/Radio Liberty*, December 17, 2020, https://www.rferl.org/a/tajikistan-afghanistan-reinforcements-taliban/31342303.html.

resurgence, hundreds to thousands of Afghan fighters and refugees flooded into Tajikistan, giving Rahmon yet another reason to crack down and thereby breed more religious opposition.

The Effect of the Taliban's Return to Power

Escalating instability in Afghanistan after the withdrawal of all U.S. and NATO forces in 2021 has exacerbated the risk of regional instability. Within Afghanistan, not only the Taliban but also the growth of ISIS-K and al-Qaeda pose threats to the region. Ideas of Islamic justice—through an Islamic state or caliphate—have continued to inspire some Central Asians.

Despite the collapse of the caliphate in Syria and Iraq, ISIS's branch organizations have survived and even grown, and ISIS-K benefited from the U.S. withdrawal from Afghanistan. As we have seen, ISIS-K has two main sources of fighters: those already waging jihad in Afghanistan, such as the IMU and JA, and, after 2017, those migrating from ISIS's fallen caliphate to Afghanistan (in some cases, returning to Afghanistan). Indeed, Central Asian fighters in Syria and Iraq have rarely gone home for fear of incarceration and torture; instead, some joined ISIS-K. As discussed in Chapter 14, at its height in 2016–17, the number of ISIS-K fighters was estimated at up to six thousand. Before the Taliban took power, over 1,800 ISIS-K members had been killed,[22] and U.S. forces and the Afghan National Army had reduced ISIS-K to under 2,200 fighters.[23] More than 1,400 ISIS-K militants who had surrendered to NATO or Afghan forces between October 2019 and March 2020 were being held prisoner by President Ashraf Ghani's government in summer 2021.[24] As the Taliban seized power and broke open prisons, including the massive Pul-e-Charkhi facility and the Bagram base's Parwan Prison, they freed thousands of militants. While they had intended to release Taliban and al-Qaeda fighters, not their rival Islamists, the Taliban inadvertently released ISIS-K members as well. ISIS-K assaults, such as one on a

[22] UN Security Council, "Ninth Report of the Analytical Support and Sanctions Monitoring Team Submitted Pursuant to Resolution 2255 (2015) Concerning the Taliban and Other Associated Individuals and Entities Constituting a Threat to the Peace, Stability and Security of Afghanistan," S/2018/466, May 30, 2018, 13; "Afghanistan: Who Are Islamic State Khorasan Province Militants?," *BBC News*, October 11, 2021, https://www.bbc.com/news/world-asia-58333533; "Explainer: ISIS-Khorasan in Afghanistan," Wilson Center, August 27, 2021, https://www.wilsoncenter.org/article/explainer-isis-khorasan-afghanistan.

[23] UN Security Council, "Twenty-Seventh Report of the Analytical Support and Sanctions Monitoring Team Submitted Pursuant to Resolution 2368 (2017) Concerning ISIL (Da'esh), Al-Qaida and Associated Individuals and Entities," S/2021/68, February 3, 2021, 15.

[24] UN Security Council, "Eleventh Report of the Analytical Support and Sanctions Monitoring Team Submitted Pursuant to Resolution 2501 (2019) Concerning the Taliban and Other Associated Individuals and Entities Constituting a Threat to the peace, stability and security of Afghanistan," S/2020/415, May 27, 2020, 17.

prison in Nangarhar, released another thousand prisoners, including hundreds of ISIS-K fighters.[25]

Throughout the debate about the U.S. withdrawal, in the Obama, Trump, and Biden administrations, many argued that the Taliban's return to power was uncertain and would likely take time. The U.S.-Taliban agreement of February 2020 pledged the Taliban to rid Afghanistan of terrorists threatening the United States. Some assumed that the Taliban would and could uphold that agreement. Many also believed that ISIS-K, including its Central Asian adherents, was by then too weak to pose a serious threat to the United States, Afghanistan, or the region. All those assumptions were shattered in August 2021. The Taliban seized political power upon rolling into Kabul on August 15, before the United States had even completed its withdrawal. On August 26, an ISIS-K militant broken out of Parwan Prison used a suicide bomb to kill thirteen U.S. troops and at least 172 Afghans during the frantic American evacuation from Kabul Airport.[26] Another eighteen U.S. service members and more than 150 others were wounded. As the United States still reeled from the attack, ISIS-K published its inaugural English-language magazine, the *Voice of Khorasan*, which featured a glorified martyrdom profile of Abdul Rahman al-Logari, the suicide bomber who had carried out the strike.[27]

ISIS-K suicide attacks across Afghanistan, including strikes on schools and Shia mosques, have continued. In a briefing to the UN Security Council (UNSC) three months after the Taliban took power, Deborah Lyons, the UN Secretary General's Special Representative (SRSG) to Afghanistan reported, "Once limited to a few provinces and Kabul, ISILKP [ISIS-K] now seems to be present in nearly all provinces and increasingly active. The number of attacks has increased significantly. . . . In 2020—sixty; so far this year [through mid-November 2021]—334 attacks [were] attributed to ISILKP or, in fact, claimed by ISILKP."[28] Lyons continued, "[T]he reality of the current situation threatens to heighten the risk of extremism. The continued deterioration of the formal economy will provide impetus to the informal economy, including illicit drugs, arms flows and human trafficking. The ongoing paralysis of the banking sector will push more of the financial system into unaccountable and unregulated informal money exchanges which can only help facilitate terrorism, trafficking, and further drug smuggling. These pathologies will first affect Afghanistan but then they will

[25] Abdul Sayed, "ISIS-K Is Ready to Fight the Taliban: Here's How the Group Became a Major Threat in Afghanistan," *Washington Post*, August 29, 2021.

[26] "Eric Schmitt and Helene Cooper, Lone ISIS Bomber Carried Out Attack at Kabul Airport, Pentagon Says," *New York Times*, February 4, 2022.

[27] Bridget Johnson, "Inaugural Magazine from ISIS Khorasan Declares Taliban Can 'Become Our Brother,'" *HS Today*, February 7, 2022.

[28] "SRSG Lyons Briefing to the UNSC on the Situation in Afghanistan," UNAMA, https://unama.unmissions.org/srsg-lyons-briefing-unsc-situation-afghanistan-3, November 17, 2021.

infect the region."[29] Some sources put ISIS-K at about 3,500 fighters in late 2021, while others suggested its numbers had climbed to 5,000 or more.[30] Going forward, the example of Iraq after Saddam Hussein's fall in 2003 indicates that other likely sources for ISIS-K recruits are former Afghan National Army and police forces who fled their posts as the Taliban took control; joining ISIS-K would offer protection and jobs. Khalil Hamraz, the spokesman for the Taliban's intelligence directorate, openly acknowledged that his group's military takeover has strengthened ISIS-K.[31]

Its resurgence has negative implications for the region. For the first time since its inception, ISIS-K launched an attack on Uzbekistan's heavily fortified border in April 2022. The rocket strike, claimed by ISIS-K on social media, was denied by Uzbek authorities in an attempt to appear in control and deny the group a propaganda win.[32] If ISIS-K continues to demonstrate its commitment to establishing a caliphate, and if the Taliban continues to fail at providing basic services, other foreign fighters in Afghanistan, including Central Asians, are likely to join ISIS-K's ranks.

ISIS-K is hardly the only or the major threat from Afghanistan since August 2021. A July 2022 UNSC report assessed al-Qaeda as once again positioned to be the leader of global jihad.[33] Even before the fall of Kabul, it was already apparent that al-Qaeda had remained in Afghanistan and that the Taliban had no intention of evicting its ally. The UNSC reported in both 2020 and 2021 that up to six hundred al-Qaeda fighters were spread across eleven to fifteen Afghan provinces.[34] The Taliban controlled thirty-four provinces, and al-Qaeda once again enjoyed safe harbor and the space to train, recruit, and plan strikes.[35] Some counterterrorism analysts argued that the terrorist group would regain its ability to strike globally after the U.S. withdrawal.[36] The depth of the Taliban–al-Qaeda

[29] "SRSG Lyons Briefing to the UNSC."

[30] Susannah George, "Taliban Sends 1,300 Fighters to Eastern Afghanistan to Battle Islamic State," *Washington Post*, November 22, 2021; Sayed, "ISIS-K Is Ready to Fight the Taliban."

[31] George, "Taliban Sends 1,300 Fighters."

[32] Ayaz Gul, "Uzbekistan Dismisses Islamic State's Claim of Cross-Border Attack," *Voice of America*, April 19, 2022, https://www.voanews.com/a/uzbekistan-dismisses-islamic-state-s-claim-of-cross-border-attack-/6535868.html.

[33] UN Security Council, "Thirtieth Report of the Analytical Support and Sanctions Monitoring Team Submitted Pursuant to Resolution 2610 (2021) Concerning ISIL (Da'esh), Al-Qaida and Associated Individuals and Entities," S/2022/547, July 15, 2022, 5–6, 16; Jeff Seldin, "Al-Qaida Positioned to Surpass Islamic State among Jihadis," *Voice of America*, July 19, 2022 https://www.voanews.com/a/al-qaida-positioned-to-surpass-islamic-state-among-jihadis-/6665672.html.

[34] UN Security Council, "Eleventh Report of the Analytical Support and Sanctions Monitoring Team Submitted Pursuant to Resolution 2501 (2019) Concerning the Taliban and Other Associated Individuals and Entities Constituting a Threat to the Peace, Stability and Security of Afghanistan," S/2020/415, May 27, 2020, 11–12.

[35] Bill Roggio, "Department of Defense Continues to Downplay Taliban and Al Qaeda Threat in Afghanistan," *FDD's Long War Journal*, May 19, 2022.

[36] Roggio, "Department of Defense Continues to Downplay."

connection was exemplified by the location of Ayman al-Zawahiri when he was killed by a CIA drone strike on July 31, 2022; he was in Kabul, in close communication with the Taliban leadership.[37] The UNSC had recently reported that al-Qaeda "plays an advisory role with the Taliban and the groups remain close."[38] Contrary to the public assessments of the Biden administration, some counterterrorism experts argued that al-Qaeda operatives or their affiliates held significant administrative positions in at least eight Afghan provinces; these included Central Asians.[39]

As it regrouped, al-Qaeda continued to work closely, both in Afghanistan and in Syria, with a faction of the IMU and IJU. So too, some KIB fighters, who had once left Afghanistan to join al-Qaeda in Syria, returned; they remain allied with al-Qaeda there. Other Central Asian and Uyghur groups, including those once trained by the IMU—such as the Turkistan Islamic Party, the East Turkestan Islamic Movement (ETIM), and JA—remained affiliated with al-Qaeda and particularly active in northern Afghanistan. In a clear breach of its promise to evict terrorist foreign fighters, and angering Tajikistan's government, the Taliban placed five heavily ethnic Tajik districts in the northern Badakhshan province under the control of a Tajik national who was a commander in JA.[40]

Meanwhile, hundreds to thousands of Central Asian foreign fighters—especially KTJ and KIB—were still waging jihad in Idlib through 2022. They continued under various factions of al-Qaeda's umbrella there, which was at least ten thousand strong.[41] Should these fighters leave Syria, they would have both the motive and the opportunity to return once again to the protection of al-Qaeda within a Taliban-controlled Afghanistan. In fact, six months after the Taliban's return to power, a UNSC report warned about the ongoing threat from these Central Asian fighters in both Syria and Afghanistan. In Afghanistan, the report stated, they were "experiencing greater freedom of movement. . . .[They] have embraced the Taliban takeover," and they "look forward to international recognition of the Taliban," expecting that "refugee status and passports" from Afghanistan will enable them to travel internationally.[42]

[37] Eric Schmitt, "US Says Al-Qaeda Has Not Regrouped in Afghanistan," *New York Times*, August 13, 2022; Bill Roggio, "U.S. Kills Al Qaeda Emir Ayman al Zawahiri in Drone Strike," *FDD's Long War Journal*, August 1, 2022.

[38] UN Security Council, "Thirtieth Report of the Analytical Support and Sanctions Monitoring Team Submitted Pursuant to Resolution 2610 (2021) concerning ISIL (Da'esh), Al-Qaida and Associated Individuals and Entities," S/2022/547, July 15, 2022, 16.

[39] Schmitt, "US Says Al-Qaeda Has Not Regrouped."

[40] Bill Roggio and Andrew Tobin, "Tajik Terrorist Serves as Taliban Commander in Northern Afghanistan," *FDD's Long War Journal*, May 25, 2022.

[41] UN Security Council, "Thirtieth Report of the Analytical Support and Sanctions Monitoring Team," 12.

[42] UN Security Council, "Twenty-ninth Report of the Analytical Support and Sanctions Monitoring Team Submitted Pursuant to Resolution 2368 (2017) Concerning ISIL (Da'esh), Al-Qaida and Associated Individuals and Entities," S/2022/83, February 3, 2022, 16–17.

In short, the evolving situation in Afghanistan has provided safe harbor to Central Asian Islamists fleeing religious repression and seeking space to network and mobilize. Moreover, the Taliban victory in Afghanistan and the growth of al-Qaeda and ISIS-K there, despite years of U.S. efforts to eliminate them, and despite successful U.S. strikes on their leadership, has sent a clear message to would-be radicals and their followers: Islamism has won.

Beyond Central Asia

A brief look beyond post-Soviet Central Asia demonstrates that Islamism's emergence in some other cases, especially cases of secular authoritarian regimes, has aligned with the framework proposed by this book; state threats to or repression of religion, together with the spread of Islamist ideology among religious entrepreneurs, has driven Islamist emergence and mobilization.

In the Caucasus, for example, Islamism gained significant traction in Chechnya and Dagestan in the 1990s. There, the story is similar to Uzbekistan's or Tajikistan's: Soviet oppression of Islam, in addition to Stalin's forced deportation of Chechens in the 1940s, created anti-Soviet resentment and politicized Islamic and national identity.[43] When associational space increased, Islamist ideas, networks, and funding spread from both the Middle East and Afghanistan. Although elites driven by nationalism emerged first, by the mid- to late 1990s, in the context of the devasting war waged on Chechnya by Russian President Boris Yeltsin (1994–96), Islam increasingly became a focal point and source of opposition mobilization against the Russian state. In 1995, a Saudi known as Ibn al-Khattab, the same former Afghan Arab fighter and affiliate of Osama Bin Laden who aided the Tajik Islamist opposition, introduced Salafi jihadism to Chechnya. "A jihadist Che Guevara," Ibn al-Khattab took up the anti-Russian struggle and helped "transform the war into one of the most important jihadist movements of our time."[44] Chechen militias became increasingly Islamized, and under their pressure the Chechen leadership adopted *shariat* law in 1997. After Putin relaunched the Chechen war in 1999 to eliminate "terrorists," decimating the region and bringing the overall death toll to 150,000 to 200,000, the Chechen leadership, Dagestanis, and broader Caucasian resistance became more radicalized, calling for militant jihad.[45] They were heavily influenced by Salafi jihadist ideas,

[43] Norman Naimark, *Fires of Hatred: Ethnic Cleansing in Twentieth-Century Europe* (London: Harvard University Press, 2001); Anna Politkovskaya, *A Small Corner of Hell: Dispatches from Chechnya* (Chicago: University of Chicago Press, 2003), 2.

[44] Byman, *Road Warriors*, 18, 80–81.

[45] James Hughes, *Chechnya: From Nationalism to Jihad* (Philadelphia: University of Pennsylvania Press, 2007), 94–128.

money, training, and foreign fighters.[46] Forming the Islamic Emirate of the Caucasus, they fought for about thirteen years against Putin; the movement ultimately dwindled as its fighters joined ISIS's caliphate in Syria and Iraq.[47]

Understanding the connection between repression of Islam and Islamist opposition also helps to explain the origins of the mujahidin in Afghanistan in 1979. The mujahidin movement, a loose collection of Afghani Islamist organizations, first emerged in opposition to the Soviet-style, antireligious modernization campaign of the communist People's Democratic Party of Afghanistan's and multiplied once the USSR invaded to back the new party. Faced with repression of their Muslim faith and practice, a core element of their national identity, tens of thousands mobilized with the mujahidin, who ultimately drove the USSR out of Afghanistan in 1989.[48] As in Chechnya, a weak state and war created the associational space necessary to spread new ideas and mobilize networks. Puritanical Islamist interpretations and money from Saudi Arabia and Pakistan further radicalized elements of the mujahidin. By 1989, they were victorious and the Afghan jihad offered a model for Islamist militants globally. A decade later, at the onset of the twenty-year U.S. war in Afghanistan, the Taliban likewise used religion again to draw on Afghan identity and mobilize fighters against the United States. As we have seen, the Taliban, al-Qaeda, and the IMU all portrayed the United States as a foreign oppressor waging war on Islam.[49]

Likewise, the Uyghur nationalist movement initially emerged in response to communist China's suppression of ethnic and cultural identity.[50] Communist repression of Muslim belief and practice escalated after 9/11. Chinese policy turned to mass deportations of Uyghurs to labor camps, reminiscent of Stalin's Gulag, and has led to what some scholars have called "cultural genocide."[51] This contention unsurprisingly generated a militant Islamist offshoot; some Uyghurs fled to Afghanistan, where they encountered Salafi jihadist ideas and turned to al-Qaeda for support. They trained with the IMU and Chechens and formed the ETIM. Like the IMU and IJU, ETIM shifted its attention to Syria and Iraq to fight for a caliphate in the 2010s.[52]

[46] Byman, *Road Warriors*, 95–97.

[47] Hassan and Weiss, *ISIS*, 280–81.

[48] Mohammad Kakar, *Afghanistan: The Soviet Invasion and the Afghan Response, 1979–1982* (London: University of California Press, 1997); Ali Ahmad Jalali, *A Military History of Afghanistan* (Lawrence: University of Kansas Press, 2017).

[49] Carter Malkasian, *The American War in Afghanistan* (Oxford: Oxford University Press, 2021), 24, 349; David Edwards, *Caravan of Martyrs: Sacrifice and Suicide Bombing in Afghanistan* (Berkeley: University of California Press, 2019).

[50] David Brophy, *Uyghur Nation: Reform and Revolution on the Russia-China Frontier* (Cambridge, MA: Harvard University Press, 2016).

[51] Sean Roberts, *The War on the Uyghurs: China's Internal Campaign against a Muslim Minority* (Princeton, NJ: Princeton University Press, 2020); Adeeb Khalid, *Central Asia: A New History for the Imperial Conquests to the Present* (Princeton, NJ: Princeton University Press, 2021), 495.

[52] Animesh Roul, "Al-Qaeda and Islamic State Reinvigorating East Turkistan Jihad," *Jamestown Foundation, Terrorism Monitor* 17, no. 10 (May 17, 2019).

More broadly, my arguments speak to the many other cases of religious repression and forced secularization by a secular authoritarian state in the twentieth and twenty-first centuries. Turkey, Iraq, Algeria, Egypt, Tunisia, and Iran, among other cases, share some similarities with Central Asia in the birth and evolution of Islamist movements in the twentieth century. Instead of Soviet atheist oppression, the marginalization and repression of Islam under either colonial and postcolonial rule or secular, modernizing states played a driving role there in generating Islamism. Religious entrepreneurs in these countries drew inspiration from various religio-political ideologies. As in Central Asia, they developed and disseminated Islamist ideologies to attract and mobilize society in pursuit of Islamic ideas of justice.

Only a handful of Muslim-majority cases have embarked on a path similar to that of Kyrgyzstan in the 1990s: liberalization of politics and religion. In Indonesia, a country boasting the largest Muslim population in the world and a democratic political system since 1998, religious freedom has been widespread. President Suharto's previous government had repressed communism, not Islam.[53] Islamic faith and practice have been vibrant and pluralist.[54] Muslim civic and political activism has thrived, including Nahdlatul Ulama, the largest Muslim civic organization in the world.[55] Islam and politics are not wholly without controversy, however, especially in certain provinces where debate over *shariat* law has emerged. Moreover, Muslim activists are often intolerant and opposed to an individualistic, liberal democracy.[56] As in Kyrgyzstan and its neighbors, Islamist voices do exist and have been slowly growing, with some radicalization. In response to the state's increased hostility to and closure of any manifestation of political Islam, and influenced by the diffusion of extremist ideologies, including those of Hizb ut-Tahrir Indonesia and al-Qaeda, Islamist intolerance and vigilantism in Indonesia began to escalate.[57] The vigilante group Islamic Defenders' Front emerged as contention over Islam escalated. Nonetheless, in both Kyrgyzstan and Indonesia, most Muslim leaders promote a Muslim-style democracy rather than espouse the ideas of Islamism. The trajectories of both Indonesia and Kyrgyzstan, two very distinct Muslim-majority countries, offer some cause for optimism. They convincingly demonstrate that religious

[53] Vedi Hadiz, "Indonesian Political Islam: Capitalist Development and the Legacies of the Cold War," *Journal of Current Southeast Asian Affairs* 30, no. 1 (2011): 3–38.

[54] Jeremy Menchik, "Crafting Indonesian Democracy: Inclusion-Moderation and the Sacralizing of the Postcolonial State," in *Democratic Transition in the Muslim World*, ed. Alfred Stepan (New York: Columbia University Press, 2018), 163–200.

[55] Hefner, *Civil Islam*.

[56] Jeremy Menchik, *Islam and Democracy in Indonesia: Tolerance Without Liberalism* (New York: Cambridge University Press, 2016).

[57] Zachary Abuza, *Political Islam and Violence in Indonesia* (London: Routledge, 2006).

liberalization and pluralism allow the flourishing of civil Islam while discouraging militant Islamism.

The history of state violence against Islam, beginning under Soviet communism, has repeated itself in the three decades since the Soviet Union fell. Trends in Central Asia over the past four decades suggest that, with ongoing repressive, unjust, and corrupt governance, the familiar pattern of Islamist emergence and mobilization, and the risk of violent radicalization, will continue. In the cases examined in this work, Central Asian Islamist movements have engaged in civil war, carried out gruesome terrorist attacks at home and in Europe, struck at U.S. and NATO troops, and fought with the Taliban, al-Qaeda, ISIS, and ISIS-K, thereby threatening both regional stability and U.S. interests in Afghanistan. Defying the trend toward violent radicalization among so many Islamists swayed by al-Qaeda and ISIS, the IRPT proved to be the major proponent of democracy and just government in the region. The Islamist phenomenon—and the state policies and transnational ideas that generate it—cannot be ignored. Islamism is inseparable from unjust governance.

In making this argument, I have sought to look beyond the dynamic between the state and Islamist movements. By integrating the experiences, narratives, and views of ordinary Central Asians—on being Muslim in the Soviet era, on struggling to study Islam or merely to pray, or on their desire for a more Muslim form of democracy—we gain a perspective on religion and politics in Central Asia that goes further than headline-grabbing terrorist attacks. We have seen how the lives of so many Muslims were destroyed by repression and injustice. We will likely never know how many people vanished into Soviet, Uzbek, Tajik, and even Kyrgyz prisons. We will never know how many were starved, injected with psychotropic drugs, boiled alive, or beaten to death because of their faith and desire for religious freedom. We will never know the fate of the many courageous journalists and human rights defenders, some of whom were imprisoned or killed because they revealed the truth about this oppression. We will never know the everyday suffering of those outside the prisons, who lived in fear or paced away the hours, agonizing over the uncertain fate of their loved ones who had been arrested or just "disappeared." We will never know how many families were separated or destroyed. Someday historians will write about the brutality of Karimov and Rahmon much as they write about the suffering and death caused by Stalin.

After years of studying this region, I do know that Central Asians want a better, more just, more secure life for their children. In the end, I hope that this work brings a clearer and deeper understanding of the causes of Islamism, and serves as a witness to the story of what Central Asians have endured under Soviet and post-Soviet oppression. It is also my hope that understanding the drivers of radicalism and violence will shed light on the possibilities for integrating Islam into the public space and political debate within a democracy—enabling a more pluralist, peaceful, and prosperous future.

APPENDIX

Qualitative Research Method and Sources

Research on Islamism under Authoritarianism

Carrying out research under the postcommunist authoritarian regimes of Central Asia is not easy. The Stalinist days may be gone, but scholars face many hurdles, including powerful state security services; the legacy of fear, mistrust, and self-censorship on the part of society and state employees; academic institutions that force scholars to self-censor; the lack of reliable, published data or even accurate news; very limited archival access; and, of course, the ongoing postcommunist processes of changing languages, street signs, alphabets, names, and history books—to the confusion of locals and foreigners alike. Obtaining the necessary visas made research challenging, not to mention coups and violent conflict, precarious border crossings, internal checkpoints, police harassment, and more than a few flat tires in mountain passes. In such countries, neither auto repairs nor facts are readily available. I sought to verify every "fact" in this book, though the truth is often difficult to ascertain. All of these challenges make creative fieldwork all the more necessary for answering sensitive political questions.

There are also numerous limitations in studying Islamic movements in Eurasia and elsewhere. It was not possible to interview some types of Islamists, particularly Salafi jihadists. When interviewing ordinary citizens of Central Asia about Islam and politics, decades of repression of both Islam and free speech meant that some underreported their preferences for Islam's public or political role. Because all Islamist movements were banned (except the IRPT before late 2015), people were highly unlikely to express open support for Islamists. Face-to-face qualitative interviews, oral histories, and focus groups are imperfect tools. Researching Islamist politics in authoritarian contexts is unquestionably a challenge. It is therefore critical to integrate findings from multiple methods and sources: various types of interviews, participant observation, textual and video primary sources, surveys, and comparative historical analysis. Given the importance of the topic at hand, both for the populations of Eurasia and for Western policymakers, I deemed the challenge of conducting such research one worth taking.

Combining Elite Interviews and Political Ethnography

In my research, I integrated political ethnography—both participant observation and informal communications—with face-to-face open-ended interviews, semi-structured interviews, and oral histories. I also used focus groups, and compared those findings with the results of two surveys in Kyrgyzstan (2006, 2010).[1] Each of these varied methods

[1] Due to space constraints, the survey analysis is being published separately.

provides important forms of data and insights for obtaining answers to complex questions about people's religious identity, attitudes toward Islam and political Islam, and motivations for forming, joining, or supporting different Islamist groups.

I conducted the research for this project in Tajikistan, Uzbekistan, and Kyrgyzstan during multiple extended trips between January 2003 and June 2019. I made two research trips to Russia to obtain historical and ethnographic sources, to consult with Central Asianists at the Russian Academy of Sciences, and to collect comparative data on the Caucasus. Over the years of this project, from its very early stages to its conclusion, I carried out 378 open-ended interviews with respondents who included members of the IRPT, members of HTI, mosque community leaders, Islamic teachers, representatives of Islamic NGOs, state imams and state religious officials, *madrasa* teachers, Tablighi Jamaat members, parliamentary deputies, and government officials. I conducted further interviews with experts (academics inside Central Asia, journalists, U.S. embassy personnel, analysts in the U.S. Department of Defense, U.S. Department of State, OSCE, Freedom House, and United Nations Development Programme). Finally, political ethnography included visits to mosques attended by Central Asians in Moscow and neighborhoods of Central Asian migrants in Istanbul. These interviews and observations helped to shape my understanding of the grievances of both Islamists and ordinary Muslims, and to trace the dynamic contention between the state and Islamist actors.

Focus Groups, Oral Histories, and Semi-Structured Interviews

Throughout this study, I have employed various qualitative methods to explore the views of ordinary people rather than merely those of Islamist movement activists and the government. We need to understand what Central Asian students, businessmen, and housewives think about Islam's role in society and the state. I conducted three types of nonelite interviews: oral histories, semi-structured individual interviews, and focus groups. My goal was to assess the extent to which Islam survived the Soviet era; how ordinary people practiced, believed, or thought about being Muslim under communism and postcommunism; to what extent Islamist ideas were congruent with societal norms about Islam; and how people viewed government.

Chapter 4 relies on twenty-five oral histories (with male communal elders, elderly women, and local religious figures) as well as semi-structured interviews with communal leaders. The oral histories sought to uncover memories and experiences of the Soviet era, particularly the 1960s to 1980s. Chapters 4, 7, 10, and 13 draw on 154 individual, semi-structured interviews (fifty-four in Uzbekistan, fifty in Kyrgyzstan, and fifty in Tajikistan) to gather the views of communal leaders: *mahalla* leaders, religious teachers and leaders, businessmen who contribute to a mosque community, local government officials, and local journalists—all people influential at the local level. They discussed Islamic belief and practice in the Soviet and post-Soviet periods, corruption, democracy, governance, and a range of Islamist ideas (from *shariat* courts to militant jihad). These interviewees often influenced the views of ordinary Muslims in their communities.

Chapters 7, 10, and 13 draw primarily on my analysis of the discourse that took place in focus group interviews. Focus groups lasted two to three hours each. Using focus group transcripts that ranged from about twenty-five to fifty pages, I traced conversations about a range of topics: the meaning of Muslim rituals and practices; views about democracy, blasphemy, and *shariat*; understandings of jihad and views about when it might be justified. Overall, I assessed whether any congruence exists between the core Islamist ideas and the Central Asian societies of Tajikistan, Uzbekistan, and Kyrgyzstan.

Like other interviews, focus groups do not randomly sample the population, so the data they provide is not statistically meaningful. Nonetheless, focus groups can be representative. In my study, local colleagues and I conducted 79 focus groups: 76 with Muslim participants (19 in Tajikistan, 32 in Uzbekistan, and 25 Kyrgyzstan) and 3 groups with non-Muslims. In total, focus groups included 787 respondents, the size of many small surveys (223 participants in Kyrgyzstan, 306 in Uzbekistan, 258 in Tajikistan). Focus groups took place in seven regions in each country. Groups were composed of similar individuals (the same gender and similar age, class, and education level) to maximize participants' comfort in responding (see Table A.1). Having fellow students, workers, housewives, or others of similar social status simulated in some ways the conditions in which individuals shape their religious and political views in the context of their community. Muslim groups included individuals who self-identified as Muslim and self-reported having at least occasionally fasted or prayed. They represented the vast majority of society claiming to be Muslim believers. According to Pew data, 89 percent of Kyrgyzstanis, 97 percent of Uzbekistanis, and 99 percent of Tajikistanis identify as Muslim.[2]

Strengths and Limitations of Interviews

All data is partial and has potential bias. Yet unlike survey data, the various types of interviews used (oral histories, focus group discussions, semi-structured interviews with communal leaders, and elite interviews) offer contextualized responses which reveal nuances and contradictions. In facilitating and analyzing a large number of focus groups, we can form insights from the overall trends and discussions, which often reveal strong norms about Islam and politics or about other religious and political grievances in Tajik, Uzbek, and Kyrgyz society. Where there is significant disagreement or ambivalence within and across groups, these discussions reveal the absence of a norm, or perhaps shifting norms. Islamic norms are neither fixed nor uniform. As opposed to most studies, which focus unilaterally on Islamist party elites and their platforms and actions, this study seeks to identify whether and why specific elements of Islamist platforms might attract popular support.

With the advice of local sociologists, I formulated questions to minimize fear. I offered concrete examples to discuss. While participants sometimes offered a direct opinion about specific Islamist groups, my local assistants (trained sociologists) and I never asked about direct support; we asked indirectly "whether and why others" in their community supported such groups. Most questions focused on ideas and experiences ("What is better about independence?"; "How did you learn your faith?"; "Do you want your children to take religious lessons, and where/how?"; "What role should Islam play in family, society, or politics?"; "What does *shariat* mean?"; "What is democracy, and what do you think about it?") rather than on specific Islamists.

[2] Pew Research Center, "The World's Muslims: Religion, Politics and Society," April 20, 2013, https://www.pewresearch.org/religion/2013/04/30/the-worlds-muslims-religion-politics-society-overview/.

Table A.1 Focus Group Interviews

Focus Group Number	Gender	Occupation	Ethnicity	Age	Year	Location
TAJ-FG#1	M	University students	Tajik	20–24	2009	Dushanbe
TAJ-FG#2	F	University students	Tajik	20–24	2009	Dushanbe
TAJ-FG#3	M	Small business owners	Tajik	25–35	2009	Dushanbe
TAJ-FG#4	F	White-collar workers	Tajik	25–35	2009	Dushanbe
TAJ-FG#5	M	Small business owners	Tajik	35–50	2009	Isfara
TAJ-FG#6	F	University students	Tajik	25–35	2009	Khujand
TAJ-FG#7	M	University students	Tajik	20–24	2009	Khujand
TAJ-FG#8	M	White-collar workers	Tajik	25–35	2009	Khujand
TAJ-FG#9	F	University students	Tajik	21–24	2009	Qurghonteppa
TAJ-FG#10	M	Migrant laborers	Tajik	25–35	2009	Qurghonteppa
TAJ-FG#11	M	White-collar workers	Tajik	35–50	2009	Qarotegin/ Gharm
TAJ-FG#12	M	Small business owners	Tajik	25–35	2009	Qarotegin/ Gharm
TAJ-FG#13	M	Migrant laborers	Tajik	25–35	2009	Kulob
TAJ-FG#14	M	Small business owners	Tajik	35–50	2009	Kulob
TAJ-FG#15	F	University students	Tajik	20–24	2013	Dushanbe
TAJ-FG#16	M	Blue-collar workers	Tajik	35–45	2013	Dushanbe
TAJ-FG#17	M	University students	Tajik	20–25	2013	Khujand
TAJ-FG#18	F	White-collar workers	Tajik	35–50	2013	Khujand
TAJ-FG#19	M	Small business owners	Tajik	20–30	2013	Dushanbe

Table A.1 Continued

Focus Group Number	Gender	Occupation	Ethnicity	Age	Year	Location
UZ-FG#1	M	Small business owners	Mixed	30–55	2005	Tashkent
UZ-FG#2	F	White-collar workers	Mixed	30–55	2005	Tashkent
UZ-FG#3	F	Small business owners/ entrepreneurs	Uzbek	35–55	2005	Marg'ilon, Ferghana region
UZ-FG#4	F	Small business owners/traders	Uzbek	20–29	2005	Tashkent
UZ-FG#5	M	Blue-collar workers	Uzbek	20–29	2005	Marg'ilon, Ferghana region
UZ-FG#6	M	White-collar workers	Uzbek	40–49	2005	Marg'ilon, Ferghana region
UZ-FG#7	F	Small business owners	Uzbek	30–39	2005	Qashqadaryo
UZ-FG#8	M	Blue-collar workers	Uzbek	20–29	2005	Qashqadaryo
UZ-FG#9	M	White-collar workers	Uzbek	35–55	2005	Namangan
UZ-FG#10	M	University/ institute students	Uzbek	18–25	2005	Namangan
UZ-FG#11	F	Blue-collar workers, housewives	Uzbek	30–39	2005	Namangan
UZ-FG#12	F	University/ institute students	Uzbek	18–25	2005	Urganch
UZ-FG#13	M	Small business owners	Uzbek	30–39	2005	Urganch
UZ-FG#14	M	Migrants/blue-collar workers	Uzbek	20–29	2005	Urganch
UZ-FG#15	F	University students	Uzbek	18–25	2005	Bukhara
UZ-FG#16	M	Wealthy entrepreneurs	Tajik	35–55	2005	Bukhara

Table A.1 Continued

Focus Group Number	Gender	Occupation	Ethnicity	Age	Year	Location
UZ-FG#17	M	Blue-collar workers	Uzbek	35–55	2005	Bukhara
UZ-FG#18	M	Migrants/blue-collar workers	Uzbek	20–29	2005	Tashkent
UZ-FG#19	F	University students	Uzbek	18–25	2005	Tashkent
UZ-FG#20	F	White-collar workers	Uzbek	35–55	2005	Andijon
UZ-FG#21	F	Blue-collar workers	Uzbek	20–34	2005	Andijon
UZ-FG#22	M	University/ institute students	Uzbek	18–25	2005	Andijon
UZ-FG#23	F	Small business owners/ entrepreneurs	Uzbek	35–50	2005	Tashkent
UZ-FG#24	M	Migrants	Uzbek	24–35	2005	Tashkent
UZ-FG#25	M	University students	Uzbek	20–27	2013	Tashkent
UZ-FG#26	F	White-collar workers	Uzbek	35–45	2013	Ferghana
UZ-FG#27	F	University students	Uzbek	18–25	2013	Ferghana
UZ-FG#28	M	Small business owners/ entrepreneurs	Uzbek	25–35	2013	Ferghana
UZ-FG#29	M	Blue-collar workers	Uzbek	35–45	2013	Termiz
UZ-FG#30	F	Blue-collar workers	Uzbek	35–45	2013	Termiz
UZ-FG#31	M	White-collar workers	Uzbek	20–25	2013	Termiz
UZ-FG#32	M	White-collar workers (some unemployed)	Uzbek	35–45	2013	Tashkent
UZ-FG#33	F	University students	Uzbek	18–25	2013	Tashkent
UZ-FG#34	M	Small business owners/traders	Uzbek	35–45	2013	Tashkent

Table A.1 Continued

Focus Group Number	Gender	Occupation	Ethnicity	Age	Year	Location
KY-FG#1	M	Migrant laborers	Tajik	40–49	2005	Batken
KY-FG#2	M	Agricultural/ blue-collar workers/traders	Kyrgyz	20–29	2005	Batken
KY-FG#3	M	University students	Uzbek	20–23	2005	Jalalabat
KY-FG#4	F	White-collar workers	Kyrgyz	20–29	2005	Jalalabat
KY-FG#5	M	Small business owners	Uzbek	40–49	2005	Jalalabat
KY-FG#6	F	University students	Kyrgyz	20–23	2005	Osh
KY-FG#7	F	Small business owners	Uzbek	40–49	2005	Osh
KY-FG#8	Mixed	White-collar workers	Mixed	Mixed	2005	Osh
KY-FG#9	M	Small business owners	Uzbek	20–29	2005	Osh
KY-FG#10	M	Agricultural labor	Kyrgyz	20–29	2005	Issyk-Kul
KY-FG#11	F	Small business owners	Kyrgyz	40–49	2005	Issyk-Kul
KY-FG#12	F	University students	Kyrgyz	20–23	2005	Bishkek
KY-FG#13	M	Rural migrants/ blue-collar workers	Kyrgyz	20–29	2005	Bishkek
KY-FG#14	F	White-collar workers	Mixed: Uzbek, Dungan	30–39	2005	Bishkek
KY-FG#15	M	White-collar workers	Kyrgyz	30–39	2007	Bishkek
KY-FG#16	M	Small business owners	Kyrgyz	30–39	2007	Bishkek
KY-FG#17	F	White-collar workers	Kyrgyz	30–39	2007	Bishkek

Table A.1 Continued

Focus Group Number	Gender	Occupation	Ethnicity	Age	Year	Location
KY-FG#18	F	University students	Kyrgyz	20–23	2007	Bishkek
KY-FG#19	F	White-collar workers/ housewives	Uzbek	40–49	2007	Osh
KY-FG#20	M	University students	Uzbek	20–23	2007	Osh
KY-FG#21	F	Small business owners/traders	Kyrgyz	30–39	2007	Jalalabat
KY-FG#22	M	Small business owners	Kyrgyz	40–49	2007	Jalalabat
KY-FG#23	F	Small business owners/traders	Uzbek	30–39	2007	Kara-Suu
KY-FG#24	M	Small business owners	Kyrgyz	20–29	2007	Kara-Suu
KY-FG#25	M	Migrant labor/ blue-collar workers	Mixed: Uzbek, Uyghur	20–29	2007	Bishkek
KY-FG#26	F	Small business owners/traders	Kyrgyz	20–29	2007	Osh

Focus group participants and other interview respondents were recruited by snowballing, used pseudonyms, and were audio recorded but not videotaped, to ease their worries and minimize risk.[3] Overall, participants were active in responding to questions, and groups typically continued for two to three hours.

Focus groups present both strengths and challenges in facilitating participant discussion of sensitive political issues. By the 2000s, widespread fear of explicitly discussing political Islam meant that it was impossible to ask directly about support for political Islam in a survey. However, posing indirect questions about political, economic, and religious grievances, as well as various theological and social claims (e.g., the need for purism, anti-Semitism) and political propositions (an Islamic state, *shariat* as law) of Islamists, in the context of qualitative open-ended interviews and focus groups, was feasible. We could also assess sympathy toward Islamist groups like HTI by asking about court decisions against them. The focus groups also provided individual-level data useful in further assessing the alternative theories about Islamist support. For example, because participants in seventy-six groups self-identified

3 Mahmood, *Politics of Piety*.

as practicing Muslims but most opposed militant jihad, these focus groups challenge essentialist theories, which expect practicing Muslims uniformly to support jihad. Focus groups also debunk the theory that economic frustration drives popular support of radical Islamism. Such frustration was almost universal among the participants, but supporters of a caliphate or an Islamic state were a small minority. Those who supported a secular political order were poor or economically frustrated. Discussions did offer qualitative evidence at the local and individual level of analysis that support my core argument: religious repression politicizes religious identity, making one receptive to ideas and the emotional messaging that intertwines identity and values with religiously framed solutions to injustice. Frustration with repression and injustice was higher in certain regions and was usually coupled with sympathy for Islamist ideas. These results further dispel any notions that Soviet secularization ever deeply penetrated small towns and rural regions, much less that it had an irreversible grip on Central Asia.

None of the interview responses can be easily quantified because open-ended questions allow room for complicated, nuanced, and often uncertain or even contradictory responses. Yet, each of the types of interviews helped uncover meaning—the meaning of complicated concepts such as democracy, *shariat*, and jihad. Unlike surveys, interview responses reveal how people think, react, and talk about injustice and repression. Unlike ethnography, these various types of interviews reveal whether the meaning given to democracy or a norm about Islamic funerals discussed by one participant is shared by others across towns, regions, and countries and across gender, age, or class divisions.

My study draws on my own extensive interviews and field observations, as well as interviews and surveys carried out by my local research assistants. By conducting interviews both directly and through proxies, whom I trained, I controlled for response bias related to my identity as an American citizen, and I also expanded the scope and therefore the representative nature of the study. I composed the questionnaires in Russian, my partners edited them, and we translated and back-translated into each of the local languages. We conducted pilot interviews and pilot focus groups in each country and for each round of fieldwork. We adjusted as necessary to account for lack of clarity, fear, or other issues that arose.

Almost all focus groups and about half of the semi-structured interviews were conducted by my assistants and transcribed. Where possible in the capital cities and in other large cities, I observed some of the focus groups, acting as "note-taker." In smaller regions, my presence may have severely biased the results. All the semi-structured interviews and focus groups conducted by my assistants were audio recorded and transcribed. This allowed me to gather insight from the full discussion or interview responses when I was not present. I could then systematically compare responses across interviews. We did not retain focus group participants' names or addresses after the interview so as to ensure that responses were fully anonymous.

I read each transcript in full. My assistants (both native Uzbek and Tajik) also read about 75 percent of the transcripts. We each took notes and roughly coded the interviews categorically (not quantitatively) according to various criteria of interest (such as whether the respondents were favorable to Christianity and Judaism or favorable to aspects of democracy). We discussed any areas of ambiguity and assessed, together with the actual moderator, whether the respondents seemed open and honest or reluctant and fearful.

Ultimately, I did not use any quantitative measurements in the analysis, because doing so loses either the richness and depth or the fluidity and ambiguity of many responses. Instead, I translated substantial portions of each interview for use in qualitative analysis in the text. I did all of the analysis of the interview transcripts of all focus groups and interviews, which number thousands of pages.

Overall, such interviews proved to be the optimal method for understanding religious identity, practices, and political attitudes. Respondents were far more at ease in the context of a conversation, sharing tea and bread for several hours—as the culture demands—with a guest and scholar.

Carrying Out Waves of Interviews, Focus Groups, and Surveys over Time

The timing of the fieldwork was determined by funding and research leaves, but also my intent to capture change over time, under differing political and religious conditions. In each country, focus groups and interviews took place in several rounds.

In Kyrgyzstan, I conducted two rounds of focus groups, interviews, and surveys: first, under the late Akayev regime and early post-Akayev period, when religion was relatively free; and second, under Bakiyev's growing authoritarianism and religious repression. The second survey was originally intended to take place during the Bakiyev regime in spring 2010. Because of the overthrow of Bakiyev in April 2010, I postponed the survey until fall 2010. Conditions were not completely stable by then, but the survey team was able to work with minimal disruption. It was clear that religious and ethnic repression in the south was not only continuing but escalating, even while a "democratizing" transition appeared to be underway in the north. The survey was able to capture the change in religious repression—a core interest of the Kyrgyzstan chapters. In Kyrgyzstan, interview respondents in the south were notably less open after the 2010 anti-Uzbek pogroms, but all focus groups had concluded before then. Subsequent interviews with activists took place during multiple field research trips through 2019.

In Uzbekistan, I conducted interviews with experts, NGOs, journalists, human rights activists, government officials, and religious personnel from 2002 through 2005. The first round of focus groups and interviews took place before the Andijon massacre, and respondents/participants were openly critical, reflecting a period of willingness to contest Karimov's regime. The May 2005 government crackdown evicted most foreigners, including scholars, from the country, and necessitated a pause in the research there. The second round of focus groups took place well after Andijon; I sought to establish continuity over time but limited my questions due to the more restrictive political environment. Oral histories, focused mainly on the Soviet era, took place in 2014.

I carried out elite interviews with government officials and IRPT activists, as well as oral histories, during four research trips to Tajikistan between 2004 and 2013. My research assistants conducted focus groups and semi-structured interviews there in two waves as well, first when religion was somewhat freer and the IRPT was beginning to revive, and again after religious restrictions had increased and the IRPT faced increasing political pressures. Tajik participants were generally open, since we completed all fieldwork before the IRPT was banned.

Doing research in an authoritarian context is fraught with risks. I have abided by Institutional Review Board guidelines and have additionally taken steps to conceal identities and views of those who spoke with me and my research assistants. The names of nonactivist/nonelite interviewees and the dates of the interviews have been obscured or changed to protect the anonymity of all those participating in the interviews. All names used in references to focus groups, the semi-structured interviews, and oral histories are pseudonyms. Although some journalists and activists gave me permission to use their names, in many cases I have not done so, given the large numbers who have been threatened, prosecuted, or killed for political reasons over the past three decades. In Table A.1, as in the text, all precise interview dates have been obscured to preserve anonymity.

Glossary

adat customary law

adhan the call to prayer

ayah Qur'anic verse

ayil village (also *qishloq*)

azan call to prayer

bai wealthy person (*boy* in Uzbek; written *bai* in transliteration)

bay'ah oath

bid'ah innovation

chachvon face veil of woven horsehair

choyxona teahouse

da'wat invitation or calling to Islam

da'watchi one who proselytizes Islam

domla/domullo/domlo/damulla religious teacher

duo prayer

emir title for ruler or military commander

eshon Sufi master

fard al-Ayn in Islamic law an obligation of each individual Muslim, a pillar of Islam

fatwa nonbinding legal opinion issued by a jurisconsult (*mufti*)

farz Islamic duty, obligation

fikr opinion

fiqh the science of Islamic law and jurisprudence

fitna disorder

ghazavat holy war

glasnost openness; reform program under Gorbachev

hadith record of the traditions and sayings of the Prophet Muhammad

hafiz person who has memorized the entire Qu'ran

haji a Muslim who has made the pilgrimage to Mecca

hajj the pilgrimage to Mecca during the holy month; fifth pillar of Islam *hakimiyya* Allah's sovereignty on earth

halal permitted according to religious law

halka (or *doira*) secretive network of cells

haram sinful, forbidden acts in Islam

hijab a head, face, or body covering worn in public

hijra migration

hofiz master singer of traditional songs

hokim governor

hudud (pl. *of hud*) mandatory punishments in the Qur'an and *hadith*, but rarely applied due to strict evidentiary standards

hujra religious study circle

hujum assault

hutba sermon

imam religious leader

iman profession of faith

ishan Sufi master

jahiliyya time of ignorance, before Islam's emergence

jamaat party, society, or congregation

janaza Islamic funeral rites

jihad striving

juma Friday

juma namaz Friday prayers

kafir (pl. *kuffar*) infidel

Khalifah Caliphate

khoja sacred lineage

kolkhoz Soviet collective farm

korenizatsiia Soviet nationalities policy

kufr denial of "the Truth"

kulak wealthy peasant, persecuted by Stalin

madrasa Islamic religious school

mahalla neighborhood

maktab Islamic primary school

mazar shrine

mazhab schools of thought in Islam

mudarris instructor in a *madrasa*

muezzin a male Muslim who issues *adhan* (the call to prayer)

mufti Muslim legal scholar capable of issuing a nonbinding *fatwa*; also the chief Islamic authority in SADUM, the Muslim Board of Uzbekistan, and the Spiritual Administration of Muslims of Kyrgyzstan

muftiyat alternative name for SADUM, the Soviet religious administration

muhajir an immigrant to a new land; used in the Qur'an to refer to those who have followed the Prophet

mujahid (pl. *mujahidin*) one who wages jihad; a warrior of God

mullah religious leader

munafiq false Muslim, hypocrite, or a Muslim who hides his disbelief

murid follower, disciple in a Sufi order

murtadd apostate

Musulmonchilik Muslimness (*Musulmoniy* in Tajik)

namaz prayer

nasheed religious song, chant

Navruz Persian New Year

nike (Kyrgyz) Islamic marriage

nikoh (Tajik/Uzbek) Islamic marriage

O'zbekchilik Uzbekness

okrug district

oqsoqol literally, "white beard"; village or neighborhood elder

otin, otincha female Islamic teacher

paranji body veil

perestroika liberalizing reforms under Gorbachev

pir Sufi master

qadimist conservative, traditionalist

qazi Islamic judge of a *shariat* court

qo'rboshi commander

Qori a person who recites the Qur'an

Qozikalon highest Muslim authority in Tajik SSR

Qoziyot Tajik branch of SADUM

Qur'an the book of Islamic revelation

raikom district committee

raion district

Ramadan Islamic holiday marking the end of the fasting month

sadaqa voluntary charity

samizdat clandestine publications, produced within the country

shahada Muslim profession of faith; one of Islam's five pillars

shahid martyr

shariat path or ideal Islamic law as expressed in the Qur'an and Muhammad's example

shaykh honorific title for a spiritual leader, Sufi master

shirk the sin of polytheism or idolatry

shura council

sovkhoz Soviet state farm

sunna practices and traditions of Muhammad for Muslims to follow

sunnat to'yi (Tajik/Uzbek) Islamic circumcision celebrations

sunnöt toi (Kyrgyz) Islamic circumcision celebrations

sura verse of the Qur'an

tafsir the science of explanation of and commentary on the Qur'an

taghut false god or idol; also applied to tyrannical rulers

takfir pronouncement of someone as an unbeliever (*kafir*) or no longer Muslim

talaq divorce

tamizdat clandestine publications, produced outside the country

tariqat Sufi order, brotherhood; a Sufi missionary

tavba repentance

tawhid absolute monotheism, oneness, and unity of God

ulama religious scholars

umma the community of Muslims

urf-adat customs and customary laws of a society

ustod (or *ustoz*) teacher, master

usul religious methodological principle

usul al-fiqh the science of the sources of Islamic law and its relation to legal rulings

Wahhabi a member of a puritanical Muslim sect founded in Arabia in the eighteenth century

waqf a public or private religious endowment of property

xalq people

zakat compulsory charitable giving of a portion of one's salary

zikr Sufi devotional recitation ritual in remembrance of God

ziyarat religious pilgrimage

Index

For the benefit of digital users, indexed terms that span two pages (e.g., 52–53) may, on occasion, appear on only one of those pages.
Tables and figures are indicated by *t* and *f* following the page number